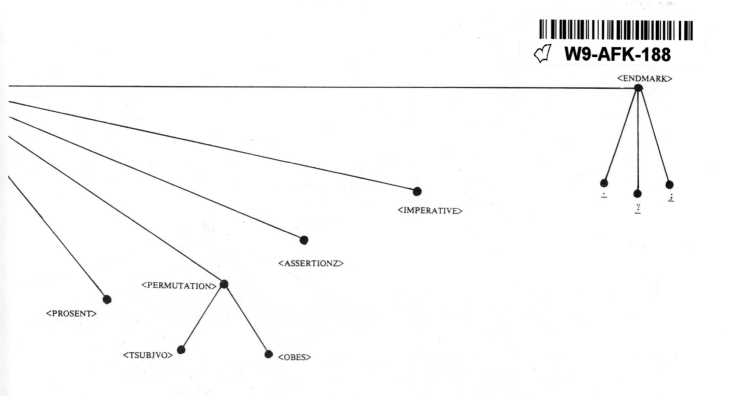

[64 options; see App. 1,
def. 8.1, and App. 4]

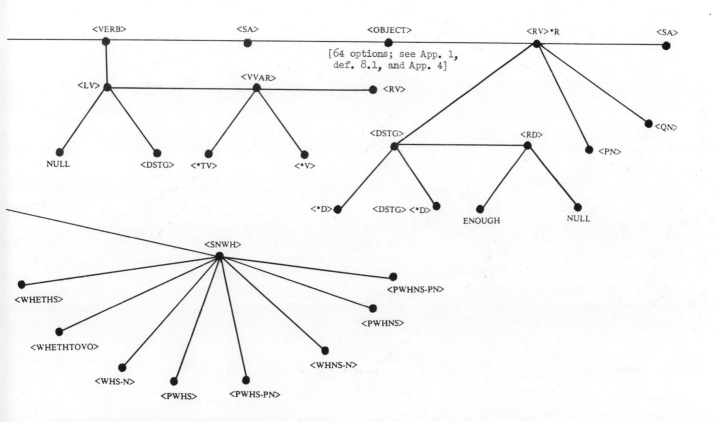

Natural Language Information Processing
A Computer Grammar of English and Its Applications

Natural Language Information Processing
A Computer Grammar of English and Its Applications

Naomi Sager

New York University

1981

Addison-Wesley Publishing Company, Inc.

Advanced Book Program
Reading, Massachusetts 01867

London · Amsterdam · Don Mills, Ontario · Sydney · Tokyo

The end-paper diagrams illustrate the different ways of constructing an English sentence according to the computer grammar presented in the book. Starting with SENTENCE, each path through the diagrams generates a structural analysis, or "parse tree," of a class of English sentences. Horizontal lines are followed left to right and branches are followed to their terminations. At points where lines radiate like spokes of a wheel, a choice of path is made. Terminations of the form <*X> represent word classes; e.g.,<*N> for NOUN. Terminations of the form <X> represent linguistic strings (Chapter 1); they are defined in Chapter 4 and Appendix 1. Only the ASSERTION string, the major sentence type of English, is shown in full. The diagrams are intended as a quick reference guide to the description of the grammar in Part 2.

Designed by Judith Clifford.

Library of Congress Cataloging in Publication Data

Sager, Naomi.
 Natural language information processing.

 Bibliography: p.
 Includes index.
 1. English language—Data processing. 2. Linguistic String Parser (Computer grammar) I. Title.
PE1074.5.S3   420'.72   80-25191
ISBN 0-201-06769-2

ABCDEFGHIJK-HA-89876543210

Contents

*prepared by Susanne Wolff

Preface

This book presents a grammar of English that is used in a computer system for analyzing free-text English input. The distinguishing properties of the grammar are three:

1. It contains a reasonably full coverage of English.
2. It is based on patterns of word combination (syntax).
3. It reveals an essential relation between the grammar and the information, so that the syntactic processing of a sentence produces a standard arrangement of the information in the sentence.

Because of these properties, the grammar makes possible the computerized analysis of English text and the organization and extraction of information from the natural language material.

A natural language information processing system based on the use of the grammar has been developed by the Linguistic String Project (LSP) at New York University. The system has been programmed in three versions, starting with the first implementation of the parser and grammar in 1964–5. The latest version, written in FORTRAN, operates on the Control Data 6600 at the Courant Institute of Mathematical Sciences of New York University. The system now includes, in addition to the basic parser and grammar, an English transformational component and the facility to convert the output of the syntactic analyzer into the information structures of specific subject areas (as described in Chapters 8 and 9). Although the main focus has been on processing scientific articles and technical reports, the program and the grammar are general enough to apply to other types of English material and, with appropriate modifications, to other languages also (see Sec. 10.2).

The book is divided into three parts. Part 1 presents the basis for language computation. It discusses how language differs from its near neighbors, mathematics and logic, and summarizes a theory of sentence structure suited for computation. It also introduces the English-like programming language in which the computer form of the grammar is written.

Part 2 presents the computer grammar of English in considerable detail, supplemented by material in the appendices. Appendix 1 gives the full listing of the grammar except for certain portions noted in the introduction to Appendix 1. Appendix 2 is an alphabetic guide to the mnemonics of the definitions used to specify the major grammatical constructions of English. Appendix 3 gives the definitions of lexical attributes used in classifying English words. Appendix 4 is a further guide to the grammar, listing with brief descriptions all the detailed grammatical tests (''restrictions''). Finally, an index to all the technical terms in Part 2 is given.

Part 3 of the book describes informational applications of the system, which work mainly with narrative medical documents. Part 3 also describes how the grammar can be used in education.

In the years of development of the LSP language processing system, and, more recently, in informational applications of the system, I have had the active collaboration of colleagues of the Linguistic String Project. Many features of the system are due to their individual and collective contributions. While I have tried to acknowledge these features by references throughout the text, the references do not convey how much the final elaboration and functioning of the LSP system has depended on the day-to-day, and year-to-year, cooperative effort of the individuals named here, and others who have come and gone, leaving their contribution. I am glad to have this opportunity to acknowledge my debt to Carol Raze Friedman, Ralph Grishman, Lynette Hirschman, Eileen Fitzpatrick, Judith Clifford, Morris Salkoff, Beatrice Bookchin, Richard Schoen, Barbara Anderson, Cynthia Insolio Benn, Catherine Christenson, Guy Story, Elaine Marsh, Susanne Wolff, and Carolyn White. In addition, I am grateful to Judith Clifford and Cynthia Insolio Benn for yeoman work on the manuscript.

The research reported here on the structure and processing of natural language information has been supported by a number of projects of the National Science Foundation and the National Library of Medicine. I am particularly appreciative of the early support given this work by the Division of Information Science and Technology (then the Office of Science Information Service) of the National Science Foundation, at a time when practical applications of the research were still far in the future. Also, at an early stage of the work, endorsement by the Board of Regents of the National Library of Medicine helped to initiate applied work in a medical context. A large part of the recent work has been supported by research grants SIS 75-22945 and DSI 77-24530 from the Division of Information Science and Technology of the National Science Foundation; the research on medical document processing reported here was supported in part by NIH grant LM 02616 from the National Library of Medicine.

Naomi Sager

List of Illustrations

Figure

List of Tables

Table

Part 1
GOALS and TOOLS

Chapter 1 Introduction

1.1 The Goals of Natural Language Processing

Natural language processing is now a topic of interest in diverse academic and applied fields. Computer scientists, educators, psychologists, linguists, information specialists, medical administrators, file managers, and also nonspecialists are asking how far the computer can go in interpreting "natural," or human, language (as opposed to artificial languages, such as programming languages or mathematics). Clearly, many useful tasks could be performed if the computer could be programmed to extract the content of a message that has been delivered to it or stored in it in natural language form.

For example, it would be helpful for the large number of people who could profit from the use of a computer in their work, but are not programmers, if they could instruct the computer in English, or use English to explain what they wanted, and by an interactive process arrive at an executable program to perform their task.[1] Should the program, in turn, control a physical process, we have the picture of a language-instructed machine.[2]

Educators who see pedagogic value as well as practicality in computer-aided instruction (CAI) would like the students to be able to interact with the computerized lesson material in a natural manner; that is, to be able to ask questions and test understandings by typing into the computer their own freely composed sentences.[3] In another area, designers of computerized search systems are concerned that future systems be more "user oriented" (ACM Panel 1971). Of great use, for example, would be a facility whereby scientists and others who need access to large natural language data bases could state their information request to the system directly, in their own words, without the need to translate it into the fixed forms of a formal query language.[4]

The potential uses of natural language processing mentioned so far are "front end" operations; they would enable the user to communicate in natural language with material stored in computer memory. That material might be of the types mentioned—the elements of a computer program, lesson materials, or stored texts; or, to cite a different application, the material might be a table of numerical data, or of scientific data. The user would then use natural language to pose questions that could be answered automatically from the tables.[5]

But another concern is the nature of the stored material on which computer programs can operate. Question-answering systems that operate on numerical data bases in particular areas of information can supply a useful service where such data bases exist. Only a small fraction of the information that scientists, engineers, administrators, and others need is available in this form, however. Rather, textual material, in books, journal articles, reports, notes, records (medical records, for instance), files of correspondence—all manner of written material—records information for future use. Such bodies of material are increasing so rapidly that the term "information explosion" has become common parlance.

Text searching is already in use in a number of systems that have access to natural language in data bases, such as the titles and abstracts of articles in addition to index terms and key words. Text processing in this context means scanning the natural language material for the occurrence of particular alphanumeric strings or logical combinations of them, where these strings may be words, parts of words, or phrases possibly separated by some number of words deemed irrelevant for the retrieval. These expressions can become part of the computer form of the information request that is used in computer search of the data base. A "match" of a given expression with strings in a title or abstract (or other items characterizing the document) is a sign that the document in question may be relevant to the request. Those concerned with information retrieval are the first to acknowledge that terms or strings taken in isolation or in Boolean logical combination are a crude approximation to informational content. But text scanning is fast, and by scanning figure captions and table headings as well as titles and abstracts, it has been shown that the performance of programs of this type can be greatly improved (O'Connor 1975).

Text processing in one form or another will undoubtedly be employed in information systems in the future because the machine readable form of natural language documents is becoming available as a by-product of other technological processes. F. W. Lancaster foresees that:

> More and more data bases will exist in natural-language form and, as more efficient and economical mass storage devices are developed, full text searching will become the norm in information retrieval operations. The pattern is more or less inevitable: more data bases in natural language form because "publication" itself will be electronic; more searching of data bases directly by scientists because these files will be readily accessible through terminals in offices and homes; more need for a natural language search approach because the person who is not an information specialist will not want to learn the idiosyncracies of a conventional controlled vocabulary and, even if he were willing to master one controlled vocabulary, the range of data bases that will be readily accessible to him virtually precludes the conventional controlled vocabulary approach.

> Those concerned with the design of information systems should now be concentrating
> on functional requirements for the user-oriented, natural language systems of the future.
> . . . It seems entirely probable that, because future systems will be natural language systems
> and must be simple for the non-information-specialist to use, linguistic techniques may
> have much more to offer the system designer than they have in the past (Lancaster 1977:
> 39–40).

The increasing role of computers in the daily information processing functions of many
institutions also creates a need for natural language processing, and in some cases creates the
data base for it. Most files are in natural language and many operations on those files are of
a routine nature. If some of these operations could be performed by computer on the
original natural language text of the documents, it would be worthwhile for the institution to
have the documents stored in machine readable form. Existing techniques of data capture
(by magnetic typewriters, for example) can produce paper copy and machine readable copy
in the same operation. Improved optical readers are under constant development. The creation of files in machine readable form is thus an option that will be available to many institutions in the future.

In some cases, natural language files have already been put into machine readable form,
not for purposes of processing the contents by computer but for convenience of access and
storage. The existence of the files in computerized form then raises the question of whether
further data processing operations can be carried out on them without having to transfer the
information manually into pre-set formats. An example of this process is the case of a
hospital that computerizes its patient files for quick back-up to the written charts and for
transactional purposes; then, finding itself with this large natural language data base, seeks
computer techniques for processing the contents of the documents to obtain the summaries
and other information required for health care evaluation and for clinical research. We are
bound to see a pressure of this sort arising wherever natural language files are computerized.
Once information is available in computer readable form, users inevitably want the computer to process it.

A question thus arises as to whether there are computer techniques for operating on the
information in natural language files without the need for persons to code the information in
the documents. The answer is yes. The program and grammar presented in this book have
been adapted for such use by adding additional stages of processing to the initial grammatical analysis. The techniques have been tested on medical records written in free narrative. Documents were analyzed by computer and the sentences automatically mapped into
tablelike forms that contain the same information as the texts. From these tables, as is shown
in Chapters 8 and 9, questions about the document content can be answered automatically
and summaries of the different kinds of information in the documents can be automatically
generated.

The techniques used in these applications start with automatic grammatical analyses of
text sentences. The programs then reduce the number of alternative grammatical forms for
the same information so as to arrive at more regular informational representations of the
text sentences. Finally, words of similar informational standing in the given type of material

are transferred to correspondingly labeled slots in an information table developed for the given field of application (as described in 8.1.1). The informational word classes and the table definition for a given application are based on grammatical and word co-occurrence analysis of a sample of the documents to be processed.

This process is not simple, to be sure. In a computer program that analyzes natural language material, there is no way of avoiding complex operations on complex data structures. The surprising thing is that it can be done at all. With the methods that are now being developed for natural language processing, a computer can be programmed to perform operations that, if one did not see how the process was built up step by step, one would think could only be done by human beings with knowledge of both the language and the subject matter.

1.2   Properties of Language

There are reasons why natural language can be processed by computer programs. Overtly, in its written form it is composed of linearly arranged discrete entities that, like the symbols of mathematics and various codes, occur only in particular combinations. For this reason a grammar, which specifies the rules of combination of the elements in well-formed sentences of the language, can in principle be used in a procedure to recognize the syntactic structure of sentences. Such a procedure will produce a structural description of a sentence (or more than one description if the sentence is ambiguous) that shows how the sentence was composed of elements specified by the grammar, combined according to the stated rules of sentence formation. In this respect natural language resembles its near neighbors, the formal languages of mathematics, logic, and programming, for some of which recognition procedures have been devised. But there are significant differences between natural languages and formal languages that have made the computer analysis of natural language a special area of research.

1.2.1   *Grammatical Subclasses and Selection*

The symbols in syntactic formulas for natural language represent word classes (e.g., N is noun, TV tensed verb). A sentence is represented by a string of such symbols in which a word from each of the classes is substituted for the corresponding class symbol in the string, analogous to the substitution of values for variables in mathematics. However, in natural language not every such word substitution into a correct sentence formula results in an equally acceptable sentence, as though in mathematics the equation $(a + b)^2 = a^2 + 2ab + b^2$ were to be more true for some numbers than others. Thus, *Engineers demonstrated equipment* is a well-formed assertion of the N TV N type, whereas *Engineers demonstrated students,* while grammatical, is a highly unlikely assertion. No matter how refined the word classes represented by formula symbols are made, some differences in the acceptability of particular combinations of words resulting from the substitution of words for class symbols in formulas remains.

As a result of the differences in acceptability of the word sequences, a natural language grammar contains constraints that refer to subclasses of the major classes. For computation, words must be assigned attributes that indicate subclass memberships, and analysis procedures must be equipped with the ability to access the lexical entries for words and to eliminate readings in which words are assigned syntactic roles incompatible with their subclass memberships. Otherwise, ungrammatical input strings may be accepted as sentences (*Engineers demonstrates equipment*), and wrong or unlikely analyses of word sequences in correct sentences may be obtained (the assertion *The students demonstrated during the visit* analyzed like the noun phrase *the equipment demonstrated during the visit*).

In some cases the unacceptability of particular word combinations is grammatical in character (sharp yes–no) as in the example *Engineers demonstrates . . . ,* where number agreement between subject and verb is violated. However, over and above what can be captured in grammatical constraints the acceptability of word combinations is graded and dependent on the universe of discourse or the situational context. Thus, *John walks to school* is normal and *John breathes to school* marginal, while *John floats to school* would be acceptable if John's school is on a waterway and someone gives his boat a strong schoolward push in the morning. For a given word *w,* the set of words with which *w* commonly co-occurs in a given syntactic relation is called (following the linguist Bloomfield [1933]) the **selection** of *w* in that relation; for example, if *w* is a verb, then it has a selection of subject nouns, and if also transitive then also a selection of object nouns.

The selection of a word is closely related to its meaning. If two words in the same grammatical class were to have identical selections they would be exact synonyms; conversely, if they have few linguistic environments in common, their meanings are very different. Selection is difficult to state precisely for the words of a whole language and differs markedly from subject matter to subject matter (consider the varied uses of the word *subject* itself). In particular domains, however, especially those where the vocabulary is limited and usage is regular, selectional classes can be defined precisely and selectional rules have virtually the force of grammatical constraints. In medicine: *The patient developed a cough,* but not *A cough developed the patient*.

1.2.2 *Syntactic Ambiguity*

When the sentences of a language are described in terms of permitted sequences of symbols, it may happen that an acceptable symbol sequence can be derived in more than one way by the rules of the grammar. We call this **syntactic ambiguity.** In the case of natural language, where the symbols represent word classes, a syntactically ambiguous string means that a sequence of words that by virtue of their class memberships constitute an instance of the string has more than one analysis.[6] Sometimes this corresponds to a perceived ambiguity, as, for example, in the two readings of *They are visiting relatives;* the reading in which *visiting* is a left modifier of *relatives* has the relatives doing the visiting, whereas the reading in which *are visiting* is a verb string corresponds to an interpretation in which those who are doing the visiting are different from the relatives.

Very often, because word sequences belonging to the same word class sequence have differing acceptability, only one of several syntactic readings of a given word sequence is perceived as the correct analysis; only one is the intended reading. In computerized sentence analysis, thus, the computer "sees" readings of which the human reader is unaware. In processing a medical document, for example, one computer analysis of the sentence *This morning mother noted swollen hands* created for us the concept of a "morning mother."

To guide the computer to the correct syntactic analysis, and beyond this (where possible) to the intended analysis, we add more detailed rules, called **restrictions,** as to what are acceptable word combinations. Restrictions are needed not only to select the correct and intended final analysis but to limit the creation of many alternative analyses of subsequences of symbols within the sentence string. These **local ambiguities** can cause so much wasted time in the course of the analysis as to preclude in some cases the obtaining of a final analysis altogether.

1.2.3 *Implicit Elements*

In addition to treating the words that are present in a discourse, a natural language processor has to deal with the phenomenon that some words are present in "zeroed" form, that is, are not physically present but are reconstructible from the context, as is *agree* after *do* in *They agree and we do too.* The missing words are repetitions of words that occurred previously in the sentence in corresponding syntactic positions. A related phenomenon in natural language is **reference:** some words refer to other words or stretches of the discourse. The most familiar referentials are the personal pronouns, but the phenomenon includes phrases like *this process, the foregoing,* and simply *this,* referring to a preceding sentence or passage. To complete the analysis and to perform content-oriented tasks, the zeroed words must be supplied and the antecedents of referentials must be identified.

1.2.4 *Meaning*

Important as it is to have an effective grammar for language computation, grammar alone is not sufficient for applications. Somewhere, somehow, the system has to come to grips with the specific content of the texts under analysis. For some investigators, the explication of the meaning of the texts is the goal of computational work with language, and they see their computational systems as potential models for human cognitive processes (Schank 1975, Lindsay et al. 1977). Although goals may differ, a common feature of much contemporary language research in artificial intelligence and computational linguistics is the use of semantic models that have their origin outside of the syntactic analysis of the text material. Some researchers would obviate syntactic analysis altogether if possible, or at least keep it to a minimum (Charniak and Wilks 1976).

Although universal semantic systems are probably beyond reach, it is still possible to develop limited semantic representations for restricted areas of knowledge. A combined syntactic-semantic notational system for summarizing the contents of articles in endocrinology was developed by one investigator[7] in order to manage a large file of the literature in this field. In the fields of medical computing and medical applications of artificial intelligence, there is research in modeling disease processes as a basis for providing computerized consultation on treatment and diagnosis.[8] There is also a successful system for automatically coding pathology reports based on a classification of the nomenclature of pathology into major semantic categories.[9] These efforts have not based their semantic categories on formal linguistic analysis of texts in their field, nor have they had the goal of applying their categories to textual material in the field by means of computerized analysis. In contrast, the use of linguistic methodology for the derivation of semantic categories in a subject area, and the use of these categories for automatic analysis of texts in the subject area are the long-range goals of the work described in this book. These two different approaches to linguistic computation should complement each other in the development of practical applications of natural language processing.

1.3   Computer Parsing

The type of analysis one obtains for a sentence depends directly on the theory of sentence structure, or type of grammar, one uses to obtain the analysis. In the work described here we use a characterization of language structure called linguistic string analysis that was developed specifically for computerized syntactic analysis of texts and was used in an early form as the basis for the first computer program to analyze English sentences (Harris et al. 1959, Harris 1962). Briefly, linguistic string analysis asserts that every sentence is built from one elementary sentence, which is called the center string, by the insertion of adjunct strings (modifiers) at specified points in the center string or inserted adjunct strings. Thus, to take a simple example, the sentence *I know a printer who does fine work* has as center string *I know a printer* to which has been adjoined to the right of the noun *printer* the adjunct string *who does work,* to which the adjunct string *fine* has been adjoined to the left of the noun *work*. A more complete description of string analysis is given in Sec. 1.4.

The virtue of string analysis for computation is that the structural components of a sentence under string analysis are precisely the units to which syntactic and semantic constraints apply, so that the translation of these constraints into computer operations on the sentence is straightforward. Also, these same units of the sentence decomposition are directly related to the information carried by the sentence, so the string analysis constitutes the first approximation to an informational analysis of the sentence that later can be refined and specialized for informational applications.

To start with a more familiar notion, we can take as a point of departure the old-fashioned activity of diagramming a sentence. In one simple version[10] the modifiers in a given sentence are each written on a line underneath the element they modify, with a vertical line showing where the modifier enters the sentence. A sentence diagram or parse of this type—done by hand—is shown in Fig. 1.1. On the top line are the words of the main clause: *The force depends on the concentration.* The first modifier (*with which a heart beats*) is written on a line just below and enters just after—that is, to the right of—the first noun (*force*). The first modifier itself contains a modifier (*isolated*) entering to the left of *heart*. There appear to be two prepositional modifiers of *concentration: of Ca* and *in the medium,* although the latter might be considered a modifier of *Ca* (the calcium which is in the medium). The noun *medium* has the modifier *which surrounds it,* in which *it* is a pronoun standing for *isolated heart.* As far as it goes, this is clearly a sensible breakdown of the sentence into parts, one in which the top line carries the central assertion of the sentence and each modifier adds some factual detail to the information in the line directly above it.

Figure 1.2 shows the analysis obtained by a computer program (the Linguistic String Project, or LSP, parser) for the same sentence. This branching type of diagram is called a **string parse tree.** The term "parse" has an up-to-date definition. It is not the same activity as old-fashioned sentence parsing although it has the same purpose, namely to show how the sentence was built up according to rules of the grammar. In computer work on language analysis, a parse is the output of a program that obtains such an analysis, which is often exhibited in the form of a tree, called a parse tree. The string parse tree will become more familiar to the reader as the book progresses. For the moment the reader should only note that despite the obvious differences between the two representations of the sentence in Figs. 1.1 and 1.2 there are striking similarities. Let us ignore for the moment the details of the elaborate structure displayed in the computer parse tree shown in Fig. 1.2 and note only that it consists of several major horizontal layers. Each layer consists of groups of elements occupying tree positions called nodes. Some of these nodes originate branches that stretch downward and terminate at symbols connected to words of the sentence. If we skim intermediate steps and read the words in each major horizontal layer of the computer parse tree, we read approximately the same word sequences that appear on different lines of the hand-done sentence diagram. The similarity between the sentence diagram and the string

Fig. 1.1 Sentence diagram for *The force with which an isolated heart beats depends on the concentration of Ca in the medium which surrounds it.*

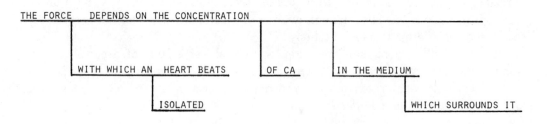

THE FORCE WITH WHICH AN ISOLATED HEART BEATS DEPENDS ON THE CONCENTRATION OF CA

IN THE MEDIUM WHICH SURROUNDS IT

THE FORCE   DEPENDS ON THE CONCENTRATION

WITH WHICH AN   HEART BEATS   OF CA   IN THE MEDIUM

ISOLATED   WHICH SURROUNDS IT

(IT = ISOLATED HEART)

parse tree thus lies in the way the sequence of sentence words is segmented into component word strings. In the sentence diagram the process of arriving at the segmentation is not shown (and indeed is intuitive). In the string parse tree, however, the major steps in arriving at the segmentation are explicitly represented by the nodes of the parse tree; each node, from the topmost node, SENTENCE, down to the sequence of nodes to which the words of the sentence are attached, represents a choice made among alternative ways of building a sentence, stated in the computer grammar. (Note that, to save space the illustrations of computer-generated parse trees in this book do not show the NULLs and empty SA nodes.)

At this point one might ask why the vast apparatus of computer technology and years of research effort should be required to arrive at the same result as can be obtained by a (bright and responsible) twelve-year-old practicing an old-fashioned method of English grammar. The answer lies in the requirements of formal analysis. When a person does the analysis, he or she may draw on experience that is not entirely embodied in the stated procedure, and the procedure may still be workable even if it is not entirely precise. But a formal procedure, such as a computer program, cannot rely on understanding the sentence, or on the familiarity of certain word combinations, or on a feeling for what constitutes a grammatical sentence of the language. It can only work with sequences of marks and formal (combinatorial) rules concerning the marks, that is, with the form of the utterance (hence the term "formal"). Since the words of the language are far too many to deal with individually, they are grouped into classes, which can then be represented by symbols. Rules are then stated as to which combinations of symbols are well formed. The achievement of formal grammatical analysis is to arrive at the explicit equivalent of a manual analysis, and in some cases at an even more refined and semantically revealing analysis, solely by operations on the symbols for word classes and their combinations—that is, on the constructs used to specify which are the well-formed sequences of symbols that conform to the grammatical sentences of the language.

The practical advantages of a computer program over manual analysis in the case where large amounts of data are to be processed are too well known to be repeated here. The problems in computerizing textual analysis are not all solved. Nevertheless it is clear that if the many complex operations required to obtain a linguistic analysis of texts could be performed at speeds comparable to those now achieved for arithmetic operations, and if the analysis could be sharpened so that it represented the intellectual content in ways suited for further processing, then a new technology of information handling would be in sight. In such an application computer parsing of sentences would be only one part of a larger process, but a crucial one, in the analysis of the information contained in texts. Its importance lies in the fact that it makes an informationally relevant division of the sentence into parts and it identifies the grammatical relations that tie these parts together and are themselves part of the information carried by the sentence. In the case of the LSP system, the string parse trees that are obtained for sentences, along with grammatical information that is stored in the course of analysis, make the output suitable for input to a second component that utilizes linguistic transformations (cf. Chapter 7) to sharpen the informational character of the representation. To this a stage of processing special to the field of application can be applied to provide

Fig. 1.2   Computer parse tree. Note that in this and all other figures showing computer outputs of the parsing program a convention to save space in printing out the parse trees has been utilized. NULLs and empty SA nodes are not printed.

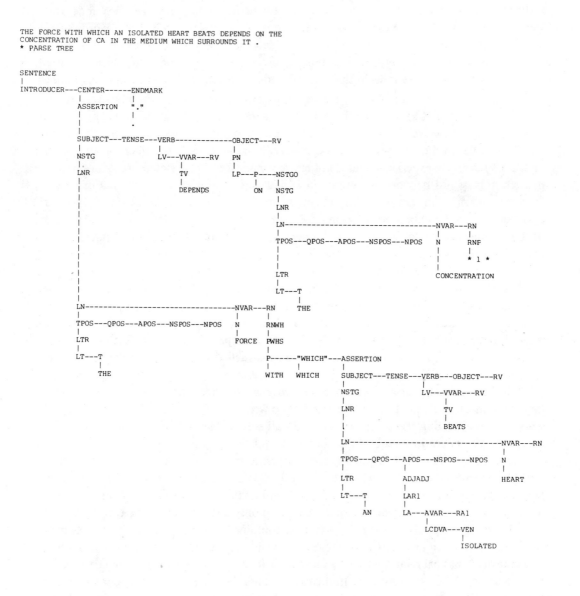

```
THE FORCE WITH WHICH AN ISOLATED HEART BEATS DEPENDS ON THE
CONCENTRATION OF CA IN THE MEDIUM WHICH SURROUNDS IT .
* PARSE TREE


SENTENCE
|
INTRODUCER---CENTER------ENDMARK
             |           |
             ASSERTION   "."
             |           |
             |           .
             |
             SUBJECT---TENSE---VERB------------OBJECT---RV
             |                 |               |
             NSTG              LV---VVAR---RV  PN
             |                 |              |
             LNR               TV             LP---P----NSTGO
             |                 |              |    |    |
             |                 DEPENDS        ON   NSTG
             |                                     |
             |                                     LNR
             |                                     |
             |                                     LN-----------------------------------NVAR---RN
             |                                     |                                     |      |
             |                                     TPOS---QPOS---APOS---NSPOS---NPOS     N      RNF
             |                                     |                                     |      |
             |                                     |                                     |      * 1 *
             |                                     |                                     |
             |                                     LTR                                   CONCENTRATION
             |                                     |
             |                                     LT---T
             |                                     |
             LN-----------------------------------NVAR---RN    THE
             |                                     |      |
             TPOS---QPOS---APOS---NSPOS---NPOS     N      RNWH
             |                                     |      |
             LTR                                   FORCE  PWHS
             |                                            |
             LT---T                                       P------"WHICH"---ASSERTION
             |                                            |      |         |
             THE                                          WITH   WHICH     SUBJECT---TENSE---VERB---OBJECT---RV
                                                                           |                 |
                                                                           NSTG              LV---VVAR---RV
                                                                           |                 |
                                                                           LNR               TV
                                                                           |                 |
                                                                           |                 BEATS
                                                                           |
                                                                           LN-----------------------------------NVAR---RN
                                                                           |                                     |      |
                                                                           TPOS---QPOS---APOS---NSPOS---NPOS     N
                                                                           |                 |                   |
                                                                           LTR               ADJADJ              HEART
                                                                           |                 |
                                                                           LT---T            LAR1
                                                                           |                 |
                                                                           AN                LA---AVAR---RA1
                                                                                                   |
                                                                                                   LCDVA---VEN
                                                                                                           |
                                                                                                           ISOLATED
```

```
THE FORCE WITH WHICH AN ISOLATED HEART BEATS DEPENDS ON THE
CONCENTRATION OF CA IN THE MEDIUM WHICH SURROUNDS IT .
* PARSE TREE
```

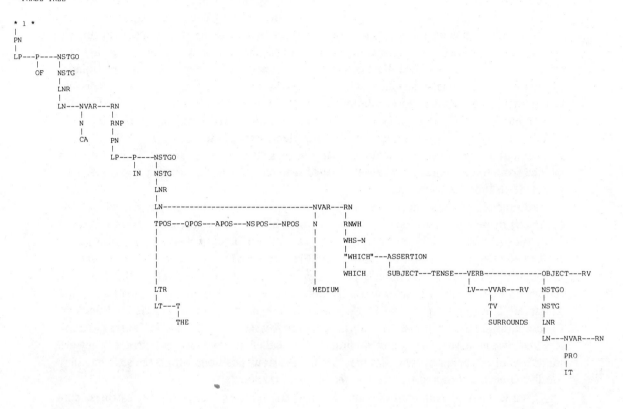

a labeling and alignment of sentence parts carrying comparable information. Step by step, by grammatical means, we arrive at a regular representation of the informational units in the text and their interrelation.

1.4   Linguistic String Analysis

It is an observable property of sentences of a language that they are composed in a regular way of component word strings, where the word strings are all of a few types. A convenient way of representing these types is as a sequence of symbols, called a **linguistic string,** where each symbol is either a particular word (standing for itself) or the name of a major word class of the language, such as N for noun, TV for tensed (inflected) verb, VEN for past participle, VING for verb with *-ing* suffix, V for infinitive verb, ADJ for adjective, D for adverb, T for article, and so forth. A simple sentence, such as *The heart beats,* for example, can be represented by the sequence T N TV"." (The quotation marks around the endpoint period indicate that it is a literal term, not representing anything else.) This sequence belongs to a type called an **elementary center string;** it represents a sentence in its simplest form. No words can be deleted from this elementary sentence in such a way as to leave again a sentence; it cannot be reduced. Particular sequences, called **adjunct strings,** can be adjoined, or inserted, at various points in a string so that the result, a nonelementary, or derived, center string, represents a more complex sentence. For example, T VEN N TV "." represents the sentence *The isolated heart beats.,* in which VEN is an adjunct string one symbol in length that has been adjoined to the left of N in the elementary center string T N TV "." In a nonelementary sentence, what remains after a word string that is an adjunct string has been deleted from the sentence, is still a well-formed sentence. The center strings are ASSERTION, QUESTION, IMPERATIVE, and so on.

Adjunct strings, too, may be either elementary or derived. Thus the past participle VEN (*isolated*) in the preceding example is elementary, but in the sentence *The freshly isolated heart beats.,* represented by T D VEN N TV "." , the adverbial adjunct (*freshly*) is adjoined to the left of VEN and the resulting sequence D VEN adjoining N is no longer an elementary adjunct string. Elementary adjunct strings may be longer than one symbol. Most of the modifiers familiar to us from English grammar correspond to adjunct strings in a string grammar. Thus, the relative clauses (*the man whom we met*) are among the right adjuncts of the noun, as are prepositional phrases (*the store on 8th street*). Subordinate clauses (*because it rained, when leaving*) are counted among the so-called **sentence adjunct strings.** They are modifiers of a whole sentence that may occur in various positions within the sentence they modify (*Because it rained we left, We left because it rained*).

Simple rules of combination can be stated for building complex center strings, corresponding to complex sentences, out of elementary center and adjunct strings. One simply classifies the adjunct strings according to the position in which each occurs within another string—for example, to the left of a noun or to the right of the verb. We thus arrive at the definition of **adjunct sets,** conveniently divided into the types: LX, strings that occur to the left of the word class X (for example, the left adjuncts of the noun are labeled LN); RX, strings that occur to the right of a word class X; SA, sentence adjuncts, strings that occur to the left or right of any element X of a string (but if X has left or right adjuncts, then to the left or right of these). Conjunctional strings are here treated as adjuncts.

One way of stating the rules of string combination is in terms of these defined sets: If a string α is a member of a set A (where A is the set of center strings, or SA, or LX or RX for some X) and if an adjunct string β is inserted into α in accordance with the classification of β as LX, RX, or SA, then the resulting string α' is again a member of the set A. Thus, if $\alpha' = X_1 X_2$, a center string, and $\beta = X_3 X_4$, a member of the set LX$_2$ (where X_1, X_2, X_3, X_4 are word classes), then $\alpha' = X_1X_3X_4X_2$ is again a center string. Built up in this way, the set of center strings represents all the sentences of the language that can be formed by adjunction, by the addition of modifiers either to other modifiers or to the main clause.

Besides center and adjunct strings there is an important class of sequences that occur regularly as subparts of center or adjunct strings. For example, in the sentence *For the heart to beat requires energy,* it is convenient to recognize the sequence *for* T N *to* V, corresponding to the word string *for the heart to beat* as a separate element of the center string. The class of sequences that includes *for* T N *to* V, is called **sentence nominalization strings**; these are sentences that have been changed in order to occupy noun positions. Sentencelike internally except for the form of the verb and certain other changes in form, they nevertheless occur in positions analogous to those in which nouns occur in other sentences, for example as the subject or object of a verb. We assimilate sentence nominalization strings into the derivation of the center strings of the language by broadening slightly the definition of a linguistic string. Instead of saying strings are composed exclusively of words or word classes, as stated earlier, we will henceforth understand a linguistic string to be a sequence of one or more words, word classes, or named grammatical positions, where a named position, such as SUBJECT in the string SUBJECT TV "." or in the string SUBJECT TV N ".", stands for a disjunction of sequences consisting of words, word classes, or named positions, and where the disjunctions are sets of alternative values that may be substituted for the named position. Such a definition will include all the elementary strings defined previously, along with strings that have strings as elements. For example, if we define SUBJECT to be either T N or the sentence nominalization string consisting of the sequence *for* T N *to* V, then the center string SUBJECT TV N "." stands for the sequences T N TV N "." and *for* T N *to* V TV N ".", which are obtained simply by substituting for SUBJECT each of its values in turn. This enlarged center string represents elementary sentences such as *The heart requires energy.*, as well as sentences containing a sentence nominalization as the subject of the main verb, such as *For the heart to beat requires energy.*, and many others.

This is all the apparatus that is needed to describe the string structure of sentences of the language. One starts with the linguistic strings defined a priori for the language, as sequences of one or more words, word classes, or named positions. The strings are classified as to their occurrence as center strings, as sentence nominalization strings, or as adjunct strings of different types (LX, RX, SA, for word classes X of the grammar). **Adjunction** is the operation of inserting an adjunct string into another string either to left or right of a word class X or between two elements of the string according to whether the adjunct string is a member of LX, RX, or SA, as stated in the derivation rule for adjunction given previously. **Substitution** is the operation of substituting for a named position one of its values, that is, replacing the named position by a sequence consisting of words, word classes, or named positions. Starting with the set of elementary center strings, by repeated application of the operations of adjunction and substitution one can generate a set of structures, the elementary and derived center strings, which correspond to the sentences of the language.

Linguistic string analysis is presented here as a method of constructing, or generating, well-formed sentence structures from certain axiomatically given linguistic strings. This description presents the strings in a form that will make it easy to understand the organization of the computer grammar in later chapters. However, string analysis could instead have been presented as the result of applying an experimental procedure to the sentences of the language whereby one starts with sentences and by an experimental procedure arrives at the linguistic strings of the grammar. This alternative procedure is based on **excision**[11] as follows: Starting with a given sentence S (it is convenient to proceed from right to left) one excises a word or a contiguous word sequence from S (call the excised portion E) if the residue R ($R = S - E$) is again a grammatical sentence. One repeats this for each successive R_i (where $S = R_0$, and the residues are numbered consecutively) until no more excisions are possible. Each E is a component elementary word string. It turns out that over many sentences all the component elementary word strings fall into a small number of types on the basis of their grammatical form (their word class composition in terms of noun, verb, and so on), and on the point in R at which they were excised (for example, to the right of a noun, or to the right of a verb). A crucial part of the procedure is a control on whether R_{i-1} is essentially the same sentence as R_i except for the subtraction of detail. This is not the case, for example, when *a fool* is excised from *They will consider him a fool*. Also certain "automatic" changes in shape accompany some excisions (such as change in number suffix). The adjunct strings emerge from this procedure rather straightforwardly, the sentence-nominalization strings only by positing a hierarchy of rather more extensive automatic changes. This procedure is illustrated in Figs. 10.7 and 10.8, where it is discussed in connection with methods of teaching language structure.

1.5   A System for Natural Language Information Processing

The Linguistic String Project has developed a system for informational applications of natural language processing, operating on texts of considerable linguistic complexity.[12] Texts are accepted as written with no restrictions on the grammar or vocabulary of the input, except that the syntactic properties of the text words must be included in the lexicon. The components of the system are as follows:

1.   An implemented grammar of English (described in this book);
2.   A parsing program that produces syntactic analyses of input sentences, utilizing the aforementioned grammar and components (3), (4), and (5);
3.   A word dictionary, now comprising about 9,500 words (with a larger back-up dictionary of partially classified words), which provides parts of speech and syntactic subclass information for each word, the classifications reflecting the use of the words in English as a whole, exclusive of colloquial or purely literary usage;
4.   A programming language especially designed for writing natural language grammars;
5.   Procedures for transforming string parse trees into informationally equivalent, less varied, structures, utilizing (a) transformations valid for all English sentences, and (b) transformations specific to specialized subject matters;

6. Programs for text and dictionary work (concordance, dictionary update, and other functions) and a clustering program that operates on grammatically analyzed sentences of a subfield to generate semantic word classes for the subfield.

Of these components, this book describes in greatest detail the grammar since it provides the basis for further applications. As will be shown, the type of grammar used, linguistic string analysis, provides an analysis of each sentence into component word-strings that are at the same time both the grammatical and informational units of the sentence. Further operations refine and specialize the outputs of the string analysis program to obtain the desired informational representation of sentences. In this system, there is no call upon a special independent semantic component in order to achieve highly sophisticated information processing. The string parse tree and subsequent operations of transforming and labeling its components are the means of providing an informational characterization of the input texts.

NOTES

1. This is the goal of some of the research in automatic programming, such as is described in Heidorn 1976 and in the references cited there.

2. Programs for controlling machine tools and other devices exist [e.g., APT 1967], but the instructions are not written in natural language. In a well-known experiment in artificial intelligence a simulated robot was instructed to move blocks into different arrangements, using English-language instructions in a conversational mode. The vocabulary of the instructions was limited to that needed for operating in the blocks "microworld" (Winograd 1972).

3. Powerful CAI systems such as the PLATO system (Sherwood 1974), have operated effectively with only rudimentary language processing capabilities. But there is no doubt that even more interesting lessons could be devised if the student could participate more actively.

4. A bibliographic retrieval system with a natural language user interface is described in Hillman 1973.

5. Question-answering systems of this type have been developed for business statistics (Plath 1976), for data on the composition of lunar rocks (Woods et al. 1972) and for other structured data bases (L. R. Harris 1977, Hendrix 1978, Waltz 1978). A question-answering system in which the data are also in natural language is described in Grishman and Hirschman 1978 and in Grishman 1979. A large part of natural language research within artificial intelligence (AI) is concerned with the goal of improved man–machine communication. An overview of research in this field as of February 1977 is to be found in Waltz 1977, in which investigators provided a summary of their current projects. An earlier survey of question-answering systems is Simmons 1970. Issues are discussed in Petrick 1976. Related work in speech recognition is described in Walker 1978.

6. Another source of syntactic ambiguity in natural language is the fact that some words are in more than one class (e.g., *visit* is a noun, a tensed verb, and an infinitive verb, depending on the context). As a result a word sequence may conform to more than one sentence formula.

7. Hans Selye; description of the system is in Selye and Ember 1974.

8. For example see Amarel 1974. An interactive consultation program on drug administration is described in Shortliffe 1976.

9. The nomenclature in question is SNOP (Systematized Nomenclature of Pathology) of the College of American Pathologists, recently extended to other branches of medicine and now called SNOMED. The automatic coding system referred to was developed at NIH and is described in Dunham et al. 1978. Linguistic issues in medical computing are discussed in Pratt 1973.

10. Other methods of sentence diagramming, with historical references, can be found in Householder 1972.

11. Proposed by Henry Hiż (1961) and described in Chapter 2 of Harris 1962.

12. The algorithm and first statement of the grammar were given in Sager 1960. An experimental implementation in IPLV was completed in 1965 (Sager et al. 1965) and a fast assembly language version for the IBM 7094 was written by Carol Raze in 1966 (Sager et al. 1966, Raze 1967). Output parses obtained for several scientific articles by the early programs were printed in Bookchin 1968. The grammar was first documented in Sager 1968 and Salkoff and Sager 1969. The present program in FORTRAN was written by Ralph Grishman. It is described in Grishman et al. 1973 and in Grishman 1973, with details given in Grishman 1974b, 1976. The lexical component is described in Fitzpatrick and Sager 1974, based in part on prior work of Barbara Anderson, with contributions by Judith Clifford and Richard Schoen. The programming language for the grammar is described in Chapter 3, drawing on Sager and Grishman 1975, and in Grishman 1974a. The transformational part of the program is described in Hobbs and Grishman 1976; English transformations and sublanguage information-formatting transformations are described in Sager and Hirschman 1979 and in Hirschman and Sager 1981.

Chapter 2 Computer Representation of Linguistic Data

2.1 Requirements of a Natural Language Parser

The major components of a computer system for analyzing the structure of sentences are (1) a set of categories and subcategories for the words of the language and a lexicon in which each word is assigned the categories and subcategories that apply to it; (2) a grammar of the language, using the same categories and subcategories as the lexicon and whatever constructs are required by the type of grammar used to specify the well-formed sentence structures of the language; (3) an analysis procedure, or parsing program, whose inputs are the text to be processed, the lexicon, and the grammar, and whose output for each sentence is a structural description of the sentence, showing how the sentence was constructed according to the rules of the grammar. Often this account is presented in the form of a parse tree, such as the one shown in Fig. 1.2, but other output forms are possible, such as parenthesization of word groups in the input string.

The designer of the system must make various linguistic and technical decisions with regard to these components. Some decisions will necessitate constructing auxiliary apparatus. For example, with regard to the lexical component, one must decide whether the words of the text are to be broken up into morphemes (roughly stems and affixes) or treated as whole words. In the former case, a deaffixation program for stripping the affixes from words may be desirable. In the latter case, some method of cross-referencing words that have the same stem (for example, *walk, walks, walking, walked*) must be envisioned. There is also a question as to whether all text words must be given their grammatical classification in advance of the analysis process. Some investigators have described a sentence analysis program that uses a dictionary containing only a small number of grammatical words and affixes and requires no preclassification of the majority of text words (Bratley et al.,1967). This would be a tremendous advantage in applications of the program, since the dictionary burden—the necessity of classifying text words in advance of processing—is one of the heavy costs in using linguistic processing. Unfortunately, it turns out that the program that does not have a considerable number of the text words preclassified (particularly the verbs) yields many incorrect analyses for each sentence. The LSP is currently investigating ways in which correct parses can be obtained when a number of words (those not already in the LSP lexicon) are not coded prior to parsing. Instead, the relevant categories are deduced from context.

With regard to the grammar, a central question is how to organize the mass of detail in a grammar of a natural language. Without sufficient detail the grammar is inadequate. But simple proliferation of the rules to handle more and more detailed cases makes the grammar unintelligible. This consideration bears on the question of how the grammar is to be represented in the computer. There are also a number of particularly complex areas in natural language grammar (for example, conjunctional constructions and ellipsis) that present a special and difficult problem for machine analysis.

Lastly there is the question of the parsing procedure itself. A number of parsing procedures, or algorithms, have been developed for artificial languages, that is, higher level programming languages, such as ALGOL and FORTRAN. The parsing procedure is used as part of the translation of programs written in the higher-level programming language into machine language instructions by means of a syntax-directed compiler (Lewis and Stearns 1968). Some of these parsing algorithms utilize a specification of the syntax of the programming language that has a clear relevance to the problem of specifying natural language structure. But the type of grammar used by these algorithms falls short of what is needed for natural language. They require that all wellformedness requirements, which are statements as to what constitutes a correctly formed sentence of the language, be stated as formal definitions or, equivalently, as context-free rewrite rules, which are rules stating that a particular symbol may be replaced in any of its occurrences by another symbol or sequence of symbols from the alphabet specified for the system. In order to use such a grammar for natural language, we would have to fractionate the basic parts of speech, such as noun, verb, and so on into many smaller classes that express particular combinations of properties, for example a class of nouns that are singular and countable (*book*), a class of nouns that are singular and human (*man*), and so on. In terms of this large alphabet of symbols, the grammar would then consist of a very large number of seemingly unrelated (but actually similar) formulas in each area of the grammar. Such a characterization rapidly becomes unwieldy as well as opaque (Gross 1972). However, by appropriate additions to the means of specifying the grammar and to the basic parsing algorithm, an algorithm designed for artificial languages can be adapted for parsing natural language.

Assuming the appropriate enrichments can be made, there is still a question as to what strategy should be employed by the algorithm. One can first collect well-formed subparts and try to fit them together to make a well-formed whole (the strategy employed in so-called bottom-up parsing), or one can generate the set of sentence structures with a view to finding one that fits the given sentence (the strategy employed in so-called top-down parsing). Whichever parsing strategy is adopted, a major question is still the design of auxiliary mechanisms and their integration into the parsing process, since only a small part of the analytical task is accomplished by the methods of standard (context-free) parsing procedures.

In the pages to follow, the solutions to these problems as they have been developed within the framework of the Linguistic String Program system will be traced. First, the main features will be illustrated with simple examples. Then the principles of a more general solution for the full treatment of the language data will be described.

2.1.1   *The Lexicon*

The LSP lexicon is organized on a word basis. The major word classes in the LSP lexicon and grammar are N noun, NS possessive noun, PRO pronoun, ADJ adjective, Q quantifier, T article, TV tensed verb, V tenseless verb (infinitive), VING present participle, VEN past participle, W modal or tense word, D adverb, P preposition, DP particle, CS1–CS7 subordinate conjunctions. Other connectives, including *wh*-words, and coordinate and comparative conjunctions, because of their individual properties, appear in the grammar as literals. Approximately 150 subclasses of the major classes are currently recognized, of which about one-sixth are classses (such as case-marked pronouns) with a fixed number of members, hence are not used in classifying new words. About one-half of the remaining subclasses are concerned with specifying which object strings are permissible for a given verb; for example, *exist* takes no object string (written NULLOBJ), whereas *require* may occur with a noun string as its object (written NSTGO) as in . . . *requires energy*. This type of information appears in the lexical entries for verbs under the heading OBJLIST. Definitions of the major subclasses are given in Appendix 3.

The word categories of the grammar can be arranged in a hierarchical structure, with the major word classes divided into subcategories and the subcategories in turn divided into further subcategories. The lexical entry for a given word reflects this hierarchy and can be represented by a tree structure similar to the one used for the sentence parse tree. For example, a simplified lexical entry for the verb *require* might be

REQUIRE   V: (OBJLIST: (NSTGO)), TV: (OBJLIST: (NSTGO), PLURAL).

In tree form:

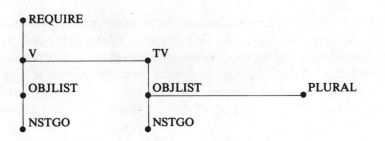

This shows that *require* is in two major classes V (infinitive, as in *to require energy*) and TV (tensed verb, as in *They require energy*). As a member of either class, *require* has the possibility of occurring with an NSTGO object (*energy* in the preceding examples). This is indicated by V and TV each having the attribute OBJLIST with value NSTGO. In addition the TV category has the attribute PLURAL (*They require . . . , Ⱥ It require . . .*). (The symbol Ⱥ preceding a word sequence indicates that the sequence is not a well-formed sentence or in some contexts not a well-formed phrase.) To avoid writing the shared attribute OBJLIST twice, we could write an equivalent dictionary entry as follows:

REQUIRE   V: .12, TV: .12, PLURAL.

.12 =   OBJLIST: (NSTGO).

Here .12 is an arbitrary number that names the location of the shared sublist.

To obtain the benefits of morphemic analysis, words with a common stem (such as *walk, walks, walking, walked*) share lists of common properties, and words with similar morphological properties are written in a standard format, or canonical form, which can be referred to by a single symbol in the lexicon; for example, the entries for *respond, require, exist*, are all written in a canonical form VTVPL for words that are multiply classified as V (infinitive), TV present PLural. A sample dictionary that uses canonical forms is shown in Fig. 2.1 along with a tree structure representation of the entry. Up-arrows in Fig. 2.1 indicate that sublists may be shared (down-arrows are quotation marks). The canonical form (VTVPL) that precedes REQUIRE is defined in the midsection of the figure. It is

(VTVPL) = V: .12, TV .12, PLURAL.

If the definition of VTVPL is substituted for its occurrence in the entry for REQUIRE (and is placed after REQUIRE) we obtain

REQUIRE   V: .12, TV: .12, PLURAL.

This is just the form needed for supplying the subclass (attribute) lists of *require* in its various forms.

2.1.2   *The Grammar*

The LSP grammar is divided into two main components to accord with a major division of the linguistic data: (1) a statement of basic sentence constructions down to the level of major word classes and (2) a statement of detailed wellformedness constraints (restrictions) as to the subclasses of words that can occur together within the same construction or in grammatically rated constructions. For our purposes the basic constructions are **linguistic strings** and the grammatical relations are adjunction and substitution. These terms were defined in

Fig. 2.1   Sample entries from the Linguistic String Project lexicon.

```
(VTVPL) REQUIRE
.12 = OBJLIST: .3, VSENT2, VSENT3.
.3  = NSTGO, VINGSTG, C1SHOULD, NTOVO, PNTHATSVO: .15
.15 = PVAL: (↓OF↓).

(TVSI) REQUIRES ↑.

(ING) REQUIRING ↑.

(TVVEN) REQUIRED ↑.
.14 = OBJLIST: .3, VSENT2, VSENT3, POBJLIST: .4.
.4  = TOVO, PN: .15, NULLOBJ.


          Canonical forms used in sample entries

(VTVPL) = V: .12, TV: .12, PLURAL.

(TVSI) = TV: .12, SINGULAR.

(ING) = VING: .12.

(TVVEN) = TV: .12, VEN: .14.
```

Tree diagram of entry for require

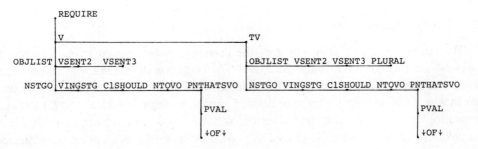

the statement of linguistic string theory in Chapter 1, but the string theory presented there covered only the first component of the grammar. There was no attempt to say which word sequences were well-formed sentences beyond the requirement that the corresponding word class sequence should conform to a sequence that could be generated from an elementary center string by the operations of adjunction and substitution. Thus, at this level of specification, T N TV"." stands equally well for well-formed sentences such as *The heart beats* and the nonsentence word sequences such as *The heart utilizes*. Yet a great part of grammatical description is concerned with just such details as whether a given verb requires an object, as does *utilize,* or whether the subject and verb in a clause agree in number (*The heart utilizes energy, Ã The heart utilize energy*). These restrictions represent a whole new level of grammatical specification.

It turns out that when the grammar is divided into the two major components, strings and restrictions, it is possible to use one of the standard parsing algorithms in conjunction with the first component to obtain the gross syntactic structure of the sentence, that is, to obtain its decomposition into component linguistic strings. When this analysis is recorded in the form of a parse tree, the restrictions can then be stated as procedures that examine the parse tree and test whether the words associated with particular nodes have certain properties required for detailed wellformedness, such as agreement in number or syntactic and semantic subclass compatibility.

To bring these two parts together, the standard parsing algorithm is equipped with a "restriction interpreter" that causes the restriction procedures to be executed on the parse tree. In addition there are several ways in which the parser interacts with the grammar so as to coordinate the two levels of wellformedness determination. With regard to parsing strategy, the LSP uses a top-down algorithm (to be explained presently), augmented by a saving mechanism that allows once-constructed subtrees to be re-used in alternative parse-tree contexts. The LSP grammar has also been formulated in a form suitable for use with a bottom-up parser (Hobbs 1974).

2.2 A Small Computable String Grammar

2.2.1 *BNF Component*

To represent the first component of the grammar in the computer, we use the BNF (Backus–Naur form) metalanguage (Backus 1960). This form of syntax specification is particularly well suited for use in context-free parsing algorithms. It consists of a set of definitions in which each syntactic type to be defined appears in angle brackets (<X>), followed by the symbol "::=", followed by its definition, followed by a period. Each definition is a sequence of one or more options separated by vertical lines, where each option is a sequence of one or more elements. An element may be a word (a literal) or a syntactic type. For some applications, such as natural language, it is convenient to have another type of element, a lexical type, written <*X>, where X is a set of words with similar syntactic properties. Thus, <*N> can represent the noun class, <*TV> the class of tensed verbs, <*T> the article class, and so on.

We can easily write the first component of the string grammar in BNF definitions. A BNF definition in a string grammar of English will consist of a sequence of elements, each of which is either a literal (an English word or mark of punctuation), or a syntactic type, such as <SUBJECT>, or else a lexical type representing a word class (also called a terminal symbol or atomic), for example, <*N> standing for noun class. The center string <SUBJECT> TV ".", which was introduced in Chapter 1, could be written as follows:

<CENTER> ::= <SUBJECT> <*TV> "." .

and the named position SUBJECT:

<SUBJECT> :: = <*T> <*N> | <FOR-TO> .

<FOR-TO>   :: = FOR <*T> <*N> TO <*V> .

These three definitions constitute a primitive BNF grammar that can be used by a top-down parsing algorithm, provided we supply a small lexicon in which major word classifications are drawn from the set N, TV, V of terminal symbols of the grammar. Words can also appear in the lexicon without classification if the grammar treats them only as literals, as are *for* and *to* in the following example lexicon; where they are not classed as prepositions but only in accord with their appearance as literals in the FOR-TO definition.

A suitable small lexicon for this primitive BNF grammar might be

the   T.

heart   N.

responded   TV.

responds   TV.

respond   V/TV.

helps   TV.

for   .

to   .

Using this small grammar and lexicon we can illustrate how a top-down parser constructs a structural representation of a sentence by describing the main steps it would take in analyzing the simple sentence *The heart responded*.

The parser first creates a node corresponding to the root definition of the grammar (here CENTER):

• CENTER

It then begins to create a sequence of nodes corresponding to the elements of the definition of CENTER. Inside the machine, nodes of the parse tree are connected by pointers (stored addresses). These are represented in the parse-tree diagram by lines connecting the nodes. The parser builds the nodes corresponding to a sequence of elements one by one, completing the subtree beneath each element node before it starts the next one. Thus, we first have:

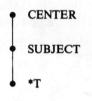

To build the subtree under SUBJECT a choice among the options in the definition of SUB-JECT must be made; the first option is tried first; other options will be tried if the parse fails to build a subtree under SUBJECT whose terminal nodes match classifications of the initial sentence words, or if alternative analyses are sought. A node corresponding to the first element of the sequence constituting the first option of SUBJECT is created:

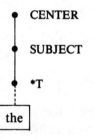

Having reached an atomic node, the name of the node (T) is compared with the classification(s) of the current sentence word; here the word is *the*, having classification T. This constitutes a match, so a pointer is created from the atomic node T to the lexical entry for *the*. Details regarding this connection need not concern us yet; we can indicate the connection by a dotted line from the atomic node to the sentence word, shown in a box. The current word now becomes *heart*, and the following parse tree appears:

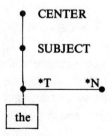

The parser must now complete the sequence <*T> <*N> in the definition of SUBJECT, so a second atomic node is created:

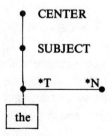

Again the atomic node is compared with the classifications of the current sentence word, and again there is a match. A pointer is created from the atomic node N to the lexical entry for *heart*:

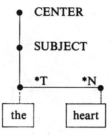

The SUBJECT node is now satisfied, so the parser begins on the next element after SUBJECT in CENTER:

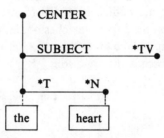

The atomic node TV matches the classification TV of *responded* and thereby satisfies the second element of CENTER. A pointer to the lexical entry for *responded* is created and the current word becomes ".":

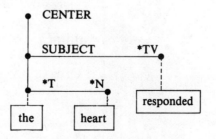

The third element of the CENTER is ".", which matches the literal ".", thereby finishing the CENTER string. The input sentence has been proved to be a center string, hence well formed, and the final parse tree is:

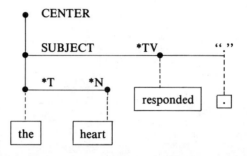

However, the job is not finished since there may be another well-formed parse tree (indicating that the sentence is ambiguous). The program begins to back up in the same way it would have done if an atomic node had failed to match a classification of the current sentence word. In backing up the parser detaches nodes in the reverse order of their creation until it finds one that corresponds to an option of a definition where the definition contains an untried option. We thus reach the situation:

CENTER

SUBJECT

and are ready to try the second option of SUBJECT, the string FOR-TO. A node corresponding to this string is built as the value of SUBJECT, and a node corresponding to the first element (FOR) for the string is constructed:

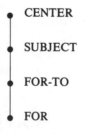

CENTER

SUBJECT

FOR-TO

FOR

At this point all the sentence words have been detached from the parse tree, so the current word is again *the*. The node whose name is the literal FOR is compared with *the*, but these are not identical, so the node FOR is detached. Since there are no more options of SUBJECT, the node SUBJECT is detached; and since there are no more options of CENTER the CENTER node is detached. The parsing process is terminated and the program prints out: NO MORE PARSES.

2.2.2   *Restriction Component*

We come now to the second component of the grammar, the restrictions. This is a good deal more complicated to explain, because the restrictions deal precisely with the features that distinguish a natural language from the far more simple artificial languages for which parsing algorithms like the one presented were designed. It was already noted that without a restriction component the two word sequences *The heart beats* and *The heart utilizes* would receive the same analysis despite the fact that the first is a well-formed sentence and the second is not. As another example, using our small BNF grammar, we would obtain the same parse tree for the two word sequences *For the heart to respond helps*, and *For the heart to help responds*, the second being hardly a sentence of English. (The first is not a very comfortable sentence of English since the object of *helps* can only be supplied by the context, but most people would accept it as a grammatical sentence and it can serve as our example.) The difficulty with the second sequence is that *respond* is not the kind of verb that occurs with a nominalized sentence like the FOR-TO string as its subject. There are a number of subclasses of verbs, nouns, and adjectives in English that have precisely this property that *respond* lacks. In the LSP grammar these have the form VSENTn, NSENTn, ASENTn, where n is a digit. Let us use VSENT1 temporarily to stand for all verbs that can take a nominalized sentence as their subject. The verb *help* is in this subclass, but the verb *respond* is not.

The intent in formulating a restriction for the computer grammar is thus to distinguish between two parse trees that are identical except for properties of the particular words associated with atomic nodes of the parse tree. For example, we want to accept the parse tree corresponding to *For the heart to respond helps* shown in Fig. 2.2 and reject the parse tree corresponding to *For the heart to help responds* shown in Fig. 2.3. In our small grammar the only difference in this case is that the lexical entry for *helps* contains the subclass VSENT1, whereas the entry for *responds* does not. This difference is illustrated in the parse tree of Fig. 2.2 by drawing a line from the atomic node *TV associated with *helps* to the subcategory VSENT1 of the TV category of *helps*. This line represents a real connection made by the parser between the parse tree and lexical entries. Each lexical entry is a treelike structure. When in the course of building a parse tree for a sentence the parser matches an atomic node in the parse tree with a major category of the current sentence word, the parser creates a pointer from the atomic node to the subcategory tree of the matching category in the word's lexical entry. This, in effect, makes the subcategory tree in the lexicon into a subtree of the atomic node in the parse tree. The parser can then test the parse tree for the presence of particular attributes of the words associated with the terminal nodes of the parse tree.

Fig. 2.2 Accepted parse tree.

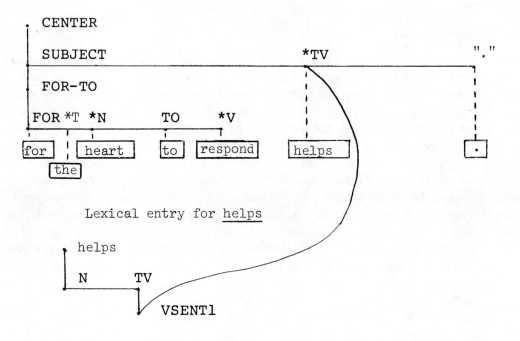

Lexical entry for <u>helps</u>

Fig. 2.3 Rejected parse tree.

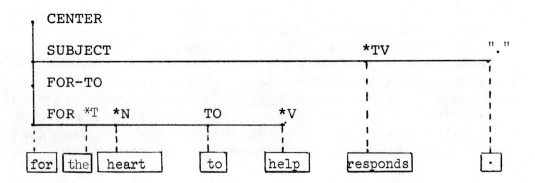

We can now develop a simple restriction that will accept the parse tree of Fig. 2.2 and reject the parse tree of Fig. 2.3. This restriction will illustrate in an elementary way how grammatical rules are turned into operations on the parse tree (a description of the actual restriction apparatus follows in Secs. 2.4 and 2.5 and in Chapter 3). A fairly general statement of the grammatical constraint in this restriction is: If the subject is a nominalized sentence, then the verb is of the type that accepts a nominalized sentence as subject. A statement of this constraint as it applies specifically to the parse trees in Figs. 2.2 and 2.3 is: In the CENTER string, if the value of the SUBJECT is FOR-TO, then TV has the attribute VSENT1.

The restriction is to be a procedure, that is, a sequence of operations that can be executed on the parse tree. We assume that the parsing algorithm has been equipped with a restriction interpreter that can recognize that certain sequences of characters stand for particular operations, and on recognizing such a sequence can cause the operations to be executed. A minimal set of several types of operations will suffice for the simple restriction:

1. Tree-climbing operations: UP, DOWN, LEFT, RIGHT, for locating the nodes that are to be tested. We assume the restriction interpreter is equipped with a pointer that can be moved by the tree-climbing operations. We refer to these operations informally by saying "We are now at . . ." or "The program now moves to . . ." or the like. If the operation can be executed, success is indicated by recording " + ", if not, by recording " − ".
2. Node-testing operations: TEST FOR **N**, TEST FOR ATTRIBUTE **A**, where N is a variable ranging over node names and A is a variable ranging over attributes of atomic nodes. The node test returns a value " + " if the current node has the name N; otherwise it returns " − ". The attribute test returns " + " if the program finds the attribute A associated with the atomic node; otherwise it returns " − ".
3. Logical operators, IF p THEN q, where p and q are any sequence of one or more operations or logical operators. (Sequences of more than one operation or operator should be enclosed in parentheses and the individual operations or operators separated by semicolons.) The sequence returns a value " + " if every part of the sequence returned " + "; otherwise the value is " − ". The test IF p THEN q returns " + " unless p returns " + " and q returns " − ". The test q begins at the same node as the test p. (The other logical operators AND, OR, NOT, need not be defined for this restriction.)

We can now write our restriction in a computable form. Let us call it WELLFORMED SENTENCE NOMINALIZATION, or simply WSN for short, and assume that it will be executed starting at the node CENTER as soon as a subtree for CENTER has been completed:

WSN = IF (DOWN; DOWN; TEST FOR FOR-TO)
          THEN (DOWN; RIGHT; TEST FOR ATTRIBUTE VSENT1).

If the final result of executing a restriction on a parse tree is a returned value " + ", then the restriction succeeds and the parse tree is accepted. However, if the final returned value is " − ", the restriction fails and the parse tree is rejected. Executed on the parse tree of Fig. 2.2 the restriction succeeds and the parse tree is accepted. Executed on the parse tree of Fig. 2.3, the restriction fails and the parse tree is rejected.

2.3   A Small Grammar vs. a Large Grammar

How does the actual LSP grammar, which is intended for use in computerized text analysis, differ from the small illustrative grammar just described? In principal, only in magnitude. The large LSP grammar has a BNF component consisting of 180 definitions (exclusive of conjunctional strings) as opposed to the 3 definitions in the BNF component of the illustrative grammar. The restriction component of the large LSP grammar has about 180 restrictions, in contrast with the lone WSN restriction in the illustrative grammar, but here the contrast is not so much in the number of restrictions as in their size and complexity. For example, the WSN restriction in the large grammar (WSN1), which corresponds in linguistic intent to the foregoing illustrative WSN restriction, must cover many additional occurrences similar to the one handled by the WSN restriction. The following list presents just a few of these additions.

1.   Other sentence nominalization strings besides FOR-TO are subject to a similiar restriction; consider *That she is here surprises them,* ≠ *That she is here surrounds them, Whether life exists on other planets intrigues them,* ≠ *Whether life exists on other planets impedes them.*

2.   Not only verbs are restricted (consider *surprises* versus *surrounds*) but also predicates: *That she is here is true,* ≠ *That she is here is blue.* The predicates may be adjectives, as in the preceding example sentence; adjectival *Ving* (*Whether life exists on other planets is intriguing,* ≠ *Whether life exists on other planets is believing*); predicate nouns (*That she is here is a fact,* ≠ *That she is here is a tract*); or prepositional phrases (*That they replicate is of interest,* ≠ *That they replicate is of imprint*).

3.   Not all verbs or predicates that occur with one sentence nominalization string occur with others; ≠ *Whether life exists on other planets surprises them.*

4.   The same restriction applies in strings other than ASSERTION, where the exact form or the order of the subject, verb, and object elements differs from that in ASSERTION; an example, though rare, is the following: *Is whether life exists on other planets of scientific interest only?*

5.   Some verbs in the passive voice take sentence nominalizations as subject: *That they replicate is known.* This construction must be distinguished from other constructions and from occurrences of the same verb in the active voice: ≠ *That they replicate knows* . . . .

6.   The restriction should apply to subject-verb and subject-predicate pairs even if the subject is separated from the relevant verb or predicate by intervening verbs and

predicates: *That they replicate is apt to be considered of lesser interest and is less well known.*

7. The restriction should also apply to those *wh*-strings in which the implicit subject of the verb or predicate within the *wh*-string is (or would be) a nominalized sentence: *They replicate rapidly, which is considered surprising.*

When all of these additions are incorporated into one restriction, the result is a considerable body of code. The grammar writer who tries to write this restriction as a sequence of tree-climbing operations (UP, DOWN, LEFT, RIGHT), node-testing operations, and logical operators of the types defined for the illustrative restriction faces a formidable task. Aside from the length of the restriction, the tediousness of the task, and the numerous opportunities for error, the grammar writer will be frustrated by the fact that so many parts of the restriction are similar to each other or to parts of other restrictions. Particularly is this true of the portions of the restriction that locate particular nodes. The path to a predicate noun will be slightly different from the path to a predicate adjective; the position of the subject with respect to the verb or predicate in a QUESTION will be slightly different from that in an ASSERTION, and so on. When the entire restriction is finally written and debugged, the writer of the restriction may with justification be pleased, but others will with equal justification be overwhelmed by the prospect of modifying or changing such restrictions, as they inevitably must as long as the grammar is evolving. Even if the grammar is "perfect" and "complete," which obviously is impossible, it is still only a stage in a longer process. Therefore, it should not be inaccessible as later stages are developed. All this leads the grammar writer to seek generalizations that will organize the large body of code represented by the restrictions into more convenient, reusable subparts. This situation is well known to programmers and invites the use of parameterized subroutines and functions in place of stretches of similar code. As far as possible linguistic restrictions should similarly be composed of high-level units of code, each covering a number of situations with common features.

The evolution of the LSP grammar reflects this process. Earlier versions had more detailed coding of the restrictions. Once the computer grammar was implemented and tested, it was possible to survey the resulting grammar in order to propose generalizations for reducing the amount of hand-coding. In this endeavor the members of the Linguistic String Project worked from "both ends"—from theory, because we knew the essential relations of string grammar, and from practice, because we had before us a computer grammar that had already been found adequate for parsing texts. The latter served as a control and a source of additional ideas in planning the generalized operations. The result was a higher-level language, particularly suited for writing computer grammars with restrictions.

The next two sections will be devoted to describing the generalizations that were introduced into the LSP grammar in order to make this labor-saving innovation possible. The result is also intended to make restrictions more readable and easier to modify.

2.4   Types of Definitions

The simple BNF grammar and restriction presented in Sec. 2.2 sufficed to illustrate in principle how the two components of the computer grammar are used to arrive at a correct grammatical analysis of a sentence. But the division of the linguistic data into these two components does not by itself solve the problem of how to represent a large grammar succinctly and effectively. For this we need a two-level specification of the grammar, but first we must introduce some notational conventions that regularize the syntax in the BNF component. Although their use would appear to be only a matter of convenience, their effect is to make possible the definition of a powerful metalanguage for writing the rest of the grammar. It will be shown that this two-step approach achieves a very great simplification and reduction of the grammar. In place of thousands of rules that would be required without such a generalization we have a few hundred rules that suffice for the analysis of complicated text sentences.

BNF definitions are divided into different types depending on their role in the string grammar. The three main types are STRING definitions, ADJSET (**adjunct set**) definitions, and LXR definitions, illustrated in Fig. 2.4 by definitions from the BNF component of the LSP grammar. Unfamiliar symbols in the figure will be explained later. For now we are concerned mainly with the form of the definitions. STRING definitions have a single option consisting of a sequence of elements. Some of these elements, like SUBJECT, TENSE, VERB, and OBJECT in ASSERTION are "required," in the sense that they must subsume sentence words except under stated conditions. The other elements of STRING definitions are of the type ADJSET. ADJSET definitions have several options, which are the names of string definitions or sets of string definitions. Every ADJSET definition contains a NULL option, which when attached to the parse tree is automatically satisfied without subsuming any sentence words. This NULL option represents the fact that the strings named in ADJSET definitions are optional additions to the sentence. (In definitions of the *R type, such as <SA> *R in Fig. 2.4, the NULL option is added during compiling, as will be explained.) The two types of definitions STRING and ADJSET correspond to the **linguistic strings** and **adjunct sets** introduced in Sec. 1.3.

ADJSET definitions include the ubiquitous sentence adjunct set SA and all the left and right adjunct sets of the grammar. The latter are collected into two ADJSET subtypes LX and RX, where X stands for a major word class, such as N, V, TV. The left and right adjunct sets are introduced into the grammar in a regular way by means of definitions of the LXR type. Everywhere that a given word class X can appear in the grammar we place a reference to the corresponding LXR definition in place of X. The form of these definitions is

<LXR> ::= <LX> <*X> <RX>.

<LX>   ::= <OPTION>|<OPTION>|. . .|<OPTION>|NULL.

<RX>   ::= <OPTION>|<OPTION>|. . .|<OPTION>|NULL.

Fig. 2.4   Types of definitions in the BNF component of the grammar.

TYPE STRING

        <ASSERTION> ::= <SA><SUBJECT><SA><TENSE><SA><VERB>

                    <SA><OBJECT><RV><SA>.

TYPE ADJSET

        <SA>*R ::= <*INT>|<DSTG><RD>|<PN>|<PA>|<NSTGT>|

                <PSUBJ>|<RNSUBJ>|<LCS><CSSTG>|

                -<OBJBESA>|-<SOBJBESA>|<VINGO>|<VENPASS>|

                <SAWH>|<TOVO>|<NVSA>.

        <LV> ::= NULL|<DSTG>.

        <RV>*R ::=<DSTG><RD>|<PN>|<QN>|<SN>.

TYPE LXR

        <LVINGR> ::= <LV><*VING><RV>.

Here, each option in an LX/RX definition stands for a possible left/right adjunct of X, and NULL represents the fact that X may occur without adjuncts. For example, LVINGR in Fig. 2.4 stands for a verb in V*ing* form with optional left and right adjuncts of the verb (*driving, just driving at a normal pace*). This manner of introducing left and right adjunction greatly simplifies the complex calculations required by restrictions and conjunctions, as will be seen in later chapters.

    In some cases, in place of an <*X> in an LXR definition we have an element of the type <XVAR>, whose values include <*X> and usually at least one other ATOMIC type node. XVAR represents local variants of X, like a compound adjective in place of a simple adjective.

    To represent the fact that the operation of adjunction is repeatable for some adjunct sets, we introduce a special notation into the way of writing BNF definitions. The adjoining of a sentence adjunct, for example, is a repeatable operation, as in *However, since yesterday it has been raining,* where *however* and *since yesterday* are both sentence adjuncts; also the right adjuncts of N are repeatable, as in *the man from Stockholm who was invited.* In defining a repeatable adjunct set Y, the grammar writer writes a definition of the form:

<Y> *R ::= <OPTION>|<OPTION>|...|<OPTION>.

in which no NULL option is included. When the grammar is compiled—that is, translated into a form more suitable for the machine—this definition is replaced by three definitions of the following form:

<Y>   ::= <Y1> <Y2>| NULL.

<Y1>   ::= <OPTION>|<OPTION>|...|<OPTION>.

<Y2>   ::= NULL |^v <Y1>|<Y2>.

These recursive definitions are only a computational device; the linguistic relation is one of repeated adjunction on the same host. Here the symbol ^{v} stands for a restriction that requires that a particular switch be on before the second option of Y2 can be used. This switch is called the REPETITION (or REP) switch and controls whether repetition of adjunction is to be accepted. More will be said later about the use of switches in the grammar.

2.5   Locating Relations[1]

The reader may well wonder at this point what is gained by this additional level of abstraction. Not only do we have a classification of the linguistic data represented by the grammar itself, but we have introduced a classification of the grammatical classifications, almost as though we intended to write a grammar of the grammar. And indeed that is precisely our intention. When operations on the parse tree can be defined in terms of **types of definitions** instead of individually named definitions, we obtain a powerful language for linguistic computation.

In general, the problem of natural language computation is not so much one of formally stating grammatical constraints as of locating the arguments of the constraints in any sentence in which they apply. The solution here is to define a small set of "locating relations" such that if any two words in a sentence have any grammatical constraint operating between them, they will be related by one of the locating relations or a particular product of them. The locating relations are then implemented as routines of the grammar, and restriction tests are written in terms of these higher-level routines instead of individual tree-climbing operations.

The locating relations are defined in terms of the types of definitions noted previously, and the type ATOMIC (terminal symbol of the tree, which corresponds to a major word class) of the BNF grammar. Their computable form can thus be stated as operations on types of tree nodes, referred to a generalized tree module. The generalized tree module (Fig. 2.5) has as its root a node of type STRING, and extends down each branch to the first node, which is either of type ATOMIC or of type STRING. The bounding string nodes are each the root of a similar module. The parse tree for any given sentence is composed entirely of such modules.

Fig. 2.5 Parse tree module.

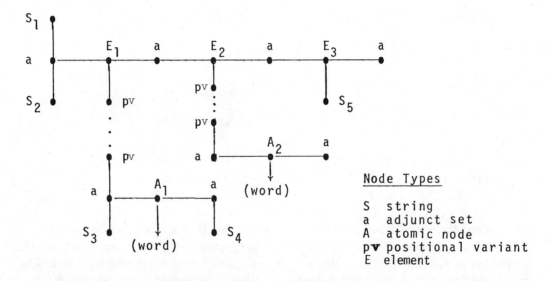

The essential locating relations[2] are listed in Table 2.1, where they are illustrated by statements applying to the tree module of Fig. 2.5. The string node that is the root node of the module is the **immediate string** of all the other nodes in the module. Basic to all string analysis is the notion of an **element** of a string. The daughter nodes of any node of type STRING are defined to be the elements of that string, and **coelements** of each other.[3] An extension to this definition is made for the case where a string occurs as an element of another string, as does ASSERTION in the definition of THATS or WHS−N. In this case, the included string (such as ASSERTION) is said to be occuring as a **string segment**. All such strings are on the list TYPE STGSEG. When they are so occurring their elements are considered to be elements of the including string as well. Thus, in Fig. 1.2, the SUBJECT node (*the isolated heart*) is by definition an element of ASSERTION, and because this ASSERTION occurs as a string segment in WHS−N, SUBJECT is also, by the extended definition of the element relation, an element of WHS−N.[4]

In the full BNF English grammar, elements of a string definition are rarely individual words or lexical types, but, rather, nodes of the positional variant type since the various ways

Table 2.1

Locating Relations

Locating Relations	Example in Fig. 2.5
IMMEDIATE STRING	S_1 is the immediate string of every node (except S_1) in the module of Fig. 2.5
ELEMENT	S_1 has element E_1 (also E_2, E_3) E_1 is element of S_1
COELEMENT	E_1 has coelement E_2,E_3
CORE	E_1 has core A_1 E_3 has core S_5
LEFT ADJUNCT	A_1 has left adjunct S_3
RIGHT ADJUNCT	A_1 has right adjunct S_4
HOST STRING	S_1 is the host string of S_2
HOST	A_1 is the host of S_3,S_4

of satisfying the same element position in similar strings have been collected into one definition, such as SUBJECT. However, grammatical and semantic constraints apply not to constructs but to words in a sentence that are in a particular grammatical relation. This means that in addition to the relation "element of a string," defined as the daughter node of a STRING type node, it is important to keep track of the word or word-string that satisfies the element in the sentence. This correspondence is expressed by the **core** relation. The precise definition is that the core of a node α (α any type of node except STRING, ATOMIC, or WORD) is the unique node of type ATOMIC or of type STRING in the subtree below α that is not below a node of type ADJSET in that subtree or is not LN.[5]

Figure 2.6 can be used to illustrate the locating relations. The node ASSERTION, which is of type STRING, has elements: SUBJECT, TENSE, VERB, OBJECT, RV and one SA[3]. The core of the node SUBECT (and below SUBJECT, of NSTG and LNR) is the atomic node *N (the noun *medium*). The core of the VERB is *TV (the tensed verb *contains*), and the core of the node OBJECT (and below OBJECT of NSTGO, NSTG, and LNR) is *N (the noun *calcium*). The cores of the other elements of ASSERTION are each the atomic node *NULL, not shown in Fig. 2.6. Note that words corresponding to the successive core nodes of the nonadjunct elements of the ASSERTION string form an elementary "telegraphic" sentence (*medium contains calcium*), which conveys the rudimentary information in the sentence. This is important in later applications of the analysis.

Fig. 2.6   Parse tree illustrating locating relations.

```
THE MEDIUM WHICH SURROUNDS THE HEART UNDOUBTEDLY CONTAINS CALCIUM .
* PARSE TREE
```

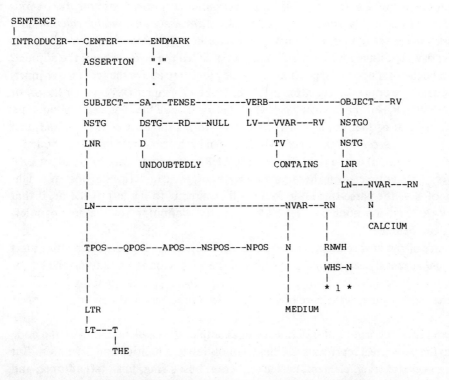

```
THE MEDIUM WHICH SURROUNDS THE HEART UNDOUBTEDLY CONTAINS CALCIUM .
* PARSE TREE (CONTINUATION)
```

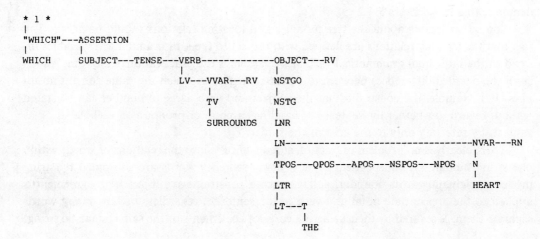

While element, coelement, and core concern the elements within a single linguistic string, constraints also apply among words in two different elementary strings. The most common relation between the two strings is that of host–adjunct: One string is a sentence adjunct of the other string or is the adjunct of a particular word in the other string. For example, in the sentence of Fig. 2.6 *The medium which surrounds the heart undoubtedly contains calcium, undoubtedly* is an adverbial sentence adjunct of *the medium contains calcium,* and *which surrounds the heart* is a right adjunct of *medium* in *the medium contains calcium.*

The string that is adjoined by a sentence adjunct is called the **host string** of the adjunct. It is defined to be the first node of type STRING in the parse tree above the sentence adjunct. In Fig. 2.6 the sentence adjunct is the atomic *D (*undoubtedly*) under DSTG under the SA of ASSERTION. ASSERTION is the host-string of D. An atomic node that has a left or right adjunct is called the **host** of that adjunct. Thus *N (*medium*) is the host of the right adjunct string WHS – N (*which surrounds the heart*), which is seen in the parse tree under the node RN (right adjuncts of the noun) to the right of NVAR in LNR. Since by the use of standard LXR definitions every right adjunct string lies under an RX node, we can define the host of a right adjunct string of X as the parse-tree node found either directly to the left of RX or, if that node is an XVAR, then one node below XVAR. A similar definition for the host of a left adjunct string can be made.

The converse of the host relations for left and right adjunct strings are the relations **left adjunct** and **right adjunct**. Seen from the position of the atomic node *X that has the left or right adjunct, the left adjunct is the core of the LX node that is just to the left of *X (or of XVAR), and the right adjunct is the core of the RX node, found just to the right of *X (or of XVAR).

Other useful relations can be also defined. For example, the **value** of a node α (the node just below α in the parse tree) represents the choice of option in a multioption definition. But the relations **immediate string, element, coelement, core, host string, host, left adjunct,** and **right adjunct** are the essential relations in the metalanguage for string grammar; they make possible a concise computable statement of a wide variety of linguistic constraints, as will be demonstrated in Chapters 5–7.

Some final points about the tree modules and locating relations should be noted. The fact that the locating relations are defined with respect to types of grammatical variables instead of the individual grammatical variables overcomes the practical difficulty that results from the detailed differences between different sentences in which the same constraint applies. For example, the constraint that the subject and verb agree in number can be stated without regard to whether the sentence at hand has a noun or pronoun or a whole string as subject, by referring only to the core of the subject.

There clearly is no problem of "action at a distance" since the relations of words within one string module are independent of how many sentence words are subsumed by string modules originating at its boundaries. That such a constraint as subject–verb agreement is applied to the appropriate noun and verb in the sentence, regardless of how many words separate them, is assured by their being the cores of coelements of the same linguistic string.

An additional important fact for computation is that except for a few cases (treated by extended scope routines, described in Chapter 3), grammatical constraints operate within one module or two adjacent modules related by adjunction. This means that constraints are largely local.

It should be noted finally that the locating relations are not a device that just happens to work. The amount of detail in natural language description is so great that to be effective a method for computing language structure must reflect the relevant properties of language itself. In this case the tree module and the locating relations are based on a fundamental property of language. Since there is no a priori distance defined for natural language (analogous to bars and rests in music), it follows that if language can have a constructive grammar then there must exist some characterization of the well-formed sentences that is based on purely contiguous relations (Harris 1968). In this characterization, all grammatical events can be stated as occurring between particular elements at a point in the constructive history, or derivation, of the sentence when these elements are adjacent. Linguistic strings are units of syntactic description for which this property of contiguity of operation holds. Inside the string the contiguity results from placing element next to element. Among strings, the contiguity results from adjoining a string to the left or right or at an interior point of a host string. Since the tree modules represent linguistic strings, they preserve the property of contiguity of operations.

2.6 Locating Routines

It is probably already clear to the reader that the locating relations among node types described in the preceding section can be quite readily translated into procedures to be executed on the parse tree. We call such procedures locating routines. By introducing locating routines into the grammar we have the following result: When a restriction must test a node that has the relation right adjunct, or core, or host, or any of the other defined relations to the given node, instead of writing out the instructions for locating that node, the restriction writer simply writes the name of the appropriate linguistic relation. Then when the restriction is being executed, the restriction interpreter turns to the routine of that name and executes the instructions that locate the desired node.

The brevity that is achieved in the grammar in using the locating routines will be appreciated when it is noted that in the present LSP English grammar there are on the order of 1,000 calls on the small set of locating routines, and each routine represents a sizeable body of code. The greatest gain, however, is in the power of expression for linguistic computations. Consider the hypothesis that if any two words W_1, W_2 in a sentence have a grammatical relation to each other, then in a string parse of the sentence, W_2 can be reached from W_1 by executing a basic locating routine or a sequence of such routines. In other words, this small set of routines suffices to express the parse-tree relations of linguistic interest in the analysis of sentences. It will be seen, for example, in the chapter on transformations that the same locating routines used in the restrictions can be used to identify the component parts of transformational resultants so that the transformations can then be reversed.

Several of the locating routines take arguments; for example, the coelement routine must be supplied the name of a node so that the routine knows at which element to stop when scanning across sibling nodes. Thus, one writes COELEMENT VERB, for example, to arrive at the node VERB from, say, the SUBJECT or OBJECT node of an ASSERTION string. The same is true for the ELEMENT routine; one would write ELEMENT SUBJECT to go from the ASSERTION node to the SUBJECT node. The power of routines is greatly extended by allowing routines to be arguments of routines. The most common occurrence of this kind in restrictions is used to obtain the core of an element which is itself located by a routine. Thus, one might write CORE OF COELEMENT VERB if the intention was, when starting at, say, the SUBJECT in ASSERTION, to reach the atomic node that satisfied the VERB element in the ASSERTION string. This is used in the subject–verb agreement restriction, for example. Note that we have adopted English syntax to state the argument of a routine; in CORE OF COELE-MENT VERB, the part following OF is the first routine to be executed; when this part has been successfully executed, the CORE routine is executed starting at the node that was reached by executing the first routine (COELEMENT VERB). As in English, OF-phrases can be strung out for as long as needed.

2.7   A Formal Metalanguage

The last step in the development of an appropriate tool for specifying the syntax of a natural language is to ''put it all together'' in the form of a programming language. Such a language will, it is hoped, make the task of writing a computer grammar less formidable. Using it we should be able to define new structures, routines, and restrictions as needed, with a minimum of effort devoted to translating ideas into code. Drawing on our own experience we at the LSP concluded that BNF is a most suitable form for defining syntactic construc-tions, that procedural statements are perhaps the best way to define routines, and that English declarative syntax is the most comfortable vehicle for expressing restrictions on the parse tree. Our version of the appropriate tool is then a programming language, called the Restriction Language, which provides all three modes of expression.

The English syntax incorporated into the Restriction Language is based on a simple sub-ject–predicate statement form in which the subject has the function of locating a node in the parse tree to which some test is to be applied, and the predicate states the test to be made. The locating of the proper node by the restriction subject is done by invoking locating routines. Logical combinations of statements are also expressed in English syntax, using the implicit parenthesization provided by the English word pairs BOTH-AND, EITHER-OR, IF-THEN, and other expressions.

A full description of the Restriction Language will follow in Chapter 3. For now, the use of the language for writing restrictions can be illustrated by showing one way in which the simple WSN restriction of Section 2.2 could be written in a general form, using the Restriction Language:

WSN = IN ASSERTION:
                   IF THE VALUE OF THE ELEMENT SUBJECT IS SN,
                   THEN THE CORE OF THE ELEMENT VERB HAS ATTRIBUTE VSENT1
                        OR VSENT2 OR VSENT3.

Fig. 2.7   Parse tree tested by restriction WSN.

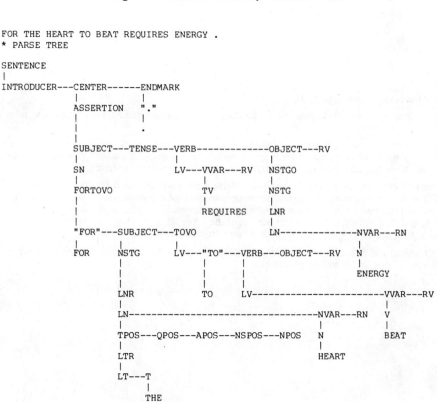

```
FOR THE HEART TO BEAT REQUIRES ENERGY .
* PARSE TREE

SENTENCE
|
INTRODUCER---CENTER------ENDMARK
            |          |
            ASSERTION   "."
            |          |
            |           .
            |
            SUBJECT---TENSE---VERB------------OBJECT---RV
            |                 |              |
            SN                LV---VVAR---RV NSTGO
            |                      |        |
            FORTOVO                TV       NSTG
            |                      |        |
            |                      REQUIRES LNR
            |                               |
            "FOR"---SUBJECT---TOVO          LN------------NVAR---RN
            |       |         |             |                    |
            FOR     NSTG      LV---"TO"---VERB---OBJECT---RV   N
                    |         |      |       |         |
                    |         |      |       |         |       ENERGY
                    |         |      |       |         |
                    LNR       TO     LV--------------------------VVAR---RV
                    |                                            |
                    LN--------------------------------NVAR---RN  V
                    |                                 |          |
                    TPOS---QPOS---APOS---NSPOS---NPOS N          BEAT
                    |                                 |
                    LTR                               HEART
                    |
                    LT---T
                         |
                         THE
```

(SN is the set of sentence nominalization strings in the grammar (definition 5.11 in Appendix 1). VSENT1, VSENT2, and VSENT3 are the verb subclasses (defined in Appendix 3), which can occur with SN subject. See Fig. 3.1 and discussion for extension to cases of embedding.) This restriction would be executed beginning at the ASSERTION node of a string parse tree. In executing restrictions the convention is that if there are two statements under a logical operator (for example, IF p THEN q) then the execution of the second statement begins at the same node of the parse tree as the execution of the first statement. The foregoing WSN restriction can be executed with correct results on any subtree originating at ASSERTION. If executed on the parse tree of Fig. 2.7 it will succeed for the reason that the core of the VERB in ASSERTION does indeed have one of the required attributes (VSENT2). If executed on the parse tree of Fig. 2.6 the restriction will succeed trivially since the premise is false. Note that the computable source form of the WSN restriction written in Restriction Language is very close to the general, informal, statement of the grammatical constraint with which the discussion of this restriction was introduced in Sec. 2.2. The burden of translating the brief English statement of the grammatical constraint into a fairly substantial body of tree-climbing and testing operations has been shifted from the grammar writer to the Restriction Language compiler.

NOTES

1. This section is based upon Sager 1972a.

2. All restrictions could be written using only the locating relations called essential. For convenience, other locating relations have been defined.

3. This definition makes SA an element of ASSERTION contrary to the spirit of string grammar, where adjunct sets are optional insertions and the string elements are all nonoptional. Computational simplicity is gained by adjusting the definitions of the locating relations to the particular representation of the grammar.

4. An extension of the definitions of element and coelement has also been made for the case where a string definition contains an element consisting of a disjunction of options enclosed in parentheses. In the parse tree, the chosen option is treated as an element of the linguistic string, and as a coelement of all other elements of the linguistic string. Thus in Fig. 1.3, the literal WHICH is shown as an element of the string WSN – N, though in the definition of WHS – N (definition 15.3 in Appendix 1) WHICH is an option of an unnamed parenthesized element.

5. The left adjuncts of N are ordered, hence stringlike in this property. LN is therefore on the TYPE STRING list but should not be taken as the core of an element.

Chapter 3 The Restriction Language[1]

The Restriction Language (RL) was introduced in order to provide a programming language especially suited for specifying a large grammar of a natural language. A compiler for the language is presently operative on the Control Data 6600 and functions as part of the most recent implementation of the LSP system for parsing English scientific texts. It will be recalled from the previous chapter that the LSP grammar has two principal components: a BNF (or context-free) grammar and a set of restrictions. The context-free grammar associates with each input sentence a set (possibly empty) of parse trees. The restrictions state conditions on a parse tree that must be met in order for the tree to be accepted as a correct analysis of the input sentence. The restrictions are used to express detailed wellformedness constraints that are not conveniently statable in the context-free component. These may be contextual constraints on the linking of different subtrees or may involve attributes of the particular lexical items that are associated with terminal symbols of the parse tree.

The language is a generalization of procedures that proved effective in the first two implementations of the parsing system. In these implementations the entire grammar (context-free definitions, restrictions, and word dictionary) was written in a uniform list-structure format that was easy to convert to internal list structure but imposed a considerable burden on the grammar writer with regard to the size and form of the grammar. This was particularly true of the restriction component, which ran to thousands of lines and was not easy to read or to modify. A principal aim in the most recent implementation, therefore, was to develop a higher level language especially suitable for writing restrictions. A simple example of a restriction was shown in the previous chapter, illustrating in a small way the expressive power of the language. Here, the basic constructions of the language and some of its special features are introduced so that the syntax and semantics of the restrictions of the full English grammar can be understood.

3.1   Types of Restrictions

Before going on to the syntax of restriction statements it is necessary to know how restrictions are identified and how their execution is invoked. These two questions are related. It was noted earlier that the parsing program tries to eliminate incorrect analyses of a sentence as early in the parsing process as possible. This applies to the execution of restrictions as well as to the building of the parse tree. Some restrictions can be formulated so that they examine only positions in the parse tree that lie above or to the left of a node about to be constructed. This is true of restrictions that govern the selection of particular ADJSET options depending on certain properties of the host or host-string. It is also true of such constructions as the "it" form of sentences (*It requires energy for the heart to beat*), where the subject must be *it* before an SN string can be accepted in the predicate. This condition can be checked before embarking on the rather lengthy procedure of trying to build an SN string. Restrictions that can be executed before any elements of the definition have been attached to the tree are called DISQUALIFY restrictions and are signaled by the prefix D in the restriction name; in the full grammar for example, DSN2 is the restriction that controls the acceptance of an SN string in the predicate. By contrast, restrictions that "look down" into the parse tree, which cannot be executed until some element of the definition is completed, are called WELLFORMEDNESS restrictions, and receive the prefix W. The example WSN restriction in Sec. 2.7 is of this type. An acceptable name for this restriction name is WSN or WSN-TEST or any sequence of alphanumeric characters (up to twenty characters) beginning with a W.

In general, we wish to execute a given restriction as soon as the parts of the parse tree that are examined by the restriction have been constructed. For example, if a restriction concerns only the subtree under SUBJECT, then in building the parse tree for ASSERTION, the restriction should be executed as soon as the subtree under SUBJECT is built; there would be no point in trying to build subtrees corresponding to the remaining elements of ASSERTION if the whole ASSERTION parse tree may be discarded because a local constraint on the SUBJECT was not satisfied. We state at which node a given restriction is to be executed by writing the name of the node preceded by IN and followed by a colon at the beginning of the restriction:

IN SUBJECT :

This portion of the restriction is called the HOUSING and stretches from the equals sign through the colon, as was seen in the SN restriction developed in the last chapter:[2]

WSN = IN ASSERTION: IF THE VALUE OF THE ELEMENT SUBJECT IS SN,
                    THEN THE CORE OF THE ELEMENT VERB HAS ATTRIBUTE
                    VSENT1 OR VSENT2 OR VSENT3.

The same restriction can be housed in several BNF definitions by listing the definitions, separated by commas, before the colon. The housing may also specify after what element or option of a definition the restriction should be executed. For example we can improve the efficiency of the WSN restriction above by having it executed after the VERB subtree is completed, since no further elements of ASSERTION are examined by the restriction. The housing in this case would be:

IN ASSERTION AFTER VERB:

In the case of a DISQUALIFY restriction we can single out the particular option affected by writing a housing of the form

IN definition RE option:

3.2   Principal Constructions of the Restriction Language

The chief form of statement in the Restriction Language is a declarative sentence consisting of a subject and a predicate. The subject and predicate can take various forms. Statements may be combined with logical connectives, and register references and assignments can be inserted in statements. Some statement forms do not fit the subject–predicate mold, such as the imperative forms used in the routines.

3.2.1   *The Subject of an RL Statement*

The subject of a Restriction Language statement generally locates a node, attribute, or sentence word that is then tested by the predicate. Since the routines carry the burden of locating nodes in the parse tree, the routine invocation is the most frequently used type of subject. If a routine has no argument, it is invoked by simply writing its name:

CORE

If a routine takes an argument, the argument is written immediately after the routine name:

COELEMENT VERB

If a node name appears alone, without any routine name:

SUBJECT

the routine called STARTAT is invoked with the node name as argument. STARTAT examines the current node and the nodes one level below the current node for the node name given as argument. For example, in the foregoing WSN restriction, ELEMENT SUBJECT and ELEMENT VERB can be replaced, respectively, by SUBJECT and VERB:

WSN-ALT1 = IN ASSERTION: IF THE VALUE OF THE SUBJECT IS SN,
                          THEN THE CORE OF THE VERB HAS ATTRIBUTE
                          VSENT1 OR VSENT2 OR VSENT3.

Here the STARTAT routine does the work of the ELEMENT routine in the former version.

Frequently more than one routine must be executed to get from the starting point to the node to be tested. As was shown previously, this can be accomplished by combining several routine calls with the word OF. For example,

CORE OF THE COELEMENT VERB OF SUBJECT

would first execute STARTAT with argument SUBJECT, then it would execute COELEMENT with argument VERB (which would begin where STARTAT finished) and finally it would execute CORE (which would begin at VERB, where COELEMENT VERB finished). If any routine invoked by a statement fails, execution of the entire statement is immediately terminated with a failure indication. Operations are also provided for locating a word in the sentence, such as the first or last word subsumed by a node or the current word that is to be matched in the parsing process.

3.2.2   *The Predicate of an RL Statement*

The predicate tests whether the entity located by the subject of the RL statement has a particular property. The chief types of tests that can be made are the following:

1.   Test of node name. One can test if the node that was located has a certain name by using the IS predicate:

VALUE OF SUBJECT IS SN.

Any set of node names can be defined as a **type** of node. One can then test whether the name of the current node is in a given set by using the IS OF TYPE predicate:

PRESENT-ELEMENT IS OF TYPE ADJSET.

2.   Test for attribute. To test if an atomic node or an attribute has a particular attribute, the HAS ATTRIBUTE predicate can be used:

CORE OF VERB HAS ATTRIBUTE PLURAL.

Alternatively, an IS predicate can be used:

CORE OF VERB IS PLURAL.

It is frequently necessary to test both the name of an atomic node and one of its attributes, or an attribute and one of the attributes of the attribute. Such conditions can be expressed succinctly by following the atomic node name or attribute by a colon (read ''which has attribute'') and the second attribute[3]:

CORE OF OBJECT IS N:PLURAL.
CORE OF OBJECT HAS ATTRIBUTE ASENT1:AFORTO.

3. Test for name of word. The IS predicate also serves to test the name of the word matched to an atomic node:

CORE IS ↓THE↓.

The same predicate serves to test the name of a word located in the sentence by the subject of a restriction statement.

CURRENT WORD IS ↓THE↓.

4. Test for subsumed word. The SUBSUMES predicate tests whether any of the words subsumed by a node meets a stated condition. Any test that can be applied to a single sentence word (test for name, for category, or for category and attribute) can also be used in the SUBSUMES predicate:

PRESENT-ELEMENT SUBSUMES ↓,↓.
PRESENT-ELEMENT SUBSUMES ADJ:ASENTI:AFORTO.

5. No test. Occasionally one only wants to determine whether a node specified in the subject can be located in the parse tree; no further test on that node is required. For this purpose RL provides the EXISTS predicate, which in itself always succeeds (the statement fails only if the subject fails).

6. Parse tree tests. Though any condition regarding the structure of the parse tree can be expressed entirely in the subject of a statement, sometimes it is convenient to do so by means of a predicate. For example, to determine whether a given node occurs as part of a tree dominated by SUBJECT, one can execute

IMMEDIATE SUBJECT EXISTS.

where IMMEDIATE is a routine that looks upward in the parse tree for the node named in the argument. One can alternatively invoke the routine using a HAS predicate:

SN HAS IMMEDIATE SUBJECT.

In the case of a few routines there is an alternative wording that is much more natural in the predicate position; for the routine IMMEDIATE, for example, one can write

SN IS OCCURRING AS SUBJECT.

The negation of any predicate may be expressed simply by adding NOT to the verb:

PRESENT-ELEMENT IS NOT SN.
PRESENT-ELEMENT DOES NOT SUBSUME ↓,↓.

Wherever a word or symbol may appear in a predicate, the disjunction of two or more words or symbols may appear instead:[4]

VALUE OF SUBJECT IS SN OR VINGSTG.
SUBJECT DOES NOT SUBSUME ↓A↓ OR ↓AN↓ :

A few of the tests that must be made in the grammar do not fit neatly into the subject–predicate organization, and so are included as separate types of statements. One of these is THERE IS . . . AHEAD, which tests whether any sentence word not yet matched by a node in the parse tree meets a stated condition; for example,

THERE IS A ↓TO↓ AHEAD.

This statement is used in optimization restrictions, to avoid trying an option if a required word or category or attribute is not present in the remainder of the sentence. For example, the following is an optimization restriction of the grammar:

DOPT9 = IN TOVO, FORTOVO, NTOVO: THERE IS A ↓TO↓ AHEAD.

3.2.3   Connectives

The RL provides a full range of connectives for specifying logical combinations of statements and thereby in effect for specifying the flow of control within a restriction. The logical operators include NOT, AND, OR, NOR, and IF . . . THEN . . . , and can be nested to any depth. The operator evaluates only as many statements as are required to determine the value of the operator; thus, in an occurrence of p AND q, if p fails the entire statement fails, and q is not executed. Iteration operators, for constructing loops with a termination test either at the beginning or end, are also available, although in the current grammar they are used only inside the routines.

When the logical operators AND, OR, and NOR have only two arguments, they are written: BOTH p AND q, EITHER p OR q, and NEITHER p NOR q. When they have more than two arguments, the arguments are preceded by ALL OF . . . , ONE OF . . . , or NONE OF . . . , optionally followed by ARE TRUE or IS TRUE. To avoid run-on sentences and ambiguity in this case, the arguments are given names, beginning with a dollar sign. For example, the grammar restriction (WSN1) corresponding to our simple WSN restriction reads in part:

ONE OF $PREDICATE, $SENTENTIAL-VERB, $EVENT-VERB IS TRUE.

Naming is not restricted to arguments of ALL OF . . . , ONE OF . . . , NONE OF . . . . Any RL statement may be assigned a name beginning with a $ and then referenced from any point in another statement where the original statement could appear. If the named statement is to be referenced from a restriction other than the one in which the statement appears, the name is placed on the GLOBAL list in the LIST section of the grammar.

3.2.4   *Relocating Devices and Registers*

Any construction that can be used in the subject of a statement to locate a node can also be used in an AT . . . or IN . . . phrase before a statement, to specify where a statement should begin. For example, an alternative formulation of the WSN restriction WSN-ALT1, presented earlier, is:


```
WSN-ALT2  =  IN ASSERTION: AT SUBJECT,
                IF THE VALUE IS SN
                THEN THE CORE OF THE COELEMENT VERB HAS ATTRIBUTE
                    VSENT1 OR VSENT2 OR VSENT3.
```


Registers are the variables of the RL. A register may be assigned a value by writing its name (an X followed by an integer) after any RL subject, predicate, or routine invocation. The value assigned to the register is a pointer to the node, attribute, or word at which the restriction is located after the given subject, predicate, or routine is executed. The register may be referenced by using it in the subject of a statement or in an AT phrase. Registers are used frequently in the grammar in order to avoid having to locate the same node several times in one restriction. Often the first statement in a restriction contains register assignments for nodes that will be referenced in statements to follow. For example, the first part of WSN1 reads (in part):

WSN1 = IN ASSERTION: IF ELEMENT SUBJECT X10 HAS VALUE SN,
                            THEN ONE OF $PREDICATE, $SENTENTIAL VERB,
                            $EVENT VERB IS TRUE.

After the IF clause in this statement is executed, the register X10 will contain a pointer to the SUBJECT node in ASSERTION. The statement $PREDICATE begins:

$PREDICATE = AT X10 . . .

The reference to X10 immediately positions the restriction interpreter at the SUBJECT node, without the need to reexecute the ELEMENT routine.

There is also a device available for causing the second (or third or fourth) argument of a logical operator to begin at the node where the execution of the previous argument ended. To signal this an arrow is placed before the connective word preceding the second argument; for example,

IF . . . → THEN . . .

If no arrow appears, the second argument will begin at the same node as the first argument.

3.2.5   *Commands*

The declarative statement format, which has proven so convenient for stating the restrictions, is not particularly suitable for the routines, especially the low-level routines that deal in terms of elementary tree motion and testing operators. The RL therefore provides an imperative format, similar to that used in procedural languages, primarily for routines. In this format each statement or command specifies an individual elementary operation, such as GO UP, GO DOWN, GO LEFT, GO RIGHT (in the parse tree); TEST FOR SUBJECT; STORE IN X5; DO CORE (routine invocation). Commands may be strung together with semicolons (this is equivalent in effect to combining them with BOTH . . . AND . . . ; or ALL OF . . .). A simple example of a restriction containing such a sequence of commands was seen in the previous chapter, in Sec. 2.2.2.

Two commands that are used frequently in routines are ASCEND TO *argument,* and DESCEND TO *argument.* The argument in these commands is the name of a node, or a disjunction of node names, or the name of a list of nodes. The ASCEND command looks upward in the parse tree for the argument but is blocked from ascending through either a STRING or ATOMIC type node unless that node appears as a second (optional) argument of the command, in the form PASSING THROUGH *argument.* The command may also specify non-STRING or -ATOMIC nodes that are to block the ascent, using the form NOT PASSING

THROUGH *argument*. The command DESCEND TO *argument* performs a breadth-first search of the subtree below the current node with the same provisos and options as the ASCEND command; that is, it does not descend through STRING or ATOMIC nodes unless specifically instructed to do so, and may be instructed not to pass through other nodes as well. These two commands have been a part of all implementations of the LSP and are basic to the operation of the locating routines. For example, the DESCEND command does the main work in the CORE routine, shown in Sec. 3.3.1.

Among the commands, several are concerned specifically with the generation of conjunction strings and the execution of restrictions on conjunctional strings with ellipsis (STACK command). Several others are used in transforming the parse tree. These commands are discussed in the chapters on conjunctions and transformations.

3.2.6.   *Monitoring the Parsing Process*

Although the foregoing discussion would indicate that the restrictions evaluate each parse tree independent of the course of the parsing process to that point, this is not quite correct. Both for reasons of efficiency and to avoid unlikely analyses when more common analyses are available, several statements are included that can monitor the overall parsing process. The simplest such statement tests whether

A PARSE HAS BEEN OBTAINED.

The parser also provides a more sophisticated method of selecting a preferred analysis by defining nested subsets of the English grammar. The input sentence is first analyzed with respect to the smallest subset, a grammar containing the common English constructions. If no parse is obtained, the sentence is reanalyzed with respect to the next larger subset, which includes some infrequent constructions. This process is repeated until an analysis is obtained or the entire grammar has been used. These subsets are specified in the grammar by including restrictions that test one of a set of switches. These switches are all off in the initial attempt at analyzing a sentence, and are turned on one by one in the subsequent stages of the process. Because of the richness of the grammar, this mechanism also makes an important contribution to parsing efficiency. The current grammar defines two subsets; the smaller, the "nonrare" grammar, is still adequate for most of the sentences in scientific texts. As a result, the time lost on reanalyzing the more unusual sentences is less than the time saved in analyzing the more common sentence types with a smaller grammar. Further information on switches is included in the chapters on the grammar.

One further statement provided in the RL makes it possible to find out how far the context-free parser has backed up into the sentence since the last parse tree for the sentence was found. This test (for the so-called MIN WORD) is used as part of a scheme to avoid generating several parse trees in cases of permanent predictable ambiguity, such as when an adjunct string can be attached at several points in the tree. This device is discussed in Secs. 1.3.2 and 5.4.1.

3.2.7   *Node Attributes*

The RL includes a facility for assigning and testing node attributes. A node attribute is in effect a variable associated with a particular node in the parse tree; these variables may be assigned either the value true or false or a pointer to some other node in the parse tree. Unlike assignments to registers, node attributes are not erased when a restriction is finished. Node attributes simplify the task of writing the grammar and can make the restrictions and routines much more efficient. For example, if a lengthy routine is frequently executed, one can save time by recording the node located by the routine as a node attribute of the starting node the first time the routine is executed at that node, and referring to the node attribute thereafter. Another application arises when one wants to know whether a particular node occurs in some subtree. Rather than search the entire subtree, one can assign a node attribute to the root of the subtree when the node in question is attached, and test that node attribute later.

A complication arises because a restriction housed on one node can assign an attribute to some other node. An instance of this arises in the relative clause construction. When an ASSERTION string occurs in a relative clause, the "omitted" element (for example the OB-JECT in "what I eat" and the SUBJECT in "what eats me") is marked by assigning it the value NULLWH. When the ASSERTION is completed, a restriction checks that precisely one element has been omitted. This could be done by having the restriction search all possible points of omission. A more efficient procedure, employed in the LSP grammar, is to have a restriction housed on NULLWH assign the node attribute DIDOMIT to the ASSERTION node. The restriction on the ASSERTION need then merely check for the presence of this attribute.

Suppose, however, that the sentence contained a clause without omission, such as *that I eat cheese*. The parser might try the value NULLWH for OBJECT (and hence assign DIDOMIT to the ASSERTION). Because of this (incorrect) choice, the parser would eventually get stuck, unable to complete the parse; it would then back up and try an alternate option for OBJECT (in this case, *cheese*). At this point the node attribute DIDOMIT should be removed, since the ASSERTION no longer contains an omission. This erasure is performed automatically by the parser.

3.3   **Routines**

In previous implementations of the LSP system, and in some other linguistic parsing programs, (such as Woods 1975), the node arguments of wellformedness tests and of other linguistic operations are obtained by explicit sequences of basic tree operations. As we noted earlier, the argument-locating task in the present LSP system is accomplished by a small set of generalized linguistic locating routines defined as a separate component of the grammar. Relatively few routines are required because the parse tree is composed of string modules that can stand in only a few possible relations to each other: a string node S_i is either a center string, or is adjoined to an element of some other string S_j, or is a sentence nominalization string within S_j. These relations may be local or extended over several operations of adjunction or substitution. For example, in the sentence *It is essential that John leave,* the string *that John leave* is the first (and only) nominalization string in the assertion whose subject is *it,* whereas in the sentence *It seems to be considered essential that John leave* the same string is at several string levels remove from the *it* subject of the assertion. The locating routines are accordingly divided into two groups: basic locating routines and extended-scope routines. The former operate within one string subtree or between two string subtrees directly related by adjunction or substitution. The latter handle sentence nominalization strings and adjunct strings at an arbitrary depth of embedding.

3.3.1   *Basic Locating Routines*[5]

There are about thirty basic routines in the grammar. Described here in detail are several that illustrate the locating relations discussed earlier (in Secs. 2.5 and 2.6).

CORE Routine

ROUTINE CORE –	=	DO $CORE-PATH.
$CORE-PATH	=	ONE OF $AT-ATOM, $DESCEND-TO-ATOM, $DESCEND-TO-STRING IS TRUE. (GLOBAL)
$AT-ATOM	=	TEST FOR ATOM.
$DESCEND-TO-ATOM	=	DESCEND TO ATOM NOT PASSING THROUGH ADJSET1.
$DESCEND-TO-STRING	=	DESCEND TO STRING NOT PASSING THROUGH ADJSET1; IF TEST FOR LN THEN $RIGHT-TO-CORE.
$RIGHT-TO-CORE	=	ITERATE GO RIGHT UNTIL TEST FOR CONJ-NODE FAILS; DO CORE – .

The CORE routine locates the sentence word corresponding to a higher level grammatical element E by descending to a terminal node (''atom'') from E. This is done by $DESCEND-TO-ATOM. When CORE descends from E it does not look at structures that are adjuncts, which are on list ADJSET1. Thus for the sentence *For the heart to beat requires energy* shown in Fig. 2.7 the routine CORE, starting at the node SUBJECT in the FORTOVO string, will not search below the left-adjunct node LN (arriving mistakenly at *the*) and will arrive at N (the noun *heart*). Sometimes the starting location of CORE will be an atomic node. This is provided for by $AT-ATOM, which tests whether the current node is an atomic node, the routine's first test. Sometimes a string occurs as the core of an element in place of a noun (*for the heart to beat*), as is the case in Fig. 2.7 for the element SUBJECT in ASSERTION. This situation is provided for by $DESCEND-TO-STRING. Thus CORE starting at the SUBJECT of ASSERTION in Fig. 2.7 will locate the string FORTOVO.[6]

ELEMENT Routine

ROUTINE ELEMENT   (X) =   EITHER DO DOWN1   (X) OR $STRING-SEGMENT.

$STRING-SEGMENT   =   DO DOWN1   (STGSEG); DO DOWN1   (X).

ROUTINE DOWN1   (X)   =   GO DOWN; ITERATET GO RIGHT UNTIL TEST
                                              FOR X SUCCEEDS.

It is assumed that ELEMENT starts at a node Y and that X is an element of the string corresponding to Y. Thus ELEMENT locates X by searching the level below Y. This is done by
routine DOWN1(X), which first goes to the level below Y by executing the command GO
DOWN and then searches the nodes on that level until it finds X. The latter step is accomplished by an iterate command: ITERATET GO RIGHT UNTIL TEST FOR X SUCCEEDS.
The ITERATET command begins by executing the test portion of the command. In Fig. 2.7
the execution of ELEMENT(SUBJECT), starting at the string node ASSERTION, will locate
the node SUBJECT. Sometimes the definition of a string Y contains an element X that is the
name of another string of the grammar. This is the case in Fig. 2.7 where TOVO, a defined
string of the grammar, appears as a string segment of FORTOVO. In this situation not all the
elements of FORTOVO are on one level below FORTOVO but some are one level below the
string segment TOVO of FORTOVO. $STRING-SEGMENT, therefore, searches one level below
Y for a node on the string-segment list STGSEG and if it finds one, it searches for X one level
below the string segment. In Fig. 2.7, ELEMENT(OBJECT), starting at FORTOVO, first
locates TOVO by executing DOWN1(STGSEG) and then locates OBJECT by executing
DOWN1(OBJECT).

3.3.2 *Extended-Scope Routines*

VERB-COELEMENT Routine.   In many restrictions we wish to reach the verbal sibling
of the SUBJECT or OBJECT node. Because the verbal element has a different name and a different substructure in different strings, we find it convenient to define a routine VERB-
COELEMENT to locate the desired verbal sibling in all cases.

ROUTINE VERB-COELEMENT – = DO $NEXT-VERB – .

$NEXT-VERB – = DO $1; DO $2.   (GLOBAL)

$1   =   THE PRESENT-ELEMENT – HAS COELEMENT – VERB OR
              LVING OR LVENR OR LVR OR VERB1 X7.

$2   =   IF X7 IS VERB1 WHERE VALUE IS NOT LTVR THEN
              PRESENT-ELEMENT – HAS COELEMENT – VERB2 X7.

$1 locates the verbal sibling of the starting node by invoking the COELEMENT routine
with a disjunction of verb-type nodes as its argument. It then stores the result in register X7.
Registers are cleared at the end of a restriction execution. $2 tests whether the verbal sibling
in X7 is the first part (VERB1) of a two-part verb that appears in permuted forms such as the

yes–no question and the permuted center string (*Nor has he left*). When the value of VERB1 is not LTVR (that is, not *have* or *be* in a tensed form), the verb is found in the second verb position (VERB2). In such a case VERB2 is stored in X7 so that the routine exits with this value. The reason for this is that $NEXT-VERB is a global statement and its use in another context requires that the routine exit with a verbal element stored in X7.

DEEPEST-COVERB Routine. The DEEPEST-COVERB routine applies to situations in which a constraint applies to a subject and verb, but an arbitrary number of embeddings may separate the subject from the verb. For example, the WSN restriction that applies to *That he left surprised them* applies equally well to *That he left seems to have surprised them, That he left was thought to seem to have surprised them,* and so on. The DEEPEST-COVERB routine iterates through the embedded constructions to arrive at the verb element to which the constraint applies.

ROUTINE DEEPEST-COVERB – = ITERATE $NEXT-VERB – UNTIL $OBJ-HAS-VERB FAILS.

($NEXT-VERB – is defined in VERB-COELEMENT routine)

$OBJ-HAS-VERB = BOTH $VERBAL – → AND PRESENT-STRING HAS ELEMENT – OBJECT OR PASSOBJ.

$VERBAL = IF PRESENT-ELEMENT – HAS COELEMENT – OBJECT OR PASSOBJ → THEN EITHER CORE – X3 IS VO OR VINGO OR VENO OR TOVO OR TOBE OR VENPASS WHERE X3 IS NOT OCCURRING IN SN, OR $ASPECTUAL IS TRUE.

$ASPECTUAL = BOTH X3 IS ADJ: AASP, AND RIGHT ADJUNCT OF X3 IS TOVO.

A quick view of how the DEEPEST-COVERB routine operates is the following: Each execution of the iterate command looks first for a verbal coelement using the global statement of the VERB-COELEMENT routine. Assuming it finds a verbal element it then examines the object position to see whether it contains a verb-containing string ($OBJ-HAS-VERB). If it does, i.e. $VERBAL succeeds, the routine goes to that verb-containing object string and in turn to the object position of that string, so that it is ready for the next iteration. The details of $VERBAL will concern us later. First it may be helpful to see how the routine operates as part of a restriction. Consider the parse tree for the sentence *That he left seems to have surprised them,* shown in Fig. 3.1, and the restriction:

WSN-DEEPEST = IN ASSERTION: AT SUBJECT
IF THE VALUE IS SN
THEN THE CORE OF THE DEEPEST-COVERB HAS
ATTRIBUTE VSENT1 OR VSENT2 OR VSENT3.

The restriction is invoked at ASSERTION but is immediately relocated to the node SUBJECT by the phrase AT SUBJECT. It then tests whether the node below SUBJECT (the value of SUB-

JECT) is SN, which it is in Fig. 3.1. Then starting again at the SUBJECT node it executes the DEEPEST-COVERB routine and, in a manner that we shall trace presently, finds that the deepest coverb is LVENR in the string VENO. It then executes the CORE routine at the node LVENR and reaches the atomic node VEN (*surprised*), which it tests for the attribute VSENT1.

Fig. 3.1   Parse tree tested by restriction WSN-DEEPEST.

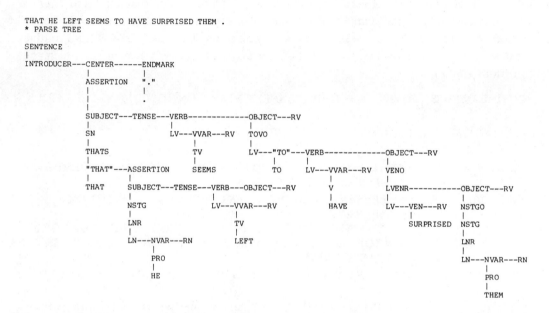

```
THAT HE LEFT SEEMS TO HAVE SURPRISED THEM .
* PARSE TREE

SENTENCE
|
INTRODUCER---CENTER------ENDMARK
             |           |
             ASSERTION   "."
             |           |
             |           .
             |
             SUBJECT---TENSE---VERB------------OBJECT---RV
             |                 |              |
             SN                LV---VVAR---RV TOVO
             |                 !            |
             THATS             TV           LV---"TO"---VERB------------OBJECT---RV
             |                 |            |          |              |
             "THAT"---ASSERTION SEEMS       TO         LV---VVAR---RV VENO
             |        |                                |              |
             THAT     SUBJECT---TENSE---VERB---OBJECT---RV V              LVENR----------OBJECT---RV
                      |                 |      |         |              |              |
                      NSTG              LV---VVAR---RV   HAVE           LV---VEN---RV  NSTGO
                      |                 |                               |              |
                      LNR               TV                             SURPRISED      NSTG
                      |                 |                                              |
                      LN---NVAR---RN    LEFT                                           LNR
                           |                                                           |
                           PRO                                                         LN---NVAR---RN
                           |                                                                |
                           HE                                                               PRO
                                                                                            |
                                                                                            THEM
```

Referring now to the DEEPEST-COVERB routine as it applies in Fig. 3.1, we begin the ITERATE command by executing $NEXT-VERB starting from the SUBJECT node. The SUBJECT node has a coelement VERB so $1 of $NEXT-VERB exits "+" with the node VERB stored in X7. $2 of $NEXT-VERB succeeds trivially since the node stored in X7 is VERB not VERB1; thus $NEXT-VERB succeeds and the DEEPEST-COVERB routine starts $OBJ-HAS-VERB at the node VERB. If $OBJ-HAS-VERB fails, the ITERATE command will be successfully completed and the DEEPEST-COVERB routine will return VERB as the value of the deepest coverb; this would be correct in a sentence with only one embedding (*that he left surprised them*). However, the sentence in Fig. 3.1 contains several embeddings and the first execution of $OBJ-HAS-VERB therefore succeeds. In $OBJ-HAS-VERB, the first of the two conjoined statements ($VERBAL) looks ahead to see if the next object position contains one of the named verb-containing strings as the core of the object position or (via $ASPECTUAL) has an aspectual adjective as its core with a TOVO string adjoined to the right of the adjective (*That he left is apt to surprise them*); if either is true, the second part of $OBJ-HAS-VERB moves to the object position in that verb-containing string. (The arrow preceding a conjoined restriction statement causes that statement to be executed starting at the location where the preceding statement ended.) In Fig. 3.1 the object position following VERB (the node OBJECT) has the core TOVO, which is one of the named verb-containing strings, so the routine moves first to TOVO, which it stores in X3, and from there to the OBJECT node in TOVO. It is now ready for a new cycle of the ITERATE command. This time $NEXT-VERB, starting from the OBJECT node in TOVO, returns with the VERB node in TOVO as the current value of the deepest coverb; from this point $OBJ-HAS-VERB moves to the OBJECT node following VERB in TOVO and finds that its core is the verb-containing string VENO (which it stores in X3). Starting from the node VENO the second half of $OBJ-HAS-VERB results in a move to the OBJECT node in VENO, from which the third cycle of the ITERATE command begins. $NEXT-VERB takes us to LVENR in VENO and $OBJ-HAS-VERB tests whether the core of the OBJECT node in VENO is one of the named verb-containing strings; this time the test fails since the core of the OBJECT is the atomic PRO. The routine then tests whether the core is an aspectual adjective; it fails, so $VERBAL fails and $OBJ-HAS-VERB fails. The ITERATE command is completed and the routine returns VENO as the current (and final) value of the deepest coverb.

A routine called the DEEPEST-COPRED is an extension of the DEEPEST-COVERB routine to the case where the deepest coverb is *be;* in this case the constraint in question usually applies to the adjective or noun occurring as the object of *be,* so the DEEPEST-COPRED returns the core of the object of *be* (OBJBE) as its value. For example, WSN1 uses the DEEPEST-COPRED routine to check the wellformedness of predicates occurring with an SN string as subject (for example, *For him to leave is easy, ̸А For him to leave is eager*). For a detailed example of the operation of the DEEPEST-COPRED routine, see the note cited following WAGREE2 in Sec. 5.2.

A routine called the ULTIMATE-SUBJECT is similar to the DEEPEST-COVERB routine but ascends rather than descends. One extended-scope routine called the ULTIMATE-OBJECT can extend over a wider range of embeddings than the DEEPEST-COVERB, DEEPEST-COPRED, and ULTIMATE-SUBJECT routines. The situations to which it applies involve relative clauses and conjunctions. The operation of the ULTIMATE-OBJECT routine is traced in detail in Sec. 5.8. The following examples illustrate the situations to which the various extended-scope routines apply:

1. Routine DEEPEST-COVERB
    John will *leave* on Sunday.
    John plans to try to arrange to *leave* on Sunday.
    John is known to have tried to arrange to *leave* on Sunday.
    (Subject of *leave* is *John.*)

2. Routine ULTIMATE-SUBJECT
    It is advisable *for John to leave.*
    It can be taken as likely *that John will leave.*
    It seems to have been considered advisable *that John leave.*
    (Embedded sentence about John requires *it* as ultimate subject.)

3.   Routine ULTIMATE-OBJECT

the *man* whom I *met* (   )

the *man* whom I plan to try to arrange to *meet* (   )

the *man* whom it was suggested they thought I should plan to arrange to *meet* (   )

(Object of *met* and *meet* is *man.*)

He will *go* and she *can* (   ) too.

He will *go* and she thinks you said that *she* can (   ) too.

He will *go* and she thinks you said you were willing to try to get John to agree that she *can* (   ) too.

(*go* is zeroed after *can.*)

NOTES

1. Sager 1972a. This chapter, exclusive of Sec. 3.3, is based upon parts of Sager and Grishman 1975, largely written by R. Grishman.

2. The articles A, AN, THE are ignored by the RL compiler and may be inserted freely to enhance readability. In writing a restriction it is helpful to align two-part operators so that the logical structure is apparent, as is done here with IF-THEN.

3. ASENT1 applies to an adjective like *easy,* which can take a sentence nominalization string as subject; AFORTO is the subclass of ASENT1 that occurs in particular with the strings FORTOVO and TOVO: *To get the right analysis is not easy.*

4. The fact that disjunction may be expressed in predicates whereas conjunction requires the combining of entire statements is a consequence of the list structure into which the RL is translated: each elementary test operation takes a list of symbols as its argument, and succeeds if any one of the symbols can be found. In practice, testing for a conjunction of symbols is a rare occurrence in the grammar, so this has proved no inconvenience.

5. This section is adapted from Raze 1976; the routines of the grammar were written by Carol Raze Friedman. Routines are listed in Appendix 1 following the BNF definitions and lists. Conjunction routines are not included, and only the versions of the basic routines that do not include stacking (see Chapter 6) are listed. The names of these routines are appended with a minus sign. Several nonstacking routines are shown here; in the discussion the minus sign will be dropped since the functioning of the stacking and nonstacking versions is the same except in conjunctional constructions.

6. The portion ''IF TEST FOR LN THEN $RIGHT-TO-CORE'' is needed for the rare occurrence of a string node as the core of NVAR (namely, NQ as value of NAMESTG, as in *Page 2 is missing*). In this case $AT-ATOM and $DESCEND-TO-ATOM both fail in the execution of CORE at the LNR dominating NAMESTG. However, $DESCEND-TO-STRING will locate LN as the first node on the TYPE STRING list (see note 5 of Chapter 2). It must then move to the right from LN to NVAR and execute CORE− at NVAR, skipping any intervening conjunction nodes that may have been inserted.

Part 2
A COMPUTER
STRING GRAMMAR
of ENGLISH

Chapter 4   The BNF Component of the Grammar

This chapter will describe a set of BNF definitions for the major constructions of English in a string grammar of English, in particular, the grammar used in the LSP system. Since the notation of BNF definitions is equivalent to that of context-free productions, it may seem at first glance that the BNF component defines a phrase structure grammar of the type that has become familiar in the form Sentence → Noun Phrase + Verb Phrase; Noun Phrase → Determiner + Noun, and so on. But the BNF definitions of the string grammar belong to classes that reflect the categories of string analysis. In particular, we define the center strings, sentence nominalization strings, adjunct strings, and adjunct sets of a string grammar of English, along with some convenient auxiliary groupings of the definitions. As we have seen, the classification of the definitions into the types of string grammar such as STRING and ADJSET leads to a modular structure of the parse tree and makes possible the formulation of generalized routines for operating on the parse tree.

The plan of this chapter is to follow quite closely the order of the definitions in the listing of the BNF component of the grammar in Appendix 1. The numbering of the chapter sections corresponds to the numbering of the sections of BNF definitions in the grammar. Thus, Sec. 4.4 of this chapter will describe the definitions in Sec. 4.4 of the BNF portion of the listing. Individual definitions are numbered correspondingly within each section of the

Naomi Sager, Natural Language Information Processing: A Computer Grammar of English and Its Applications
Copyright © 1981 by Addison-Wesley Publishing Company, Inc., Advanced Book Program.   ISBN 0-201-06769-2
All rights reserved. No part of this publication may be reproduced, stored in a retrieval system, or transmitted, in any form or by any means, electronic, mechanical photocopying, recording, or otherwise, without the prior permission of the publisher.

listing and each section of this chapter. To avoid any confusion between references to sections in the text and references to definitions, chapter cross-references are written, for example, as "Sec. 4.4" and numerical cross-references of the type "4.4" are reserved for the serialized BNF definitions in the listing of the grammar. As an aid to identifying the elements used in the BNF definitions, an alphabetic index explaining the mnemonics and giving the serial number of each definition is supplied in Appendix 2.

The definitions within each section will be discussed mainly from the point of view of their coverage: what occurrences are analyzed as instances of the definition. In addition, the main restrictions that limit in detail the sequences covered by a given definition will be mentioned when the definition is discussed, and the code name of the restrictions will be noted in parenthesis (for example, WSN1). This chapter can thus also serve as a guide to the restriction component of the grammar, which is described in detail in Chapter 5 and is listed in Appendix 1. A number of word subclasses important for distinguishing well-formed occurrences of the definitions will be mentioned, and their computer names (written in small capital letters) will be noted parenthetically. Definitions of the word subclasses are given in Appendix 3.

With these notational conventions established we may now consider the BNF definitions for English.

4.1   Sentence

<SENTENCE>	::= <INTRODUCER> <CENTER> <ENDMARK>.	1.1
<INTRODUCER>	::= NULL|AND|OR |BUT | – FOR.	1.2
<CENTER>	::= <ASSERTION>|<QUESTION> |<PROSENT>| <PERMUTATION> | –<ASSERTIONZ> |<IMPERATIVE>.	1.3
<ENDMARK>	::= '.' |'?' |';'.	1.4

These definitions state that the syntactic type SENTENCE is composed of a sequence of three syntactic types: an INTRODUCER followed by a CENTER followed by an ENDMARK. The INTRODUCER may be NULL or one of the words AND, OR, BUT, FOR (where FOR is considered rare, as signified by the prefixed minus sign; see Sec. 4.1.1). The CENTER may be an ASSERTION, or a QUESTION or a PROSENT (pronoun for a sentence), or a PERMUTATION or an ASSERTIONZ (zeroed ASSERTION), or an IMPERATIVE; these are also syntactic types and require further definition. The ENDMARK is a period, or a question mark, or a semicolon.

In defining the center string, or main clause, of a sentence, the two levels SENTENCE and CENTER are introduced for several reasons. One reason is that a center string without final punctuation may occur as part of another string, as does the assertion *he is here* in *I know that he is here.* Another reason is that a sentence may consist of two or more conjoined center strings that are followed by a single endmark: *Voice is generally thought of as a purely individual matter, yet is it quite correct to say that the voice is given us at birth and maintain-*

ed unmodified throughout life?[1] We therefore place all the center strings (without final punctuation) into the syntactic type CENTER, and the different possible endmarks into the type ENDMARK. A restriction then ensures that only well-formed combinations of values of CENTER and ENDMARK occur; for example, a questionmark after QUESTION (WPOS23).

The definition of SENTENCE also provides for the occurrences of an initial introducerword: *And physicists are made of atoms., But, for the scientist, these are matters of little moment.* These words often serve as a connective to a preceding sentence. The occurrence of an introducer word is optional, as indicated by the NULL option in the definition of INTRODUCER.

4.1.1 *RARE options*

In INTRODUCER it will be noticed that the option FOR is preceded by a minus sign. A minus sign preceding an option X in the definition of Y signifies that X is considered "rare" as a value for Y in the present grammar. This means that the option X will not be used unless no parse can be obtained using the grammar without the options marked rare. If in analyzing a sentence the parser reaches "NO MORE PARSES" and no previous parse has been obtained, a switch called the rare switch goes on and the parsing procedure is repeated from the beginning of the sentence, this time using the complete grammar including the options marked rare. The minus sign preceding an option invokes a disqualify restriction that says that the option can be used only if the rare switch is on. For example, the restriction on FOR as an option of INTRODUCER, if written out in Restriction Language, would read: IN INTRODUCER RE OPTION FOR: THE RARE SWITCH IS ON. References to the RARE switch may also be made as part of more complex restrictions such as WCOM10.

The reason for introducing levels of grammatical operation is perhaps obvious: Many sentences use only a portion of the full grammar. A particular portion P might be adequate for, say eighty out of one hundred sentences of a text. The time needed to analyze these eighty sentences can be cut significantly by using P instead of the full grammar. A low time limit can be set when P is used. The other twenty sentences, of course, will fail when analyzed using P, and they will have to be run again using the full grammar. These sentences, however, are likely to be time-consuming in any case; a larger gain has been made in cutting the computing time on the eighty simpler sentences.

In this grammar an option may be considered rare for either linguistic or computational reasons. Linguistically, it may simply be of rare occurrence in the language as a whole, or in the type of discourse to which the program is being applied. The center string ASSERTIONZ, for example (as in *He left and fast* in Sec. 4.2) is relatively rare in scientific writing. Sometimes the trouble that an option will cause in the computation is the dominant consideration. Trouble, here, means the amount of local ambiguity a symbol introduces, and the time consequently spent during parsing in following alternate paths that ultimately fail. For example, the introducer *for* (*For the whole evolutionary process, both cosmic and organic, is one*) is not linguistically rare to the extent that occurrences of the center string ASSERTIONZ are. But *for* is a word that can begin a number of different strings, several of which can also begin sentences; compare, for example (1) *For this reason language is an unusually favorable domain for the study of the general tendency of cultural behavior to work out all sorts of formal elaborations . . .* ; (2) *For this reason to seem pertinent to the reader, it is necessary to realize that . . .* ; (3) *For this reason to seem pertinent to the reader requires the addition of some background material.* In these examples, the word *for* begins, respectively: (1) a prepositional phrase occurring as adjunct of the sentence; (2) a FORTOVO string (6.2) occurring as adjunct of the sentence; (3) a FORTOVO string occurring as subject of the sentence. Clearly, a sentence that begins with *for* followed by a noun phrase is at least three ways ambiguous from the start, without counting the possibilities due to taking *for* as a sentence introducer, leaving the noun phrase following *for* to be analyzed as the first element of the CENTER string. Since there are many ways of starting a CENTER string with a noun phrase, *for* as introducer is clearly troublesome. Considering that it is also not of very frequent occurrence, the final judgment is to call it rare.

4.2   Center Strings

<ASSERTION>	::= <SA> <SUBJECT> <SA> <TENSE> <SA> <VERB> <SA> <OBJECT> <RV> <SA>.	2.1
<QUESTION>	::= <SA> (<YESNOQ>|<WHQ-N>|<WHQ>|<PWHQ-PN>| <PWHQ>|<WHNQ-N>|<PWHNQ-PN>|<PWHNQ>).	2.2
<PROSENT>	::= THIS <SA> .	2.3
<PERMUTATION>	::= <TSUBJVO>|<OBES> .	2.4
<ASSERTIONZ>	::= <*NULLC> <SAZ> .	2.5
<IMPERATIVE>	::= <SA> [PLEASE] [DO |DO NOT |↓DON↓↓T↓] <VO> [PLEASE] .	2.6

(Note: VO is defined in Sec. 7 of Appendix 1, VERBAL AND VERBAL OBJECT STRINGS; SAZ is defined in Sec. 9, SENTENCE ADJUNCT STRINGS.)

Examples of the ASSERTION center are numerous; for example, *This sentence is an example.* Sentences of the type *There is noone home* and *It is true that he left* are analyzed by this grammar as instances of ASSERTION although they could be treated as special center strings. The considerations behind this decision are summarized in 4.2.1. To accommodate these occurrences, the definition of SUBJECT contains the literal THERE as an option, and *it* is required as the core of the SUBJECT for complement occurrences of sentence nominalization strings in the predicate (DSN2,4,5).

Many restrictions that concern the overall wellformedness of sentences are housed in ASSERTION, as well as in strings that can be said to be derived from ASSERTION. Among these restrictions are subject–verb agreement (WAGREE1), subject–predicate agreement (WAGREE2), constraints on collective and reciprocal verbs (WAGREE3), selectional (word-choice) restrictions on the subject, verb, and object (WSEL1, WSEL2), wellformedness of sentence nominalization strings in the subject (WSN1), and wellformedness of *there* as the value of the subject (WVC9).

The main question forms encountered in scientific writing and therefore included in the computer grammar are the yes–no question (YESNOQ) and the *wh*-question, but not all forms.[2] The latter are represented in the computer grammar by strings whose names contain the letters WHQ; these are defined in Sec. 4.3. The option PROSENT stands for prosentence, the analogue of pronoun for a sentence; the proword in question is *this* in such occurrences as *And this though every speaker will accept utterances that he has not heard before.* The word *this* in the prosent occurrences is usually preceded by *and* (DPOS13)[3] and is followed by a sentence adjunct.

Sentence forms in which the elements of the ASSERTION are permuted are not frequent in scientific writing, but they do occur. In one form, TSUBJVO, the order is tense, **subj**ect, **v**erb, **o**bject (*In no case do the advantages which these properties confer seem to be trivial; Nor could Sherrington find any support for the suggestion that impulses from stretched areas of skin played a decisive, or even important role*). Usually the tense element is preceded by a negative word or phrase (WVC7) like *in no case, nor* in the preceding examples. A more frequently encountered permutation reverses the positions of the subject and object of *be*, so that the order is **o**bject, **be**, **s**ubject (OBES): *At stake is the future of public education in New York, But even more fierce was the struggle for jobs between the similar crafts and trades.*

In the CENTER position in a conjunctional string we often find zeroed (or, implicit) elements: *He left and she too [left].* The most extreme is one in which the entire center string preceding the conjunction can be said to occur in zeroed form after the conjunctions (*He left and fast = He left and [he left] fast*). The zeroed occurrence is indicated by what type of adjunct occurs after the conjunction, usually a particular member of RV or SA. In computing the structure of sentences of this type, the place of the CENTER in the conjunction string is held by ASSERTIONZ having as value the null element NULLC followed by the adjunct set SAZ. This center is only acceptable as a conjunct of an ASSERTION center (Ⱥ *Will he leave and fast?*) with the conjunction *and* or *but* (DZERO1).

The imperative construction is characterized by the tenseless form of the verb and such special features as an optional *please* (*Please turn to page 74, Watch your language, please*), and an optional emphatic *do* (*Do stay*). *Do* is also present in the imperative as in the carrier of the negative morpheme *not, – n't* (*Don't be late*). Note that in the imperative, *do* can occur before *be* (*Do be sensible*), but elsewhere this sequence is not allowed (WVC2): Ⱥ *But I did be sensible.* In the imperative string, there are also constraints on the occurrence of reflexive pronouns; these constraints show that the implicit subject of the infinitive verb is *you: Don't tire yourself,* Ⱥ *Don't tire himself.* However, these restrictions are not included in the computer grammar because of the infrequent occurrence of both reflexive pronouns and the imperative form in scientific writing.

The definitions of ASSERTION, QUESTION, and IMPERATIVE provide for an initial optional sentence adjunct, e.g. a subordinate clause like *when it rains* in *When it rains it pours,*

When it rains do you feel gloomy?, *When it rains take care in driving*. An initial sentence adjunct is very unlikely in the other center string forms.

Aside from the types of centers defined in the computer grammar, quite a number of special center forms could be added to the grammar, particularly if texts containing conversational discourse were to be analyzed. A fairly frequent form, even in scientific writing, is the noun phrase standing alone, usually preceded by *hence, thus* (classed as interjection INT in the string lexicon), or an introducer word: *Thus the need for prepositions when variables are used for which we substitute sentences and not names of sentences, And now the conclusion*.

A prepositional phrase or other adjunct can sometimes occur alone (*At last!*). There are many forms of exclamatory expressions, some of them parts of fuller sentences and some of them unqiue forms[4]: *If I only had the nerve!*, *What a good man he was !*, *How I would like to go to a sunny place now!*, *Happy the man who . . . .* Shortened forms of fuller sentences occur in literary contexts and in conversation, the shortening resulting from the dropping of *it is* (*Useless for him to attempt to be gay, Better to be out of it all*) and repetition zeroing following the tense element: *But they are, I will*. There are of course the expressions *Hello, Goodbye, Sorry, Here goes*, and so on in normal conversation. Most special forms and idioms can be related to grammatically well-formed sentences (sometimes by extended analysis) but a few are quite special (*The more the merrier*). For the computer grammar most of these departures would have to be defined as special strings.

4.2.1   There *and* it *forms*

Contrary to the treatment in the LSP grammar, there are a number of reasons for defining a special center string for sentences of the type *There is a man waiting in the lobby, There is an additional problem, however*. The main reason is that the underlying sentence obtained by transformational analysis has as its subject the portion immediately following the verb *be*. Thus, *There is a man waiting in the lobby* can be transformed into *A man is waiting in the lobby*. The form of the special center string would be:

<THERESTG>   ::= THERE <TENSE> <SA> <VERB> <SA> <SUBJECT>
                        <SA> <OBJECT> <RV> <SA>.

An immediate difficulty with this string is the fact that the OBJECT position is often empty. This is the case in *There is an additional problem, however*, where the subject of *is* is the noun phrase *an additional problem* and no object of *is* appears in the sentence. The same is true of *There was destined to be a lengthening of women's skirts after they had become short enough*, where the subject of *was destined to be* is the sentence nominalization string *a lengthening of women's skirts*. In the computer grammar these two subject sequences would be instances, respectively, of the two options NSTG and VINGSTG of SUBJECT (5.1).

If a THERESTG such as the preceding one were defined in the string grammar, some restriction on the verb would also be necessary; only a few verbs besides *be* occur in this string (*seem, come, appear, happen, result, follow, arise,* and a few others): *There came a time when he no longer cared, There has resulted a considerable change in the views on women's proper role;* ⚡*There wrote a man a letter.* Locating (discovering) the proper verb to which this restriction applies is not a simple matter in the THERESTG formulation, as is illustrated by the example *There was destined to be a lengthening of women's skirts* . . . . In this sentence the verb in question is the second occurrence of *be* (after *was destined to*), not the first occurrence *was*; the portion immediately following *was* is not the subject: ⚡*Destined to be a lengthening of women's skirts was* . . . parallel to *An additional problem is* . . . .

Despite the clear advantages in defining a string in close correspondence to a transformational analysis of *there-* sentences, there are various reasons for analyzing *there* in these cases as a (quasi) subject of the ASSERTION string,[5] as is presently done in the computer string grammar. Chief among these reasons is the fact that *there* appears in the subject position not only in the ASSERTION string but in many strings whose forms can be related to the ASSERTION, such as the YESNOQ (*Can there be any question?*); the *wh*-question (*What is there for dinner?*); the tag question (*There will be trouble, won't there?*); the permutation centers (*Never has there been such a rapid change in England*); sentence nominalization strings occurring as subject, object, or predicate, such as FORTOVO (6.2) (*It was impossible for there to be order.*), NTOBE (8C.1A) (*I don't want there to be any confusion*), PSVINGO (8A.5) (*. . . account for there being something rather odd*), SVO (8C.2) (*. . . insist there be a lawyer present*), as sentence adjunct SOBJBESA (9.9) (*There being no witnesses present, it was impossible to say*), as the headless relative clause S-N in RN (15.13) (*Money is just about the most useful thing there is*), and others. The inclusion of *there* as subject enables all these occurrences of the *there*-form to be analyzed by the string in question without additions to the definition. If the *there*-form is handled as a special permuted center, then an option for the *there*-form must be added to every one of the string definitions noted. This situation illustrates the fact that it is often convenient to divide the linguistic analysis into two stages: to treat the given forms by string analysis and the transformational relations by an additional step of analysis. The optimal dividing line between the two stages is not always obvious. In the case of the *there*-form, there is a great saving in the size of the grammar by deferring the transformational statement to a later time.

But if *there* is the subject, how is the remainder of the sentence to be analyzed? A natural candidate for analyzing this part is the VERB + OBJECT of the ASSERTION when *there* is taken as the value of SUBJECT. Since the verb in a *there*-sentence is usually *be* or a *be*-like verb (WVC9), the question is whether the portion following *there is* in these occurrences is an acceptable object of *be*. In fact, it most often is. Very often it can be analyzed as a noun object of *be* followed by a right adjunct of N; for example, *a man waiting in the lobby* in *there is a man waiting in the lobby*, can be seen as *a man* with adjunct *waiting in the lobby*. This is not surprising since a host N with its right adjunct *α* can in general be related to a sentence of the form N is *α: A man waiting in the lobby ↔ A man is waiting in the lobby*. Though there are some difficulties in deriving the set RN from the objects of *be*, the two sets have many members in common, so that the set RN does very nicely as an interim analysis of the object portion of the *there*-center.

There are even some detailed observations that support the N + RN analysis in preference to the SUBJECT + OBJECT of *be* analysis. For example, the relative clause is not an object of *be*, yet it appears after *there is N* in *there*-sentences: *There is a problem which needs our attention, ∄ A problem is which needs our attention*. Of course the entire phrase *a problem which needs our attention* could be taken as the subject of *be*, leaving an empty object as in the shorter *There is an additional problem*, but then the question arises with regard to many sentences: When should one split the sequence following *there is* into SUBJECT + OBJECT of *be* and when consider it all to be within the SUBJECT? This question would arise with regard to *There is a man waiting in the lobby*, for example. We also find the contrary case: An element occurs as an object of *be* but not after *there is* and not as RN. For example, an adjective with no adjuncts has that property: *The girl is lovely, ∄ There is a girl lovely, ∄ The girl lovely is here.*

Some of the same considerations discussed in detail with regard to the *there*-form apply to the *it*-form in such sentences as *It seems certain that he is dead, We thought it probable that the accusation would be refuted, It occurred to me there was no time to lose.* Here, too, the transformational subject of the predicate or verb appears after the predicate or verb (after *certain, probable, occurred to me*), and the position of the subject is occupied by a particular word (*it*). As in the case of *there*, it would be possible to define special strings in which the element SUBJECT appears after the verb and *it* appears before the verb, but this would expand the grammar considerably, since the *it*-form also occurs in many different string shapes; as in the YESNOQ (*Can it possibly not have occurred to him that others would be substantially inconvenienced?*), in the permutation centers (*Nor can it have escaped his notice that . . .*) in the sentence nominalization strings such as SOBJBE (*I make it a rule never to look into a newspaper*), and others. A similar decision to that made with regard to *there*-sentences was made in the string grammar: *It* is taken as the subject and the remainder of the sentence is analyzed as a VERB + OBJECT + adjuncts. In particular the sentence nominalization strings occurring after the verb or predicate noun or predicate adjective are handled as special subsets of the respective adjunct sets RV, RN, RA. Restrictions ensure that the subject is then *it: It occurred to me there was no time to lose, ∄ He occurred to me there was no time to lose*, and so on (DSN2, DSN4, DSN5). This treatment does not prejudice later transformational analysis; the wellformedness tests DSN2, DSN4, DSN5 in fact establish that the conditions for reversing the "*it*-permutation" transformation apply. The actual undoing of the permutation can be done when the rest of the string analysis of the sentence has been completed.

4.3   Question Centers[6]

\<YESNOQ\>	::= \<VERB1\> \<SUBJECT\> \<RW\> \<SA\> \<VERB2\> \<OBJECT\> \<RV\> \<SA\> \<ORNOT\>.	3.1
\<ORNOT\>	::= OR NOT|NULL.	3.2
\<WHQ-N\>	::= (WHO|WHOM|WHICH|WHAT|WHOSE) (\<YESNOQ\>| \<ASSERTION\>).	3.3

<WHQ>	::= (WHERE |WHEN |HOW |WHY) <YESNOQ>.	3.4
<PWHQ-PN>	::= <*P> (WHOM |WHICH |WHAT |WHOSE) <YESNOQ>.	3.5
<PWHQ>	::= <*P> (WHOM |WHICH |WHAT |WHOSE) <YESNOQ>.	3.6
<WHNQ-N>	::= <WHN> (<YESNOQ> | <ASSERTION>).	3.7
<WHN>	::= <LNR> |− <VINGOFN>.	3.7A
<PWHNQ-PN>	::= <*P> <WHN> <YESNOQ>.	3.8
<PWHNQ>	::= <*P> <WHN> <YESNOQ>.	3.9

In the question forms, the tense element generally appears before the subject. This can be seen in the yes–no question YESNOQ (3.1) in such examples as *Will he come?, Is she staying? Have they left?* and in *wh*-questions, such as *Who will come? Who is staying?, Who has left?* The permuted tense element is either a word in the modal class that contains *will, can, may, shall, should, would, could, might, must, ought* or is incorporated into a tensed form of *do, be,* or *have.* In the BNF definition of the YESNOQ the position for the permuted tense is VERB1 (7.13). When the value of VERB1 is a modal, then the remaining verb position VERB2 (7.14) has the infinitive verb form as its value (DVC3). If the tense element is a suffix (*-s, -ed,* or ∅), then when it is permuted to the front in the question form, *do* becomes the carrier of the tense: *Did they answer?,*[7] *Ⱥ Answered they?, Ⱥ -ed they answer?.* The tensed forms of *have* and *be* occur in the VERB1 position (WVC5) when functioning either as auxiliaries (*Has she gone?, Is she leaving?*) or as true verbs: *Has he any money?, Is she a student?* In both cases the portion following the subject is analyzed as an object string and the value of VERB2 is NULL (DVC4). *Not* (in the adjunct set RW) is distinguished in the question form by occurring optionally in two positions, directly after the tense element, that is, in TENSE, as in *Might not such considerations have a bearing on the decision?, Can't we avoid such long discussions?,* or after the SUBJECT, as in *Does it not seem strange that . . . ?.*

The *wh*-questions are composed of a *wh*-word (a word beginning with *wh*- or the word *how*) or a phrase containing such a word, followed by a base question form. The base form is the YESNOQ string or (in a restricted environment) the ASSERTION string. WHQ − N (read "WHQ minus N") stands for a *wh*-question that contains a null element in some position of the question center where in the corresponding assertion a noun or noun-position string would ordinarily occur. The interpretation of the null element in the question center is that it indicates the syntactic role of the answer phrase. Thus, in the analysis of *What did you select?* the null element (indicated by ()) is the value of the object position governed by the verb *select: What did you select()?.* If the answer is *a book,* a transformation of the question to an assertion, along with the substitution of *a book* for the null element due to *wh,* yields *You selected a book.*

The use of the base question form YESNOQ in the definitions of the *wh*-question strings is a measure of economy. As a result, the null element due to *wh* appears as the value of an element in the YESNOQ string: *Did you select* ()?. A possible linguistic interpretation is that there exists an intermediate yes–no question with an indefinite element: *Did you select (something)?*.

An analysis similar to that given for WHQ – N applies to questions that begin with a preposition and a *wh*-word. PWHQ – PN is exactly analogous to WHQ – N except that a preposition precedes the *wh*-word and the null element stands in place of a prepositional phrase PN. The preposition of the nulled PN is the one appearing at the head of the string. Thus, *On whom did you rely?* is analyzed as containing the sequence P (*on*) + *wh*-word (*whom*), followed by a YESNOQ with a null element in place of the PN object of *rely* (*on* N): *On whom did you rely* ()?. Again the interpretation is that an answer to the question (say, *on John*), if substituted for the null element in the object position in the question, would assume its correct syntactic role in the complete answer obtained by transforming the question into its corresponding assertion form: *You relied on John*.

The strings WHQ, PWHQ, and PWHNQ also contain elements that have a null value, but in these cases the element is an optional one, an adjunct string. In WHQ the type of adjunct is indicated by the *wh*-word *where, when, how,* or *why* at the head of the string: *Where/when/how/why are you going?*. The answer might be a PN string: *to the movies/in an hour/by bus/for distraction;* but it could also be an adjunct of a different form, particularly if the question word is *how* or *why: by taking a bus/to relax a little*. When the null element due to *wh* occupies the place of an adjunct string, the computer string grammar lets the NULL option of the adjunct set stand for the null due to *wh* so as to minimize the computation with null elements in the parsing. To distinguish a *wh*-string of this type (such as WHQ) from those in which a required string element has a null value (such as WHQ – N), the string name in the former type has no minus element.

In *wh*-questions and other *wh*-strings the *wh*-word can also occur in an adjectival position: *Whose book did you borrow?*. To retain the integrity of the noun phrase, we do not separate *whose* from *book* in the analysis but, rather, make a slot for the *wh*-word within the noun phrase and say that the entire noun phrase containing the *wh*-word (*whose book*) appears as the first element of the string, in the analogous position to *what* in *What did you select?* and to *on whom* in *On whom did you rely?*. The remainder of the string then has the same form as in the other *wh*-questions, namely a YESNOQ string with a null element as value for one element within the string. In particular, the null element must occur in a noun position; the mnemonic string name therefore contains " – N", and the full name WHNQ – N indicates that a *wh*-word plus a noun (WHN) precedes the main body of the question Q – N. The adjectival *wh*-word can also occur in a noun-position string based on the V*ing* form of the verb: *Which handling of the problem is more suitable?*. Accordingly, the first element WHN of the string WHNQ – N contains two options: LNR (a noun with its left and right adjuncts (5.3)) and VINGOFN (the nounlike V*ing* string (5.10)).

As a final group of this type, we have the *wh*-questions in which the *wh*-word is adjectival (the base form is the one indicated by WHNQ) and the overall form is prepositional; that is a preposition precedes the *wh*-word and the nulled element is a prepositional phrase: *On whose notes did you rely?, From which airport did you send the wire?.* The former example is an instance of the string PWHNQ – PN, in which the nulled PN is the object of *rely: On whose notes did you rely* ()?; the second example is an instance of PWHNQ, where the nulled PN is taken as an adjunct of *send*. It is considered an adjunct because the assertion without the PN is still a well-formed sentence: *You sent the wire.*

In the question form WHQ – N it will be noted that two options are provided in the second element position: YESNOQ and ASSERTION. The need for the ASSERTION option arises in the analysis of certain *wh*-questions in which the null element is in the subject position: *Who* () *came in?* The tense element here does not permute to before the subject (perhaps because the subject position is empty), so there is no need for a tense-permuted question center (YESNOQ) in order to analyze this form. It is more direct to analyze such a sentence as *Who came in?* as consisting of a *wh*-word + an ASSERTION in which a null element occurs in the subject position + a questionmark. However, the existence of both permuted and unpermuted center options creates a redundant analysis in the case where the verb is *have* or *be* and the subject is nulled; for example, the question *Who is here?* can be analyzed by either the YESNOQ option (*Who is* () *here?*) or by the ASSERTION option (*Who* () *is here?*). Since these analyses are equivalent, one option (ASSERTION) is excluded when the verb is *have* or *be* (WWH53). Since the ASSERTION option applies only to strings with subject omission (the informal term for the occurrence of a null element due to *wh* is omission), it can never follow the *wh*-word *whom*: *Ậ Whom came in?* (WWH54).

4.4   Permutation Centers

<TSUBJVO>   ::= (NEITHER|NOR |<DSTG>|<PN>) <SA> <VERB1>   4.1
                 <SUBJECT> <SA> <VERB2> <OBJECT> <RV> <SA>.

<OBES>   ::= (<PN>|<ASTG>|<DSTG>|<VENPASS>) <SA>   4.2
                 <TENSE> <SA> <VERB> <SA> <SUBJECT> <SA>.

The computer string grammar contains a rudimentary treatment of inverted assertion forms, consisting of the two strings TSUBJVO and OBES. Preceding the tense element VERB1 (7.13) in TSUBJVO we expect a negative element, either one of the words *neither, nor,* or an adverb string DSTG (9.2) or a prepositional string PN (8A.3), where the string occurrence contains a word with a negative marker: *Never has there been any sign of an adaptive remedial change, Only in one case was the value higher than 0.04* (*only* is analyzed as containing a negative element: *In only one case = In no case but one case*). The restriction that requires a negative first element (WVC7) is not an ideal treatment of the phrases that support permutation, though it covers many cases. For one thing, the attribute NEGATIVE, which is assigned to words that facilitate permutation, is not very well defined. Like many parts of the grammar, this area is "roughed out" in the interests of obtaining a broad coverage, with the hope that time and added resources will enable us to make further refinements later.

The permutation of the subject and object around *be* (OBES) is encountered rather frequently in certain authors. Not all objects of *be* appear in the preverb position. The more common ones are the prepositional phrase PN (*Of critical importance is the fact that all data, with no exceptions, are consistent with the final structure as proposed in Table III*); the adjective with its adjuncts called ASTG (8.8) (*Far more constant than the temperature is the alkalinity of sea water*[8]); the passive string called VENPASS (7.7) (*Somewhat reduced in importance thereby are the observations regarding . . .*), the adverb string DSTG (*Here is a variety that baffles description*). It is possible for the verb *be* to appear as the second or third verb in a series (*Far more important seems to be . . .*), but this is so rarely encountered that after some years this provision being carried in OBES has recently been dropped. The present string carries a restriction that the core of the VERB in OBES must be a form of *be* (WVC6).

In addition to the inverted forms presently implemented in the computer grammar, mention should be made of the center strings in which a part or the whole of the object string appears at the head of the center string; this is not infrequent with prepositional phrases that are tied closely to the verb (these are treated as objects of the verb by the string grammar): *On such calculations, our lives depend, To these may be added the phenomena of radio-activity; Out of properties of univeral matter and the characteristics of universal energy has arisen mechanism; From this relationship, therefore, follows the conclusion, fully established by experiment, that whenever in such a solution . . . .* Although less frequent, such permutations can occur for many other object strings of the grammar. There would be no difficulty in adding these strings to the grammar, but thus far the textual material has not required it. Permutations within two-part object strings are defined as alternative object strings.

A shortened form of the assertion with permuted subject and tense occurs in conjunction and comparative strings: *He left and so did she, Mammals have generally been conceded to possess a much wider "plasticity" and "adaptability" of coordination than do amphibians.* These strings are defined in the section on conjunction and comparative strings.

4.5   Subject Strings

    <SUBJECT>   ::= <NSTG>|<VINGSTG>|<SN>|<*NULLWH>|THERE.   5.1

The definition of SUBJECT (5.1) states the different options for filling the subject position in a string. The subject may be a noun string NSTG (5.2), like *fashion* in *Fashion is a custom in the guise of a departure from custom*, or it may be a nounlike sentence nominalization string based on the verb form *Ving,* the VINGSTG (5.8) as in the sentence *Seeing things to eat always makes me feel hungry.* Alternatively, it can be a more "centerlike" or "weak" nominalization string from the set SN (5.11), as in *That he is dead seems tolerably certain,* where the subject is a THATS string (6.1), or *To exploit a person is to make money out of her without giving her an equivalent return,* where the subject (and also the object) is the infinitive string TOVO (7.12) consisting of **to** + **V**erb + **O**bject. Two other options of SUB-JECT are the null element *NULLWH and the word *there*. We have already seen evidence of the null element due to *wh* in the *wh*-question in Sec. 4.3 (*Who () came in?*); the conditions for accepting the *NULLWH as the value of SUBJECT are given by a restriction (WWH2). *There* is analyzed as the subject in such sentences as *There were three hundred people elbowing and jostling one another* and *There is nothing to forgive,* for the reasons summarized in Sec. 4.2.2.

4.5.1   *Noun String and Names*

<NSTG>	::= <LNR>|<NWHSTG>.	5.2
<LNR>	::= <LN> <NVAR> <RN>.	5.3
<NVAR>	::= <*N>|<*PRO>|<*VING>|<NAMESTG>|<*NULLN>.	5.4
<NAMESTG>	::= <LNAMER>|<NQ>.	5.6
<LNAMER>	::= <LNAME> <*N> <RNAME>.	5.7

The option NSTG covers a wide variety of noun-position occurrences. The main ones are covered by the definition LNR (5.3), consisting of a noun (or one of its local variants) with its left and right adjuncts. The variants include proper names, pronouns, and compound nouns. In the latter case, the head of the compound, or in our terminology the core of LNR, is a noun or a V*ing* word. Thus, *log book* and *log rolling* are both instances of LNR; in the former the value of NVAR in LNR is *N (*book*) and in the latter it is *VING (*rolling*).[9] For purposes of describing certain sequences that occupy the same position as a noun but consist only of members of LN not followed by a noun (like *the poor, each*), the grammar provides a null element *NULLN of NVAR, standing for a real noun that could occur after the given sequence. The missing noun is either a classifier noun (*one, thing, person*) or a more specific noun that can be supplied by the context: *Each expressed a different option* (each person), *Of six samples tested, five were pure* (five samples). The *NULLN could be dispensed with, of course, by simply defining new subject strings consisting of particular sequences of members of LN. Using the *NULLN analysis, the specific sequences permitted before a *NULLN are stated in a restriction (DN1).

Pronouns occur in the same positions as nouns, and occur with limited left and right adjuncts of the noun (*Only she can help you, He who hesitates is lost*). On the left, only a small subclass of adverbs (DLTPRO) occurs (WN11). On the right, some RN strings are more comfortable with particular pronouns, and an attempt to grade the likeliness of particular PRO + RN combinations is made in restrictions DN52–DN56. A more important restriction on pronoun occurrences concerns whether the pronoun should be nominative or accusative: *He went, We saw him go* (WPOS5, WPOS6).

Proper names and namelike sequences can occur in the position of nouns, and, like pronouns, take limited left and right adjuncts: *A certain Mr. Smith from Toronto called.* Names have an internal structure that is represented by the definition NAMESTG (5.6). Proper names are covered by an LXR definition, the option LNAMER of NAMESTG (left adjuncts of NAME + **NAME** + right adjuncts of NAME (5.7)), in which the left adjuncts, LNAME (14.13), include an optional title noun (*Dr., Ms., Mrs., President*) and an optional sequence of names or initials preceding the last name. The right adjuncts, RNAME (13.7), are such items as *Jr., Ph.D., M.D.* The parse tree for *Dr. Francis P. Jones, M.D.* is shown in Fig. 4.1.

In addition to their internal structure, names can have left and right adjuncts drawn from LN and RN. This is illustrated in Fig. 4.2, which shows the parse tree for *the recently appointed Dr. Francis P. Jones, M.D., a pharmacologist.* RN here is the apposition string APPOS. Note that if no restrictions are placed on LN and RN as adjuncts of names, the sequence *Francis Jones* can be analyzed in several ways: as an instance of NAMESTG similar to that in Fig. 4.2, and also as NAMESTG = *Jones* with LN = *Francis* (in NPOS, as though *Francis Jones* were a compound noun), and again as NAMESTG = *Francis* with an appositional right adjunct *Jones*, similar to *my friend Jones.* These possibilities in the context-free grammar are rejected by restrictions (WN11, WN13).

Fig. 4.1 **Parse tree showing NAMESTG.**

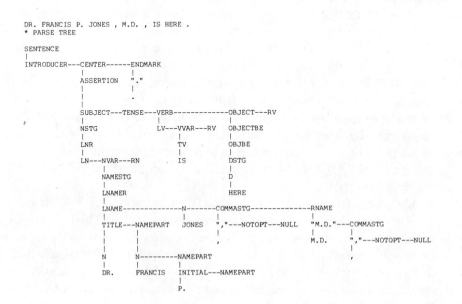

Fig. 4.2   Parse tree showing NAMESTG with left and right adjuncts.

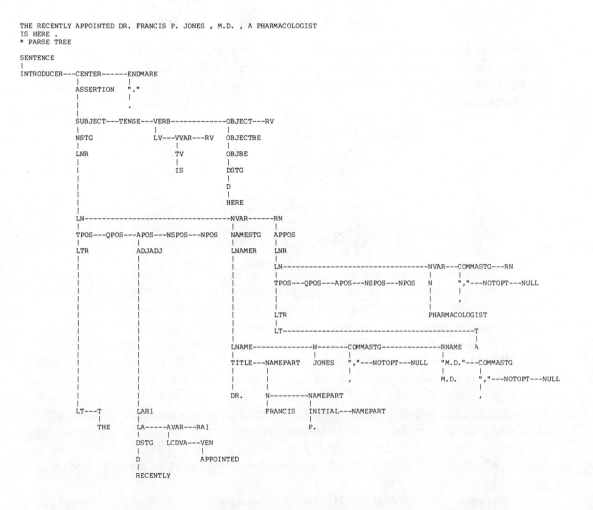

The second option NQ of **NAMESTG** arises as follows: In scientific writing one frequently encounters phrases like *Series 1, Table A, Figure 3*, which have the form of a noun followed by a number or a letter. The name of this string in the string grammars is NQ, which stands for **n**oun + **q**uantifier (12.20). It occurs both as a noun phrase, as in *A schematic diagram is shown in Figure 3,* and as a left adjunct of a noun, as in *the Series 1 values.* In its noun phrase occurrence it is like a name, and so it has been placed in NAMESTG as a second option. The nouns that occur in the N position of NQ are not a sharply defined class, but it is nevertheless efficient to place in a subclass NPREQ (**n**ouns **p**receding **Q**) those nouns occurring most frequently in this position, and to require this type of noun in a well-formed occurrence of NQ (WN12).

4.5.2   *Noun-Replacing* wh-*strings*

$$<\text{NWHSTG}> \quad ::= <\text{WHATS}-\text{N}> \mid <\text{WHERES}> \mid <\text{WHEVERS}-\text{N}>. \qquad 5.5$$

Wh-strings can occur in a noun position in two ways, represented in the string grammar by the two sets SNWH (sentence **n**ominalization **wh**-string (6.5)), an option of SN (5.11), and NWHSTG (**n**oun-equivalent **wh**-**str**ing (5.5)). These two types can be illustrated by the following contrasting examples:[10]

What was lost in the war can never be determined.

(WHS – N in SNWH)

What was lost in the war can never be regained.

(WHATS – N in NWHSTG)

An NWHSTG replaces a particular noun (or string), whereas an SNWH is a nominalization of a sentence under *whether . . . or . . .* or one of the other *wh*-words or *wh*-phrases, like *what, who, whom, which, how much.* We find NWHSTGs in sentences that assert what the missing noun or string is: *What he loves is (are) bananas, What he loves to do is walk;* or in sentences that assert something about the missing noun or string, as in *What she cooks always tastes good, What happened next will make your hair stand on end.* Note that a concrete verb or predicate on a *what*-string subject shows that the *what*-string is an NWHSTG and not an SNWH: *Ⱥ Whether she cooks X or Y or Z tastes good.* Conversely, if the verb or predicate of a *what*-string is not definite in this regard—that is if it can have as its subject either a nominalized sentence or a concrete noun—then ambiguity results: *What the* Times *critic says is decisive.* In the SNWH reading, whether the critic approves or disapproves will have a decisive effect, whereas in the NWHSTG reading some particular point the critic made was particularly persuasive.

The present definition of NWHSTG in the computer grammar has three quite limited options.[11] WHATS – N (15.9) covers occurrences headed by *what*: **What follows** *is a summary,* **What I ate last night** *made me sick.* WHERES (15.10) covers occurrences headed by *where:* **Where he went wrong** *is in putting himself above the law.* WHEVERS – N (15.15) covers N-omitting strings headed by words of the form *wh-ever*, in particular, the more frequent ones *whoever, whomever, whichever, whatever, whosoever:* **Whoever comes** *is welcome; I'll give the book to* **whoever comes** *for it.*

4.5.3   *Nounlike Sentence Nominalizations*

We come now to sentence nominalizations other than those headed by *wh*-words. English is rich in such forms. They range from strong nominalizations in which the central

word is morphologically a noun (*The loss of the key by John was mentioned*), to those differing from complete sentences only in the addition of a preceding word such as *that*: *That
John lost the key was mentioned*. In between there are various grades of "nounlikeness"
correlating in various respects with particular semantic interpretations. The strongest
nominalizations are so nounlike that for purposes of the string analysis they are best handled
as nouns with left and right adjuncts, as instances of LNR. The subject and object of the
nominalized verb or adjective in these forms have the external shape of adjuncts. The subject, for example, can have the form N's (*my friend's return*), *by* N (*the discovery of germanium by Winkler*), *of* N (*the fitness of the environment*). The object often appears in the
form PN, with P either *of* or a preposition that is characteristic for the given verb or adjective: *the rational classification of chemical properties, every conceivable change from one
form of energy to another.* In addition, like adjuncts, these adjunctlike sequences may be
dropped in almost all cases. For example, *change* occcurs without *from . . . to* in *Not every
conceivable change is possible.* But is should be noted that unlike adjuncts, the optionality of
these sequences is sometimes limited, and sometimes their absence means that the core word
is occurring in a different sense.

4.5.4   V*ing* Strings

<VINGSTG>   ::= <NSVINGO>|<VINGOFN>.   5.8

<NSVINGO>   ::= <TPOS>< VINGO>.   5.9

<VINGOFN>   ::= <LN>< LVINGR> (OF|NULL) <OBJECT> <RV> <SA>.   5.10

The situation is somewhat more favorable for defining a sentence nominalization string
in the case of nominalizations based on the V*ing* form of the verb: *John's losing of the key,
the losing of the key by John, John's losing the key.* Some of the features of the strong
sentence nominalizations are also found in the V*ing* forms, for example the adjunctlike
shapes of the subject and object: N*'s, by* N, *of* N, PN. Compare, for example, *John's loss of
the key* with *John's losing of the key*, and *The loss of the key by John* with *The losing of the
key by John.* However, the V*ing* forms are just that much more regular with respect to an
assumed underlying declarative sentence as to suggest that the string definitions for the V*ing*
forms should reflect that relation. Thus, the V*ing*-based forms are defined as verb-containing
strings in the computer grammar, VINGSTG (5.8), whereas the similar, but less regular,
derived-noun forms are treated as LNR.

Some of the differences between V*ing* forms and derived-noun (V*n*) forms are these.
There is more regularity as to the appropriate preposition before the object noun following a
V*ing* than following a derived-noun V*n*. In transitive V*ing* occurrences, if the object noun
phrase is preceded by a preposition, then that preposition is *of*. However, in a V*n* sequence,
if the object of V*n* begins with a noun phrase preceded by a preposition then either *of* or
some other preposition particular to the V*n* precedes the object: *John's loving of Mary, Ḁ*

John's loving for Mary, but both *John's love of Mary* and *John's love for Mary*. In the V*n* form sometimes a new preposition (not *of*) is introduced, or the preposition that usually occurs with the verb is replaced by another, something that does not happen in the V*ing* forms: *Mary's instructions to John that he must be more prompt,* ≠ *Mary's instructing to John that he must be more prompt; Mary's sympathy for those people,* ≠ *Mary's sympathizing for those people*, but both *Mary's sympathy with those people*, and *Mary's sympathizing with those people*. A similar situation arises in cases where an *of* is introduced between the two parts of a two-part object in the V*n* case but not in the V*ing* case: *Mary explained to John what happened, Mary's explaining to John what happened, Mary's explanation to John of what happened,* but only marginally if at all: *Mary's explaining to John of what happened.*[12]

The occurrences of V*ing* sequences are thus more regular than those based on V*n* and more readily support verb-containing string definitions. The next problem is to compare the different V*ing* sequences and determine which belong in separate definitions. Both form and potential ambiguity are considerations. When there are contrasting differences in the outward form of the V*ing* occurrences we are able to set up different string definitions to cover the contrasting occurrences. It then turns out that some of the noncontrasting occurrences of these defined strings, the cases where the different definitions cover the same word sequence, correlate with a perceived ambiguity, and it is possible to associate the differences in the interpretation of the word sequence with the different string analyses (examples will be given). The converse is not always the case, however. Not every ambiguity is associated with different string parses, because some ambiguities correlate with different transformational analyses of the same string form, and some ambiguities relate only to the meanings of the individual words.

Two V*ing* string forms that can be distinguished on the basis of contrasting occurrences are the more nounlike VINGOFN string (**V*ing* of N** (5.10)) and the less nounlike NSVINGO (**N*'s* V*ing* O***bject*, 5.9). Adverb modifiers of the verb generally have adjectival form in VINGOFN (*their punctual answering of letters*, and adverbial form in NSVINGO (*their answering letters punctually,* ≠ *Their punctual answering letters*). This difference is represented in the definitions by placing LN to the left of VING in VINGOFN but not in NSVINGO. However, adverbial modifiers that occur in prepositional form, such as PN of manner, may occur as postobject RV in VINGOFN: *their playing of the second movement at a slow tempo*. Another contrast is that the articles *the* and *a, an* generally occur with the VINGOFN form rather than the NSVINGO form (*the answering of letters,* ≠ *the answering letters*),[13] and certain other words that occur in the article position are also more comfortable in the VINGOFN form than the NSVINGO form, among them *each, every, some, either, neither, any: each rewriting of the preface,* ≠ *each rewriting the preface*. (WSN10 and WSN11 tailor the article position accordingly.)

Both VINGOFN and NSVINGO accept a genitive form for the subject of VING: *John's writing of poetry, John's writing poetry*. The genitive may be a possessive noun N*'s* with its left and right adjuncts, LNSR (12.4), or a possessive noun (*his, their*). Both of these occur in the same position as articles vis-a-vis other left adjuncts of N or VING (*his generous giving,* *his generous gift*). These occurrences are all covered by the definition of TPOS (article **posi**-tion (12.2)) in the BNF grammar. In NSVINGO TPOS appears as an element; in VINGOFN it appears within the element LN, which precedes VING in the string definition.

Contrasting VING occurrences are also seen in the OBJECT position when the object is one that begins with (or is) a noun phrase. (This noun phrase will be referred to simply as N.) The VINGOFN string expects an *of* before an N object (*their answering of our letters),* whereas the NSVINGO string does not (*their answering our letters*). Another contrast is in the range of values of OBJECT. In general the NSVINGO string accepts the same range and form of object strings for the V*ing* word as are accepted in the ASSERTION for tensed forms of the same verb. For example, THATS: *His parents strongly preferred **that he remain in college;** his parents' strongly preferring **that he remain in college.** In contrast, the V*ing* word in the VINGOFN string occurs almost exclusively with object strings that begin with N or PN.[14] This preference is pronounced if a derived noun (V*n*) form of the same verb exists in the language (*his parents' strong **preference** that he remain in college;* uncomfortable: *his parents' strong **preferring** that he remain in college*). However, when there is no corresponding V*n* form in the language, V*ing* may have a wider range of objects: *his parents' insistent urging that he remain in college.*[15]

There are certain V*ing* occurrences that have none of the contrasting features of VINGOFN versus NSVINGO. For example, *his driving* could be analyzed as an occurrence of either string since only N*'s* (*his*) appears to the left of V*ing* (*driving*) and there is no noun object to occur with an *of* (VINGOFN) or without an *of* (NSVINGO). Such a sequence is potentially ambiguous, as can be seen in *His driving worries his mother,* where in one interpretation it is the fact of his driving under some circumstance that worries his mother (NSVINGO), and in another interperation it is the manner of his driving that is worrisome (VINGOFN). Sometimes the predicate of the VINGSTG subject disambiguates such noncontrasting occurrences, since not all predicates occurring with VINGOFN as subject can occur equally well with NSVINGO as subject: *His phrasing of the idea was clear, ≠ His phrasing the idea was clear.* In this example *clear* is a predicate of manner, which is a type favoring VINGOFN occurrences. We can therefore expect that a noncontrasting (potentially ambiguous) V*ing* occurrence will not in fact be ambiguous if the predicate is either sharply manner or sharply fact. Thus, *His speaking was impressive* is ambiguous (the fact that he spoke versus his manner of speaking), whereas *His speaking took courage* (fact) and *His speaking was garbled* (manner) are both unambiguous. Unfortunately, it has not been possible thus far to classify predicates as to fact versus manner in the computer word dictionary. We are therefore left with many cases where an occurrence of a VINGSTG is not in fact ambiguous, but the computer has no way of checking this fact. Until finer word classes for predicates or further disambiguating techniques are developed, noncontrasting VINGSTG occurrences are shunted into the NSVINGO string (WSN10, WSN11).

Another ambiguity arises because some V*ing* words have an occurrence in which they represent the product or result of the V action: *Her cooking tastes good.* If the environment is not clearly fact, manner, or result, then ambiguity results, as in *Her cooking is marvelous.*

Here the fact reading is equivalent to "It is marvelous that she is cooking." The manner reading states that her way of cooking (her skill) is marvelous. Finally, the result reading states that the product of her cooking tastes marvelous. No separate string has been defined for the result nominalization.

4.6   Sentence Nominalization Strings

In the spectrum of sentence nominalization strings from most nounlike to least nounlike, the least nounlike have been collected into the set SN (5.11).

<SN>	::= <THATS>|<FORTOVO>|<TOVO>| –<SVINGO>| <C1SHOULD>|<SNWH>.	5.11
<THATS>	::= THAT <ASSERTION>.	6.1
<FORTOVO>	::= FOR <SUBJECT > <SA> <TOVO>.	6.2
<SVINGO>	::= <SUBJECT> <SA> <VINGO>.	6.3
<C1SHOULD>	::= (THAT | – NULL) <ASSERTION>.	6.4
<SNWH>	::= <WHETHS>|<WHETHTOVO>|<WHS-N>| <PWHS>|<PWHS-PN>|<WHNS-N>|<PWHNS>| <PWHNS-PN>.	6.5

These strings are also named individually as options of OBJECT, but we shall present them here as subject strings, giving mainly examples of their occurrence as SUBJECT.

The classical representative of these so-called weak nominalizations is the form consisting of *that* + a declarative sentence, THATS (6.1): *That this simplifies the chronologic problem is obvious*. In the LSP grammar this has the form:

<THATS> ::= THAT <ASSERTION>.

Slightly less nounlike because the verb loses the tense is the string FORTOVO (**for** + subject + *to* + verb + object (6.2): *For it to dawn upon her consciousness that she wished for something, was definitely to renounce that wish*. Here, the verb takes the infinitive form and the subject is preceded by *for*. When the subject is indefinite, the portion *for* + subject can be dropped, so that TOVO (7.12) is the string form: *to keep in love* in *Falling in love and winning love are often difficult tasks; but to keep in love is also a business of some importance*.

The subjunctive form in English is represented in the computer grammar by the string C1SHOULD (6.4). The name contains C1, an old LSP name for ASSERTION, and *should*, the only tense word allowed in this string. Occurrences of this string are either tenseless or contain the tense word *should*(WSN4): *That he be honest is the only requirement, That he* (*should*) *write to his father is absolutely imperative.* This string has the form

$$\text{<C1SHOULD>} \quad ::= \text{(THAT} \mid -\text{NULL)} \text{ <ASSERTION>.}$$

The NULL alternative to THAT indicates that in some positions (in particular, the object position) the THAT may be absent, though this is rare in scientific writing: *This would require (that)   X be zero.*[16] A restriction (WSN5) ensures that a *that* is present in subject occurrences.[17]

A rather rare subject string SVINGO (subject + **V***ing* + **o**bject (6.3)) is one in which the subject of VING does not take a genitive form: *Is the lady bothering you any reason for you to come bothering me?, Parliament breaking up immediately after gave the officials a good excuse for doing nothing more.* This string rarely has a pronoun in subject position (WSN9): *Ⱥ Him leaving early is a surprise, Someone leaving early is a disturbance* (considered rare).

Though it is rare (DSN8), an SN string can in principle be the value of the SUBJECT in an SN string. For example, SVINGO is the value of the SUBJECT in SVINGO in the (rare) sentence *His leaving passing unnoticed surprised me.* Similarly THATS (with one THAT suppressed) is the value of the SUBJECT in a THATS string in *That he left passed unnoticed surprised me.* The grammar must therefore be able to provide for such occurrences, though this raises an interesting question for the top-down parser. In calling upon SN as the value of SUBJECT in an SN string such as SVINGO, whose first element is SUBJECT containing again the option SN, the prospect of an "infinite loop" is encountered. Definitions with this property are therefore named on a TYPE RECURSIVE list, and are handled specially.[18]

The sentence-nominalization *wh*-string, SNWH (6.5) was contrasted earlier with occurrences of the noun-equivalent NWHSTG (5.5), as in *What he eats is a mystery* (SNWH) versus *What he eats is what he can get* (NWHSTG). In scientific writing SNWH strings occur when questions are posed for discussion or inquiry, or philosophically: *In what respect and how far life is destined ever to remain a scientific riddle can only be surmised.* The form of these strings is in many cases identical to *wh*-strings that occur as right adjuncts of the noun (relative clauses). These strings are therefore all defined in a special section, 15, of the grammar. The particular *wh*-strings that occur as SNWH are named as options of the SNWH definition.

4.7   Verb and Verbal Object Strings

<VERB>	::= <LV> <VVAR> <RV>.	7.1
<VVAR>	::= <*TV>|<*V>.	7.1A
<LTVR>	::= <LW> <*TV> <RW>.	7.2
<TENSE>	::= <LW> <*W> <RW>|NULL.	7.3
<LVR>	::= <LV> <*V> <RV>.	7.4

\<VENO\>	::= \<LVENR\> \<SA\> \<OBJECT\> \<RV\>.	7.5
\<LVENR\>	::= \<LV\> \<*VEN\> \<RV\>.	7.6
\<VENPASS\>	::= \<LVSA\> \<LVENR\> \<SA\> \<PASSOBJ\> \<RV\> \<SA\>.	7.7
\<LVSA\>	::= NULL |\<DSTG\>.	7.8
\<VINGO\>	::= \<LVSA\> \<LVINGR\> \<SA\> \<OBJECT\> \<RV\> \<SA\>.	7.9
\<LVINGR\>	::= \<LV\> \<*VING\> \<RV\>.	7.10
\<VO\>	::= \<LVR\> \<SA\> \<OBJECT\> \<RV\> \<SA\>.	7.11
\<TOVO\>	::= \<LV\> TO \<VERB\> \<SA\> \<OBJECT\> \<RV\> \<SA\>.	7.12
\<TOBE\>	::= \<LV\> TO \<VERB\> \<SA\> \<OBJECT\> \<RV\> \<SA\>.	7.12A
\<VERB1\>	::= \<TENSE\> |\<LTVR\>.	7.13
\<VERB2\>	::= \<LVR\> \<SA\> |NULL.	71.4

(Note: For definitions of OBJECT and PASSOBJ, refer to Appendix 1.)

The set of definitions for the verb position follows from two main decisions on how to treat the verb computationally. One of these decisions concerns the tense of the main verb and the other concerns extended verbal sequences, such as are found in compound tenses (*be* V*ing, have* V*en*) and aspectuals of the type exemplified by *begin to* V, *begin* V*ing*. With regard to the treatment of tense, verbs that carry a tense suffix *-ed, -s,* or zero (present plural) are in the major word class TV as distinct from the infinitive V; that is, the tense suffix is not separated from the verb. The modals, along with auxiliary occurrences of *do*, constitute a separate word class W. Thus *They walk* is represented by PRO TV, and *They will walk* by PRO W V. As a result of these lexical classes the ASSERTION and other center strings must accommodate the affixed tense and the separate-word tense differently. In the former case, the element VERB in ASSERTION is satisfied by a single word TV, possibly with adjuncts. In the latter case, two element positions are required, TENSE and VERB in ASSERTION, with the possibility that sentence adjuncts may intervene (*He will certainly walk*); the TENSE element is satisfied by a W word and the VERB element by the infinitive V. A restriction (WVC1) ensures that TENSE is empty preceding a tensed main verb TV (∄*He will walks*), and that an infinitive V does not occur as the main verb unless the preceding TENSE element is not empty (∄ *He walk*). In the yes–no question center YESNOQ (3.1) the elements corresponding to TENSE and VERB are VERB1 and VERB2. VERB1 differs from TENSE in providing the additional option LTVR covering tensed forms of *have* and *be*, which can precede the subject in questions (Sec. 4.3) and which take tense adjuncts in place of verb adjuncts.

With regard to the treatment of extended verbal sequences it should be noted that the compound tenses (*He is walking, He has walked, He has been walking,* and so on) are only the tip of the iceberg when it comes to expressing aspect and other local modifications of the verb, such as *He began walking, He tried to walk, He is trying to begin to walk.* Rather than define two mechanisms, one for the conventional compound tenses *be* V*ing* and *have* V*en*, and another for the more numerous and more complex aspectual (and other) operators on the verb, it was decided to make a uniform treatment of all verbal sequences occurring after the inflected verb or after the sequence W V(modal + infinitive). The elements TENSE and VERB of ASSERTION, and the elements VERB1 and VERB2 of YESNOQ, cover the first inflected verb TV or sequence W V, and all subsequent verbal elements are analyzed as object strings. This places all recursion of verbal elements into the object position and facilitates the definition of routines that can "look through" aspectual and other operators on the verb (see DEEPEST-COVERB in Sec. 3.3). It also prepares the way for a uniform transformational treatment of all operators on the verb and sentence.

In accord with this decision the set of definitions classed as verbal includes a number of object string definitions. They appear as options of OBJECT in section 8 of the BNF grammar, but they are defined here because of their role in extending the verb. VENO (7.5) covers the past participle V*en* + object: *He has sold his soul to the devil.* VINGO (7.9) covers the present participle V*ing* + object: *I'm losing my mind, She succeeded in being accepted.* TOVO (7.12) covers *to* + V + object: *He began to worry, She loves to swim.* VENPASS (7.7) covers the passive string: *He was held prisoner.* The way in which this analysis appears in the parse tree can be seen in Fig. 3.1.[19]

This way of treating compound tenses is reflected in the lexical entries for *have, be,* and *do.* The OBJLIST attribute (defined at the beginning of Sec. 4.8) for *have* contains VENO, indicating that this is an acceptable value of OBJECT following a verb element whose core is one of the forms of *have.* Because of the unique properties of the verb *be,* its object specification is a definition of the grammar, OBJECTBE (8.3), described in Sec. 4.8.1; OBJECTBE contains VINGO and VENPASS among its options. The OBJLIST attribute of *be* in the lexicon accordingly consists of the sole entry OBJECTBE. *Do* is in the modal class W as well as in the major verb classes, V, TV, VING, VEN, which cover its occurrences in, for example, *He hates to do his homework, She has done all the painting of the woodwork alone.* Of course, the grammar must ensure that only well-formed occurrences of sequences of *have, be, do* are accepted (∄ *He is having gone*). This is done by restrictions (WVC2, WVC3).

The definitions of the VERB and TENSE elements and of the VING and VEN and V elements in the verbal object strings all have standard LXR forms, though in some cases, such as VERB and TENSE, we have retained the more conventional names. These LXR definitions are VERB (7.1), LTVR (7.2), TENSE (7.3), LVR (7.4), LVENR (7.6), LVINGR (7.10), VERB1 (7.13), VERB2 (7.14). In these definitions (except LTVR, which takes tense adjuncts) the left adjunct slot is filled by LV, the left adjuncts of the verb (14.2), and the right adjunct slot by RV, the right adjuncts of the verb (13.5). The main left and right adjuncts of verbs are adverbs of different types. The right adjuncts also include prepositional phrases (*they left in a hurry*) and, for some verbs, quantity expressions (*He ran twenty yards*).

4.8   Object Strings

There are presently close to sixty object strings defined in the LSP grammar. Particular verbs occur only with a subset of these strings. In parsing a sentence, it would be time-consuming to try all the options in the definition of OBJECT (8.1) after every verb. We therefore list for every verb in the lexicon the object strings that can occur with that verb; these appear in the verb's lexical entry as the values of the attribute OBJLIST. When the node OBJECT is to be built, the options of OBJECT are compared to the values of OBJLIST in the lexical entry for the verb governing OBJECT, and only those named in both lists are tried (DVC1). A similar restriction is applied at the object position PASSOBJ (8.2) in the passive string VENPASS (7.7), calling on the attribute POBJLIST of the verb (DVC2). The foregoing provision in the grammar means that the job of classifying verbs for the LSP lexicon requires a considerable knowledge of the grammar. Object string occurrences are not always immediately distinguishable from other occurrences of the same word sequences, that is, from word sequence occurrences that have a different analysis in the grammar. It is thus in establishing the diagnostic frames to be used in classifying verbs for the lexicon that the most careful statements regarding the intent of each object string definition are made. This work is embodied in the OBJLIST definitions in Appendix 3. The summary here is therefore limited to the main object string types.

4.8.1   *Objects of* be

<OBJECTBE>	::= <VENPASS>|<VINGO>|<OBJBE>|<SN>| −<VINGSTG>|<TOVO>|−<ASSERTION>| −<BEINGO>|<EMBEDDEDQ>.	8.3
<OBJBE>	::= <ASTG>|<NSTG>|<PN>|<DSTG>| <*NULLWH>.	8.4
<BEINGO>	::= <LV> BEING (<LAR>|<NSTG>).	8.5
<ASTG>	::= <LAR>|<LQNR>.	8.8
<LAR>	::= <LA> <AVAR> <RA>.	8.9
<EMBEDDEDQ>	::= [↓:↓] <QUESTION>.	8.10

Let us begin the coverage of word strings in the predicate position with the definition OBJECTBE (8.3). This definition is only invoked following actual occurrences of forms of *be*. It covers the use of *be* as an auxiliary verb, and in other constructions to be described, as well as in true predicate occurrences covered by the option OBJBE (8.4), where *be* is followed by an adjective (*The earth is round*), a noun (*Glucagon is a protein*), a prepositional phrase (*The book is on the table*), or an adverb (*Spring is here*). The corresponding options of OBJBE are ASTG (8.8), NSTG (5.2), PN (8A.3), and DSTG (9.2). OBJBE is also an element of predicate-based strings that lack an explicit verb *be*.[20]

ASTG covers occurrences of adjectives (*young, free*), adjectival V*ing* and V*en* (*very surprising, badly behaved*), compound advectives (*dust free*), compound V*ing*/V*en* adjectives (*high flying, high strung*); it also covers measure sequences like *seven inches long, two inches in diameter*, which are instances of the string QN (12.17). All of these may occur with appropriate left and right adjuncts so that the definition of ASTG consists of two options: LAR (8.9), in which AVAR (12.14) covers all the adjective variants, and LQNR (12.15) consisting of QN with quantitative left and right adjuncts.

The NSTG option of OBJBE covers predicates of a classificatory nature (*Man is a mammal*); these agree with the subject noun in number. However, other uses of *be* + N are also covered, and the predicate nouns in these occurrences do not always agree with the subject (*The solution is more policemen, Her paintings are a delight*), often because of the zeroing of another verb (*The solution is [to have] more policemen*) or to other transformations that lead to an *is* form (WAGREE2). Count-noun constraints are lifted in predicate occurrences of a subclass of nouns (NCOUNT3): *He is president, We elected him president, He remained president, A President is here* (WN9).

PN is not a frequently occurring object of *be* in scientific writing except in PNs preceding sentential complements: *It is often of importance to determine the relative percentages of isotopes in natural elements*. These will be discussed presently. Adverbial predicates are covered by the option DSTG in OBJBE, where the adverb in DSTG is limited to a subclass DPRED: *He is here, He is well* (WPOS1H). These are not frequent in scientific writing.

In addition to the predicates in elementary sentences, the options of OBJBE cover occurrences of sentential complements in predicate position, following an adjective or noun in one of the subclasses ASENT1, ASENT3, NSENT1-3, NSENTP: *It is true that he came, They are anxious for you to attend, It is a fact that he came, It is of interest how they voted* (DSN5). These complement strings are in the set SN (Sec. 4.6). To cover their occurrence in the predicate, SN appears as an option of RA, RN and RV.

The NSTG option of OBJBE also serves to cover occurrences of the type *It is* N (*that/wh*-) S – N where S – N stands for a sentence from which N has been "extracted," that is, an occurrence of an ASSERTION string with a *NULLWH in the N position: *It is John that you saw*. The N in NSTG in this case need not agree with the subject *it* (assuming *it* to be singular): *It is the proteins which concern us here* (WAGREE2). The portion (*that/wh*) S – N has the same form as some of the *wh*-strings in RN and is analyzed that way by the present LSP grammar.[21]

Leaving the "inner" objects of *be*·OBJBE we come first to occurrences of *be* as a verbal element in the progressive tense form *be* V*ing* and as a carrier of the passive. Both of these usages are seen in the LSP grammar as occurrences of the verb *be* followed by an object string: VINGO (7.9) in the case of the progressive tense, and VENPASS (7.7) in the case of the passive, as was noted in Sec. 4.7. The verb *be* does not itself occur in the progressive tense—that is, in the V*ing* form preceded by *be*—except as part of the passive (*They are being* *watched*) or with restricted subject and object, where it takes on a special sense: *He is **being foolish, He is being a pest,** ⅟ The ball is **being round***. Because of the rarity of the latter, it is efficient to define a special object string BEINGO (8.5) for these occurrences.

The other main occurrence of *be* is with some form of nominalized sentence as its object. This may be a string from the set SN (*An additional difficulty is **that we have no money***) or one of the V*ing* forms from the set VINGSTG (5.8): *An added worry is **meeting the deadline***. The subject, of course, is restricted: ⅟ *An additional person is that we have no money* (DSN1). The SN strings based on the infinitive (TOVO and FORTOVO) occur as the object of *be* with the same restrictions on the subject as other SN strings, but in addition they occur pairwise around *be: to live is to love* (WSN3). An embedded question, EMBEDDEDQ (8.10) can follow *be*, provided the subject is an NSENT noun of the type that occurs with *wh*-complements: *The question is: **Can they obtain the 2/3 majority?*** (DSN12).

A last note on OBJECTBE pertains to occurrences of the *is to* form: *He is to leave on Sunday*. Only tensed forms of *be* are involved: ⅟ *He will be to leave on Sunday*. For this reason tensed forms of *be* + *to* (*is to, was to*) could be entered as idioms having the classification W, that is, in the modal class. Rather, in the present LSP grammar the infinitive string TOVO is listed as an option of OBJECTBE (in addition to its occurrence in the SN option of OBJECTBE), with a restriction (DPOS1) limiting its acceptance to occurrences following a tensed form of *be*.

4.8.2   *Basic Object Strings*

We may group together under the heading basic object strings options of OBJECT that for the most part are the object forms remaining in elementary sentences after all transformations have been reversed. These are generally short (exclusive of adjuncts) and exclude sentence nominalization strings.[22]

The basic object strings include NSTGO (8.6), which covers the direct object (*We saw John, We saw him);* NN (8.7), covering the indirect object (*We gave him a book*); PN (8A.3), covering direct objects preceded by a preposition (*They rely on John*), NPN and its inverted variant PNN (8A.8, 8A.9) as in *One can correlate suicide rates with rainy weather, One can correlate with outside factors many psychologically determined behaviors and states;* the particle DP such as *on* in *He carried on alone* (the string DP1 (8B.1)); forms of DP + N and DP + N + PN as in *They broke up the meeting,* DP2 (8B.2); *They broke it up,* DP3 (8B.3); *The breaking up of the meeting,* DP4, (8B.4); *She moved in on him,* DP1PN (8B.6); *I mixed up one string with a similar one,* DP2PN (8B.7); *I mixed it up with another one,* DP3PN (8B.8); *the mixing up of one with another,* DP4PN (8B.9).

These object strings, while basic in the sense mentioned before, are string forms that cover a large number of subtypes, many of which can be associated with transformations. A number of the different subtypes, and some of the transformational sources, have been cited in the definitions of OBJLIST attributes in Sec. IV of Appendix 3 and in greater detail in

Sager 1968. These attributes bear the same names as the object strings and many details regarding each object string will be found in the attribute definitions.

4.8.3   *Sentence Nominalization Strings in OBJECT*

A large variety of forms of embedded sentences are found in the object position in English sentences. All of the sentence nominalization strings that occur in the subject position (SN and VINGSTG) occur in the object, and there are new types that occur only in the object. In addition, many of these forms occur with a noun or PN preceding the embedded sentence (*I told him you were coming*) and these must be accounted for by explicit definition. All in all, with the SN and VINGSTG options, and counting the sentential options of basic object string definitions as new definitions, there are some forty object strings in the LSP grammar that are concerned specifically with covering sentence nominalization forms.

We may start with the basic object strings, which by extension cover V*ing*-based nominalization strings in the noun positions. Extending the PN form in this way we have the strings PVINGSTG (8A.4): *He talked about (our) raising money;* PSVINGO (8A.5): *He talked about them raising money, He spoke about there being no alternatives;* PVINGO (8A.6): *They succeeded in taking control,* and ⫫ *They succeeded in our taking control;* PSNWH (8A.7): *We asked about whether visas would be issued.*

Extensions of the NPN string to cover V*ing* occurrences in part repeat the above four strings (8A.4–7), each here preceded by an object noun. Thus, NPVINGSTG (8A.12): *He told them about our raising money;* NPSVINGO (8A.13): *He told us about them raising money, He informed us about there being no raises;* NPVINGO (8A.14): *She restrained him from borrowing money,* and ⫫ *She restrained him from our borrowing money;* NPSNWH (8A.15): *We asked him about whether visas would be issued.* However, these forms also cover cases where the verb is like *attribute* and the first noun position in the NPN form stands for an event or is a derived noun while the second noun position contains a VINGSTG: *They attributed his depression to his wife's leaving him.* The NPN form also can be extended by having a VINGSTG in the first noun position, with either a noun or VINGSTG or SVINGO in the second noun position: *They reported his not tolerating medicine to the doctor, They attributed her leaving to there being no chances for advancement.* These NPN extensions are all covered by VINGSTGPN (8A.10), and its inverted form PNVINGSTG (8A.11): *They reported to the doctor his not tolerating medication and refusing food.*

In a similar way, the basic DP strings are extended to include VINGSTG in the noun position of DP2-4: *They kept up their writing to the President* (DP2); and further by adding the options PVINGSTG and PSVINGO in the PN position of DP1PN, DP2PN, DP3PN, DP4PN (8B.6–9): *They traced back his breathing difficulties to early heavy smoking of cigarettes* (DP2PN). DP can also precede an SN string in the object: *They let out that a change of government would not be frowned on.* This is covered by the string DPSN (8B.5).

The object nominalization strings that are neither extensions of basic object strings nor simple repeats of the subject nominalization strings SN and VINGSTG can be divided into those forms that are new in the object position and those consisting of an SN string preceded

by an object N or PN. The former are the strings NTOVO (8C.1): *They asked him to come,
They promised him to come*; NTOBE (8C.1A): *They consider her to be well qualified;* SVO
(8C.2): *They let him be first;* STOVO − N (8C.8): *They have paying their workers to consider;*
and the strings based on a subject-predicate without *be: We consider it a matter of honor*
(8D.1–8). The object strings consisting of an N or PN followed by an SN string are NTHATS:
I told him that I would go (8C.3); NSNWH: *I asked her whether I should go* (8C.4);
PNTHATS: *She suggested to me that I might go* (8C.5); PNTHATSVO: *They required of him
that he be on time* (8C.6); PNSNWH: *They inquired of him whether they might enter* (8C.7).
This latter set are amply illustrated in Appendix 3.

4.9   Sentence Adjunct Strings

$$\text{<SA>*R} \quad ::= \quad \text{<PDATE>|<*INT>|<DSTG> <RD>|<PN>|} \qquad 9.1$$

          <PA>|<NSTG>|<RSUBJ>|<RNSUBJ>|<LCS> <CSSTG>|
          −<OBJBESA>|−<SOBJBESA>|<VINGO>|<VENPASS>|
          <TOVO>|IN ORDER <TOVO>|−<SAWH>|−<NVSA>|
          <COMPAR> .

As the reader is by now probably aware, the set SA of sentence adjuncts is distinguished
by its occurrence practically everywhere.[23] These adjuncts are not tied to any particular element in the host string and are therefore for the most part acceptable in different positions in
the strings they adjoin. But not all positions are equally comfortable, and not all SA strings
are equally acceptable in the different positions[24] (DPOS2, DPOS3, DPOS4, DPOS5, DPOS10,
DPOS12). Nor do all SA strings adjoin the same other strings (DPOS7, DPOS8, DPOS9). For
example, short strings like PN, which are not clearly ''centerlike''[25] are less likely to be adjoined by the longer sentence adjunct strings than are the centerlike strings. Thus, in *We
took refuge in his car because it was raining,* the string *because it was raining* is more likely to
be an adjunct of the ASSERTION *We took refuge* than of the PN *in his car.* But this is not a
hard and fast rule, as the following (*New York Times*) sentence illustrates: *A businessman I
interviewed in his car because, he said, ''I'm fairly certain they don't have the car bugged,''
told this story about himself.*

4.9.1   *Short Sentence Adjuncts*

The options of SA that have been referred to as short sentence adjuncts are: PDATE
(**preposition** + **date**), e.g. *on Jan. 3, 1979;* *INT (interjections), e.g. *moreover, thus;* DSTG
RD (**adverb string** (9.2) + optional right adjunct *enough*), e.g. *interestingly enough, generally, soon;* PN (8A.3), e.g. *in principle, at high temperatures;* PA (**P** + **a**djective, (9.3)), e.g. *in
general, at first;* NSTGT (**NSTG** of time (9.4)), e.g. *today, nearly a century ago;* RSUBJ (**r**ight
adjuncts of **subj**ect at a distance (9.5)), e.g. *(we) have ourselves wondered;* NVSA (**n**oun +
verb in **SA**(9.11)), e.g. *Noone, they say, is perfect.*

The category *INT (interjections) covers words like *however, moreover, alas, therefore,
thus, also,* which differ from other sentence adverbs (like *generally, naturally*) in that they

cannot themselves be left-adjoined by other adverbs: *quite naturally, Ⱥ quite alas.*INT can often be interpreted as a connective to another sentence. Its freedom of occurrence is greater than other sentence adjuncts; for example, it can intervene between a host and its adjunct (*Any attempt, therefore, which may be made here*), but these latter possibilities are not presently covered by the LSP grammar.

The adverbs that can occur in sentence adjunct position form a large and diverse class. Only a few subtypes are distinguished in the current LSP grammar. For example, the adverb subclass DMANNER, which occurs in the frame TV (OBJ) DMANNER cannot occur in SA position to the left of W (*Ⱥ He slowly can run on a muddy track*), whereas other DSAs can (*He generally can run on a muddy track*).

The different types of PNs that occur in sentence adjunct positions are too numerous and too varied to be recognized on syntactic grounds. In a further specialization of the grammar for scientific writing, the PNs stating experimental conditions could be recognized by the occurrence of small noun subclasses, the occurrence of measure sequences, and other special features: *at constant temperature, at 120 degrees Centigrade.* But a solution to the problem of assigning PN occurrences to their proper slot (SA, RN, RV, RA, as adjunct of a particular N, and so on) requires yet more subject matter specialization.

The option PA covers many P + adjective equivalents of adverbs (*in general = generally*) and many where the relation to the adverb is less direct (*at last, lastly*). The adjective in the string PA is in the adjective subclass AINPA, and the main prepositions are *in* and *at* (WPOS11).

NSTGT covers time expressions consisting of a time noun NTIME1 that is supported by an appropriate left or right adjunct: *Three years ago he left, Ⱥ Three years he left* (WPOS10, DPOS6), or a time noun NTIME2, which can stand in the SA position alone: *Yesterday he returned.* The left and right adjuncts of N that can support NTIME1 occurrences as SA are in the subclass TIMETAG of their major category adjective, adverb, or preposition (see ATIMETAG in Appendix 3).

There is a small set RSUBJ of strings that occur in sentence adjunct positions (but not pre-SUBJECT, DPOS4A) and agree in number and person with the subject N or a more proximate object N of the host string: *They themselves were impressed with the discovery; They were themselves impressed with the discovery; They were impressed with the discovery themselves,* also *They were impressed with the discovery itself.* This set of strings contains the pronoun subclass PROSELF and a small number of words that appear elsewhere in the grammar as articles or quantifiers such as *some, any, neither, each, all, both.* These words have been given the subclassification QROVING. A restriction (WQ6) checks that an article or quantifier occurring as RSUBJ is in subclass QROVING. Another restriction (WPOS7) checks that a pronoun occurring as RSUBJ is in subclass PROSELF. Yet another restriction (WAGREE7) checks that a pronoun or quantifier occurring as RSUBJ agrees in number with the associated noun. The QROVING words in RSUBJ may be followed by a PN where the P is usually *of: We are all of us guilty.* Since *all* is also a degree adverb, ambiguity may result in certain occurrences where *all* can be analyzed as RSUBJ: *We think they are all wrong.*

Another ambiguity concerns the occurrence of PROSELF as RSUBJ versus its occurrence as indirect object or adjunct after certain verbs: *He picked himself a winner, He had himself judged in a similar competition*. But these ambiguities are rare because RSUBJ hardly ever occurs in the postverb position unless the verb is *be*.

The string NVSA (**noun + verb** in **SA** (9.11)) covers such occurrences as *we believe* in *This result, we believe, has not been previously reported; He is, we believe, the candidate most likely to receive the nomination; He will receive the nomination, we believe*. This string does not occur in string-initial position (DPOS12); in that position the same sequence would be analyzed as occurring with a sentential object and the nuance associated with the SA occurrences is lost: *We believe (that) he will receive the nomination*. The NVSA string consists of noun + verb where the verb is the subclass VSENT3 (*we believe*) or of a subject + predicate that support a THATS complement, as in *it seems, it is true, it is thought: He will be nominated, it seems; He received the nomination, it is true, but he is not likely to win the election it is thought*. A more elaborate treatment of these sequences than the present NVSA string would cover all possible segments of this type, including nested verbal sequences (*There are, Bullins seems to be telling us, values still left in the Southland*).[26]

4.9.2   *Longer Sentence Adjuncts*

The longer SA strings comprise certain *wh*-strings that appear in SA (the option SAWH (9.10)): *He received the nomination, which surprised many people;* subordinate conjunction strings with their optional adverbial left adjunct (the option LCS CSSTG and definition CSSTG (9.7)): *just when we thought the worst was over;* the string TOVO (7.12) occurring mainly as a shortened form of *in order* **to + V + o**bject: *One must eat to live,* but also otherwise: *To state it in another fashion, such results suggest the existence of a specific plant hormone that causes flowering;* strings based on the subject–predicate form (options OBJBESA (9.8), SOBJBESA (9.9), VINGO (7.9) and VENPASS (7.7)): *An ambitious undertaking, this study lasted over 20 years; These exceptions noted, the general statement is as follows; Considering the gamut of aquatic plants and animals, the important species harvested are but relatively few in numbers; Rendered latent at the place of evaporation, it is turned back into actual heat at the point of condensation*. In addition to these strings the SA set covers the *so–that* type of comparative (COMPAR (9.1B)): *The supply of whales fell so low that their expeditions became unprofitable;* and adjuncts of a noun subject that occur in postobject position (RNSUBJ (9.6)): *A man called who didn't leave his name*.

The *wh*-strings in SA are of two types. One type, the string SAWHICHSTG (15.14) in SAWH, represents a relative clause in which the portion that is "relativized" is a sentence, or, in string terms, the SAWHICHSTG is a *wh*-string with omission in which the "omitted" element is a sentential string, in particular a THATS string in subject·position. Thus, *He received the nomination, which surprised many people* can be expanded to: *He received the nomination, and (the fact) that he received the nomination surprised many people,* similar to the expansion of a sentence with a relative clause: *This event, which surprised many people, had a singular history* expanded into *This event had a singular history and this (same) event surprised many people.* In accord with this analysis, the verb in the SAWHICHSTG is singular (WAGREE6), as is the case when a string is the subject, and the SAWHICHSTG occurs only after its host string (DPOS5), just as a relative occurs only after its host noun. The SAWHICHSTG sometimes contrasts with a *wh*-string in RN adjoining a noun, as in such sentences as *They played some modern compositions, which is always surprising* versus *They played some modern compositions, which are always surprising.* When the verb in the RN string is singular there may be ambiguity: *They played some modern music, which is always surprising.*

The other type of *wh*-string in SA represents sentences that state disjunctions, explicitly or implicitly. The first such string is WHETHS (15.1): ***Whether they like it or not,*** *they must become increasingly concerned with the many anthropological, sociological and psychological problems which invade the field of language.* Since WHETHS occurs in subject, object, and complement positions as well as in SA, the definition of WHETHS contains a choice of *wh*-words. However, only the *wh*-word *whether* is permissible when the string occurs as SA (WPOS28). As a sentence adjunct, the WHETHS string expresses disjunction by the occurrence of an *or*-string, or an occurrence of *or not* in one of two possible positions: *whether they like it **or only tolerate it,** whether **or not** they like it, whether they like it **or not*** (WSN7). A shorter version of the WHETHS string not presently implemented, has the same restrictions but comprises only predicates, exemplified by such occurrences as: *Such dark bodies, **whether extinct suns or planets,** are . . . ; When other substances, **whether soluble or insoluble, crystalline or colloidal,** are brought into contact with it, we see . . . .*

The string WHEVERS – N (*wh*-word with suffix *-ever* + S – N (15.15)) is exemplified by: ***Whatever methods are used for the isolation, purification, and maintenance of a pure bacterial strain,*** *the appearance of heritable changes cannot be avoided.* Here, disjunction is carried by the *wh-ever* words, as in *whatever method,* which is equivalent to *whether method 1, or method 2, or method 3, ...* This string is N-omitting—that is, it is of the type in which the contained ASSERTION has a NULLWH in one of the N positions. Thus, *whatever methods are used* is analyzed as a *wh*-containing noun phrase *whatever methods* followed by an instance of ASSERTION in which the SUBJECT element has the value NULLWH.[27]

All of the longer sentence adjunct strings introduce a new, subordinate, sentence into the main sentence. Most frequently there is a connective present, as is the case in the *wh*-strings just described and in the subordinate conjunction strings described separately below. Strings based on a subject–predicate type sentence can occur without an explicit connective, unless the presence of a preceding or following comma (or in spoken English, the intonation) is considered to be the connective. These strings will now be considered in greater detail.

The string SOBJBESA covers occurrences in sentence adjunct position of a subject of *be* followed by a predicate from the set OBJBE, optionally followed by a sentence adjunct, or one of two other options (VINGO and VENPASS) of OBJECTBE. For example, in *We came upon mothers and young swimming side by side, **the baby whale rising and falling in a rhythm that exactly matched that of its parent,*** the final portion of the sentence (*the baby whale rising . . .*) is an occurrence of SOBJBESA in which the option VINGO (*rising . . .*)

follows its subject (*the baby whale*); in *Most of our root crops are produced by two families, the carrot family and the turnip family, **both of them excellent examples with many related forms that immediately come to mind,*** the portion beginning *both of them* is an occurrence of SOBJBESA in which the option OBJBE (with value NSTG: *excellent examples . . .)* follows its subject (*both of them*); and in *The heritage consists of information, **apparently all of it concerned, directly or indirectly, with the construction of protein molecules,*** the final portion beginning with *apparently* is an occurrence of SOBJBESA in which the subject (*all of it*) is followed by the option VENPASS (*concerned . . . with . . .*).[28]

The string OBJBESA, along with the SA options VINGO and VENPASS, cover occurrences of the predicate OBJBE or VINGO or VENPASS without either the subject of *be* or the verb *be* preceding it. Examples of OBJBE occurring as a sentence adjunct are very rare in scientific writing: ***One of the oldest of the arts,*** *toxicology is emerging as one of the newest sciences.* VINGO and VENPASS occur more frequently: *The external ear has disappeared, **leaving simply a hole about the diameter of a pencil lead; Stripped of flesh,** the skeleton of a whale has a profile quite different from the living animal.* As we noted earlier, OBJBE is defined so as to cover occurrences of sentential complements in the predicate (via SN in RA and RN). However, in occurrences of OBJBE in OBJBESA, complements that require expletive *it* as subject are excluded; *true that he was here, of interest that he was here*, for example, cannot be occurrences of OBJBE as a sentence adjunct (DSN2, DSN5).[29] All of the SA strings SOBJBESA, OBJBESA, VINGO, and VENPASS, which are based on a subject–predicate sentence without *be* and occur without an explicit connective, are usually set off from the rest of the sentence by a comma or commas (DCOM3, WCOM6). In the case of SOBJBESA and OBJBESA the comma (or commas) is mandatory, and in the case of VINGO and VENPASS it is virtually required in the string-initial SA position, and in other positions often serves to distinguish the sentence adjunct occurrence from other occurrences of VINGO and VENPASS.[30]

It should be noted that there is another type of adjunct occurrence of OBJBE, VINGO, and VENPASS in the postobject position (or postverb position, since this string occurs mainly with intransitive verbs): *He died a Catholic, He returned a hero; He returned **embittered**; He lay **smiling**; He lived all his life **detesting and protesting religion**.* These contrast with OBJBESA in that they are not preceded by a comma: *Ⱥ He lived all his life, detesting and protesting religion.* Also these adjuncts do not occur in other than postobject position: *Ⱥ A Catholic, he died.* The same word sequence may occur in other positions, but then the interpretation is different: contrast *A Catholic, he opposed changing the state divorce laws.* The postobject strings have the sense of an unstated connective "in the state of," but this impression does not suffice to define the strings for the grammar, and their implementation awaits a more thorough linguistic analysis of the form.

4.10   Subordinate Conjunction Strings

    <SUB0>   ::= <*CSO> <OBJBE> <SA> .   10.1

\<SUB1\>	::= \<*CS1\> \<ASSERTION\> .	10.2
\<SUB2\>	::= (\<*CS2\>|AS|THAN) \<VENPASS\> .	10.3
\<SUB3\>	::= \<*CS3\> \<VINGO\> .	10.4
\<SUB4\>	::= \<*CS4\> \<VINGSTG\> .	10.5
\<SUB5\>	::= \<*CS5\> \<SVINGO\> .	10.6
\<SUB6\>	::= \<*CS6\> \<SOBJBE\> .	10.7
\<SUB7\>	::= \<*CS7\> \<SVEN\> .	10.8
\<SUB8\>	::= \<*CS8\> \<Q-INVERT\> .	10.9
\<SUB9\>	::= SHOULD \<SVO\> .	10.10

The subordinate conjunction strings have been divided according to their external form, but all of them can be viewed as containing an ASSERTION that has some elements either zeroed or changed in form. Fortunately, the string segments following the subordinate conjunctions are for the most part already familiar from their occurrence in other parts of the grammar already described. A partial list of the conjunctions occurring in each of the subordinate conjunction strings is given in Table 4.1.

Table 4.1
Members of Subordinate Conjunction Classes (Partial List)

CS0:	*as, if, although, though, when, unless, since, while, as if, once*
CS1:	*because, for, since, when, where, if, as, after, before, whereas, unless, until, once, while, though, although, as though, except[a], whenever[b], wherever[b], so that*
CS2:	*unless, until, if, when, once, while, though, although, as though, as if, since, as, where*
CS3[c]:	*while, although, though, as though, once, as if, if, unless, by*
CS4:	*since, after, before, during, until, besides, prior to, according to, upon, with, in*
CS5:	*with, without, what with* (same list for CS6, CS7)

[a]. Marginal: *He was there except no one saw him.*

[b]. These could instead be made options of the first element of a new SA string WHEVERS, similar to WHEVERS–N in SAWH but not requiring a NULLWH.

[c]. Only CS that do not also occur as the head of SUB4: *while driving, Ⱥ while his driving.*

SUB0 covers occurrences of a subordinate conjunction in the class CS0 followed by a predicate of the type defined in OBJBE (noun, adjective, PN, adverb): *Whales, as prey, are prize packages; Please answer by Monday, if possible; Once at home, he changed his mind about the offer; He answers his own letters when here*. Not all members of CS0 occur with the adjective predicate: *As a young man he loved sports,* but *Ậ As young, he loved sports* (DPOS18); and only indefinite pronouns occurring with an adjunct are acceptable as pronoun predicates in SUB0: *As someone who has contributed to peace in our time he can be honored; Ậ As someone he can be honored; Ậ As him he can be honored* (WPOS8, WPOS9B).

Usually, the implicit (zeroed) subject of the predicate in SUB0 is the same as the subject of the host string (*whales are prey* from *Whales, as prey, . . .*). This is not the case for sentential predicates (such as *possible, true, convenient*) since in these cases the entire host sentence is the implicit subject of the SUB0 predicate: *Please answer by Monday if* (*for you to answer by Monday is*) *possible.* Except for the sentential case just noted, we can assume that the subject of the host string is the subject of the SUB0 predicate whenever SUB0 occurs in the presubject SA position, or, in fact, in any SA position except the postobject position. In the postobject position the zeroed subject in SUB0 may refer to either the subject or the object in the host string: *He loved Mary as a young man, He loved Mary as a young woman;*[31] but subject-zeroing is by far the most likely of the two. The actual linking of the predicate in SUB0 to the words in the sentence that are understood (implicitly) to be the subject of the SUB0 predicate is left for the transformational stage of analysis, which follows the string analysis.

SUB1 is by far the most frequently occurring subordinate conjunction string. It contains a complete ASSERTION: *When a whale surfaces and exhales, there is a visible spout.* However, the ASSERTION in SUB1 may end after the TENSE element, or after the VERB if the core of the VERB is *have* or *be: She left shortly after you did; They are going because you are*. This is a type of zeroing in which the verb of the main clause occurs implicitly in the subordinate clause (*They are going because you are (going)*), and in order for this zeroing to take place, there must be a parallel construction in the host string and subordinate string, similar to that required for zeroing under coordinating conjunctions. The zeroing may be deferred to a similar situation in a nested object string: *They are going because they think that you are.* The zeroing in an object string may also take place after *to*; the *to* is in parallel construction with a tense element of the host string: *He went because he wanted to (go).* Here *went* = past + *go,* and *to go = to + go.* Different from zeroing under coordinating conjunctions, this zeroing in subordinate conjunction strings is not dependent on the position in the host string in which the conjunctional string occurs. For example, it may be string initial, whereas coordinate conjunction strings never are: *If you want to, you may go; Ậ And you want to, you may go.* SUB1, with or without zeroing, occurs readily in all SA positions. However, a small subset of CS1 (e.g. *for*) is unacceptable in the string-initial SA position: *Because he hated school he joined the army, Ậ For he hated school he joined the army.* (DPOS2).

SUB2 covers subordinate occurrences of a passive string, in which the grammatical subject and the verb *be* are zeroed: *Once weaned, Gigi learned to take food from the hands of people swimming beside her.*[32] In SUB2, as in most of the SA strings in which the subject does not appear explicitly, the implicit subject is usually the same as the subject of the host string. Thus, in the preceding example *Once weaned,* adjoined to the host string, *Gigi learned . . . ,* contains the implicit occurrence of *Gigi* as the grammatical subject of (*was*) *weaned.* Again, as in the case of SUB0, the object, rather than the subject, in the host string may be the implicit subject in SUB2, but these occurrences (or second readings) are rare, if not marginal: *We forward letters **when properly addressed.***

SUB3 and SUB4 cover subordinate conjunction strings based on the V*ing* form of the verb occurring either with an explicit subject in adjunct form (N's, *of* N, *by* N) or with an implicit subject. SUB3 occurrences are distinguished from SUB4 occurrences by the requirement that the implicit subject of VINGO be the same as the subject or object in the host string:[33] *She made a wide sweep around the boat, **as though orienting herself**.* These contrast with SUB4 occurrences, in which a new explicit subject of the V*ing* verb may be introduced (but need not be): ***Since their leaving,** things haven't been the same.* In some cases the implicit subject of V*ing* in SUB4 may be different from the subject or object in the host string: *Radio and television coverage was prohibited **during the signing of the pact**; This episode convinced Kinney that **with gentle handling** a baby whale could be captured and kept indefinitely.* In these examples, the subject of *signing* and *handling* are not repetitions from the host string.

A peculiar type of zeroing, which has not been well described, occurs in SUB4. A transitive V*ing* verb in SUB4 may occur without its noun object, and the object is then understood to be the same as the subject or object in the host string: *This figure changes its organization with prolonged viewing.* Here, the verb *viewing* requires an object, which is satisfied by an implicit occurrence of *this figure.* Similarly, *hearing* has *new music* as its implicit object in *One grows to like the new music on continued hearing;* and *distilling* has *the water* as its implicit object in *The water was purified by distilling.* A special restriction is required for this type of zeroing after V*ing.*

SUB5–SUB7 cover occurrences of a subordinate conjunction (CS5) followed by an ASSERTION-based string in which the SUBJECT element is not transformed into an adjunct shape as in SUB3–SUB4, while the remainder is a reduced or transformed version of the VERB + OBJECT position of the ASSERTION. We thus find after the conjunction (e.g., *with, without*) the by now familiar SVINGO (subject + **VINGO** (6.3)): *They adjourned **with no decision being taken**;* SOBJBE (subject + **OBJBE** (8D.1)): *They adjourned **with many members of the committee in disagreement**;* SVEN (subject + **VENPASS** (8D.2)): *They adjourned **without a decision taken.*** It can be seen that SUB5–SUB7 cover occurrences similar in form to those covered by SOBJBESA, discussed in the preceding section, except that in the case of SUB5–7 these occurrences are preceded by a prepositionlike subordinate conjunction (CS5). Compare: *We overtook a whale surging along, **its broad back awash and gleaming** (SOBJBESA) with *We overtook a whale surging along **with its broad back awash and gleaming** (SUB6). SUB8 contains Q-INVERT in which the tense word or modal precedes the subject, and the verb and object are zeroed: *He left early **as did she.*** In SUB9 the modal *should* precedes the subject: ***Should you find a tick on yourself** and if red spots appear on your wrists and ankles, you may have Rocky mountain spotted fever.*

4.11   RN, Right Adjuncts of N

`<RN>*R`	`::= <VENPASS>│<RNP>│<RNWH>│<THATS–N>│`
	`<S–N>│<SN>│<VINGO>│<TOVO>│<TOVO–N>│`
	`<FORTOVO–N>│<ADJINRN>│<DSTG>│<APPOS>│`
	`WHATSOEVER│<EMBEDDEDQ> .`
		11.1

`<RNP>`	`::= <PDATE>│<PN>│<PNVINGSTG>│ –<PSVINGO>│` `<PSNWH> .`	11.2
`<RNWH>`	`::= <PWHS>│<PWHS-PN>│<WHS-N>│<WHENS>│` `<WHNS-N>│<PWHNS–PN>│ –<PWHNS> .`	11.3
`<TOVO–N>`	`::= <TOVO> .`	11.4
`<FORTOVO–N>`	`::= <FORTOVO> .`	11.5
`<ADJINRN>`	`::= <LAR>│<LQNR> .`	11.6
`<APPOS>`	`::= <LNR> .`	11.7

The set RN of right adjuncts of the noun shares many members in common with the objects of *be*, OBJECTBE (8.3) and its subset OBJBE (8.2). This is not surprising in view of the fact that many N + RN occurrences can be transformationally related to sentences of the form N *is* RN, as *Glucagon, a small protein* is related to *Glucagon is a small protein*. To see the extent of this correspondence and also its limitations, we compare briefly the options of RN with those of OBJECTBE and OBJBE. The RN options VENPASS, VINGO, TOVO, SN, and EMBEDDEDQ correspond to the options having the same names in OBJECTBE. The RN options APPOS (**appos**ition (11.7)), ADJINRN (**adj**ective **in RN** (11.6)), RNP (**RN P**repositional strings (11.2)), and DSTG correspond grossly to the OBJBE options NSTG, ASTG, PN, and DSTG, respectively. The remaining options of RN do not correspond to options of OBJECTBE or OBJBE. Four are concerned with relative clauses, namely RNWH, THATS–N, S–N and WHATSOEVER; and two with infinitive-based forms that are similar to relative clauses in their N-omitting feature (FORTOVO–N (11.5) and TOVO–N (11.4)).

To see the correspondences between RN and OBJECTBE, let us compare the content of corresponding definitions and consider a few examples in which the same word sequence appears as RN and as an object of *be*. Appositional strings (APPOS) in RN cover the same types of sequences as LNR in the NSTG option of OBJBE: *his mother, Mary Jones; His mother is Mary Jones*. Like predicate nouns, appositive nouns agree with the host noun (WAGREE5), with the same exceptions as were stated for predicate nouns: *her paintings, a delight to the eye*. Additional restrictions on APPOS are needed in order to distinguish it from other noun sequences (DCOM4, WCOM10, DN57). The definition of ADJINRN has the same options as ASTG in OBJBE, and covers the same occurrences except for restrictions relating to length (WN50) and complement occurrence (DSN2): *the earth, seemingly round*, . . . (LAR in

ADJINRN), *The earth is seemingly round* (LAR in ASTG in OBJBE); *A capsule seven inches long and two inches in diameter* (LQNR in ADJINRN), *The capsule is seven inches long and two inches in diameter* (LQNR in ASTG in OBJBE). RNP in RN refers to prepositional strings, of which the main member is PN: *the book on the table* (PN in RN) related to *The book is on the table* (PN in OBJBE). Similarly, DSTG in RN (*the people here*) is related to DSTG in OBJBE (*the people are here*). VENPASSS and VINGO occurrences in RN are similar to those described in Sec. 4.7 and the beginning of Sec. 4.8: *those persons held prisoner by the junta regime* (VENPASS in RN) related to *those persons are held prisoner by the junta regime* (VEN-PASS in OBJECTBE); *persons being watched* (VINGO in RN) related to *Persons are being watched* (VINGO in OBJECTBE.[34]

Continuing with the comparison of RN with OBJECTBE, the option TOVO in RN is related to the TOVO option in OBJECTBE that covers *is to* forms: *The man to do the job is John* (TOVO in RN) related to *A man is to do the job* (TOVO in OBJECTBE) + *the man is John*. The two TOVO-related forms in RN that do not also appear in OBJECTBE (FORTOVO – N and TOVO – N) have definitions that appear to be identical to those of TOVO and FORTOVO, respectively. However, in each of the RN strings one N position must be satisfied by a NULLWH: *The man for you to see ( ) is John, The man to see ( ) is John*. The explanation and interpretation of such occurrences is that the "omitted" noun element in each of these RN strings (the object of *see* in both examples) has been extracted from the sentence appearing in adjunct form and is shared by the two component sentences: *You should see a man* + *the man is John*.[35] The N-omitting string then appears as an adjunct of the extracted noun (*man* in the foregoing examples). While these N-omitting TOVO strings are not listed in OBJECTBE, there is a marginal, or literary, occurrence in that position (*A hole is to dig, A ball is to throw*); in these cases (not covered by the LSP grammar) the extracted noun appears as the subject of *be*, in much the same manner as in other extraction strings noted as objects of *be*.

The relative clauses in RN bear special mention. Not only are they perhaps the most frequently used device for introducing a subordinate assertion into a main sentence, but they are theoretically important as a step in the transformational description of all adjunct strings. The discussion here is brief, leaving for the sections on *wh*-strings and *wh*-restrictions further details regarding the form of these strings and the computational mechanism for checking wellformedness.

The adjunct *wh*-strings in RNWH have the same overall form as the *wh*-question (Sec. 4.3), the N-equivalent *wh*-strings (NWHSTG, Sec. 4.5) and the sentential *wh*-strings (SNWH, Sec. 4.6), with some differences in detail as will be noted. In addition, RN contains strings of the same type that are not present in the other sets of *wh*-strings, like THATS – N (*a man that I know*), S – N (*a man I know*), WHATSOEVER (*any man whatsoever*). Not included in the present LSP grammar are similar strings covering such examples as: *the book, the title of which attracted attention; questions, the answering of which seemed natural enough; until the divinity of Jesus became a dogma, which to dispute was death, which to doubt was infamy; the marriage to Miss Smith, to decide which he went to Europe; a jar of my making*. It is planned to add these strings as needed.

The options of RNWH include the same options that appear in the definition of SNWH except for WHETHS and WHETHTOVO. However, *what* is not a string head in RN occurrences of *wh*-strings (DWH51). Examples of RN occurrences of *wh*-strings are *an instrument package which could store and transmit data* (WHS – N); *the means by which its output can be adjusted* (PWHS); *data on which scientists rely* (PWHS – PN); *the baby whale, whose mother swam attentively close by* (WHNS – N); *a whaler from whose early observations much can be learned* (PWHNS); *a man on whose judgments one can rely* (PWHNS – PN). In addition RNWH contains the string WHENS, which covers such occurrences as: *the exact hour* (*when*) *he left*, and *the next season, when nine vessels were there;* and also occurrences with *where: the place where these events occurred*. In WHENS, *when* can be dropped but not *where*; in such a case no comma precedes WHENS (*⊅ We know the day, he arrived*); also the host of WHENS must be a time noun for occurrences with *when* or NULL as string head (WCOM8). No parallel requirement for a place noun as host of *where* occurrences can be made, however, since place nouns are less well defined and *where* strings cover many situations besides place: *the case where x approaches zero; situations where this solution is inapplicable.* (*When* also occurs marginally in these constructions but we have not included them: *the case when x approaches zero.*)

The string THATS – N (*the mechanisms that govern the construction of the nervous system*) is a *wh*-string in all respects except that *that*, rather than a *wh*-word, is the connective. Local ambiguity of THATS – N and THATS following a sentential noun is unavoidable; for example, over the stretch *the fact that he cites* in *the fact that he cites authorities*. This costs computing time, but in all but the rare cases of real syntactic ambiguity (*the statement that he read*) the local ambiguity is resolved when the computation of the string is complete since the THATS – N string carries a restriction (as do all N-omitting or PN-omitting strings) that checks that in the construction of the parse tree corresponding to this string, a properly placed NULLWH has been accepted (WWH1).

The "headless" *wh*-string S – N (*the number of compounds it can form*) is restricted in various ways. There is no subject-omission in S – N; that is, the grammar does not include older usages of the contact clause: *There is a fatality attends the actions of some men, My father had a daughter lov'd a man.* As a practical measure, S – N is considered rare unless its first element (the subject) begins with a pronoun, an article or a name (*a book they recommend, a book the public ignored, a book Marx wrote when he was young* (DN51)). If not for a restriction of this type, compound nouns and other phrases would be broken up, and long fruitless computations trying to construct ASSERTION strings would be undertaken many times in a sentence. In this vein, another restriction (DN50) limits the types of host noun phrases that can be adjoined by S – N. It is also helpful to make use of the fact that S – N is not preceded by a comma: *⊅ A book, they recommend, is now available* (DCOM1). This restriction also applies to RN strings TOVO, TOVO – N, FORTOVO – N and WHATSOEVER.

It was noted in connection with the objects of *be* that the sentence nominalization strings SN appear as an option of RN in order to cover complement occurrences of SN strings following sentential nouns (*fact, feature*) in such sentences as *It is a very interesting fact that the principle of linguistic transfer is not entirely absent even among the unlettered people of the world, It is an extraordinary feature of the genetic material that genes with a closely related function are occasionally (but not always) located close together.* These strings also occur in apposition (as adjunct) to some of the subclasses of sentential nouns in other noun positions, as in *The fact that almost any word or phrase can be made to take on an infinite variety of meanings seems to indicate . . . ; . . . and the related fact that the nucleic acids and proteins of all species are built out of the same building blocks; . . . in spite of the fact that . . .* , and so on. The sentential nouns are subclassed into NSENT1, NSENT2, NSENT3, and NSENTP (see Appendix 3) on the basis of gross syntactic features, such as whether they take SN strings in apposition or as predicates or as either (in different sentences) or as both (in the same sentence). This gives a rough semantic division also. The NSENT1–NSENT3 nouns are further subclassified with regard to which SN string they occur with. These properties are checked by restrictions (DSN3, DSN5).

VINGSTG sentence nominalization strings also occur as right adjuncts of N, but preceded by a preposition, often *of: It is difficult to overestimate the significance of knowing the genetic code, The fact of a man being a poisoner is nothing against his prose, The question of how the enzyme recognizes the beginning and end of each gene.* The strings corresponding to these examples appear, respectively, as the options PVINGSTG (8A.4), PSVINGO (8A.5), PSNWH (8A.7) of RNP (11.2). A wider range of nouns can occur as the host of these strings than as the host of the SN strings, and thus far the LSP grammar has not restricted the host N occurring with these forms. A rough survey of the types of nouns (including nominalized verbs and adjectives) that can be adjoined by the P + V*ing* sentence nominalizations is illustrated by the following examples: pure NSENT1 (*fact, feature, theory*): *the fact of a man being a poisoner;* nominalized VSENT1 (*surprise, shock*): *his shock at there having been no provision for medical aid by the administration;* nominalized VSENT3 (*thought, hope*) and sense-V (*feeling, sight*): *The woman by the rail rose in confusion at the sight of the strangers coming in;* NSENT2 and nominalized VSENT2 (*evidence, proof, indication*): *an indication of their being willing to drop charges;* nominalized aspectual verb VASP (*beginning, end, attempt, appearance*); *the appearance of being willing to negotiate;* nominalized aspectual adjective AASP (*ability, readiness*): *his ability in doing mathematics problems* (but these occur more commonly with TOVO: *his ability to do mathematics problems*); nominalizations of other adjective subclasses: *his fatigue at (after) conducting so many interviews;* and other subclasses, as in *an edifying tableau of Mercy pleading with Justice* or *the value of islands as observation-posts for studying the mystery of bird migration.*

4.12 LN, Left Adjuncts of N

A striking feature of the left adjuncts of N is that they are ordered. The gross order classes correspond to roughly distinct morphologic classes: articles T, quantifiers Q, adjectives ADJ, possessive nouns N's of type,[36] nouns N, occurring before the host, or core, N in the order: T Q ADJ N's-of-type N. Not all classes occur in every LN sequence. Thus, we have *these three prominent citizens* (T Q ADJ N),[37] not *three these prominent citizens* (Q T ADJ N); *many chemical agents* (Q ADJ N), not *chemical many agents* (ADJ Q N); *apparent diffusion coefficients* (ADJ N N), not *diffusion apparent coefficients* (N ADJ N), and so forth.

The order classes illustrated are represented in the LSP grammar by a sequence of position elements in the definition of LN:

$$\text{<LN>} ::= \text{<TPOS> <QPOS> <APOS> <NSPOS> <NPOS>} . \qquad 12.1$$

Each position contains a number of variants, which in turn may have left adjuncts (rarely, short right adjuncts like *enough*): *a very strong bond, a strong enough bond.* Adjunction in APOS and NPOS is repeatable (*an easy, accurate manner; the Raleigh fringe patterns*). In the portion of the noun phrase stretching from APOS through NPOS there appears to be a finer set of ordered positions such that a particular interpretation attaches to the words filling these positions vis-à-vis words in neighboring positions.[38] This can be demonstrated by changing the characteristic order of two neighboring words, where this is possible within the gross fixed order classes, and observing that each of the interchanged words assumes the semantic character of the other in the original sequence. For example, compare *Chinese red cabbage* with *red Chinese cabbage*; the word closest to the core noun *cabbage* carries the connotation of type, whereas the word closer to the adjective slot is descriptive (the type *red cabbage* that is Chinese, or the type *Chinese cabbage* that is red). (A second reading of *red Chinese cabbage* shows *red* as an adjunct of *Chinese*.) Recognizing the subtleties due to ordering within the adjective and noun positions in LN is still beyond computer capabilities.

4.12.1 *Article Position*

The article position TPOS can be filled by a number of different words or word sequences:

<TPOS>	:: = <LTR>|<WHLN>|<LNAMESR>|<LNSR>|<HOWQSTG> .	12.2
<LTR>	::= <LT> (<*T>|NULL) .	12.3
<LNAMESR>	::= <LNAME> <*NS> .	12.3A
<LNSR>	::= <LN> <*NS> .	12.4
<WHLN>	::= WHOSE|WHICH|WHAT|WHATEVER|WHICHEVER WHOSOEVER|<HOWQASTG> .	12.5
<HOWQASTG>	::= HOW (MUCH|MANY|<*ADJ>) [OF] <*T> .	12.6
<HOWQSTG>	::= HOW (MUCH|MANY) .	12.7

In the definition of TPOS, the option LTR (12.3) covers occurrences of the definite and indefinite articles *the, a, an,* and a number of words that have been assimilated into the article category, as shown in Table 4.2. These words all satisfy the restriction on the occurrence of singular countable nouns (NCOUNT1–NCOUNT3) as the core of LNR; namely that such nouns be preceded by some determiner or an indefinite article (WN9). Some of the article words in LTR can be preceded by particular quantifiers or adverbs (in LT (14.8)). The acceptable Q T and D T sequences can almost be listed as individual word sequences, for example *many a* (*time*), *many the* (*time*), *all the* (*time*), *Ⱥ all a* (*time*); *scarcely a* (*whisper*), *Ⱥ scarcely the* (*whisper*). However, a rough coverage by subclasses has been possible, with restrictions checking for well-formed sequences. These restrictions are noted in Table 4.2 and Table 4.3; the latter shows the quantifier subclasses.

The presence of a NULL in the core position of LTR requires some explanation. Several adverbs (*only, even*) that occur preceding an article (*even an approximation*) also occur preceding a noun or pronoun: *even bacteria, even they*. These words can be considered to adjoin the whole sequence from the article through the core noun, which is also what a pronoun substitutes for. We could therefore define these to be left adjuncts of the entire LNR (where LN no longer contains these words). This might be a better linguistic analysis, but it sacrifices the regularity obtained by treating these words as part of a standard LXR definition within a linearly ordered sequence of adjuncts in LN. These adverbs (called DLTPRO, adverbs to the left of T and PRO) are therefore placed in LTR, where they are allowed preceding either an article or a NULL core of LTR. This is the only purpose for a NULL core in LTR and the NULL core is accepted only if DLTPRO precedes it (WN3).

WHLN (12.5) occurs in those *wh*-strings in which the *wh*-word replaces an adjective or stands for a word classified by the host N: *whose book, what book*. In these strings the whole noun phrase (or V*ing* string) containing the *wh*-word appears in the position where a sole *wh*-word appears in similar strings: *With whose signature was it sent*? (PWNQ), *On what evidence was the conviction based*? (PWNQ – PN), . . . *an expository method, which method was adopted* (WHNS – N in RN).

Both linguistic and computational considerations led to placing these *wh*-words in the article position of LN. Vis-à-vis other left adjuncts of N, they occur in the article position (preceding Q ADJ N's-of-type N) and do not occur when an article is present: compare *whose many large oil paintings* with *the many large oil paintings; Ⱥ the whose many . . . , Ⱥ whose the many . . . .* These *wh*-words also function as articles in satisfying the count-noun restriction: *The book fell, Whose book fell?, Ⱥ Book fell* (WN9).

Computationally, it is desirable that the substructure LN N (a noun with its left adjuncts) be autonomous, that it invoke no restrictions referring to the structure of the sentence outside LN N, since then such a unit, once constructed, can be saved and later tried in different parse tree contexts, with no danger that a constraint that was satisfied in the first context will not be satisfied in the new context. Definitions and restrictions in the machine grammar are therefore formulated in such a way as to preserve the autonomy of structures wherever possible. The inclusion of *wh*-words in LN in anticipation of the operation of the count-noun restriction is a case in point. If *whose*, for example, were not included in LN, then in an instance of LN N where N is a count-noun and no article is present, the count-noun restriction would be obliged to check that the N is not occcurring in a *wh*-string before it could reject N as the core of LNR, thus violating the autonomy of LN N, and making it impossible to save the LN N substructure.

Table 4.2

Article Subclasses

INDEF:	*a, an*
	INDEF can be preceded by QMANY or QHALF or DLT: *many a man, such an occurrence, Half a loaf is better than none, hardly a soul* (WN1, WPOS1G).
	INDEF is not one of those articles that can precede V*ing* in the string NSVINGO: *A̸ A receiving letters cheers one up* (WSN10).
DEF:	*the*
	DEF can be preceded by QMANY or QHALF: *all the people, both the two parties* (WN1). An adjective preceded by DEF can occupy the noun position (without a following N): *the hungry, the poor* (DN1). DEF cannot precede V*ing* in NSVINGO: *A̸ The sending telegrams doesn't help* (WSN10).
TPOSS:	*my, your, her, his, its, their, our*
	TPOSS can be preceded by QMANY or QHALF: *Both our tickets are void* (WN1).
TDEM:	*this, that, these, those*
	TDEM can be preceded by QMANY or QHALF: *Double this amount is needed* (WN1); it can stand alone in the noun position: *Those are mine* (DN1). TDEM plural, when standing alone in the noun position, occurs rather readily with the right adjunct S−N, in contrast with other articles in this position: *Those you saw were specially chosen* (DN50).
TQUAN:	*some, either, neither, any, each*
	TQUAN can stand alone in the noun position: *Neither is true* (DN1). Standing alone in the noun position it can occur with S−N, but it is rather rare: *Some you saw were randomly chosen* (DN50). TQUAN is disqualified (as too rare) preceding V*ing* in NSVINGO: *Some sending letters might help* (WSN10).
EACHEVRY:	*every, each*
	EACHEVRY enables a plural noun to occur as subject of a singular verb: *Each man, woman, and child is important in our work, A̸ A man, woman, and child is important in our work* (WAGREE1).

Table 4.3

Quantifier Subclasses

QHALF: *half, double, triple, . . .*
           QHALF can precede article subclasses INDEF, DEF, TPOSS, TDEM but not
           TQUAN, EACHEVRY: *Half a minute will be enough, double the amount, Half
           your life is gone, Nearly triple this amount is needed* (WN1, WN2).

QALL: *all, both*
           QALL can precede DEF, TPOS, or TDEM, but not INDEF, TQUAN, EACHEVRY:
           All his money is gone, ⌀ All a group is here (WN1, WN2).

QMANY: *many, such*
           QMANY can precede INDEF but not other article subclasses: *Many a man has
           lost his head over that* (WN1, WN2).

QROVING: *all, both, none*
           QROVING occurs as ''roving'' adjuncts of an N-subject or a more proximate N:
           *They are all here, We boiled them all for ten minutes, They are none of them of
           any use* (WQ6).

QNUMBER: numbers (words or numerals)
           e.g., *1, 3, ninety, thousand;*
           numbers > 1 are PLURAL (WQ4, WQ5).

Having once opted for *wh*-words in LN, one must ensure that occurrences of LN containing these *wh*-words fall in particular strings and not others: *What book on the subject can you recommend?* but *⌀ What book was very informative* (as assertion); and one must make sure that *wh*-strings that rely on LN to provide the *wh*-word do indeed contain a *wh*-word in each occurrence. These strings all contain the element WHN (3.7A).[39] The constraint is then very simple: TPOS can have the value WHLN only if occurring in an LN in WHN (WWH51), and in an occurrence of WHN, TPOS in LN must have the value WHLN (WWH52).

In addition to the *wh*-words in WHLN in TPOS there are several sequences beginning with *how* (HOWQASTG (12.6)) exemplified by such sequences as *how much this factor influences the reaction, how much of the structure and function of the chloroplast is governed by DNA, how many of the marine invertebrates are migratory, how large a molecule it is.* With particular values of T, some of these sequences can occur without a following noun (preceding NULLN, DN1): *How many ( ) of these there are is not known.*

The word class N's is found in two different positions to the left of N: in the article position, that is, preceding Q, ADJ, or N (*Man's physical structure, this country's 1700 intentional food additives currently in use*), and early in the N-position, that is, following most adjectives and preceding most LN nouns (*a portable children's swimming pool*). The latter most often carry the signification of type so that we have called them "N's-of-type." N's in the article position is represented by the option LNSR (12.4) in TPOS; N's-of-type is represented by *NS in NPOS (12.21). N's in TPOS can have almost the same left adjuncts as a host N: *the federal old-age insurance program, the federal old-age insurance program's supporters;* in fact, one can look upon LN N's as a sequence LN N to which *'s* is added. Certain RN strings are sometimes also included before *'s*, as in apposition: *my son Sam's wife* (but these are not included in LNSR). Since TPOS is the first element in LN, and TPOS can have the value LNSR, which in turn begins with LN, LNSR is left-recursive, as it should be for the analysis of such sequences as *my uncle's first cousin's next-door neighbors' house*. If the first N of an N's sequence in TPOS is a singular count-noun (*uncle's*), then its left adjuncts must contain a nonempty TPOS or the quantifier *one* so as to satisfy the count-noun restriction (WN9) as it applies to the core N's of LNSR: *my uncle's neighbors' house, Ⱥ uncle's neighbors' house.*[40] N's also agrees in number with its left adjunct (not including *his, their*, and so on): *this lady's neighbors, Ⱥ these lady's neighbors* (WAGREE4).

The existence of two N's positions is indicated in examples where both N's are present, separated by intervening material: *the city's newly established children's court*: and by sequences where the adjuncts preceding N's do not (by meaning) adjoin N's: *a freshly laundered nurse's uniform.* Also certain sequences of N's do not analyze as nested occurrences of LN N's in TPOS; *the printer's printer's error* does not imply (in one analysis) that the printer himself employed a printer. A TPOS occurrence of LN N's has agreement in number between the article and N's, as noted previously, so that a singular article followed by a plural N's cannot be analyzed as a TPOS LN N's: *a children's court.* Genealogical relations are expressed as nested LN N's: *John's children's children* are his grandchildren, but a *children's children's court* is not a grandchildren's court.[41]

Though rare, one can find instances of N's N in which N's is a count-noun but is not preceded by a nonempty TPOS as would be required by LN N's in TPOS: *Woman's talk bores me.* This assures that N's is occurring as a postadjective N's-of-type. One would expect to find further examples of this sort in which N is plural (*doctor's bills*), but these seem to occur rarely. Rather, we find *a doctor's bills* or *doctors' bills.*

The fact that the postadjective N's has the interpretation of "type" does not mean that the LN N's in TPOS cannot express a similar meaning, usually with T = *a* (sometimes T = *the*): *a woman's gentle heart.*[42] In our analysis, the cases of *a N's N* where N's is not singular must be analyzed as containing an N's-of-type because the article and noun do not agree in number (thus violating WAGREE4): ***a children's court, a teachers' register, a fools' paradise, a bankers' order, a boys' club, a girls' high school, a women's weekly.*** Where a conflict in number does not occur, as in *a* N's N (N's singular), or in N's N (N's plural), other grounds would be required to decide between the two analyses: ***a cardinal's hat, a doctor's certificate, a bookmaker's runner, a solicitor's office, a gull's nest, children's clothes, men's outfitters, women's magazines, birds' eggs.***[43]

Possessive time nouns also seem to occur in either the preadjective N's position (TPOS) or the postadjective N's-of-type position (NSPOS); as in TPOS: *an hour's hurried housework, his week's beer consumption;* in NSPOS: *a good night's sleep, an honest day's work*. In some cases the *'s* is absent: contrast *in a few years' time* with *in a hundred years time*. Similarly: *the company('s) officers, the hospital gardens*.[44] Proper names do not occur as N's-of-type (DN3).

4.12.2   *Quantifier Position*

In the major order classes of LN, the quantifier class, which includes numerals (*1,296*), number words (*three hundred*) and other quantity words (*several, many*), follow the article class and precede the adjective class: *the 1,700 intentional food additives, the many necessary adjustments*. These words and word sequences are covered by the definition of QPOS (12.8) in LN:

<QPOS>	::= NULL|<LQR> .	12.8
<LQR>	::= <LQ> <QVAR> <RQ> .	12.9
<QVAR>	::= <*Q>|<CPDNUMBR> .	12.10
<CPDNUMBR>	::= <*Q> <*Q>|<CPDNUMBR> <*Q>|<*Q> <FRACTION>|<FRACTION> .	12.11
<FRACTION>	::= <*Q> ↓/↓ <*Q> .	12.11A

LQR (12.9) is a standard LXR type definition, permitting limited left and right adjuncts of the core quantifier or number (*approximately two hundred, ten odd, ten or so*). The core position of LQR is a single word Q that is either a number word (*two, hundred*) or a quantifier word (*all, many*); or it is a numeral, classed as Q, or a sequence of number words comprising a compound number (CPDNUMBR, 12.10): *two hundred, two hundred thousand*. Compound numbers are always plural whereas the Q value of QVAR may be singular (*one*) or plural (*two, 3, many*) or neither (*Half is plenty, Half are absent*), depending on the lexical category assigned. This particular property of quantifiers is important in testing for agreement within LN: ∄ *This three compounds* (WAGREE9); between LN and its host N: ∄ *These three compound* (WAGREE4); between subject and verb: ∄ *Many is acceptable* (WAGREE1); between subject and predicate: ∄ *Many are a qualified candidate* (WAGREE2); between subject or object and collective verb: ∄ *One book gathers* (WAGREE3), and so on.

Thus far the LSP has not found it necessary to include a precise definition of well-formed number-word sequences although the small subgrammar of these sequences is quite simple. Rather, the computer grammar simply accepts repeated number words or numerals (both subclassed as QNUMBER), relying on the conjunction mechanism to supply *and* where needed (*two hundred and fifty* = Q Q and Q).

Many of the quantifier words have such individual features that one would be justified in treating each one as a unique grammatical entity. For recognition purposes one would then list the well-formed sequences of these words and of these words in combination with the article words. We tried, rather, to fit the quantifier words into the overall form of the grammar, and in particular into the order classes of LN, by defining quantifier subclasses and restricting their occurrence in various ways (see Table 4.2).

The left adjuncts LQ (14.3) of the quantifiers are for the most part degree adverbs, such as *nearly, almost, precisely, about, just, scarcely, hardly, merely,* which also occur in other adjunct sets: *nearly three hundred readings, They nearly reached the peak value.* However, there are detailed differences among the quantifiers with regard to which adverbs are acceptable: *precisely five, ₳ precisely many, increasingly many, ₳ increasingly five.* We have not tried to detail these combinations in the computer grammar.

An interesting departure from the prevailing correlation of morphologic class with order class is the appearance of a subclass of adjectives (and of V*ing* and V*en*) to the left of Q in some occurrences: *an additional five qualified persons,*[45] *the following three items*. This subclass (APREQ) can also occur following the quantifier: (*five additional qualified persons, the three following items*), but in some cases there is a change in meaning with the shift: *the first five postulates* versus *the five first postulates*. This indicates that the left adjunct of N may be viewed as nested outward from the host N: the five postulates who are first versus the first postulates who are five (in number).

4.12.3   *Adjective Position*

The adjective position APOS (12.12) has a rich substructure resulting from diverse transformational sources (see, for example, Vendler 1968). The detailedly different forms that result from the operation of the transformations nevertheless conform to a relatively simple gross structure, which is described in the definitions for APOS and its substituents (12.12–12.20). The fact that a number of adjectives (or V*ing* or V*en*, or QN strings) can be strung out into a long sequence (*the more rigorous Dowex 50 column chromatographic method*) is expressed by the recursive definition ADJADJ (12.12A):

<APOS>	::= <ADJADJ>|NULL .	12.12
<ADJADJ>	::= <LAR1>|<LQNR>|<ADJADJ> (<LAR1>|<LQNR>) .	12.12A
<LAR1>	::= <LA> <AVAR> <RA1> .	12.13
<AVAR>	::= <LCDA> <*ADJ>|<LCDVA> (<*VING>|<*VEN>) .	12.14

The first option LAR1 of ADJADJ covers adjectives, V*ing* or V*en* words occurring singly or as part of compounds (*opaque, invading, sealed, electron-opaque, cell-invading, vacuum sealed*), each with optional left and right adjuncts. The definition of LAR1 is a standard LXR definition in which AVAR covers the core sequences. The left adjuncts LA (14.4) are adverbial (*very beautiful, previously existing, generally known*), restricted as to which occur with adjectives and which with V*ing* or V*en* (WPOS4). The set of right adjuncts RA1 (13.4) is a reduced version of RA (13.3), the set of right adjuncts of predicate adjectives appearing in the option LAR (8.9) of ASTG in OBJBE—so reduced, in fact, that only the option *enough* remains: *a long enough period*. Noncompound V*ing* words occurring in APOS are assumed to bear an underlying relation of predicate or verb with respect to the host N as subject: *a surprising fact* (the fact surprises), *the revolving planets* (planets revolve). A restriction (DSEL1) checks whether the host N is indeed a suitable noun subject for the verb V (appearing here as V*ing*). A V*en* word occurring not as a part of a compound is assumed to be capable of appearing in a passive construction (even if occurring adjectivally rather than as a passive in APOS): *∄ an existed theorem* (WPOS14). There is a known set of V*en* occurrences for which this is not true: *the departed guests, a fallen woman, the elapsed time*. Thus far we have not provided for them, preferring to screen V*en* occurrences by the crude test in WPOS14 without checking for the small set of words that form the exception to the rule and that do not occur frequently in scientific writing.

The compound adjectives based on adjective words have a left part (LCDA (14.9)), which for the most part is a noun (*satin smooth, electron-opaque*). The compound adjectives based on V*ing* and V*en* have as left parts (LCDVA (14.10)) either a noun, an adverb, or an adjective:[46] *ear splitting, well meaning, sweet smelling, hand-picked, over-determined, large-boned*. The V*ing* and V*en* compound adjectives for the most part occur with a host N and with adverbs that are different from those with which the same V*ing* or V*en* word occurs when not in a compound: *a very hard working programmer, a working program, ∄ a very working program*. Although the adverb and host restrictions on compound adjectives are not tested for in the present LSP grammar, some internal constraints are applied to the N-V*ing* compound adjective. It is assumed that the most frequently encountered form will be the productive one resulting from a transformation in which the object N of a verb V appears as the left part of a compound adjective N V*ing*, where V*ing* is V + *ing*: *The sound splits the ears, an ear splitting sound*. A restriction (WSEL4) applies a rough test of whether N in N V*ing* is a suitable noun object for V.

The second option of ADJADJ is LQNR:

<LQNR>	::= <LQ> <QNPOS> <RQ> .	12.15
<QNPOS>	::= <QN>|<NQ>|<QNS> .	12.16
<QNS>	::= <LQR> <*NS> .	12.16A
<QN>	::= <LQR> <PERUNIT> <*N> (<QNREP>|NULL) <PER UNIT> <SCALESTG> .	12.17

<PERUNIT>	::= (PER|↓|↓) <*N>|PERCENT|PER CENT|NULL .	12.17A
<QNREP>	::= <Q–CONJ> .	12.17B
<SCALESTG>	::= <*ADJ>|<PN>|NULL .	12.19
<NQ>	::= <*N> <QLETTER> .	12.20
<QLETTER>	::= <LQR>|<*N> .	12.20A

The definitions 12.15–12.20 account in a rough way for the sequences that occur in the adjective position (for example, among adjectives in an adjectival sequence) but that are not based on adjectives, V*ing*, or V*en: a dozen **one inch** galvanized wood screws, a **two mile** jog, the first **90-day** test period, a **number 3** Phillips screwdriver, The **Table A** entries*. These are mainly of two types: measure sequences described by the string QN (12.17) like *one inch, two mile*, and *90-day* in the preceding examples, and named or numbered items of a series, like *number 3, Table A* in the examples, which are covered by the string NQ (12.20). NQ was described in connection with its occurrence as an option of NAMESTG, in Sec. 4.5.

The string QN consists of a number (LQR (12.9)) followed by an optional *per unit* phrase, followed by a noun (*6 per cent solution*), followed optionally by another QN (QNREP, as in *3 pounds 2 ounces*), followed optionally by a *per unit* phrase (*3 miles per hour*), followed optionally by a phrase denoting the scale or dimension of the measurement (SCALESTG): *a two inch long line*. *Long* in this example is an instance of *ADJ in SCALESTG.

The QN string occurs in a number of string positions: in APOS of LN, as described here (*a two inch long line*); as an option of ADJINRN in RN: *a line two inches long, a line two inches in length*; as an option of ASTG in OBJBE: *The line is two inches long/two inches in length*; preceding certain prepositions as an option of LP (14.5): *two inches above the shelf*; as a verb adjunct or option of RV (13.5): *She swam 50 yards, He kicked the ball fifty yards*; and as the object of certain verbs: *It measures fifty yards*. Occurrences in these different positions are restricted in certain ways and differ in detail, as specified in restrictions DQ1–DQ4, WQ1–WQ3, and WQ7. Thus, WQ1 requires that Q and N in QN agree in number in all but the LN position: *The line measures two inches,* ⱥ *The line measures two inch,* ⱥ *a line two inch long;* in LN the N of QN is singular: *a two inch line, a thousand volume library,* ⱥ *a two inches line,* ⱥ *a thousand volumes library*. In most instances of QN, the N is a well-known unit word (*inch(es), degree(s), mile(s)*), classed as NUNIT in the lexicon. A part of WQ1 requires that N in QN be in the subclass NUNIT in all QN positions except in LN, where there appears to be more freedom of occurrence: *a thousand volume library,* ?*The library is a thousand volumes, a ten apartment unit,* ?*The unit is ten apartments* (rather, *has* a thousand volumes, *has* ten apartments).

An NUNIT noun occurring as the N in QN can be followed by a dimension or scale expression, that is, by SCALESTG (12.19) like *high* in *an 800 foot high building,* ⱥ *an 800 liquid high building* (DQ3). The *ADJ and PN options of SCALESTG contain particular adjective and noun subclasses (ASCALE, NSCALE), checked by WQ2, WQ3.[47] However, in addition to the ASCALE adjectives in SCALESTG, comparative adjectives are freely permitted (WQ2), covering such occurrences as *It's 2 degrees colder* (*cold ≠* ASCALE).

Further adjustments of the QN and SCALESTG definitions to cover occurrences in different positions include a restriction (DQ2) that excludes the PN option of SCALESTG from occurring in QN in LN: *Ⱥ a two inch in length line;* a restriction (part of DQ3) that excludes both the *ADJ and PN options of SCALESTG from occurring in QN in LP: *Ⱥ He hung it 2 inches in height above the shelf*; and a restriction (DQ1) requiring that a non-null option of SCALESTG follow the N of QN when QN is occurring in RN: *a line two inches long, Ⱥ a line two inches*. This is part of the length requirement on adjectives occurring to the right of N (WN50). Except for this constraint, occurrences of SCALESTG are optional, represented by the option NULL in SCALESTG.

The line between the adjective and noun positions in LN is not sharp. Color words, for example, occur at the border between APOS and NPOS, that is, after most adjectives (*a large round red ball, Ⱥ a red large round ball, ?a large red round ball*) and before the first nouns in NPOS:[48] *a locked black steel filing cabinet, Ⱥ a locked steel black filing cabinet* unless *steel* is an adjunct of *black*. They have both adjective and noun properties. Like nouns they occur alone or with an indefinite article (*Red is my favorite color, A red is preferable*) and have adjective and noun left adjuncts (not as a compound adjective, according to stress data): *a pale blue sky, a sky blue sky*. Although color words are not very important in the science texts we have treated, they are interesting from the point of view of the order classes in LN; at the level of fine order classes, the border between Q and ADJ and between ADJ and N has intermingling of subclasses from the two major classes.

4.12.4   *Noun and N's-of-Type Position*

In the sequences covered by NPOS (12.22), nouns or V*ing* that when spoken have adjectival stress precede those that are part of compound nouns: *a farewell courtesy call, a steel filing cabinet*. Roughly, the order is nouns of material followed by nouns of type followed by compound nouns (*wire-mesh moving-belt chicken feeders*), but this is only an approximate description. It does not, for example, characterize the noun sequence in *Coal lies in the deep-mine mountain coal counties of Appalachia from Pennsylvania to Alabama*. The N's-of-type generally precedes the pure N or V*ing* left adjuncts of N: *a women's fashion weekly;* hence NSPOS precedes NPOS in LN. But this order is not always maintained: *a district children's court*. Again, the finer shading is not in terms of gross morphologic divisions.

The computer grammar covers these delicately ordered sequences crudely:

<NSPOS>   ::= NULL|<*NS> .   12.21

<NPOS>   ::= NULL|<NNN> .   12.22

<NNN>   ::= <LCDN> <*N>|<NNN> <LCDN> <*N> |–<LCDN>
               <*VING>|–<NNN> <LCDN> <*VING> .   12.22A

The non-null option of NSPOS is only the word class NS, restricted so as not to allow possessive proper names (DN3). N's-of-type can have left adjuncts (*a predominantly women's occupation*) but this is so rare that we have not included it in NSPOS.

The non-null option NNN of NPOS is recursively defined. All different types of N and V*ing* occurrences in this position are covered by this definition, but some are rare. Limited left adjuncts of these N and V*ing* words are allowed for in LCDN (14.11): *an organic chemistry textbook, his foreign service tour.*

4.13   Right Adjuncts Other Than RN

Most of the remaining adjunct sets, both right and left, contain the adverb string DSTG:

          \<DSTG\>   ::= \<*D\>|\<DSTG\> \<*D\> .   9.2

The definition covering adverb occurrences is left-recursive,[49] expressing the fact that adverbs can be left-adjoined by other adverbs (*a very nearly perfectly convincing argument*). Only certain adverb subclasses may be left adjuncts of adverbs, so that a restriction (WPOS21) checks that the leftmost adverb in a nest is in one of these subclasses (DSA, DLP, DVERY, DLCOMP): *a seemingly generally accepted view* (*seemingly* = DSA); *a quite generally accepted view* (*quite* = DLP); *a very generally accepted view* (*very* = DVERY); *a far more widely held view* (*far* = DLCOMP, a left adjunct of the comparative marked word; *≠ a far widely held view*). These four subclasses are approximately coextensive with the adverbs that can left-adjoin other adverbs. The left-recursive definition of DSTG covers truly left-nesting adverb chains, and also those that might better be interpreted as repeated adjunction (or comma conjunction) to the left of a common host (*a rapidly, irreversibly failing heart*), or as left-nesting adverbs adjoined to an adverb + host pair, as in *really quite intelligent*, taking *really* as adjunct of *quite intelligent*, rather than of *quite*. The task of obtaining a deeper analysis of adverb sequences (and adverb adjuncts in general), like that of analyzing noun sequences to the left of a host noun requires detailed transformational analysis. The necessary detailed linguistic treatment of adverbs is not yet available in the literature.

In the LSP grammar, adverbs are for the most part subclassified on the basis of the string position in which they occur. There is therefore in many cases a simple correspondence between the name of the adverb subclass (like DRV) and the adjunct position (RV) in which the adverb subclass normally occurs. Table 4.4 lists the adverb subclasses, the position in which they occur, and several characteristic examples. For the most part simple restrictions suffice to check that an adverb occurring as the core of DSTG in a particular syntactic position has the required subclassification (WPOS1A–R). Several more complex situations (adjuncts of the verb, and adverbs in the noun phrase) are handled by individual restrictions (WPOS2, 3, 4).

Table 4.4

Adverb Subclasses

A.   Subclasses Defined by Position

Adverb Subclass	Adjunct Set	Examples
DSA	SA, sentence adjuncts	*Soon* he left. He *soon* left. He left *soon*.
DRW	RW, right adjuncts of tense	He will *not* go. He is *not* leaving.
DLV	LV, left adjuncts of verb	He *simply* failed. He *almost* passed.
DLA	LA, left adjuncts of adjective	*very* young, *quite* nice
DLW	LW, left adjuncts of tense	He *just* can't sing.
DLQ	LQ, left adjuncts of quantifier	*not* many, *almost* 13, *very* few
DLP	LP, left adjuncts of preposition	*almost* out the door, *way* off the road
DLCS	LCS, left adjuncts of subordinating conjunction	The meeting was canceled *merely* because it rained.
DLT	LT, left adjuncts of article	*Scarcely* a soul was about. *Hardly* a man survived.
DLTPRO	LT, left adjuncts of article and pronouns	*only* the best *even* she
DPERM	adverb of tense–subject permutation	*Seldom* has he behaved so well. *Long* may he reign.
DPRED	object of *be*	He's *here*. They are *behind*.
DRN	RN, right adjuncts of noun	the man *there* the time *before*
DLCOMP	left adjuncts of comparative adjectives and adverbs	*much* nicer *far* more potent

Table 4.4

Adverb Subclasses (continued)

B.   Subclasses Defined by Selection with Verb

Adverb Subclass	Adjunct Set	Examples
DMANNER	SA, sentence adjuncts with verb-adverb selection	*Slowly*, he rose to his feet. He prayed *hopefully*.
DLOC3	RV, right adjuncts of verbs of motion	The rock fell *down*. John walked *out*.
DEVAL	object D or D in ND object of evaluative verbs	He did *well*. They treat them *badly*.
DLOC1	object D or D in ND object of locative verbs	She lives *there*. She put it *there*.
DRV	RV, right adjuncts of verb with verb-adverb selection (also occurs postobject, and to the left of V*en* or V*ing* in LN)	He writes *poorly*. It is a *poorly* written text. It was a *lightly* falling rain.

The set of the right adjuncts of the verb RV has several options.

$$\text{<RV>*R} ::= \text{<DSTG> <RD>|<PN>|<QN>|<SN>} .   \qquad 13.5$$

It contains in addition to DSTG the strings PN and QN, and the set SN. With regard to the PN option, some prepositions rarely occur as the value of P in a PN adjunct of the verb (*of, to*); and some are preferred as sentence adjuncts (*since, during, prior to, throughout, about*) (WPOS17).[50] Also, if a PN occurring in postverbal position can be analyzed as an object of the verb, the parsing program will accept this as a preferred analysis (WPOS15). Thus, in *He compared the samples with the previous lot*, the program will analyze *with the previous lot* as part of the object of *compare*, and consider RARE the reading in which the PN beginning with *with* is taken as an adjunct, as in *He compared the samples with reluctance*. The measure string QN (*He threw the ball 10 feet*) was described in Sec. 4.12 since it also occurs as an alternative option to adjectives in APOS. The SN option of RV covers sentence complements in the set SN occurring after the verb + object (*It surprised me that she was there*). This option is accepted as a value of RV only in the postobject RV position, and there are constraints on the verb and ultimate subject (DSN4). Adjunction of RV strings is limitedly repeatable, as indicated by the notation <RV>*R: *He proceeded carefully at a snail's pace.*

Table 4.5

Predicate Adjective Sequences

Subject		Predicate		Examples	Restriction
1. N		ADJ	PN	The garden is free of weeds. They are ripe for conquest. He is necessary for their support. It is not consistent with his abilities.	
2. N		ADJ	PN	He is good at chess.	
3. N		ADJ	PVINGO (P = *at, in*)	He is good at playing chess. And: Ⱥ He is good at our playing chess.	
4. N		ADJ: AASP	TOVO	He is prone to act rashly.	DSN7
5. N		ADJ	TOVO	He is young to travel alone.	
6. N	ADJ:ASENT1:AFORTO:SUBJEXT		TOVO	John is foolish to go.	DSN2
7. N		ADJ:ASENT3	SN, ASSERTION, TOVO	John is happy to go. John is happy that you will go. John is happy you will go.	DSN2
8. It		ADJ:ASENT1	SN	It is true that he was here. It is doubtful whether he was here. It is easy for John to do the job.	DSN2
9. N	ADJ:ASENT1:AFORTO:OBJEXT		(FOR)TOVO – N	The job is easy for John to do. That is astonishing to hear.	DSN6
10. N		ADJ	TOVO – N	She is ravishing to look at. (ADJ ≠ ADJ: ASENT1: Ⱥ To look at her is ravishing)	
11. N		ADJ	PVINGSTG PSVINGO	I am tired of his talking so much. They are overjoyed at there being so many children present.	

Predicate adjectives can be followed by a variety of sequences, illustrated in Table 4.5, all of which are covered by the definition of **RA**.

<RA>   ::= <SN>|–<ASSERTION>|<PN>|<PVINGSTG>|<PSVINGO>|
               <TOVO – N>|<FORTOVO – N>|<TOVO>|ENOUGH|NULL .   13.3

Where a subclass of ADJ is noted in Table 4.5, a restriction in the grammar checks for this subclass in occurrences of the given type of sequence. In the case of sentential complements (line 8 in Table 4.5) it is also required that the subject be *it* (DSN2). The case described in line 3 is not represented by an option PVINGO in RA because the subclass that would distinguish this occurrence from PVINGSTG occurrences (line 11) has not been stated, though it is clearly adverbial in origin (*He plays chess well*). The examples of PN (line 1), illustrate that this form has many different sources.

4.14   Left Adjuncts Other Than LN

Most left adjunct sets consist of the option DSTG, standing for occurrences of adverbs. The subclasses of adverbs permitted in different string positions is controlled by restrictions (WPOS1A–WPOS1Q). Mainly, there is a one-to-one relation between subclass and position as was noted in describing adverb subclasses in Table 4.4. However, in the case of LA, several subclass of adverbs are permitted because of the different types of adjectival words or sequences that can fill the core position AVAR. Thus, a restriction on LA (WPOS3) permits sentence adverbs DSA (*generally true*), verb adjuncts DRV (*poorly written*), adjuncts of adjectives and adjectival V*ing* DLA (*very true, very amusing*); and adjuncts of the comparative-marked adjectives (*considerably better, Ⱥ considerably good*). Another restriction (WPOS4) restricts the combinations of adverb subclass + host (*poorly written, Ⱥ poorly true; very true, Ⱥ very written*).

Prepositions P and subordinating conjunctions CS have adverbial left adjuncts LP (14.5), LCS (14.6), respectively: *just before noon, just after you left*. In addition to the option DSTG, LP contains QN: *They camped **several hundred yards** beyond the bend in the creek*. Most of the left-adjunct sets that occur within the noun phrase have been discussed in connection with their host words in LN (Sec. 4.12): LT (14.8) and LPRO (14.7) in connection with the article position TPOS; LQ (14.3) and ADJPREQ (14.3A) in connection with quantifiers in QPOS; LCDA (14.9) and LCDVA (14.10) in connection with compound adjectives in APOS; LCDN (14.11) in connection with compound nouns in NPOS. The definitions for LNAME (14.13), TITLE (14.15), and NAMEPART (14.15) were discussed in connection with noun subjects (Sec. 4.5) and illustrated in Fig. 4.1.

4.15   *Wh*-Strings

Wh-strings appear in five different ways in the grammar. They occur as interrogative sentence nominalization strings SNWH (Sec. 4.6), as *wh*-questions and WHQ strings (Sec. 4.3), as noun-equivalent *wh*-strings NWHSTG (Sec. 4.5), as right adjuncts (relative clauses) RNWH of the noun (Sec. 4.11) and as sentence adjunct *wh*-strings SAWH (Sec. 4.9). SNWH and *wh*-question are closely related, as one might expect from such occurrences as *The question whether he knew was raised* (SNWH in SN in RN), and *This raised the question: What did he know?* (EMBEDDEDQ in RN), in addition to the pure *wh*-question *What did he know?*. The overlap in the sets of *wh*-words suggests that NWHSTG and RNWH are related.

This is plausible in view of the possibility of substituting *that which* for *what* in many NWHSTG occurrences, thus transforming it into a sequence of host + RNWH adjunct: *I eat what she cooks, I eat that which she cooks.* The absence of *who(m), whose, which* from the *wh*-words in NWHSTG results from the more common use of the locutions *the one who* (or *the person who*), *the one which* (or *that which*), for example, *The one which you chose was blue, ⊅ Which you chose was blue.*.

A characteristic of *wh*-strings is the feature that in our implemented grammar is expressed by "omission," the absence of word values for a particular element (usually N or PN) of a string when that string occurs as part of a *wh*-string. This property has been discussed previously (see Sec. 4.3), so that the notion of "*wh*-strings with omission" is by now familiar. In our present grammar, only those strings that omit a "required element" (as opposed to an adjunct) use the mechanism of omission. Thus, in *the cover which she designed ( )*, the NSTGO object of *designed* is satisfied by NULLWH, the mark of omission; whereas in *the book for which she designed the cover,* no NULLWH appears since *for which* stands for an omitted adjunct of *cover*. From a transformational point of view, this differential treatment is unbalanced, since in reversing the *wh*-transformation both types of omitted elements have to be restored. However, from a computational point of view, this division is justified. A plethora of null elements creates problems for the parser. We use null elements when we need them to obtain well-formed parses (as in the case with NULLWH values of required elements) or when the refinement of locating the implicit elements is not too costly (NULLN, NULLRECIP). But where there is a choice and the deeper analysis can be obtained more efficiently in the transformational stage of analysis, we defer the more complete analysis until that stage.

The element NULLWH therefore occurs in the BNF grammar as an option of SUBJECT (*the man who ( ) came*); as an option of NSTGO occurring as object (*the man we saw ( )*); or as part of an object string (*a man whom you can rely on ( )*; *the wall they painted ( ) red*); or as part of an adjunct PN (*the book she designed the cover for ( ) (RN)*; *the knife which he cut the meat with ( ) (RV)*); and as an option of OBJBE (*try to remain the good student you were ( )*). The conditions for accepting NULLWH in these positions are tested by restrictions WWH2, 3, 4, 5.

Omission can of course take place within embedded strings (*the book which we thought you said it was important for everyone to read ( )*) or at the end of a chain of nested PN adjuncts (*the chart which we have a copy of a copy of ( )*). These types of distancing are handled by extended-scope routines, the ULTIMATE-OBJECT and ULTIMATE-HOST routines. The operation of these routines will be illustrated in connection with the *wh*-restrictions in Sec. 5.8.2.

Omission in a conjunctional string is required in some cases where the conjunctional string occurs in a *wh*-string: *The man I met ( ) and talked to ( ), ⊅ The man I met ( ) and talked to the man.* However, not all conjuncts in *wh*-strings require omission: *a person whom John and Mary both like ( )*. The omission requirement must therefore be imposed on conjunctional strings in certain positions in *wh*-strings. Embeddings and nestings may also

Table 4.6

Comparativelike Strings

Marker	Linked SA-Occurrence*		
enough occurring as Q	Enough were present (*for the meeting*) *to begin*.[a] We have enough *to eat*[b] We have enough *for everybody*.[c] We have enough *for staying longer*.[d]	Enough people came (*so*) that they held the meeting.[e,f]	Enough were present so as to hold the meeting[g,h]
occurring in RA in RV	It was light enough *to see*.[a] It rained quite enough *to please everybody*.[a]	They made it clear enough (*so*) that the meaning could not be misunderstood.[e,f]	They made it clear enough as to dispel all doubts.[g,h]
too occurring as D	It was too much to ask.[b]		
such occurring as prearticle quantifier in TPOS		There was such a (*large*) crowd (*that*) we couldn't find them.[e,g]	It was arranged in such a manner (*so*) as to leave no room for complaint.[g,h] He was such a man as you won't find again easily.[i] He was such as you.[j]
so occurring as D		So many were there (*that*) we couldn't find them.[e,g] There was so large a crowd (*that*) we . . .[e,g]	It was so clean as to . . .[h] He was so able a man as one hardly sees nowadays.[i]

*SA string occurrence in examples as follows: *a.* FORTOVO or TOVO; *b.* FORTOVO – N or TOVO – N; *c.* PN (P = *for*); *d.* PVINGO (P = *for*); *e.* THATS or SUB1 (CS1 = *so that*); *f.* ASSERTION; *g.* *so as* TOVO; *h.* as TOVO; *i.* as S – N; *j.* PN (P = *as*).

occur in the conjoined strings: *the man I met ( ) and thought I would like to talk to ( ), ≠* *The man I met ( ) and thought I would like to talk to the man*. A general device for handling omission in conjunctional strings is described in connection with the *wh*-restrictions in Chapter 5.

4.16 Conjunction and Comparative Strings

In addition to the conjunction and comparative strings that are dynamically generated as described in Chapter 6, there are comparativelike strings that the grammar partially covers with existing definitions in LN and SA. Table 4.6 shows examples of these strings. Like comparative strings, these strings depend on the prior occurrence of a "marker," usually in LN. The string that is signaled by the marker occurs in final sentence-adjunct position. Some of the occurrences are therefore covered by strings that exist in SA to analyze other types of occurrences, for example TOVO in SA (*He did it to please you*) can also cover *Were there enough presents to please you*? (similar to the first example in the first column of Table 4.6). The string THATS (column 2) does not usually occur as SA without a preceding *so*; it is therefore included in SA in such a way that it can be restricted, namely as an option of COMPAR. Since most of the other strings in Table 4.6 are already defined in the grammar for other purposes, they can be added to COMPAR as needed.

NOTES

1. The main sources for examples aside from those made up to illustrate a particular point are *The Selected Writings of Edward Sapir* (1949), where the sentences appear in context, not as examples, Otto Jesperson's *Modern English Grammar* (1961), *Present-day English Syntax* by G. Scheurweghs (1959), *The New York Times,* and articles in the fields of biochemistry, physics, ethology, and pharmacology that have been used in applications of the string program.

2. Thus, this grammar does not include questions that have the form of an assertion plus question intonation (*He's here*?) or the tag question (*He was here, wasn't he*?) although the taglike forms that contain conjunctions (*Is it true, or isn't it*?) are obtained by the usual conjunction process. A straightforward extension of existing mechanisms for treating zeroing under conjunctions would accommodate short forms like *Will you? Hasn't he*?. For applications to colloquial English, one could add more short forms (*What? Your name? How tell the difference?*) and the nonpermuted *wh*-forms (*He went where? How did I manage what?*). Since questions are signaled by the presence of a questionmark these additions would not burden the parsing process. A useful detailed treatment of the question is found in Bollinger 1957. See also Jesperson 1961: Vol. I, p. 25, and Harris 1978.

3. But not always: "This in spite of the fact that other Negroes have gone to their death or prison condemned by juries of white persona only" (from an address by Earl Warren).

4. No attempt to catalogue the wealth of such forms will be made here. For coverage with regard to almost any aspect of English grammar there is no better source than Otto Jespersen's *Modern English Grammar* (1961).

5. Only some of these reasons are noted here. Others are given in Jespersen 1961 (Vol. VII, Secs. 3.1, 3.2; see particularly 3.1.).

6. Definitions 3.5 and 3.6 are differentiated by restrictions.

7. Auxiliary occurrences of *do* have therefore been incorporated into the modal class (see Sec. 4.7).

8. The inverted form is frequently associated with the comparative.

9. Since *VING as part of a VINGSTG may also be a right adjunct of N (*There is a log rolling down the hill*), steps are taken to eliminate false ambiguities where it can be shown that the structural demands of the two readings are in conflict (WN10).

10. From Jerry Hobbs's description of the LSP English grammar in Hobbs 1974.

11. A more extensive set of definitions for this type is given in an earlier presentation of the grammar in Sager 1968.

12. The description of the forms of the object in *Vn* nominalization strings, and a number of the examples are drawn from Sec. 1.7.3 of Anderson 1970.

13. But Jesperson, op. cit., Vol. V, Sec. 9.3₄ gives examples to the contrary.

14. A NULL in place of "OF" is allowed in the VINGOFN string when the object is PN. See the definition of VINGOFN and WSN11.

15. The NSVINGO and VINGOFN examples here contrast in that NSVINGO takes adverbs (*strongly*) whereas VINGOFN takes adjectives (*strong, insistent*). See subsequent discussion.

16. The NULL is also computationally troublesome in this position, since it opens the door to an attempted computation of a full ASSERTION when probably, if a noun phrase follows the verb, it is not the subject of an ASSERTION but a noun phrase object: *This would require extensive changes* versus *This would require extensive changes be made.*

17. The string THATS could have been defined similarly to C1SHOULD: <THATS> ::= (THAT/NULL) <ASSERTION>, since *that* is often dropped in object position: *I know (that) she was here.* However, this solution was rejected because a number of frequently occurring verbs are not equally comfortable in both forms: *Note that X is zero* versus *Note X is zero.* In the specification of permitted object strings for a verb in the lexicon, THATS and ASSERTION are listed as needed; for example, *know* has both, whereas *record* has only THATS.

18. A definition D on the TYPE RECURSIVE list has this constraint when it is invoked at sentence word w_i: If a node corresponding to D is successfully built starting at sentence word w_i, this fact is recorded along with the depth of nesting n in D (initially 0). In order to begin building an instance of D starting at word w_i at depth $n + 1$ in D, there must have been a successful completion of D at depth n starting at w_i.

19. In the definitions of VINGO and VENPASS an initial element LVSA covers sentence adjuncts that occur before VING or VEN in adjunct occurrences of these strings: *Suddenly feeling dizzy, he reached for the hand rail.* The string TOBE (7.12A) occurs only as an element of the object string NTOBE (8C.1A). VO appears only in the IMPERATIVE center string.

20. In particular OBJBE is an element of the object strings ASOBJBE (*as* + **OBJBE**), SASOBJBE (subject + *as* + **OBJBE**), NASOBJBE (object N + *as* + **OBJBE**), SOBJBE (subject + **OBJBE**)—see Appendix 3—and of the sentence adjunct strings OBJBESA (**OBJBE in SA** (9.8)) and SOBJBESA (**SOBJBE** in SA (9.9)). All of these strings are based on a subject–predicate form without the verb *be*.

21. A more general treatment of extraction is possible based on the form *It is X (that/wh) S-X,* where X is an option of OBJBE, and S-X is an occurrence of ASSERTION with *NULLWH satisfying an X position: *It is here that we disagree* (X = predicate adverb), *It is of proteins which we speak* (X = PN). Only the more limited N-extraction has been implemented in the present LSP grammar.

22. However, the noun string NSTGO covers nominalizations based on a derived noun, or nominal, as was discussed in Sec. 4.5.

23. In the current computer grammar shown in Appendix 1, the definition of SA is written with options in parentheses and explicit NULL, instead of the *R convention. This allows no repetition, places NULL as the first option, and still creates the type of structure expected by the restrictions written when the *R definition was in use.

24. The presence or absence of a comma also affects acceptability (DCOM3, WCOM5, WCOM6).

25. The centerlike strings are named on the TYPE CENTERLIKE in the LISTS section of the grammar.

26. This was done in the IPL and FAP implementations of the grammar.

27. This analysis may seem strange in view of the fact that in *whatever methods are used,* the noun phrase *whatever methods* can be considered to be already present in the subject position before *are used.* However, in other cases, the *wh*-containing noun phrase is not in its regular place in the ASSERTION: *whatever methods one follows;* hence the more general treatment used in the LSP grammar.

28. *Concerned*, here, is not a true passive as evidenced by the fact that (*is*) *concerned with* could be replaced by *concerns* with no subject–object reversal. A small class of V*en* words (like *concerned with, engaged in*) have this property though they have the string structure of VENPASS.

29. The operation of DSN2 and DSN5 is rather subtle in this case. The exclusion of sentential complements in RA or RN occurring within OBJBE in OBJBESA comes about by the failure of the ULTIMATE-SUBJECT ROUTINE in the global restriction-part $SUBJIT, which checks that the ultimate subject is *it*. This will not prevent, for example, *anxious for him to succeed* as OBJBESA because no test for *it* is invoked when the adjective is ASENT3 (*anxious*) as opposed to ASENT1 (*true*).

30. In an occurrence of VINGO or VENPASS preceded by a comma and following a noun it is often difficult to distinguish the sentence adjunct occurrence from an occurrence of a reduced nonrestrictive relative clause having the same form. Thus, the sequence *reduced in price* can only be a sentence adjunct in *Reduced in price, these items are sold in discount stores,* since relative clauses do not precede their host noun. But in the sentence *These items, reduced in price, are sold in discount stores,* the same sequence may be either an SA or RN, though the semantic distinction is slight. In the position where VINGO and VENPASS can be either RN or SA, the occurrences without a preceding comma are taken as RN and those with a preceding comma as SA (DCOM3A).

31. Strings headed by *as* have more freedom of occurrence and more different interpretations than strings headed by other members of CS0. Note that in the examples *as a young man* can be permuted to the presubject SA position, but *as a young woman* cannot. Several different adjunct strings headed by *as* could be defined (e.g. *as* N as prepositional phrases, in addition to *as* as CS0) but the distinctions are not easy to define precisely. In addition, *as* also appears in the grammar in several other capacities: in the object strings ASOBJBE, NASOBJBE, SASOBJBE, and in the *as–as* comparative (*He is as effective on the courts as a young man*). In the string analysis we have tried to cover all *as* occurrences with a small number of definitions, leaving the interpretation of the forms to the transformational stage of analysis.

32. SUB2, with string head THAN or AS, is also used to cover certain comparative strings based on VENPASS; *It is more dangerous **than first thought**, The side effects are not as **minor as claimed***.

33. Except for the sentential predicates (e.g. *though surprising*), where the entire host string is the implicit subject, as noted in connection with SUB0.

34. But *persons having been watched* has no OBJECTBE counterpart: ⍉ *Persons are having been watched*. The use of the definite article in the examples is only for readability and is not intended as an example of correct transformational decomposition.

35. The FORTOVO form (and its occurrence in reduced form as TOVO) is transformationally related to the subjunctive: For N to V Obj↔N should V Obj (*for you to see a man↔You should see a man*).

36. The N's-of-type class is defined and illustrated below. Throughout this section N's will be substituted in place of the computer designation NS for possessive noun so that the contrast of the possessive noun with the nonpossessive noun will be clear.

37. *This, that, these, those* are in the article subclass TDEM (article **dem**onstrative) because of their occurrence in the article position *vis-a-vis* other left adjuncts of the noun. Occurring alone (*This is true, These are many*) they are analyzed as adjuncts of a NULLN that carries their referential status.

38. For an account of detailed ordering in the adjective position and the transformational sources, see Vendler 1968.

39. The names of these strings also contain "WHN", they are WHNS – N, WHNQ – N, PWHNS – PN, PWNQ – PN, PWHNS, PWHNQ.

40. Since *neighbors'* is plural it does not require a preceding article. Therefore it is the count-noun *uncle* of *uncle's* that requires the article, showing that the count-noun restriction applies to the N of LN N's.

41. This example is due to H. Hiž.

42. Fries called these "descriptive uses of the inflected genitive" (1940: 75). He distinguished at least a half-dozen different meanings associated with occurrences of N's before N.

43. From oral data, N's-of-type seems often to carry compound-noun stress. Thus, the spoken *these children's clothes* is not ambiguous.

44. Fries called these the suppressed genitive (Fries 1940: 258).

45. Notice that *an* does not agree in number with the noun *persons*, which is its apparent host, nor is it tied to *additional* since E *an additional qualified persons* (similar to *a few qualified persons*). Only a few words in the APREQ subclass have this property, i.e. *additional, extra,* possibly reduced from *an additional* (*group of*), *an extra* (*group of*). Reduction may account for other aberrant quantifier occurrences, e.g. *all* Q from *all* (*of the*) Q, since generally quantifier words do not form a sequence: *all five,* Ⱥ *several five.*

46. A quantifier can occur here but has not been included: *three-toed, 2-headed.*

47. Also particular words in ASCALE, NSCALE go with particular words in NUNIT: *long, length,* with *inches, feet.* This is not checked by the LSP restrictions at present. The unit and scale words vary from one subscience to another so that these dictionary categories must be expanded according to the field of application in order to use the QN restrictions of the grammar.

48. But color words may precede adjectives of material, type, or provenience, which are usually noun-derived: *a white wooden cabinet, a blue hand-blown bottle, a typical gray English sky.*

49. Alternatively, a standard LXR type definition can be defined in which LD, the left adjuncts of D, is left-recursive. At some point this part of the grammar will be rewritten in standard form.

50. The division between RV PNs and SA PNs is somewhat arbitrary. The criterion of mobility to other positions for SA PNs sometimes conflicts with our sense that PNs and adverbs expressing time, place, and experimental conditions should be SA, whereas manner PNs and manner adverbs are more closely related to the verb and should be RV. At best these assignments are partial steps to a more refined analysis, and without the adverb restrictions, strange parses result.

Chapter 5   The Restriction Component of the Grammar

The need for restrictions follows from elementary considerations regarding natural language. The amount of detail required for an effective treatment of sentences, even a crude one, is very large. It is also well known that no matter how much detail is incorporated into a grammar there is always more that can be added. And for particular applications, constraints due to the subject matter must be added. There is thus a need for a component of the grammar capable of handling a large and increasing amount of detail.

The device used in the LSP system is to define **restrictions,** individual tests for determining whether the parse tree that is being constructed to represent the analysis of the sentence is correct in detail, given the properties of the individual sentence words noted in the the computer lexicon. The restriction framework is also used for special functions, such as the optimization of the grammar, the generation of conjunction strings, and the cross-referencing of elements for later use in transforming the sentence.

The Restriction Language (RL), the programming language that was described in Chapter 3, is the vehicle for expressing restrictions and transformations in the LSP system. In designing the language, we hoped that when the restrictions were written in RL they would "speak for themselves"; that is, they would require a minimum of translation into English in order for the user to understand what each restriction is intended to do and how it does it. The restrictions fall short of our expectations, particularly the longer, more complicated ones, which require considerable technical and linguistic explanation in order to understand their operation. As a minimal aid in the grammar, each restriction is preceded by comments that state the motivation and give linguistic examples. A one-line summary of the intent of every restriction is provided in Appendix 4.

Some general remarks about restrictions are in order before beginning the specific descriptions. The restriction component of the LSP grammar was developed early in the work of the Linguistic String Project. Restrictions, conceived as tests to be applied to the structures generated by the analyses, were a central feature of the original LSP algorithm, and the major restrictions in the present grammar were a part of the first implemented grammar. Since an attempt was being made to write a relatively complete grammar of English, many constraints were translated into restriction code ''on principle,'' rather than as practical necessity dictated.

We have also learned from working with the parser. Sometimes unwanted parses lead directly to new restrictions. More often, they point to amusing ''misinterpretations'' on the part of the machine, alternate parses not easy to eliminate except by ad hoc rules. Interestingly enough, the ''misinterpretations'' by the machine are not always due to the absence of selectional restrictions at this stage in the process, as might be expected. Sometimes it is a matter of choosing the more likely syntactic combinations (choosing between *We have measured potentials*. and *We have measured potentials*, for example). But these preferences are not easily expressed as constraints on the parse tree. As a result, the main body of grammatical restrictions has remained relatively constant over the years.

Since the restrictions were for the most part written to express known grammatical constraints and not as the need arose out of failures in parsing, the question arises as to whether all the restrictions in the grammar are necessary. There is certainly a danger that a purist attitude may lead one to include detailed tests that increase the cost (the time) of parsing without proportionally increasing the effectiveness of the parsing. Success in the rare situation in which some detailed constraint applies may not be worth the time needed to test for that situation in the many sentences in which the constraint does not apply. This question arises in part because of the examples that are used to illustrate the linguistic intent of a restriction. In order to demonstrate the existence of a linguistic constraint we contrast a well-formed sentence with a nonsentence word sequence differing from the well-formed sentence only in the absence of the constraint. For example, to illustrate agreement of subject and verb in the case where the verb is singular, we might have the following examples: *She walks,* which contrasts with *They walks*. This does not mean that we expect to parse nonsentences of the type *They walks*. Rather, in some well-formed sentence (*They sometimes on Sunday walks meet friends*) there may be a partial analysis that would, perhaps temporarily, place two words in a grammatical relation that is not well formed in the given sentence (*they* = subject, *walks* = main verb, *on Sunday* = PN); the existence of the restriction ensures that this path will be quickly rejected by the parser.

Still, some restrictions are certainly more effective than others in eliminating false paths. One monitoring device we have used to evaluate the relative utility of restrictions registers each failure of a given wellformedness restriction. Each failure means an incorrect path is being blocked, so the higher the failure rate for a given restriction, the more effective it is in the parsing process. The agreement restrictions, particularly subject–verb agreement (WAGREE1), and the count-noun restriction (WN9) consistently register high scores. But we have found that particular restrictions, which may not have high failure scores, are nevertheless critically important in certain kinds of sentences. It also happens that, occasionally, due to a small technical error we are treated to an "unplanned experiment" in which one or more restrictions unexpectedly fails to operate. The usual result is a large number of unwanted parses. We are therefore cautious about reducing the restriction component until we have a quantitative study of the relative effectiveness of the restrictions, one of the projects we hope to undertake when time permits.

Another question that might be raised is how thoroughly the grammar has been tested. The same question arises in regard to any large computer program. In the case of the LSP grammar, almost every logical path in every restriction was tested, using trivial test sentences for each path. This was necessary because very little in the way of error diagnostics can be applied during the parsing process. Because of the inherent ambiguity of the language, a parse subtree may be rejected, correctly, on the way to a correct parse, or wrongly, due to an error in some restriction. There are thousands of necessary subtree rejections in the course of analyzing a single text sentence. The error diagnostics problem then is how to distinguish "good" rejections from "bad" ones, or, how to distinguish restriction failures due to temporary incorrect parse trees from restriction failures due to incorrect restrictions. Text sentences are too complicated for this purpose. We can be sure that a restriction is functioning correctly in a text sentence only if it has previously been found to do so in all types of situations that may be encountered. We therefore test each logical path with a trivially simple sentence (like *He walks, Ⱥ They walks*).

Some final remarks on the strategy of restrictions: It will be noted throughout the restriction component of the grammar that restrictions are formulated mainly in negative statements. We rule out non-well-formed combinations rather than test for well-formed combinations. For example, in the negative formulation of agreement restrictions, we test that the subject of a definitely singular verb is not plural, rather than (in a positive formulation) that a singular verb requires a singular subject. In some types of restrictions, such as agreement, the work done in the restriction is about the same in either the positive or the negative formulation. The difference in these cases is only in the lexical component. Thus, the lexical categorization that goes with a negative formulation assigns no number attribute SINGULAR or PLURAL (rather than both SINGULAR and PLURAL) to words that are neither definitely singular nor definitely plural, for example nouns such as *fish, series* (*this fish, these fish, this series, these series*) or past tense verbs like *walked, sang* (*she walked, they walked, she sang, they sang*). This shortens lexical entries. In some types of restrictions, such as selection, the negative formulation considerably lightens the burden attached to adding new subclasses to the grammar. For example, the selection restrictions WSEL1, WSEL2 rule out certain noun subclasses as the subject or object of particular verbs. Using the negative formulation, we may add a new noun subclass to the grammar without being forced to say which verbs occur with the new subclass as subject or object. We may wish to add this information to each verb entry, but the grammar will continue to function without these additions to the lexicon, whereas in a positive formulation we would have to add this information before the selection restrictions would accept well-formed subject-verb-object sequences involving words in the new subclass. When the English grammar is specialized for a particular subject matter application, the selection rules can be much stronger than in the all-English grammar and a positive formulation is preferable.

Another strategy question concerns the fact that several different restrictions may require the same information about the sentence. For example, a number of different configurations of sentence complements require that the subject of the sentence be *it: It seems that he left, It is likely that he left.* The test for this is written once, and the name of the restriction substatement ($SUBJIT) is placed on the TYPE GLOBAL list. It can then be invoked as needed in other restrictions.

In a given sentence tree, information obtained by a restriction with regard to a particular parse subtree may be needed later in the analysis. The results of such a restriction test can be stored as an attribute of the root node of the given parse subtree. Node attributes are also a convenient way to pass information along in the parse tree. At one time we considered writing the entire restriction component in the style of attributes—as operations on information passed upward automatically via a node-attribute passing system. This method is excellent for agreement restrictions but is not well suited to the rest of the grammar. In most restrictions, the information calculated by a restriction is needed only in particular types of sentences. In view of the large size of the grammar the obligatory node-attribute passing system would result in storing and passing along much unneeded information.

5.1   The Organization of Restrictions

There are different ways in which restrictions can be organized. We have chosen to group together restrictions that are linguistically related, either by type of construction or by type of constraint. Restrictions are divided into the following groups (numbered as in Appendix 1):

1. Agreement restrictions   (WAGREEn)
2. Comma restrictions   (DCOMn, WCOMn)
3. Comparative restrictions   (DCOMPn, WCOMPn)
4. Conjunction restrictions   (DCONJn, WCONJn)
5. Minword restrictions   (DMINn)
6. Noun phrase restrictions   (DNn, WNn)
7. Optimization restrictions   (DOPTn)
8. Position restrictions   (DPOSn, WPOSn)
9. Quantifier restrictions   (DQn, WQn)
10. Selection restrictions   (DSELn, WSELn)
11. Sentence nominalization restrictions   (DSNn, WSNn)
12. Verb and center string restrictions   (DVCn, WVCn)
13. *Wh*-string restrictions   (DWHn, WWHn)
14. Zeroing restrictions   (WZEROn)

Groups 2, 3, 4, 6, 9, 11, 12, 13 are of the type that concern a particular linguistic element or construction. Thus are covered the comma, comparatives, coordinate conjunctions, the noun phrase, quantifiers, sentence nominalizations (exclusive of *wh*-complements), tense-verb constraints, and *wh*-strings of all kinds. Groups 1, 8, 10, 14 each control a particular type of linguistic constraint. Thus, all agreement restricitons are in one section, even if they concern the noun phrase or other constructions named by special sections. The so-called position restrictions cover a miscellany of constraints that are not clearly of other stated types, though by and large they check for particular subclasses in particular positions or contexts (say, a particular preposition depending on the governing verb, (WPOS15)). Selection restrictions concern the appropriateness of the combinations of word choices in given syntactic relations. Zeroing restrictions concern the wellformedness of conjunctional strings with ellipsis and lay the groundwork for recovering the implicit word-occurrences in these strings. Minword and optimization restrictions are concerned with increasing the efficiency of parsing and limiting the number of alternative analyses (see Sec. 5.4). To illustrate the style and content of restrictions, a few sections of the restriction component are presented in detail here, in the order in which they appear in Appendix 1. We begin with the agreement restrictions. These are relatively intricate and illustrate the level of linguistic detail that is incorporated into restrictions. The reader may prefer to start with the simpler restrictions of Sec. 5.6.

5.2   Agreement Restrictions

WAGREE1: *Subject and verb agree in number.*   This restriction will be traced in considerable detail in order to illustrate the use of the Restriction Language as well as to explain the linguistic motivation for the component tests.

        WAGREE1 = IN ASSERTION AFTER VERB:
                IF BOTH $VB AND $SUBJ ARE TRUE
                THEN BOTH $SINGAGREE AND $PLURAGREE ARE TRUE.

The first character, W, of the name WAGREE1 indicates that the restriction is a **wellformedness** test and is executed after the parse tree corresponding to the element specified in the housing portion of the restriction has been constructed. The housing portion, IN ASSERTION AFTER VERB, states that the restriction is attached to the VERB element of ASSERTION. Thus, this wellformedness restriction will be executed after the VERB subtree in ASSERTION is completed. The execution of a restriction starts at the node named just after IN—here, at ASSERTION.

The main restriction sentence is an implication: IF **restriction test** THEN **restriction test** where both restriction tests in this case have the form BOTH **address** AND **address.** (An address is any alphanumeric sequence preceded by a dollar sign.) Each of the component tests of the implication start at the initial node position—here, ASSERTION. In the premise, the test at the first address $VB has two functions.

$VB = EITHER CORE X2 OF VERB X20 IS TV: SINGULAR OR PLURAL,
      OR BOTH X20 HAS COELEMENT TENSE →
      AND CORE X2 OF TENSE IS SINGULAR OR PLURAL.   (GLOBAL)

The first function is to screen out cases where the verb does not discriminate between singular and plural subjects, since in these cases the restriction should exit "+" immediately. As was noted previously, the attributes SINGULAR and PLURAL in this grammar mean "definitely singular" and "definitely plural," respectively; their presence in the context of executing an agreement restriction therefore means that further tests must be executed, and their absence means that no tests need be done. Thus, if the main verb (core of VERB, for example TV *walks* in Fig. 5.1a) is number-discriminating, e.g. *walks* or *walk* (not infinitive), the subject must be checked for agreement, e.g. *She walks, Ⱥ They walks, They walk, Ⱥ She walk;* but if it is not number-discriminating, e.g. *walked* (*she walked, they walked*), then no agreement test need be made.

In $VB this screening has two parts. First, the VERB element is tested by executing CORE X2 OF VERB X20 IS TV: SINGULAR OR PLURAL, as follows: The test starts at ASSERTION, where the restriction is housed, and first searches the elements of ASSERTION for VERB. (The presence of a node name in argument position invokes the routine STARTAT (see Chapter 3), which makes this search.) The node VERB is stored in the register X20. Then the CORE routine is executed, starting at VERB, and the result is stored in X2; in Fig. 5.1a, the CORE routine would arrive at *TV (*walks*) and store it in X2. Then the core is tested for the attribute SINGULAR or PLURAL.

The second part of the screening process is executed in case the first part fails; if the core verb is not number-discriminating, there is the possibility in this grammar that the tense word, if it is a form of *do*,[1] is: *She does not generally walk, Ⱥ They does not generally walk, They do not walk, Ⱥ She do not walk*. This situation is illustrated in Fig. 5.1b. The test is executed starting at the VERB node (stored in X20); the COELEMENT routine scans the other elements of ASSERTION to find TENSE, where it executes the CORE routine and tests whether the core word has the attribute SINGULAR or PLURAL. (The arrow between TENSE and AND indicates that the test under AND will begin at the node TENSE.)

Figure 5.1 also illustrates the second function of $VB, which is to make register assignments to nodes that will be referred to again in the course of the restriction. For example, the node VERB, which was stored in X20, is used immediately in the second part of $VB. The use of registers greatly increases efficiency.

The second test $SUBJ of the premise has the sole function to store the core of the SUBJECT in a register (X1) for convenience of access later in the restriction.[2]

$SUBJ = AT X20, THE CORE – X1 OF THE
        COELEMENT – SUBJECT EXISTS.   (GLOBAL)

The SUBJECT node is assigned to a register before the subparts of the restriction are invoked not only for economy within WAGREE1 but because the subparts are global and may be used in other restrictions where the tests are applied to different nodes. For example, in the course of WAGREE3, the core of the OBJECT is assigned to X1 and the global subpart $NOTSINGX1 defined in WAGREE1, below, then applies to the core of the OBJECT rather than to the core of the SUBJECT, as here.

Fig. 5.1   Register assignments after the execution of $VB and $SUBJ in WAGREE1.

a.   Inflected main verb.

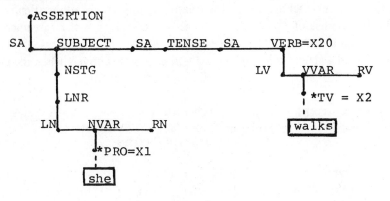

b.   Inflected tense word.

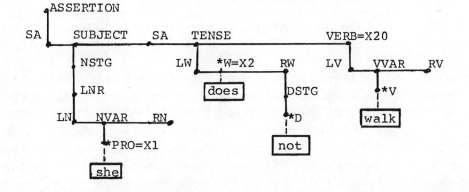

The execution of $SUBJ begins at ASSERTION, as do all subparts of WAGREE1, unless otherwise specified. However, the first operation, signaled by "AT X20," redirects the restriction to the register X20, which contains the node VERB. The statement in $SUBJ thus effectively starts at VERB in ASSERTION. At VERB the COELEMENT routine with argument SUBJECT is executed; the COELEMENT routine searches the siblings of the node where it is executed for the one named as argument. Here, the routine arrives at the node SUBJECT, where the CORE routine is executed, and the node reached is stored in X1. In the parse trees of Fig. 5.1, the path traversed in the execution of $SUBJ is from VERB to SUBJECT to the atomic PRO lying below SUBJECT; then PRO is stored in X1. The predicate EXISTS does not initiate further operations; its function is solely to complete the required subject–predicate form of restriction sentences. The minus sign appended to CORE indicates that if a second core value is present due to conjunction (*she and he, she and her brother*), the second (or third, or fourth) value will not be "stacked," as is otherwise done in the case of conjunction (see Chapter 6). In agreement restrictions we wish to check for the presence of a conjunction explicitly, since the presence of *and* may change a singular subject to plural. We therefore do not want to use the powerful stacking device for treating conjunctions automatically.

If the tests in the premise of WAGREE1 are both successful, then the agreement tests proper, $SINGAGREE and $PLURAGREE, are executed. Both tests are executed, but only one applies nontrivially in a given case. $SINGAGREE applies substantively when the verb or tense word is SINGULAR, and $PLURAGREE applies when it is PLURAL.

$SINGAGREE = IF X2 IS SINGULAR
            THEN BOTH AT X1 NOT $PLURN
                AND $NOTPLURSUBJ.   (GLOBAL)

$SINGAGREE first tests whether the verb element stored in X2 has the attribute SINGULAR. If it does, then the two further tests NOT $PLURN and $NOTPLURSUBJ are executed. The negation of $PLURN tests that a noun phrase subject is not plural, and $NOTPLURSUBJ tests that the subject as a whole is not plural due to conjoinings not covered in $PLURN.

$PLURN = EITHER PRESENT-ELEMENT– IS PLURAL
         OR THE LEFT-ADJUNCT– OF THE PRESENT-ELEMENT– IS LN
            WHERE ONE OF $TPLUR, $QPLUR, $A-HUNDRED IS TRUE.
                                                    (GLOBAL)

(For an explanation of $A-HUNDRED, see description of $SINGN in $PLURAGREE.)

The cases covered by $PLURN are illustrated by the parse trees in Fig. 5.2, which show different configurations for a plural noun phrase. This global test is used in WAGREE1, 2, 5, and 7, with in some cases different register assignments. (Hence the use of PRESENT-ELEMENT– instead of a named register in $PLURN.) $PLURN is directed to cases where X1 (the core of the subject, assigned in $SUBJ) is the core of a noun phrase LNR (as opposed to cases where X1 is a string). It tests that a parse subtree corresponding to LNR is definitely plural. First, X1 may itself be PLURAL (*they, samples* in Fig. 5.2a). If X1 is PLURAL, $PLURN signals success immediately, and the second test under EITHER . . . OR . . . in $PLURN is not executed. In WAGREE1, the negation of $PLURN changes the success signal to failure, so that $SINGAGREE, and hence WAGREE1, fail in this case, as they should for a sentence like *A̸ They walks*. However, if X1 is not PLURAL, then it is possible that the left adjuncts determine a plural noun phrase (Fig. 5.2b–g). For example the core might be a noun that is not SINGULAR or PLURAL (*fish, series*) or a NULLN, preceded by a plural article or quantifier: *This series converges, Ⱥ These series converges, One was tested, Ⱥ One hundred was tested.* [3]

Fig. 5.2 Parse trees for plural noun phrases, tested by $ANDSING

a. The core of the noun phrase is PLURAL.

b. The core of TPOS is PLURAL.

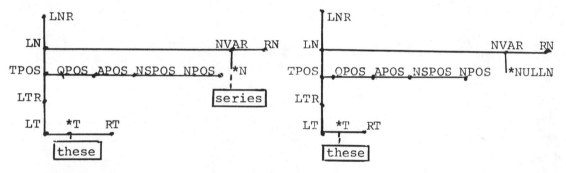

c. TPOS has a parallel postconjunction element; the conjunction is *and*.

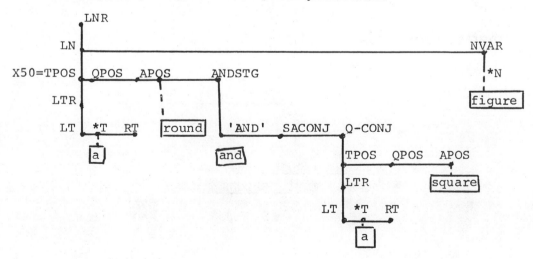

d. The core of QPOS is PLURAL.

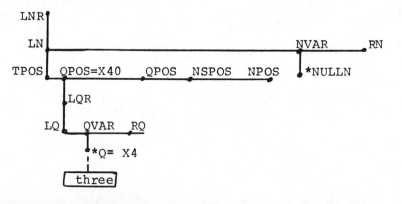

e. The core of QPOS is CPDNUMBR.

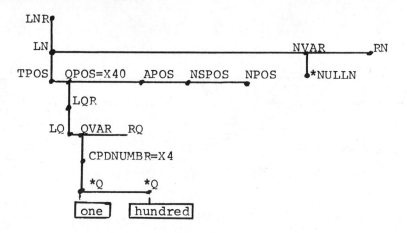

f. The core of QPOS has a conjunct.

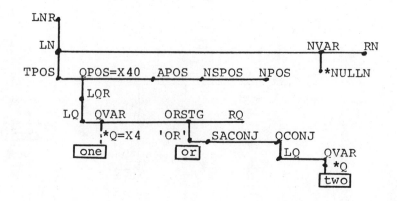

g. QPOS has a parallel postconjunction element; the conjunction is *and*.

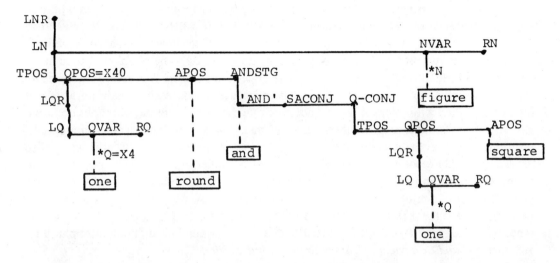

   The tests for a plural noun phrase due to the left adjuncts of N are $TPLUR and $QPLUR:

$TPLUR = AT ELEMENT – TPOS X50
        EITHER $TPLUR-TEST
        OR $CONJUNCT-IS-AND IS TRUE.

$TPLUR-TEST = CORE – [OF TPOS] IS PLURAL.   (GLOBAL)

$CONJUNCT-IS-AND = BOTH ITERATE $POSTCONJ →
                   AND IT IS OCCURRING IN ANDSTG.

$POSTCONJ = THE PRESENT-ELEMENT – HAS NODE ATTRIBUTE
             POSTCONJELEM.   (GLOBAL)

$QPLUR = AT ELEMENT – QPOS EITHER $QPLUR-TEST
                          OR $CONJUNCT-IS-AND IS TRUE.

$QPLUR-TEST = ONE OF $1, $2, $3 IS TRUE.   (GLOBAL)
   $1 = THE CORE – [OF QPOS] X4 IS PLURAL.
   $2 = EITHER X4 IS Q-OF
        OR X4 IS CPDNUMBR
           WHERE VALUE IS NOT FRACTION.
   $3 = X4 HAS CORE-CONJUNCT.

$A-HUNDRED = BOTH CORE – OF ELEMENT-TPOS IS ↓A↓
             AND IN ELEMENT – QPOS EITHER CORE – X4 IS ↓FEW↓
             OR ↓DOZEN↓ OR ↓HUNDRED↓ OR ↓THOUSAND↓
             OR ↓MILLION↓ OR ↓BILLION↓,
                     OR LEFT-ADJUNCT OF X4
             IS ADJPREQ.

Parse trees for the situations covered by $TPLUR are illustrated in Figs. 5.2b and c. Figure 5.2b shows two cases where a plural core of TPOS (*these*) determines a plural noun phrase, hence will cause $PLURN to succeed, and NOT $PLURN in $SINGAGREE in WAGREE1 to fail, as it should for, say, *These series converges.* Figure 5.2c shows a situation in which a conjunction (see Chapter 6) within LN causes the noun phrase to be plural even though the core noun is SINGULAR: *A round and a square figure were drawn, Ⱥ A round and a square figure was drawn.* The conjoined LN sequences in such a case each contain an article or quantifier; other conjoinings in LN do not as a rule determine a plural noun phrase: *a red and blue flag.* To determine whether a given element has a conjoined element in a parallel position within a conjoined construction, the program tests for an attribute called POSTCONJELEM (**post-conj**unction **elem**ent), which would already have been assigned to the given element in just such a case. The test is iterated in $CONJUNCT-IS-AND to cover a possible chain of conjuncts. In $CONJUNCT-IS-AND it is also required that the conjunction be *and,* which in the present representation of conjunction strings is equivalent to the occurrence of the conjunct (Q-CONJ) in an ANDSTG. Other conjunctions do not confer plurality: *Whether a round or a square figure is drawn is immaterial.*

Parse trees illustrating the cases covered by $QPLUR are in Figs. 5.2d–g. Figures 5.2d, e, and f correspond respectively to the tests $1–$3. Tests $1 and $2 follow directly from the way the quantifier position QPOS in LN was defined (Sec. 4.12): A single-word quantifier or number is SINGULAR or PLURAL depending on its lexical properties; the string CPDNUMBR is plural. Test $3 (Fig. 5.2f) treats the situation where the core of QPOS has a conjunct (called a CORE-CONJUNCT to distinguish it from a parallel-position conjunct due to conjoining at a higher level, as in Figs. 5.2c and g). The conjunction can be *and* (*two hundred and fifty fish were caught, Ⱥ Two hundred and fifty fish was caught*), or *or* (*two or three hundred were caught, Ⱥ Two or three hundred was caught*). A puzzling case with *or* is the occurrence of *One or . . . : One or two are missing, ?One or two is missing, ?One or two is sufficient for our purpose.* All other *or* occurrences among quantifiers appear to be plural, so we have taken them all to be plural, ignoring this possible exception. Similarly, we have not made an exception for a singular occurrence with conjunction *but: Not two but one fish was caught, ?One but not two fish was/were caught.* Figure 5.2g illustrates the case parallel to Fig. 5.2c, where the plural feature derives from conjoining at the level of LN ($CONJUNCT-IS-AND). In Fig. 5.2c the parallel elements are TPOS, whereas in Fig. 5.2g the parallel elements are QPOS.

The foregoing tests were concerned with plural noun phrases where there was one core of the noun phrase. Either the core itself was plural or the left adjuncts of the core contained conjunctional strings that conferred a plural number on the whole noun phrase. A subject may also be plural due to the conjunction of noun phrase cores or the conjunction of mixed types of subject constructions. These cases are illustrated by the parse trees in Figs. 5.3 and 5.4, to which the global test $NOTPLURSUBJ applies.

$NOTPLURSUBJ = BOTH $ANDSING AND NOT $ANDSUBJ ARE TRUE.   (GLOBAL)

Fig. 5.3   Parse trees tested by $ANDSING.

a.   Conjoined cores; noun phrase is plural.

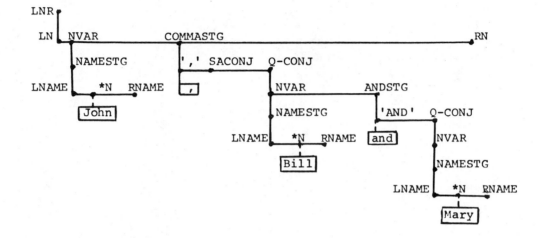

b.   Conjoined cores; noun phrase is singular.

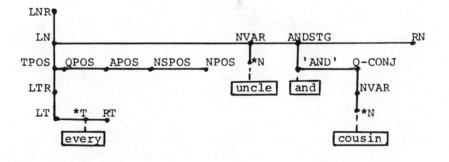

Fig. 5.4   Conjunction on the level of SUBJECT, tested by $ANDSUBJ.

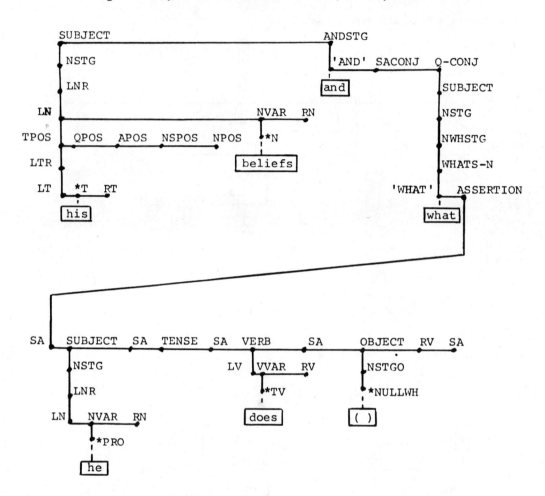

The test $ANDSING covers the most frequent type of plural subject due to conjunction, namely conjoined noun phrase cores: *John, Bill and Mary are here* (Fig. 5.3a), *≠ John, Bill and Mary is here*. It also provides for an exception to the rule that conjoined cores with the conjunction *and* determine a plural noun phrase;[4] in the case where conjoined cores in the SUBJECT are preceded by *each* or *every*, the verb is singular: *Every man and every child was filled with joy, Every uncle and cousin was named in the will* (Fig. 5.3b). The test reads:

$ANDSING = AT X1, IF $CORE-HAS-AND
                    THEN IN THE LEFT-ADJUNCT – OF X1,
                    THE CORE OF TPOS IS T:EACHEVRY.   (GLOBAL)

This test gives the conditions for considering a noun phrase with conjoined cores, where the last conjunction is *and,* to be singular. Thus, if it fails, which is possible only if cores conjoined by *and* are not preceded by *each* or *every,* the noun phrase will correctly be considered plural.

The test $ANDSING begins at X1 (in WAGREE1, the core of the SUBJECT) and first checks whether the core has an *and*-conjunct. If it does, then the noun phrase is deemed plural unless X1 has an article left adjunct *each* or *every* (the sole members of the subclass EACHEVRY shown in Table 4.2). The conjunction test is:

$CORE-HAS-AND = BOTH ITERATE CORE-CONJUNCT EXISTS →
           AND PRESENT-ELEMENT – IS OCCURRING IN ANDSTG.
                                     (GLOBAL)

The Restriction Language prose here is awkward but efficient. A mixture of declarative and procedural syntax has been used; the first test under BOTH . . . AND . . . is an iterate command whose argument is a declarative sentence CORE-CONJUNCT EXISTS. The CORE-CONJUNCT routine checks that the core of an element has a conjunct at the core level. As in other agreement tests, a test is made that the conjunction is *and;* that is, the last conjunct reached in an iteration of the core-conjunct routine must be under an ANDSTG node. In Fig. 5.3a the last conjunct is the node Q-CONJ, which subsumes *Mary,* and which is occurring in an ANDSTG as required by the test $CORE-HAS-AND.

In addition to conjunction at the core level, a plural subject results when the core of the SUBJECT is a conjunction of a string and an LNR construction: *His beliefs and what he does are in conflict.* The parse tree for the SUBJECT in this example is shown in Fig. 5.4.[5] The test for this type of subject construction, is the test $ANDSUBJ:

$ANDSUBJ = AT X20 CO-CONJ SUBJECT EXISTS
           WHERE IT IS OCCURRING IN ANDSTG.   (GLOBAL)

The $ANDSUBJ test starts at the VERB (stored in X20); the CO-CONJ routine with argument SUBJECT looks for a coelement SUBJECT and checks whether it has a parallel postconjunction element, as illustrated in Fig. 5.4, or a chain of such conjoined elements. If it does, and if the final conjunction is *and,* then the test $ANDSUBJ succeeds. This indicates a plural subject, and consequently the tests $NOTPLURSUBJ and $SINGAGREE fail, causing WAGREE1 to fail. This would happen in the case of Fig. 5.4 if the parse tree under SUBJECT were being tested as a possible subject for a singular verb, such as *is:* *⚓ His beliefs and what he does is in conflict.*

The previous example may sound marginally acceptable. If so, this may be related to the fact that when two strings are conjoined in the subject position, it is possible to have a singular verb, although a plural verb is more likely: *To know of a crime and not to report it is a violation of the law.* Because of this possibility, we allow conjoined strings as the subject of either singular or plural verbs; that is, $NOTPLURSUBJ in $SINGAGREE in WAGREE1 does not exclude conjoined strings as the subject of singular verbs. This leniency could easily be extended to the mixed type of conjuncts illustrated in Fig. 5.4 by simply dropping NOT $ANDSUBJ from $NOTPLURSUBJ. The test $ANDSUBJ has a more central role in $PLURAGREE, which will be considered next.

The second half of the subject–verb agreement restriction considers the case where the verb or tensed word is definitely plural and where as a consequence the subject should not be singular: *They walk, A̸ He walk, They don't walk, A̸ He don't walk.*

$$\text{\$PLURAGREE = IF X2 IS PLURAL THEN EITHER \$SUBJNOTSG}$$
$$\text{OR X1 is }\downarrow\text{I}\downarrow.\qquad\text{(GLOBAL)}$$

For the reason for the clause "OR X1 IS ↓I↓" see the first note for this chapter. This clause accepts occurrences such as *I walk, I don't walk*—occurrences with a first person singular subject and a present tense verb, which in the LSP lexicon is classed as PLURAL. Since "I" is a rare subject in science texts this classification is a better treatment than requiring that every occurrence of present tense verb forms like *walk* and *do* be tested for a possible subject *I* in order to determine number. The test is made only in the case where the more common agreement test fails. In texts where *I* is not expected to occur the test can be dropped; the agreement restriction will still apply to these verb forms, which would not be the case if they did not carry the PLURAL attribute.

The main body of the $PLURAGREE test is in the test $SUBJNOTSG (**subject is not singular**), a global test used in WAGREE1, 2, 3 and 7.

$$\text{\$SUBJNOTSG = EITHER \$NOTSINGX1 OR \$ANDSUBJ IS TRUE.}\qquad\text{(GLOBAL)}$$

The second test $ANDSUBJ under EITHER . . . OR . . . is the same test for a higher level conjoined SUBJECT (Fig. 5.4) that was made in $NOTPLURSUBJ as a part of $SINGAGREE. In $SINGAGREE the test was used (perhaps too stringently) to rule out subjects with higher level conjoining as subjects of singular verbs, whereas here we wish to accept such subjects as appropriate for plural verbs; for example, we wish to accept *His beliefs and what he does are in conflict.*

The frequently occurring cases of a singular subject are all covered by the test $NOTSINGX1. This global test is used in WAGREE1, 3, 5, 7, 8 (and in WAGREE2 also as part of $SUBJNOTSG). It reads:

$$\text{\$NOTSINGX1 = AT X1 EITHER BOTH NOT \$SINGN}$$
$$\text{AND NOT \$SINGSTRING}$$
$$\text{OR EITHER \$CORE-HAS-AND}$$
$$\text{OR \$DIMINISHER IS TRUE.}\qquad\text{(GLOBAL)}$$

Briefly, this says that the construction whose core is X1 is not definitely singular, or is compatible with a plural verb, if (1) the core with its left adjuncts is not a singular noun phrase, not *she, salt, a sample, this series, this, one,* (for example none of the parse trees in Fig. 5.5); or (2) the core is not a string that is inherently singular appearing without a conjunct, like A̸

Whether he lied are of consequence (not a parse tree of the type shown in Fig. 5.6); or (3) the core has an *and*-conjunct: *John, Bill and Mary are here, ≠ John are here* (Fig. 5.3a); or (4) the core is a type of noun called "diminisher," which specifies a portion of an object or set: *A large **part** of his constituency are nonvoters.*

Fig. 5.5   Parse trees for singular noun phrases, tested by $SINGN.

a.   The core of the noun phrase is SINGULAR.

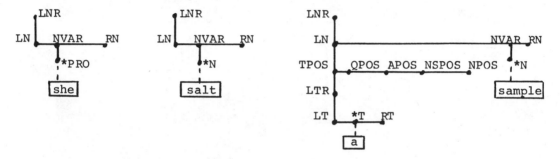

b.   The core of TPOS is SINGULAR.

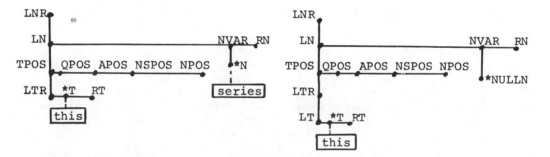

c.   The core of QPOS is SINGULAR (and not conjoined).

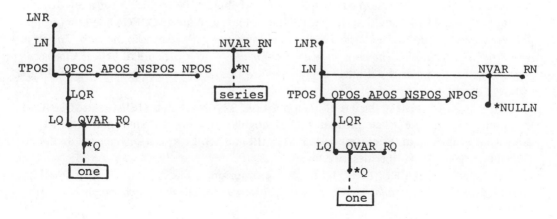

Fig. 5.6   Parse tree for a definitely singular string, tested by $SINGSTRING.

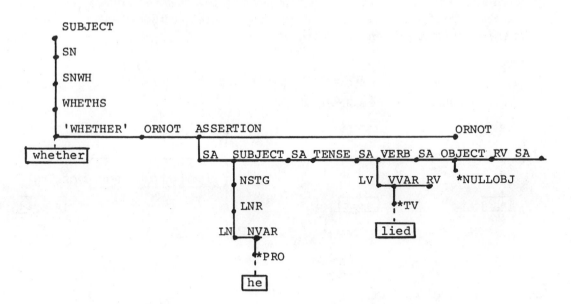

The first of the preceding cases is covered by the negation of the test $SINGN.

$SINGN = EITHER PRESENT-ELEMENT – X15 IS SINGULAR
WHERE X15 IS NOT AGGREGATE
OR EITHER X15 IS VING WHERE IT IS NOT PLURAL,
OR THE LEFT-ADJUNCT – OF X15 IS LN WHERE
BOTH NOT $A-HUNDRED
AND EITHER $TSING
OR $QSING IS TRUE.   (GLOBAL)

In most respects, $SINGN parallels $PLURN, which has already been described in detail. However, where $PLURN checked for a PLURAL attribute $SINGN checks for a SINGULAR attribute (Fig. 5.5a). In addition, if the singular noun is also an AGGREGATE noun (*group, family, crew*), it is not to be considered definitely singular with respect to the verb: *The crew was hired in a fortnight, The crew were all dead drunk.* And if the core of LNR is VING (*car washing*), it is considered definitely singular unless marked PLURAL in the lexicon: *A̶ Car washing are expensive.*

With regard to tests in the left-adjunct position, SINGN calls on $TSING and $QSING to determine whether the article or quantifier is singular. The tests $TSING and $QSING are somewhat simpler than the corresponding $TPLUR and $QPLUR, but sufficiently similar so that they will not be further described here.

The global test $A-HUNDRED takes care of occurrences like *A hundred were tested, A thousand sheep were inoculated, An additional ten are required,* the only anomaly here being that *a* is still taken in the article position instead of in close association with the quantifier in QPOS, as would be the case if *a hundred,* for example, were analyzed like *one hundred.* Such a change in the grammar and lexicon would be desirable.[6] In the meantime, *a* appears as a singular article accompanying a plural quantifier like *hundred* or *thousand,* so that an exception must be made in the agreement of subject and verb (WAGREE1), of article and host noun (WAGREE4), and of article and quantifier (WAGREE9).

The test $SINGSTRING checks for configurations in which the core of the SUBJECT is a string and is definitely singular because it is not conjoined and is not of a type that can occur with either a singular or a plural verb.

$$\text{\$SINGSTRING} = \text{BOTH X1 IS OF TYPE STRING}$$
$$\text{AND AT X1 NEITHER DESCEND TO Q-CONJ}$$
$$\text{NOR X1 IS WHATS} - \text{N.} \qquad \text{(GLOBAL)}$$

The negation of this test succeeds immediately if the core (X1) is not a string, which will happen for the cases covered by the preceding tests. If the core is a string it may or may not be well formed with a plural verb: *What we observe are small indentations in the cell wall.* Other strings, however, do not occur with a plural verb unless they are conjoined: *Whether he knew and whether he lied are unknown, Whether he knew and whether he lied is not certain, Ã Whether he knew are not certain.* The absence of a parallel test in $SINGAGREE for the case of a singular verb occurring with conjoined strings as subject reflects the fact that conjoined or unconjoined strings can occur with a singular verb: *Where he goes and what he does are not matters in question, Where he goes and what he does is a mystery, That he lied and that he lied to cover the lies is by now common knowledge.*

The test $DIMINISHER names a few of the main nouns that in the singular often occur as the grammatical subject of plural verbs.

$$\text{\$DIMINISHER} = \text{PRESENT-ELEMENT IS } \downarrow\text{NUMBER}\downarrow \text{ OR } \downarrow\text{FRACTION}\downarrow \text{ OR } \downarrow\text{PART}\downarrow.$$

Often these words are followed by *of* N in which N is a plural or aggregate noun, but these *of* N phrases are often dropped in situations where they can be reconstructed from the context: *A small fraction (of the samples tested) were found to contain albumin, A large number were negative, A large part of the forest lands are now denuded.* These occurrences are similar to those in which an aggregate noun occurs in place of a "diminisher" noun (*A majority (of the people) disapprove of his action*) and to those in which a quantifier occupies this place: *Many (of them) were involved.* The aggregate case has been handled by making an exception for AGGREGATE nouns in $SINGN. (The quantifier case is not an exception to agreement.) When the "diminisher" class is better defined, $DIMINISHER will be replaced by a subclass check, similar to that for AGGREGATE nouns.

WAGREE1A: Agreement in Question. This restriction is similar to WAGREE1 except that the housing and the register assignments are adjusted to the configuration of elements in the YESNOQ string: (1) The restriction is executed after the SUBJECT node is completed, instead of as in ASSERTION after the VERB node, because in the yes–no question the subject follows the verb; (2) only the tense element (here VERB1) is tested, since the only number-discriminating verb elements in the yes–no question are inflected forms of *have* and *be* (cores of option LTVR of VERB1) or of *do* (core of option TENSE of VERB1): *Has he gone?* versus *Have he gone?*, *Is she coming?* versus *Is they coming?*, *Did they leave?* versus *Does they leave?*. The actual tests for agreement are the global restriction subparts $SINGAGREE and $PLURAGREE defined in WAGREE1.

WAGREE1B: Agreement in permuted subject–predicate string. This restriction is identical to WAGREE1 except for the housing; it is executed after the SUBJECT node is completed because of the permutation of verb and subject elements in OBES: *Of greater interest is the observation that . . . , Of greater interest are the observation that . . . .*

WAGREE2: Subject and predicate noun agree in number. This restriction checks for agreement between the subject of *be* and a noun object of *be* in center strings and in strings where the verb *be* may be present in the form V*ing*, V, *to* V, and so on. This coverage is expressed in the strings named in the housing.

WAGREE2 = IN ASSERTION, YESNOQ, TSUBJVO, SVINGO, FORTOVO, NTOVO, SVO:

Thus, ASSERTION: *He is a carpenter, He is carpenters;* YESNOQ: *Is he a carpenter?, Is he carpenters?;* TSUBJVO: *Neither was he a wealthy man, Neither was he wealthy men;* SVINGO: *This left him being the winner, This left him being the winners;* FORTOVO: *For a woman to be a carpenter is still rare, For a woman to be carpenters is still rare;* NTOVO: *The would like him to be a doctor, They would like him to be doctors;* SVO: *They let him be an assistant, They let him be assistants.*
Following the housing portion is the restriction text[7]:

```
IF BOTH EXTENDED-CORE – X1 OF ELEMENT – SUBJECT X10 IS NOT ↓IT↓
    AND AT X10 DEEPEST-COPRED X6 HAS VALUE NSTG WHERE CORE IS
        NOT EMPTY,
THEN BOTH AT X10, VERB-COELEMENT X20 EXISTS
    AND AT CORE – X3 OF X6 EITHER BOTH $SINGTEST
                                    AND $PLURTEST
                OR $MIXED.                              (GLOBAL)
```

Like WAGREE1, the form of the restriction is an implication in which the premise does some screening and sets up register assignments, and the conclusion does the actual tests for agreement. The screening in this case eliminates occurrences in which the grammatical subject is *it* due to "extraction" (Sec. 4.8, objects of *be*): *It is carpenters we need.* In this case the subject *it* need not agree with the noun object of *be*. The register assignments include the placing of the core of the SUBJECT in X1 and the node SUBJECT in X10. In addition the DEEPEST-COPRED routine is executed; this routine will find OBJBE in the object position following any number of embeddings that do not introduce a new subject. This OBJBE is stored in X6, provided the value of OBJBE is NSTG, indicating the presence of a predicate noun. The core of NSTG is then put in X3. Thus, in addition to the examples given for the strings named in the housing, the restriction will test each of these strings in cases where embeddings distance the subject from the predicate noun: *He proved to be a rascal, Ǎ He proved to be rascals; They would like him to want to be considered a good doctor, Ǎ They would like him to want to be considered good doctors; He is thought to have been considered a good teacher, Ǎ He is thought to have been considered good teachers.* The DEEPEST-COPRED routine operates in these examples (see next subsection).

The tests $SINGTEST and $PLURTEST use global parts of $SINGAGREE and $PLURAGREE from WAGREE1. The logical arrangement of tests is different, however. In WAGREE2 it is more convenient to test the subject first and then, if the subject is definitely singular or plural, to check the predicate for agreement. In WAGREE1, the order was the reverse; first the verb was tested and then the subject was checked for agreement with the verb.

Another difference between WAGREE2 and WAGREE1 concerns the status of exceptions to agreement. There are very few exceptions to subject–verb agreement (WAGREE1), although there is some confusion about what number verb should be used with certain subjects, as in *A number of persons is/are here.* There are more deviations in agreement between subject and predicate nouns. These are due to a variety of sources lumped together rather imperfectly in the escape test $MIXED, which applies in WAGREE2 and WAGREE5 (apposition).

```
$MIXED = EITHER $RARE
         OR EITHER X3 IS NSENT1 OR NSENT2 OR NSENT3,
            OR X1 IS NSENT1 OR NSENT2 OR NSENT3.              (GLOBAL)
```

In addition to the type of exception found in WAGREE1, which also appears in WAGREE2 (*A number of persons are/is here., A number of persons are carpenters*) certain nouns often appear in the singular connecting a plural noun to a subsequent noun or nominalized sentence: *The nucleus contains the **chromosomes, which are the site** of DNA and RNA synthesis; These **cases are a perfect example** of what is commonly referred to as "deviant behavior."* In the absence of a well-defined subclass to include such words as *site, example, illustration, case* and in another sense *matter, area, subject, object* (*These **discrepancies are a matter** of the highest importance/ are a subject of concern/ are the object of much current attention,* and so on), these cases are caught under the heading $RARE. The global $RARE test ($RARE = THE RARE SWITCH IS ON) also covers other cases, such as *be* occurring in the sense of *constitutes: **Public executions** had long grown to **be a scandal** to the country.* Another type of exception is stated explicitly in $MIXED. This type is illustrated by such sentences as *These boys are a problem, The solution is fewer and lower taxes* (Sec. 4.8, objects of *be,* NSTG), in which one of the nouns in question is a sentence classifier (NSENT1, NSENT2, or NSENT3): *problem, solution.*

Aside from exceptions, the body of the restriction is in the global parts $SINGTEST, $PLURTEST, which have a parallel structure. We begin with $SINGTEST.

$SINGTEST = IF $SUBJSING THEN AT X3 NOT $PLURN.   (GLOBAL)
$SUBJSING = BOTH $NOTPLURSUBJ [WAGREE1]
                AND AT X1 EITHER $SINGN [WAGREE1]
                          OR $SINGSTRING [WAGREE1].

The premise $SUBJSING of $SINGTEST determines whether the subject is definitely singular. This is done by first checking that there are no conjoinings that would make the subject plural ($SUBJNOTPLUR; see WAGREE1 and Figs. 5.3a, 5.4) and then testing for one of the configurations of a singular noun phrase ($SINGN, Fig. 5.5) or a singular string ($SINGSTRING, Fig. 5.6). If $SUBJSING succeeds, then the predicate noun is checked to see that it is not plural (*Ⱥ John is carpenters*); that is, at X3, which holds the core of the predicate NSTG, the test NOT $PLURN is executed. (It will be recalled that the global test $PLURN is neutral with regard to the use of registers since all its subtests begin at the PRESENT-ELEMENT – .)

It will be noticed that no test for conjunction is made in the predicate position, although tests for conjunction in the subject were included in $SUBJSING. This is because a conjunction of nouns with *and* in the predicate position does not necessarily determine plural number but may only be carrying multiple predications: *John is a carpenter and a mechanic*. However, in the subject position, a comparable *and* construction does determine plural number: *A carpenter and a mechanic are the supervisors, Ⱥ A carpenter and a mechanic are the supervisor* (but possibly without repeated article: *?A carpenter and mechanic is the supervisor*).

$PLURTEST follows the same logic as $SINGTEST. The overall form is an implication in which the premise tests whether the subject is plural. The conclusion is executed only if the subject is plural, and tests that the predicate noun is not singular.

$PLURTEST = IF $SUBJPLUR THEN AT X3 EITHER NOT $SINGN OR EITHER
                $CORE-HAS-AND [WAGREE1] OR $DIMINISHER [WAGREE1]. (GLOBAL)
$SUBJPLUR = AT X1
                ONE OF $PLURN [WAGREE1], $SCORE-HAS-AND [WAGREE1],
                $ANDSUBJ [WAGREE1] IS TRUE.

The subject is plural if any one of three conditions obtains: (1) The subject is a plural noun phrase ($PLURN, Fig. 5.2); (2) the core of the subject noun phrase is conjoined by an *and*-string ($CORE-HAS-AND; Fig. 5.3a); (3) the subject is conjoined at a higher level ($ANDSUBJ, Fig. 5.4). Corresponding to these three cases are the following examples: (1) *They are carpenters, Ⱥ They are a carpenter;* (2) *John, Bill and Mary are carpenters, Ⱥ John, Bill and Mary are a carpenter;* (3) *The population explosion and what this means for the future of mankind were the central topics of the conference.* Note that again, as in WAGREE1, the conjunction of strings (as opposed to nouns) in the subject position is not taken as an indication of plural number. It most often does indicate plurality (*Whether he knew and when he knew were central questions*), but it may instead indicate a conjunction of events (nominalized sentences) which are considered as a unit: *Whether he knew and when he knew was a paradigm of the investigation.* The same is true in a more limited way of (3), but the further shade of unlikeliness of combining unlike syntactic forms makes it possible to rule against this case in the restriction. Should this "rule" be broken, there is always the escape test $MIXED to check, and perhaps accept, the occurrence.

The operation of the routine DEEPEST-COPRED in WAGREE2.   As an example of the operation of the DEEPEST-COPRED routine (see Appendix 1 under EXTENDED-SCOPE ROUTINES) we will examine the sentences *He seems to be a good teacher* and *He is thought to have been considered a good teacher,* to which the restriction WAGREE2 applies. The parse trees for the ASSERTION centers of these sentences are shown in Fig. 5.7 and Fig. 5.8. In WAGREE2, the routine DEEPEST-COPRED is invoked at the node SUBJECT of the string that houses the restriction; in Figs. 5.7 and 5.8 this node is SUBJECT in ASSERTION. The restriction must find the predicate noun that is constrained to agree with the subject in ASSERTION; in Figs. 5.7 and 5.8, the noun *teacher,* which is the core of OBJBE (the deepest copredicate), should agree with *he,* the core of the subject of the assertion: ⧸*A He is good teachers.*

The definition of the DEEPEST-COPRED routine has three options: $DEEPBE (the **deep**est verb is *be*); $ZEROBE (the string containing the subject and predicate to be tested has a **zero**ed verb *be*); $PASSOBJBE (the deepest embedded string is passive and has the **pass**ive object **OBJBE**). The alternatives $DEEPBE (*He seems to be a good teacher.*) and $PASSOB-JBE (*He is thought to have been considered a good teacher.*) use the DEEPEST-COVERB routine to descend from the starting OBJECT node through any number of embeddings to reach the last (deepest) verb node. In Fig. 5.7, the core of this node is *be,* and in Fig. 5.8 it is *considered.* If the core of the deepest coverb is *be* or a *be*-replacer (VBE or BEREP) then $DEEPBE continues to the OBJECT node where it descends to OBJBE. This is the case in Fig. 5.7 (*He seems to be a good teacher*), where the DEEPEST-COVERB routine iterates through VERB in ASSERTION (core = *seems*) to VERB in TOVO (core = *be*) in the manner detailed in Chapter 3 in connection with Fig. 3.4. Then $DEEPBE continues with the execution of the COELEMENT routine with argument OBJECT, starting at VERB in TOVO. At OBJECT it descends to OBJBE by executing the command DESCEND with argument OBJBE; OBJBE is then the deepest copredicate of the subject (core = *he*) in the assertion.

In Fig. 5.8, where the deepest coverb is LVENR (core = *considered*), $DEEPBE fails since the core of the deepest coverb is not *be* or a *be*-replacer verb. However, before failing, it stores the deepest coverb in X7. $PASSOBJBE picks up from there, testing whether the deepest coverb is an element of the passive string VENPASS, as is the case in Fig. 5.8. In VENPASS, the object element is PASSOBJ rather than OBJECT, so the corresponding continuation is to execute the COELEMENT routine with argument PASSOBJ, starting at LVENR in VENPASS. At PASSOBJ, DESCEND is executed with argument OBJBE, to complete the DEEPEST-COPRED routine.[8]

The alternative $ZEROBE of the DEEPEST-COPRED routine could be used in WAGREE2 to handle such occurrences as *They consider him a good teacher* (Fig. 5.9) because this portion of the routine is directed toward precisely those subject–predicate strings (illustrated by SOBJBE: *him a good teacher*) in which the verb *be* has been zeroed, that is, does not appear explicitly. These strings have the element OBJBE, which would be located by $ZEROBE starting from one of the elements (not OBJBE) of these strings and executing the COELEMENT routine with argument OBJBE. However, in WAGREE2, we do not use the DEEPEST-COPRED routine for this case because it is more efficient to locate OBJBE directly, as part of the restriction statement in a second form of WAGREE2 (WAGREE2A).[9]

WAGREE2A and WAGREE2B: Subject–predicate agreement in SOBJBE, SASOBJBE. These restrictions cover such occurrences as *They consider him a good teacher* (Fig. 5.9) versus Ⱥ *They consider him good teachers,* and *They treat him as an equal* versus Ⱥ *They treat him as equals.*[10] The definitions of SOBJBE and SASOBJBE (8D.1 and 8D.6) differ from those covered by WAGREE2 in such a way that the statement "AFTER OBJECT" in WAGREE2 is replaced by "AFTER OBJBE" in WAGREE2A, and the preliminary tests following the housing are simplified. These strings cover subject–predicate occurrences directly; they have no verb, which is assumed to be *be,* so that the object position is known to have the form OBJBE, and it is not necessary to start with the element OBJECT and narrow it down to OBJBE (via the option OBJECTBE with chosen option OBJBE) as in the strings treated by WAGREE2. This specificity requires a correspondingly specific housing statement, however.

Fig. 5.7   Parse tree with embedding, tested by WAGREE2, using DEEPEST-COPRED routine.

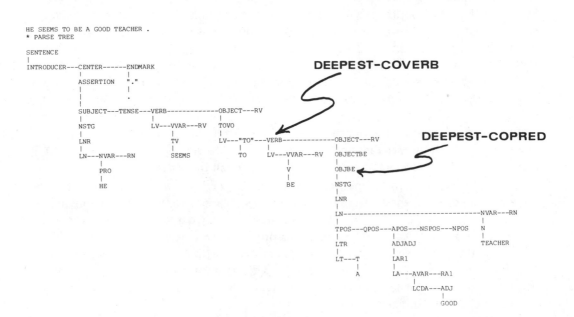

Fig. 5.8 Parse tree with deeper embedding, tested by WAGREE2 using DEEPEST-COPRED routine.

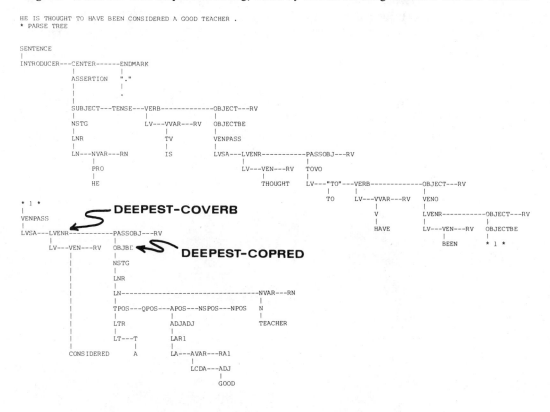

Fig. 5.9 Parse tree tested by WAGREE2A.

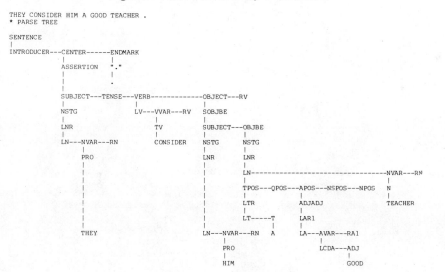

WAGREE3: Reciprocal and collective verbs.   This restriction follows directly from the definitions of two verb subclasses, the reciprocal verbs, which take the object NULLRECIP (see OBJLIST: (NULLRECIP), in Sec. IV of Appendix 3) and the collective verbs (VCOLLEC-TIVE in Sec. VI of Appendix 3). The reciprocal verbs are defined in such a way as to include two types of verbs: verbs that are unambiguously reciprocal when they occur in the environments where reciprocal verbs occur, like *meet: John and Mary met (each other), Ⱥ John met, Ⱥ Mary met;* and those (*fight, talk, love*) that in these same environments have an analysis as a reciprocal verb (*John and Bill fought = John and Bill fought each other*) but possibly also as a nonreciprocal verb (*John and Bill fought* (in the last war)). Parse trees illustrating the two analyses of verbs of the latter type are shown in Fig. 5.10.

Fig. 5.10   Reciprocal and nonreciprocal verb occurrences.

a.   Parse tree with *fought* as a reciprocal verb.

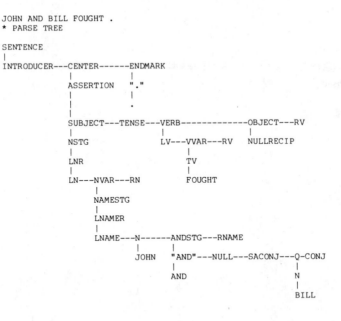

```
JOHN AND BILL FOUGHT .
* PARSE TREE

SENTENCE
|
INTRODUCER---CENTER------ENDMARK
            |          |
            ASSERTION  "."
            |          |
            |          .
            |
            SUBJECT---TENSE---VERB------------OBJECT---RV
            |                 |                 |
            NSTG              LV---VVAR---RV   NULLRECIP
            |                      |
            LNR                    TV
            |                      |
            LN---NVAR---RN         FOUGHT
                 |
                 NAMESTG
                 |
                 LNAMER
                 |
                 LNAME---N------ANDSTG---RNAME
                         |      |
                         JOHN   "AND"---NULL---SACONJ---Q-CONJ
                                |                       |
                                AND                     N
                                                        |
                                                        BILL
```

b. Parse tree with *fought* as a nonreciprocal verb.

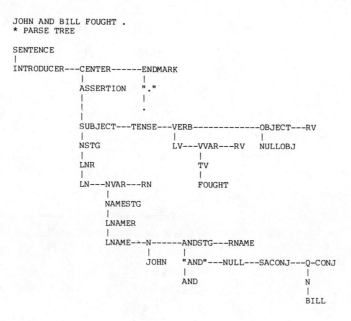

```
JOHN AND BILL FOUGHT .
* PARSE TREE

SENTENCE
 |
INTRODUCER---CENTER------ENDMARK
             |           |
             ASSERTION   "."
             |           |
             |           .
             |
             SUBJECT---TENSE---VERB------------OBJECT---RV
             |                 |                 |
             NSTG              LV---VVAR---RV    NULLOBJ
             |                      |
             LNR                    TV
             |                      |
             LN---NVAR---RN         FOUGHT
                  |
                  NAMESTG
                  |
                  LNAMER
                  |
                  LNAME--➤-N------ANDSTG---RNAME
                  |        |
                  JOHN    "AND"---NULL---SACONJ---Q-CONJ
                          |                       |
                          AND                     N
                                                  |
                                                  BILL
```

The collective verbs are those that, when occurring transitively, require that the noun object be either plural or conjoined or else an aggregate or collective noun: *He collects stamps, ☀ He collects a stamp, He collected a crowd* (AGGREGATE), *These outputs are only collecting dust* (NCOLLECTIVE). The collective verbs often occur with the required type of object appearing in the subject position instead of the object position: *Dust collects on these old outputs.*[11] Parse trees for occurrences of collective verbs are shown in Fig. 5.11.

The restriction WAGREE3 is directed more toward obtaining a correct and revealing parse of sentences containing reciprocal or collective verbs than toward eliminating false paths in the course of parsing, as is the case for example with WAGREE1 and WAGREE2. It applies substantively only when a reciprocal or collective verb occurs in a sentence, and these occurrences are not very frequent. When such verbs do occur, however, this restriction is essential; otherwise, wrong parses will be obtained, so that, for example, *Robinson Crusoe met Friday* would have two parses, and *John and Mary met* would have a second analysis expandable into *John met and Mary met.*

Fig. 5.11   Collective verb occurrences.

a.   With AGGREGATE noun object.

```
HE COLLECTED A CROWD .
* PARSE TREE

SENTENCE
|
INTRODUCER---CENTER------ENDMARK
            |           |
            ASSERTION   "."
            |           |
            |           .
            |
            SUBJECT---TENSE---VERB------------OBJECT---RV
            |                 |              |
            NSTG              LV---VVAR---RV NSTGO
            |                 |             |
            LNR               TV            NSTG
            |                 |             |
            LN---NVAR---RN    COLLECTED     LNR
                 |                          |
                 PRO                        LN-----------------------------------NVAR---RN
                 |                          |                                    |
                 HE                         TPOS---QPOS---APOS---NSPOS---NPOS     N
                                            |                                    |
                                            LTR                                  CROWD
                                            |
                                            LT---T
                                                 |
                                                 A
```

b.   With NCOLLECTIVE subject.

```
HYDROGEN COLLECTS AT THE CATHODE .
* PARSE TREE

SENTENCE
|
INTRODUCER---CENTER------ENDMARK
            |           |
            ASSERTION   "."
            |           |
            |           .
            |
            SUBJECT---TENSE---VERB---OBJECT---RV
            |                 |      |
            NSTG              LV---VVAR---RV
            |                 |      |
            LNR               TV     PN---NULL
            |                 |      |
            |                 |      LP---P----NSTGO
            |                 |      |    |    |
            LN---NVAR---RN    COLLECTS  AT   NSTG
                 |                           |
                 N                           LNR
                 |                           |
                 HYDROGEN                    LN-----------------------------------NVAR---RN
                                             |                                    |
                                             TPOS---QPOS---APOS---NSPOS---NPOS     N
                                             |                                    |
                                             LTR                                  CATHODE
                                             |
                                             LT---T
                                                  |
                                                  THE
```

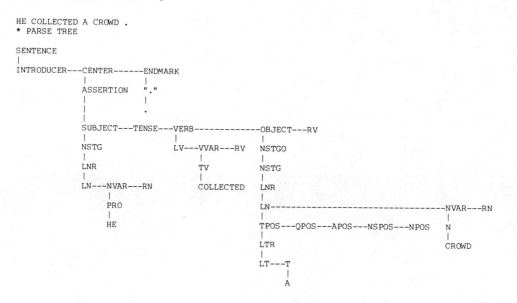

The following remarks pertain to the text of WAGREE3 as it appears in Appendix 1. The main restriction sentence (from WAGREE3 to the first period) has the same form as the previous WAGREE restrictions: A housing portion is followed by preliminary tests that set up register assignments. The housing states the strings to which the restriction applies, here all the verb-containing strings like ASSERTION: *John and Mary met, * John met;* YESNOQ: *Did the group disperse? * Did John disperse?* (but perhaps *Did John disperse with the others?*); SVINGO: *They saw the leaves scattering in the wind, * They saw a leaf scattering;* SVO: *Don't let dust gather, * Don't let a bug gather;* FORTOVO: *They prefer for a large group to collect; * They prefer for a woman to collect;*[12] *The police required the truckers to disperse, * The police required a trucker to disperse;* NTOBE: *The delegates are said to be waiting to convene, * The delegate is said to be waiting to convene;* STOVO – N: *They have the boys constantly arguing to contend with* (well-formed reciprocal and well-formed nonreciprocal, that is, arguing with each other or arguing with others); TSUBJVO: *Nor did they ever marry* (well-formed reciprocal and well-formed nonreciprocal, that is, marry each other, or marry separately.).

The test for a reciprocal verb is $RECIP. The first step of $RECIP is to see whether NULLRECIP has been accepted as the core value of the OBJECT. Since NULLRECIP appears on the OBJLIST of reciprocal verbs only, its presence signifies a potentially well-formed reciprocal occurrence that should be tested further. (DVC1 would have ruled out NULLRECIP as the object of any verb that did not have NULLRECIP as a value of OBJLIST in the verb's lexical entry.) If this part of $RECIP fails, indicating that the verb is not reciprocal, then $RECIP exists ' + ' and no further tests are done. In Fig. 5.7a, $RECIP would find NULLRECIP as the core of the OBJECT following the VERB whose core is *fought,* since *fought* is a reciprocal verb (in one of its occurrences). After finding that the verb is reciprocal and has a null object, $RECIP tests that the subject is not definitely singular, via the global test $SUBJNOTSG, defined in WAGREE1. For example, none of the parse trees shown in Figs. 5.5 and 5.6, which are rejected by NOT $SINGN in $NOTSINGX1 in $SUBJNOTSG, would be accepted as the subject of a verb occurring with NULLRECIP as its object: * *She meets, * * Salt meets,* not *The sample we used differs* as a reciprocal occurrence (contrast with *Sample A and Sample B differ* (*from each other*)), not *This series agrees* as a reciprocal occurrence (only acceptable as occurring with a deleted object: *This series agrees* (*with others*)), and so on. Examples could be given for all the subtests of $SUBNOTSG. The typical reciprocal situation, with a pair of subjects conjoined by *and* (*John and Mary met [each other] recently*), is tested by $CORE-HAS-AND in $NOTSINGX1.

The test $COLL has two parts. $COLLECTIVE-SUBJ accepts such occurrences as *People collected on street corners* and *Dust gathers in corners,* in which the subject is not definitely singular ($SUBJNOTSG) or else is NCOLLECTIVE (*dust*). The test $COLLECTIVE-OBJ, illustrated by the examples in the introduction to WAGREE3, tests the object of a collective verb. If the OBJECT has the value NSTGO, a noun phrase object, then a similar test to the one applied to the subject in $COLLECTIVE-SUBJ is applied to the object. The core should not be definitely singular as tested by $NOTSINGX1 (* *He collected a stamp*), or else it must be NCOLLECTIVE (*It collects dust*). Another acceptable possibility is that the object has a higher-level conjunct (*We'll collect Molly and whoever else wants to come*); the test for this is similar to $ANDSUBJ in $SUBNOTSG, the only difference being that the argument of the routine CO-CONJ is OBJECT instead of SUBJECT.

WAGREE4: LN and N agree in number.   A singular or plural core of LNR can only have left adjuncts that agree with it in number: *this book, ₳ these book* (tested by $SING); *these books, ₳ this books* (tested by $PLUR).

$SING tests for a singular core of LNR in just the same manner as the global test $SINGN defined in WAGREE1; that is, it tests whether the core has the attribute SINGULAR (*book, group*) or whether it is VING (*saving* in *life saving*). Unlike $SINGN it makes no exception for AGGREGATE nouns (*crew*) since these nouns must agree with their left adjuncts (*one crew, ₳ two crew*), even though they may occur with a plural verb (*The crew were hired in a fortnight*). If the core is definitely singular, then $SING tests that neither the article adjuncts nor the quantifier adjuncts are plural (NEITHER $PLURT NOR $PLURQ). $PLURT and $PLURQ are just like $TPLUR and $QPLUR of WAGREE1, except that they include only the tests that are local to a single LN occurrence, illustrated in Figs. 5.2b, 5.2d, 5.2e, 5.2f, and exclude those that test conjoined LNs (Figs. 5.2c and 5.2g).

$PLUR tests for a plural core of LNR just as $PLURN in WAGREE1 does, namely by testing whether the core has the attribute PLURAL. Note that plural number due to the conjoining of cores does not allow left adjuncts to be plural: *₳ These boy and girl*. If the core is PLURAL then neither article nor quantifier left adjuncts should be singular (NEITHER $SINGT NOR $SINGQ; Figs. 5.5b and 5.5c): *₳ one boys*. However, the sequences like *a hundred* treated by the global test $A-HUNDRED are, of course, plural: *₳ a hundred boys*.

WAGREE5: Host and apposition noun agree in number.   This restriction is a virtual repeat of WAGREE2 (subject–predicate agreement), applied to the core of LNR with its left adjuncts as the first argument and an apposition phrase (APPOS in RN) as the second argument. Thus, *John, a carpenter* occurring as a noun with appositional right adjunct is tested for agreement in the same way by WAGREE5 that *John is a carpenter* is tested by WAGREE2. In some appositional occurrences, like *the drug digoxin,* it may seem that the proper analogy is the reverse: *Digoxin is a drug;* but for the purpose of applying agreement constraints the order of the two noun phrases is immaterial. Note that the presence of an *and* in the appositional phrase does not determine plural number in WAGREE5 (*John, a professional carpenter and an amateur musician*), just as an *and* in the predicate does not determine plural number in the tests of WAGREE2. The same exceptions covered by $MIXED in WAGREE2 apply to host + apposition constructions, treated in WAGREE5: *The suggested solution, more policemen, was opposed by some members of the Council.*

WAGREE6: Agreement of SAWHICHSTG with its absent string host.[13]   This restriction accepts such occurrences as *He left, which is surprising* and rejects such nonsentences as *₳ He left, which are surprising.* The analysis of the SAWHICHSTG given in Sec. 4.9 is that the SAWHICHSTG (*which is surprising*) is a relative clause whose host, instead of being a noun, as is the usual case for relative clauses, is in this case the host string (the center ASSERTION *He left*). Since such a string is singular, the verb must not be plural.

WAGREE7: Agreement of roving adjuncts with their host.   RSUBJ (9.5), the set of so-called **roving** adjuncts of the **subj**ect, appears as an option of SA because it may occur in different positions within a string (see Sec. 4.9). The pronoun core of RSUBJ is constrained to agree in number with the subject (occasionally the object) noun in the host string: *He is himself uncertain, ≠ He is themselves uncertain, He is uncertain himself, ≠ He is uncertain themselves, They themselves saw it, ≠ He themselves saw it, We like the book and the man himself.* The quantifier core of RSUBJ is not tested by WAGREE7 because the agreement constraints for the quantifier words in the RSUBJ positions are more complex than for their occurrence elsewhere, for example in LN, perhaps due to a zeroing of *of* N:PLURAL following the quantifier: *The men are each (of them) in a different category* (*each* in RSUBJ), *≠ each men* (*each* in LN). The loss due to not testing these rare occurrences is slight.

The first restriction sentence of WAGREE7 screens for a pronoun core of RSUBJ and makes register assignments. Since the most likely situation is that RSUBJ modifies the subject, the test $SUBJAGREE is done first. Only if this fails will the object be tested (not an airtight restriction, but only reflexive pronouns are allowed as the core of RSUBJ (WPOS7) and sentences with reflexive pronouns are rarely ambiguous). $SUBJAGREE uses tests defined in WAGREE1, with the role of the core verb in WAGREE1 being taken by the core of RSUBJ in $SUBJAGREE. Thus, $SINGAGREE applies when the core of RSUBJ is SINGULAR, and $SUBJNOTSG (the main test in $PLURAGREE) applies when the core is PLURAL. $OBJAGREE also uses tests from WAGREE1 except where the mention of the OBJECT element is necessary (as in the test for higher-level conjoining). Also the contents of register X1 are changed from the core of the SUBJECT to the core of the OBJECT so that the same tests used in $SUBJAGREE can be invoked in $OBJAGREE. The use of the full machinery of WAGREE1 in the simpler case covered by WAGREE7 is a bit heavy handed. However, the generality is justified by the saving in human time that results from writing and debugging one set of tests for all agreement phenomena. There is also the chance that some sentence will make use of the full apparatus, for example: *Whether it was illegal and who is to judge are themselves important questions.*

WAGREE8: Prepositions requiring plural.   This restriction applies the global test $NOTSINGX1 and a test for higher level conjoining to the noun element (NSTGO) of noun-containing prepositional strings when the preposition is *between* or *among: between us, ≠ between him; among us, ≠ among her.* The only complexity arises because the restriction applies to two different configurations, the PN string (tested by $PN and $NSTG-NOT-SING) and *wh*-strings containing the element WHN (tested by $PWH and $WH-NOT-SING). The latter are listed in the housing portion of the restriction; WHN in these strings may be illustrated by (*the house*) *between whose front and back doors, ≠* (*the house*) *between whose front door*[14]; . . . , *between which periods he was unemployed, ≠ between which period; among whose papers many unpublished manuscripts were found, ≠ among whose paper.*

WAGREE9: The left adjuncts of N agree in number.   The need for WAGREE9 as a separate restriction arises when the core of LNR is neither SINGULAR nor PLURAL; the left

adjuncts must still agree: *these two, Ⱥ this two.* This restriction can be looked at as a basic
test for locally singular or plural left adjuncts of the noun. It uses all and only those parts of
the LN tests defined in WAGREE1 that are within one LN; that is, there are not tests for conjoined LNs that confer plural number on the subject, but aside from this the tests applied to
TPOS and QPOS are identical to those in $TSING, $QSING, $TPLUR, $QPLUR in WAGREE1.

5.3   Comma Restrictions

The comma is a difficult element to handle because not all its occurrences can be
described within a grammar. Some occurrences are conjunctional, for example the comma
after *Iceland* in *Several countries, including Iceland, Norway, and South Africa, have no
factory ships.* These commas have a regular grammatical description. But other occurrences
are not so regular. For example, the comma before *and* in the preceding example is entirely
optional, and the comma before *including* is significant, but not syntactically required. If,
on the other hand, a comma were to be placed between *several* and *countries,* it would be
clearly ungrammatical.

In parsing a sentence with the Linguistic String Project's present grammar of English,
an occurrence of a comma in a sentence under analysis is first tried as a conjunction via the
Special Process mechanism described in Chapter 6. If no conjunctional analysis is possible
and there is no other call on a comma from the BNF grammar, the comma is accepted
automatically (as punctuation), and is attached under COMMASTG in the parse tree.
Ungrammatical and unlikely occurrences are ruled out by restrictions, which state that an occurrence of a given string is not well formed if it is preceded (or not preceded, or followed, or
not followed) in the sentence by a comma. Some of these restrictions are purely grammatical,
and others rest on what is likely to be common practice. We have found that despite the
uncertain grammatical status of some of these constraints in English, without them many
strange analyses of sentences result.

The situation handled by the comma restrictions can be summarized as follows:

1. Situations where a preceding comma is not allowed. These may be divided into the
    case where an adjunct string is not to be preceded by a comma (DCOM1, WCOM8,
    DCOM6; also the test $NOCOMMA in DSN2) and the case where an element of a
    string is not to be preceded by a comma, in particular, the elements VERB
    (DCOM2), NVAR (WCOM2), OBJECT or PASSOBJ (WCOM4), N of QN (WCOM2A),
    QNREP (DCOM5), LVINGR of VINGOFN (WCOM2B).
2. Situations where a preceding comma is to be expected (DCOM3; also portions of
    DPOS5, DPOS18, DPOS20).
3. Situations where a following comma is not allowed (WCOM1, WCOM1A,
    WCOM1B).
4. Situations where a following comma is to be expected (WCOM3, WCOM3A,
    WCOM6).
5. Special situations: apposition (DCOM4, WCOM10), sentence adjuncts between
    string elements (WCOM3A, WCOM5, WCOM7).

A few restrictions from each group will be described here.

DCOM1: RN strings with no preceding comma.   The strings named in the housing of DCOM1[15] are not accepted directly following a comma. They are of two types. The strings S – N and WHATSOEVER never occur with a preceding comma: ⚠ *The boy, I met, was a student;* ⚠ *No objection, whatsoever, was sustained.* The strings TOVO, TOVO – N, and FORTOVO – N, which appear in several parts of the grammar,[16] are restricted here only in their RN occurrences. TOVO – N and FORTOVO – N do not occur with a comma separating them from the host noun (or noun variant): *the man to see,* ⚠ *the man, to see.* In the case of TOVO, it is necessary to distinguish RN occurrences from SA occurrences. For example, after the subject noun we may have TOVO as a right adjunct of N: *The desire to tell the truth is lacking;* or as a sentence adjunct: *The desire, to tell the truth, is lacking.* In the latter case the adjunct is most often set off by commas.

DCOM2: No comma before verb.   A comma cannot be placed before a main verb unless there is a special reason for it: ⚠ *Such reasons, exist.* In this restriction, a comma is allowed just preceding the element VERB of ASSERTION only if one of three conditions holds. The first condition is stated in the global test $INCONJSTG, found in WCOM2A. $INCONJSTG distinguishes conjunctional occurrences of the comma from punctuational occurrences by testing whether the given element (here, VERB) is occurring as part of a conjunction string Q-CONJ. If it is, the comma is allowed and the remaining tests, which apply to the punctuational comma, are not executed. This case is illustrated in Fig. 5.12.

Fig. 5.12 Parse tree when DCOM2 is executed at current word *guard* in *They feed the young, guard them, and train them to live alone.*

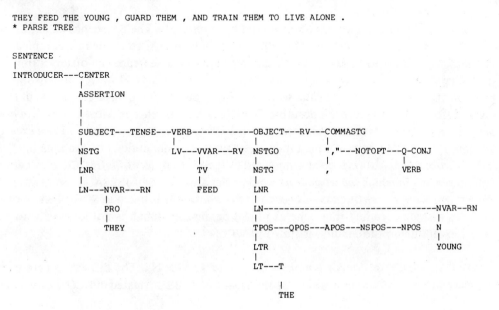

```
THEY FEED THE YOUNG , GUARD THEM , AND TRAIN THEM TO LIVE ALONE .
* PARSE TREE


SENTENCE
|
INTRODUCER---CENTER
             |
             ASSERTION
             |
             |
             |
             SUBJECT---TENSE---VERB------------OBJECT---RV---COMMASTG
             |                  |              |             |
             NSTG               LV---VVAR---RV NSTGO         ","---NOTOPT---Q-CONJ
             |                       |         |             |              |
             LNR                     TV        NSTG          ,              VERB
             |                       |         |
             LN---NVAR---RN          FEED      LNR
                  |                            |
                  PRO                          LN-------------------------------NVAR--RN
                  |                            |                                N
                  THEY                         TPOS---QPOS---APOS---NSPOS---NPOS |
                                               |                                YOUNG
                                               LTR
                                               |
                                               LT---T
                                                    |
                                                    THE
```

Figure 5.12 also illustrates a situation in which DCOM2 succeeds trivially, without even reaching the test $INCONJSTG. Since DCOM2 is executed whenever the node VERB is attached, it is executed at the VERB node in the main ASSERTION, when the current word is *feed*. Since the preceding word in the sentence is not a comma, the restriction is quickly satisfied.

If $INCONJSTG fails, the next test $PREVSA (**prev**ious **SA**) in DCOM2 is executed. This global test accounts for such commas as the one appearing before *have* in the sentence *Baleen whales, too, have been recorded as trying to help each other in moments of distress,* where the comma in question follows an occurrence of an SA string (here the atomic *INT = *too*). It also accounts for a comma between an SA occurrence and the VERB in a conjunctional string, for example the comma before *pulled* in *Donahoo dived over the side and, when the sling was released, pulled the canvas clear.* In the case of an SA occurrence after a conjunction, the name of the SA node is SACONJ. The test $PREVSA thus tests for a preceding, nonempty SA or SACONJ node. If the test succeeds, the comma is considered well formed, and DCOM2 succeeds without executing the remaining test $RN.

If the comma preceding the VERB is neither conjunctional ($INCONJSTG) nor due to a preceding SA ($PREVSA) then it may be due to a preceding RN string ($RN) as in the sentence *A mystery of the whale's ear is that the semicircular canals, which provide a sense of balance, are remarkably small,* where the comma before *are* is of this type. The test $RN applies specifically to an RN comma appearing before the element VERB of ASSERTION, since this is the verb element most likely to be preceded by a long, comma-enclosed adjunct. (A simple variation of the restriction could be formulated for other verb-containing strings.) The premise of $RN "IF VERB IS NOT OCCURRING IN OBES" exempts the string OBES (*Most important is the fact* . . .) from the tests in $RN. The reason is simply that the SUBJECT node, assumed to be present in the tests in $RN, has not yet been constructed in the OBES string when the restrictions on the VERB are executed.[17]

DCOM3: SA strings that require a preceding comma.[18]   The SA strings OBJBESA and SOBJBESA, named in the housing of DCOM3 are usually set off from the rest of sentence by commas, as was noted in Sec. 4.9. At the beginning of a sentence (or of any string), no preceding comma is required; only a following comma (WCOM6). However, in any other SA position, DCOM3 demands that the word preceding one of the named strings should be a comma (for example before the postobject SOBJBESA occurrence in *Most of our root crops are produced by two families, the carrot family and the turnip family, **both of them excellent examples** . . .*). This restriction eliminates certain false ambiguities, for example in (1) *He left his work done, his work done* is analyzed as the SVEN object of *left;* DCOM3 prevents a second reading in which *his work done* would be analyzed as SOBJBESA. By contrast, in (2) *He left, his work done,* DCOM3 succeeds and *his work done* is taken as SOBJBESA; WCOM4 excludes a second reading (the same as in (1)) because a comma is not allowed before an object except under the conditions stated in WCOM4.

DCOM3A: DCOM3 for SA options VINGO and VENPASS.   The difference here is that VINGO and VENPASS, as opposed to OBJBESA and SOBJBESA treated in DCOM3, are not exclusively sentence-adjunct strings, but also occur in other positions, for example as RN. The comma helps to distinguish the SA occurrence from the RN occurrence in positions where both may occur, as after a noun object of a verb. Contrast: (1) *We met a guest leaving the party,* where the most likely reading is the one in which *leaving the party* is an instance of VINGO in RN (a guest who was leaving the party); with (1) *We met a guest, leaving the party.* In (2), we would take *leaving the party,* preceded by a comma, as an instance of SA (when leaving the party). The SA analysis does not imply that the subject of *leaving* is the same as the subject of *met,* though this is the most frequent situation. In the operation of the restriction, a comma is required before any SA occurrence of VINGO or VENPASS except in post-object position when the object is not a noun phrase (*He walked off leaving puzzled looks behind him*).

DCOM3B: DCOM3 for SA option TOVO.   The *to* in the TOVO string in SA is a shortened form of *in order to.* To distinguish the sentence adjunct TOVO from other TOVO occurrences it is usually preceded by a comma in positions where there might be local ambiguity (*The desire, to tell the truth, is lacking* versus *The desire to tell the truth is lacking*). Thus, DCOM3B requires a comma before TOVO as SA string unless TOVO is occurring postobject, where the comma is often not found (and where ambiguity is infrequent): *He did it to please his parents.*

DCOM4 and WCOM10: Commaless apposition.   One of the difficult problems in text parsing is to determine the length of a noun phrase when a string of sentence words are all potential candidates for inclusion in it. We face this problem often because so many words are in both the TV and N classes, like *walk, work.* One path through the grammar may cause the main verb of the sentence, if it is such a TV/N word, to be gobbled up by the subject noun phrase, creating a temporary false analysis: *Sewage treatment needs an isolated location* and *In this way stringed instruments like the harp may have been started thousands of years ago.*[19] The problem is compounded when the grammar permits the occurrence of two adjacent noun phrases, as in commaless apposition. Here the problem is not whether the noun phrase stretches (falsely) over the candidate verb word, as in the preceding example, but whether the noun phrase, however long it stretches, should in fact be divided into two noun phrases, the second in apposition to the first. For example, *the enzyme ATPase* has the intended analysis as the noun phrase *the enzyme* with apposition *ATPase,* and another structural analysis as the noun *ATPase* with left adjuncts *the enzyme,* similar to *the membrane ATPase.* In this example the resolution of the structural ambiguity requires constraints on subject matter; what the parsing can do is to set up the correct structural alternatives and eliminate ones that are grammatically incorrect or extremely unlikely.

The purpose of DCOM4 and WCOM10 is to limit acceptance of commaless apposition to the most frequent situations: (1) the apposition noun is a proper name (*the painter Picasso*); (1) the host noun is a classifier of the apposition noun (*the enzyme ATPase*). In the latter case the first noun should be preceded by an article or other element of TPOS (unlikely are *enzyme ATPase; sugar glucose*). With regard to classifier nouns, two main types are recognized, designated NCLASSIFIER1 and NCLASSIFIER2. NCLASSIFIER1 words are the term classifiers of English, words like *term, word, symbol,* which are characteristically used with apposition to introduce nomenclature. NCLASSIFIER2 introduces into the grammar the fact of the existence of subject-specific classifier words, without specifying the particular classifier-classificand pairs for any given subject matter. Thus, in developing a lexicon for a particular application, if one wants to analyze correctly appositional sequences of the type *the enzyme ATPase,* one should add the attribute NCLASSIFIER2 to the noun entries of the words most likely to be general types in the given subject matter. For example, for analyzing cell-level pharmacology articles, NCLASSIFIER2 words included *drug, agent, enzyme, protein, molecule, ion.*

5.4   MINWORD and Optimization Restrictions[20]

The MINWORD and optimization restrictions are not part of English grammar. They are practical measures taken to speed the parsing process and to control the volume of output due to syntactic ambiguity, without losing information.

5.4.1   *MINWORD Restrictions*

The motivation for the MINWORD restrictions can be illustrated by the familiar problem of correctly assigning a prepositional phrase to the element it modifies in the sentence; for example, in *I know a man with a car from France,* there are at least three ways of assigning *from France:* (1) as a modifier of *car* (a car that is from France); in the string grammar, the PN is in RN where *France* is the core of the LNR containing RN; (2) as a modifier of *man,* (a man from France); here the PN is in RN where *man* is the core of the LNR containing RN; (3) as a modifier of the verb *know* or of the statement whose verb is *know* (the knowing is from (being in) France); in the string grammar the PN is in RV or SA. Many examples of this type of ambiguity can easily be constructed, reflecting a true situation in text analysis. Without subject-matter or textual constraints, the number of correct syntactic readings of an ordinary sentence in scientific writing quickly exceeds manageable bounds, since every combination of the different modifier–host assignments gives rise to another reading.

This type of syntactic ambiguity creates a practical problem for text processing. In very limited domains, the system designer can sometimes state in advance a relatively complete semantics for the topic, and on this basis make reasonable guesses as to the correct readings. However, for most subject matters, no such a priori semantic specification is available. An approach in this case is to limit the number of parses in such a way that alternative readings are automatically recoverable when needed for more refined processing.

To do this we observe that the type of ambiguity illustrated at the beginning of this subsection is limited in each instance to a particular segment of the sentence (for example, *from France*), analyzed as a particular string of the grammar in adjunct status (a PN string in this case). The ambiguity, as far as the grammar is concerned, consists in the fact that in each different reading the adjunct string is occurring as a member of a different adjunct set (RN or SA or RV) or else as a member of the same adjunct set as in a previous reading but in association with a different host (RN with host N_1 (*man*) or host N_2 (*car*)). This observation leads to a relatively simple device for limiting the number of parses to one for each family of parses due to alternative analyses of the same adjunct string.

The device works as follows: When the first parse is obtained, the program scans the parse tree for nodes named on the MINWORD list. This list contains the names of adjunct strings that can appear in different adjunct sets or can have multiple host assignments, as described before. At each such node, the program creates a MINWORD attribute (MAT) having the form MAT:*x:y* where *x* is the name of the given node and *y* is the name of the adjunct set in which the given node is occurring, that is, the immediate parent node of the adjunct string node. Thus, in the parse tree of Fig. 5.13 the MINWORD attribute MAT:PN:RNP. is attached to the word *from*.

Fig. 5.13 Attribute assignment for use by DMIN1 in an ambiguous sentence.

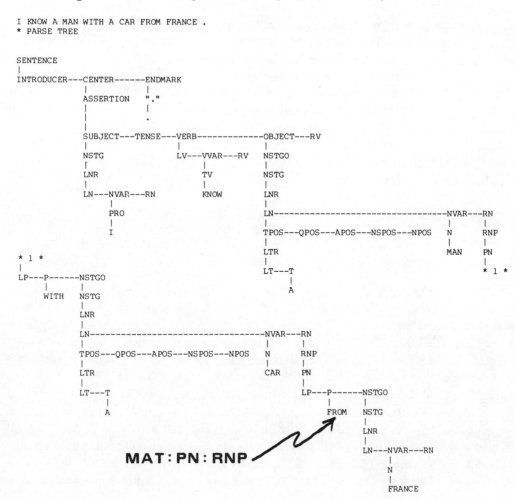

The parser now begins to back up through the parse tree, detaching nodes in the reverse order of their creation, trying to create an alternative parse tree by constructing nodes corresponding to previously unused options of the BNF grammar. When it detaches an atomic node (a terminal node associated with a sentence word) the sentence-word index W is diminished by one. Thus, in backing up after obtaining a parse for an n-word sentence, W will have the value n when the last (nth) word of the sentence is about to be re-analyzed. Later, it will have the value $n - 1$, and so on, eventually reaching W = 1. In the course of the parser's destroying and rebuilding nodes to obtain another analysis, W will increase and decrease many times. At all times, however, there will be a minimal value of W, indicating how far back into the sentence the undoing process has reached in at least one of its backing-up efforts to date. We call the sentence word at the minimal value of W the MINWORD. MINWORD values are monotonically decreasing.

The usefulness of the MINWORD is this: If the sentence word index has the same value as the MINWORD, say m for the mth sentence word ($1 \leqslant m \leqslant n$), then the parser is assured that no change has been made in the parse tree for words 1 through $m - 1$. If now at word m it begins to build an adjunct string node of the same type (like PN) as one it has previously built starting at word m (but this time as a member of a different adjunct set or as adjunct of a different host) then except for rare circumstances a successful alternative parse of the sentence will be generated that differs from other parses solely in that it assigns a particular adjunct string a different syntactic status in the sentence. This alternative assignment is established by the execution of the MINWORD restriction on the given parse tree. There is no need to construct each alternative parse tree, since its difference from a given parse tree is known, so the MINWORD restrictions prevent these alternative parse trees from being built.[21]

To illustrate, the MINWORD restriction on PN occurrences is as follows[22]:

> DMIN1 = IN ( )SA, ( )RV, RNP, RA, OBJECT, PASSOBJ RE PN:
> IF \$MINPAR THEN THE CURRENT WORD IS NOT
> MAT: PN: SA OR RV OR RNP OR RA OR OBJECT OR PASSOBJ.
> \$MINPAR = THIS IS THE MIN WORD.   (GLOBAL)

When the parser backs up after obtaining the parse tree shown in Fig. 5.13, it will first detach "." and try to create a node that can begin with ".", corresponding to an unused option first of ENDMARK (no match), then of SA (not shown; also no match), then of RV (no match), then of RN to the right of NVAR (*France*), the last node created in the subtree under OBJECT (no match). The parser then detaches *France* and backs up into NVAR and LN. Again failing to complete a sentence parse, it backs up further and detaches *P (*from*), which becomes the current word and also the MINWORD, since no earlier sentence words have yet been detached to give the MINWORD a lower value. Unused options of LP are tried without success; then the node PN in RNP is detached and other options of RNP and RN are tried, but none will succeed in this case. RN gets a NULL value, thereby satisfying its parent LNR, and in turn the NSTG above LNR, the NSTGO above NSTG, the PN and NSTGO, and the RNP, whose value now is again PN, with the change that the PN subsumes *with a car* rather than *with a car from*

France. If the parser can now go forward and find an analysis for the detached words *from France.* it will produce a second parse for the sentence.

In going forward, the parser could try for a second PN in the same RN that subsumes *with a car,* via the recursive definitions that were generated by the compiler for the *R definition RN; this would correspond to the interpretation: the man who has a car is from France. However, in the LSP system the repeating option of *R definitions is not used unless the REP (etition) switch is on; so in this case the parser will ascend above RN to the postobject RV in ASSERTION. Here DMIN1 will be executed just before a node corresponding to the option PN in RV is to be constructed.

The test in DMIN1 is an implication: If the current word is also the MINWORD, then it is checked for the presence of a MINWORD attribute, which shows that the current word once before started a subtree of the same type as the one about to be constructed, in which case the option is disqualified. In the case of Fig. 5.13, when a PN in RV is about to be built and the current word is *from,* this word is the MINWORD and has the MINWORD attribute MAT: PN: RNP. This is one of the possible values of the MINWORD attribute tested for in DMIN1. Therefore, the PN node will not be constructed at RV. Similarly, when the parser now advances to SA, with the current word still *from,* DMIN1 will again be executed with regard to the option PN, and again this option will be rejected. If in this sentence the first PN to be constructed starting with the word *from* had been in the SA position (say, by reordering the options in RN to have NULL the first option), then *from* would have the MINWORD attribute MAT: PN: SA, and in backing up, DMIN1 would be executed at RNP. Again, *from* would be the MINWORD and would be carrying a MINWORD attribute tested for by DMIN1, so DIMIN1 would fail and *from France* would not be rebuilt a second time.

5.4.2 *Optimization Restrictions*

Optimization restrictions save parsing time by testing sentence words not yet attached to the parse tree for characteristics required by a node about to be constructed. Some restrictions test the current word to see if it is in a word class that could possibly start the node in question (DOPT1, DOPT8, DOPT18–DOPT21). Since many definitions contain a distinctive word class, word subclass, or literal, which need not be a property of the first sentence word subsumed by the node, many optimization restrictions are look-aheads: they scan the remaining words of the sentence for one that has the required property (DOPT4–7, DOPT9–17). A few optimization restrictions disqualify an option if there are not sufficient remaining sentence words to constitute a minimal occurrence of the option (DOPT2–3).

For the most part, the optimization restrictions are self-explanatory. One special feature requires explanation. Most tests of the current word have the form: EITHER *test* OR $SCOPE; where $SCOPE is a global test:

$$\text{\$SCOPE = THE CURRENT WORD IS A SCOPEWORD.} \qquad \text{(GLOBAL)}$$

A scope word is the first word of a pair such as *either–or, both–and, neither–nor,* in which the second word is a coordinating conjunction, and the segment marked off by the word pair is structurally similar to the conjunctional string. A scope word can occur in many positions where the grammar requires or permits a particular grammatical element. For example (DOPT1A), an adverb string DSTG is permitted in SA positions (as is *now* in *Now we need a mathematician*); but in place of an adverb we may find as the first word of DSTG a scope word (like *both* in *Both now and later we will need a mathematician*), signaling a forthcoming conjunction and marking off the scope of the construction that will be "repeated" by the conjunction string (here, after *and* a second adverb). Without the $SCOPE alternative, the optimization restrictions would rule out many well-formed sentences.

5.5   Noun Phrase and Quantifier Restrictions[24]

5.5.1   *Noun Phrase Restrictions*

In both the DN and WN restrictions, those numbered 1–49 treat LN and NVAR, and those with numbers 50 or greater treat RN. For the most part, the disqualify restrictions (DN) are concerned with eliminating unlikely analyses in advance of constructing their component subtrees, whereas the wellformedness restrictions (WN) treat the grammatical constraints proper.

DN1: Conditions for accepting NULLN as core of LNR.   As noted in Sec. 4.5 in the description of NSTG, it is convenient to analyze certain LN sequences that occur without a following noun as instances of LN NVAR, where NVAR has the value NULLN (as does *three* in *Three are missing*). The restriction DN1, which tests LN for the appropriate sequences preceding NULLN, begins with some pretests to assure that LN is not empty (it would be inefficient to set up all the registers and do whatever else is necessary for testing parts of LN if LN is empty) and that NPOS is empty (the test $NNULL) to assure that the left part of a compound noun is not taken as a complete noun phrase. The allowed sequences terminating in an adjective or adjective variant are specified in $ADJ; those terminating in a quantifier are specified in $Q, and those terminating in a word in the TPOS position are specified in $ART.

$ADJ allows various sequences of the type article + adjective drawn from TPOS and APOS, like *The latter* in *The latter is the more likely case.* In place of an adjective there may be a VING or VEN word: *the most convincing (of the three arguments), the following, the given, the wounded;* the ADJ, VING, or VEN may have left adjuncts or be part of a compound adjective as is permitted in the APOS of LN, and may be preceded by QPOS as well as TPOS (*the many wounded*). Because of the danger that NULLN will cause unwanted alternative parses by splitting normal noun phrases btween the adjective and head noun, currently only the most likely ADJ, VING, and VEN words are allowed. These include comparatives and superlatives (*The stronger survive, The best is yet to come*) and words that are in the subclass APREQ (defined in Appendix 3 as an adjective subclass, but applying also to VING and VEN) such as *the following, the given, the first, the second, the last.* These stringent subclass restraints can easily be eliminated for more literary texts.

A recursively generated APOS before NULLN is considered rare: *The fierce strong survive* (though: *the hungry poor*). The test for this is:

EITHER $RARE OR VALUE OF VALUE OF X3 [APOS] IS NOT ADJADJ.

The particular core values of TPOS that support an occurrence of APOS without a head noun are (1) the definite article T:DEF, as in the foregoing examples; (2) a possessive adjective, called by us T:TPOSS, as in *Their wounded were evacuated, Our own is a different approach*, (3) a possessive noun, as in *the enemy's wounded, the country's aged.*[25] The word *another* is accepted in place of an article + adjective sequence, because *another* is itself morphologically composed of an article + adjective.

$Q accounts for quantifiers as in **Two hundred** *were present,* **Many** *are the different species that have developed such devices*. An example with left adjuncts of Q present and TPOS also not empty is **More than half the two hundred** *present (were from outside the district)*.

$ART allows for the core of TPOS to be a possessive noun NS (*Theirs was accepted*), or T:DEM (*this, that, these, those*) or T:TQUAN (*some, either, neither, any, each;* as in **Neither** *can win,* **Some** *are lucky*) or a *wh*-string of the type HOWQ in TPOS (**How much** *do you want?*, **How much** *is uncertain*.).

DN2, DN3.   These restrictions are required because of the fact that a particular grammatical element appears in more than one place in the grammar, and the different occurrences have slightly different properties.[26] In DN2, the element in question is LQ. When occurring in LQR in QPOS, it may have ADJPREQ (14.31) as its value (*last* in *the last three hundred hired*), but when it occurs in LQR in LT in LTR in TPOS, that is, as a left adjunct of a prearticle quantifier, this option is excluded. Thus, LQ in TPOS may be an adverb (*almost* in *almost all the last three hundred hired*) but not an adjective ADJ:APREQ like *last* (∄ *last all the three hundred hired*).

In the case of DN3, the element in question is the word class NS. As noted in Sec. 4.12, a possessive noun occurs in two different positions among the ordered left adjuncts of the noun, in TPOS and in NSPOS. The NSPOS occurrences are more restricted, and convey the notion of "type": *a women's weekly*. Thus, possessive proper names do not occur in NSPOS: *a women's weekly,* ∄ *a Josephine's weekly*.

DN4.   This is a restriction of the kind one would find only in a computer grammar, aimed at unlikely unwanted alternative parses only a machine would see. One can construct ambiguous examples: *The poor people respect work*. One reading has SUBJECT = *the poor people,* and the VERB + OBJECT = *respect work*. A second reading (if DN1$ADJ is relaxed to allow *the poor* to occur before NULLN) has SUBJECT = *the poor* (whom) *people respect* and the VERB + OBJECT = *work*. The second reading, in which the parser accepts a NULLN when the current word is a noun, is disqualified by DN4.

DN50, DN51. Two restrictions are aimed at reducing unlikely readings due to the headless relative clause S–N, exemplified by *people respect* in the DN4 example. DN50 treats the case where S–N follows NULLN, as in the example just cited, and specifies which LN sequences (from among those accepted by DN1) can be followed by S–N. In particular:

$QPOS accepts a sequence ending in a quantifier: *The five we tested had special problems.* $TPOS1 accepts an occurrence of *these* or *those* (T:TDEM, PLURAL): *Those you are looking at are not for sale.* SINGULAR members of T:TDEM are considered unlikely here, as in *This he brought is most useful.*

$TPOS2 accepts an occurrence of one of the words in T:TQUAN (see DN1$ART): *Some we require are not available,* but these are considered rare before S–N.

DN51 specifies what the first element of S–N should consist of.

$PRO accepts a pronoun (*the best we can offer*).

$T accepts a word in any one of the article subclasses but not the indefinite article: *an environment **this** plant is partial to,* but not *an environment a plant could thrive on.* The line between what is likely and unlikely is thin here.

$N accepts a noun that is COLLECTIVE (this includes chemical names): *the things **people** believe, the substances **oxygen** combines with,* or a proper name (*the paper **Jones** published*). Noncollective plural nouns are excluded (*the play **critics** preferred*) because they initiate many false paths and are infrequent in scientific writing. The S–N construction as a whole is not widely used in published texts.

DN51 also refuses an S–N within an S–N (*the book you read **John** recommended*) via the test $S–N, and it requires that the host noun be determined, that is, that it have a preceding article or quantifier (*I bought the books John suggested,* more likely than *I bought books John suggested*). The test ($HOST) for this is simply that TPOS or QPOS be nonempty.

DN52–DN56. There are five restrictions on options of RN as adjuncts of pronouns. DN52 and DN53 disqualify most of the options of RN if the host is a pronoun (except indefinite pronouns) or a name. (The corresponding restriction on LN with pronoun or name as host is WN11.)

SN	*It that he said the truth is true.*
ADJINRN	*Anyone free to leave would leave.*
	He free to leave is hesitating.
S–N	*Something he saw frightened him.*
	It he saw frightened him.
TOVO–N	*There's noone (for you) to see here.*
FORTOVO–N	*She (for you) to see is Mary.*
TOVO	*Someone to do the job will come on Monday.*
	They to do the job are waiting.

VENPASS	*Anyone selected can win.*
	Ⱥ He selected won.
VINGO	*Anyone not wishing to cause a disturbance should leave.*
	Ⱥ They not wishing to cause a disturbance withdrew.
	(no comma after *they*)
WHATSOEVER	*anything whatsoever*
	Ⱥ they whatsoever
PVINGSTG	*Something for settling the nerves may help.*
	Ⱥ They for settling the question are here.
PSVINGO	*Ⱥ It for the money's absence not being noticed is this.*
PSNWH	*Ⱥ He of whether to buy or not is at the door.*

DN54–DN56 allow certain RN strings to adjoin the personal pronouns *we, you* (although for scientific writing these adjoinings should perhaps be considered rare) and some also to adjoin indefinite pronouns.

APPOS	*we the people, you the listeners* (only personal pronouns)
DSTG	*we here, someone here* (personal or indefinite pronouns)
PN	*we of the nominating committee, someone on the nominating committee, something of this nature* (personal or indefinite pronouns)

The relative clause options RNWH and THATS – N are allowed without restriction as adjuncts of pronouns (*he who hesitates*) but probably could be restricted similar to the adjuncts in the foregoing list.

DN57.   Disqualifying an apposition string as adjunct to an apposition string, DN57 has an important use in constructions of the form: N, N, N, *and* N. These are most often a string of conjuncts with none of them apposition strings. However, the second N in some cases is in apposition to the first N; *Russell, a logician, a philosopher and a political writer.* In such a case the third N is not another apposition string adjoined to the second N.

DN58.   The host N of P-*wh* adjunct strings should be the appropriate subtype of an NSENT word: *the question of how groups enter new ways of life.*

WN1–WN8.   These restrictions are on particular positions within LN, starting with TPOS (WN1-3), then QPOS (WN4-5), then APOS (WN6-7) and NPOS (WN8). These restrictions follow from the definitions of article and quantifier subclasses given in Tables 4.2 and 4.3 of Sec. 4.14, and other considerations noted in that section and in the annotation of the restrictions in Appendix 1.

WN9–WN17.　Constraints WN9–WN17 affect the core of LNR.[27]

WN9: Count-noun restriction.　Some singular nouns as the core of LNR require a preceding article or other determiner: *The bed fell, A̸ Bed fell.* These are called countable nouns or count nouns. There are different types (defined in Appendix 3). All count nouns are NCOUNT1; NCOUNT2 and NCOUNT3 are subtypes of NCOUNT1 that may occur without a preceding determiner in stated environments.

In the operation of WN9, when a singular count noun is found to be the core of LNR, first a search for a preceding determiner in LN is made via the tests $TPOS, $QPOS, $APOS.

$TPOS	*a bed, the bed, his bed, his roommate's bed* (NS), *whose bed* (WHLN) as in *the fellow whose bed fell*
$QPOS	*One bed is as good as another.*
$APOS	*Another bed.*[28]
$COUNT2	*He is sick in bed.*

Bed, in the example for $COUNT2, is NCOUNT2, with the preposition *in* specified as the value of its NCOUNT2 attribute in its word dictionary entry. This is used in the $PNTEST to verify that *bed* is occurring in a prepositional phrase whose preposition is *in* when the restriction is being executed. If it is, then WN9 is satisfied even though no preceding determiner is present (Fig. 5.14).

$COUNT3	*They elected him Congressman, but now he is President. Congressman* and *President* are both NCOUNT3; in their occurrences in the example both are occurring in OBJBE (Fig. 5.15).
$COUNT4	In areas of specialized usage there are exceptions to the count noun restriction that are characteristic for that area. For example, in the medical literature we may find *This is true of brain and nerve* (meaning brain and nerve tissue). In ordinary usage *brain* and *nerve* are NCOUNT1. We have left room for such words to be classed as NCOUNT4, where the words assigned NCOUNT4 will be different in different applications. Via the test $COUNT4, WN9 accepts any NCOUNT4 word as the core of LNR, with no requirements on the LN position. It should be noted that not all exceptions to the count-noun restriction are accounted for in WN9, for example, *Book after book slid down the chute* (*book* NCOUNT1).

WN10:　Restriction on VING as core of LNR.　We draw the line between VINGSTG occurrences of VING and LNR occurrences at the point where a compound noun is formed. For example, we analyze *planting* as the VING in the string NSVINGO in *Their planting trees is desirable* and *Planting is difficult;* as the VING in VINGOFN in *The planting of trees is*

desirable and in *The planting is going well* (see discussion in Sec. 4.5); but we take VING as the core of LNR in *tree planting.*[29] To minimize wrong analyses such as misinterpreting *child fretting* as a compound noun in LNR with VING core in *I saw a child fretting over candy,* we require that the VING core of LNR be (as verb) one that can take a noun object; that is, it has NSTGO as a value of its OBJLIST attribute in the word dictionary. (A selectional constraint is also applied to N VING compound nouns by WSEL3.)

WN11: Restriction on pronoun and name as core of LNR. $NAME specifies that a name is not the head of a compound noun ($NPOSNULL) nor of an N's-of-type ($NSPOSNULL) (*a garden party, Ⱥ a garden Mary, a children's bike, Ⱥ a children's Mike*) and further that it is unlikely (rare) to have an article, quantifier, or adjective preceding a name. Thus, *a certain Dr. Smith* will be treated as rare.

$PRO specifies that all left-adjunct positions except TPOS be empty before a pronoun (*Ⱥ a certain him*) and that in TPOS, only an occurrence of a DLTPRO adverb is acceptable (*only she, Ⱥ only a she, Ⱥ The she,* and so on).

Fig. 5.14   Operation of the count noun restriction WN9 when the core of LNR is NCOUNT2.

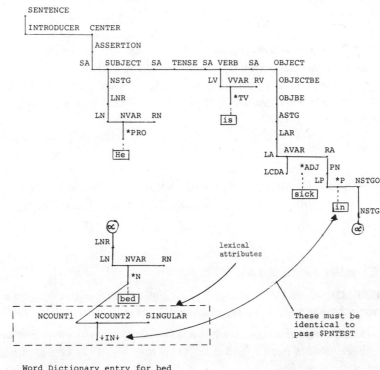

Fig. 5.15   Parse tree tested by WN9, where the core of LNR is NCOUNT3.

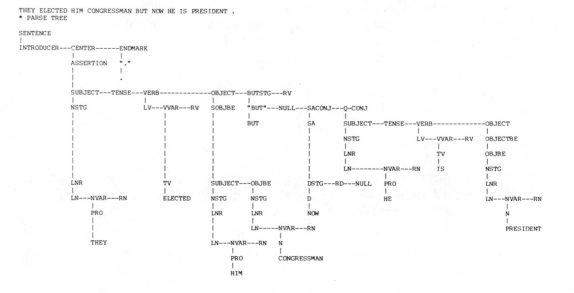

WN12, WN13, WN14–16, 16A: More on names.   Since a noun that is a name (N:NAME) becomes the core of LNR via NAMESTG as value of NVAR, WN12 prevents NVAR from taking an N with attribute NAME as value. This would be redundant.

WN13 prevents breaking up a proper name or title + name into a noun with an appositional right adjunct; *Smith* is rejected as the core of APPOS in *Mary Smith* and *Doctor Smith,* but not in *my friend Smith.*[30]

WN14–WN16 and WN16A require the proper noun subclasses in the different parts of NAMESTG.

WN50–WN53: Some details regarding several RN strings.   WN50 is a restriction on the adjective string as a right adjunct of a noun; ADJINRN must meet one of the following conditions:

$LEFTADJ, where the adjective has left adjuncts, making the adjective phrase "heavy": *a point not far distant.*

$RIGHTADJ, where the adjective has a right adjunct: *a student good at math, a person necessary for their support, strawberries fresh from the field.*

$CONJOIN, where the adjective has a conjunct: *good men true and brave, many children hungry and in need of aid.* Conjuncts may be of the comparative type also: *women as capable as she.*

$QNSTG, where the adjective string is, in fact, a QN string: *a table two feet long.*

$AINRN, where the adjective is in the subclass AINRN of those adjectives that can occur without adjuncts in ADJINRN: *the Congressmen present, this book alone would* . . . .

$INDEF, where the host is an indefinite pronoun: *something sweet.*

WN51 restricts PN as RN; certain prepositions occur only with certain subclasses of N. WN52 is a restriction on APPOS; APPOS should not have a null core. Like DN4 and DN50, this restriction is aimed at eliminating false readings due to the breaking up of normal noun phrases by NULLN. But note that this restriction excludes certain sequences we might in some sentences wish to analyze as LN + NULLN + APPOS: *A few samples, five ( ) in number, were not tested.* DN1 may allow a certain LN NULLN sequence, but if it occurs within an apposition noun phrase, the more restrictive WN52 will reject it because it has a NULLN core.

WN53 keeps TOVO – N in an RN in subject position from capturing the main verb TV (mistaking a TV/N word for an N) and from other false capturings by requiring that the upcoming main verb be a form of *be* or *be* – replacer. Thus, TOVO – N: *the problems to work on are . . .;* not TOVO – N: *the facts to keep on record . . . .*

5.5.2 *Quantifier Restrictions*

In this grammar, quantifier restrictions are mainly concerned with the quantified measure sequences one finds in natural science texts, consisting of a number (or quantifier word) followed by a unit of measure and possibly an expression giving the scale or dimension of the measure. This is the QN string (*three centimeters in length*) described in connection with APOS in LN in Sec. 4.12. The restrictions of this type are DQ2–DQ4, WQ1–WQ3, WQ7–WQ9, WQ13, and WQ14. The string NQ, also described in the APOS section, is restricted by WQ10–WQ12. Of the remaining quantifier restrictions, WQ4 and WQ5 concern details of the definitions NUMBRSRG and CPDNUMBR covering numbers in both word and symbolic forms, discussed in connection with QPOS in Sec. 4.12. WQ6 concerns "roving" quantifiers, like *all* in *We are all coming.*

Recall that in this grammar a number of words ordinarily thought of as quantifiers, such as *each, any, some,* are because of their positions of occurrence vis à vis other words in the noun phrase, classed as T: TQUAN rather than as Q. Tables 4.2 and 4.3 and restrictions WN1–WN5, as well as the discussion of RSUBJ in Sec. 4.9 are all concerned in one way or another with treating these words. We have tried to obtain the widest possible coverage of quantifier-containing sequences and to limit redundant and spurious analyses. However, we do not claim that the parses obtained are easily related to underlying source sentences that capture the correct interpretation, as is the case in many other parts of the string grammar.

5.6 **Selection Restrictions**

Not all grammatically correct sentences are equally likely. *A bear hibernates* is not a surprising sentence, whereas *A fact hibernates,* at the least, requires explanation. A word is said to have a wide selection if it occurs with very many other words, as does the verb *be,* and a narrow selection if it occurs with only a few or with a special subset, as does *hibernate.* Selection restrictions aim to use such differences among words to decide which is a more likely parse among equally valid syntactic analyses, for example to accept *The bear hibernates* and reject *Ḁ The fact hibernates.*

Clearly, selection restrictions are not grammatical constraints of the usual type, where there is a clear answer: "Yes it is well formed," or: "No, it is not well formed;" and where there are clear-cut word subclasses, which behave in a regular way with respect to the constraint. In addition, unlike grammatical constraints that operate in the same way over the whole language (barring certain dialect differences), selectional constraints vary, depending on the area of discourse. What is normally acceptable in one context may be outlandish in another and vice versa. Consider, for example, the different linguistic environments of *field* in agriculture, sports, physics, and computer science.

Should one include selectional constraints in a grammar at all? The practical answer, of course, is yes, since in the difficult task of computerized language analysis one uses everything one can. However, such restrictions are effective only to the extent that selectional subclasses can be formulated for the material. Thus, for the language as a whole, which includes literature, fairy tales, and other forms, there are very few sets of words that can be regularly excluded as, say, the subject or object of particular verbs. For science writing as a whole, some constraints of this type can be stated in terms of gross noun subclasses, such as the LSP classes NHUMAN, NONHUMAN, NTIME (time nouns), and NSENT (sentence classifiers, like *fact*). Thus (as a rule), *The patient refused food, Ḁ The fact refused food,* where *refuse* is classed in the lexicon as a verb not likely to take an NSENT noun as subject.

Selectional constraints are much stronger and more reliable when the language material concerns a narrow subject matter, as is the case in subfields of science, where a limited vocabulary is used in a regular way, and where a body of knowledge, assumed to be known by both writers and readers, severely limits what can be sensibly said. In a science subfield, selectional constraints have virtually the force of grammatical restrictions, as is demonstrated in the applications described in Chapters 8 and 9.

The selectional restrictions in the LSP grammar are independent of the particular words and word subclasses checked for co-occurrence compatibility by the restrictions. The restrictions compare attribute lists that they obtain for particular words from their entries in the word dictionary. Thus, the same restriction can be used at different levels of selectional specificity (whole language, science language, science sublanguage) by adding or deleting items on the relevant attribute lists of words in the lexicon. The attribute lists in question are those labeled NOTNOBJ (**not** an appropriate **n**oun **obj**ect) and NOTNSUBJ (**not** an appropriate **n**oun **subj**ect).[31]

WSEL1, WSEL5, WSEL6: Suitable object N for a given verb.   The effect of WSEL1 is illustrated by the parse trees in Fig. 5.16 and 5.17 for the sentence *The children cook Tuesdays.* Figure 5.16 shows the one and only parse obtained for this sentence by the parser, using the present LSP lexicon. In this parse, *Tuesdays* is a time adjunct on the assertion *The children cook*. Figure 5.17 shows the state of the parse tree for this sentence when the parser has found an alternative slot for *Tuesdays,* namely as the object of *cook* (as in *The children cook fritters*), but is prevented from accepting this analysis by WSEL1, using the lexical entries for *cook* and *Tuesdays* shown in Fig. 5.18.

It will be seen in Fig. 5.18 that *Tuesdays* has the category N (noun) with the attribute NTIME2 among other attributes, and that the verb *cook* has the category TV (tensed verb), with attribute NOTNOBJ (among others), whose attributes in turn are NTIME1, NTIME2, NSENT1, NSENT2, NSENT3, and NHUMAN. Since the values of NOTNOBJ for a given verb are those noun subclasses of the grammar that are not appropriate noun objects of the given verb, the appearance of NTIME2 as an attribute of NOTNOBJ in the entry for *cook* indicates that nouns having the attribute NTIME2 (such as *Tuesdays*) are not acceptable as the noun object of forms of *cook*.

The text of WSEL1 is as follows:

    WSEL1   =   IN OBJECT AFTER NSTGO:
                      IF ALL OF $OBJECT-NOUN, $GOVENING-VERB,
                          $FORBIDDEN-NOUN-LIST ARE TRUE,
                      THEN $NO-COMMON IS TRUE.

    $OBJECT-NOUN = THE CORE X3 OF THE OBJECT X10
                      IS N OR PRO.

    $GOVERNING-VERB = AT X10 THE VERB-COELEMENT
                          X4 EXISTS.

    $FORBIDDEN-NOUN-LIST = THE CORE OF X4 HAS
                          THE ATTRIBUTE NOTNOBJ X5.

    $NO-COMMON = LISTS X3 AND X5 HAVE NO COMMON ATTRIBUTE.

The housing portion, IN OBJECT AFTER NSTGO, tells us that this restriction will be executed in every string of the grammar which has an OBJECT element, whenever the verb governing the OBJECT position has a noun phrase as object (NSTGO). There are thirty object-containing strings in the grammar, exclusive of conjunctional strings, so that WSEL1 has a wide applicability.

The body of the restriction is an implication with three conjoined premises and one conclusion. The first premise, $OBJECT-NOUN, tests whether the core of the object[32] is a noun or pronoun, and in addition stores a pointer to the node OBJECT in register X10 and a pointer to the core in register X3. Operating on the tree in Fig. 5.17, this will place in X3 a pointer to the atomic node N (*Tuesdays*). Should this first premise fail, the restriction is satisfied and a success signal will be returned to the parser. This is as it should be, since if the object is not a noun or pronoun the object cannot be in an unacceptable noun or pronoun subclass.

Fig. 5.16 Parse tree tested by WSEL1, where the verb and the object noun are compatible.

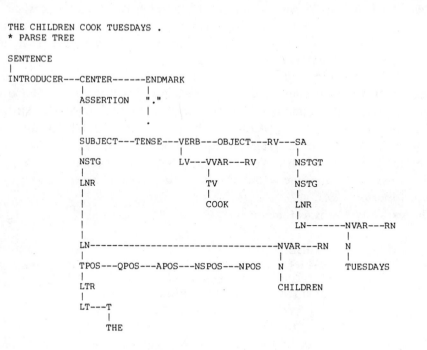

```
THE CHILDREN COOK TUESDAYS .
* PARSE TREE

SENTENCE
|
INTRODUCER---CENTER------ENDMARK
             |              |
             ASSERTION     "."
             |              |
             |              .
             |
             SUBJECT---TENSE---VERB---OBJECT---RV---SA
             |                 |                     |
             NSTG              LV---VVAR---RV         NSTGT
             |                      |                 |
             LNR                    TV                NSTG
             |                      |                 |
             |                      COOK              LNR
             |                                        |
             |                                        LN-------NVAR---RN
             |                                                  |
             LN-------------------------------NVAR---RN         N
             |                                  |               |
             TPOS---QPOS---APOS---NSPOS---NPOS  N               TUESDAYS
             |                                  |
             LTR                                CHILDREN
             |
             LT---T
                  |
                  THE
```

Fig. 5.17 Partial parse tree rejected by WSEL1.

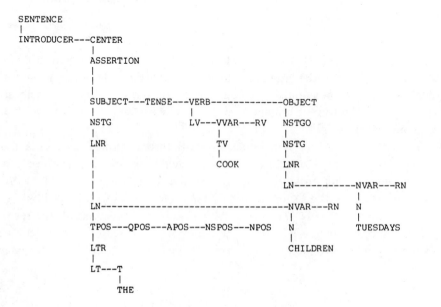

```
THE CHILDREN COOK TUESDAYS .

SENTENCE
|
INTRODUCER---CENTER
             |
             ASSERTION
             |
             |
             |
             SUBJECT---TENSE---VERB------------OBJECT
             |                 |               |
             NSTG              LV---VVAR---RV   NSTGO
             |                      |           |
             LNR                    TV          NSTG
             |                      |           |
             |                      COOK        LNR
             |                                  |
             |                                  LN-----------NVAR---RN
             |                                                |
             LN-------------------------------NVAR---RN       N
             |                                  |             |
             TPOS---QPOS---APOS---NSPOS---NPOS  N             TUESDAYS
             |                                  |
             LTR                                CHILDREN
             |
             LT---T
                  |
                  THE
```

Fig. 5.18 Lexical entries for *cook* and *Tuesdays* used by WSEL1 in example.

```
(NVTV)       COOK.
.11     =    NCOUNT1, NHUMAN.
.12     =    OBJLIST:  .3, NOTNOBJ:  .1, NOTNSUBJ:  .2, VENDADJ.
.1      =    NHUMAN, NSENT1, NSENT2, NSENT3, NTIME1, NTIME2.
.2      =    NONHUMAN, NSENT1, NSENT2, NSENT3, NTIME1, NTIME2.
.3      =    DSTG, NN, NPN:  .5, NSTGO, NULLOBJ, PNN:  .5.
.5      =    PVAL:  (!FOR!).


(TVVEN)      COOKED  ↑.
.14     =    OBJLIST:  .3, NOTNOBJ:  .1, NOTNSUBJ:  .2, VENDADJ, POBJLIST:  .4.
.4      =    NSTGO, PN:  .5, NULLOBJ.

(ING)        COOKING  ↑.

(NTV)        COOKS  ↑.




(NSIX)       TUESDAY.
.11     =    NONHUMAN, NTIME2.

(NPLX)       TUESDAYS  ↑.


note: (NVTV)  =  N:  .11, SINGULAR, V:  .12, TV:  .12, PLURAL.
      (NTV)   =  N:  .11, PLURAL, TV:  .12, SINGULAR.
      (TVVEN) =  TV:  .12, VEN:  .14.
      (ING)   =  VING:  .12.
      (NSIX)  =  N:  .11, SINGULAR.
      (NPLX)  =  N:  .11, PLURAL.
```

The second premise, $GOVERNING-VERB, also has as its aim to locate and store a node on which further processing will be done. This node is the verbal sibling of OBJECT, in this case, VERB. In other strings the verbal element may have a different name and different substructure (say a VING form, as in *is cooking*), so that it is convenient to use a generalized routine, VERB-COELEMENT, which locates the desired verbal sibling in all cases. The $GOVERNING-VERB test, applied to the tree in Fig. 5.17, starts at OBJECT (the value of X10), executes the VERB-COELEMENT routine, which brings it to the node VERB, and stores a pointer to VERB in X4. Again, if this test fails, the restriction is trivially satisfied, since this means there is no governing verb present.

The third premise, $FORBIDDEN-NOUN-LIST, invokes the CORE routine starting at the node VERB (the value of X4) to obtain the governing verb itself (here TV, *cook*). It then searches the attribute list of category TV in the dictionary definition of *cook* for NOTNOBJ. If the search is successful, a pointer to the attribute NOTNOBJ is placed in X5.

The conclusion, $NO-COMMON, compares the attribute list of category N of *Tuesdays* (the value of X3) with the attribute list of NOTNOBJ in *cook* (the value of X5). If these lists have no element in common then *Tuesdays* is acceptable as an object of *cook*. In this case they have the attribute NTIME2 in common, so that the test $NO-COMMON fails, and the partial parse tree shown in Fig. 5.17 is rejected.

The same selectional constraint that applies to a verb and its noun object in the active voice, tested by WSEL1, applies to the same verb and its noun object when they are occurring in a passive construction, except that the noun no longer appears in the object position. An important case of this type, where the verb appears as a passive adjunct of the noun, is tested by WSEL5. The passive structure itself, where the subject of *be* + VEN must be an acceptable object of the root V, is tested by WSEL8.

WSEL2: Suitable subject N for a given verb.   This restriction is similar to WSEL1, but checks the subject noun, rather than the object noun, of the co-occurring verb. Thus, in the sentence *The patient ate well Monday but Tuesday refused food,* a second analysis, which would have *Tuesday* the subject of *refused* is rejected because the NOTNSUBJ attribute of *refused* contains NTIME2 as one of its values. (A parse with the noun *well* taken as the object of *ate* is rejected by WN9.) It should be noted that WSEL2 uses the extended-scope routine DEEPEST-COVERB to locate the verb that is selectionally related to the subject noun, since there may be intervening verbs between these two elements, as in *The patient ate well Monday but Tuesday was reported to have refused food.* In this sentence, the core of the DEEPEST-COVERB is *refused.* Because the DEEPEST-COVERB routine does not test whether the verb element it locates is occurring in an active or a passive construction (e.g. *was refused* as opposed to *have refused*), this test is made within WSEL2 by $NOTPASS.

WSEL3, WSEL4, WSEL6: Selectional restrictions on N VING.   WSEL3 and WSEL4 test an N VING sequence in LN for verb–object co-occurrence compatibility; e.g. *fire fighting* is seen as related to *X fights fire(s).* WSEL3 treats the compound noun occurrence of N VING (*Fire fighting is a dangerous occupation*), while WSEL4 treats the same sequences occurring adjectivally (*fire fighting equipment*). WSEL6 tests N and VING for subject–verb co-occurrence compatibility; for example, *a gentleman dining here,* where VING is in the RN string VINGO, is seen as related to *A gentleman is dining here.*

These restrictions can be criticized because only the most productive (most frequent) type of compound is covered (not *folk dancing* or *arc welding*). We are led to use these crude restrictions because of the many syntactic possibilities for N VING sequences. Consider the simple sentence *We saw a fire fighting brigade returning.* Without selectional constraints, there is a reading in which the noun *fire* has a right adjunct VINGO, with VING = *fighting;* that is, the fire is fighting something (the something is "brigade returning"). Assume that *fight* requires an animate subject and that a noun subclass INANIMATE appears both as a value of the NOTNSUBJ attribute of *fighting,* and also as a noun subclass of *fire.* This would enable WSEL6 to reject this unlikely reading. Also *brigade returning* is a highly unlikely compound noun. Since *brigade* is classed as NHUMAN, and the transitive occurrence of *return*[33] has NHUMAN as value of NOTNOBJ (*⊅ He returned Mary,* though possibly in everyday speech *He returned the children at 6 o'clock*), WSEL3 will reject this compound noun in examples like the one above—in *We saw a brigade returning, They reported seeing a man returning,* as opposed to *We protested the cross burning* (where *cross* is the object of *burn*).

WSEL7: Selectional restriction on VING N and VEN N. Generally, a VING word tht occurs adjectivally adjoining a noun (*dining* in *a dining gentleman*) has a selectional relation to that noun, which is the same relation it would have if the noun were occurring as the subject of a verbal occurrence of VING (*a gentleman is dining,* or *a gentleman dines*). There are exceptions, of course (*a fighting spirit*), but on the whole the restriction WSEL7, which checks that the head noun N in this VING N construction is not a forbidden subject for the verb VING, works very well. It should be stressed that the VING N construction checked by WSEL7, in which VING occurs in APOS in LN, is not the same as the compound noun VING N construction (*washing machine, dining room*), in which VING occurs in NPOS in LN. WSEL7 is not applied to the latter, since the selectional constraints there are not those of subject–verb but rather are similar to those in N P X's Ving (*a room for (someone's) dining*).

The test for a forbidden subject of VING in WSEL7 compares the attribute list NOTNSUBJ of every VING word occurring in APOS in N with the list of subclasses of the N word about to be accepted as the host of LN (that is, as the value of NVAR, following LN). If these lists have no attribute in common, then the host N is not a forbidden subject of any of these VING words. An illustration of this type of test was given for WSEL1 earlier. WSEL7 includes a similar test applied to VEN words in APOS using the attribute NOTNOBJ of VEN in place of NOTNSUBJ of VING (see annotation of WSEL7 in Appendix 1).

5.7 Sentence Nominalization Restrictions

This set of restrictions is mainly concerned with the correct placing of sentential complements in the sentence and the correct choice of verb or predicate adjective or predicate noun to occur with these complements. In terms of the BNF definitions of the LSP grammar, these restrictions are concerned with the strings named as options of SN (5.11) and of VINGSTG (5.8). A brief description of the function of these restrictions follows.

DSN1 and WSN1 deal with SN strings occurring as the subject or object of the verb *be,* for example as subject (WSN1): *That he is dead seems tolerably certain,* and as object (DSN1): *The trouble is that we have no money.*

DSN2–6, DSN13, and WSN2 treat SN strings in the post-verb or post-predicate position. DSN2 controls acceptance of SN strings in RA: *It seems tolerably certain that he is dead, It is not desirable for you to stay, She is anxious for you to leave.* DSN3 makes the choice of SN string in RA or in RN more refined depending on the sub-subclass of the adjective or noun host. DSN4 and WSN2 control acceptance of SN strings after a verb of the VSENT type. DSN5 controls SN strings following a noun, and DSN13 treats the verbs like *seems* and *appears* that have *it* as subject and SN as object. DSN4: *It surprised us that he left, It was not known whether they were present;* DSN5: *It is of interest that they knew; the fact that . . . , the question whether . . . ,* in all environments; DSN6: *She is easy to please.* DSN13: *It seems that . . . .*

DSN7 and DSN12 treat two forms that are not strings in SN but are related to them. DSN7: *She is eager to please;* DSN12: *This posed the question: Who else knew?*

DSN8 is a computationally important restriction expressing the unlikeliness of finding an SN string as the subject within an SN string, as in ***Whether for him to stay or not is what we should discuss is debatable.***

DSN9–12 and WSN3–9 treat specific features of individual sentence nominalization strings, while WSN10–11 are concerned with dividing the VINGSTG terrain between NSVINGO and VINGOFN, discussed in some detail in Sec. 4.5.

As an example of the DSN restrictions DSN2 will be described in some detail, and as an example of the WSN restrictions, how WSN1 achieves the objectives stated in Sec. 2.3 will be traced for this type of restriction.

DSN2: Conditions for accepting SN following a predicate adjective.   DSN2 is one of the restrictions concerned with the placing of sentential complements (SN strings in the LSP grammar) of the type illustrated by *that he came, for him to leave, whether they left or not.* In order for an occurrence of an SN string following a predicate adjective to be well formed (as is *It is true that he came*), various conditions must be satisfied, as stated in the text of DSN2 in Appendix 1. The first condition is stated in the restriction subpart $HOST. When executed, $HOST tests whether the adjectival element associated with the SN string is of the appropriate subclass (*It is round that he came*). This adjectival element stands in the relation of *host* to the SN string in question. The execution of the HOST routine starting at the SN node locates the adjectival element that is to be tested. This can be illustrated by referring to the ASSERTION parse tree for the sentence *It is true that he came,* shown in Fig. 5.19.

Fig. 5.19   Parse tree tested by DSN2; SN string follows predicate adjective.

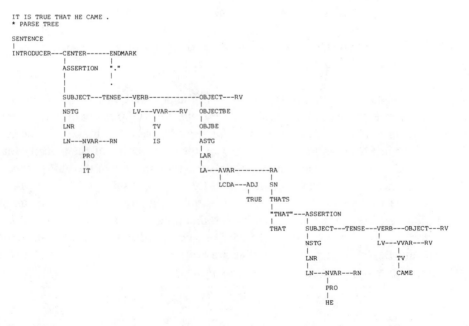

In the upper right portion of Fig. 5.19, several levels below the OBJECT node of ASSER-
TION is the LXR-type node LAR, standing for an adjective (or other adjectival element, such
as VING or a compound adjective) with its left and right adjuncts. The adjectival element in
this case is the terminal symbol ADJ (*true*), and the value of the right adjunct (RA) node is
SN. Given the three-element standard form for all LXR type definitions, the routine HOST
goes from any node in either the rightmost or leftmost subtree of an LXR configuration to
the core of the center element. Thus, its execution starting from SN ends at ADJ, the correct
element to be tested.

The test $NOCOMMA rules out for example ⧸*A It is true, that he came,* in which a comma
intervenes between the predicate adjective and the complement. The execution of THE
PRECEDING WORD locates the sentence word last attached to the parse tree. DSN2 is
executed when the option SN of RA is about to be attached, so in *It is true, that he came* THE
PRECEDING WORD is ",".

The test $NOT-ADJINRN rules out SN occurrences following an adjective which is occur-
curring as a right adjunct of a noun. Thus, it would be well formed to have an adjective in
this position followed by adjuncts other than SN (*The implication, clear to all, was that he
was present*) but not by an SN string (⧸*A The implication, clear that he was present, was
understood by all*). In the BNF part of the English grammar, there is a definition ADJINRN
for the occurrence of an adjective with its optional adjuncts (LAR) as a right adjunct of a
noun. Hence, in order to verify that an SN in RA is not occurring in this position, the test
$NOT-ADJINRN employs the predicate IS NOT OCCURRING IN ADJINRN. This predicate
looks upward in the parse tree for ADJINRN (but not above the first STRING-type node); if
an ADJINRN is found the restriction fails.

The remaining tests of DSN2, $IT, $SUBJIT, and $HUMAN apply constraints to the sub-
ject, depending on which subclass of adjective or VING is present in the predicate adjective
position. The comments preceding DSN2 in Appendix 1 give some indication as to these
subclasses, and detailed definitions of the subclasses mentioned are to be found in Appendix
3. The most interesting feature in the test $SUBJIT is the use of the routine ULTIMATE-
SUBJECT. By means of this routine, the same restriction DSN2 that checks that the subject is
it in *It is true that he came,* also checks for *it* in *It seems to be true that he came,* in *It seems to
be considered to have appeared probable that he came,* and so on, to any arbitrary depth of
embedding.

WSN1: Correct verb or predicate for SN subject.   Early in Chapter 2 a simple version of
WSN1 was developed. Then the contrast between a simple illustrative restriction and a real
restriction of the grammar was illustrated by stating how the simple WSN restriction would
have to be expanded to cover a variety of sentence nominalization strings occurring in a
variety of syntactic environments, where both these factors influenced which particular
noun, verb, and adjective subclasses could occur with particular SN strings. These additions
were summarized in seven points; we are now in a position to see how each of these additions
is realized in WSN1.

1. Coverage of different sentence nominalization strings is accomplished by referring to the set SN of sentence nominalization strings rather than to each string by name. Thus, the premise of the implication that constitutes the main test in WSN1 begins: IF EITHER ELEMENT SUBJECT X10 HAS VALUE SN, OR . . . . (The OR-clause concerns item (7) in this list.) A particular instance of such a construction is seen in the ASSERTION parse tree for *That he left seems to have surprised them,* in Fig. 3.4.

2. Only particular subclasses of verbs, nouns, and adjectives occur with SN subjects. This is handled by the tests in the conclusion of the main implication begun previously. The implication concludes:

> . . . THEN ONE OF $PREDICATE, $SENTENTIAL-VERB,
> $EVENT-VERB IS TRUE.

$PREDICATE covers, *That she is here is true, А̸ That she is here is blue,* and the other examples given in (2) of the seven points listed in Chapter 2. The different kinds of predicates are detailed in $ADJPRED, $VINGPRED, $NPRED, $PNPRED, testing for subclasses of the ASENT and NSENT type (see the subclass definitions in Appendix 3). An escape clause $RARE is provided, because not all cases of predicate nouns are covered, for example action classifiers (*activity* in *To read was considered sinful activity*), and nominalized adjectives (*To get to the top will be perfect joy*).[34] A puzzling detail in the $PREDICATE test is the requirement that THE CORE OF THE DEEPEST-COPRED IS NOT OCCURRING IN SN. The core of the deepest-copred is a string TOVO in a sentence like *To live is to suffer.* We do not want to rule out such sentences by requiring an adjective or noun, and so on in the predicate position, so we defer this (less likely) construction to a later part of the restriction, the end of $VSENT in $SENTENTIAL-VERB. This clause is rarely reached in the execution of the restriction.[35]

$SENTENTIAL-VERB allows three types of VSENT verbs with SN subjects. It also allows for constructions in which the VSENT is nominalized and appears grammatically as the object of one of the verbs in a small subclass VMOD: *has an effect* in place of *affects, makes trouble for us* in place of *troubles us.* In addition, there are similar constructions where the noun is not derived from a VSENT verb but from an ASENT adjective (*presents difficulties*). The verb (e.g. *present*) in these cases is also classed in VMOD. Yet more special are particular expressions involving a verb that ordinarily does not have a sentential subject, but with a particular choice of object noun or PN or DP can do so, e.g. *came to our attention, came to light, drives one crazy, clamors for analysis.* These border on the idiomatic but are not entirely frozen word sequences. As an interim solution, the verbs in question are given the attribute VEXP, so that at least the sentences containing these expressions will not be rejected by WSN1. All these verb subclasses are tested for in $VSENT.

3. Matching particular SN strings with particular verbs or predicates is presently done by other restrictions, not WSN1. For verbs, the restrictions DVC1 and DVC2 trim the options of OBJECT according to what is specified as values of OBJLIST in the lexical entry for each

particular verb. For predicates the selection is made by DSN3 (but presently only when the SN string occurs following the predicate adjective or noun).

4. Extension of the test to other strings besides ASSERTION. This is accomplished by naming the other strings to which the constraints apply in the housing of the restriction: IN ASSERTION, YESNOQ, SVINGO, and so on, causing the restriction to be executed whenever a parse tree for one of these strings is constructed. The use of the same restriction in different constructions is possible because in defining strings the widest possible use is made of the same elements as appear in ASSERTION, such as SUBJECT, OBJECT. This also makes for a simple conversion of these strings to an underlying ASSERTION form by the transformational component of the program.

5. Passive versus active is checked by the test $PASSIVE in $SENTENTIAL-VERB, which tests that verbs like *know, assume* in subclass VSENT3 are occurring in the passive when they have a sentential subject (*Ⱥ That he was here knows . . .*). The sentence-connecting verbs VSENT2 are exempted, since they do so occur (*That he was here evidences that . . ., That he was here is evidenced by . . .*).

6. Extension to cases of embedded verbs and predicates. Thus, in addition to . . . *is true,* ($PREDICATE in item (2)) also *seems to have been assumed to be true,* and in addition to . . .*surprised them* ($SENTENTIAL-VERB), also *could be said to have surprised them,* and the like. This is accomplished by using the DEEPEST-COPRED routine in $PREDICATE, which also delivers the deepest-coverb (in register X7) for use in $SENTENTIAL-VERB. The operation of these extended scope routines is discussed in connection with Fig. 3.4.

7. A sentential subject can occur implicitly. Consider the text sentence *Furthermore, the maximal diastolic potential was also reduced, which could result in a more rapid firing,* for which the ASSERTION parse tree is shown in Fig. 5.20. here, the value of SUBJECT in the ASSERTION under SAWHICHSTG is not SN, but NULLWH. However, we recognize that the NULLWH refers back to the preceding ASSERTION, which the SAWHICHSTG adjoins. The constraints on the verb in the SAWHICHSTG are therefore the same as those that apply to an ASSERTION having a sentential string physically present as the subject. To accommodate this situation, the premise of WSN1 asks that the value of SUBJECT be either SN or else a NULLWH occurring in SAWHICHSTG. The rest of WSN1 need not take account of which of these two conditions was the case.

One test relevant to SAWHICHSTG alone is made in $WHICH-STRING. This test results form the fact that certain comparatives have the same form and environments as the SAWHICHSTG and have been assimilated into this string definition by simply allowing *than* or *as* in place of *which*. (E.g. compare the sentence in Fig. 5.20 with *Furthermore, the maximum diastolic potential was less reduced than would appear in a more rapid firing.*) But the choice of verb subclasses in some cases imposes a requirement that the string begin with *which;* hence the test in $WHICH-STRING. One type of verb that seems to be favored by SAWHICHSTG and is therefore looked for is the EVENT verb (*happen, occur*): *He again exercised the Presidential veto, which Congressional leaders are beginning to feel **happens** far too often.*

Fig. 5.20   Parse tree tested by WSN1; SN string is subject.

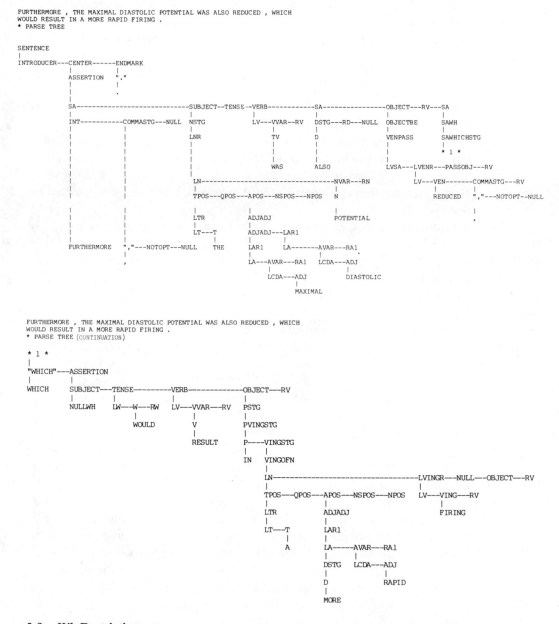

```
FURTHERMORE , THE MAXIMAL DIASTOLIC POTENTIAL WAS ALSO REDUCED , WHICH
WOULD RESULT IN A MORE RAPID FIRING .
* PARSE TREE


SENTENCE
   |
INTRODUCER---CENTER------ENDMARK
              |            |
            ASSERTION    "."
              |            |
              |            .
              |
            SA----------------------------SUBJECT--TENSE--VERB------------SA----------------OBJECT---RV--SA
              |                              |       |     |               |                   |          |
            INT----------COMMASTG---NULL    NSTG    LV---VVAR--RV   DSTG---RD---NULL  OBJECTBE         SAWH
              |            |                  |       |   |          |                   |             |
              |            |                 LNR     TV           D               VENPASS          SAWHICHSTG
              |            |                  |       |           |                   |                 |
              |            |                  |       |   WAS   ALSO                  |               * 1 *
              |            |                  |       |                         LVSA---LVENR---PASSOBJ---RV
              |            |                 LN------------------------------NVAR---RN        |
              |            |                  |                                         LV----VEN-------COMMASTG---RV
              |            |                 TPOS---QPOS---APOS---NSPOS---NPOS   N             |
              |            |                  |       |           |           |           REDUCED    ","---NOTOPT--NULL
              |            |                 LTR             ADJADJ       POTENTIAL                         |
              |            |                  |               |                                            ,
              |            |                 LT---T         ADJADJ---LAR1
           FURTHERMORE   ","---NOTOPT---NULL  THE            LAR1        LA-------AVAR---RA1
                          |                                  |           |                .
                          ,                                 LA---AVAR---RA1  LCDA---ADJ
                                                             |               |
                                                          LCDA---ADJ     DIASTOLIC
                                                             |
                                                          MAXIMAL
```

```
FURTHERMORE , THE MAXIMAL DIASTOLIC POTENTIAL WAS ALSO REDUCED , WHICH
WOULD RESULT IN A MORE RAPID FIRING .
* PARSE TREE (CONTINUATION)


* 1 *
  |
"WHICH"---ASSERTION
  |          |
WHICH     SUBJECT---TENSE---------VERB------------OBJECT---RV
            |         |             |               |
          NULLWH    LW---W---RW   LV---VVAR---RV   PSTG
                      |             |               |
                    WOULD           V             PVINGSTG
                      |             |               |
                    RESULT          P----VINGSTG
                                    |    |
                                   IN   VINGOFN
                                         |
                                        LN-------------------------------------LVINGR---NULL--OBJECT---RV
                                         |                                         |
                                        TPOS---QPOS---APOS---NSPOS---NPOS   LV--VING---RV
                                         |                  |                   |
                                        LTR              ADJADJ              FIRING
                                         |                  |
                                        LT---T            LAR1
                                         |                  |
                                         A                LA-----AVAR---RA1
                                                           |        |
                                                          DSTG    LCDA---ADJ
                                                           |        |
                                                           D      RAPID
                                                           |
                                                          MORE
```

5.8   *Wh* Restrictions

The striking feature of *wh*-strings, and one that requires careful control by means of restrictions, is the presence of a null element NULLWH in the parse subtree dominated by the node corresponding to the *wh*-string definition. The NULLWH can be interpreted as a place-holder for a sentence word or words that would satisfy the element whose value is NULLWH, were the *wh*-string to be transformed into an ASSERTION. Thus, we analyze *the house that Jack built* as being related to *Jack built a house.* In the parse tree for *the house that Jack built* (Fig. 5.21a), NULLWH is the value of NSTGO under OBJECT in the ASSERTION portion of the *wh*–string THATS-N[36]; it holds the place for a noun-string object of the verb governing ing the OBJECT node (here, the verb *built*). We say that the noun object in such a case has been "omitted" (see Sec. 4.3 and 4.15). The transformational component of the grammar later fills in the omitted words; that is, it reconstructs the ASSERTION underlying the *wh*-string, as illustrated in Fig. 5.21b.

Fig. 5.21a   Parse tree showing NULLWH marking omission in *wh*-string.

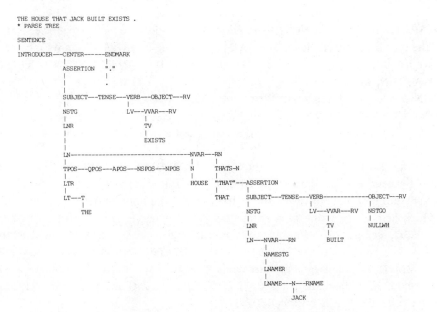

Fig. 5.21b   ASSERTION parse tree reconstructed from tree containing NULLWH.

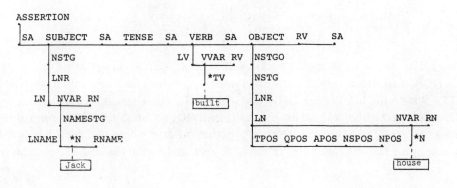

The task of the WH restrictions is to accept only well-formed occurrences of NULLWH, and, in the cases where the sentence contains the words that should be substituted for NULLWH, to store a pointer that will aid in locating them. Linguistic aspects of *wh*-strings were dealt with in Chapter 4. Here we will treat the mechanisms by which omission is controlled and the elements that are related via *wh* are identified in the parse tree.

5.8.1   *Accepting NULLWH*

Let us start by constructing a simple WH-restriction that applies to the parse tree in Fig. 5.21a. In the parse subtree under OBJECT in Fig. 5.21a, NULLWH is the value of NSTGO. The restriction should test whether NULLWH is an acceptable value of NSTGO.

WWH-SIMPLE = IN NSTGO AFTER NULLWH:
ALL OF $PATH-TO-WH-STRING, $NO-PREVIOUS-OMISSION, $ACCEPT ARE TRUE.

The $PATH-TO-WH-STRING test should look upward in the parse tree to see if there is a node of the type that should have a NULLWH as the value of an NSTGO in its subtree. These strings are listed in the grammer under the heading TYPE N-OMITTING-WH-STRING. The string THATS – N, which subsumes *that Jack built* in Fig. 5.21a, is on the list N-OMITTING-WH-STRING. The PATH test might then read:

$PATH-TO-WH-STRING = IMMEDIATE-STRING IS OF TYPE N-OMITTING-WH-STRING.

It will be recalled from Chapter 3 that the routine IMMEDIATE-STRING ascends in the parse tree until it meets a node of the type STRING. In Fig. 5.21a we should like it to reach THATS – N from NSTGO. However, the first STRING type node above NULLWH is ASSERTION, which here is occurring as a segment of the string THATS – N (for string segment, TYPE STGSEG, see Sec. 2.5). We want to "look through" the segment ASSERTION to reach THATS – N. The routine to use in place of IMMEDIATE-STRING in cases of this sort is NONSEG-IMMEDSTG (**nonseg**ment **immed**iate **str**ing). This routine ascends to a STRING type node and then to the node just above it if the first STRING node is on the TYPE STGSEG list and the node above it is on the TYPE STRING list.[37]

The revised PATH test might then be as follows:

$NONSEG-PATH = NONSEG-IMMEDSTG X5 IS OF TYPE
N-OMITTING-WH-STRING.

In Fig. 5.21a, the new $NONSEG-PATH will start at NSTGO under OBJECT, ascend to ASSERTION, and from ASSERTION to THATS – N, which is then stored in X5. Since THATS – N is on the list TYPE N-OMITTING-WH-STRING the test succeeds.

The second test in WH-SIMPLE is $NO-PREVIOUS-OMISSION. This rules out such sequences as *Jack the house that built,* a hypothetical case where *that built* has two omissions, one in the SUBJECT element, referring to *Jack* and one in the OBJECT element referring to *house*. To rule out such false analyses, there must be some means of recording when an omission (the accepting of a NULLWH node) is made. Let us assume that when a NULLWH is accepted as the value of NSTGO, a node attribute DIDOMIT is created at the node corresponding to the N-omitting *wh*-string, the node that "gave permission" for the omission. In Fig. 5.21a, this node is THATS – N, which was stored in register X5. The test $NO-PREVIOUS-OMISSION then need only test for the attribute DIDOMIT at X5. This would be written in Restriction Language as follows:

$NO-PREVIOUS-OMISSION = IT IS NOT THE CASE THAT X5 HAS
THE NODE ATTRIBUTE DIDOMIT.

In this RL statement, the portion HAS THE NODE ATTRIBUTE DIDOMIT invokes an operator that checks the current node for the node attribute given as its argument, here DIDOMIT.

It only remains to provide for assigning the DIDOMIT attribute to the *wh*-string node when NULLWH is accepted, and to leave the address of NULLWH so that the *Wh* transformation can fill in the appropriate words. These actions are accomplished by $ACCEPT, the last test of WWH-SIMPLE:

$ACCEPT = BOTH PRESENT-ELEMENT – HAS VALUE NULLWH X0
AND IN X5 ASSIGN PRESENT STRING
THE NODE ATTRIBUTE DIDOMIT.

As a result of the first clause of $ACCEPT, the address of NULLWH is placed in a special register X0, which is used by the node-attribute assigning operator in creating a pointer as the value for the node attribute DIDOMIT. This is expected by the WH transformation. The second clause causes the *wh*-string node (stored in X5) to be assigned the node attribute DIDOMIT with a value that is the contents of X0, here the address of NULLWH. The node attribute assigning operation is a complex one (see Chapter 3) because it has to provide for automatic erasure of the attribute at the node carrying the assigned attribute (here the N-omitting *wh*-string) when the node that initiated the assigning of the attribute (here NULLWH) is detached in the course of the parser's backing up. However, all this is done behind the scenes; the restriction writer need only call for the assigning of the node attribute, as is done in $ACCEPT.

We have now seen in a simple form the three main steps in determining when to accept a NULLWH: (1) check that the NULLWH is in the scope of an omitting string; (2) check that no previous omission took place; (3) place a tag on the omitting string, showing that an omission has now been accepted. These three tests are included in all the restrictions that control the acceptance of NULLWH in different element positions in the grammar, namely WWH2 (NULLWH as value of SUBJECT), WWH3 (NULLWH as value of NSTGO in object or adjunct), WWH4 (NULLWH as value of OBJBE), WWH5 (NULLWH as value of PN). In these restrictions the tests corresponding to those in WWH-SIMPLE are $PATH (in place of $PATH-

TO-WH-STRING), $NOTAG (in place of $NO-PREVIOUS-OMISSION), and $ACCEPT (identical to ACCEPT in WWH-SIMPLE). The first two of these are more elaborate than the tests in WWH-SIMPLE because they provide for embedding in *wh*-strings, for conjunctions in *wh*-strings, and for special features of individual strings (treated in $PRETEST and $POSTEST). Before going on to these more complex situations, one more elementary requirement must be stated.

Consider the ill-formed sequence *the house that Jack built the house.* Here no NULLWH has been accepted within the scope of THATS – N. It is not sufficient to allow for accepting a NULLWH. We must also check that when a node corresponding to an omitting string is completed, its subtree does indeed contain a NULLWH. This is quite simple, since all that is required is that the node have been assigned the attribute DIDOMIT. Thus we have for the N-omitting case:

WWH1 = IN N-OMITTING-WH-STRING: PRESENT-STRING
              HAS NODE ATTRIBUTE DIDOMIT.

This restriction is housed in all the strings named on the TYPE N-OMITTING-WH-STRING list. The combined effect of WWH1 and the test $NOTAG assures that there is exactly one and only one NULLWH in every omitting string (exclusive of NULLWH in conjunction strings within an omitting string).

5.8.2   *Embedding*

What if instead of *the house that Jack built* the sentence to be analyzed contained *the house that Jack was said to have built* (Fig. 5.22), or *the house that it seems Jack was said to have arranged to have someone else build,* or a similar even longer sentence? All of these are handled by adding to the PATH test of WWH-SIMPLE, an option called $NESTED, which provides a path to the *wh*-string from a NULLWH in an embedded string.

$NONSEG-NEST-PATH = EITHER $NONSEG OR $NESTED.
$NONSEG = NONSEG-IMMEDSTG X5 IS OF THE TYPE N-OMITTING-WH-STRING.
$NESTED = BOTH X5 IS OF THE TYPE OMITTING-OBJECT-STG
              AND THE NONSEG-IMMEDSTG X5 OF THE ULTIMATE-OBJECT
              IS OF THE TYPE N-OMITTING-WH-STRING.

The path in $NESTED is executed only if $NONSEG fails. Its operation can be illustrated by tracing the execution of $NONSEG-NEST-PATH in the parse tree in Fig. 5.22.

Starting at the NSTGO above NULLWH in Fig. 5.22, the test $NONSEG locates the NONSEG-IMMEDSTG of NSTGO (VENO), stores it in X5, and tests whether it is of the type that requires an omission. VENO is not of that type, so $NONSEG fails and $NESTED is executed. $NESTED starts by testing whether the node in X5 is of the type OMITTING-OBJECT-STG. Not every object string can support omissions, so a list of those that can do so is supplied in the grammar.[38] VENO is on this list.

Fig. 5.22   Parse tree showing embedding in a *wh*-string.

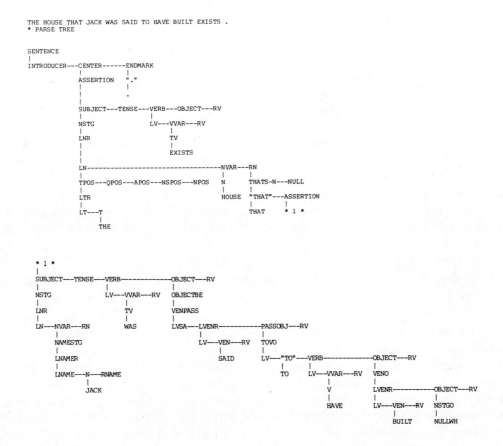

```
THE HOUSE THAT JACK WAS SAID TO HAVE BUILT EXISTS .
* PARSE TREE


SENTENCE
|
INTRODUCER---CENTER------ENDMARK
            |            |
            ASSERTION    "."
            |            .
            |            .
            |
            SUBJECT---TENSE---VERB---OBJECT---RV
            |                 |
            NSTG              LV---VVAR---RV
            |                      |
            LNR                    TV
            |                      |
            |                      EXISTS
            |
            LN----------------------------------NVAR---RN
            |                                   |      |
            TPOS---QPOS---APOS---NSPOS---NPOS   N      THATS-N---NULL
            |                                   |      |
            LTR                                 HOUSE  "THAT"---ASSERTION
            |                                   |      |
            LT---T                              THAT   * 1 *
                 |
                 THE



* 1 *
|
SUBJECT---TENSE---VERB-------------OBJECT---RV
|                 |                |
NSTG              LV---VVAR---RV   OBJECTBE
|                      |           |
LNR                    TV          VENPASS
|                      |           |
LN---NVAR---RN         WAS         LVSA---LVENR----------PASSOBJ---RV
     |                                   |              |
     NAMESTG                             LV---VEN---RV  TOVO
     |                                        |        |
     LNAMER                                   SAID     LV---"TO"---VERB-------------OBJECT---RV
     |                                                      |      |              |
     LNAME---N---RNAME                                      TO     LV---VVAR---RV  VENO
             |                                                          |         |
             JACK                                                       V         LVENR----------OBJECT---RV
                                                                        |         |              |
                                                                        HAVE      LV---VEN---RV   NSTGO
                                                                                       |         |
                                                                                       BUILT     NULLWH
```

The next step in $NESTED is to climb out of the nest of object strings that separate NULLWH from the *wh*-string node carrying the omission requirement. In Fig. 5.22, the climb is from VENO, through TOVO and VENPASS, to the OBJECT node in the ASSERTION segment of THATS – N. From this OBJECT node the path to the omitting string THATS – N is the same as though there had been no embedding, as if we were back in the simple case *The house that Jack built,* for which the test $NONSEG sufficed. Accordingly, the difference between the path to the omitting string in $NESTED and that in $NONSEG is the invoking in $NESTED of the ULTIMATE-OBJECT routine before ascending to the omitting string; the ULTIMATE-OBJECT routine performs an ascent through any number of embedded object strings (and certain adjunct strings) that can separate NULLWH from the string node requiring the omission.

The operation of the ULTIMATE-OBJECT routine is as follows. The routine has two parts. The first (up to the first semicolon) covers nested object strings and can be illustrated with reference to Fig. 5.22. The second portion, for adjunct strings, will be taken up afterward.

```
ROUTINE ULTIMATE-OBJECT =
    EITHER ITERATE $ASCEND OR TEST FOR OBJECT OR PASSOBJ;
    EITHER $ADJUNCT OR TRUE.
$ASCEND = ASCEND TO OBJECT OR PASSOBJ
    PASSING THROUGH TRANSMITTING-OBJ-STG
    NOT PASSING THROUGH ADJSET.
```

The ASCEND operator moves upward in the parse tree to a node named as its argument (here OBJECT or PASSOBJ), but it stops when it meets a STRING type node unless the node is named or is on a list that is named as the argument of PASSING THROUGH (here the list TRANSMITTING-OBJ-STG). It also stops if it meets a node that is named or is on a list that is named as argument of NOT PASSING THROUGH (here, the list ADJSET). The command ITERATE $ASCEND, causes this procedure to be repeated at each OBJECT or PASSOBJ node reached. Thus, in Fig. 5.22, the ULTIMATE-OBJECT routine ascends first from NSTGO to the OBJECT in VENO, then to the OBJECT node just above VENO, then through the object string TOVO to PASSOBJ, and then, on the last successful iteration of $ASCEND, through VENPASS to the OBJECT node in the ASSERTION segment of THATS – N. (VENO, TOVO, and VENPASS are all named on the list TRANSMITTING-OBJ-STG.[39]

The second part of the ULTIMATE-OBJECT routine covers cases where the embedded string is under an adjunct set node, that is, a node on the ADJSET list. This case is illustrated by *the house that it was reported that Jack was able to build,* shown in Fig. 5.23. Here *to build* is a TOVO string in the adjunct set RA, and *that Jack was able to build* is an SN string under the adjunct set node RV after *reported*. The ADJSET node in both cases blocks the upward ascent of $ASCEND. As a result the second part of the ULTIMATE-OBJECT routine (the part after the semicolon) is executed in both cases. This part of the routine invokes $AD-JUNCT to obtain an upward ascent through an adjunct string, but if $ADJUNCT fails, there is an automatic success (TRUE) without upward movement so that the ULTIMATE-OBJECT can exit with a value.

```
$ADJUNCT = ONE OF $ASP, $SNRA, $SNRN, $SN-IN-RV IS TRUE;
    DO $UPAGAIN.
```

Four cases of transmitting adjunct strings are covered by $ADJUNCT. $ASP (for **aspec**-tual adjective, e.g. *able*) and $SN-IN-RV are the ones that come into play in the parse tree of Fig. 5.23. The other two cases are not different in principle.[40] In executing the ULTIMATE-OBJECT routine on the parse tree in Fig. 5.23, $ADJUNCT is first invoked when the restriction interpreter is looking at the OBJECT node in TOVO (*to build*), having been blocked in its further ascent by the ADJSET node RA. The test $ASP in $ADJUNCT applies:

```
$ASP = NONSEGWH X6 IS TOVO WHERE TOVO IS OCCURRING AS RA X40.
```

The routine NONSEGWH[41] goes from the OBJECT node in TOVO to the node TOVO, and from there up to RA (because of OCCURRING AS RA). It stores TOVO in X6 and RA in X40. Control reverts to $ADJUNCT, whose next instruction is DO $UPAGAIN.

$$\$UPAGAIN = \text{GO TO X40; DO ULTIMATE-OBJECT.}$$

Fig. 5.23 Parse tree showing deeper embedding in a *wh*-string.

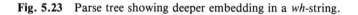

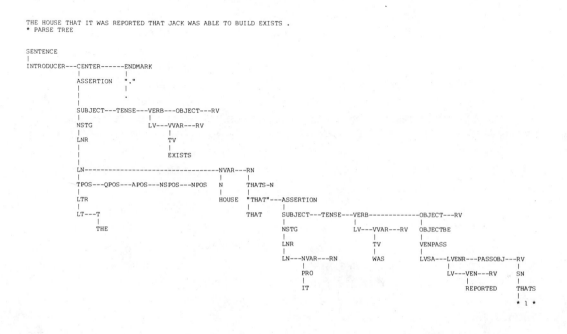

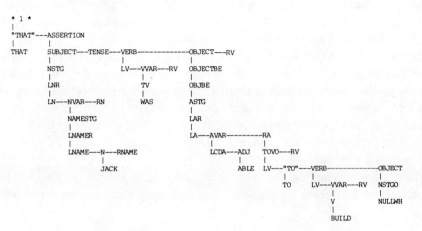

The second execution of ULTIMATE-OBJECT thus begins at RA (X40). ITERATE $ASCEND goes to the OBJECT node dominating RA, and tries to ascend further through ASSERTION (which is on the TRANSMITTING-OBJ-STG list) but is blocked by the ADJSET node RV. This brings it to the execution of $ADJUNCT again, this time starting at the OB-JECT node in ASSERTION UNDER SN. $ASP fails (but stores ASSERTION in X6). This time the test $SN-IN-RV applies:

$SN-IN-RV = BOTH X6 IS OCCURRING AS SN →
                AND SN IS OCCURRING AS RV
                WHERE PREVIOUS-ELEMENT – IS OBJECT OR PASSOBJ X40.

The result of executing $SN-IN-RV is to verify that a further ascent is correct and to store in X40 the PASSOBJ node preceding RV in VENPASS. From this PASSOBJ node, $UPAGAIN initiates a new cycle of ULTIMATE-OBJECT. This time ITERATE $ASCEND is not blocked by an ADJSET node and reaches the OBJECT node in the ASSERTION just under THATS – N. This is as far as it can go. No $ADJUNCT test applies so the alternative TRUE to $ADJUNCT automatically satisfies the final clause of the routine. The final node that was reached, the OBJECT node in the ASSERTION segment of THATS – N, is the ULTIMATE-OBJECT in this case.

5.8.3   Conjunctions in wh-Strings

Conjunction strings within omitting wh-strings also require omission. Thus, *the house that Jack built and Mary furnished,* where *furnished* (like *built*) lacks its noun object, is a well-formed noun phrase, whereas *the house that Jack built and Mary furnished the house,* where the conjunction string contains a complete ASSERTION with no omission, is not well-formed.

Since there may be any number of conjuncts in a sentence, some method of keeping track of the number of omissions versus the number of conjuncts must be supplied. Since each conjunct within an omitting string requires exactly one omission,[42] the simplest method is to keep the count locally, that is, to pass the omission requirement to each conjunct and check that each conjunct has satisfied the requirement. To see how this would work, suppose that each conjunct node Q-CONJ within the scope of an omitting wh-string is assigned the node attribute MUSTOMIT as soon as the conjunct node is created. Now suppose that in building the Q-CONJ subtree a node is created one of whose options is NULLWH. The PATH test that looks upward for a node requiring omission should be satisfied under these conditions when it reaches a Q-CONJ node carrying the MUSTOMIT attribute (provided there is not already a DIDOMIT attribute assigned, and all other tests are satisfied). In other words, the Q-CONJ node is a surrogate wh-node.

To have a uniform method for both the initial wh-node and the Q-CONJ surrogates, we use the MUSTOMIT attribute throughout. The first thing that happens when a node corresponding to an omitting string is created is the assignment of the MUSTOMIT attribute by a simple restriction[43]:

> DWH1 = IN N-OMITTING-WH-STRING: ASSIGN PRESENT STRING
> THE NODE ATTRIBUTE MUSTOMIT.

Correspondingly, the final part of the path to the omitting string is a test for the MUSTOMIT attribute rather than for an N-OMITTING-WH-STRING. For example, the path in the *wh* restrictions of the grammar reads:

> $PATH = $HERE OR $NESTED.
> $HERE = X5 HAS THE NODE ATTRIBUTE MUSTOMIT.

$NESTED is similarly revised. The same MUSTOMIT-DIDOMIT device can be used for conjuncts within omitting strings. In principle, if the conjunct is occurring under a string node that has been assigned DIDOMIT, then the conjunct should be assigned MUSTOMIT. This principle works, but it has to be elaborated slightly because of the effects of zeroing in conjunctional strings.

Zeroing (or ellipsis) in conjunctional strings results in segments that are structurally incomplete when compared with the string they conjoin. For example, compare *the house that Jack built and that he later sold* with *the house that Jack built and later sold;* in the latter sentence the conjunct lacks the word *that* and lacks a subject (which is understood to be *Jack*). The conjunct is structurally incomplete when compared to the THATS – N string it conjoins, and the elements that are "missing" in the conjunct are said to be present in zero form, because they can easily be filled in by reference to the corresponding nonzero elements in the string that the conjunct conjoins. There are different ways of handling this phenomenon. Briefly, in the LSP grammar, we posit as few null elements as possible during parsing, and fill in as many of the missing words as desirable (for a given application) during transformational analysis. This means that in parsing *the house that Jack built and later sold* (Fig. 5.24), there will be no null elements created in the conjunctional string to fill out the positions of THAT and of SUBJECT; this is done later by the transformation that expands conjunctional strings.

As a result of the decision to minimize null elements, the assigning of MUSTOMIT to conjunctional strings must take account of certain truncated conjunctional strings that, because of the truncation, do not require omission, even though the string they conjoin is an omitting string. The rule is that only postobject conjunctional strings receive the MUSTOMIT attribute (again, only if the string or conjunct they conjoin has the attribute DIDOMIT). If the conjunct can be placed after subject, tense or verb element, then the NULLWH is "shared" by having a common OBJECT node (as in Fig. 5.24). If the objects are dissimilar, however, or if embeddings intervene, then each conjunct requires a NULLWH, as in *the house that Jack built and intends to rent,* shown in Fig. 5.25. The restriction that assigns MUSTOMIT to Q-CONJ is DWH1B.[44]

Fig. 5.24 Parse tree showing conjunction under *wh*.

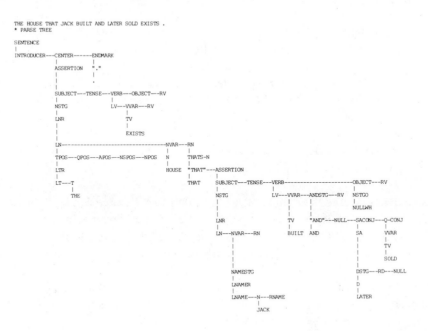

Fig. 5.25 Parse tree showing embedding and conjunction under *wh*.

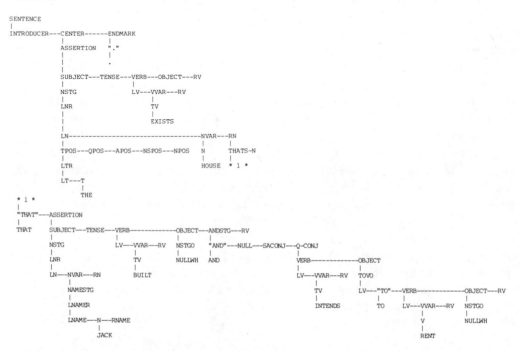

NOTES

1. Sec. 4.7. *Do* is classed both as tense word W and true verb. In both classes, the form *does* is SINGULAR and *do* (not infinitive) is PLURAL. Note that a special handling of subject *I* in $PLURAGREE permits us to class *do* and all third person present plural verbs (*walk, sing*) as definitely PLURAL, so as to maximize the utility of the subject–verb agreement restriction.

2. A minus sign at the end of the name indicates that the routine does not cause the restriction that invoked the routine to be reexecuted on conjuncts (no "stacking," see Sec. 6.3). In the grammar listed in Appendix 1, $SUBJ uses the routine $EXTENDED-CORE – in place of CORE –. The new routine jumps to the host if the value of SUBJECT is *NULLWH. For NULLWH see Sec. 5.8.

3. A plural quantifier can be the subject of a singular verb when appearing as the name of a number: (*The number*) *one hundred was tested;* or when it occurs as the subject of *is* in the sense of *constitutes: Three is a crowd.* The restriction does not allow for these exceptions at present.

4. There are exceptions not covered by the restriction, illustrated by such examples as: *An anomaly and a scandal was removed from our legislation, Life and literature is so poor in these islands, The happiness and perfection of both depends on good will.*

5. In Fig. 5.4, *does* is not occurring as a tense word but structurally as a verb. Also *what he does* is shown as an instance of WHATS – N in NWHSTG, with the interpretation that the string is replacing nameable actions, that which he does. Technically, there is another analysis of this word sequence as an instance of WHS – N in SNWH, which has the same form as WHATS – N when the *wh*-word is *what.*

6. The change requires restrictions governing the multiple classification of *a* as both T and Q (as Q, *a = one*) and special handling for such expressions as *an additional* Q, and *an extra* Q (Q a number greater than 1).

7. See note 2.

8. In Fig. 5.8 OBJBE is the passive object of *considered* (the value of PASSOBJ) because *considered* has the active object SOBJBE (subject + **OBJBE**); OBJBE (*a good teacher*) is what is left in the object position following *considered* when a passive (*He was considered a good teacher*) is made from the active form (*They considered him a good teacher*) in which the object is SOBJBE. Details of the PASSOBJ-OBJECT relation are in Sec. V of Appendix 3.

9. While $ZEROBE is not used here, within WSN1 it locates OBJBE in such occurrences as *One might find it surprising that* . . . (*it surprising that* . . . = SOBJBE). The inefficiency of using DEEPEST-COPRED for these infrequent occurrences is negligible and doing so saves writing a specially housed restriction for the embedded *it* construction.

10. SOBJBESA should also be included here: *His father a well known pianist and composer, he early had access to* . . . , *Å His father well known pianists and composers, he* . . . . This addition requires a change in the definition of SOBJBESA, replacing the element NSTG by SUBJECT, with some restrictions.

11. When a collective verb occurs with conjoined nouns, the correct number of such conjoined nouns appears to be three or more: *John, Mary and Bill gather in the Commons Room at noon, ?John and Bill gather in the Commons Room at noon.* The definition of a collective noun (see NCOLLECTIVE in Appendix 3) is such that chemical nouns, like *salt, hydrogen,* are NCOLLECTIVE: *Hydrogen collects at the cathode.*

12. Possibly ambiguous with a well-formed occurrence of *collect* as a transitive verb with deleted object (*With respect to pledged donations, they prefer for a woman to collect* (them).)

13. This restriction could be eliminated by a slight adjustment in WAGREE1. The present use of EXTENDED-CORE – in WAGREE1 (see note 2) has the effect that when a restriction tries to descend through the node whose value is NULLWH, the descent is redirected to the host noun; thus, *the man who was here* is accepted by WAGREE1, and *the man who were here* is rejected. In the case of the SAWHICHSTG, the restriction (WAGREE1) should be redirected to the host string, where the test $SINGSTRING (or NOT $SINGSTRING) would apply. However, the generality of WAGREE1 is hardly needed for this special situation, and a special restriction (WAGREE6) does the job more efficiently.

14. But we might have: *between whose front door and back.* We have not taken account as yet of A N and A constructions where a second occurrence of N may be inferred.

15. The housing portion of DCOM1 contains the symbol ( )RN. Parentheses are prefixed to a reference to an adjunct definition in the housing of a restriction if that definition is repeatable (Sec. 2.3), indicated by the presence of *R in the BNF definition.

16. TOVO appears in RN, SA, RA, and OBJECT; TOVO – N and FORTOVO – N in the adjunct sets RN and RA.

17. The statement in $RN that the "COELEMENT TENSE IS EMPTY" entails a rather elaborate explanation. The intent of the $RN test is to rule out a comma between the SUBJECT and VERB (*Å Such reasons, exist*) unless the SUBJECT node contains a right adjunct of N, in which case a comma would be justified. To find a comma due to an RN string abutting on the VERB requires that no tense word intervene between the SUBJECT and VERB, that is, that the node TENSE is empty, and that the SA nodes preceding and following the empty TENSE also be empty. If, in the case we are considering, where a comma precedes the VERB, the post-TENSE (pre-VERB) SA node is not empty (as tested by $PREVSA), then the test $RN will never be reached, so that at the execution of $RN we are assured that this SA node is empty. A test that the pre-TENSE SA node is also empty should be made. This is being incorporated into a rewrite of DCOM2.

18. A preceding comma is also required (by WPOS18) in SA occurrences of PN, and (by WPOS20) in SA occurrences of TOVO, when the string also qualifies as the object of the preceding verb. For example, contrast *He learned to please his parents* (TOVO as object) with *He learned, to please his parents* (TOVO as SA); contrast *He gave a book to our son* (PN as part of NPN object) with *He gave a book, to our surprise* (PN as SA). The comma is not a foolproof indicator of syntactic status, but it helps. Also tucked away in another restriction (DPOS5), the SAWHICHSTG in SAWH in SA requires a preceding comma (*He left, which surprised us*).

19. *May* as a noun is the month of May. Since capital letters are not distinguished in the input, the words *may* (the modal) and *May* (the month) are homographs.

20. The COMPARATIVE and CONJUNCTION restrictions that are found in the full grammar between the COMMA and the MINWORD sections are not being presented in this book. Brief descriptions are given in Appendix 4. Some features are discussed in Chapter 6.

21. To be fully logical, the MINWORD restrictions should be executed after the adjunct string subtree is recreated; that is, they should be wellformedness restrictions instead of disqualify restrictions. Then a check could be made that the created subtree subsumes the same number of words as a previously constructed adjunct subtree of the same type, starting at the same word. It is possible, but highly unlikely, that an adjunct string of different length could be constructed and the words not subsumed by both versions somehow fitted into a different analysis of the sentence. We have ignored this rare possibility in order to gain efficiency.

22. OBJECT and PASSOBJ are included because object occurrences of PN are favored over adjunct occurrences when the conditions for an object occurrence are met. The conditions for accepting a PN as object of a given verb include a check that the preposition occurring in PN is one of those listed in the word dictionary entry as likely in a PN object of that verb. WPOS15 assures that such PNs will be taken as object occurrences in preference to adjunct occurrences in some positions. DMINI prevents second readings as adjuncts in these and other positions.

23. An optimization restriction DOPT19 prevents the building of subtrees corresponding to options of RN, SA, RV when the current word is an endmark. These efforts would fail in any case, but optimization avoids an unnecessary amount of node attaching and detaching.

24. It should be noted that a section of restrictions, the POSITION RESTRICTIONS, which fall alphabetically between the NOUN and QUANTIFIER sections, has been omitted from the listing in Appendix 1 and will not be described here. Brief descriptions of the restrictions are given in Appendix 4.

25. Note that by the stringent demands on ADJ, VING, and VEN words, the examples here with words like *aged, wounded, meek* would be considered rare.

26. Restrictions of this type are called position restrictions. They are found in the section of that name, except for those concerning the noun, conjunctions, or other elements that have their own section.

27. The conditions for accepting NULLN as the value of NVAR (that is, as the core of LNR) are given in DN1.

28. *Another* is treated uniquely because it combines an article with an adjective. We class it as an adjective because it occurs conjoined with adjectives (*Another and better solution is . . .*). Also it occurs as ADJ:APREQ, as in *Another three persons arrived*. It is treated as a literal in WN9 and DN1 to avoid defining a special subclass for its occurrence as a determiner.

29. In addition, some VING words are also classed as nouns (as is *filling* in *I have a gold filling*); see under major word classes in Appendix 3. Such a multiply classified word is rejected as the VING in NSVINGO or VINGOFN when it also fits the LNR analysis.

30. Occupational titles + names, like *Doctor Smith*, could be taken as N + APPOS, as one would analyze *the painter Picasso*, that is, the doctor who is Smith, the painter who is Picasso. But we have assimilated titles into the definition of NAMESTG so that we will have the same analysis for, *Dr.* as for *Doctor*, and for *Dr. and Mrs.* in *Dr. and Mrs. Smith*. This makes the N + APPOS reading redundant. See also discussion of Fig. 4.1.

31. At present, these attributes are assigned independently. That is, the particular noun subclasses excluded as subjects of a given verb are excluded for all occurrences of the verb regardless with what object the verb is occurring, and similarly the exclusion of particular noun subclasses as objects of a given verb does not take account of what the subject is. This is admittedly crude, since selection takes place within a complete assertion.

32. The present grammar (Appendix 1) uses EXTENDED-CORE in place of CORE here so as to apply selectional constraints within a *wh*-string by rerouting the CORE routine to the host if the core is NULLWH. For example, in *the meal on Tuesdays which they cook . . .* , the *wh*-string *which they cook* as an adjunct of *Tuesdays* will be rejected because the EXTENDED-CORE routine executed at OBJECT will be rerouted to the host *Tuesdays*.

33. In *He left a private and returned a corporal, returned* is not analyzed as occurring transitively.

34. Some of these nouns take *of* and a VING nominalization instead of straight apposition, which is the criterion for NSENT1 and NSENT2, e.g. *The joy of getting to the top,* rather than *the joy to get to the top,* a small difference in form that at the moment puts them beyond the reach of the SN restrictions.

35. The wellformedness of the ''to live is to suffer'' construction is tested by WSN3.

36. Several strings, including THATS – N and S – N, do not begin with a word containing *wh* but do function like other *wh*-strings and are included in the *wh*-string class.

37. The routine NONSEGWH, which is the one actually used in WH restrictions, has yet one other feature. It does not use an automatic iterative jump through conjunctional strings that is included in all other routines. The reason is that the full WH restrictions make the conjunction-check themselves.

38. Some strings are excluded from the N-OMITTING-OBJECT-STG list because they are definitely not well formed when containing a NULLWH, e.g. DP4: *The sending in of the troops was questioned, ≠ The troops which the sending in of was questioned . . .* (though a form where the *wh* word occupies the NULLWH position is acceptable: *The troops, the sending in of which was questioned . . .*). Also, some object *wh*-strings that already have omission are excluded: *I asked about what the letter contained, ≠ The letter which I asked about what contained.* In all, over thirty object strings are excluded, some only because they are unlikely with omission rather than ill formed with omission.

39. This list is almost the same as the OMITTING-OBJ-STG list. The differences are too detailed to go into here.

40. $SNRA covers such occurrences as *the house that it is probable Jack built* where *Jack built* (with omitted N-object) is an ASSERTION in SN in RA, and RA adjoins the predicate adjective *probable.* $SNRN covers similar cases where the predicate is a noun or PN, e.g. *the house that it is a fact Jack built* and *the house that it is to his advantage that Jack should build.* The check that the predicate adjective or predicate noun is one that can be followed by an SN occurrence is made by DSN2, DSN3, and DSN5.

41. See note 37.

42. This statement will be modified in subsequent explanation.

43. The restriction shown here is for the N-omitting case. The PN-omitting case is similar throughout, but uses the attribute pair MUSTOMPN and DIDOMPN. See in Appendix 1, DWH1A, WWH5.

44. One feature of DWH1B may be puzzling. A particular problem arises when NULLWH occurs in the SUBJECT element of a string that has a conjunct (*the man who built the house and rented it*). We force the conjunct to have a SUBJECT element (Test $1 in DWH1B) because otherwise it could be well formed without omission. By requiring a subject in this case, the omission requirement in postobject conjuncts is uniform.

Chapter 6   The Treatment of Conjunctions[1]

One particularly intricate problem in the computer parsing of natural language texts is the complexity introduced into the parsing system by coordinate and comparative conjunctions. This complexity is due to the richness of conjunctional constructions and to the material implicit in sentences containing conjunctions. The computational problem can be divided into three parts: (1) generating parse trees that cover the occurrences of conjunction-headed strings in sentences, (2) locating words in the sentences that are repeated implicitly in a ''zeroed,'' or elided, form in particular positions in conjunction strings, and (3) reconstructing the complete sentences underlying conjunctional occurrences when the application requires such an expansion.

As algorithmic solution to problem 1, whereby the parser generates conjunction strings based on preceding parse-tree structures, has been a constant feature of the LSP system since its first implementations (Sager 1967). Similar devices have also been described more recently in the framework of other parsing systems (for example, Woods 1973). This chapter describes the method of generating strings and the computational solution to problems 2 and 3 of the LSP system. In the solution to 2 and 3, a mechanism called ''stacking'' locates the positions of zeroed elements in conjunction strings and cross-references them to the corresponding elements in the head construction. Constraints can then be applied to elided conjuncts as though they were expanded. When a correct parse is obtained, the expansion into complete underlying structures is carried out, following the pointers that have been set up during the parsing.

The strategy of treating ellipsis in two steps—locating zeroed elements and later carrying out the physical expansion—is important for a solution to conjunctions for several reasons. First, it is costly and often fruitless to expand a conjunctional string until one is sure one has a good parse. Second, to get a good parse one has to execute restrictions on the generated parse tree including the conjunction subtrees, and this requires locating zeroed elements. Third, the decision as to which conjunctional constructions should be expanded is application-specific.

6.1   The Generation of Conjunction Strings

Constructions containing coordinate conjunctions CONJ have the overall form: *A* CONJ *B,* where *A* and *B* are structures of the same type in the grammar. In linguistic string grammar, *A* and *B* are particular elements or sequences of elements in linguistic strings, or adjunct strings from the same adjunct set: An element or a sequence of elements in a string occurrence may be conjoined by a conjunctional string consisting of the conjunction followed by another occurrence of the same type of string element (or elements) as precedes the conjunction (for example *the checking **and monitoring** of the data by the computer, other chemicals that maintain the fertility of the sea **or affect its life cycles**). Most conjunctional occurrences have strict structural identity of *A* and *B* (for example VING AND VING *in checking and monitoring*), but in certain positions, a certain range of forms is found to conjoin (*slowly and with great care, It is terrible to be **old and considered useless**, Patient is doing well and in no distress*). When conjuncts differ in form, they are usually members of the same set of strings. More pressing is the question of which subclasses in conjuncts of the same form make well-formed sequences. This depends largely on the area of discourse.

Computationally, to include all the conjunctional strings of a large grammar in the grammar definitions would complicate the grammar and increase its size beyond practical limits. Instead, the LSP uses a mechanism called the special process (SP) mechanism that allows conjunction strings to be defined dynamically during parsing. This way, whenever a conjunction occurs, only those conjunction strings that might occur in the given parse tree context will be generated.

The SP mechanism is a general device for dynamic syntax generation[2] that works in the following way. Various words in the language (coordinate and comparative conjunctions, comma, parentheses) are classed as SPWORDs in the lexicon. When an SPWORD becomes the current sentence word, a new element is inserted into the definition currently being processed. The definition of the inserted element is named as the attribute of SPWORD in the word's lexical entry. It calls on definitions already in the grammar and may also cause options to be generated with reference to structures built up in the course of the analysis, as is done in the case of conjunction strings. The SP definitions for coordinate conjunctions all contain an option with the element Q-CONJ, which is specified by a restriction as follows: Given that the SP-node has been inserted following the *m*th element X_m in a grammar definition, the options of Q-CONJ are

$$X_m \mid X_{m-1}X_m \mid X_{m-2}X_{m-1}X_m \mid \ldots \mid X_1 \ldots X_{m-1}X_m \quad .$$

That is, the restriction carries out structural repetition of the segments that end in X_m in the given definition.

For example, the lexical entry for *and* is

$$\text{AND} \qquad \text{SPWORD:} \quad (\text{ANDSTG}).$$

If *and* is the current word when LNR is being processed,

$$\text{<LNR>} :: = \text{<LN> <NVAR> <RN>}.$$

say, when NVAR has just been completed, the definitions that will be used by the parser are, first, the definition of ANDSTG given in the BNF section of the grammar

$$\text{<ANDSTG> ::= AND [NOT] <SACONJ> <Q-CONJ>}. \qquad\qquad 6.1$$

and second, the definition of Q-CONJ, which will be generated for this situation according to the foregoing scheme by the GENERATE operator under the control of the restriction DCONJ4:

$$\text{<Q-CONJ> :: = <NVAR> / <LN> <NVAR>}.$$

If RN in LNR had just been completed instead of NVAR, the definition of Q-CONJ would have been

$$\text{<Q-CONJ> :: = <NVAR> / <LN> <NVAR> / <LN> <NVAR> <RN>}.$$

The parse tree that results from using the second option of Q-CONJ in the definition of ANDSTG in LNR is seen in Fig. 6.1 in the LNR under SUBJECT (*persistent neck stiffness and low grade temp*). (The sentence in Fig. 6.1 was parsed with the LSP medical grammar. The root definition is again SENTENCE, but it has been redefined so as to accommodate sentences with more than one center string (called TEXTLETs). TEXTLET leads to the familiar definition of SENTENCE, renamed OLD-SENTENCE. The medical grammar contains most of the English grammar plus a coverage of many forms with deletion (for example, *lungs clear*). In the parse tree, *low grade* is a compound noun occurring in adjective position—that is, in the subtree dominated by APOS in LN.)

The SP mechanism is initiated as soon as an SPWORD becomes current, and it operates level by level, moving upward in the parse tree as the grammar permits. Suppose the SPWORD is *and*. A node ANDSTG is created immediately to the right of the node most recently completed. In the sentence of Fig. 6.1 this node would first be N (*stiffness*). However, there is a restriction (DCONJ5) in the present grammar that limits the insertion of a special process node to being directly below a node of type LXR or STRING. This restriction

Fig. 6.1   Parse of sentence with conjunction.

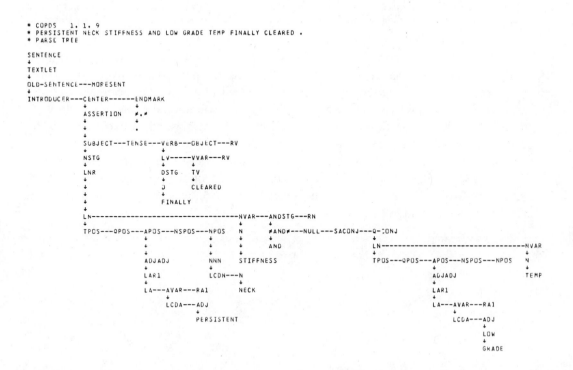

avoids redundancies created by conjoining at intermediate levels and regularizes the points of conjunction in the parse tree. In Fig. 6.1 the first place that ANDSTG can be placed is on the level above this N, that is, after NVAR, where it appears in the tree.

But suppose the generated options on a particular level fail or the global context later invalidates the local analysis and the conjunction subtree has to be dismantled (as would be the case for LNR of Fig. 6.1 if the sentence had been, for example, *Patient had persistent neck stiffness and low grade temp was noted.*) Then, the SPWORD is tried as a non-SPWORD on the same level as it was tried as an SPWORD, using the ordinary grammar (for example, *but* as adverb in the *They found but one*). If this too fails, and if the parser finds itself at the end of a nested construction, then the SP mechanism ascends one level and repeats the entire process. Such an ascent and repeat generation of Q-CONJ would take place in the analysis of *Patient had persistent neck stiffness and low grade temp was noted.* ANDSTG would appear in the parse tree after the element OBJECT of ASSERTION, and the generated Q-CONJ in ANDSTG would contain the elements SUBJECT (*low grade temp*), VERB (*was*), and OBJECT (*noted*).

In addition to the special process mechanism, another device is used by the LSP system for some cases of zeroing. Some conjunctional strings differ from the usual form of conjunctional occurrences in that the zeroed elements are not contiguous to the conjunction as in the type just described. For example, in *They liked the device but others did not*, the verb and object *like the device* have been zeroed in the conjunctional string; the positions of the zeroed verb and object in *but others did not* do not immediately follow *but*, but follow the tense position (*did*). This type of conjunctional occurrence is covered in the LSP grammar by a node called NULLC. The NULLC is automatically satisfied without subsuming a sentence word if certain conditions are met that are stated in restrictions.[3] When NULLC occurs in a parse tree, it represents the fact that a required element of a string has been deleted in the conjunct in such a position that the resulting parse tree will not have similar structures on either side of the conjunction unless nodes are created that have null values. Thus, in the parse of the example sentence, shown in Fig. 6.2, the VERB and OBJECT of the ASSERTION following *but* both have the value NULLC (not printed). The strings joined by the conjunction (Q-CONJ and its immediate string) both contain the required elements of ASSERTION, namely, SUBJECT, TENSE, VERB, and OBJECT. (TENSE is empty when the tense is morphologically bound to the verb.)

Fig. 6.2   Parse tree using NULLC.

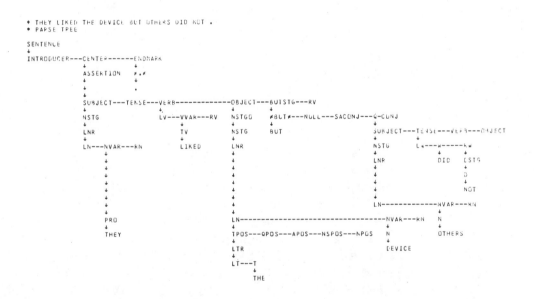

Before a NULLC node is accepted, several types of constraints must be satisfied. The general conditions for acceptance of a NULLC node are as follows:

1. It must be within a conjunctional string.
2. The preconjunctional element that corresponds to the deleted element must subsume some sentence word(s).

3.   The zeroing pattern must be one of a few types known to be acceptable for con-junctional strings with this type of zeroing. (Examples of the most common zero-ing patterns will be given.)

Thus, in the example sentence shown in Fig. 6.2, the verb of the assertion following *but* will have the value NULLC, and conditions 1–3 are met as follows:

1.   NULLC is in a conjunctional string—the string headed by *but*.
2.   The corresponding preconjunctional verb subsumes *liked*.
3.   The NULLC verb is not contiguous to the conjunction *but*, but follows the tense in the conjunctional string, this construction being one of the allowed patterns of zeroing.

The restriction governing the acceptance of NULLC in a given position assigns to the NULLC node the node attribute LINKC, whose value points to the preconjunctional structure that would have been repeated. Once the LINKC attribute is assigned, any constraint can locate this structure and thus identify the words that have been deleted.

The LSP grammar covers the most common patterns of zeroing of the noncontiguous-to-CONJ type, illustrated for the ASSERTION by the following sentences:

> *He laughed and she also.*
>   zeroed TENSE, VERB, OBJECT

> *He laughed but she didn't.*
>   zeroed VERB, OBJECT

> *He chose a rose and she a poppy.*
>   zeroed TENSE, VERB,

> *He should have gone but didn't* also *but hasn't, but couldn't.*
>   zeroed SUBJECT, VERB, OBJECT

> *He left and fast.*
>   zeroed SUBJECT, TENSE, VERB, OBJECT
>   (for a subset of verb and sentence adjuncts)

6.2   Features of Specific Conjunction Strings

6.2.1   *Scope Markers*

In terms of the operation of structural repetition by which conjunctional strings are ob-tained, the words *either* (as part of *either-or*), *neither* (as part of *neither-nor*), and *both* (as part of *both-and*) can be seen to mark the point in the host string beyond which elements cannot be "repeated" in the conjunctional string; for example, *John both wrote and cor-rected a paper,* ≠ *John both wrote and Mary corrected a paper.* That is, the first word of the pair functions as a "SCOPEWORD" for the generation or the options of Q-CONJ in the conjunction string headed by the second word of the pair. Since a SCOPEWORD can occur almost anywhere in the sentence as long as an appropriately placed CONJ string occurs later, a Special Process interrupts the analysis when a SCOPEWORD becomes the current word and inserts it into the parse tree, setting up a requirement for the appropriate CONJ to occur on the same level as the SCOPEWORD. If this requirement is not met, the same procedure is tried on other levels. The word having the SCOPEWORD classification is also tried as a nonspecial word if it has other word-class memberships (as in *Either is true, Both are present*).

6.2.2 Comma Conjunctions

The comma is troublesome because in some of its occurrences it is a conjunction (as in the string *X, X and X*) whereas in others it is a punctuation mark and as such not used with great regularity. In computer parsing the comma is first tried as a conjunction. If that fails, then it is accepted as punctuation. The words following the comma must then be analyzed by the ordinary grammar. In addition, particular strings that either should or should not be set off by punctuation commas carry their own restrictions to this effect, as does *The children asleep, they* . . . (Sec. 5.2)

6.2.3 Comparatives

The comparative forms in English are particularly rich structurally, and one way to handle them is to see their resemblance to strings and processes already defined. Accordingly, the Special Process definition that is initiated by *than* (when preceded by *more, less,* or *X-er,* where *X* is an adjective or one of a few adverbs) or by *as* (when preceded by adverbial *as*) contains several options:

1. Conjunctional. Compare, for example, the phrases or sentences in the following two columns:

men and women	*more men than women*
People will buy the book and read it.	*More people will buy the book than read it.*
	People will more (often) buy a book than read it.
	but *People buy more books than read them.*

With a few restrictions that depend on the placing of the comparative marker in the host string, the large body of comparative strings can be obtained using the same set of strings (options of Q-CONJ) as are generated in the conjunctional Special Process.

2. *wh*-like. There exists in the grammar a *wh*-string that adjoins a whole sentence, as in *The crowd dispersed quietly, which they had not expected.* When the ultimate verb is this string is such as can occur with *that S* as its object (S = sentence), there is a similar comparative string:

The crowd dispersed quietly,	*The crowd dispersed more*
which they had not expected.	*quietly than they had expected.*

The *wh*-string that adjoins an N also has a comparative analogue.

The boxes which we asked for	*More boxes than we asked for*
have arrived.	*have arrived.*

Than and *as* can therefore be placed in the same class as *which* (as heading the same strings) and handled by the ordinary grammar, with the restriction that *then* and *as* each be preceded in the sentence by the appropriate comparative marker, and with certain restrictions on the strings headed by *than* and *as* versus *which*. There is also a shortened form of the passive strings of this type (headed only by the comparative string heads); for example, *More people than expected were there, The crowd dispersed more quietly than expected.*

3. N *is* A strings. As a right adjunct of N, a comparative marked adjective behaves (in string terms) as though it were preceded not by N alone but by N *is* A (A = adjective), from which the various Q-CONJ strings can be obtained:

Someone smarter than I could solve the problem.
Someone smarter than I am could solve the problem.
Someone smarter than I am patient could solve the problem.

4. Inverted assertion. This option covers the comparative strings in which the subject appears after the tense element (including *have, be,* or *do*). For example, (from a text):

Mammals have generally been conceded to possess a much wider "plasticity"
and "adaptability" of coordination than do amphibians.

5. Special zeroing, for small adverb subclasses: *more beautiful than ever, more people than ever.*

6.3   Restrictions under Conjunctions

A sentence with a conjunction presents a problem for the application of detailed constraints (restrictions) to the parse tree, an essential part of the parsing process. The tree structure will be different from that assumed by the restriction; conjunctional strings will have been inserted and the conjunctional strings themselves may be truncated versions of defined strings. To appreciate what this problem means, one must keep in mind that a grammar like that of the LSP for processing English text sentences is very large by comparison with grammars used in most other natural language processing systems, which are directed to particular subsets of English. The LSP parsing grammar consists of approximately 3,500 lines. The restrictions constitute by far the largest part of the grammar, and without them, text parsing is out of the question. In addition, we have found that roughly one-third of all text sentences contain coordinate or comparative conjunctions, many times in complicated interrelation. It is therefore essential that there be a means for executing restrictions on sentences containing conjunctions.

One solution to this problem is to rewrite all the restrictions so that they test for conjunctions and accommodate truncated segments. This was done in earlier versions of the grammar (Salkoff and Sager 1969), but it involved a large amount of detailed work and both increased and complicated the grammar greatly. As an alternative, it might be thought that truncated segments should be expanded when they are parsed, so that the restrictions will always operate on complete strings. But this is not possible as a general rule without vastly complicating the parsing process. The solution employed, then, is to execute restrictions on conjunctional strings in the form in which they appear in the parse tree, but in the case of truncated strings to locate the elements that would be present if the string were expanded. The actual expansion is done later, using information obtained during the execution of the restriction.

The execution of the restriction on the conjunctional sequence is initiated automatically if a restriction is applied to a structure that contains a conjunct. The mechanism called stacking temporarily saves the conjunct (or the relvevant subpart of it) so that the restriction can be reexecuted on it after the restriction has been executed on the structure into which the conjunct was inserted. The restriction will not exit with an indication of success unless it succeeds on all the saved conjunctional structures as well as on the initial structure for which the restriction was invoked.

As a simple example of stacking, consider the operation of the selectional restriction WSEL1 on the sentence, *They demonstrated the device and students observed.* WSEL1 (described in detail in Sec. 5.6) is housed in OBJECT and is executed just before a noun phrase is accepted as the object of a given verb: the core noun must not be in a subclass that is listed as a value of the NOTNOBJ attribute of the verb. In this instance the restriction is executed on an OBJECT node that subsumes *the device and students observed* when this sequence has been analyzed as a single noun phrase containing a conjunct. (One sees a conjunct of similar form in, for example *The teachers and students observed gave their consent.*) WSEL1 rejects this analysis because *students* (NHUMAN) is not an appropriate object noun for the verb *demonstrate*. NHUMAN appears as a value of the NOTNOBJ attribute of *demonstrate* in the lexicon.

A trace of the execution of WSEL1 in this situation is shown in Fig. 6.3. It will be seen from the trace that when the CORE[4] routine is executed, stacking causes the core noun

Fig. 6.3   Trace of WSEL1 showing stacking of conjuncts and reexecution of restriction.

```
WSEL1 BEING EXECUTED IN OBJECT WHICH SUBSUMES  THE DEVICE AND STUDENTS OBSERVED ...
    IMPLY( AND( ( STARTAT(  ( OBJECT )  ) -> OBJECT=THE DEVICE AND STUDENTS OBSERVED
            ... ) + STORE( X10 ) + ( EXTENDED-CORE -> N=DEVICE ) + STORE( X3 ) +
            IS( ( N PRO ) ) + LOOK( X10 -> OBJECT=THE DEVICE AND STUDENTS OBSERVED
            ... ) + ( VERB-COELEMENT -> VERB=DEMONSTRATED ) + STORE( X4 ) + LOOK(
            X4 => VERB=DEMONSTRATED ) + ( CORE -> TV=DEMONSTRATED ) + ATTRB( (
            NOTNOBJ ) ) + STORE( X5 ) + ) + NOT( COMMONAT( LOOK( X3 -> N=DEVICE
            ) + LOOK( X5 ) + ) - ) + )

RESTRICTION RESTARTED DUE TO STACKING AT NODE N
WHICH SUBSUMES STUDENTS
        -> N=STUDENTS ) + STORE( X3 ) + IS( ( N PRO ) ) + LOOK( X10 -> OBJECT=THE
            DEVICE AND STUDENTS OBSERVED ... ) + ( VERB-COELEMENT -> VERB=DEMONSTRATED
            ) + STORE( X4 ) + LOOK( X4 -> VERB=DEMONSTRATED ) + ( CORE -> TV=
            DEMONSTRATED ) + ATTRB( ( NOTNOBJ ) ) + STORE( X5 ) + ) + NOT(
            COMMONAT( LOOK( X3 -> N=STUDENTS ) + LOOK( X5 ) + ) + ) - ) -

WSEL1 FAILED AT NODE OBJECT WHICH SUBSUMES  THE DEVICE AND STUDENTS OBSERVED ...

THEY DEMONSTRATED THE DEVICE AND STUDENTS OBSERVED .

    PARSE   1


1. SENTENCE  = INTRODUCER  CENTER  ENDMARK
                            2.


2. ASSERTION = SA  SUBJECT   SA  TENSE   SA  VERB            SA  OBJECT      ANDSTG    RV
                   THEY                      DEMONSTRATED         3. DEVICE    AND 4.
                   SA


3. LN        = TPOS  OPOS  APOS  NSPOS  NPOS
               THE


4. Q-CCNJ    = SUBJECT    SA  TENSE  SA  VERB       SA  OBJECT
               STUDENTS                  OBSERVED

    Note:  Each executed routine or operator is printed with its argument(s)
           in parenthesis.  The parenthetical expression of the form (X -> Y=Z)
           is not an argument, but tells what node Y, subsuming words Z, was
           reached in the immediately previous execution of the routine X.
           If an operation succeeds, + is printed; otherwise -.
```

(*students*) of the conjunct to be saved for a reexecution of the restriction with this value of CORE. When the restriction succeeds for the sequence *demonstrated the device,* it is reexecuted for the sequence *demonstrated students,* resuming at the point immediately after the call to the routine CORE, which invoked stacking. In the example, the reexecution fails, so the entire restriction fails. The correct (and only) parse obtained for the sentence is shown at the bottom of Fig. 6.3 in the short form of the output.

Modification of the nonconjunction grammar to incorporate stacking fortunately could be done by modifying a small number of routines used by restrictions, rather than by modifying the restrictions themselves. The routines that were modified are those that locate a basic linguistic structure in the parse tree, such as the routines CORE, HOST, ELEMENT, LEFT-ADJUNCT. When a conjunction is present, the routines invoke stacking and also assign the node attributes PRECONJELEM and POSTCONJELEM, pointing, respectively, from the conjunct to the parallel element in the preconjunction string and from the element in the preconjunction string that has the conjunct to the conjunct. These pointers are later used in the conjunction-expansion transformation.

In addition to modifications for stacking, the routines were also modified to function properly in the nonconjunction grammar for new situations due to conjunctions. In a sentence with a conjunction, the routine may be operating in a structure into which conjunctional strings have been inserted, or the routine may be operating in a truncated version of a defined string or host–adjunct sequence. For example, the RIGHT-ADJUNCT routine is assumed to start at a node X in an LXR type structure. Without conjunctions, the RIGHT-ADJUNCT routine goes one node to the right from X to arrive at the right adjunct position of X. But if a conjunct has been inserted to the right of X, as in Fig. 6.1 in LNR (*and low grade temp*), the RIGHT-ADJUNCT routine must move two nodes to the right (that is, it must pass through the conjunctional node) to arrive at the correct position. All necessary modifications to the routines for conjunctions are described in detail in Raze 1976.

6.4   Automatic Expansion of Conjunction Strings with Ellipsis

Making explicit the implicit word occurrences in text sentences is an important step in preparing a natural language data base for information retrieval or other information processing. This is accomplished with regard to ellipsis in conjunction strings by a conjunction-expansion transformation, which is part of the transformational component of the grammar. Without discussing how the expansion is carried out, we can illustrate its effect on a simple sentence from a corpus of medical records analyzed by the LSP.

The parse tree for the sentence *Persistent neck stiffness and low grade temp finally cleared* was shown in Fig. 6.1. The final goal of processing this sentence (and all others in the corpus) is to map the words of the sentence into the appropriate columns of a medical "information format" (see Chapter 8) in such a way that each row of the format represents a reported medical fact or event. The tabular rearrangement of the sentence parts makes it possible to retrieve specific facts automatically and to generate statistical summaries over many case reports. As a first step in this process, after parsing, incomplete strings are filled out so that the rows of the table will not lack any information that was present in the sentences.

Figure 6.4 shows the effect of executing the conjunction-expansion transformation on the sentence in Fig. 6.1. (The transformed parse tree is not printed when the expansion is done as part of information formatting.) The conjoined noun phrases (*persistent neck stiffness and low grade temp*), which were the SUBJECT of one ASSERTION in the parse, are now each the subject of a complete ASSERTION. The second ASSERTION is created by the conjunction transformation. At the time the tree in Fig. 6.4 was computed, the tense transformation had also been executed on each ASSERTION so that *cleared* became *clear past*.

Fig. 6.4 Expansion of medical sentence with conjunction.

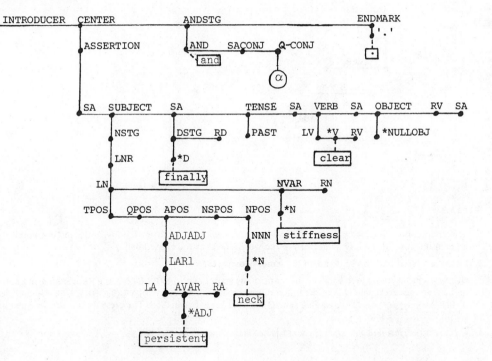

Expansion of medical sentence with conjunction

COPDS 1.1.9

PERSISTENT NECK STIFFNESS AND LOW GRADE TEMP FINALLY CLEARED.

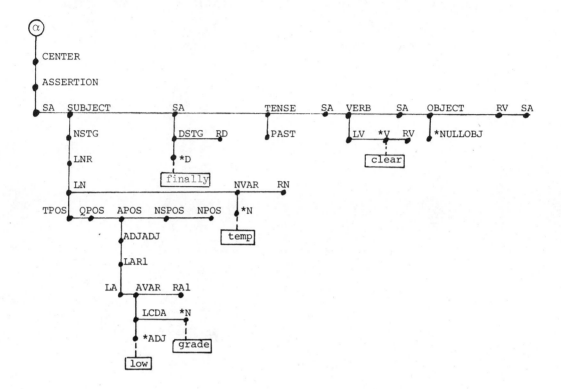

NOTES

1. This chapter is adapted from Sager 1967 and Raze 1976. The routines, restrictions, and transformations governing conjunctions in the LSP grammar are the work of Carol Raze Friedman.

2. First introduced into the LSP system by James Morris (1966).

3. NULLC elements, and the restrictions that control the acceptance of NULLC (Zeroing Restrictions) are not shown in the grammar in Appendix 1. In the full grammar, NULLC is an option of VERB, OBJECT, TENSE and elements of LN. An early version of the zeroing restrictions is given in Sager 1968. The present set is documented in Raze 1976.

4. EXTENDED-CORE replaces CORE in WSEL1. See end of note 2 in Chapter 5.

Chapter 7   The Transformational Component of the Grammar

Transformational analysis, one of the major advances in linguistics during the past three decades, has a direct bearing on the possibility of performing computerized information processing on texts. In moving from automatic sentence analysis to informational applications of the analysis, it is important to eliminate, as far as possible, alternative grammatical forms for the same information, and to expand sentences with ellipses so that like portions of sentences can be aligned. Both of these operations can be carried out in a general way over any English discourse, using paraphrastic English transformations operating on the output of the string parsing program.

7.1   Transformational Analysis

Transformational analysis was introduced into linguistics by Zellig S. Harris in 1952 as an outgrowth of his work on discourse structure (Harris 1952). In that work it was clear that many sentences and sentence parts, while differing in grammatical form, were similar in content and, in fact, contained virtually the same vocabulary items except for certain grammatical words or affixes: *which, by, -ing,* and so forth. When two or more such forms satisfied certain grammatical conditions they were called transforms of each other. The forms were understood to be sequences of variables of the type N noun, V verb, and so on (called variables because their values are different words in different sentences) and grammatical words or affixes, called constants of the transformation. A classic example is the active–passive transformation.

$$N_1 \text{ tV } N_2 \leftrightarrow N_2 \text{ t } \textit{be V-en by } N_1.$$

Here N_1, t (tense), V, and N_2 are the variables and *be, -en* (past participle marker), and *by,* are the grammatical constants. For example, if N_1 has the value *Withering,* t the value *-ed* ("past"), V the value *use,* and N_2 the value *digitalis,* we have the transformational relation between two sentences:

Withering used digitalis in 1784. ↔ *Digitalis was used by Withering in 1784.*

Note that the information content is the same in both forms although a shift in emphasis or other stylistic change may be introduced by the transformation.

It is obvious that there are many ways of expressing the same content. If we limit our considerations to just those cases where the vocabulary except for grammatical constants is kept constant, there are still many forms available for stylistic variation and for combining a given assertion with others to form a single sentence. One may nominalize a sentence, for example, so that is has a form that can occupy the position of a noun in another sentence. Ignoring the tense in *The heart beats,* we may put this sentence in the form *For the heart to beat* to make it the subject of *requires energy* in *For the heart to beat requires energy.* One may make certain permutations and additions of constants, as in *It requires energy for the heart to beat;* and one may combine two sentences by turning one into a modifier of the other. For example, from *The heart responds* and *The heart beats* we may form *The heart which beats responds, The heart which responds beats, The beating heart responds,* and so on, all retaining the two starting notions intact while they are combined in different ways.

Oddly enough, although some of these relations among sentences and sentence parts were noted by linguists in the past, there was never an attempt to treat them systematically before their introduction in 1952 in the service of regularizing discourse analysis. The reason may be that linguistics until 1950 was thoroughly occupied with achieving an adequate description of the structure of the sentence, and it was not until the problem of structure beyond the domain of one sentence was tackled that the question of the relation among sentences came under study. Moreover, the extent of these relations in language had not been appreciated. It came as a surprise in 1955 therefore, that it proved possible to construct the entire body of grammar on the basis of the transformational relation of sentences and sentence parts (Harris 1957). In this type of analysis a sentence is decomposed into elementary source sentences ("kernel sentences") plus transformations operating on the elementary sentences or on already transformed sentences. Some transformations, such as the active–passive, and the replacing of a particular noun by a pronoun, are purely paraphrastic; that is, they add no information and are only a rearrangement of parts or a change in the shape of words. Others add a fixed increment of meaning to the operand sentence, the same addition of meaning to all operand sentences; for example, *seems* in *The heart seems to respond, The child seems to understand;* these are called incremental transformations.[1]

There are various ways of displaying the transformational decomposition of a sentence. A decomposition lattice[2] shows how the underlying elementary sentences (kernel sentences) are successively transformed and combined to make the final sentence. A decomposition lattice for the sentence *The force with which an isolated heart beats depends on the concentration of calcium in the medium which surrounds it* is shown in Fig. 7.1. Each node in the decomposition lattice introduces one change in the sentence or the sentence part(s) represented by the branch(es) leading into that node. If two branches lead into a node, the node represents a binary connective, such as *and* or *wh* (see node 3 in Fig. 7.1) By convention, the primary sentence under a binary connective is written on a branch above the branch corresponding to the secondary (modifier) sentence. In Fig. 7.1, K1 is the primary sentence and K2 the secondary sentence. If only one branch leads into a node, the node represents a unary change that either is paraphrastic, for example, the passive transformation (node 1 in Fig. 7.1), or is incremental, and adds an element of meaning.

The LSP computer output for a transformational decomposition keeps a record of the transformations recognized in the sentence, but in a different form from that in the decomposition lattice. Each reverse transformation that was applied is represented by a node (having prefix T-) apearing above the structure that resulted from the application of the reverse transformation.[3] In addition, the substructure of each component is shown in Polish notation, with verb (or preposition or predicate adjective) in the role of operator, and the subject and object(s) of the verb (or analagous element) appearing as its ordered arguments. A decomposition of this type for the sentence of Fig. 7.1 is shown in Fig. 7.2.

For some applications what is of interest is not so much which particular transformations operated in the composition of the sentence as the relations among words in the component elementary sentences. Another output form is then convenient, in which the nodes that name the transformations are eliminated and each nonparaphrastic operator is shown as a node dominating its argument nodes. The result is a dependency-tree structure of the type shown in Fig. 7.3 for the same sentence as appeared in Figs. 7.1 and 7.2. This is the form used, for example, as input to a clustering program that has developed for generating semantic word classes of a subfield (Hirschman, Grishman, and Sager 1975). In the clustering program, words are compared with respect to what other words they occur with in the operator-operand relation in transformationally decomposed sentences of a sample corpus. Having the decomposition represented in the dependence tree form makes it possible to calculate word co-occurrence frequencies, since all the operator-operand occurrences of the same root word can be read directly off the tree; thus we have *beat* as verb operator on *heart* as subject in *a heart beats, a heart which beats, the beating heart, the beating of the heart, for the heart to beat, a heart beating,* for example.

Transformational analysis also provides a means of reducing the number of variant forms in sentences and for this reason is an important step toward obtaining a uniform representation of the information in related texts. If two sentences contain the same infor-

Fig. 7.1 Decomposition lattice for the sentence *The force with which an isolated heart beats depends on the concentration of Ca in the medium which surrounds it.*

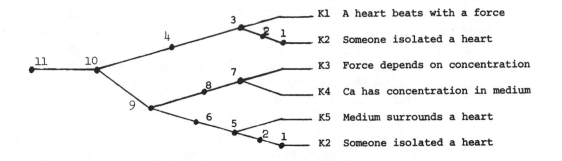

1. PASSIVE(K2) → <u>A heart was isolated by someone</u>

2. ZEROING OF INDEFINITE(1) → <u>A heart was isolated</u>

3. WH(K1, 2; <u>heart</u>) → <u>A heart which was isolated beats with a force</u>

4. ZEROING of <u>wh</u> + <u>is</u> in 3 and permutation to left of N → <u>An isolated heart beats with a force</u>

5. WH(K5, 2; <u>heart</u>) → <u>Medium surrounds a heart which was isolated</u>

6. ZEROING of <u>wh</u> + <u>is</u> in 5 and permutation to left of N → <u>Medium surrounds an isolated heart</u>

7. WH(K3, K4; <u>concentration</u>) → <u>Force depends on concentration which Ca has in medium</u>

8. In 7: N_1 <u>has</u> N_2 → N_2 of N_1 → <u>Force depends on concentration of Ca in medium</u>

9. WH(8, 6; <u>medium</u>) → <u>Force depends on concentration of Ca in the medium which surrounds the isolated heart</u>

10. WH(9, 4; <u>force</u>) → <u>The force with which an isolated heart beats depends on the concentration of Ca in the medium which surrounds the isolated heart</u>

11. PRONOUN (10; <u>The isolated heart</u>) → <u>The force with which an isolated heart beats depends on the concentration of Ca in the medium which surrounds it.</u>

Fig. 7.2 Transformational decompostion tree for the sentence *The force with which an isolated heart beats depends on the concentration of Ca in the medium which surrounds it.*

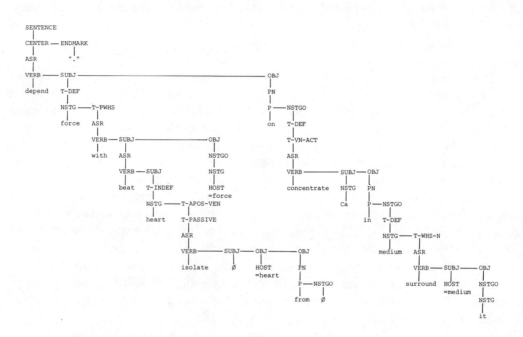

Fig. 7.3 Transformational decomposition in the form of a dependency tree.

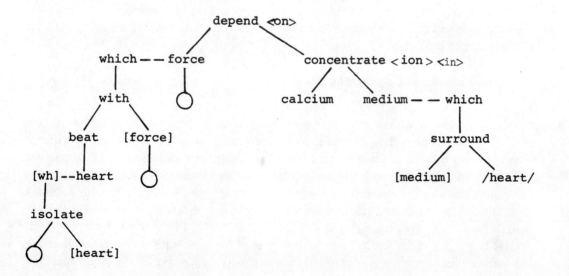

mation presented in different styles, or if they overlap in their information content, then the information they carry in common will appear in the transformational analysis of the sentences as identical component elementary sentences with the same incremental transformations; they will differ only in the paraphrastic transformations in the decomposition. This means in principle that sentences can be compared in a standard fashion for sameness or overlap in content.

It should be noted that the transformational approach to sentence structure presented in this chapter differs in particular ways from the more widely known form in which Noam Chomsky adapted transformations to a generative style of grammatical description (Chomsky 1956, 1957, 1964). In the Chomsky system the source forms (deep structure) of a sentence are phrase structure trees, and the transformations are defined as operating on this abstract type of tree structure. The final phrase structure after all transformations have been applied is called the surface structure. It is interpreted by the phonological and semantic components of the grammar. Broadly speaking, the deep structure and surface structure of a sentence correspond, respectively, to the transformational decomposition and string analysis of the sentence, but this comparison overlooks important differences in theory. From a computational point of view, the chief difference between the two formulations lies in whether the source forms of a sentence have a direct representation as word strings (elementary sentences), and whether the resultant of each transformation operating in the sentence is assumed to have a word string representation that is a sentence of the language. In the original Harris formulation of transformations such a relation exists and is the basis for the ability to recognize and reverse the transformations in an orderly way. In the Chomsky system, such a relation is not maintained or assumed. The intermediate stages of generation and transformation are abstract; words can be interpreted only in the final surface structure. The problem of recognizing the resultant of a transformation in a sentence is thereby considerably more difficult than in the Harris system, which, for this reason, is used by the LSP in preference to the Chomsky formulation.

7.2 Transformational Computation

Automatic transformational decomposition can be accomplished by first performing a "surface" analysis and then applying reverse transformations to the output of the surface analysis. This is done in the LSP system using string analysis followed by transformational decomposition (Hobbs and Grishman 1976). The transformations in the LSP system are combined with other components in a question-answering system (Grishman and Hirschman 1978) that includes the generation of natural language answers to the posed questions (Grishman 1979). Another question-answering system that uses transformations is the REQUEST (now QAS) system developed at IBM (Petrick 1976, Plath 1976). In that system, natural language queries that apply to a data base of business statistics or similar data are first parsed with a covering grammar and then analyzed transformationally in an algorithm due to Petrick. A strictly transformational approach to sentence decomposition is provided in an algorithm developed by Joshi and D. Hiž (Joshi and Hiž 1965, Hiž and Joshi 1967).

Joshi's procedure recognizes the trace left in the sentence by each successive transformation that operated to produce the sentence and undoes the transformations in a bottom-up fashion, starting with the deepest-nested trace. Many of the traces are the same as features that are recognized in string analysis or in the subsequent transformational decomposition performed in the LSP system. Joshi has also provided a unified formal theory that combines the features of string and transformational analysis (Joshi, Kosaraju, and Yamada 1972).

The string parse contains a great deal of the information that is needed in order to arrive at a transformational decomposition. Partly this is because of the inherent relation between string and transformational analysis. Partly it is the result of a conscious attempt to build into the parsing grammar such node names and node attributes as would facilitate a subsequent stage of transformational analysis.

As to the former, the strings into which a given sentence is decomposed by the string grammar can to a large extent be identified with the elementary sentences of that sentence in a transformational decomposition. In most cases the relation is direct: the center string is the main kernel sentence of the given sentence or one to which unary transformations (like the passive or the *it*-transformation) have been applied; and each adjunct string can be filled out to the corresponding kernel sentence (or kernel sentence plus unary transformations) by adding to the adjunct a distinguished word from the string to which the adjunct has been adjoined. This word is precisely the one that is defined to be the HOST of the adjunct string in the computer string grammar. In some cases the host word is the core of a nominalized sentence, in which case the denominalized sentence is the distinguished element to be supplied to the adjunct string. Examples of host nouns supplied to adjunct strings in the transformational decompostion are the words *force, heart,* and *medium* in Fig. 7.2; and in the same figure, an example of a denominalized sentence in place of a host noun is *concentrate* with its arguments *Ca* and *in medium.*

In the case of certain quantifiers, quantity sequences, and some other elements, the relation of string to transformation is less direct but often resolvable within locally adjoined or conjoined strings. The most complicated problem is determinng the antecedent of pronouns and other referentials. Within one sentence the string relations between pronoun and antecedent can be stated succinctly, but the algorithm for deciding which of several syntactic possibilities is the intended antecedent involves additional considerations. For example, in Fig. 7.2 the pronoun *it* has for antecedent the noun *heart.* In the string parse tree (Fig. 1.3) of this sentence the relations of *heart* to *it* starting at PRO (*it*) is: AT CORE OF COELEMENT SUBJECT OF ULTIMATE-OBJECT, CORE OF SUBJECT OF RIGHT-ADJUNCT [is antecedent]. With small adjustments in the routines for the way adjunct strings appear in the transformational decomposition as opposed to the string-parse, the execution of the same sequence of routines will lead from *it* to *heart* in the transformational tree. The problem then resolves into stating the constraints that eliminate other (and nearer) syntactic candidates, namely *Ca* and *force.* We would have to resort to sublanguage selectional priorities in this case ("FLUID-class *surround* TISSUE-class" being more likely than "FLUID-class *surround* ION-class,*" with virtual exclusion of "FLUID-class *surround* QUANT-class").

The policy of anticipating in the parsing phase the information that is needed for transformational decomposition is expressed in the LSP system in several ways. First, in the BNF component, virtually all of the verb-containing strings are defined in such a way as to name explicitly the SUBJECT and OBJECT elements of the underlying ASSERTION, even if the given string departs in significant respects from the ASSERTION form (for example, the VING strings or QUESTIONs). Also, predicate occurrences are labeled as such (OBJBE) in all positions of occurrence, whether adjunct or object, and whether the verb *be* occurs explicitly or implicitly. Care was also taken in defining the more than fifty object strings to reflect whether the main subject is repeated or not, and to distinguish object strings that may look alike but have different sources (see NASOBJBE versus SASOBJBE in Appendix 3, for example). Similarly, the *wh*-strings that are interrogative-related are distinguished from those that refer to a specific noun (SNWH versus NWHSTG). And the passive string is explicitly identified both in object and in adjunct occurrences (VENPASS), as are a number of different null elements that indicate different transformational sources (NULLN, NULLOBJ, NULLRECIP, NULLWH, NULLC), all different from the NULL representing optional adjunction.

Restrictions do a considerable amount of the job of locating elements that are later needed in reverse transformations. For example, the restrictions that control the NULLWH and NULLC elements go to elaborate lengths to identify and store pointers to the words in the sentence that are later to replace the NULL element in question (for example, the node attributes PRECONJELEM and POSTCONJELEM in the case of conjuncts). As another example, the occurrence of the *it*-transformation, which causes a sentence nominalization string to occur after the verb or predicate instead of in subject position, is established during the execution of the sentence nominalization restrictions.

The routines of the grammar are especially important in computing transformations. The basic linguistic relations embodied in locating routines apply, with slight modifications in the transformational decomposition. Even more important, the routines are well suited to the task of stating the conditions in the parse tree that are required in order for a given reverse transformation to apply. These conditions are stated in the same way that restrictions are, as tests of the parse tree. They test for node names and attributes, and they traverse the parse tree in the same giant steps (CORE, COELEMENT, HOST, RIGHT-ADJUNCT, and so on) as proved so effective in restrictions.

The typical form of a transformation is

IF structural condition THEN structural change.

The structural condition is written in Restriction Language using the operations and routines described in Chapter 3. The structural change is written in an extension of the Restriction Language described in Hobbs and Grishman 1976 and in greater detail in Grishman 1974a. Very briefly, the means by which the parse tree is rearranged and new structures built are via REPLACE, DELETE, and INSERT commands. The sequencing of transformations is specified by the user using a TRANSFORM command. When the common root form of a word is desired in a structure instead of the form that appears at an atomic node of the parse tree (thus replacing TV by the infinitive V, for example) the specification "CLASS *category* of *atomic node*" (e.g. CLASS V of TV) in the statement of structural change causes the word dictionary group of the word at the atomic node to be searched for a word of the stated CLASS; a new atomic node of this CLASS with its associated word is then substituted for the original one.

The major operational transformations in the present LSP system are the relative clause expansion, the conjunctional expansion, the comparative transformation, the denominalizing transformation (for nouns of verbal origin), the passive transformation, the adjective transformation, numerous nominalization-string transformations (such as VING string, FORTOVO) and a considerable number of smaller transformations concerning specific forms. Examples of the results of the operation of the transformations in the service of information formatting can be seen in the following chapter.

NOTES

1. This terminology is from Harris 1964, which is reprinted in Harris 1970 along with a number of other papers important in the development of linguistic transformations.

2. Harris 1968, Sec. 4.4, and in greater detail in Harris 1970.

3 . An exception is the conjunction EXPAND transformation. The ASSERTION resulting from the expansion appears under the node Q-CONJ, as in Fig. 6.4.

Part 3
APPLICATIONS

Chapter 8   Information Formatting

Until recently, natural language processing in information retrieval meant primarily the scanning of large amounts of machine readable natural language material for the occurrence of particular word string combinations. Such methods, although they may be suitable for document retrieval from large data bases, do not provide a characterization of the contents of documents adequate for more complex informational operations such as checking for the presence of specific facts or comparing or summarizing specific kinds of information in particular documents or collections of documents. Yet the need for computer programs that can perform such operations is growing. Not only are scientists often interested in extracting and compiling information from diverse data sources, but many institutions today have large natural language files containing information that must be accessed and processed for a variety of purposes, often in a routine manner. Some of this material is already in machine readable form, and it is likely that more will become so, especially if computer programs can take over some of the burden of processing the textual content.

This chapter and the chapter following describe how the language processing system described in Parts 1 and 2 is applied to practical information tasks involving natural language documents, particularly those of the type found in files of reports, such as medical records. An additional stage of processing, which relies on special word classes defined for the field of application, is added to the parsing and transformation components described earlier. This three-step process transforms the sentences in a file of documents in a particular subject area into informationally equivalent tablelike forms, called **information formats.** When the information is arranged in this way, it is possible for a computer to retrieve

Naomi Sager, Natural Language Information Processing: A Computer Grammar of English and Its Applications
Copyright © 1981 by Addison-Wesley Publishing Company, Inc., Advanced Book Program.   ISBN 0-201-06769-2

specific facts, checking whether the desired relation holds between terms, and to generate numerical summaries of the different types of information in documents in the file.

It should be noted from the outset that information formats for a subject area are not defined on semantic grounds based on knowledge of the subject matter. Although we check our results with consultants who know the particular subfield of application, we do not ask such experts to propose, a priori, an organization of information for that subfield, which we would then implement in the hope that it would suffice for analyzing subfield texts. First of all, there would be no guarantee that a computer could map sentences into the proposed structure. Second, experts might well disagree as to what are the most important relations to be included in the format. Last, as it happens, experts on the level needed for such work are simply not available. For all these reasons, but mainly because the purpose of the LSP was to find methods that would be generally applicable and would be assured to work, our processing of documents is based on regularities that are inherent in the textual material. For each subfield of application we analyze a sample of the documents to find the syntactic and lexical regularities over and above those of English grammar that are special to the subfield. These textual regularities on the subfield level in conjunction with English syntactical relations correspond in a direct way to the information carried by subfield texts.

The methods of analysis referred to here are essentially those of descriptive (or distributional) linguistics, only here applied to a distinguished subset of the language, called a **sublanguage** (Harris 1968: Sec. 5.9, Bross, Shapiro, and Anderson 1972, Kittredge 1981, Lehrberger 1981). The methods are successful when applied to discourse in a narrowly defined subject area, preferably even a document type, in which the main purpose is to record factual information. It is then possible to describe the textual regularities, that is, the main sublanguage word classes and their patterns of co-occurrence, in the form of a **sublanguage grammar;** and for computer applications, in the form of information formats (Sager 1972b, Sager 1975, Sager 1977, Hirschman and Sager 1981). A word of caution: Unless the special conditions of a sublanguage are present, computerized information formatting may not be practicable.

Information formats are a particularly useful way of representing the textual regularities. In the formats the parts of different sentences that carry the same kind of information appear as entries in a single column, which is very important for retrieval, and the informational relations among entities in a particular occurrence can be checked by reference to the column headings under which the entries lie. What is perhaps the most important feature is the fact that once the information format for an area is specified on the basis of an analysis of a sample set of documents, the format can be implemented and subsequent documents of the same type can be automatically mapped into it. From the freely written natural language documents we thus obtain a structured form of the information that is suitable for computerized data processing.

To introduce the methods, the next section will draw upon an experiment in which information-formatting and retrieval programs were applied to a set of English-language radiology reports. First, the language processing system mapped the sentences of the reports into the information format by the three-step process (parse, transform, map into format). Then, a second program obtained answers to specific questions about the contents of the reports by processing the formatted sentences. A numerical summary of specified types of facts reported in the documents was also computer-generated from the formatted sentences.

8.1   Processing Radiology Reports[1]

The radiology corpus consisted of the reports from the first thirteen patients in a follow-up study of cancer patients who had undergone mastectomy. To illustrate the main features of information formats, Fig. 8.1 shows a simplified radiology format applied to two short X-ray report sentences. We call each unit set off by periods a sentence even if, as is often the case in file material, the verb or some other required grammatical element is missing. The deleted words are either grammatical elements (like the verb *be*) that are also absent in common English constructions (as in *They found **the X-rays negative for metastasis***) or are words with distinguished status in the sublanguage (like *X-rays* as deleted subject of *not done* in a radiology report). The deletion patterns found in medical reports and their adaptation for use in the LSP grammar to parse radiology reports are found in Anderson, Bross, and Sager 1975).

Fig. 8.1   Simple radiology format.

	TEST			FINDING	
	TEST	TEST-LOC	DATE	VERB	FINDING
1)	films	chest	1-31-68	--	post radiation fibrosis
	films	chest	3-26-68	--	post radiation fibrosis
2)	scan	liver	1-29-69	was	normal

1. 1-31-68 and 3-28-68 chest films--post radiation fibrosis.

2. Liver scan 1-29-69 was normal.

As Fig. 8.1 illustrates, an information format has rows and columns like a numerical table, but the table entries are words or phrases rather than numbers. Each column contains the words or phrases that carry the same kind of information in the texts; for example in Fig. 8.1 the type of test is in column 1, the location of the test in column 2, and so on. All the words in the sentence are placed somewhere in the format (or are printed out with a message that they were "LEFTOVERS"). Thus, no information is lost, and the original sentences, or paraphrases of them, can be reconstructed from the format entries.

8.1.1   *Specifying the Information Format*

The relation between a word's characteristic (most frequent) environments and its meaning makes it possible to establish the relevant word classes for representing textual information. Using techniques from structural linguistics, word classes that reflect the specialized use of language (the sublanguage) of the discipline are built up from an analysis of a sample corpus. Words that occur in identical or similar environments are placed in the same sublanguage class. For example, in the sentences of Fig. 8.2, if we group together the head nouns occurring as subject of *show*, we find both *X-ray* and *film* (ignoring suffixes) occurring in this environment. If we look at a larger subset of the corpus we find that *X-ray* and *film* share a number of other environments (together with the words *scan, plate, mammograph*); these words form a subclass of nouns in texts of this subfield, based on the similarity of their environments. They also share an element of meaning, which is related to their similarity of distribution.

Continuing to group words together on the basis of common environments we obtain a number of sublanguage word classes (on the whole, subclasses of the major English classes noun, verb, and so forth) that occur together in particular syntactic combinations; for example, in the radiology material, a TEST noun + a SHOW verb + a MEDical FINDing noun (*film shows clouding, X-rays indicate metastasis*). These word class patterns are the basis for defining the information format. As a rule, we provide a column for each sublanguage word class that enters into a pattern and one or more columns for each of the informationally important word classes of English that play a role in the sublanguage, such as negation, time, quantity expressions, modals. In an instance of a formatted sentence, only a few columns will be nonempty; in most cases, this is sufficient to identify the pattern.[2] Figure 8.2 shows the information format for the radiology material with four report sentences as they appear in the format.

8.1.2   *Transferring the Information into the Format*

The formatting program operates in three steps on each successive text sentence. First the sentence is parsed with the LSP English grammar, to provide the syntactic structure of the sentence. (The English grammar has been extended to cover the incomplete sentences, or "fragments" found in notes and records.) Next the parsed sentence is regularized by applying certain information-preserving English transformations. The most important of these are the conjunction expansion (expanding two conjoined elements into two conjoined assertions—see example 4 in Fig. 8.2), and the relative clause transformation, which replaces a

Fig. 8.2 Sample formatted radiology sentences.

1. NOT DONE.

2. CHEST FILM 10-22 SHOWED NO CHANGE.

3. X-RAYS TAKEN 1-24 NEGATIVE FOR METASTASIS.

4. 3-2-65 CHEST FILM SHOWS CLOUDING ALONG LEFT THORAX AND PLEURAL THICKENING.

	TEST				FINDING					REGION	
NO-TEST	TESTN	TESTLOC	VERB-DONE	TESTDATE	NEG	BE-SHOW	CHANGE	STATUS	MED-FIND	POS	PT-BODY
1) NOT	X-RAY	CHEST	DONE	BETWEEN 4-22-64 and 6-10-64							
2)	FILM	CHEST		10-22-64	NO	SHOWED	CHANGE (SINCE 8-5-64)				
3)	X-RAYS		TAKEN	1-24-65				NEGATIVE	(FOR) METASTASIS		
4)	FILM	CHEST		3-2-65		SHOWS			CLOUDING	ALONG	(LEFT) THORAX
	FILM	CHEST		3-2-65		SHOWS			THICKENING		PLEURAL

Left adjuncts are placed in ( ) above the head noun; right adjuncts below the head noun.

relative pronoun by its antecedent; thus *fracture which may be pathological* becomes *fracture such that fracture may be pathological*. The parsed, regularized sentences are then moved, piece by piece, into the appropriate format slots by special formatting transformations. This last step involves rules specific to the language of the subfield (the specific sublanguage); the first two steps are general and would be used in the formatting of any sublanguage.

Because of the way in which the format is constructed, there is a close correspondence between word class membership and format column. However, for the cases where there is not a one-to-one correspondence between word class and format column, syntactic information is required in order to determine in which format slot a word should be placed. For example there is only one slot (TESTN) for words of the class TESTN (*X-ray, film*). Therefore the program needs only the word class membership to know where in the format to put word *X-ray*. However, there are two format slots for negatives, NO-TEST (negating the existence of a test) and NEG (negating the finding). If the input contains a negative, we determine which of these slots it should go into as illustrated by the following examples:

1. In the phrase *no metastasis, no* goes into NEG because it modifies a MED-FINDing noun.

2.   In *no X-rays* were taken, *no* goes into NO-TEST because it modifies a TESTN noun.

The formatting transformations move the words of a sentence into the appropriate format columns; they make use of information about the syntactic environment of a word where necessary to determine the appropriate format slot. Figure 8.2 shows the formatted sentences produced by this three-step process of parsing, application of English transformations, and application of formatting transformations.

8.1.3   *Filling in Implicit Information*

After the sentences have been automatically converted into tabular form by the formatting procedure, the implicit information available from context must be filled in to complete the informational representation.

One type of filling in has already been done: the English transformations have regularized conjunctional constructions, creating conjoined full assertions (see example 4 in the table). In addition, antecedents for pronouns and other types of referential expressions must be located and copied into the appropriate slots, as also the information that was omitted because it was clear from context.

The following example illustrates how the antecedent for a referential expression is found. In the phrase *11-5-62 no change from previous chest X-ray,* the phrase *since previous chest X-ray* refers to an earlier X-ray. *Previous* is the referential time expression; the program must find its antecedent, namely an exact date that identifies the chest X-ray being referred to. To do this, it searches backward in the formatted sentences to find the first sentence that has TESTN = *X-ray* or a synonym, TESTLOC = *chest,* and TESTDATE less than 11-5-62. If it finds such a line in the format, it has found the antecedent for *previous chest X-ray,* and can regularize it in the format by adding the specific date. If no antecedent is found for a referential expression, then an error message is printed out.

Certain pieces of information are omitted in the original text because they repeat words of a preceding sentence that sets the topic for the following sentences. For example given two sentences, *Chest films 10-15 infiltrate clear, Lung scarring still present,* the missing TEST information can be filled in for the second sentence by noting that it continues the topic (*chest films 10-15*) of the first sentence. We thus obtain a parallel "filled in" second sentence: *chest film 10-15 lung scarring still present.* (The "filling in" is actually done on the formatted sentences; the full text is used here merely for illustrative purposes.)

In other cases information is missing and there is no appropriate preceding sentence to set the topic, as is the case when an entire report consists of the phrase *Not done.* In such cases the program supplies certain "default" values characteristic of the subfield. For example in radiology reports, if a test name is omitted, and there is no preceding sentence setting the topic, then the default value for TESTN is *X-ray: Not done → X-ray not done.*

8.1.4 *Fact Retrieval from Information Formats*

Among specialists in information retrieval, the ability of a system to supply a user with specific information in response to an information request, as opposed to a complete document or citation that may be relevant to the request, is sometimes referred to as "fact retrieval" in contradistinction to "document retrieval" or "bibliographic retrieval." By linking the natural language information-formatting system described here to a retrieval program that can search the format columns of the data base for particular combinations of entries, we achieve a fact retrieval program that operates on natural language information.

The principal feature of the formats that facilitates this processing is that a specific type of information can be directly located by looking under the corresponding column heading. An additional feature is that the columns have been so defined that all entries in a given column have the same directionality. For example, in the radiology formats any entry in the CHANGE column is a word that indicates that a change has taken place. If a word occurs in a report that indicates the absence of change (such as *unchanged* or *same*), it will be factored into an entry in the NEG column of FINDING and the word *change* in the CHANGE column. As a result, some questions about a record can be answered by simply testing for the presence or absence of an entry in a particular column. More detailed questions, of course, can still test the value of a particular entry.

To verify that the formats are a suitable structure for fact retrieval, several routines that operate on the formatted radiology reports were programmed. A number of questions, such as whether any X-ray was taken in a given period and when it was done, could be answered directly by examining one or two format columns. A somewhat more complicated question is whether a report contains any abnormal or suspicious findings. A report contains such findings if any format line of the report contains such findings. Thus the problem reduces to the slightly simpler question, does a format line contain any abnormal or suspicious findings? This is answered by the following procedure:

A. If NO-TEST column is filled (no test was done), answer is *no;* else

B. If STATUS column (a column for normal findings) is filled and NEG column is empty, answer is *no;* else

C. If STATUS column is filled and NEG column is filled (e.g., *not normal*), answer is *yes;* else

D. If CHANGE column is filled (and value of column is not a word indicating improvement) and NEG column is empty (unnegated change), answer is *yes;* else

E. If CHANGE column is filled and NEG column is filled (no change), locate the format lines reporting the earlier test against which the current test is being compared and apply the procedure to those format lines. The answer obtained for those earlier lines is the appropriate answer for the current format line, since no change is reported. Else

F. If MED-FIND column is filled and NEG column is empty, answer is *yes.*

G. Otherwise answer is *no.*

This procedure gives the following results for the four formatted sentences of Fig. 8.2.

1. No (test A)
2. Answer obtained for formats for test of 8-5-64 (test E)
3. No (test B)
4. Yes (test F)

Figure 8.3 shows a summary table that was obtained automatically by processing the formatted radiology reports. Natural language processing was essential in calculating the recurrence column. The date of recurrence was defined by medical consultants to be the date of the first report of metastases. The logic for obtaining this information from the formatted reports is similar to that in the procedure just described. Such statistics are routinely required in research projects, but they normally involve a review of all the reports by doctors or data clerks.

8.2   Processing Clinical Narrative

A second, more ambitious, experiment in information formatting was begun in 1975, applying the LSP system to narrative documents in patient records. A sample of both out-patient and inpatient documents was analyzed manually and an information format was developed for the material. This format was implemented, and the grammar was expanded to cover additional "fragment" forms seen in these documents.

8.2.1   *Form of the Input Data*

The corpus of medical documents used in this development was obtained in machine-readable form from the Pediatrics Service of Bellevue Hospital. The computer-based health information system in use there at the time was part of a program to provide comprehensive health care to children and youth (Lyman, Tick, and Korein 1968, Lyman 1977). The form of the medical record in the system had pre-set paragraph and subparagraph headings within which any amount of free narrative was accepted (Korein 1970). Physician reports of out-patient visits, examinations, and hospitalizations were either handwritten or dictated and were keyed in on-line by medical typists with computer prompting of the paragraph structure appropriate to the type of document being entered. Documents were batch-processed daily and made available in whole or in part at sites of patient care.

From among the many document types in the system, it was decided to concentrate on hospital discharge summaries because of their comprehensive coverage of medical events and their importance for applications. A page from a pediatric discharge summary (PDS) is shown in Fig. 8.4. Although these documents contain a considerable range of types of information and vary in individual style, they still evidence the restricted and repetitive features of a sublanguage. Thus it was possible to establish the specialized word classes and the patterns of the word class co-occurrence from which the information format for this sublanguage could be defined.

Fig. 8.3   Computer-generated summary table.

PATIENT	SURGERY-DATE	REPORTS	POSITIVE-RECURRENCE	LOCATION	TIME-AFTER-SURGERY
30	04-17-67	8	YES	RIBS FEMORAL PELVIS VERTEBRAE SKULL	1 YEAR 9 MONTHS 11 DAYS
00	09-09-67	15	NONE	NIL	4 YEARS 7 MONTHS 3 DAYS
03	12-04-61	22	NONE	NIL	6 YEARS 11 MONTHS 4 DAYS
01	11-09-61	27	NONE	NIL	7 YEARS 2 MONTHS 4 DAYS
15	01-31-64	20	NONE	NIL	6 YEARS 0 MONTHS 15 DAYS
20	12-02-64	17	NONE	NIL	4 YEARS 7 MONTHS 26 DAYS
19	07-28-64	8	YES	PULMONARY	1 YEARS 4 MONTHS 1 DAY
21	04-13-65	13	NONE	NIL	4 YEARS 4 MONTHS 5 DAYS
24	08-26-65	15	NONE	NIL	3 YEARS 10 MONTHS 4 DAYS
26	12-08-65	10	NONE	NIL	2 YEARS 9 MONTHS 16 DAYS
27	03-17-66	11	NONE	NIL	3 YEARS 2 MONTHS 2 DAYS
08	02-20-62	23	NONE	NIL	7 YEARS 11 MONTHS 13 DAYS
09	03-02-62	24	NONE	NIL	9 YEARS 1 MONTHS 4 DAYS

TOTALS

TOTAL NUMBER OF PATIENTS 13
AVERAGE NUMBER OF REPORTS PER PATIENT 16
AVERAGE TIME BETWEEN VISITS 3 MONTHS
NUMBER OF PATIENTS WITH RECURRENCE 2
AVERAGE TIME - SURGERY TO RECURRENCE 18 MONTHS
NUMBER OF PATIENTS WITHOUT RECURRENCE 11
AVERAGE TIME TO LAST XRAY 65 MONTHS

Fig. 8.4   First page of a pediatric discharge summary (PDS).

```
(PDS)
IDENTIFICATION NO -
        HOSPITAL - PEDIATRIC DISCHARGE SUMMARY
NAME -                             SEX - F
DATE OF ADMISSION -                DATE OF DISCHARGE -
LOCATION -
BIRTH DATE -
##
DOCUMENT NUMBER

(REFERRING PHYSICIAN) -

(REASON FOR ADMISSION) - FEVER, COUGH, CHEST PAIN FOR 1 DAY.

(PERTINENT HISTORY)
  PRESENT ILLNESS - PATIENT DEVELOPED COUGH AND FEVER YESTERDAY.  THIS
  MORNING COMPLAINED OF RIGHT CHEST PAIN.  DURING EMERGENCY ROOM VISIT,
  RALES WERE HEARD AT RIGHT BASE.  TEMPERATURE WAS 102.6.  THERE HAS
  BEEN NO VOMITING OR DIARRHEA. CHEST XRAY SHOWED INFILTRATE IN RLL.
  SIGNIFICANT PAST HISTORY - PATIENT WITH SICKLE CELL DISEASE AND
  FREQUENT INFECTIONS, ESPECIALLY PNEUMONIA.  HAS HAD INFREQUENT
  APLASTIC CRISIS. TAKES PENICILLIN PROPHYLAXIS AND FOLIC ACID.
  PATIENT HAS 7 LIVING SIBS, 3 HAVE SICKLE CELL TRAIT.  ONE MALE SIB
  DIED IN CAR ACCIDENT.  HE HAD SEVERE SICKLE CELL DISEASE.  BOTH
  PARENTS HAVE TRAIT.

(EXAMINATION ON ADMISSION) - TMP 102.5, PU 144, RR 40,  WEIGHT 15 LBS.
  PATIENT WELL DEVELOPED, THIN.  IN MINIMAL RESPIRATORY DISTRESS.
  DECREASED BREATH SOUNDS AT BASE OF RIGHT LUNG AND SOME FINE RALES
  HEARD.  SYSTOLIC HEART MURMUR HEARD AT LEFT STERNAL BORDER. LIVER
  PALPABLE 4 CM, SPLEEN 2 CM.  FEW SHOTTY ANTERIOR AND POSTERIOR NODES.
  NO JAUNDICE.

(IMPRESSION ON ADMISSION) - PNEUMONIA.

(COURSE IN HOSPITAL) - PATIENT WAS GIVEN 1 PENICILLIN INJECTION AND
THEN STARTED ON AMPICILLIN 500 MG IV Q 6 HR.  OXYGEN THERAPY AND MIST
WERE GIVEN DURING THE FIRST FEW DAYS OF HOSPITALIZATION.  DURING THE
FIRST 6 DAYS PATIENT HAD FEVER OVER 101 DEGREES.  REPEAT CULTURES
FAILED TO CONFIRM A PATHOGEN.  TRANSFUSIONS WERE GIVEN ON 2 OCCASIONS
BECAUSE OF REDUCED HCT AND RETIC COUNT.  ERYTHROMYCIN WAS ADDED TO THE
AMPICILLIN ON THE 4TH HOSPITAL DAY.  DURING THE LAST WEEK OF
HOSPITALIZATION PATIENT WAS AFEBRILE, ACTIVE AND EATING WELL. RETIC
COUNT REMAINED DEPRESSED, 0.2% TO 5%, AND PREVENTED PATIENT FROM BEING
DISCHARGED WHEN SIGNS OF PNEUMONIA WERE GONE.

(STATUS AT DISCHARGE) - AFEBRILE.  LUNGS CLEAR.  EATING WELL.  RETICS
ON DAY BEFORE DISCHARGE WERE 9.2%.

(LABORATORY DATA)
  HEMATOLOGY - ADMISSION HCT 22.6%; RETICS 18%.  WBC 26,100 WITH 90%
  SEGS.
  URINE - URINALYSIS NORMAL.
  BLOOD CHEMISTRIES - NORMAL FOLLOWING HYDRATION.  BILIRUBIN 2.9 TOTAL.
  BACTERIOLOGY - NO PATHOGENS GROWN.
  OTHER - LUNG SCAN ON HOSPITAL DAY 4 SHOWED DEFECTS IN RML AND RLL AND
```

8.2.2 *Information Format for Clinical Narrative*

A schematic of the information format for clinical narrative is shown in Fig. 8.5.[4] It is perhaps easier to understand this information format by first considering groups of columns that constitute subunits of the larger all-inclusive table. We found it convenient to group together into one subunit all the columns concerned with TREATMENT and into another all those describing the PATIENT STATUS. Another subunit, headed PATIENT (PT), comprises the columns containing references to the patient and basic patient data such as age and sex. Further subdivisions within these major groupings have also been defined, so that the format for each sentence as represented in the machine is a tree structure. Later the trees are "flattened" to obtain a table of the type that was illustrated for the radiology material in Fig. 8.2.

Fig. 8.5 Format tree for hospital discharge summaries.

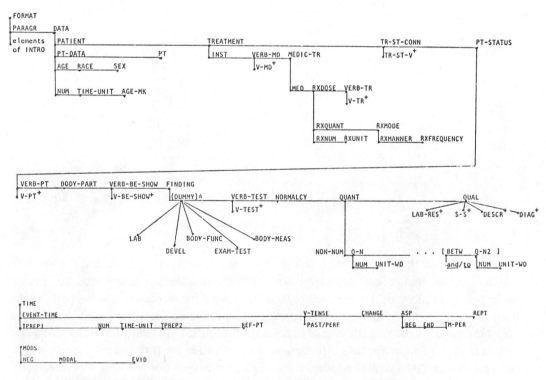

* The node DUMMY is replaced by one of its options, unless it is empty.

+ Nodes with + can have sister nodes MODS and TIME.

The **PATIENT STATUS** subunit of the format is illustrated by the output shown in Fig. 8.6 for the second sentence of the history paragraph of the document in Fig. 8.4. The printout begins with the code designation for the sentence, here HIPDS 8.1.2 (**HI**story paragraph of **P**ediatric **D**ischarge **S**ummary, **8**th document in set, **1**st subparagraph, **2**nd sentence). This is followed by the input sentence: *This morning complained of right chest pain,* followed by the word "LEFTOVERS" heading the list of sentence words not placed anywhere in the information format. (This is usually empty.) The format tree itself has a root node FORMAT, which in the case of Fig. 8.6 leads directly to DATA, and from there to the PATIENT STATUS subtree. To shorten the output, all empty nodes in the FORMAT TREE are suppressed. Thus, the formatted sentence shown in Figs. 8.6–8.10 have slightly different configurations; inside the computer the information format has a fixed structure.

Fig. 8.6   Information-formatting output for HIPDS 8.1.2.

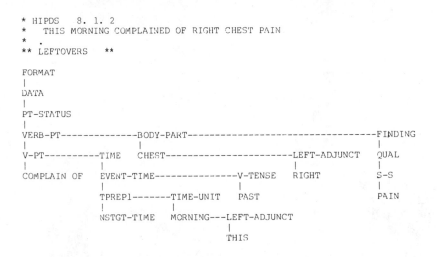

Looking into the **PATIENT STATUS (PT-STATUS)** subtree of the format as it appears in Fig. 8.6, we see that it has three elements: VERB-PT for occurrences of verbs that have a patient-word as subject (here *complain of*), BODY-PART for words designating parts of the body (here *right chest*), and FINDING for the whole range of items that might be asserted about the patient's state. In the case of Fig. 8.6 the finding is QUALitative, of the type sign or system (S-S), here *pain*. The time information is associated in the format with the verb occurrence; that is, a TIME subtree appears to the right of the verb slot V-PT. In this case, TIME has two elements EVENT-TIME and V-TENSE (for the tense of the verb). EVENT-TIME has place for a preposition under TPREP1, which here has the value NSTGT-TIME (from the parse tree node NSTGT for **noun string t**ime modifier), and place for the TIME-UNIT, which here is *morning* modified by the left adjunct *this*.

When the formatted sentence in Fig. 8.6 is combined with the others from the document in a document information table, it will occupy a single line of the table, e.g.,

CODE	V-PT	BODY-PART	S-S	EVENT-TIME
HIPDS 8.1.2	*complain of*	*chest, right*	*pain*	*morning, this*

However, to obtain this simple structuring of the information we must subject the sentence to the three stages of processing described earlier: parsing, to give the syntactic structure of the sentence; transformational decomposition, to regularize the parse tree; formatting transformations, to move syntactic units from the regularized parse tree into the format tree, retaining syntactic connections where needed, as in time information and negation.

A summary of these three steps as they apply to the sentence HIPDS 8.1.2 is the following. The parse identifies *this morning* as a time-phrase sentence adjunct (NSTGT) occurring before the subjectless fragment string *Complained of right chest pain*. Note that a selectional restriction applying between a subject noun and its verb was needed to rule out *this morning* as the subject of *complained of* in an analysis of this sentence as an instance of ASSERTION.[5] The transformational decomposition, operating on the output parse tree, fills out the fragment string to a full ASSERTION. It supplies a SUBJECT node and strips off the tense from the verb, placing the tense marker PAST as the value of the TENSE node in the ASSERTION subtree. The information-formatting transformations examine the medical subclassifications of the words under particular nodes of the regularized parse tree and transfer them to the appropriate format slots. In this case, a transformation recognizes *complain of* as patient-verb and places it in the V-PT slot of the format. Another transformation finds that the core noun *pain* of the object noun phrase *right chest pain* is a sign or symptom word and places it in the S-S slot. The left adjunct *chest*, modifying *pain*, is then examined and found to be a body-part word, so it is moved, along with its left adjunct *right,* into the BODY-PART slot. The time information in NSTGT (*this morning*) is transferred to the EVENT-TIME section of the format and associated with the V-PT verb *complained of*.[6]

Having seen one instance of the PATIENT-STATUS subtree, we may now consider a sentence that contains two instances of this structure joined by a connective. The first sentence of the history paragraph in Fig. 8.4 (HIPDS 8.1.1 *Patient developed cough and fever yesterday*) is such a sentence. The formatting output for this sentence is shown in Fig. 8.7. A CONNECTIVE slot precedes the two FORMAT instances, with the first of the two FORMATs being the one that corresponds to the first of the two sentence occurrences. (In an occurrence of a connective between a main clause and a subordinate string, the FORMAT for the main clause is first.)

Fig. 8.7   Information-formatting output for HIPDS 8.1.1.

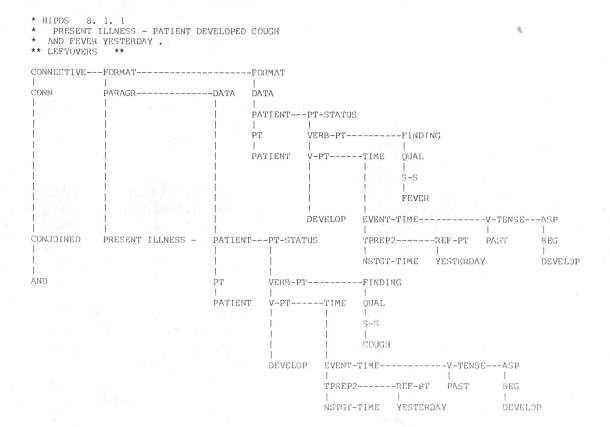

```
* HIPDS   8. 1. 1
*    PRESENT ILLNESS - PATIENT DEVELOPED COUGH
*    AND FEVER YESTERDAY .
** LEFTOVERS   **

CONNECTIVE---FORMAT--------------------FORMAT
|              |                       |
CONN           PARAGR-------------DATA  DATA
|              |                   |    |
|              |                   |    PATIENT---PT-STATUS
|              |                   |    |         |
|              |                   |    PT        VERB-PT----------FINDING
|              |                   |    |         |               |
|              |                   |    PATIENT   V-PT------TIME   QUAL
|              |                   |              |         |      |
|              |                   |              |         |      S-S
|              |                   |              |         |      |
|              |                   |              |         |      FEVER
|              |                   |              |         |
|              |                   |              DEVELOP   EVENT-TIME------------V-TENSE---ASP
|              |                   |                        |               |        |
CONJOINED      PRESENT ILLNESS -   PATIENT---PT-STATUS       TPREP2-------REF-PT   PAST   BEG
|              |                   |         |              |               |              |
|              |                   |         |              NSTGT-TIME   YESTERDAY        DEVELOP
|              |                   |         |
AND            PT                  VERB-PT----------FINDING
               |                   |               |
               PATIENT             V-PT------TIME   QUAL
                                   |         |      |
                                   |         |      S-S
                                   |         |      |
                                   |         |      COUGH
                                   |         |
                                   DEVELOP   EVENT-TIME------------V-TENSE---ASP
                                             |               |        |
                                             TPREP2-------REF-PT   PAST   BEG
                                             |               |              |
                                             NSTGT-TIME   YESTERDAY        DEVELOP
```

In the first **FORMAT** subtree in Fig. 8.7, the first subnode is **PARAGR**, to cover the paragraph heading that appeared just before this sentence in the document. The **DATA** in this **FORMAT** subtree contains a **PATIENT** unit (just the word *patient* under the heading **PT**) and a **PT-STATUS** unit. Here, **PT-STATUS** has a **FINDING** portion that contains a **QUAL** node leading to an **S-S** node (here, *cough*). And, as in the preceding figure, it has a **V-PT** node with associated time information. The verb in this case is *develop*, which, in addition to its major sublanguage classification, carries time-aspect information. Thus, in the **TIME** subtree attached to the right of the verb slot **V-PT**, *develop* appears again as the entry under **BEG** (for beginning-indicator) under **ASP** (for verb-aspect).

A feature to notice in the formatting of a sentence with a conjunction is the effect of the transformational expansion of the conjunct. The words that were repeated implicitly in the conjunct (here the verb *developed* and the associated time information *yesterday*) are copied into corresponding positions in the second **FORMAT** occurrence.

Another type of connective is illustrated by the formatting output for HIPDS 8.1.3, shown in Fig. 8.8. Here the first FORMAT subtree following the CONNECTIVE corresponds to the main clause (*rales were heard at the right base*) and the second FORMAT, represents the medical-event information in the time expression *during emergency room visit*. The TIME subtree of the first FORMAT carries the EVENT-TIME prepositional phrase *during visit*. However, this time phrase also tells us that there was in fact an emergency room visit, so the phrase is formatted as a second assertion. The connective in this case is an implicit relative clause (the event was during a visit that was an emergency room visit), which is expanded so as to repeat the antecedent time-reference point (*visit*). All this stored information is abbreviated in the subnode under CONN of CONNECTIVE.

Fig. 8.8   Information-formatting output for HIPDS 8.1.3.

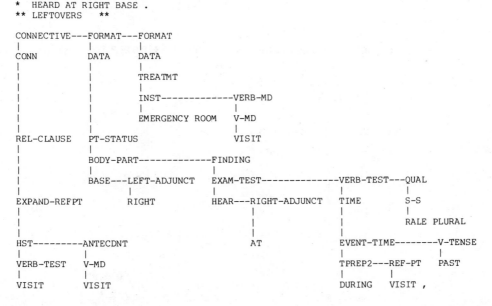

```
*  HIPDS    8. 1. 3
*    DURING EMERGENCY ROOM VISIT , RALES WERE
*  HEARD AT RIGHT BASE .
** LEFTOVERS    **


CONNECTIVE---FORMAT---FORMAT
|              |         |
CONN          DATA      DATA
|              |         |
|              |        TREATMT
|              |         |
|              |        INST-------------VERB-MD
|              |         |                |
|              |        EMERGENCY ROOM   V-MD
|              |                          |
REL-CLAUSE    PT-STATUS                  VISIT
|              |
|             BODY-PART------------FINDING
|              |                     |
|             BASE---LEFT-ADJUNCT   EXAM-TEST--------------VERB-TEST---QUAL
|              |        |            |                      |          |
EXPAND-REFPT         RIGHT          HEAR---RIGHT-ADJUNCT   TIME        S-S
|                                     |                     |          |
|                                     |                     |         RALE PLURAL
|                                     |                     |
HST---------ANTECDNT                 AT                    EVENT-TIME--------V-TENSE
|            |                                              |                 |
VERB-TEST   V-MD                                           TPREP2---REF-PT   PAST
|            |                                              |        |
VISIT       VISIT                                          DURING   VISIT ,
```

The next sentence of the history narrative, HIPDS 8.1.4, brings into play another type of FINDING in the PT-STATUS unit of the format. Figure 8.9 shows the formatted version of this short sentence (*temperature was 102.6*). Under FINDING there is a node for BODY-MEASure (here *temperature*), a node VERB-TEST for V-TEST verbs (here *be*) that occur with test and measure nouns, and a QUANT node for the NUMerical finding (here *102.6*).

Fig. 8.9   Information-formatting output for HIPDS 8.1.4.

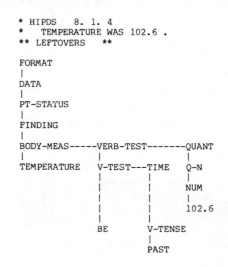

```
* HIPDS   8. 1. 4
*    TEMPERATURE WAS 102.6 .
** LEFTOVERS   **

FORMAT
|
DATA
|
PT-STATUS
|
FINDING
|
BODY-MEAS-----VERB-TEST-------QUANT
|               |             |
TEMPERATURE   V-TEST---TIME   Q-N
              |        |      |
              |        |      NUM
              |        |      |
              |        |      102.6
              |        |
              BE       V-TENSE
                       |
                       PAST
```

Fig. 8.10   Information-formatting output for HIPDS 8.1.5.

```
* HIPDS   8. 1. 5
*    THERE HAS BEEN NO VOMITING OR DIARRHEA .
** LEFTOVERS   **

CONNECTIVE---FORMAT---FORMAT
|            |        |
CONN         DATA     DATA
|            |        |
|            |        PT-STATUS
|            |        |
|            |        FINDING
|            |        |
|            |        QUAL
|            |        |
|            |        S-S--------TIME------MODS
|            |        |          |        |
|            |        DIARRHEA   V-TENSE   NEG---EVID
|            |        |          |         |     |
|            |        |          |         NO    THERE BE
|            |        |          |
CONJOINED    PT-STATUS           PRESENT PERF
|            |
AND          FINDING
             |
             QUAL
             |
             S-S--------TIME------MODS
             |          |        |
             VOMITING   V-TENSE   NEG---EVID
                        |         |     |
                        |         NO    THERE BE
                        |
                        PRESENT PERF
```

As a last example of a format-tree, the output for the next sentence, HIPDS 8.1.5 (*There has been no vomiting or diarrhea*), is shown in Fig. 8.10. Here, the interesting feature is the transformation of the connective construction *No x or y* to *No x and no y*. Also the presence of MODS covering NEGation and EVIDential status. The form *there is . . .* is seen as an EVIDential modifier, indicating positive assertion of the finding. The fact that the positive assertion is negated (by the nonempty NEG) is checked during retrieval.

8.2.3 *Information Table of a Patient Document*

When the format trees for the sentences of a document are collected, they can be compressed into an **information table** for the document. One form of such a table is illustrated in Figs. 8.11–8.13. The column heads are a selection of nodes of the format tree, mainly terminal nodes. The rows correspond to the format trees of the successive sentences, here "flattened" so that a row-column entry contains just the words that appeared in the format under the node named as column head.

Fig. 8.11 Portion of information table for admission and history paragraphs.

CODE	CONN	V-PT	BDYPART	LAB	DEVEL	EXMTEST	BDYMEAS	V-TEST	NNUM	Q-N	S-S	DESCR	DIAG	MODS	EVNTTIME	CHNGE ASP
ADPDS 8 1 1	,										FEVER				FOR 1 DAY	
ADPDS 8 1 1	,										COUGH				FOR 1 DAY	
ADPDS 8 1 1	,		CHEST								PAIN				FOR 1 DAY	
HIPDS 8 1 1	AND	DEVELOP									COUGH				NSTGT-TIME YESTERDAY	DEVELOP
HIPDS 8 1 1	AND	DEVELOP									FEVER				NSTGT-TIME YESTERDAY	DEVELOP
HIPDS 8 1 2		COMPLAIN OF	CHEST RIGHT								PAIN				NSTGT-TIME MORNING THIS	
HIPDS 8 1 3	REL-CL		BASE RIGHT		HEAR	AT					RALE PLURAL				DURING VISIT ,	
HIPDS 8 1 3	REL-CL															
HIPDS 8 1 4							TEMPERA TURE	BE	102.6							
HIPDS 8 1 5	AND										VOMITING			NO THERE BE		
HIPDS 8 1 5	AND										DIARRHEA			NO THERE BE		
HIPDS 8 1 6		CHEST RLL IN		X-RAY				SHOW			INFILTRA TE					

Fig. 8.12   Portion of information table for examination paragraph.

CODE	CONN	V–PT	BDYPART	LAB	DEVEL	EXMTEST	BDYMEAS	V–TEST	NNUM	Q–N	S–S	DESCR	DIAG	MODS	EVNTTIME	CHNGE	ASP
EXPDS 8 1 1	,						TEMPERA TURE			102.5							
EXPDS 8 1 1	,						PULSE			144							
EXPDS 8 1 1	,						RESPIRA TIUN RATE			40							
EXPDS 8 1 1	,						WEIGHT			15 POUND							
EXPDS 8 1 2	,				WELL DEVEL OPED												
EXPDS 8 1 2	,										THIN						
EXPDS 8 1 3			RESPIRATO RY							MINI MAL	DISTRESS IN						
EXPDS 8 1 4	AND		BASE AT LUNG OF RIGHT			BREATH SOUND PLURAL											DECRE ASED
EXPDS 8 1 4	AND					HEAR		FINE			RALE PLURAL SOME						
EXPDS 8 1 5			HEART LEFT STERNAL BORDER			HEAR AT					MURMUR SYSTOLIC						
EXPDS 8 1 6			LIVER			PALPABLE				4 CENTI METER							
EXPDS 8 1 6			SPLEEN							2 CENTI METER							
EXPDS 8 1 7	AND		NODE PLURAL ANTERIOR					FEW			SHOTTY						
EXPDS 8 1 7	AND		NODE PLURAL POSTERIOR					FEW			SHOTTY						
EXPDS 8 1 8												JAUNDICE NO					

Fig. 8.13   Portion of information table for course-in-hospital paragraph.

CODE	CONN	PT	V–MD	MED	RXDOSE	V–TR	MODS	EVNTTIME	CHANGE	ASP
COPDS 8 1 1	AND	PATIENT	GIVE	PENICILLIN						
COPDS 8 1 1	AND	PATIENT		AMPICILLIN	500 MILLIGRAM INTRAVENO USLY Q 6 HR					START ON
COPDS 8 1 2	AND		GIVE			THERAPY OXYGEN		DURING FEW FIRST DAY THE OF HOSPITALIZ ATION		
COPDS 8 1 2	AND		GIVE	MIST				DURING FEW FIRST DAY THE OF HOSPITALIZ ATION		
COPDS 8 1 3		PATIENT								

Figures 8.11 and 8.12 show the PT-STATUS section of the information table for sections of two paragraphs from document 8 of the corpus (PDS8, Fig. 8.4). Figure 8.11 contains the rows corresponding to the paragraph reason-for-admission and the first six sentences of the paragraph pertinent-history. The format trees for five of these sentences (HIPDS 1.1.1–1.1.5) were displayed and described in Sec. 8.2.2.

Figure 8.13 shows part of the PATIENT unit of the format (just the column PT) along with columns from the TREATMENT unit of the format for the first few sentences of the course-in-hospital paragraph. Space does not permit discussion of this portion of the format. However, it should be noted that the TIME and MODS unit of the format appears wherever an entry is of the type that can take time modifiers or modals (there are nine such nodes in the present definition of the clinical format tree). Thus, columns from this unit appear in all three figures. It should be noted that some words from the sentences will not appear in the tables because they lie in portions of the format that are not reproduced here. Thus, in Fig. 8.11, the second row of HIPDS 8.1.3 lacks *emergency room*, which is the entry under INSTitution in the TREATMENT unit of the format, and also lacks an occurrence of *visit* under V-MD in that unit.

NOTES

1. This work is described more fully in Hirschman, Grishman, and Sager 1976, Hirschman and Grishman 1977, Sager et al. 1977. In addition, a natural language question-answering system that operates on a data base of formatted radiology reports is being developed. For this, see Grishman and Hirschman 1978.

2. For a fuller discussion of the design of an information format, with particular reference to the format for hospital discharge summaries treated in Sec. 8.2, see Hirschman and Sager 1981.

3. A more detailed description of this work is contained in Sager 1978, Sager and Hirschman 1979, and Hirschman and Sager 1981.

4. From Sager and Hirschman 1979, where examples and a detailed description of the information-formatting process are given in Sec. 3 and 4 by Dr. Hirschman.

5. The restriction is WSEL2, similar to the selectional restriction WSEL1, which was explained in detail in Sec. 5.6. In the parsing of material that contains fragment strings, the full ASSERTION is tried first.

6. The treatment of time is an important part of the processing of medical documents. For this, see the work of Dr. Hirschman in Sec. 4.4 and 4.5 of Sager and Hirschman 1978 and Hirschman 1981.

Chapter 9   Applications of Medical Information Formatting

In the applications of the method of information processing described in this book—information formatting—the essential point is that the information that originally was presented in natural language has been arranged by the computer in a structured form that permits computer programs to answer complex informational queries about the contents of the documents. A retrieval program operating on formatted discharge summaries, for example, can establish not only that a given diagnosis word was mentioned, but that a diagnosis was positively asserted (or denied, or suggested). It can also supply a list of the symptoms that were manifested and their time sequence in relation to tests and treatments that were given, all by reference to the entries in the relevant columns of the format. This chapter describes several pilot applications using information-formatted patient documents. In each case, retrieval programs obtain answers to queries by searching particular columns of the format for specified entry values and checking for the presence or absence of certain other column entries in the same row of the table.[1] In addition, when called for, the relation between rows (mainly time sequences) is checked.

Section 9.1 describes an application in which documents are processed in order to determine whether the health care reported in the document meets physician-specified health care criteria. A sequence of rather complicated tests is performed on each document and those documents that do not pass the tests are flagged for manual review. Section 9.2 describes a retrieval operation in which the intent is to pull all the documents that report a specified constellation of medical events. The program generates a table summarizing the particulars of the events in the retrieved documents, such as might be useful in clinical research or in preparing a hospital staff conference.

Although these applications are different in intent and the retrieval programs differ correspondingly, the programs draw upon a common body of routines. For example, one linguistic routine used very often checks whether a given column-entry has an associated MODS entry that indicates negation or lack of certainty. Routines involving the TIME columns are frequently used, for example to determine whether an event was at or near the time of admission or discharge. An example of a routine with medical content is the one that tests for fever, which will be outlined. It is used in a negative version in the application of the health care evaluation program illustrated in Sec. 9.1, where the question is whether the patient was reported afebrile at discharge; it is used in a positive version in the retrieval program illustrated in Sec. 9.2 as part of the test for signs of infection, since fever is a sign of infection.

9.1   Health Care Evaluation[2]

Increasing concern with the quality and cost of medical services has led to a number of proposed systems for the documentation and assessment of health care. One system of wide currency is the Performance Evaluation Procedure (PEP) of the Joint Commission on Accreditation of Hospitals (JCAH 1974). A set of health care audit criteria for each disease to be audited is stated on a data sheet that is filled out by reference to the patient record. A data sheet of this type for pneumonia in sickle cell disease is shown in Fig. 9.1. For each criterion the standard (expected value) is either 100 percent (element is present) or 0 percent (element is absent). If the standard is met, the element column (EL) is checked. Sometimes alternative ways of meeting the criterion are stated. If these are present the exception (EX) column is checked. A failure to meet a criterion is registered by a check in the variation (VAR) column.

The data sheet in Fig. 9.1 was filled out by a physician working only with the discharge summary so that the results could be compared with those generated by the computer program operating on the information-formatted version of the same document. Four discharge summaries for pneumonia in sickle cell disease were available to test the programmed health care evaluation criteria for this condition. One discharge summary was used to debug the program. The remaining three summaries were then run through the program to produce evaluation charts, which were compared with the results obtained for these three documents by the physician. The computer-generated chart for PDS 8 (the document in Fig. 8.4) is shown in Fig. 9.2.

For purposes of comparison between the physician-coded and computer-generated charts, each line with an entry under EL/EX/VAR was counted as one item. The criterion for pneumonia in sickle cell disease contained 33 entries; for the three test documents, they agreed on an average of 30 of 33 entries per document (91 percent). There were a total of nine discrepancies between the manual and the computer results for the three test documents. The breakdown of the nine discrepancies can be summarized briefly as follows:

3   bugs in retrieval concerning time and negation

3   differences in the interpretation of the audit criteria by the manual coder and that given by our medical consultant at the time the computer program was written

2   superficial computer bugs

1   failure to include a term in a synonym list for a medical condition.

As an example of one of the routines used in the health care evaluation program, consider criterion 7 in Figs. 9.1 and 9.2. Under Discharge Status, criterion 7 is "afebrile," and the associated standard is 100 percent. The medical clerk is instructed to write "100 percent" if the patient record contains the assertion that the patient was afebrile at discharge or contains a recorded temperature of less than 100.2 degrees (pediatric "normal") within 48 hours of discharge. A sketch of the logic of the routine that searches the formatted discharge summary for this information is the following:

In DATA columns

Either both S-S contains *fever* or *febrile* and associated MODS has non-empty NEG
    (e.g., *no fever, afebrile*)

Or   both BODY-MEASURE contains *temperature, temp*, or *tmp* and one of the following holds:
        1. associated MODS has nonempty NEG (e.g., *no temperature*)
        2. NORMALCY is nonempty (e.g., *normal temperature*)
        3. QUANT contains a number $\leqslant 100.2$.

In TIME columns

Both   REFPT contains either *discharge* or a date that matches the given date of discharge

And   either other columns of EVENT-TIME are empty or the calculated value t of EVENT-TIME is within 48 hours of the given date of discharge
        (e.g., *the evening before discharge*).

In the document of Fig. 8.4, the paragraph status-at-discharge contains the word *afebrile*; the formatted sentence has *febrile* under S-S and the NEG column of the associated MODS unit filled with NEG-PREFIX, the representation of the prefix *a-* of *afebrile*. The first test of the DATA columns clearly applies.

With regard to the test of the TIME columns, the first test succeeds because the event-time "discharge" had been filled in from the paragraph heading "status-at-discharge" dur-

Fig. 9.1 Audit criteria: pneumonia in sickle cell disease (portion of PEP data sheet).

PNEUMONIA IN SICKLE CELL DISEASE	STD %	EL	EX		VAR
<u>Diagnosis of Pneumonia</u>					
1. Chest x-ray positive (or A + B)	100%	✓			
A. Positive throat culture					
B. Two of following in history č/or exam.					
(1) Chest pain			✓		
(2) Dyspnea or respiratory distress			✓		
(3) Rales in lung(s)			✓		
(4) Cough			✓		
(5) Rib or sternal retraction					
<u>Diagnosis of Sickle Cell Disease</u>					
2. One of following:	100%	✓			
(1) Positive sickle cell preparation					
(2) Hemoglobin electrophoresis = HgS					
(3) Statement in history "known sickler" or equivalent		✓			
<u>Special Procedures</u>					
3. Blood culture at admission	100%				✓
4. CSF culture if temp elevation persists	"				✓
5. Tuberculin test if not done in past year	"				✓
6. Monitoring of hematocrit or hemoglobin (or)	"	✓			
A. hematocrit or hemoglobin stable					
<u>Discharge Status</u>					
7. Afebrile	100%	✓			
8. Chest x-ray shows improvement	"				✓
9. Lungs clear or improved on examination	"	✓			
10. Plan for on-going care	"	✓			
11. <u>Length of Stay</u> - 4 to 10 days (or A or B)	100%				
A. Transferred or signed out or died					
B. Complications of pneumonia					✓
12. <u>Mortality</u>	0%				
<u>Complications of Pneumonia</u>					
13. Pleural fluid or Empyema	0%	✓			
CM = Aspiration					
14. Meningitis	0%	✓			
CM = Positive CSF					
15. Pneumothorax	0%	✓			
CM = Chest suction					
16. Lung Abscess	0%	✓			
CM = Antibiotics					

Fig. 9.2 Computer-generated health care evaluation chart.

```
PEP CRITERIA - PNEUMONIA IN SICKLE CELL DISEASE


                                              STD    EL    EX     VAR
(DIAGNOSIS OF PNEUMONIA)
(1 CHEST X-RAY POSITIVE (OR A + B))           100%   YES   O
(1 A POSITIVE THROAT CULTURE)                        O     O
(1 B TWO OF THE FOLLOWING IN HISTORY AND/OR EXAM)    O     YES
(1 B (1) CHEST PAIN)                                 O     YES
(1 B (2) DYSPNEA OR RESPIRATORY DISTRESS)            O     YES
(1 B (3) RALES IN LUNG (S))                          O     YES
(1 B (4) COUGH)                                      O     YES
(1 B (5) RIB OR STERNAL RETRACTION)                  O     O
(DIAGNOSIS OF SICKLE CELL DISEASE)
(2 ONE OF FOLLOWING)                          100%   YES   O
(2 (1) POSITIVE SICKLE CELL PREPARATION)             O     O
(2 (2) HEMOGLOBIN ELECTROPHORESIS = HGS)             O     O
(2 (3) STATEMENT IN HISTORY 'KNOWN SICKLER' OR EQUIVALENT)  O  YES
(SPECIAL PROCEDURES)
(3 BLOOD CULTURE AT ADMISSION)                100%   O     O      YES
(4 CSF CULTURE IF TEMP ELEVATION PERSISTS)    100%   O     O      YES
(5 TUBERCULIN TEST IF NOT DONE IN PAST YEAR)  100%   O     O      YES
(6 MONITORING OF HEMATOCRIT OR HEMOGLOBIN (OR))  100%  YES  O
(6 A HEMATOCRIT OR HEMOGLOBIN STABLE)                O     O
(DISCHARGE STATUS)
(7 AFEBRILE)                                  100%   YES   O
(8 CHEST X-RAY SHOWS IMPROVEMENT)             100%   O     O      YES
(9 LUNGS CLEAR OR IMPROVED ON EXAMINATION)    100%   YES   O
(10 PLAN FOR ONGOING CARE)                    100%   YES   O
(11 LENGTH OF STAY - 4 TO 10 DAYS)            100%   O     O      YES
(11 A TRANSFERRED OR SIGNED OUT OR DIED)             O     O
(11 B COMPLICATIONS OF PNEUMONIA)                    O     O
(12 MORTALITY)                                0%     YES   O
(COMPLICATIONS OF PNEUMONIA)
(13 PLEURAL FLUID OR EMPYEMA)                 0%     YES   O
(13 CM = ASPIRATION)                                 O     O
(14 MENINGITIS)                               0%     YES   O
(14 CM = POSITIVE CSF)                               O     O
(15 PNEUMOTHORAX)                             0%     YES   O
(15 CM = CHEST SUCTION)                              O     O
(16 LUNG ABSCESS)                             0%     YES   O
(16 CM = ANTIBIOTICS)                                O     O


(FOR EL 4 IT WAS NOTED ONLY THAT TEMPERATURE ELEVATION PERSISTS)



    ABBREVIATIONS:

        CSF = CEREBROSPINAL FLUID
        CM  = CRITICAL MANAGEMENT
```

ing a stage of format-normalization preceding retrieval. "Normalization," or "filling-in-from-context," was described in connection with formatted radiology reports in Sec. 8.1.3. A similar process is carried out on the formatted hospital discharge summaries. However, in the case of the discharge summaries, the major type of implicit information that must be made explicit is the time of each reported event, at least the time relative to other events. Not only is this information important in itself, as in this example where the time "at discharge" is part of the query. Having a time associated with each format line is important in distinguishing different events that have the same "name" (the different events named *fever* that may occur at admission, in the course in the hospitalization, at discharge).

9.2   Organization of Patient Data[3]

Suppose a collection of discharge summaries has been information-formatted. This can serve as a data base for clinical investigations. If a hospital had such a collection of documents on patients with sickle cell disease, for example, it might wish to compare its own experience with what is reported in the literature about the disease. Statements from the literature could be programmed as retrieval requests addressed to the hospital's data base of formatted discharge summaries. To demonstrate this possibility, we programmed such a retrieval on our small data base of computer-formatted hospital discharge summaries.

The literature states that the condition in sickle cell disease know as painful crisis is often precipitated by infection. The corresponding question for the data base is: In how many instances did patients hospitalized with painful crisis and sickle cell disease have evidence of possible infection prior to the onset of painful crisis? More precisely, we wish to retrieve all the discharge summaries that meet three conditions: (1) Painful crisis is reported in the document. (2) Infection or a sign of infection is reported in the document. (3) The time of the reported infection is earlier than the time of the painful crisis. "Painful crisis" and "infection" name routines that check particular columns of the format for the presence of words indicative of the condition. These lists are given by the physician. For example, the PAINFUL CRISIS word list is: CRISIS, SICKLE CELL CRISIS, PAINFUL CRISIS, HAND-FOOT SYNDROME. Using these lists, the routine PAINFUL CRISIS checks for any one of the three sets of conditions.

1. The DIAGNOSIS column contains a CRISIS-WORD, and a routine called CHECK-REAL exits '+'. This routine determined whether a column-entry is free of negation and uncertainty. This test of the syntax is important since we would not want to accept, say "no evidence of crisis" as an instance of "crisis."

2. The BODY-PART column has an EXTREMITY-WORD or ABDOMEN-WORD and the SIGN-SYMPTOM column has a PAIN-, SWELLING-, or WARM-WORD. This covers such occurrences as *She developed painful hands; slight residual swelling of both feet.* Again, the entry must not be negated or uncertain, as determined by the CHECK-REAL routine.

3. Occurrences like *Patient refuses to stand on left foot,* an indication of pain in an extremity, are caught by (3). BODY-PART has EXTREMITY-WORD (*foot*) and the DESCRIPTOR column has a MOVE-WORD (*walk, stand, stood*). This time the routine CHECK-REAL should find NEGATION.

The INFECTION routine of the retrieval program is similar in form to the PAINFUL CRISIS routine. The TIME routines are of a more general linguistic character. They assign an event-time to each row of the format, within the limits of what is stated or implied in the narrative. From this, relative time of occurrence of two events reported in the documents can be computed.

When we applied the retrieval sketched here to our small data base, four documents were retrieved and a summary table was printed; Table 9.1 is derived from the computer-generated table. It showed the document number, patient's age, the symptom of infection that preceded painful crisis, and the time of occurrence of the symptom relative to admission.

What this experiment demonstrates is the possibility of organizing patient data in different ways by dividing the patient documents into subsets according to specified criteria. When the documents are in information-formatted form, this job can be done automatically by retrieval programs of the type illustrated here. The apparatus for information-formatting is considerable, but its result is a data base of information that can be used for many purposes.

In medicine, such a data base of patient records has potential application in a number of areas, outlined in Table 9.2. In research it can be used for the identification of patterns of disease, for example features of cases of sickle cell patients who have many infections in contrast with those who do not; also genetic, familial, and environmental factors in disease can be identified.

Table 9.1

Retrieval Result

Document #	Patient Age	Sympton of Possible Infection Preceding Painful Crisis	Time of Sympton Relative to Admission
XXX570	8 MO	105 degree fever	Adm – 1 day
XXX571	1 YR	Vomiting	Adm – 18 hr
XXX572	1 YR 2 MO	Watery stool plural	Adm – 4 day
XXX574	2 YR 5 MO	Fever, anorexia	Adm – 2.5 week

Table 9.2

Potential Applications of Linguistic Processing

Research
        Identification of patterns of disease
        Identification of genetic, familial, environmental factors in disease
        Use of previous cases as controls in clinical trials
        Identification of adverse reactions to procedures and treatments

Education
        Clinical conferences—undergraduate and postgraduate

Health Care Evaluation
        Medical audit/quality assessment of performance in patient care
        Assessment of patterns of health care

From a large data base of this type, cases suitable as controls in clinical trials could be located, and adverse correlates of particular treatments could be established.

In education, conferences could profit from comparing the hospital's own experience with the literature, as illustrated in the retrieval described in this section.

In health care, retrieval programs operating on formatted discharge summaries can determine whether discharge summaries meet audit criteria for quality assessment, as described in Sec. 9.1.[5]

NOTES

1. More precisely, the programs operate on the format trees in "unflattened" form. The row-column concept is still applicable, though in fact the operations are tree searches.

2. Description of this application appears in Sager and Lyman 1978, Hirschman, Sager, and Lyman 1979, Hirschman, Story, and Marsh forthcoming.

3. A fuller presentation of this work is given in Sager, Hirschman, and Lyman 1978.

4. From Sager and Hirschman 1979, where examples and a detailed description of the information-formatting process are given in Sec. 3 and 4 by Dr. Hirschman.

5. I am indebted to Dr. Lyman for discussions of the potential applications of linguistic processing in medical documentation.

Chapter 10　Applications in Teaching

The size and complexity of the Linguistic String Project grammar, described in Part 2, may seem forbidding to the reader who is thinking of applications in teaching or in other specialized domains. It is therefore important to point out that the grammar need not be used in its entirety. In addition to its use in automatic language processing, the grammar can be viewed as a resource to be drawn upon for particular uses. In computational applications, the value of having a large tested grammar available is that parts of the grammar can be added as needed with the assurance that the parts will fit together without redundancy or conflict. This avoids a difficulty that small systems face on expansion; it often happens that the initial implementation works well for the initial corpus but becomes unwieldy as more and more sentence types are covered. Similarly, in teaching a language, it is important to provide a framework in which newly learned rules and constructions can be related in an orderly fashion to those already mastered.

The string grammar, in the manner in which it has been implemented, is a naturally appropriate tool in this respect. Whether it is used in conjunction with a computer or purely as source material, one can start with a very elementary grammar and build it up step by step, using the BNF definitions as the basis for selecting what each stage of the grammar development should cover. This approach has been used successfully in teaching computational linguistics. In teaching languages it affords a rational method for teaching the principles of sentence construction and for introducing in a graded manner the means of enriching the basic language structures.

Naomi Sager, Natural Language Information Processing:　A Computer Grammar of English and Its Applications

Copyright © 1981 by Addison-Wesley Publishing Company, Inc., Advanced Book Program.　　ISBN 0-201-06769-2

10.1   **Computational Linguistics**

There are a number of ways in which the material in this book and related materials developed by the Linguistic String Project[1] can be used for teaching computational linguistics, on both the introductory and the advanced level. Students need not have a background in either computer science or linguistics in order to understand the principles of language analysis and to use the computer for language processing. One can build up the concepts of language structure in a logical way, drawing on the students' own knowledge of the language in relation to the constructs of string and transformational analysis. At New York University students who have never used a computer before learn quite quickly how to write a small computer grammar and how to do computer parsing as a basis for further linguistic and computational projects. Depending on the interests of students, the various applications of automated language processing in information systems, artificial intelligence, medical computing, and other areas can be then explored in more advanced courses.

One method students seem to enjoy and to learn from is to start with a very small grammar and build it up gradually, first in the whole class and then on an individual basis or in small groups. Figure 10.1 shows a very simple grammar and lexicon that can be used for this purpose. When these are input to the LSP system with the proper control cards, parses are obtained for such sentences as *My cat eats fish, What a cat eats eats fish, Happy cats generally eat what they fish, Cats fish to eat,* and so on. Important points about language analysis and about computer language processing are raised by the machine performance in parsing such sentences with the simple grammar. A trace of the parsing process illustrates how a top-down parser works and how the lexical categories of words are coordinated with the grammar in natural language parsing. The parses themselves illustrate the limits of context-free parsing and the need for restrictions since some wrong analyses will be obtained and many wrong sentences can be parsed with the same grammar. The particular grammar shown in Fig. 10.1 also illustrates the "PN problem" (see Sec. 5.4) since it provides for prepositional phrases in several syntactic slots. The parses for a sentence such as *My cat eats fish with fins* can stimulate a lively discussion of ambiguity and serve as the starting point for an analysis of different types and sources of ambiguity. (It should be noted that *even* and *only* were not given the adverb (D) classification in the introductory lexicon shown in Fig. 10.1, in order to illustrate the possible use of literals in an BNF definition, in this case in the definition LPROR.)

The first step in enriching such a simple grammar is to provide subclassifications (attributes) for the words in the lexicon and restrictions in the grammar that test for attribute compatability so as to eliminate wrong parses. For example, one might wish to develop a simple restriction that would cause the parser to reject *My cat eats they*. The Restriction Language provides a vehicle for writing restrictions. The basic RL statement types can be learned rather easily, and when the appropriate lists and simple routines are added to the simple grammar, restrictions can be written without much difficulty.

Fig. 10.1   Introductory class grammar.

```
*BNF
<SENTENCE> ::= <CENTER> ?.?.
<CENTER>    ::= <ASSERTION>.
<ASSERTION>::= <SA> <SUBJECT> <SA> <VERB> <SA> <OBJECT> <SA>.
<SA>        ::= <*D> / <*INT> / <PN> / <*NULL>.
<PN>        ::= <*P> <NSTG>.
<SUBJECT>   ::= <NSTG>.
<NSTG>      ::= <LNR> / <LPROR> / <NREP>.
<LNR>       ::= <LN> <*N> <RN>.
<LN>        ::= <TPOS> <APOS>.
<TPOS>      ::= <*T> / <*NULL>.
<APOS>      ::= <*ADJ> / <*NULL>.
<RN>        ::= <PN> / <*NULL>.
<LPROR>     ::= <LPRO> <*PRO> <RN>.
<LPRO>      ::= ONLY / EVEN / <*NULL>.
<NREP>      ::= WHAT <SUBJECT> <SA> <VERB> <SA>.
<VERB>      ::= <LTVR>.
<LTVR>      ::= <LV> <*TV> <RV>.
<LV>        ::= <*D> / <*NULL>.
<RV>        ::= <*D> / <PN> / <*NULL>.
<OBJECT>    ::= <NSTG> / <THATS> / <*NULLOBJ> / <TOVO>.
<LVR>       ::= <LV> <*V> <RV>.
<THATS>     ::= THAT <ASSERTION>.
<TOVO>      ::= TO <LVR> <SA> <OBJECT> <SA>.


*WD
+A+       T,
CAT       N,
CATS      N,
EAT       TV, V,
EATS      TV,
EGG       N,
EGGS      N,
EVEN .
FIN       N,
FINS      N,
FISH      N, TV, V,
GENERALLY D,
HAPPY     ADJ,
HE        PRO,
HER       PRO, T,
HIM       PRO,
MEAN      N, TV, V, ADJ,
MEANS     N, TV, V,
MY        T,
ONLY .
SHE       PRO,
SLEEP     TV, N, V,
SLEEPS    TV,
THAT .
THEM      PRO,
THEY      PRO,
TO        P,
WHAT .
WITH      P,
+.+ .
```

Figure 10.2 shows a set of lists and routines that may be added to a simple BNF string grammar, such as the one shown in Fig. 10.1, to equip it for parsing with restrictions. Several illustrative restrictions are also shown in Fig. 10.2, formulated with reference to the BNF definitions in Fig. 10.1 and the augmented lexicon shown in Fig. 10.3. Of these restrictions, WAGREE is a simple version of the restriction WAGREE1 of the large grammar, the restriction that checks for number agreement of subject and verb; WWH controls (in a very incomplete way) the *what*-string NREP of the simple grammar; the restriction requires a transitive verb in this string because the string is defined with implicit object omission (*what my cat eats, ≠ what my cat sleeps*). WCOUNT is a simple restriction on countable nouns (subclass NCOUNT) that is modeled on WN9 of the large grammar (*My cat generally sleeps, ≠ Cat generally sleeps*). The last sample restriction, WVERBOBJ, restricts the value of the OBJECT in any given occurrence to be one of the strings named as a value of the OBJLIST attribute of the verb governing the object position in that occurrence; thus, with this restriction in effect, and using the lexicon in Fig. 10.3 the sequence *A cat sleeps the fish* would be rejected because *the fish* would be analyzed as an instance of the NSTG option of OBJECT, but *sleeps* does not have NSTG as a value of its OBJLIST attribute (cf. DVC1 in the large grammar).

A small grammar, like that shown in Figs. 10.1–10.3, can be mastered in a relatively short time, and the student will have learned as well to read simple diagnostic traces and to debug simple errors. With this beginning and some study of the Restriction Language Manual, students can begin to develop their own grammars. Several approaches are possible. One method is to have students choose a short text and expand the grammar and the lexicon so that they cover that particular text. In order not to be too ad hoc, the description of the BNF definitions of the large grammar (Chapter 4) can be consulted and the definitions and restrictions in the students' grammar can be modeled after those in the large grammar. Novel solutions can also be tried.

An example of this approach is illustrated by a recent project of three undergraduate students[2], who expanded the grammar and the lexicon of Figs. 10.1–10.3 so that they would cover the following text from N. Tinbergen's *Social Behavior in Animals* (1953)[3].

> Another system which prevents the parents from eating their own young has been developed in Cichlid fish. They do eat young of other species. A curious learning process makes them distinguish their own young from those of other species. Ths was shown in a simple experiment by Noble.[69] He replaced the eggs of an inexperienced pair, who were breeding for the first time in their lives, by eggs of another species. When the eggs hatched, they accepted the young and raised them. Whenever they met young of their own species however they ate them! Such a pair was spoiled for ever, for next time, when they were allowed to keep they own eggs, they devoured the young when they hatched! They had learned to consider another type of young as their own.

Parses obtained for this short text by the LSP system using the large English grammar were available (in Bookchin 1968) as a guide for developing the smaller grammar and as a check on the results obtained. The small subset grammar and lexicon developed by the students for the Tinbergen text are shown in Fig. 10.4. Figure 10.5 reproduces the students' explanation of the additions in the BNF component, and Fig. 10.6 does the same for their explanation of the new restrictions.

Fig. 10.2 Lists, routines, and sample restrictions for introductory class grammar.


```
*LISTS
ATTRIBUTE = SINGULAR, PLURAL, NCOUNT, NHUMAN, OBJLIST, NOMINATIVE,
            ACCUSATIVE.
TYPE STRING = ASSERTION, PN, NREP, THATS, TOVO.
TYPE STGSEG = ASSERTION.
TYPE ADJSET = SA, LN, LPRO, LV, RN, RV.
TYPE LADJSET = LN, LPRO, LV.
TYPE RADJSET = RN, RV.
TYPE LXR = LNR, LPROR, LTVR, LVR.


*RESTR
ROUTINE STARTAT (X) = EITHER TEST FOR X OR $DOWN1.
 $DOWN1 = GO DOWN;  ITERATET GO RIGHT UNTIL TEST FOR X SUCCEEDS.
ROUTINE ISIT (X) = TEST FOR X.
ROUTINE CORE = ONE OF $1, $D, $S IS TRUE.
 $1 = TEST FOR ATOM.
 $D =DESCEND TO ATOM NOT PASSING THROUGH ADJSET.
 $S = DESCEND TO STRING NOT PASSING THROUGH ADJSET.
ROUTINE L (X) = ITERATET GO LEFT UNTIL TEST FOR X SUCCEEDS.
ROUTINE R (X) = ITERATET GO RIGHT UNTIL TEST FOR X SUCCEEDS.
ROUTINE COEL1 (X) = EITHER DO L(X) OR DO R(X).
ROUTINE COELEMENT (X) = EITHER DO COEL1(X) OR $STGSEG.
 $STGSEG = DO COEL1(STGSEG);  DO DOWN1(X).
ROUTINE DOWN1 (X) = GO DOWN;ITERATET GO RIGHT UNTIL TEST FOR X SUCCEEDS.
ROUTINE ELEMENT (X) = EITHER DO DOWN1(X) OR $STGSEG.
 $STGSEG = DO DOWN1(STGSEG);  DO DOWN1(X).
ROUTINE LEFT-ADJUNCT = DO L(LADJSET);  EITHER TEST FOR LN OR DO CORE.
ROUTINE RIGHT-ADJUNCT = DO R(RADJSET);  DO CORE.
ROUTINE HOST = EITHER $1 OR $2;  DO CORE.
 $1 = EITHER TEST FOR LADJSET OR ASCEND TO LADJSET;  GO RIGHT.
 $2 = EITHER TEST FOR RADJSET OR ASCEND TO RADJSET;  GO LEFT.
ROUTINE IMMEDIATE (X) = ASCEND TO X.

WAGREE = IN ASSERTION:  BOTH $SINGAGREE AND $PLURAGREE ARE TRUE.
 $SINGAGREE = IF THE CORE X1 OF THE VERB IS SINGULAR THEN THE CORE
              X2 OF THE SUBJECT IS NOT PLURAL.
 $PLURAGREE =  IF X1 IS PLURAL THEN BOTH THE CORE X2 OF THE SUBJECT
         IS NOT SINGULAR AND X2 IS NOT OF TYPE STRING.
WWH = IN NREP:  CORE OF VERB HAS ATTRIBUTE OBJLIST:NSTG.
WCOUNT = IN LNR : IF THE CORE IS N:NCOUNT THEN IN LEFT-ADJUNCT OF
       CORE TPOS IS NOT EMPTY.
WVERBOBJ = IN OBJECT: IF THE VALUE X1 OF OBJECT EXISTS,
                    THEN EITHER CORE OF COELEMENT VERB HAS ATTRIBUTE
                          OBJLIST: X1,
                       OR CORE OF COELEMENT LVR HAS ATTRIBUTE
                          OBJLIST: X1.
```

Fig. 10.3 Small lexicon for introductory class grammar with restrictions.

```
*WD
 ?A?    T.
 CAT   N:(SINGULAR,NCOUNT).
 CATS  N:(PLURAL).
 EAT   TV:(PLURAL,OBJLIST:(NSTG,NULLOBJ)), V:(OBJLIST:(NSTG,NULLOBJ)).
 EATS  TV:(SINGULAR,OBJLIST:(NSTG,NULLOBJ)).
 EGG   N:(SINGULAR, NCOUNT).
 EGGS  N:(PLURAL).
 EVEN .
 FIN   N:(SINGULAR, NCOUNT).
 FINS  N:(PLURAL).
 FISH  N, TV:(PLURAL,OBJLIST:(NULLOBJ)), V:(OBJLIST:(NULLOBJ)).
 GENERALLY  D.
 HAPPY  ADJ.
 HE   PRO:(SINGULAR,NOMINATIVE,NHUMAN).
 HER    PRO:(SINGULAR,ACCUSATIVE,NHUMAN), T.
 HIM  PRO:(SINGULAR,ACCUSATIVE,NHUMAN).
 MEAN  N:(SINGULAR, NCOUNT), TV:(PLURAL, OBJLIST:(THATS,NSTG,TOVO)),
      V:(OBJLIST:(THATS,NSTG,TOVO)),ADJ.
 MEANS  N:(PLURAL), TV:(SINGULAR, OBJLIST:(THATS, NSTG, TOVO)),
        V:(OBJLIST:(THATS, NSTG, TOVO)).
 MY  T.
 ONLY .
 SHE    PRO:(SINGULAR,NOMINATIVE,NHUMAN).
 SLEEP  TV:(PLURAL,OBJLIST:(NULLOBJ)), N:(SINGULAR), V:(OBJLIST:
             (NULLOBJ)).
 SLEEPS  TV:(SINGULAR,OBJLIST:(NULLOBJ)).
 THAT .
 THEM   PRO:(PLURAL,ACCUSATIVE).
 THEY   PRO:(PLURAL,NOMINATIVE).
 TO P.
 WHAT.
 WITH  P.
 ?.? .
```

As these figures show, the small subset grammar in this case did not use definitions identical with those in the large grammar but used similar methods of treating phenomena. For example, it employed a null element similar to NULLN in the large grammar in analyzing *their own* as a case of LN followed by NULL, though the construct is called LZERONR (**left** adjunct + **zero N** + **right** adjunct) and is also used for conjunctional zeroing (*They accepted the young and (   ) raised them*). The students provided a table of parsing results showing the number of parses and the parsing time for each sentence, and whether their first parse matched a parse obtained by the large system, as shown in the LSP report. In seven of the nine sentences they obtained such a parse. The average number of parses per sentence was three and one-third. The next step in this approach would be to evaluate the grammar in terms of its coverage with respect to other short texts, perhaps first from the same author, and then to expand the grammar further. The major problem to be faced in such a stepwise expansion is the treatment of conjunctions. At a certain point it becomes necessary to switch to the automatic generation of conjunction strings or the grammar becomes unwieldy and the restrictions unworkable.

Another approach to building a grammar is to work within the framework of the large grammar, that is, to call upon the routines of the large grammar rather than those of Fig. 10.2 and to develop lexical entries consistent with those in the LSP lexicon. The task then is to define a subset of the large LSP grammar that is particularly suited to a given kind of textual material. This can be done by dividing the grammatical terrain among several individuals or groups. Each working unit can be responsible for a part of the grammar, such as LN, RN, and sentence adjuncts, and can compare the coverage provided by the large grammar for that area (as detailed in Chapter 4) with the occurrences present in the textual material. When all the studies are combined, a suggested subset grammar should result. When the large grammar is edited accordingly, a sample text can be parsed with the subset grammar and compared with the results of using the large grammar. This type of project is close to real applications.

Many interesting projects can also be done to answer questions such as the following about parsing: Can lexical categories be inferred from parse tree context? Can parsing be done with incomplete lexical specification? How necessary and how efficient are restrictions? (Answering this question might entail developing a quantitative measure.) Can sentences be generated using the same components as are used in recognition? For more advanced study, numerous problems involving transformations and semantic specialization of the system remain to be solved or implemented. As applications of natural language processing become more common, many more questions on which students can work are likely to arise.

Fig. 10.4 Student project: Expansion of introductory class grammar and lexicon.

```
*OBJSWET
*
*
*
*BNF
<SENTENCE>      %%= <CENTER> ?.? .
<CENTER>        %%= <ASSERTION> [<CONJSTG>] .
<ASSERTION>     %%= <SA> <SUBJECT> <SA> <VERB> <SA> <OBJECT> <SA> .
<CONJSTG>       %%= <CONJUNCTION> <ASSERTION> .
<CONJUNCTION>   %%= <*CONJ> / ?.? [<*CONJ>] .
<SA>            %%= <SAS> <SA> / <*NULL>.
<SAS>           %%= <*D> / <*INT> / <TIMESTG> / <WHENSTG> .
<TIMESTG>       %%= <*P> <LNR> .
<WHENSTG>       %%= <*WHNWD> <ASSERTION> .
<PN>            %%= <*P> <NSTG> .
<SUBJECT>       %%= <NSTG> / <*NULLWH> .
<NSTG>          %%= <LNR> / <LPROR> / <LZERONR> / <NREP> / <NAMESTG>.
<LNR>           %%= <LN> <*N> <RN> .
<LN>            %%= <TPOS> <APOS> .
<RN>            %%= <PN> / <WHSTG> / <VINGO> / <*NULL>.
<TPOS>          %%= <*T> <TPOS> / <*NULL> .
<APOS>          %%= <*ADJ> <APOS> / <*NULL>.
<LPROR>         %%= <LPRO> <*PRO> <RN> .
<LPRO>          %%= ONLY / EVEN / <*NULL>.
<LZERONR>       %%= <LN> <ZERON> <RN>.
<ZERON>         %%= <*NULL>.
<NREP>          %%= WHAT <SUBJECT> <SA> <VERB> <SA>.
<NAMESTG>       %%= <LN> <*NAME> <RN> .
<WHSTG>         %%= <*WH> <ASSERTION> .
<VINGO>         %%= <LVINGR> <OBJECT>.
<PVINGO>        %%= <*P> <VINGO> .
<VERB>          %%= <LTVR> / <*MODAL> <LVR> .
<LTVR>          %%= <LV> <*TV> <RV> .
<LV>            %%= <*D> / <*NULL> .
<RV>            %%= <*D> / <PN> / <*NULL> .
<LVINGR>        %%= <LV> <*VING> <RV>.
<OBJECT>        %%= <NSTG> / <*NULLOBJ> / <TOVO> / <VENO> / <VINGO> /
                    <NPVINGO> / <NVO> / <VENPASS> / <THATS> .
<NPVINGO>       %%= <NSTG> <PVINGO> .
<NVO>           %%= <NSTG> <VO>.
<VO>            %%= <LVP> <OBJECT> .
<LVP>           %%= <LV> <*V> <RV> .
<THATS>         %%= THAT <ASSERTION> .
<TOVO>          %%= TO <LVR> <SA> <OBJECT> <SA> .
<VENO>          %%= <LVENR> <OBJECT> .
<LVENR>         %%= <LV> <*VEN> <RV> .
<VENPASS>       %%= <LVENP> <PASSOBJ> .
<PASSOBJ>       %%= BY <NSTG> / <*NULLOBJ>.
*LISTS
ATTRIBUTE    = SINGULAR, PLURAL, NCOUNT, NHUMAN, OBJLIST, NOMINATIVE,
               ACCUSATIVE, TIME.
TYPE STRING  = ASSERTION, PN, NREP, THATS, TOVO, CONJSTG, WHSTG,
               NPVINGO, VINGO, VENO, NVO, VENPASS, TIMESTG, NAMESTG,
               WHENSTG.
TYPE STGSEG  = ASSERTION, TPOS, APOS, SAS, SA, PVINGO, VINGO, VO.
TYPE ADJSET  = SA, LN, LPRO, LV, PN, RV.
TYPE LADJSET = LN, LPRO, LV.
TYPE RADJSET = RN, RV.
```

```
TYPE LXR      = LNR, LPROR, LTVR, LVR, LVENR, LVINGR, LZERONR .
*


*
*
*RESTR
ROUTINE STARTAT (X) = EITHER TEST FOR X OR $DOWN1.
 $DOWN1 = GO DOWN;  ITERATET GO RIGHT UNTIL TEST FOR X SUCCEEDS.
ROUTINE ISIT (X) = TEST FOR X.
ROUTINE CORE = ONE OF $1, $D, $S IS TRUE.
 $1 = TEST FOR ATOM.
 $D =DESCEND TO ATOM NOT PASSING THROUGH ADJSET.
 $S = DESCEND TO STRING NOT PASSING THROUGH ADJSET.
ROUTINE L (X) = ITERATET GO LEFT UNTIL TEST FOR X SUCCEEDS.
ROUTINE R (X) = ITERATET GO RIGHT UNTIL TEST FOR X SUCCEEDS.
ROUTINE COEL1 (X) = EITHER DO L(X) OR DO R(X).
ROUTINE COELEMENT (X) = EITHER DO COEL1(X) OR $STGSEG.
 $STGSEG = DO COEL1(STGSEG);  DO DOWN1(X).
ROUTINE DOWN1 (X) = GO DOWN;ITERATET GO RIGHT UNTIL TEST FOR X SUCCEEDS.
ROUTINE ELEMENT (X) = EITHER DO DOWN1(X) OR $STGSEG.
 $STGSEG = DO DOWN1(STGSEG);  DO DOWN1(X).
ROUTINE LEFT-ADJUNCT = DO L(LADJSET);  EITHER TEST FOR LN OR DO CORE.
ROUTINE RIGHT-ADJUNCT = DO R(RADJSET);  DO CORE.
ROUTINE HOST = EITHER $1 OR $2;  DO CORE.
 $1 = EITHER TEST FOR LADJSET OR ASCEND TO LADJSET;  GO RIGHT.
 $2 = EITHER TEST FOR RADJSET OR ASCEND TO RADJSET;  GO LEFT.
ROUTINE IMMEDIATE (X) = ASCEND TO X.
*
WAGREE    = IN ASSERTION% BOTH $SINGAGREE AND $PLURAGREE ARE TRUE.
 $SINGAGREE = IF THE CORE X1 OF THE VERB IS SINGULAR THEN THE CORE
             X2 OF THE SUBJECT IS NOT PLURAL.
 $PLURAGREE =  IF X1 IS PLURAL THEN BOTH THE CORE X2 OF THE SUBJECT
         IS NOT SINGULAR AND X2 IS NOT OF TYPE STRING.
WWH       = IN NREP% CORE OF VERB HAS ATTRIBUTE OBJLIST%NSTG.
WCOUNT    = IN LNR% IF THE CORE IS N%NCOUNT THEN IN LEFT-ADJUNCT
            OF CORE TPOS IS NOT EMPTY.
WVERBOBJ  = IN OBJECT% IF BOTH THE VALUE X1 OF OBJECT EXISTS AND
            COELEMENT VERB EXISTS THEN THE CORE OF COELEMENT VERB HAS
            ATTRIBUTE OBJLIST%X1.
WZERON1   = IN SUBJECT RE NULLWH% IMMEDIATE WHSTG OF IMMEDIATE
            ASSERTION EXISTS.
WZERON2   = IN SUBJECT RE NSTG% IT IS NOT THE CASE THAT IMMEDIATE WHSTG
            OF IMMEDIATE ASSERTION EXISTS.
WZERON1   = IN LZERONR% EITHER IN LN, BOTH TPOS IS NOT EMPTY AND APOS
            IS NOT EMPTY OR IMMEDIATE CONJSTG OF IMMEDIATE ASSERTION
            OF IMMEDIATE SUBJECT EXISTS.
WTIME     = IN TIMESTG% CORE OF LNR IS N%TIME.
WCASE1    = IN SUBJECT% IF VALUE OF NSTG IS LPROR THEN CORE OF SUBJECT
            HAS ATTRIBUTE NOMINATIVE.
WCASE2    = IN OBJECT% IF VALUE OF NSTG IS LPROR THEN CORE OF OBJECT HAS
            ATTRIBUTE ACCUSATIVE.
*WD
?.? .
?.? .
?A? T.
ACCEPTED   TV%(OBJLIST%(NSTG,THATS,VINGO,NPVINGO)).  VEN%(OBJLIST%(NSTG,
           THATS, VINGO,NPVINGO)).
ALLOWED    VEN%(OBJLIST%(TOVO,NSTG,VINGO,NPVINGO)).  TV%(OBJLIST%(NSTG,
           VINGO,NPVINGO)).
?AN? T.
AND        CONJ.
ANOTHER    T.
AS         P.
```

```
ATE        TVM (OBJLIST% (NSTG)).
REEN       VEN%(OBJLIST%(VENPASS,VINGO,NSTG,THATS)).
BREEDING      VING%(OBJLIST%(NSTG,NULLOBJ        )), N%(SINGULAR), ADJ.
BY         P.
CAT        N% (SINGULAR,NCOUNT).
CATS       N% (PLURAL).
CICHLID    ADJ.
CONSIDER   V%(OBJLIST%(NSTG,THATS,VINGO,NPVINGO)), TV%(PLURAL,
           OBJLIST%(NSTG,THATS,VINGO,NPVINGO)).
CURIOUS    ADJ.
DEVELOPED     VEN%(OBJLIST%(NULLOBJ,NSTG,VINGO,PASSOBJ)),
              TV% (OBJLIST% (NSTG,VINGO)).
DEVOURED      TV%(OBJLIST%(NSTG)), VEN% (OBJLIST%(NSTG)).
DISTINGUISH      V%(OBJLIST%(NSTG,THATS,VINGO)), TV% (PLURAL,
      OBJLIST%(NSTG,THATS,VINGO)).
DO         MODAL% (OBJLIST%(NSTG,VO)), TV% (PLURAL, OBJLIST%(NSTG)),
           V%(OBJLIST%(NSTG)).
EAT        TV%(PLURAL,OBJLIST%(NSTG,NULLOBJ,TOVO)), V%(OBJLIST%(NSTG,
           NULLOBJ,TOVO)).
EATING        VING%(OBJLIST%(NSTG,TOVO,NULLOBJ)),N%(SINGULAR), ADJ.
EATS       TV%(SINGULAR,OBJLIST%(NSTG,NULLOBJ,TOVO)).
EGG        N% (SINGULAR,NCOUNT).
EGGS       N% (PLURAL).
EVEN
EXPERIMENT        N%(SINGULAR,NCOUNT), V%(OBJLIST%(NULLOBJ,TOVO)),
                  TV%(PLURAL,OBJLIST%(NULLOBJ,TOVO)).
?FIRST?    ADJ% (TIME).
FISH       N, TV%(PLURAL,OBJLIST%(NULLOBJ)), V%(OBJLIST%(NULLOBJ)).
FOR        P.
FOREVER    D.
FROM       P.
GENERALLY  D.
HAD        TV%(OBJLIST%(VENO,NSTG,TOVO)), VEN%(OBJLIST%(NSTG,TOVO)).
HAPPY      ADJ.
HAS        TV%(SINGULAR,OBJLIST%(VENO,NSTG,TOVO)).
HATCHED       TV%(OBJLIST%(NULLOBJ,NSTG)), VEN%(OBJLIST%(NSTG,NULLOBJ)).
HE         PRO% (SINGULAR,NOMINATIVE,NHUMAN).
HER        PRO% (SINGULAR,ACCUSATIVE,NHUMAN), T.
HIM        PRO% (SINGULAR,ACCUSATIVE,NHUMAN).
HOWEVER    D.
IS         TV% (SINGULAR,OBJLIST% (NSTG)).
IN         P.

INEXPERIENCED    ADJ.
KEEP       V%(OBJLIST%(NSTG,VINGO)), TV%(PLURAL,OBJLIST%(NSTG,VINGO)).
LEARNED       VEN%(OBJLIST%(TOVO,NSTG,THATS)), TV%(OBJLIST%(NSTG,TOVO,
           THATS)).
LEARNING      ADJ, VING%(OBJLIST%(NSTG,TOVO,THATS)), N%(SINGULAR).
LIVES      N%(PLURAL), TV%(SINGULAR,OBJLIST%(NULLOBJ)).
MAKES      TV%(SINGULAR,OBJLIST%(NSTG,THATS,NVO)), N%(PLURAL).
MEAN          N%(SINGULAR, NCOUNT), TV%(PLURAL, OBJLIST%(THATS,NSTG,TOVO)),
           V%(OBJLIST%(THATS,NSTG,TOVO)),ADJ.
MEANS         N%(PLURAL), TV%(SINGULAR, OBJLIST%(THATS, NSTG, TOVO)),
           V%(OBJLIST%(THATS, NSTG, TOVO)).
MET        TV%(OBJLIST%(NSTG,NULLOBJ)), VEN%(OBJLIST%(NSTG,NULLOBJ)).
MY         T.

NEXT       ADJ% (TIME).
NOBLE      ADJ, NAME.
OF         P.
ONLY
OTHER      ADJ.
OWN        ADJ,        TV% (OBJLIST% (NSTG)), V% (OBJLIST% (NSTG)).
PAIR       N%(SINGULAR,NCOUNT), TV%(PLURAL,OBJLIST%(NSTG)).
```

```
PARENTS    N% (PLURAL).
PREVENTS     TV%(SINGULAR,ORJLIST%(NSTG,NPVINGO,VINGO       )).
PROCESS      N%(SINGULAR,NCOUNT), TV%(PLURAL,ORJLIST%(NSTG,VINGO)).
RAISED     TV%(ORJLIST%(NSTG)), VEN%(ORJLIST%(NSTG)).
REPLACED     TV%(ORJLIST%(NSTG,VINGO,NPVINGO)), VEN%(OBJLIST%(NSTG,
           VINGO,NPVINGO)).
SHE            PRO%(SINGULAR,NOMINATIVE,NHUMAN).
SHOWN      VEN%(OBJLIST%(NULLOBJ,NSTG,THATS)).
SIMPLE     ADJ.
SLEEP        TV% (PLURAL,ORJLIST% (NULLOBJ)), N% (SINGULAR),
        V% (OBJLIST% (NULLOBJ)).
SLEEPS       TV%(SINGULAR,OBJLIST%(NULLOBJ)).
SPECIES    N% (PLURAL).
SPOILED    VEN%(OBJLIST%(NULLOBJ,NSTG,VINGO,NPVINGO)),
           TV%(OBJLIST%(NSTG,VINGO,NPVINGO)).
SUCH       T.
SYSTEM     N% (SINGULAR, NCOUNT).
 THAT .
?THE?      T.
THEIR      T.
THEM         PRO%(PLURAL,ACCUSATIVE).
THEY         PRO%(PLURAL,NOMINATIVE).
THIS       PRO% (SINGULAR,NOMINATIVE), T.
THOSE        PRO%(PLURAL), T.
TIME       N% (SINGULAR,TIME), TV% (PLURAL,OBJLIST%(NSTG,VINGO)),
        V%(OBJLIST%(NSTG,VINGO)).
TO         P.
TYPE       N%(SINGULAR,NCOUNT), TV%(PLURAL,OBJLIST%(NULLOBJ,NSTG,THATS)),
           V%(OBJLIST%(NULLOBJ,NSTG,THATS)).
WAS        TV%(SINGULAR,OBJLIST%(VENPASS,VINGO,NSTG,TOVO,THATS,VENO)).
WERE       TV%(PLURAL,OBJLIST%(VINGO,VENPASS,NSTG,     TOVO,VENO      )).
WHAT       WH.
WHEN       WHNWD.
WHENEVER   WHNWD.
WHICH      WH.
WHO        WH.
WITH       P.
YOUNG        N%(PLURAL), ADJ.
*CLOSE()
```

Fig. 10.5 Student project: Notes to BNF definitions.

\<APOS\>	Definition of adjective expanded to allow for recursion, i.e. one or more contiguous adjectives now acceptable.
\<CONJUNCTION\>	Either a comma, a comma followed immediately by a conjunction \<*CONJ\> or a conjunction \<*CONJ\> alone indicates the conjunction of two assertions.
	The definition as it stands does not allow for recursion but could easily be expanded to do so.
\<LZERONR\>	An LXR-type definition created to fill zeroed-noun positions, those in which a noun is implied but does not appear. This construct distinguishes zeroed-noun positions from those which are grammatically empty (indicated in the grammar by \<*NULL\>).
\<NAMESTG\>	Specific type of \<NSTG\> designed to handle proper nouns.
	Could eventually be expanded to:
	\<LN\> \<LNAME\> \<*NAME\> \<RNAME\> \<RN\>
	in which case \<LNAME\> would cover such titles as "Mr." and "Ms." while \<RNAME\> would cover those such as "Esq." and "Sr.".
\<NPVINGO\>	Expansion on \<VINGO\> construct in combination with \<NSTG\> and \<*P\>.
\<NULLWH\>	A zeroed-noun position specific to \<WHSTG\> subjects.
	It differs from \<LZERONR\> in that it is not an LXR-type definition and so has no left- or right-adjuncts.
\<NVO\>	Combination of existing \<NSTG\> and \<VO\>.
\<PASSOBJ\>	Construction which covers limited forms of the passive object.
\<PVINGO\>	Expansion on \<VINGO\> construct in combination with existing \<*P\>.
\<SA\>	Definition of sentence adjunct expanded to allow for recursion.
\<TIMESTG\>	Signals the presence of a notion of time in a sentence. Must begin with a preposition.
	(See also WTIME restriction explanation)
\<TPOS\>	Definition of article expanded to allow for recursion.
\<VENO\>	Passive verb with object
\<VENPASS\>	Passive verb with passive object
\<WHENSTG\>	Handles strings beginning with a \<*WHNWD\> (when-word), i.e. "when" and "whenever".

Fig. 10.6 Student project: Notes to new restrictions.

DZERON1
and
DZERON2

The combination of these two disqualify
restrictions involves the choice between
options of the SUBJECT definition.

While DZERON1 limits the occurrence of
NULLWH to the subject of a WHSTG, DZERON2
allows the occurrence of NSTG as subject
in all cases but a WHSTG.

Examples:

PASS: The fish which ( ) eat their own young...

FAIL: The fish which fish eat their own young...

WZERON1

This restriction concerns the LZERONR option
of NSTG. It allows the TPOS and APOS positions of LZERONR to be empty only when preceded by a CONJSTG.

PASS: They treated them as their own (ZERON).

FAIL: They treated them as (LZERONR).

PASS: The red fish fed and (LZERONR) raised them.

FAIL: The red fish fed and the red (ZERON) raised
them.

WTIME

WTIME restricts passage of noun phrases (LNRs)
within the construction TIMESTG to those
with nouns having the attribute TIME.

PASS: They were breeding fish for the first time.

FAIL: They were breeding fish for the first experiment.

WCASE1

Given a pronoun LPROR in subject position, this
restriction requires that the pronoun be of the
nominative case.

PASS: They are Cichlid fish.

FAIL: Them are Cichlid fish.

WCASE2

Given a pronoun LPROR in object position, this
restriction requires that the pronoun be of the
accusative case.

PASS: They had learned to consider them as parents.

FAIL: They had learned to consider they as parents.

10.2 Teaching a Second Language

String analysis provides a coherent framework for presenting grammatical material. It is relatively simple, so that with its aid one can easily grasp the overall organization of the grammar and see how sentences are put together in the language. A string grammar is also easily "layered" so that, with a simple grammar as the starting point, at each stage the previous grammar is not discarded but enriched. These points apply whether English or another language is being taught and whether the language is being taught as a first or a second language.

For teaching English or another language as a second language, string analysis has the property that languages, especially Indo-European languages, are much more similar to each other in their string and transformational structure than in their classical grammatical features (types of tense, gender, case). If the grammar is organized in terms of string structure, the correspondences between the two languages can be made explicit and the student can more readily utilize knowledge of the native language in assimilating the new language.

To explore this possibility, a study was made for the U.S. Office of Education, using English and French as the two languages in question (Sager, Claris, and Clifford 1970). A relatively detailed string grammar of French was provided, using as far as possible the categories already in use in the LSP computer string grammar of English. Then a table showing the correspondence between French and English strings was prepared. The study showed how very close these two languages are in their string structures[4] and explored ways in which the structural correspondences could be demonstrated.

One interesting method for teaching string structure developed out of the excision method of discovering the strings of a language (described at the end of Sec. 1.3). We applied the method starting at the end of the sentence and moving leftward, and adopted a four-column table for presenting the results of each excision:

EXCISED WORD SEQUENCE	CORRESPONDING WORD-CLASS SEQUENCE (= linguistic string)	STRING CLASS (e.g., RN, SA)	REMAINDER OF SENTENCE

Each remainder became the sentence to be operated upon to produce the next row. The method was applied (by P. Claris in France) to a short French text and independently (by Judith Clifford in the United States) to the published translation of the same text.[5] The resulting tables were then compared. They proved to be remarkably similar, and the points of difference were instructive with regard to differences in the two languages.

Table 10.1 shows the excision analysis for the second sentence of the French text; Table 10.2 shows the excision analysis of the translated version of the same sentence. Note that the string-class notation in Table 10.1 uses subscripts to identify the particular string in the French string grammar given earlier in the report from which the figure is taken (cited earlier). Some notational differences from present conventions are: r_N = RN; C_c = coordinate conjunction; r_x = conjunctional string, occurs to the right of x; a_C = adjunct of center (sentence adjunct); a_V = adjunct of verb; Σ = subject; Ω = object; D_n = adverb of negation; ⓑ = automatic morphological change due to excision—here, in particular, plural → singular.

Table 10.1

Excision Analysis of French Sentence

BRA(F)S2:	Le mâle ne mesure qu'un à deux millimètres et vit en parasite dans l'intestin ou l'utérus de la femelle.		
1. de la femelle	PN	r_{N2} (uterus)	Le mâle ne mesure qu'un à deux millimètres et vit en parasite dans l'intestin ou l'utérus
2. ou l'uterus	$C_c N$	r_{x1} $x = N$ (intestin)	Le mâle ne mesure qu'un à deux millimètres et vit en parasite dans l'intestin
3. dans l'intestin	PN	a_{C3}	Le mâle ne mesure qu'un à deux millimètres et vit en parasite
4. en parasite	PN	a_{V1}	Le mâle ne mesure qu'un a deux millimetres et vit
5. et vit	$C_c(\Sigma)tV\Omega$	r_{x1} $x = C_1$	Le mâle ne mesure qu'un à deux millimètres
6. à deux	$a\,Q$	r_Q	Le mâle ne mesure qu'un millimètre ⓑ
7. ne . . . que	D_n	a_{C1}	Le mâle mesure un millimètre. $= C_1 = \Sigma_1\, tV\, \Omega_1$

Table 10.2

Excision Analysis of English Sentence

BRA(E)S2:   The male measures only a few millimeters and lives as a parasite in the intestine or in the uterus of the female.

1. of the female	PN	r_N (uterus)	The male measures only a few millimeters and lives as a parasite in the intestine or in the uterus
2. or in the uterus	C_cPN	r_{x1} $x = N$ (intestine)	The male measures only a few millimeters and lives as a parasite in the intestine
3. in the intestine	PN	SA* $(C_c tV)$	The male measures only a few millimeters and lives as a parasite
4. as a parasite	PN	r_V (lives)	The male measures only a few millimeters and lives
5. and lives	C_ctV	r_{x1} $x = tV$ (measures)	The male measures only a few millimeters
6. only	D	l_T (a [few])	The male measures a few millimeters

*SA = sentence adjunct

NOTES

1. Chiefly the Restriction Language Manual (Grishman 1974a), the LSP Users' Guide (Grishman 1976), and the LSP Program Manual (Grishman 1974b). These are updated periodically.

2. Barbara Hodges, Barbara St. George, and Renée Sasaki.

3. Methuen, London, p. 46.

4. Independently this point was demonstrated by work of Morris Salkoff, who was able to adapt the LSP parsing program and grammar of English for use in parsing French, with certain important additions for French (Salkoff 1973).

5. The texts were Jean Brachet, *Embryologie Chemique,* Masson, Paris, Editions De Soer, Liege, 1944, pp. 36–38; and Jean Brachet, *Chemical Embryology,* translated from the French by Lester G. Barth, Interscience, New York, 1950, pp. 28–29.

References

ACM Panel (1971). Can Present Methods for Library and Information Retrieval Service Survive?, in *Proceedings of the 1971 Annual Conference of the ACM,* pp 564–67.

Anderson, B.B. (1970). Transformationally-based English Strings and Their Word Subclasses, String Program Reports, No. 7, Linguistic String Project, New York University, New York.

Anderson, B., I.D.J. Bross, and N. Sager (1975). Grammatical Compression in Notes and Records: Analysis and Computation, *American Journal of Computational Linguistics* 2 (No. 4).

APT Part Programming (1967). IIT Research Institute, APT Long Range Program Staff, McGraw-Hill, New York.

Backus, J.W. (1960). The Syntax and Semantics of the Proposed International Algebraic Language of the Zurich ACMGAMM Conference, in *Proceedings of the International Conference on Information Processing, UNESCO,* pp. 125–32.

Bloomfield, L. (1933). *Language,* Holt, Rinehart and Winston, New York.

Bolinger, D.L. (1957). *Interrogative Structures of American English,* University of Alabama Press, University, Alabama.

Bookchin, B. (1968). Computer Outputs for Sentence Decomposition of Scientific Texts, String Program Reports, No. 3, Linguistic String Project, New York University, New York.

Bratley, P., H. Dewar, and J.P. Thorne (1967). *Nature* 216: 969.

Bross, I.D.J., A. Shapiro, and B.B. Anderson (1972). How Information Is Carried in Scientific Sublanguages, *Science* 176: 1303–7.

Charniak, E., and Y. Wilks (1976). *Computational Semantics,* Elsevier, North-Holland, New York.

Chomsky, N. (1956). Three Models for the Description of Language, *IRE Transactions in Information Theory* 2: 113–24.

Chomsky, N. (1957). *Syntactic Structures,* Mouton, The Hague.

Chomsky, N. (1964). *Aspects of the Theory of Syntax,* MIT Press, Cambridge, Massachusetts.

Dunham, G.S., M.G. Pacak, and A.W. Pratt (1978). Automatic Indexing of Pathology Data, *American Society for Information Science,* March 1978: 81–90.

Fitzpatrick, E., and N. Sager (1974). The Lexical Subclasses of the Linguistic String Parser, *American Journal of Computational Linguistics,* Microfiche 2; String Program Reports, No. 9, Linguistic String Project, New York University, New York.

Fries, C.C. (1940). *American English Grammar,* Appleton-Century-Crofts, New York.

Grishman, R. (1974a). The Restriction Language Manual, Linguistic String Project, New York University, New York.

Grishman, R. (1974b). Program Manual for the LSP System for Natural Language Processing, Linguistic String Project, New York University, New York.

Grishman, R. (1976). User's Guide to the LSP System for Natural Language Processing, Linguistic String Project, New York University, New York.

Grishman, R. (1979). Response Generation in Question-Answering Systems, in *Proceedings of the 17th Annual Meeting,* Association for Computational Linguistics, pp. 99–101.

Grishman, R., and L. Hirschman (1978). Question Answering from Natural Language Medical Data Bases, *Artificial Intelligence* 11: 25–43.

Grishman, R., N. Sager, C. Raze, and B. Bookchin (1973). The Linguistic String Parser. *AFIPS Conference Proceedings, 42,* National Computer Conference, 1973, AFIPS Press, Montvale, New Jersey, pp. 427–34.

Gross, M. (1972). *Mathematical Models in Linguistics,* Prentice-Hall, Englewood Cliffs, New Jersey.

Harris, L.R. (1977). User Oriented Data Base Query with the Robot Natural Language Query System, *International Journal of Man-Machine Studies* 9: 697–713.

Harris, Z.S. (1952). Discourse Analysis, *Language* 28: 18–23.

Harris, Z.S. (1957). Co-occurrence and Transformation in Linguistic Structure, Presidential Address, Linguistic Society of America, 1955, *Language* 33: 283–340.

Harris, Z.S. (1962). *String Analysis of Sentence Structure,* Mouton, The Hague.

Harris, Z.S. (1964). The Elementary Transformations, *Transformations and Discourse Analysis Papers,* No. 54, University of Pennsylvania, Philadelphia.

Harris, Z.S. (1968). *Mathematical Structures of Language,* Wiley Interscience, New York.

Harris, Z.S. (1970). *Papers in Structural and Transformational Linguistics,* D. Reidel, Dordrecht, Holland.

Harris, Z.S. (1978). The Interrogative in a Syntactic Framework, in *Questions,* edited by H. Hiž, D. Reidel, Dordrecht, Holland.

Harris, Z.S. et al. (1959). *Transformations and Discourse Analysis Papers,* Nos. 15–19, Department of Linguistics, University of Pennsylvania, Philadelphia.

Heidorn, G.E. (1976). Automatic Programming through Natural Language Dialogue: A Survey, *IBM Journal of Research and Development* 20: 4.

Hendrix, G.G., E.D. Sacerdoti, D. Sagalowicz, and J. Slocum (1978). Developing a Natural Language Interface to Complex Data, *ACM Transactions on Data-Base Systems* 3 (No. 2): 105–47.

Hillman, D.J. (1973). Customized User Services via Interactions with LEADERMART, *Information Storage and Retrieval* 9: 587–96.

Hirschman, L. (1981). Retrieving Time Information from Natural Language Texts, *Proceedings of the Joint British Computer Society and Association for Computing Machinery Symposium: Research and Development in Information Retrieval,* St. John's College, Cambridge, England, June 1980.

Hirschman, L., and R. Grishman (1977). Fact Retrieval from Natural Language Medical Records, in *IFIP World Conference Series on Medical Informatics 2,* edited by D.B. Shires, and H. Wolf, North-Holland, Amsterdam, pp. 247–51.

Hirschman, L., and N. Sager (1981). Automatic Information-Formatting of a Medical Sublanguage, in *Sublanguage: Studies of Language in Restricted Semantic Domains,* edited by R. Kittredge and J. Lehrberger, Walter de Gruyter, Berlin.

Hirschman, L., R. Grishman, and N. Sager (1975). Grammatically-based Automatic Word Class Formation, *Information Processing and Management* 11: 39–57.

Hirschman, L., R. Grishman, and N. Sager (1976). From Text to Structured Information: Automatic Processing of Medical Reports in, *AFIPS Conference Proceedings, 45,* National Computer Conference, 1976, AFIPS Press, Montvale, New Jersey, pp. 267–75.

Hirschman, L., N. Sager, and M. Lyman (1979). Automatic Application of Health Care Criteria to Narrative Patient Records, in *Proceedings of the Third Annual Symposium on Computer Application in Medical Care,* IEEE, New York.

Hirschman, L., G. Story, and E. Marsh (forthcoming). Automated Health Care Evaluation from Narrative Medical Records, Linguistic String Project, New York University, New York.

Hiż, H. (1961). Steps toward Grammatical Recognition, *Advances in Documentation and Library Science* III, pt. 2.

Hiż, D., and A.K. Joshi (1967). A Simple Description of an Algorithm for Transformational Analysis of English Sentences, *Transformations and Discourse Analysis Papers,* No. 67, Department of Linguistics, University of Pennsylvania, Philadelphia.

Hobbs, J.H. (1974). A Metalanguage for Expressing Grammatical Restrictions in Nodal Spans Parsing of Natural Language, Courant Computer Science Report, No. 2, New York University, New York.

Hobbs, J., and R. Grishman (1976). The Automatic Transformational Analysis of English Sentences: An Implementation, *International Journal of Computer Mathematics,* Sec. A, 5: 267–83.

Householder, F.W. (Ed.) (1972), *Syntactic Theory 1: Structuralist,* Penguin Books, Middlesex, England.

Joint Commission on Accreditation of Hospitals (1974). *PEP Primer,* 4th ed., JCAH, Chicago, Illinois.

Jespersen, O. (1961). *A Modern English Grammar,* Reprinted ed., Allen and Unwin, London.

Joshi, A.K., and D. Hiz (1965). String Representation of Transformations and a Decomposition Procedure, Transformations and Discourse Analysis Project Paper, Department of Linguistics, University of Pennsylvania, Philadelphia.

Joshi, A.K., S.R. Kosaraju, and H. Yamada (1972). String Adjunct Grammars, Parts I and II, *Information and Control* 21: 93–116 and 3: 235–60.

Kittredge, R. (1981). Textual Cohesion within Sublanguages: Implications for Automatic Analysis and Synthesis, in *Sublanguage: Studies of Language in Restricted Semantic Domains,* edited by R. Kittredge and J. Lehrberger, Walter de Gruyter, Berlin.

Korein, J. (1970). The Computerized Medical Record: The Variable Field Length Format System and its Applications, in *Information Processing of Medical Records,* edited by J. Anderson and J. M. Forsythe, North-Holland, Amsterdam, pp. 259–91.

Lancaster, F.W. (1977). The Relevance of Linguistics to Information Science, in *Natural Language in Information Processing: Perspectives and Directions for Research,* Results of a Workshop on Linguistics and Information Science, Biskops-Arnö, Sweden, May 1976, edited by D. Walker, H. Karlgren and M. Kay, FID Publication 551, Skriptor, Stockholm.

Lehrberger, J. (1981). Automatic Translation and the Concept of Sublanguage, in *Sublanguage: Studies of Language in Restricted Semantic Domains,* edited by R. Kittredge and J. Lehrberger, Walter de Gruyter, Berlin.

Lewis, P.M., II, and R.E. Stearnes (1968). Syntax-Directed Transduction, *JACM,* No. 15, 405.

Lindsay, P.H., and D.A. Norman (1977). *Human Information Processing*, Academic Press, New York.

Lyman, M. (1977). A Data Support System for Emergency Health Care, in *Proceedings of the Third Illinois Conference on Medical Information Systems,* University of Illinois at Chicago Circle, Chicago, 1977, pp. 88–97.

Lyman, M., L.J. Tick, and J. Korein (1968). Comprehensive Health Care for Children: Bellevue Pediatric Project. *New York State Journal of Medicine* 68 (No. 17): 2287.

Morris, J. (1965). The IPL String Analysis Program, in First Report on the String Analysis Programs, Department of Linguistics, University of Pennsylvania, Philadelphia; Reprinted in String Program Reports, No. 1, Linguistics String Project, New York University, New York.

O'Connor, J. (1975). Retrieval of Answer-Sentences and Answer-Figures from Papers by Text Searching, *Information Processing and Management* 11: 155–64.

Petrick, S.P. (1976). On Natural Language Based Query Systems, *IBM Journal of Research and Development* 20: 314–25.

Plath, W.J. (1976). REQUEST: A Natural Language Question Answering System, *IBM Journal of Research* 20 (No. 4): 326–35.

Pratt, A.W. (1973). Medicine, Computers and Linguistics, *Advances in Biomedical Engineering* 3: 97–140.

Raze, C. (1967). The FAP Program for String Decomposition of Scientific Texts, String Program Reports, No. 2, Linguistic String Project, New York University, New York.

Raze, C. (1976). A Computational Treatment of Coordinate Conjunctions, *American Journal of Computational Linguistics,* Microfiche 52.

Raze, C. (1976). The Parsing and Transformational Expansion of Coordinate Conjunction Strings, String Program Reports, No. 11, Linguistic String Project, New York University, New York.

Sager, N. (1960). Procedure for Left-to-Right Recognition of Sentence Structure, *Transformations and Discourse Analysis Papers,* No. 27, Department of Linguistics, University of Pennsylvania, Philadelphia.

Sager, N. (1967). Syntactic Analysis of Natural Language, in *Advances in Computers,* Vol. 8, Academic Press, New York, pp. 153–88.

Sager, N. (1968). A Computer String Grammar of English, String Program Reports, No. 4, Linguistic String Project, New York University, New York.

Sager, N. (1972b). Syntactic Formatting of Scientific Information, in *AFIPS Conference Proceedings, 41*, Fall Joint Computer Conference, 1972, AFIPS Press, Montvale, New Jersey, pp. 791–800.

Sager, N. (1972a). A Two-Stage BNF Specification of Natural Language, *Journal of Cybernetics* 2: 39–50.

Sager, N. (1975). Sublanguage Grammars in Science Information Processing, *Journal of the American Society for Information Science* 26: 10–16.

Sager, N. (1977). Information Structures in the Language of Science, in The Many Faces of Information Science, *AAAS Selected Symposium 3,* edited by Edward C. Weiss, Westview Press, Boulder, Colorado, pp. 53–73.

Sager, N. (1978). Natural Language Information Formatting: The Automatic Conversion of Texts to a Structured Data Base, in *Advances in Computers, 17,* edited by M.C. Yovits, Academic Press, New York, pp. 89–162.

Sager, N., and R. Grishman (1975). The Restriction Language for Computer Grammars of Natural Language, *Communications of the ACM* 18: 390–400.

Sager, N., and L. Hirschman (1978). Information Structures in the Language of Science: Theory and Implementation, String Program Reports, No. 12. Linguistic String Project, New York University, New York.

Sager, N., and M. Lyman, (1978). Computerized Language Processing: Implications for Health Care Evaluation, *Medical Record News* (JAMRA) 49 (No. 3): 20–30.

Sager, N., J. Morris, and M. Salkoff (1965). First Report on the String Analysis Program, Department of Linguistics, University of Pennsylvania, Philadelphia.

Sager, N., M. Salkoff, J. Morris, and C. Raze (1966). Report on the String Analysis Programs, String Program Reports, No. 1, Linguistic String Project, New York University, New York.

Sager, N., P. Claris, and J. Clifford (1970). French String Grammar, String Program Reports, No. 8, Linguistic String Project, New York University, New York.

Sager, N., L. Hirschman, R. Grishman, and C. Insolio (1977). Computer Programs for Natural Language Files, in Information Management in the 1980's, *Proceedings of the ASIS Annual Meeting,* 14 (40th Annual Meeting, 1977), Knowledge Industry Publications, White Plains, New York.

Sager, N., L. Hirschman, and M. Lyman (1978). Computerized Language Processing for Multiple Use of Narrative Discharge Summaries, in *Proceedings of the Second Annual Symposium on Computer Applications in Medical Care,* edited by F.H. Orthner, IEEE, New York, pp. 330–43.

Salkoff, M. (1973). *Une Grammaire en Chaîne du Français,* Dunod, Paris.

Salkoff, M., and N. Sager (1969). Grammatical Restrictions on the IPLV and FAP String Programs, String Program Reports, No. 5, Linguistic String Project, New York University, New York.

Sapir, E. (1949). *Selected Writings of Edward Sapir,* edited by David G. Mandelbaum, University of California Press, Berkeley.

Schank, R. (1975). *Conceptual Information Processing,* Elsevier, New York.

Scheurweghs, G. (1959). *Present-day English Syntax,* Longman's Green, London.

Selye, H., and G. Ember (1964). *Symbolic Shorthand System for Physiology and Medicine,* 4th ed., Université de Montréal.

Sherwood, B.A. (1974). *The TUTOR Language,* Computer-based Education Research Laboratory and Department of Physics, University of Illinois, Urbana.

Shortliffe, F.H. (1976). *Computer-Based Medical Consultations: MYCIN,* Elsevier, New York.

Vendler, Z. (1968). *Adjectives and Nominalizations.* Mouton, The Hague.

Walker, D.E. (1978). *Understanding Spoken Language,* The Computer Science Library, Artificial Intelligence Series, Elsevier North-Holland, New York.

Waltz, D. (1977). Natural Language Interfaces, *SIGART Newsletter* 61 (publication of ACM Special Interest Group on Artificial Intelligence), Association for Computing Machinery, New York.

Waltz, D.L. (1978). An English Language Question-Answering System for a Large Relational Data Base, *Communications of the ACM* 21 (No. 7): 526–39.

Winograd, T. (1972). *Understanding Natural Language,* Academic Press, New York.

Woods, W.A. (1970). Transition Network Grammar for Natural Language Analysis, *Communications of the ACM* 13: 591–602.

Woods, W.A. (1973). An Experimental Parsing System for Transition Network Grammars, in *Natural Language Processing,* edited by R. Rustin, Algorithmics Press, New York.

Woods, W., R.M. Kaplan, and B. Nash-Webber (1972). The Lunar Sciences Natural Language Information System: Final Report, Report No. 2378, Bolt Beranek and Newman, Cambridge, Massachusetts.

Appendices

Contents

Introduction to Appendix 1

The Linguistic String Project Computer Grammar of English

The following is a listing of the grammar of English used in the Linguistic String Project parsing system as of September 1979. The listing does not include the routines and restrictions concerned with conjunctions, comparatives, and zeroing, nor the stacking versions of the basic routines (see Chapter 6). Also not listed are a lengthy section of restrictions dealing with miscellaneous phenomena (Position Restrictions) and the entire transformational component of the grammar. Brief descriptions of all the restrictions in the grammar, including those not listed here, are given in Appendix 4.

The reader should be alerted to certain notational conventions in the listing:

1. Quote marks appear as '↓'.

2. Comments are signaled by * followed by a blank at the beginning of a line or by inclusion in [ ] within a Restriction Language statement.

3. The location of a global Restriction Language statement is given as a comment where the statement is invoked.

Some minor discrepancies between the listing and the text may be noted:

1. RT of LTR has been dropped in the computer grammar (definition 12.3) because it is always empty.

2. NPOS (definition 12.22) contains two NNN options flanking a NULL option. This is to allow NULL to be the first option for the case where there is a conjunction following a current word N or VING (the more likely reading is that the N or VING with its conjuncts belongs in NVAR), and to allow the NULL option to be last in all other cases. The acceptance of the NNN options is controlled by restrictions DOPT8A and DOPT8B.

3. Q-OF (definition 12.11B) and Q-WORD (definition 12.11C) are recent incomplete additions to the grammar (covering, for example, *thousands of years ago*); a fuller treatment is intended.

4. See Note 23, page 116.

Appendix 1   The LSP Computer Grammar of English

```
*BNF
* STRING GRAMMAR OF ENGLISH
* DEFINITIONS
* BNF
*
* 1. SENTENCE
<SENTENCE>          ::= <INTRODUCER> <CENTER> <ENDMARK>  .            1.1
<INTRODUCER>        ::= NULL / AND / OR / BUT / - FOR .               1.2
<CENTER>            ::= <ASSERTION>/<QUESTION>/<PROSENT>/
                        <PERMUTATION>/-<ASSERTIONZ>/<IMPERATIVE>.     1.3
<ENDMARK>           ::= ↓.↓ / ↓?↓ / ↓;↓  .                            1.4
* 2. CENTER STRINGS
<ASSERTION>         ::= <SA><SUBJECT><SA><TENSE><SA><VERB><SA><OBJECT><RV>
                        <SA>.                                        2.1
<QUESTION>          ::= <SA> (<YESNOQ> / <WHQ-N> / <WHQ> / <PWHQ-PN> /
                        <PWHQ> / <WHNQ-N> / <PWHNQ-PN> / <PWHNQ>).   2.2
<PROSENT>           ::= THIS <SA> .                                   2.3
<PERMUTATION>       ::= <TSUBJVO> / <OBES> .                          2.4
<ASSERTIONZ>        ::= <*NULLC> <SAZ> .                              2.5
<IMPERATIVE>        ::= <SA> [PLEASE] [DO / DO NOT / ↓DON↓↓T↓] <VO>   2.6
                        [PLEASE].
* SAZ IS DEFINED IN SECTION 9, SENTENCE ADJUNCT STRINGS
* 3.  QUESTION CENTERS
<YESNOQ>            ::= <VERB1> <SUBJECT> <PW> <SA> <VERB2>           3.1
                        <OBJECT> <RV> <SA> <ORNOT> .
<ORNOT>             ::= OR NOT / NULL  .                              3.2
<WHQ-N>             ::= (WHO / WHOM / WHICH / WHAT / WHOSE) (<YESNOQ> /
                        <ASSERTION>) .                               3.3
<WHQ>               ::= (WHERE / WHEN / HOW / WHY) <YESNOQ> .         3.4
<PWHQ-PN>           ::= <*P> (WHOM / WHICH / WHAT / WHOSE) <YESNOQ> . 3.5
<PWHQ>              ::= <*P> (WHOM / WHICH / WHAT / WHOSE) <YESNOQ> . 3.6
<WHNQ-N>            ::= <WHN> (<YESNOQ> / <ASSERTION>) .              3.7
```

Naomi Sager, Natural Language Information Processing: A Computer Grammar of English and Its Applications
Copyright © 1981 by Naomi Sager.   ISBN 0-201-06769-2

```
<WHN>              ::= <LNR> /-<VINGOFN> .                                    3.7A
<PWHNQ-PN>         ::= <*P> <WHN> <YESNOQ> .                                  3.8
<PWHNQ>            ::= <*P> <WHN> <YESNOQ> .                                  3.9
* 4.  PERMUTATION CENTERS
<TSUBJVO>          ::= (NEITHER / NOR / <DSTG> / <PN>) <SA> <VERB1>           4.1
                       <SUBJECT> <SA> <VERB2> <OBJECT><RV><SA> .
<OBES>             ::= (<ASTG>/<PN>/<DSTG>/<VENPASS>)<SA><TENSE><SA>
                       <VERB><SA><SUBJECT><SA>.                               4.2
* 5.  SUBJECT STRINGS
<SUBJECT>          ::= <NSTG> / <VINGSTG> / <SN> / <*NULLWH> / THERE .        5.1
<NSTG>             ::= <LNR> / <NWHSTG> .                                     5.2
<LNR>              ::= <LN><NVAR><RN> .                                       5.3
<NVAR>             ::= <*N>/ <*PRO>/ <*VING>/ <NAMESTG>/ <*NULLN> .           5.4
<NWHSTG>           ::= <WHATS-N>/<WHERES> / <WHEVERS-N> .                     5.5
<NAMESTG>          ::= <LNAMER> / <NQ> .                                      5.6
<LNAMER>           ::= <LNAME> <*N> <RNAME> .                                 5.7
<VINGSTG>          ::= <NSVINGO> / <VINGOFN> .                                5.8
<NSVINGO>          ::= <TPOS> <VINGO> .                                       5.9
<VINGOFN>          ::= <LN> <LVINGR> (OF/NULL) <OBJECT> <RV> <SA> .           5.10
<SN>               ::= <THATS> / <FORTOVO> / <TOVO> / -<SVINGO> /             5.11
                       <C1SHOULD> / <SNWH>.
* 6.  SENTENCE NOMINALIZATION STRINGS SN
<THATS>            ::= THAT <ASSERTION> .                                     6.1
<FORTOVO>          ::= FOR <SUBJECT> <SA> <TOVO> .                            6.2
<SVINGO>           ::= <SUBJECT> <SA> <VINGO> .                               6.3
<C1SHOULD>         ::= ( THAT / - NULL ) <ASSERTION>.                         6.4
<SNWH>             ::= <WHETHS> / <WHETHTOVO> / <WHS-N> / <PWHS> /            6.5
                       <PWHS-PN> / <WHNS-N> / <PWHNS> / <PWHNS-PN> .
* 7.  VERB AND VERBAL OBJECT STRINGS
<VERB>             ::= <LV> <VVAR> <RV> .                                     7.1
<VVAR>             ::= <*TV> / <*V> .                                         7.1A
<LTVR>             ::= <LW> <*TV> <RW> .                                      7.2
<TENSE>            ::= <LW> <*W> <RW> / NULL.                                 7.3
<LVR>              ::= <LV> <*V> <RV> .                                       7.4
<VENO>             ::= <LVENR> <SA> <OBJECT> <RV> .                           7.5
<LVENR>            ::= <LV> <*VEN> <RV> .                                     7.6
<VENPASS>          ::= <LVSA> <LVENR> <SA> <PASSOBJ> <RV> <SA> .              7.7
<LVSA>             ::= NULL / <DSTG> .                                        7.8
<VINGO>            ::= <LVSA> <LVINGR><SA><OBJECT><RV><SA> .                  7.9
<LVINGR>           ::= <LV><*VING><RV> .                                      7.10
<VO>               ::= <LVR> <SA> <OBJECT> <RV> <SA> .                        7.11
<TOVO>             ::= <LV>TO<VERB><SA><OBJECT><RV><SA>.                      7.12
<TOBE>             ::= <LV>TO<VERB><SA><OBJECT><RV><SA>.                      7.12A
<VERB1>            ::= <TENSE> / <LTVR>.                                      7.13
<VERB2>            ::= <LVR> <SA> / NULL .                                    7.14
* 8.  OBJECT STRINGS
<OBJECT>           ::= <VENO>/                                                8.1
                       <THATS> / <NPN> / <TOVO> / <PN> / <PVINGSTG> /
                       <PVINGO> / <PSNWH> / <PNN> / <PNVINGSTG> / <PSTG> /
                       <PNTHATS> / <PNSNWH> / <PNTHATSVO> / <PSVINGO> /
                       <DP2> / <DP4> / <DP2PN> / <DP4PN> / <DPSN> /
                       <DP1PN> / <DP1> /<OBJECTBE> / <VINGO> /
                       <NSTGO>/<VO>/<SASOBJBE> / <*NULLOBJ> / <NASOBJBE>/
                       <VINGSTGPN> / <NPVINGSTG> / <ASOBJBE> / <NPSVINGO>
                       / <NPVINGO> / <NPSNWH> / <DP3> / <DP3PN> /
                       <OBJBE> / <VINGSTG> / <SNWH> / <WHETHS> / <SVINGO>
                       / <C1SHOULD> / <FORTOVO> / <NTOVO> / <NTOBE> /
                       <NN> / <SOBJBE> / <SVEN> / <NA> / <ADJN> / <ND>
                       <SVO> / <ASTG> / <NTHATS> / <VENPASS>
                       / <DSTG> / <NSNWH> / <ASSERTION> / <STOVO-N> /
                       <EMBEDDEDQ> / <*NULLRECIP> / <NSVINGO> /
                       <VINGOFN>.
```

```
<PASSOBJ>            ::= <THATS>/<PN>/<PVINGSTG>/<PSVINGO>/          8.2
                         <PVINGO>/<PSNWH>/<ASOBJBE>/<PSTG>/
                         <DP1>/<P1>/<DP1P>/<DP1PN>/
                         <VINGO>/<TOVO>/<ASSERTION>/
                         <NSTGO>/<SNWH>/<OBJBE>/<VENPASS>/<ASTG>/
                         <DSTG>/<VO>/<TOBE>/<*NULLOBJ>.
* RARIFY <SN>, <EMBEDDEDQ> IN <OBJECTBE>.  2/79
<OBJECTBE>           ::= <VENPASS> / <VINGO> / <OBJBE> / - <SN> /    8.3
                         - <VINGSTG> / <TOVO> / - <ASSERTION> / - <BEINGO> /
                         - <EMBEDDEDQ> .
<OBJBE>              ::= <ASTG>/<NSTG>/<PN>/<DSTG>/-<*NULLWH>.       8.4
<BEINGO>             ::= <LV> BEING (<LAR> / <NSTG>) .               8.5
<NSTGO>              ::= <NSTG> / <*NULLWH> .                        8.6
<NN>                 ::= <NSTGO> <SA> <NSTGO> .                      8.7
<ASTG>               ::= <LAR> / <LQNR> .                            8.8
<LAR>                ::= <LA> <AVAR> <RA> .                          8.9
<EMBEDDEDQ>          ::= [↓%↓] <QUESTION> .                          8.10
* 8A.  P STRINGS
<P1>                 ::= <*P> .                                      8A.1
<PSTG>               ::= <PN> / <PVINGSTG> / <PSVINGO> .             8A.2
<PN>                 ::= <LP><*P><NSTGO> / <*NULLWH> .               8A.3
<PVINGSTG>           ::= <*P> <VINGSTG> .                            8A.4
<PSVINGO>            ::= <*P> <SVINGO> .                             8A.5
<PVINGO>             ::= <*P> <VINGO> .                              8A.6
<PSNWH>              ::= <*P> (<WHETHS> / <WHETHTOVO> / <WHS-N> ) .  8A.7
<NPN>                ::= <NSTGO> <SA> <PN> .                         8A.8
<PNN>                ::= <PN> <SA> <NSTGO> .                         8A.9
<VINGSTGPN>          ::= <VINGSTG><SA> (<PN> / <PVINGSTG> / <PSVINGO>) .   8A.10
<PNVINGSTG>          ::= (<PN>/<PVINGSTG>/ <PSVINGO> ) <SA> <VINGSTG> .    8A.11
<NPVINGSTG>          ::= <NSTGO> <SA> <PVINGSTG> .                   8A.12
<NPSVINGO>           ::= <NSTGO> <SA> <PSVINGO> .                    8A.13
<NPVINGO>            ::= <NSTGO> <SA> <PVINGO> .                     8A.14
<NPSNWH>             ::= <NSTGO> <SA> <*P> <SNWH> .                  8A.15
* 8B.   DP STRINGS
<DP1>                ::= <*DP> .                                     8B.1
<DP2>                ::= <*DP>(<NSTGO> / <VINGSTG>) .                8B.2
<DP3>                ::= (<NSTGO> / - <VINGSTG>) <*DP> .             8B.3
<DP4>                ::= <*DP>OF (<NSTGO> / <VINGSTG> ) .            8B.4
<DPSN>               ::= <*DP> <SA> <SN> .                           8B.5
<DP1PN>              ::= <*DP> <SA> ( <PN> / <PVINGSTG> / <PSVINGO> ) .   8B.6
<DP2PN>              ::= <DP2> ( <PN> / <PVINGSTG> / <PSVINGO> ) .   8B.7
<DP3PN>              ::= <DP3> ( <PN> / <PVINGSTG> / <PSVINGO> ) .   8B.8
<DP4PN>              ::= <DP4>   ( <PN> / <PVINGSTG> / <PSVINGO> ) . 8B.9
<DP1P>               ::= <*DP><*P> .                                 8B.10
* 8C.   OBJECT NOMINALIZATION STRINGS
<NTOVO>              ::= <SUBJECT> <RV> <SA> <TOVO> .                8C.1
<NTOBE>              ::= <SUBJECT> <RV> <SA> <TOBE> .                8C.1A
<SVO>                ::= <ASSERTION> .                               8C.2
<NTHATS>             ::= <NSTGO> <RV> <SA> (<THATS> / <ASSERTION>) . 8C.3
<NSNWH>              ::= <NSTGO> <RV> <SA> <SNWH> .                  8C.4
<PNTHATS>            ::= <*P> <NSTGO> <RV> <SA> (<THATS> / <ASSERTION>) .  8C.5
<PNTHATSVO>          ::= <*P>  <NSTGO> <RV> <SA> <C1SHOULD> .        8C.6
<PNSNWH>             ::= <*P> <NSTGO> <RV> <SA> <SNWH> .             8C.7
<STOVO-N>            ::= <SUBJECT> <SA> <TOVO-N> .                   8C.8
* 8D. NOMINALIZATIONS WITH ZEROED VERB BE
<SOBJBE>             ::= <SUBJECT> <SA> <OBJBE> <SA> .               8D.1
<SVEN>               ::= <SUBJECT> <SA> <VENPASS> <RV> <SA> .        8D.2
<NA>                 ::= <NSTGO> <SA> <LAR> .                        8D.3
<ADJN>               ::= <ASTG> <SA> <NSTGO>.                        8D.4
<ND>                 ::= <NSTGO> <SA> <DSTG> .                       8D.5
<SASOBJBE>           ::= <SUBJECT> <SA> AS ( <OBJBE> / - <VINGO> ) <SA> .  8D.6
<ASOBJBE>            ::= AS <OBJBE> .                                8D.7
<NASOBJBE>           ::= <NSTGO> <SA> AS <OBJBE> .                   8D.8
```

```
* 9.   SENTENCE ADJUNCT STRINGS
<SA>                ::= NULL /                                               9.1
                    ( <PDATE> / <*INT> / <DSTG> <RD> / <PN> / <PA> /
                    <NSTGT> / <RSUBJ> / <RNSUBJ> / <LCS> <CSSTG> /
                    -<OBJBESA> / -<SOBJBESA> / <SAWH> / -<NVSA> /
                    <VINGO> / <VENPASS> / <TOVO> / IN ORDER <TOVO> /
                    <COMPAR> ) NULL .
<SAZ>               ::= <DSTG> <RD> / <PN> / <PA> / <NSTGT> /                 9.1A
                    <LCS> <CSSTG> / <TOVO>.
<COMPAR>            ::= <THATS>  .                                           9.1B
<SACONJ>            ::= <SA>.                                                9.1C
<PDATE>             ::= <DATEPREP> <LDATER> .                                9.1D
<DATEPREP>          ::= ON/ IN/ OF/ SINCE/ FROM/ UNTIL/ NULL .               9.1E
<LDATER>            ::=<LDATE><DAYYEAR><RDATE>.                              9.1F
<DAYYEAR>           ::= <*Q> +/+ <*Q> +/+ <*Q> / <*DATE> / <*N> [<*Q> +,+]   9.1G
                    <*Q>.
<DSTG>              ::= <*D> / <DSTG> <*D> .                                 9.2
<PA>                ::= <LP> <*P> <*ADJ> .                                   9.3
<NSTGT>             ::= <NSTG>.                                              9.4
<RSUBJ>             ::= (<*Q> / <*T>) [<PN> / <*D> ] / <*PRO> .              9.5
<RNSUBJ>            ::= - <SN> / - <RNWH> / - <THATS-N> .                    9.6
<CSSTG>             ::= <SUB1> / <SUB2> / <SUB3> / <SUB9> / <SUB0> /
                    -<SUB5> / -<SUB6> / -<SUB7> / <SUB8> / <SUB4>.           9.7
<OBJBESA>           ::= <OBJBE> <SA> .                                       9.8
<SOBJBESA>          ::= <NSTG> <SA> (<OBJBESA> / <VENPASS> / <VINGO> ) .     9.9
<SAWH>              ::= <SAWHICHSTG> / <WHETHS> / <WHEVERS-N> .              9.10
<NVSA>              ::= <NSTG><SA> <TENSE><SA><VERB>.                        9.11
* 10.   SUBORDINATE CONJUNCTION (CS) STRINGS
<SUB0>              ::= <*CSO> <OBJBE> <SA> .                               10.1
<SUB1>              ::= <*CS1> <ASSERTION> .                                10.2
<SUB2>              ::= (<*CS2> / AS / THAN)<VENPASS> .                     10.3
<SUB3>              ::= <*CS3> <VINGO> .                                    10.4
<SUB4>              ::= <*CS4> <VINGSTG> .                                  10.5
<SUB5>              ::= <*CS5> <SVINGO> .                                   10.6
<SUB6>              ::= <*CS6> <SOBJBE> .                                   10.7
<SUB7>              ::= <*CS7> <SVEN> .                                     10.8
<SUB8>              ::= <*CS8> <Q-INVERT>.                                  10.9
<SUB9>              ::= SHOULD <SVO>.                                       10.10
* 11.   RN RIGHT ADJUNCTS OF N
<RN>*R              ::= <VENPASS> / <RNP> / <RNWH> / <THATS-N> / <S-N> /    11.1
                    <SN> / <VINGO> / <TOVO> / <TOVO-N> / <FORTOVO-N>/
                    <ADJINRN> / <DSTG> / <APPOS> / WHATSOEVER /
                    <EMBEDDEDQ> .
<RNP>               ::= <PDATE> / <PN> / <PVINGSTG> / -<PSVINGO> / <PSNWH>. 11.2
<RNWH>              ::= <PWHS> / <PWHS-PN> / <WHS-N> / <WHENS> /            11.3
                    <PWHNS-PN> / - <PWHNS> / <WHNS-N> .
<TOVO-N>            ::= <TOVO> .                                            11.4
<FORTOVO-N>         ::= <FORTOVO> .                                        11.5
<ADJINRN>           ::= <LAR> / <LQNR> .                                   11.6
<APPOS>             ::= <LNR> .                                            11.7
* 12.   LN LEFT ADJUNCTS OF N
<LN>                ::= <TPOS> <OPOS> <APOS> <NSPOS> <NPOS> .              12.1
<TPOS>              ::= <LTR> / <WHLN> / <LNAMESR> / <LNSR> / <HOWQSTG> .  12.2
<LTR>               ::= <LT> (<*T> / NULL )  .                             12.3
<LNAMESR>           ::= <LNAME> <*NS>.                                     12.3A
<LNSR>              ::= <LN> <*NS>.                                        12.4
<WHLN>              ::= WHOSE/WHICH/WHAT/WHATEVER/WHICHEVER/WHOSEVER/
                    <HOWQASTG> .                                           12.5
<HOWQASTG>          ::= HOW (MUCH / MANY / <*ADJ> ) [OF] <*T> .            12.6
<HOWQSTG>           ::= HOW (MUCH / MANY) .                                12.7
<QPOS>              ::= NULL / <LQR> .                                     12.8
<LQR>               ::= <LQ> <QVAR> <RQ> .                                 12.9
<QVAR>              ::= <*Q> / <CPDNUMBR> / <Q-OF> .                       12.10
```

```
<CPDNUMBR>          ::=<*Q> <*Q> / <CPDNUMBR> <*Q> / <*Q> <FRACTION> /     12.11
                                                      <FRACTION> .
<FRACTION>          ::= <*Q>↓/↓<*Q>.                                       12.11A
<Q-OF>              ::= <Q-WORD> OF .                                      12.11B
<Q-WORD>            ::= TENS / DOZENS / HUNDREDS / THOUSANDS / MILLIONS /  12.11C
                       BILLIONS / LOTS .
<APOS>              ::= <ADJADJ> / NULL.                                   12.12
<ADJADJ>            ::= <LAR1> / <LQNR> / <ADJADJ>( <LAR1> / <LQNR> ).     12.12A
<LAR1>              ::= <LA><AVAR><RA1> .                                  12.13
<AVAR>              ::= <LCDA> <*ADJ>/<LCDVA> (<*VING> / <*VEN>) .         12.14
<LQNR>              ::= <LQ> <QNPOS> <RQ> .                                12.15
<QNPOS>             ::= <QN>/ <NQ>/ <QNS>.                                 12.16
<QNS>               ::= <LQR><*NS>.                                        12.16A
<QN>                ::= <LQR> <PERUNIT> <*N> (<QNREP>/ NULL) <PERUNIT>     12.17
                                                   <SCALESTG>.
<PERUNIT>           ::= (PER / ↓/↓) <*N> / PERCENT/ PER CENT/↓%↓/ NULL.    12.17A
<QNREP>             ::= <Q-CONJ>.                                          12.17B
<NUMBRSTG>          ::= <*Q> / <CPDNUMBR> .                                12.18
<SCALESTG>          ::= <*ADJ> / <PN> / NULL .                             12.19
<NQ>                ::= <*N> (<LQR> / <*N> ) .                             12.20
<NSPOS>             ::= NULL  / <*NS> .                                    12.21
<NPOS>              ::= <NNN> / NULL / <NNN> .                             12.22
<NNN>               ::= <LCDN> <*N> / <NNN> <LCDN> <*N> / -<LCDN> <*VING>  12.22A
                    /-<NNN><LCDN><*VING> .
* 13.   RIGHT ADJUNCTS  -  OTHER THAN RN
<RW>                ::= <DSTG> / NULL  .                                   13.1
<RQ>                ::= OR SO / ENOUGH / NULL  .                           13.2
<RA>                ::= <SN> / - <ASSERTION> / <PN> / <PVINGSTG> /         13.3
                       <PSVINGO> / <TOVO-N> /
                       <FORTOVO-N> / <TOVO> / ENOUGH  / NULL  .
<RA1>               ::= ENOUGH   / NULL  .                                 13.4
<RV>*R              ::=  <DSTG> <RD> / <PN> / <QN> /  <SN> .               13.5
<RD>                ::= ENOUGH / NULL  .                                   13.6
<RNAME>             ::= NULL / ↓JR.↓ / ↓SR.↓ /  ↓M.D.↓ / ↓PH.D.↓/  I / II /
                       III / IV   .                                       13.7
<RDATE>             ::= <WHENS>/ <NSTGT>/ NULL.                            13.8
* 14.   LEFT ADJUNCTS  --  OTHER THAN LN
<LW>                ::= <*D> / NULL  .                                     14.1
<LV>                ::= NULL   / <DSTG> .                                  14.2
<LQ>                ::= <ADJPREQ> / <DSTG> / NULL .                        14.3
<ADJPREQ>           ::= ( NULL / VERY ) ( <*ADJ> / <*VING> / <*VEN> ) .    14.3A
<LA>                ::= <DSTG> / NULL  .                                   14.4
<LP>                ::= <DSTG> / <QN> / NULL .                             14.5
<LCS>               ::= <*D> / NULL  .                                     14.6
<LPRO>              ::= NULL   / <DSTG> .                                  14.7
<LT>                ::= NULL / <*D> / <LQR>.                               14.8
<LCDA>              ::= NULL / <*N>  .                                     14.9
<LCDVA>             ::= NULL  / -<*N> / - <*D> / - <*ADJ> .                14.10
<LCDN>              ::= NULL   / <*ADJ>/-<*Q> .                            14.11
<LDATE>             ::= NULL.                                              14.12
<LNAME>             ::= <TITLE> <NAMEPART>.                                14.13
<TITLE>             ::= <*N> / NULL.                                       14.14
<NAMEPART>          ::= ( <*N> / <*INITIAL> ) <NAMEPART> / NULL.           14.15
* 15.   WH-STRINGS
<WHETHS>            ::= (WHETHER / WHERE / WHEN / HOW / WHY / IF   )        15.1
                       <ORNOT> <ASSERTION> <ORNOT>  .
<WHETHTOVO>         ::= (WHETHER / WHERE / WHEN / HOW / WHY / IF )          15.2
                       <TOVO> .
<WHS-N>             ::= (WHO / WHOM / WHICH / WHAT / WHOSE / THAN / AS)     15.3
                       <ASSERTION> .
<PWHS>              ::= <*P> (WHOM / WHICH / WHAT / WHOSE / WHERE / WHEN)   15.4
                       <ASSERTION> .
<PWHS-PN>           ::= <*P>(WHOM /WHICH / WHAT / WHOSE)<ASSERTION> .       15.5
```

```
<WHNS-N>              ::= <WHN> <ASSERTION> .                              15.6
<PWHNS>               ::= <*P> <WHN> <ASSERTION> .                         15.7
<PWHNS-PN>            ::= <*P> <WHN> <ASSERTION>.                          15.8
<WHATS-N>             ::= WHAT <ASSERTION> .                               15.9
<WHERES>              ::= WHERE <ASSERTION> .                              15.10
<WHENS>               ::= (WHEN / WHERE / BEFORE / AFTER / NULL) <ASSERTION>.  15.11
<THATS-N>             ::= THAT <ASSERTION> .                               15.12
<S-N>                 ::= <ASSERTION> .                                    15.13
<SAWHICHSTG>          ::= (WHICH / THAN / AS) <ASSERTION> .                15.14
<WHEVERS-N>           ::= (WHOEVER / WHOMEVER / WHICHEVER / WHATEVER /     15.15
                         WHOSOEVER)<ASSERTION> .
* 16. CONJUNCTION STRINGS
<ANDSTG>              ::= AND[NOT]<SACONJ><Q-CONJ> .                       16.1
<ORSTG>               ::=OR<SACONJ><Q-CONJ> .                             16.2
<NORSTG>              ::=NOR<SACONJ><Q-CONJ>   .                           16.3
<Q-CONJ>              ::=NULL .                                            16.4
<BOTHSTG>             ::=BOTH .                                            16.5
<EITHERSTG>           ::=EITHER .                                          16.6
<NEITHERSTG>          ::= NEITHER .                                        16.7
<ASSTG>               ::= AS <SACONJ> ( <Q-CONJ> / <C-ASSERT> / <Q-INVERT>  16.8
                     /<Q-PHRASE>).
<BUTSTG>              ::= BUT[NOT]<SACONJ><Q-CONJ> .                       16.9
<COMMASTG>            ::= +,+ <NOTOPT> ( <Q-CONJ> / NULL ) .               16.10
<NOTOPT>              ::= [NOT] .                                          16.10A
<THANSTG>             ::= THAN <SACONJ>(<Q-CONJ>/<Q-ASSERT>/<Q-INVERT>/    16.11
                         <Q-PHRASE>) .
<TOSTG>               ::= TO <Q-CONJ>.                                     16.12
<DASHSTG>             ::= +-+ <Q-CONJ> .                                   16.12A
<PARENSTG>            ::= +(+ <CENTER>/ <NSTG>/ <PN> +)+ .                 16.12B
<Q-ASSERT>            ::= <ASSERTION> .                                    16.13
<Q-INVERT>            ::= <VERB1>(BEEN/<*NULL>)<SUBJECT> .                 16.14
<Q-PHRASE>            ::= EVER/USUAL/NECESSARY .                           16.15
<AND-ORSTG>           ::= +AND/OR+   <SACONJ> <Q-CONJ> .                   16.16
<AS-WELL-AS-STG>      ::=  AS WELL AS   <SACONJ> <Q-CONJ> .                16.17
<ESPECIALLY-STG>      ::= ESPECIALLY <Q-CONJ> .                           16.18
<PARTICULARLY-STG>    ::=  PARTICULARLY <Q-CONJ>.                          16.19
*LISTS
* ATOMICS [WORD CLASSES]:
* T (ARTICLE); Q (QUANTIFIER); ADJ (ADJECTIVE); D (ADVERB);
* NS (POSSESSIVE NOUN); N (NOUN); PRO (PRONOUN); P (PREPOSITION);
* V (TENSELESS VERB) ;  TV (TENSED VERB);
* VEN (PAST PARTICIPLE) ;   VING (PRESENT PARTICIPLE);
* W (TENSE WORD);  DP (ADVERB-PREPOSITION, POST-V);  WH (WH-WORD);
* INT (INTERJECTION);  CS0-CS7 (SUBORDINATE CONJUNCTIONS);
* CONJ (COORDINATING CONJUNCTION).
* ZEROS: NULL (O ADJUNCT; O VARIANT OF ELEMENT);   NULLN (O NOUN);
* NULLOBJ ( O OBJECT OF INTRANSITIVE VERB);
* NULLWH (O OF OMISSION DUE TO PRONOUNING IN WH STRING);
* NULLC (ZEROED ELEMENT IN CONJUNCTIONAL STRING).
* NOTE ON REPETITION.  USER WRITES <X> *R  ::= <OPT1> / <OPT2> / ... / <OPTN>.
* PROGRAM GENERATES  <X>  ::=  <X1><X2>/ NULL.
* <X1>  ::=  <OPT1> / <OPT2> / ... / <OPTN>.
* <X2>  ::=  NULL /  v  <X1> <X2>.               v  REP SWITCH IS ON.
*
* ATTRIBUTES
*
* WOPD ATTRIBUTES
*
* ATTRIBUTE-ADJ
ATTRIBUTE =
          AASP, ACOMPOUND, AFORTO, AINPA, AINRN, APREQ, ASCALE, ASENT1,
          ASENT2, ASENT3, ASCALE, ASHOULD, ATHAT, AWH, COMPARATIVE,
          NEGADJ, NTH, SUPERLATIVE, TIMETAG.
```

```
* ATTRIBUTE-CS
ATTRIBUTE =
        CSOAS, CS1INNER.
* ATTRIBUTE-D
ATTRIBUTE =
        DEVAL, DLA, DLCOMP, DLCS, DLOC1, DLOC2, DLOC3, DLP, DLQ, DLT,
        DLTPRO, DLV, DLW, DMANNER, DMIDDLE, DMOBILE, DPERM, DPRED, DRN,
        DRV, DRW, DSA, DSA1, DUNIV, DVERY, NEGATIVE.
* ATTRIBUTE-N
ATTRIBUTE =
        AGGREGATE, COLLECTIVE, NAME, NCLASSIFIER1, NCLASSIFIER2,
        NCOUNT1, NCOUNT2, NCOUNT3, NCOUNT4, NHUMAN, NONHUMAN, NLETTER,
        NMONTH, NPREQ, NSCALE, NSENTP, NSENT1, NSENT2, NSENT3,
        NTIME1, NTIME2, NTITLE, NUNIT, PLURAL, SINGULAR.
* ATTRIBUTE-PRO
ATTRIBUTE =
        ACCUSATIVE, INDEFINITE, NOMINATIVE, PROPOSS, PROSELF.
* ATTRIBUTE-Q
ATTRIBUTE =
        QALL, QHALF, QMANY, QNUMBER, QROVING.
* ATTRIBUTE-T
ATTRIBUTE =
        DEF, EACHEVRY, INDEF, TDEM, TPOSS, TQUAN.
* ATTRIBUTE-V
ATTRIBUTE =
        BEREP, BVAL, DPVAL, NOTNOBJ, NOTNSUBJ, OBJLIST, PAST, POBJLIST,
        PVAL, VASP, VBE, VCOLLECTIVE, VDO, VENDADJ, VEVENT, VEXP, VHAVE,
        VMANNER, VMOD, VMOTION, VSENT1, VSENT2, VSENT3, VSENT4,
        VRECIP, VVERYVING.
*
* NODE ATTRIBUTES
*
* ATTRIBUTE-COMP
ATTRIBUTE =
        AS1-MARKER, AS2-MARKER, COMP-MARKER, COMP-ITEM, THAN-MARKER.
* ATTRIBUTE-CONJ
ATTRIBUTE =
        LINKC   [NODE ATTRIBUTE FOR ZEROED ELEMENT], MATCHED,
        POSTCONJELEM, PRECONJELEM, SCOPE.
* ATTRIBUTE-WH    [FOR WH-OMISSION]
ATTRIBUTE =
        DIDOMIT, DIDOMPN, MUSTOMIT, MUSTOMPN.
*
*
*
*
* GLOBAL LISTS
*
*
* GLOBAL-A
GLOBAL =
        $ACCEPT [WWH2,3,4],
        $A-HUNDRED [WAGREE1, WAGREE4, WAGREE9],
        $ANDSING [WAGREE1, WAGREE5, WAGREE7],
        $ANDSUBJ   [WAGREE1, WAGREE2],
        $APOSNULL [DN50, WN11, WQ8, WSN11],
        $ASCNT    [CORE, CORE-CONJUNCT, LEFT-ADJUNCT-POS,
                   RIGHT-ADJUNCT-POS],
        $ASPECTUAL [DEEPEST COVERB, DEEPEST-COVERB-],
        $ASSIGN-AS2 [WCOMP6C, -6D, -6E],
        $ASSIGN-COMP-MARK    [WCOMP-Q1, WCOMP-Q1A],
        $ASSIGN-PRE-AND-POST [COEL1, PRE-POST-CONJELEM],
        $ASSIGN-THAN    [WCOMP6, 6A, 6B],
        $ASSIGN-X1 [WCOMP-ADJ, WCOMP-D, WCOMP-Q1, Q2, Q2A, Q2B, Q2C,
                    Q2D, WCOMP6] ,
```

```
          $ASSIGN-X1-AS1 [WCOMP-D, -Q2, -Q2C, -Q2D, WCOMP6C],
          $ATRNSUBJ [HOST, HOST ELEMENT],
          $AT-LADJ   [HOST, HOST-ELEMENT],
          $AT-RADJ [HOST, HOST-ELEMENT] ,
          $AT-SVO-LEVEL   [WCOMP2, WCOMP3].
* GLOBAL-B
* GLOBAL-C
GLOBAL =
          $CENTERLIKE [DPOS7, DPOS9],
          $COMP-IN-LN   [WCOMP5, WCOMP5B],
          $CORE-PATH   [CORE, CORE-, CORE-CONJUNCT, HOST],
          $CORE-HAS-AND   [WAGREE1, WAGREE2].
* GLOBAL-D
GLOBAL =
          $DIMINISHER   [WAGREE1, WAGREE2].
* GLOBAL-E
* GLOBAL-I
GLOBAL =
          $IFRN   [WWH2, WWH3],
          $IN-CONJ   [DCONJOA, DCONJOB],
          $IN-CONJA   [DCONJOI, DCONJOJ, DCONJOK],
          $INCONJSTG   [DCOM2, WCOM4],
          $IN-CONJUNCTION   [WZERO1, 2],
          $IN-OBJBE [DCONJOI, DCONJOJ].
* GLOBAL-J
* GLOBAL-L
GLOBAL =
          $LEFT-TO-HOST   [HOST-ELEMENT, PREVIOUS-ELEMENT, PREVIOUS-ELEMENT-],
          $LOCATE-COMPARATIVE   [WCOMP5, WCOMP5A, WCOMP5B].
* GLOBAL-M
GLOBAL =
          $MINPAR   [DMIN1, DMIN10 - 17, DMIN2 - 9],
          $MIXED   [WAGREE2, WAGREE2A, WAGREE5].
* GLOBAL-N
GLOBAL =
          $NEXT-VERB   [DEEPEST-COVERB, HOST-ELEMENT, VERB-COELEMENT],
          $NEXT-VERB-   [DEEPEST-COVERB-, VERB-COELEMENT-],
          $NHUMAN   [DSN2, DSN7, WPOS22, WSN8, WWH2],
          $NO-AS-MATCH   [WCOMP-,Q2,WCOMP-Q2C,-Q2D],
          $NO-COMMON   [WPOS15A, WSEL1, 5, 6, 7],
          $NOCOMMONP1   [WPOS15],
          $NO-COMP-MATCH   [WCOMP-Q2, -Q2A, -Q2B, -Q2C],
          $NOT-AFTER-COMMA   [WPOS20],
          $NOTAG   [WWH2, WWH3, WWH4],
          $NOT-EMPTY-TEST   [WCONJ3A, WZERO1, WZERO2],
          $NOTOBJ   [DPOS7, DPOS9],
          $NOTPLURSUBJ   [WAGREE1, WAGREE2],
          $NOTSINGX1   [WAGREE1,3,7,8],
          $NOT-V-OBJ-CONJ-V-OB [DCONJ7,WCONJ10],
          $NOTWHOM [WWH2,4],
          $NPOSNULL   [WN11, WQ8],
          $NSPOSNULL   [WN11, WQ8, WSN11],
          $NULLED-STRUCTURE[DCONJO,DCONJOA] .
* GLOBAL-O
* GLOBAL-P
GLOBAL =
          $PATH [WWH2,3,4],
          $PNADJ [ULTIMATE-HOST],
          $PUNCT-COMMA   [DCONJ5, DCONJ5A],
          $POST-OBJ-SA   [DCOM3A, DCOM3B, DPOS22, WPOS20, WPOS27],
          $POSTCONJ   [CORE, CORE-CONJUNCT, DPOS16, PRE-POST-CONJELEM,
                       STACK-FOR-LEFT, STACK-FOR-RIGHT, STARTAT,
                       WAGREE1, WAGREE4, WPOS23],
```

```
          $PLURAGREE   [WAGREE1, 1A, 1B],
          $PLURN   [WAGREE1, WAGREE2, WAGREE5, WAGREE7],
          $PLURTEST   [WAGREE2, WAGREE2A],
          $PRECONJ   [COEL1-, PRE-POST-CONJELEM],
          $PREV-ATOM   [DCONJ5, DCONJ8A],
          $PREV-RV-SA-EMPTY   [DPOS16, DPOS17],
          $PREVSA   [DCOM2,DCOM4].
* GLOBAL-Q
GLOBAL =
          $QPLUR-TEST   [WAGREE1, 4, 9, WMED2],
          $QPOSNULL   [WN11, WQ8, WSN11],
          $QSING-TEST   [WAGREE1, 4, 9, WMED2].
* GLOBAL-R
GLOBAL =
          $RARE   [ADJINRN, CENTER, CSSTG, C1SHOULD, DCOM4, DCONJ6,
                   DCONJ7, DCONJ9, DN1, DPOS6, DP3, INTRODUCER, LCDN,
                   LCDVA, NNN, OBJECTBE, RA, RN, RNP, RNSUBJ, RNWH, SA,
                   SAOBJBE, SN, WAGREE2, WCOM10, WCONJ4, WCONJ8, WHN,
                   WMED2, WN8, WN11, WPOS15, WPOS20, WQ1, WSN1, WSN11],
          $REDUNDCY-CHK   [DCONJOA, DCONJOB, DCONJOI, DCONJOJ,
                           DCONJOK],
          $RIGHT-TO-HOST   [FOLLOWING-ELEMENT, FOLLOWING-ELEMENT-,
                            HOST-ELEMENT],
          $REP   [RN, RV].
* GLOBAL-S
GLOBAL =
          $SA-CS34-PTEST [WPOS15A,B],
          $SAVE-NULLC-IN-X3   [WZERO1, 2, 3],
          $SCOPE   [DN3, DN51, DOPT1A, B, C, D, F, G, H, I, J, K, L, N,
                    DOPT1P, Q, R, DOPT8, DOPT11, 23, 24, 25, 27],
          $SET-LINK   [WZERO1, 2, 3, 5],
          $SINGAGREE   [WAGREE1, 1A, 1B, 7],
          $SINGN   [WAGREE1, 2, 5],
          $SINGSTRING   [WAGREE1, 2],
          $SINGTEST   [WAGREE2, 2A],
          $STACK-TEST   [DOWN1, HOST, LAST-ELEMENT, NELEMRT, STARTAT],
          $SUBJ [WAGREE1, 1B] ,
          $SUBJIT   [DSN2, 4, 5],
          $SUBJNOTSG   [WAGREE1, 3, 7],
          $SUBJ-NOT-EMPTY   [WZERO1, WZERO2],
          $SUBJ-PRED-TEST   [WAGREE2A, 2B].
* GLOBAL-T
GLOBAL =
          $TPLUR-TEST   [WAGREE1, 4, 9, WMED2],
          $TSING-TEST   [WAGREE1, 4, 9, WMED2],
          $TEST-FOR-AS1-MARK   [WCOMP5C, D, E, WCOMP6C],
          $TEST-FOR-COMP-MARK   [WCOMP5,5A,5B,WCOMP6],
          $TO-PRECONJUNCTION-Y [COEL1, COEL1-, CONJELEM, HOST-ELEMENT,
                   LEFT-ADJUNCT-POS, RIGHT-ADJUNCT-POS],
          $TYPE-LXR   [DCONJ5, 5A, 5D],
          $TYPE-RESTRCTD-STG   [DCONJ5A, 5D],
          $TYPE-STRING   [DCONJ5].
* GLOBAL-U
GLOBAL =
          $UP-THROUGH-Q   [IMMEDIATE, IMMEDIATE-NODE, IMMEDIATE-STRING, IT,
                      PRESENT-ELEMENT, PRESENT-STRING, STARTAT].
* GLOBAL-V
GLOBAL =
          $VB   [WAGREE2, 1B],
          $VERBAL   [DEEPEST-COVERB, TCONJ-VERBAL-OBJ].
* GLOBAL-W
GLOBAL =
          $WORD-TO-LEFT-OF-X1   [DCONJO, DCONJOA],
          $WORD-TO-RIGHT-OF-X2   [DCONJO, DCONJOA] .
```

```
* GLOBAL-X
*
* TYPE LISTS
*
TYPE ADJSET=
  LA, LCS, LDATE, LN, LP, LPRO, LQ, LT, LV, LVSA, LW, RA, RA1, RD, RDATE
  , RN, RQ, RV, RW, SA.
* NOTE: CONJ-NODES ARE IN ADJSET1 SO THAT CORE ROUTINE DOES NOT
*       DESCEND TO CONJ.
TYPE ADJSET1 =
  AND-ORSTG, ANDSTG, ASSTG, AS-WELL-AS-STG, BUTSTG, COMMASTG, DASHSTG,
  ESPECIALLY-STG, LA, LCDA, LCDN, LCDVA, LCS, LDATE, LN, LNAME, LP,
  LPRO, LQ, LT, LV, LVSA, LW, NORSTG, ORSTG, PARENSTG,
  PARTICULARLY-STG, QNREP, RA, RA1, RD, RDATE, RN, RQ, RV, SA,
  THANSTG, TOSTG.
TYPE ATOM=
  ADJ, CS0, CS1, CS2, CS3, CS4, CS5, CS6, CS7, CS8, D, DATE, DP,
  INITIAL, INT, N, NS, NULL, NULLC, NULLN, NULLOBJ, NULLRECIP, NULLWH,
  P, PRO, Q, T, TV, V, VEN, VING, W.
TYPE CENTERLIKE =
  ASSERTION, FORTOVO, NASOBJBE, NTOVO, NVSA, OBES, Q-CONJ, SASOBJBE,
  SOBJBE, SOBJBESA, STOVO-N, TOVO, TSUBJVO, VENPASS, YESNOQ.
TYPE CONJSTG =
  AND-ORSTG, ANDSTG, ASSTG, AS-WELL-AS-STG, BUTSTG, COMMASTG,
  ESPECIALLY-STG, ORSTG, PARTICULARLY-STG, QNREP, THANSTG.
TYPE CONJ-NODE =
  AND-ORSTG, ANDSTG, ASSTG, AS-WELL-AS-STG, BUTSTG, COMMASTG, DASHSTG,
  ESPECIALLY-STG, NORSTG, ORSTG, PARTICULARLY-STG, QNREP, THANSTG,
  TOSTG.
TYPE C-NODE =
  AND-ORSTG, ANDSTG, ASSTG, AS-WELL-AS-STG, BOTHSTG, BUTSTG, COMMASTG,
  DASHSTG, EITHERSTG, ESPECIALLY-STG, NEITHERSTG, NORSTG, ORSTG,
  PARTICULARLY-STG, QNREP, THANSTG, TOSTG.
TYPE LADJSET=
  LA, LCDA, LCDN, LCDVA, LCS, LDATE, LN, LNAME, LP, LPRO, LQ, LT, LV,
  LVSA, LW.
TYPE LXR =
  LAR, LAR1, LDATER, LNAMER, LNR, LNSR, LQR, LQNR, LTR, LTVR, LVENR,
  LVINGR, LVR, TENSE, VERB.
TYPE MINLIST =
 COMPAR, D, DSTG, LCS, NSTGT, PDATE, PN, QN, QNPOS, RSUBJ, SAWH, THATS,
 TOVO, VENPASS, VINGO, WHS-N.
TYPE N-OBJ-IN-STR = [N OR PN OBJECTS OF TYPE STRING]
  ADJN, DP2, DP3, DP4, DP1PN, DP2PN, DP3PN, DP4PN, NA, NASOBJBE, ND, NN,
  NPN, NPSNWH, NPSVINGO, NPVINGO, NPVINGSTG, NSNWH, NTHATS, PN, PNN,
  PNSNWH, PNTHATS, PNTHATSVO, PNVINGSTG, VINGSTGPN.
TYPE N-OMITTING-WH-STRING =
  FORTOVO-N, SAWHICHSTG, S-N, THATS-N, TOVO-N, WHATS-N, WHEVERS-N,
  WHNQ-N, WHNS-N, WHQ-N, WHS-N.
TYPE OMITTING-OBJECT-STG =
  ASSERTION, C1SHOULD, DP2, FORTOVO, NA, NASOBJBE, ND, NN, NPN, NPSNWH,
  NPVINGO, NPVINGSTG, NSNWH, NTHATS, NTOVO, PN, PNTHATSVO, PSVINGO,
  PVINGO, PVINGSTG, SASOBJBE, SOBJBE, SVEN, SVINGO, SVO, THATS, TOVO,
  VENO, VENPASS, VINGO, VINGSTGPN, WHETHS.
TYPE PDPOBJECT =
  DP1, DP1P, DP1PN, DP2, DP2PN, DP3, DP3PN, DP4, DP4PN, DPSN, NPN,
  NPSNWH, NPSVINGO, NPVINGO, NPVINGSTG, P1, PN, PNN, PNSNWH, PNTHATS,
  PNTHATSVO, PNVINGSTG, PSNWH, PSVINGO, PVINGO, PVINGSTG, VINGSTGPN.
TYPE PN-OMITTING-WH-STG =
  PWHNQ-PN, PWHNS-PN, PWHQ-PN, PWHS-PN.
TYPE Q-NODE =
  Q-CONJ.
TYPE RADJSET=
  RA, RA1, RD, RDATE, RN, RNAME, RQ, RV, RW.
```

```
TYPE RECURSIVE =
  ADJADJ, ASSERTION, CPDNUMBR, DSTG, LN, LNSR, NAMESTG, NNN, NVSA, SN.
TYPE REPETITIVE =
  RN, RV.
TYPE SCOPE-NODE =
  BOTHSTG, EITHERSTG, NEITHERSTG.
TYPE STRING =
  ADJINRN, ADJN, APPOS, ASOBJBE, ASSERTION,
  BEINGO, C1SHOULD, CPDNUMBR,
  DP1, DP2, DP3, DP4, DP1P, DP1PN, DP2PN, DP3PN, DP4PN, DPSN,
  FORTOVO, FORTOVO-N,
  HOWQASTG, HOWQSTG,
  IMPERATIVE,
  LN,
  NA, NASOBJBE, ND, NN, NPN, NPSNWH, NPSVINGO, NPVINGO, NPVINGSTG, NQ,
  NSNWH, NSTGT, NSVINGO, NTHATS, NTOBE, NTOVO, NUMBRSTG, NVSA,
  OBES, OBJBESA,
  P1, PA, PN, PNN, PNSNWH, PNTHATS, PNTHATSVO, PNVINGSTG, PROSENT,
  PSNWH, PSVINGO, PVINGO, PVINGSTG, PWHNQ, PWHNQ-PN, PWHNS, PWHNS-PN,
  PWHQ, PWHQ-PN, PWHS, PWHS-PN, PARENSTG, PDATE,
  Q-ASSERT, Q-CONJ, Q-INVERT, Q-PHRASE, QN, QNS, Q-OF,
  S-N, SASOBJBE, SAWHICHSTG, SENTENCE, SOBJBE, SOBJBESA, STOVO-N,
  SUB0, SUB1, SUB2, SUB3, SUB4, SUB5, SUB6, SUB7, SUB8, SUB9,
  SVEN, SVINGO, SVO,
  THATS, THATS-N, TOBE, TOVO, TOVO-N, TSUBJVO,
  VENO, VENPASS, VINGO, VINGOFN, VINGSTGPN, VO,
  WHATS-N, WHENS, WHERES, WHETHS, WHETHTOVO, WHEVERS-N, WHNQ-N, WHNS-N,
  WHQ, WHQ-N, WHS-N,
  YESNOQ .
TYPE STRINGC =
  ASSERTION.
TYPE STGSEG=
  ASSERTION, DP2, DP3, DP4, PN, PSVINGO, PVINGO, PVINGSTG, SVO, TOBE,
  TOVO, VINGO, YESNOQ.
TYPE TRANSMITTING-OBJ-STG =
  ASSERTION, C1SHOULD, DP2, FORTOVO-N, NA, ND, NN, NPN, NPSNWH,
  NPSVINGO, NPVINGO, NPVINGSTG, NTHATS, NTOVO, PN, PNTHATSVO, PSVINGO,
  PVINGO, PVINGSTG, SASOBJBE, SOBJBE, SVEN, SVO, THATS, TOVO, VENO,
  VENPASS, VINGO, WHETHS.
*
*
*
*
*RESTR
* *********  ***************************************************** ********
*                                                                        *
*                                                                        *
*                               ROUTINES                                 *
*                                                                        *
*                                                                        *
* *********  ***************************************************** ********
*
* NOTE ON CONJUNCTION:
*       GIVEN THAT X AND Y ARE ELEMENTS OF A STRING WE SAY X1 HAS A
*       CONJUNCT X2 IN THE SITUATION (X1 CONJ X2) Y OR X1 Y1 CONJ X2 Y2
*       (AND SO FORTH FOR X3,X4,ETC.). ROUTINES WHOSE NAME ENDS IN +-+ DO
*       NOT STACK. IN STACKING ROUTINES, IF THE CONJUNCTS OF X1 ARE
*       PLACED ON A RE-EXECUTION STACK THEN IF THE RESTRICTION R
*       CONTAINING THE GIVEN ROUTINE IS SUCCESSFUL ,R WILL BE
*       RE-EXECUTED SUBSTITUTING X2,X3,ETC. IN PLACE OF X1 FOR THE
*       VALUE OF THE ROUTINE .
*
```

```
*
* COEL1- :GIVEN THAT X AND Y ARE ELEMENTS OF SOME STRING.COEL1-
*    STARTS AT Y AND GOES LEFT OR RIGHT TO X.HOWEVER IF X IS IN A STRING
*    SEGMENT COEL1- WILL NOT GO TO X (COELEMENT ROUTINE DOES IT). IN A
*    SITUATION X1Y1 CONJ X2Y2, COEL1 STARTING AT Y2 WILL GO TO X2.  AND
*    IN A SITUATION XY1 CONJ Y2 COEL1- STARTING AT Y2 WILL GO TO X.
*
ROUTINE COEL1-(X) = EITHER $LEFT-OR-RIGHT OR ITERATE
        $TO-PRECONJUNCTION-Y UNTIL $LEFT-OR-RIGHT SUCCEEDS.
  $LEFT-OR-RIGHT = EITHER DO LEFTR(X) OR DO RIGHTR(X).
$TO-PRECONJUNCTION-Y = EITHER $PRECONJ OR $ASSIGN-PRECONJELEM.           (GLOBAL)
$ASSIGN-PRECONJELEM = VERIFY $LOCATE-CONJNODE;
        VERIFY $ASSIGN-PRE-AND-POST[PRE-POST-CONJELEM];
        DO $PRECONJ.
$LOCATE-CONJNODE = ASCEND TO Q-CONJ; GO UP; STORE IN X100.
$PRECONJ = THE PRESENT-ELEMENT- HAS NODE ATTRIBUTE PRECONJELEM.         (GLOBAL)
* ROUTINE COELEMENT-(X): GIVEN THAT X AND Y ARE ELEMENTS OF SOME STRING
*    COELEMENT- STARTS AT Y AND GOES TO X.  IF X IS IN A STRING SEGMENT
*    COELEMENT- WILL GO ONE LEVEL BELOW THE STRING SEGMENT TO FIND X.
*
ROUTINE COELEMENT-(X) = EITHER DO COEL1-(X) OR $STRING-SEGMENT.
$STRING-SEGMENT = DO COEL1-(STGSEG); DO ELEMENT-(X).
* ROUTINE CORE-: LOOKS FOR AN ATOMIC NODE OR STRING NODE WHICH IS EITHER
*    THE NODE CURRENTLY BEING +LOOKED AT+ OR ONE THAT LIES BELOW THIS NODE.
*    THE DESCENT DOES NOT PASS THROUGH NODES ON THE LIST ADJSET1.
*
ROUTINE CORE- = DO $CORE-PATH.
$CORE-PATH = ONE OF $AT-ATOM, $DESCEND-TO-ATOM,                         (GLOBAL)
        $DESCEND-TO-STRING IS TRUE.
$AT-ATOM = TEST FOR ATOM.
$DESCEND-TO-ATOM = DESCEND TO ATOM NOT PASSING THROUGH ADJSET1.
 $DESCEND-TO-STRING = DESCEND TO STRING NOT PASSING THROUGH ADJSET1;
                      IF TEST FOR LN THEN $RIGHT-TO-CORE .
 $RIGHT-TO-CORE = ITERATE GO RIGHT UNTIL TEST FOR CONJ-NODE FAILS;
                DO CORE- .
* DOWN1- TESTS WHETHER X IS AN ELEMENT WHICH IS ONE LEVEL BELOW THE
* NODE THE PROGRAM IS CURRENTLY +LOOKING AT+.
*
ROUTINE DOWN1-(X) = GO DOWN;ITERATET GO RIGHT UNTIL TEST FOR X SUCCEEDS.
*       ELEMENT- TESTS WHETHER X IS AN ELEMENT ONE LEVEL BELOW THE NODE
* THE PROGRAM IS CURRENTLY +LOOKING AT+. IF NOT,
* AND A STRING SEGMENT IS ONE LEVEL BELOW THE CURRENT NODE
*       THE SEARCH CONTINUES ONE LEVEL BELOW THE STRING SEGMENT NODE.
*
ROUTINE ELEMENT- = EITHER DO DOWN1-(X) OR $STRING-SEGMENT.
 $STRING-SEGMENT = DO DOWN1-(STGSEG); DO DOWN1-(X).
*       ELEMOF (X) TESTS WHETHER X IS A NODE ONE LEVEL ABOVE THE NODE THE
* PROGRAM IS CURRENTLY +LOOKING AT+. ONE STRING SEGMENT NODE
* MAY BE PASSED UP THROUGH.
*
ROUTINE ELEMOF(X) = EITHER $UP-ONE-TO-X OR $UP-TO-STRING-SEG.
$UP-ONE-TO-X = DO IMMEDIATE-NODE; TEST FOR X.
$UP-TO-STRING-SEG = DO IMMEDIATE-NODE; TEST FOR STGSEG;
        DO $UP-ONE-TO-X.
* FOLLOWING-ELEMENT- GOES RIGHT TO THE FIRST NODE WHICH IS NOT  C-NODE.
*
ROUTINE FOLLOWING-ELEMENT-    = DO $RIGHT-TO-HOST[HOST-ELEMENT].
* EXTENDED-CORE-: GOES TO THE CORE.
* IF THE CORE IS NULLWH,AND IS IN AN N-OMITTING-WH-STRING IN A RN.
* THIS ROUTINE GOES UP TO THE RN AND FROM THERE TO THE HOST NOUN .
```

```
ROUTINE EXTENDED-CORE- = DO CORE-;
                         IF BOTH PRESENT-ELEMENT- IS NULLWH
                            AND AT IMMEDIATE ASSERTION , ASCEND TO
                               RN PASSING THROUGH N-OMITTING-WH-STRING
                     ,THEN HOST- EXISTS .
* THE HOST- ROUTINE GOES TO THE CORE- OF THE HOST-ELEMENT.
*
ROUTINE HOST- = CORE- OF HOST-ELEMENT EXISTS.
* ROUTINE HOST-ELEMENT STARTS AT OR ASCENDS TO LADJSET OR RADJSET OR
*     RNSUBJ Y. IF Y IS OF TYPE RADJSET OR LADJSET IT GOES TO THE CORE
*     ELEMENT X(TO X IN AN LXR TYPE NODE). IF Y IS RNSUBJ IT ASCENDS TO
*     SA AND THEN GOES TO COELEMENT SUBJECT.
*
ROUTINE HOST-ELEMENT = EITHER TEST FOR ADJSET
                       OR ASCEND TO ADJSET;
                       ONE OF $AT-LADJ, $AT-RADJ, $ATRNSUBJ IS TRUE .
  $AT-LADJ = TEST FOR LADJSET;
             STORE IN X200;
             DO $RIGHT-TO-HOST .
$RIGHT-TO-HOST = EITHER $GO-RIGHT-PAST-C OR ITERATE                     (GLOBAL)
     $TO-PRECONJUNCTION-Y[COEL1-] UNTIL $GO-RIGHT-PAST-C SUCCEEDS.
$GO-RIGHT-PAST-C = ITERATE GO RIGHT UNTIL TEST FCR C-NODE FAILS.
  $AT-RADJ = TEST FOR RADJSET;
             STORE IN X200;
             EITHER $RV-TEST OR $LEFT-TO-HOST .
$RV-TEST = TEST FOR RV; STORE IN X100; EITHER $RV-IN-STRING OR
           EITHER DO LEFTR(VVAR) OR ITERATE $TO-PRECONJUNCTION-Y UNTIL
           DO LEFTR(VVAR) SUCCEEDS.
$LEFT-TO-HOST = EITHER $LEFT-PAST-C OR ITERATE $TO-PRECONJUNCTION-Y     (GLOBAL)
        UNTIL $LEFT-PAST-C SUCCEEDS.
$LEFT-PAST-C = ITERATE GO LEFT UNTIL TEST FOR C-NODE FAILS.
$RV-IN-STRING = GO UP; TEST FOR TYPE STRING; EITHER $RV-IN-OBJECT
        OR  $RV-IN-CENTER.
$RV-IN-OBJECT = TEST FOR NTOVO OR NTHATS OR NSNWH OR PNTHATS OR
        PNTHATSVO OR PNSNWH; ASCEND TO OBJECT PASSING THROUGH Q-CONJ;
        DO $NEXT-VERB.
$NEXT-VERB =  DO $1; DO $2.                                            (GLOBAL)
  $1 = THE PRESENT-ELEMENT- HAS COELEMENT VERB OR LVINGR OR LVENR OR LVR
          OR VERB1 X7.
  $2 = IF X7 IS VERB1 WHERE VALUE IS NOT LTVR THEN PRESENT-ELEMENT- HAS
          COELEMENT VERB2  X7.
$RV-IN-CENTER = GO TO X100; DO $NEXT-VERB.
  $ATRNSUBJ = BOTH VALUE OF SA IS RNSUBJ
              AND PRESENT-ELEMENT- HAS COELEMENT- SUBJECT .
* HOST-STRING STARTS AT OR ASCENDS TO SA.IT THEN GOES TO THE FIRST
* STRING THAT IS ABOVE.
*
  ROUTINE HOST-STRING = EITHER $2 OR $1;  DO IMMEDIATE-STRING.
$2 = TEST FOR SA.
  $1 = DO IMMEDIATE (SA).
* IMMEDIATE(X) ASCENDS TO X. NODES ON THE STRING LIST ARE NOT
*      PASSED THROUGH.IF THIS ROUTINE STARTS AT Q-CONJ IT WILL GO
*       TO THE HOST NODE(UP TWICE FROM TOP OF Q NEST).
*
ROUTINE IMMEDIATE (X) =
        DO $UP-THROUGH-Q;
        ASCEND TO X PASSING THROUGH Q-CONJ.
  $UP-THROUGH-Q = ITERATET $GO-UP-TWICE UNTIL                          (GLOBAL)
                  TEST FOR Q-CONJ FAILS.                               (GLOBAL)
  $GO-UP-TWICE = GO UP; GO UP.
* IMMEDIATE-NODE- GOES UP ONE NODE.
*
ROUTINE IMMEDIATE-NODE-=GO UP.
```

```
*  IMMEDIATE-STRING ASCENDS TO THE FIRST STRING ABOVE THE CURRENT NODE.
*      IF THIS ROUTINE STARTS AT Q-CONJ IT WILL FIRST GO TO THE HOST
*      OF Q-CONJ.
*
ROUTINE IMMEDIATE-STRING =
        DO $UP-THROUGH-Q;
        ITERATE ASCEND TO STRING UNTIL TEST FOR Q-CONJ FAILS.
*  INITIALRT TESTS THAT THERE IS NO NODE TO THE LEFT OF THE NODE THE
*  PROGRAM IS CURRENTLY ↓LOOKING AT↓.
*
ROUTINE INITIALRT = VERIFY NOT DO PREVIOUS-ELEMENT-.
*  LAST-ELEMENT:  GOES TO LEVEL BELOW THE NODE THE PROGRAM IS
*   CURRENTLY ↓LOOKING AT↓ AND GOES TO THE RIGHTMOST NODE ON
*   THAT LEVEL.C-NODES ARE IGNORED.
*
ROUTINE LAST-ELEMENT-=GO DOWN;EITHER ITERATE GO RIGHT OR TRUE;
        ITERATET GO LEFT UNTIL TEST FOR C-NODE FAILS.

*
*  ROUTINE LEFTR(X): LOOKS TO THE LEFT FOR X.
*
ROUTINE LEFTR(X)= ITERATE GO LEFT UNTIL TEST FOR X SUCCEEDS.
*  LEFT-ADJUNCT- GOES TO THE LEFT ADJUNCT POSITION X
*      (SEE ROUTINE LEFT-ADJUNCT-POS) AND THEN IF X IS NOT LN TO THE
*      CORE- OF X.
*
ROUTINE LEFT-ADJUNCT- = DO LEFT-ADJUNCT-POS; EITHER TEST FOR LN OR
        DO CORE-.
*  LEFT-ADJUNCT-POS STARTS AT A CORE NODE Y WHERE Y IS AN ELEMENT OF AN
*      LXR TYPE NODE, OR FROM THE CORE ASCENDS TO Y IF Y= AVAR,QVAR OR
*      NVAR. IT THEN GOES LEFT UNTIL IT FINDS A NODE WHICH IS ON THE
*      LADJSET LIST.
*
ROUTINE LEFT-ADJUNCT-POS = EITHER $ASCNT OR TRUE; STORE IN X200;
        EITHER DO LEFTR(LADJSET) OR ITERATE $TO-PRECONJUNCTION-Y[COEL1-]
        UNTIL DO LEFTR(LADJSET) SUCCEEDS.
$ASCNT=            GO UP;
             TEST FOR AVAR OR NVAR OR QVAR OR VVAR .
*  LOOKAHEAD BEGINS WITH THE CURRENT SENTENCE WORD AND TEST WHETHER THAT
*  WORD IS OF CLASS X ( ALSO POSSIBLY WITH ATTRIBUTES Y, ETC.).  IF NOT THE
*  PROGRAM ITERATES THROUGH THE SENTENCE WORDS UNTIL THE REQUIRED WORD IS
*  FOUND.
*
ROUTINE LOOKAHEAD = GO TO THE CURRENT WORD; ITERATET GO TO THE NEXT
                    WORD UNTIL DO X SUCCEEDS.
*  NELEMRT IS CALLED AFTER AN OPERATOR HAS GONE TO THE NTH ELEMENT
*      OF A STRING(IGNORING SPECIAL PROCESS NODES). IT STACKS THE
*      CONJUNCTS OF THAT ELEMENT.
ROUTINE NELEMRT = DO $STACK-TEST[STARTAT].
*  NONSEG-IMMEDSTG ASCENDS TO THE FIRST STRING ABOVE BUT ↓PASSES THROUGH↓
*  STRINGS ON THE LIST STGSEG, I. E. STRINGS WHICH CAN OCCUR AS A SEGMENT OF
*  ANOTHER STRING.
*
ROUTINE NONSEG-IMMEDSTG =
        DO IMMEDIATE-STRING;
        EITHER $UP-THRU-SEGMENT OR TRUE.
 $UP-THRU-SEGMENT = TEST FOR STGSEG;  DO IMMEDIATE-NODE;
                    TEST FOR STRING.

*
*  ROUTINE NONSEGWH IS A VERSION OF NONSEG-IMMEDSTG USED IN WH
*  RESTRICTIONS.
*
ROUTINE NONSEGWH = ASCEND TO STRING; EITHER $1 OR TRUE .
$1 = TEST FOR STGSEG; GO UP; TEST FOR STRING.
```

```
* THE PRESENT-ELEMENT ROUTINE DOESN+T GO ANYWHERE UNLESS IT STARTS AT
*     Q-CONJ, IN WHICH CASE IT GOES TO THE HOST NODE(UP TWICE FROM
*     TOP OF Q-NEST).
*
ROUTINE PRESENT-ELEMENT = DO $UP-THROUGH-Q [IMMEDIATE(X)] .
* PRESENT-STRING -SAME AS PRESENT-ELEMENT
*
ROUTINE PRESENT-STRING = DO $UP-THROUGH-Q [IMMEDIATE(X)] .
* PREVIOUS-ELEMENT- GOES LEFT TO THE FIRST NODE THAT IS NOT SPECIAL.
*
ROUTINE PREVIOUS-ELEMENT- = DO $LEFT-TO-HOST[HOST-ELEMENT].
*
* ROUTINE RIGHTR(X) LOOKS TO THE RIGHT FOR X.
*
ROUTINE RIGHTR(X)= ITERATE GO RIGHT UNTIL TEST FOR X SUCCEEDS.
* RIGHT-ADJUNCT- GOES TO THE CORE OF THE RIGHT-ADJUNCT POSITION.
*
ROUTINE RIGHT-ADJUNCT- = DO RIGHT-ADJUNCT-POS; DO CORE-.
* RIGHT-ADJUNCT-POS IS SIMILAR TO ROUTINE LEFT-ADJUNCT-POS EXCEPT
*     IT GOES RIGHT UNTIL IT FINDS A NODE WHICH IS ON THE LIST RADJSET.
*
ROUTINE RIGHT-ADJUNCT-POS = EITHER $ASCNT[LEFT-ADJUNCT-POS] OR TRUE;
 STORE IN X200; EITHER DO RIGHTR(RADJSET) OR ITERATE
       $TO-PRECONJUNCTION-Y[COEL1-] UNTIL DO RIGHTR(RADJSET) SUCCEEDS.
*     STARTAT (X) TESTS WHETHER THE PROGRAM IS +LOOKING AT+ THE NODE X.
* IF SO, PROGRAM REMAINS +LOOKING AT+ X.  IF NOT, PROGRAM SEARCHES FOR X ONE
* LEVEL BELOW NODE IT IS CURRENTLY +LOOKING AT+. IF IT FINDS X IT REMAINS
* +LOOKING AT+ X.
* ALL CONJUNCTS OF X ARE PLACED ON THE RE-EXECUTION STACK.
*
ROUTINE STARTAT (X) = ONE OF $DOWN1, $TEST-FOR-X, $AT-X.
  $TEST-FOR-X = TEST FOR X.
 $DOWN1=GO DOWN;ITERATET GO RIGHT UNTIL $THERE SUCCEEDS.
$THERE = TEST FOR X; DO $STACK-TEST.
$STACK-TEST = IF $POSTCONJ THEN $STACK-CONJUNCTS .                    (GLOBAL)
$POSTCONJ = THE PRESENT-ELEMENT- HAS NODE ATTRIBUTE                   (GLOBAL)
       POSTCONJELEM .
$STACK-CONJUNCTS = VERIFY ITERATE $STACK-X.
$STACK-X = DO $POSTCONJ; STACK.
$AT-X = DO $UP-THROUGH-Q[IMMEDIATE(X)];TEST FOR X.
*       SUBSUMERT SEARCHES FOR A WORD OF GIVEN CLASS [AND SUBCLASS]
* WHICH IS MATCHED TO ANY ATOMIC NODE ON THE SUBTREE BELOW THE NODE THAT THE
* PROGRAM IS CURRENTLY +LOOKING AT+, I. E. WHICH IS SUBSUMED BY THE CURRENT
* NODE.
*
ROUTINE SUBSUMERT = VERIFY $2;
                    GO TO THE WORD STARTING THE PRESENT NODE;
                    NOT TEST FOR X150;
                    ITERATET $1 UNTIL DO X SUCCEEDS.
  $1 = GO TO THE NEXT WORD; NOT TEST FOR X150.
  $2 = GO TO THE WORD FOLLOWING THE PRESENT NODE; STORE IN X150.
* IT-SAME AS PRESENT-ELEMENT
*
ROUTINE IT = DO $UP-THROUGH-Q [IMMEDIATE (X)] .
* **********  ************************************************* ********
*                                                                    *
*                                                                    *
*                     EXTENDED SCOPE ROUTINES                        *
*                                                                    *
*                                                                    ≠
* **********  ************************************************* ********
*
*
```

ROUTINE DEEPEST-COPRED = ONE OF $DEEPBE, $ZEROBE, $PASSOBJBE IS TRUE.
 $DEEPBE = DO $1; DO $2; DESCEND TO OBJBE.
$1=THE CORE OF THE DEEPEST-COVERB X7 IS VBE OR BEREP .
 $2 = X7 HAS A COELEMENT OBJECT.
 $ZEROBE = THE PRESENT-ELEMENT- HAS COELEMENT OBJBE.
 $PASSOBJBE = DO $3; DO $4; DESCEND TO OBJBE PASSING THROUGH ASOBJBE.
 $3 = X7 IS AN ELEMENT OF VENPASS.
 $4 = X7 HAS A COELEMENT PASSOBJ.
* DEEPEST-COVERB-: SAME AS DEEPEST-COVERB(SEE DESCRIPTION BELOW) EXCEPT
*   USES NON-STACKING ROUTINES .
* DEEPEST-COVERB: STARTS AT ANY ELEMENT EXCEPT THE VERB OF A
*   VERB-CONTAINING STRING (USUALLY AT THE SUBJECT) AND GOES FIRST
*   TO THE VERB IN THE STRING;IF THAT VERB HAS A VERB-CONTAINING
*   OBJECT (OR A PREDICATE CONSISTING OF AN AASP+TOVO) THEN IT
*   GOES TO THE VERB IN THAT OBJECT (OR TOVO), WHERE IT REPEATS
*   THE TEST FOR A VERB-CONTAINING OBJECT. THE ITERATION ENDS ON THE
*   VERB WHICH DOESN↓T HAVE A VERB-CONTAINING OBJECT (OR PREDICATE).
*   NOTE RE SN IN $VERBAL: THIS TEST MAKES ↓IS↓ NOT ↓SUFFER↓ THE
*   DEEPEST-COVERB IN ↓TO LIVE IS TO SUFFER↓ AND ↓HIS AIM IS NOT TO
*   SUFFER↓(1 OF 2 READINGS).
*   USER BEWARE: SHIFT OF SUBJECT-OBJECT RELATION IN THE KERNEL DUE
*   TO PASSIVE MUST BE HANDLED BY THE RESTRICTION USING THE ROUTINE.
ROUTINE DEEPEST-COVERB- = ITERATE $NEXT-VERB- UNTIL $OBJ-HAS-VERB FAILS.
 $NEXT-VERB- = DO $1; DO $2 .   (GLOBAL)
 $1 = THE PRESENT-ELEMENT- HAS COELEMENT- VERB OR LVINGR OR LVENR OR
        LVR OR VERB1 X7 .
 $2 = IF X7 IS VERB1 WHERE VALUE IS NOT LTVR THEN PRESENT-ELEMENT-
        HAS COELEMENT- VERB2 X7 .
 $OBJ-HAS-VERB = BOTH $VERBAL- ↵ AND PRESENT-STRING HAS ELEMENT- OBJECT
        OR PASSOBJ.
 $VERBAL- = IF PRESENT-ELEMENT- HAS COELEMENT- OBJECT OR PASSOBJ ↵
        THEN EITHER CORE- X3 IS VO OR VINGO OR VENO OR TOVO OR TOBE OR
        VENPASS WHERE X3 IS NOT OCCURRING IN SN, OR $ASPECTUAL IS TRUE.
 $ASPECTUAL = BOTH X3 IS ADJ: AASP AND RIGHT-ADJUNCT OF X3 IS TOVO .   (GLOBAL)
ROUTINE ULTIMATE-HOST = ITERATE $HOSTJUMP UNTIL $PNADJ FAILS.
 $HOSTJUMP = DO HOST; STORE IN X3 .
 $PNADJ = X3 IS OCCURRING IN PN WHERE PN IS OCCURRING AS RN .   (GLOBAL)
ROUTINE ULTIMATE-OBJECT = EITHER ITERATE $ASCEND OR TEST FOR OBJECT
                          OR PASSOBJ; EITHER $ADJUNCT OR TRUE .
 $ASCEND = ASCEND TO OBJECT OR PASSOBJ PASSING THROUGH
        TRANSMITTING-OBJ-STG   NOT PASSING THROUGH ADJSET .
 $ADJUNCT = ONE OF $ASP, $SNRA, $SNRN, $SN-IN-RV IS TRUE; DO $UPAGAIN .
 $SN-IN-RV = BOTH X6 IS OCCURRING AS SN ↵ AND SN IS OCCURRING AS
        RV WHERE PREVIOUS-ELEMENT- IS OBJECT OR PASSOBJ X40.
 $ASP= NONSEGWH X6 IS TOVO WHERE TOVO IS OCCURRING AS RA X40 .
 $SNRA = X6 IS OCCURRING AS SN X8 WHERE X8 IS OCCURRING AS RA X40.
 $SNRN = BOTH X6 IS OCCURRING AS SN X8 WHERE X8 IS OCCURRING AS RN X40
        AND IF X40 IS OCCURRING IN PN ↵ THEN PN IS OCCURRING AS RN OR
        OBJBE X40.
 $UPAGAIN = GO TO X40; DO ULTIMATE-OBJECT .
* ULTIMATE-SUBJECT: THE ULTIMATE-SUBJECT ROUTINE ITERATIVELY ASCENDS
*   TO OBJECT OR PASSOBJ PASSING THROUGH VERB-CONTAINING OBJECT
*   STRINGS UNTIL IT FINDS AN OBJECT THAT HAS A COELEMENT SUBJECT.
*   IT ALSO ASCENDS THROUGH PREDICATE NOUNS AND ADJECTIVES AND
*   THEIR ADJUNCTS AS LONG AS THE ADJUNCTS DO NOT CONTAIN THE
*   NODE SUBJECT. THUS THE ULTIMATE SUBJECT OF X ASCENDS TO THE
*   FIRST NODE SUBJECT ON ANY LEVEL ABOVE X IN THE PARSE TREE.
*   NOTE THAT THE DEEPEST-COVERB DESCENDS MORE NARROWLY, PASSING
*   THROUGH VERB-CONTAINING OBJECT STRINGS AND TOVO AS ADJUNCT
*   OF AASP, BUT NOT THROUGH OTHER PREDICATES OR ADJUNCTS. USE
*   DEEPEST-COVERB (NOT ULTIMATE-SUBJECT) IN SELECTIONAL RESTRIC-
*   TIONS BECAUSE ↓IT↓ IS THE ULTIMATE SUBJECT OF ↓SWIM↓ IN
*   BOTH ↓IT LIKES TO SWIM↓ AND ↓IT IS FUN TO SWIM↓. USE ULTIMATE
*   SUBJECT FOR ↓IT↓ PERMUTATIONS.
*

```
ROUTINE ULTIMATE-SUBJECT = ITERATET $UP-TO-OBJ UNTIL $COELSUBJ SUCCEEDS.
$UP-TO-OBJ = EITHER ASCEND TO OBJECT OR PASSOBJ PASSING
            THROUGH VINGO OR VENO OR VENPASS OR TOVO OR TOBE OR VO OR
            ASOBJBE OR Q-CONJ, OR ASCEND TO OBJBE PASSING THROUGH VENO
            OR VENPASS OR TOVO OR TOBE OR VO OR ASOBJBE OR Q-CONJ.
  $COELSUBJ = THE PRESENT-ELEMENT HAS COELEMENT SUBJECT OR TPOS.
ROUTINE VERB-COELEMENT- = DO $NEXT-VERB- .
* **********  *********************************************** ********
*                                                                    *
*                                                                    *
*                         CONJUNCTION ROUTINES                       *
*                                                                    *
*                                                                    *
*  *********  *******************************************************
*  *********  *******************************************************
*                                                                    *
*                           END OF ROUTINES                          *
*                                                                    *
*                                                                    *
*  *********  *******************************************************
*
*
*
*  AGREEMENT RESTRICTIONS
*
*  WAGREE1:   SUBJECT AND VERB AGREE IN NUMBER.
*             NOTE RE $NOTSINGSTRING IN $PLURAGREE: A SINGULAR VERB
*             CAN HAVE EITHER A CONJOINED OR A NON-CONJOINED STRING AS
*             SUBJECT (THEIR PROTESTING AND STRIKING WAS EFFECTIVE),
*             BUT A PLURAL VERB WITH STRING SUBJECT OCCURS ONLY IF
*             THE STRING IS CONJOINED (*THEIR PROTESTING WERE EFFECTIVE).
WAGREE1 = IN ASSERTION AFTER VERB:
       IF BOTH $VB AND $SUBJ ARE TRUE
       THEN BOTH $SINGAGREE AND $PLURAGREE ARE TRUE .
  $VB [CHECK WHETHER VERB OR TENSE HAS NUMBER ATTRIBUTE] =          (GLOBAL)
       EITHER CORE X2 OF VERB X20 IS TV:SINGULAR OR PLURAL,
       OR BOTH X20 HAS COELEMENT TENSE-
            AND CORE X2 OF TENSE IS SINGULAR OR PLURAL.            (GLOBAL)
  $SUBJ = AT X20 , EXTENDED-CORE- X1 OF COELEMENT- SUBJECT EXISTS.  (GLOBAL)
  $SINGAGREE [IF X2 (VERB OR TENSE) IS SINGULAR , THE SUBJECT MUST NOT BE(GLOBAL)
       PLURAL AND THE SUBJECT ITSELF MUST NOT BE CONJOINED BY +AND+.] =
       IF X2 IS SINGULAR
                 THEN [EITHER X1 IS NUNIT  (20 MINUTES HAS PASSED)      MED
                   OR] BOTH AT X1, NOT $PLURN
                       AND $NOTPLURSUBJ.
  $PLURN [THE NOUN OR ITS LEFT-ADJUNCT IS PLURAL.] =                (GLOBAL)
       EITHER PRESENT-ELEMENT- IS PLURAL
       OR THE LEFT-ADJUNCT- IS LN WHERE ONE OF $TPLUR,
                                              $QPLUR,
                                              $A-HUNDRED.
  $TPLUR = AT ELEMENT- TPOS X50 EITHER $TPLUR-TEST
                               OR $CONJUNCT-IS-AND IS TRUE [A ROUND AND
                                              A SQUARE FIGURE WERE DRAWN].
  $TPLUR-TEST = CORE- [OF TPOS] IS T:PLURAL.                        (GLOBAL)
  $CONJUNCT-IS-AND = BOTH ITERATE $POSTCONJ [STARTAT]-
                     AND IT IS OCCURRING IN ANDSTG.
  $QPLUR = AT ELEMENT- QPOS EITHER $QPLUR-TEST
                            OR $CONJUNCT-IS-AND [ONE GLASS AND ONE
                                          CHINA PLATE WERE SOLD].
  $QPLUR-TEST = ONE OF $1, $2, $3 IS TRUE.                          (GLOBAL)
  $1 = THE CORE- [OF QPOS] X4 IS PLURAL [THREE].
  $2 = EITHER X4 IS Q-OF [HUNDREDS OF WORDS]
       OR X4 IS CPDNUMBR [ONE HUNDRED]
```

```
            WHERE VALUE IS NOT FRACTION [THE 3/4 POINT, 1/2 WAY UP].
$3 = X4 HAS CORE-CONJUNCT [ONE OR TWO].
$A-HUNDRED = BOTH CORE- OF ELEMENT- TPOS IS +A+                          (GLOBAL)
             AND IN ELEMENT- QPOS EITHER CORE- X4 IS +FEW+ OR +DOZEN+
                                              OR +HUNDRED+ OR
                                              +THOUSAND+ OR
                                              +MILLION+ OR
                                              +BILLION+,
                          OR LEFT-ADJUNCT- OF X4 IS ADJPREQ
                                        [AN ADDITIONAL THREE].

$NOTPLURSUBJ [THE SUBJECT IS NOT PLURAL.] =                              (GLOBAL)
     BOTH $ANDSING
     AND NOT $ANDSUBJ.
$ANDSING = AT X1, IF $CORE-HAS-AND                                       (GLOBAL)
             THEN IN THE LEFT-ADJUNCT OF X1, THE CORE OF TPOS IS
             T:EACHEVRY [EVERY MAN, WOMAN, AND CHILD HAS RIGHTS].
$CORE-HAS-AND = BOTH ITERATE CORE-CONJUNCT EXISTS+                       (GLOBAL)
             AND THE PRESENT-ELEMENT- IS OCCURRING
                IN ANDSTG.
$ANDSUBJ = AT X20 [VERB OR TENSE] CO-CONJ SUBJECT EXISTS                 (GLOBAL)
             [SUBJ CONJ SUBJ VERB] WHERE IT IS OCCURRING
                IN ANDSTG.
$PLURAGREE [IF X2 (VERB OR TENSE) IS PLURAL, THE SUBJECT MUST NOT BE     (GLOBAL)
        SINGULAR UNLESS IT IS +I+.] =
        IF X2 IS PLURAL
        THEN EITHER $SUBJNOTSG
               OR X1 IS +I+.
$SUBJNOTSG = EITHER $NOTSINGX1                                           (GLOBAL)
               OR $ANDSUBJ IS TRUE.
$NOTSINGX1 [CORE IS NOT SINGULAR.] =                                     (GLOBAL)
        AT X1 EITHER BOTH NOT $SINGN
                     AND NOT $SINGSTRING
               OR EITHER $CORE-HAS-AND
                      OR $DIMINISHER IS TRUE.
$SINGN [NOUN OR ITS LEFT ADJUNCT IS SINGULAR.] =                         (GLOBAL)
        EITHER PRESENT-ELEMENT- X15 IS SINGULAR
                        WHERE X15 IS NOT AGGREGATE
        OR EITHER X15 IS VING WHERE IT IS NOT PLURAL,
           OR THE LEFT-ADJUNCT- OF X15 IS LN WHERE BOTH NOT $A-HUNDRED
                                              AND EITHER $TSING
                                                     OR $QSING IS TRUE.
$TSING [THE ARTICLE IS SINGULAR AND NOT CONJOINED BY +AND+.] =
        AT TPOS X50 BOTH $TSING-TEST
                   AND NOT $CONJUNCT-IS-AND [A GREEN OR A WHITE HAT
                                               WAS FOUND].
$TSING-TEST = THE CORE- [OF TPOS] IS T:SINGULAR.                         (GLOBAL)
$QSING [THE QUANTIFIER IS SINGULAR AND NOT CONJOINED BY +AND+.] =
        AT QPOS BOTH $QSING-TEST
                AND NOT $CONJUNCT-IS-AND [ONE GREEN AND ONE WHITE APPLE
                                            WERE SOLD].
$QSING-TEST = AT PRESENT-ELEMENT- X40 BOTH THE CORE- X4 IS SINGULAR      (GLOBAL)
                                                       [ONE]
                                 AND X4 DOES NOT HAVE
                                    CORE-CONJUNCT [ONE OR TWO].
$SINGSTRING [STRINGS ARE SINGULAR.] =                                    (GLOBAL)
        BOTH X1 IS OF TYPE STRING
        AND AT X1 NEITHER DESCEND TO Q-CONJ
                NOR X1 IS WHATS-N
                   [WHAT HE ATE WAS/WERE EELS].
$DIMINISHER = THE PRESENT-ELEMENT IS +NUMBER+ OR +FRACTION+ OR +PART+    (GLOBAL)
                   [A LARGE NUMBER ARE VOTERS].
* WAGREE1A: AGREEMENT IN QUESTION
```

```
WAGREE1A = IN YESNOQ AFTER SUBJECT : IF BOTH CORE X2 OF ELEMENT VERB1
               X20 IS TV:SINGULAR OR PLURAL, AND AT X20 CORE- X1 OF
               COELEMENT- SUBJECT EXISTS, THEN BOTH $SINGAGREE AND
               $PLURAGREE [WAGREE1] ARE TRUE.
* WAGREE1B: AGREEMENT IN SUBJECT-PREDICATE PERMUTATION
WAGREE1B = IN OBES AFTER SUBJECT: IF BOTH $VB AND $SUBJ [WAGREE1] ARE
               TRUE, THEN BOTH $SINGAGREE AND $PLURAGREE [WAGREE1] ARE TRUE.
* WAGREE2:  SUBJECT AND NOUN OBJECT OF ↓BE↓ AGREE IN NUMBER.
WAGREE2 [W96-SUBJ-PREDN] = IN ASSERTION, YESNOQ, TSUBJVO,SVINGO,
        FORTOVO, NTOVO, SVO :
        IF BOTH EXTENDED-CORE- X1 OF ELEMENT- SUBJECT X10 IS NOT ↓IT↓
           AND AT X10 DEEPEST-COPRED X6 HAS VALUE NSTG WHERE CORE IS
                    NOT EMPTY ,
        THEN BOTH AT X10 , VERB-COELEMENT X20 EXISTS
               AND AT CORE- X3 OF X6 EITHER BOTH $SINGTEST
                                            AND $PLURTEST
                                       OR $MIXED .
   $SINGTEST = IF $SUBJSING THEN AT X3 NOT $PLURN [WAGREE1].                (GLOBAL)
   $SUBJSING = BOTH $NOTPLURSUBJ [WAGREE1] AND AT X1 EITHER $SINGN
               [WAGREE1] OR $SINGSTRING [WAGREE1].
   $PLURTEST = IF $SUBJPLUR                                                 (GLOBAL)
               THEN AT X3 EITHER NOT $SINGN[WAGREE1]
                       OR EITHER $CORE-HAS-AND [WAGREE1]
                             OR $DIMINISHER [WAGREE1] IS TRUE.
   $SUBJPLUR = AT X1 ONE OF $PLURN [WAGREE1], $CORE-HAS-AND [WAGREE1],
                    $ANDSUBJ [WAGREE1] .
   $MIXED = EITHER $RARE OR EITHER X3 IS NSENT1 OR NSENT2 OR NSENT3,        (GLOBAL)
               OR X1 IS NSENT1 OR NSENT2 OR NSENT3.
* WAGREE2A: SUBJECT-PREDICATE AGREEMENT IN SOBJBE(THEY THOUGHT JOHN
*        A GOOD CARPENTER).
WAGREE2A= IN SOBJBE AFTER OBJBE: $SUBJ-PRED-TEST IS TRUE.
   $SUBJ-PRED-TEST = IF IN OBJBE X6 BOTH VALUE IS NSTG                      (GLOBAL)
                               WHERE CORE IS NOT EMPTY
                          AND COELEMENT- SUBJECT X10 EXISTS
               THEN EITHER BOTH $SINGTEST AND $PLURTEST
                       OR $MIXED.
* WAGREE2B: SUBJECT-PREDICATE AGREEMENT IN SASOBJBE(THEY TREAT HIM
*        AS AN EQUAL).
WAGREE2B= IN () SASOBJBE AFTER OBJBE: $SUBJ-PRED-TEST IS TRUE.
* WAGREE3: RECIPROCAL VERBS CAN ZERO ↓EACH OTHER↓ IN THE OBJECT,
*        TAKING INSTEAD NULLRECIP AS OBJECT (JOHN AND BILL MET (EACH
*        OTHER)). IN THIS CASE THE SUBJECT CANNOT BE SINGULAR
*        (*JOHN MET). COLLECTIVE VERBS WHEN OCCURRING WITH OBJECT
*        NULLOBJ CANNOT HAVE A SINGULAR NON-COLLECTIVE SUBJECT
*        (DUST GATHERS, *A BOOK GATHERS) AND WHEN OCCURRING WITH A NOUN
*        OBJECT CANNOT HAVE A SINGULAR NON-COLLECTIVE NOUN OBJECT
*        (THE SHELF GATHERS DUST, *THE SHELF GATHERS A BOOK).
WAGREE3 [W107-RECIP AND COLLECTIVE] = IN ASSERTION, YESNOQ, SVINGO,
        SVO, FORTOVO, NTOVO, NTOBE, STOVO-N, TSUBJVO:
        IF AT OBJECT X20 , EXTENDED-CORE- X1 OF COELEMENT SUBJECT EXISTS
        THEN BOTH $RECIP AND $COLL ARE TRUE.
   $RECIP = IF AT X20 THE DEEPEST-COVERB X5 HAS COELEMENT OBJECT X12 WHERE
               CORE IS NULLRECIP THEN $SUBJNOTSG [WAGREE1] IS TRUE.
   $COLL = IF CORE X2 OF [DEEPEST-COVERB] X5 IS VCOLLECTIVE THEN EITHER
               $COLLECTIVE-SUBJ OR $COLLECTIVE-OBJ IS TRUE.
   $COLLECTIVE-SUBJ = BOTH CORE OF X12 IS NULLOBJ AND EITHER $SUBJNOTSG
               [WAGREE1] IS TRUE OR X1 IS COLLECTIVE.
   $COLLECTIVE-OBJ = BOTH X12 HAS VALUE NSTGO AND EITHER AT CORE- X1 OF
               X12 $NOTSINGX1 [WAGREE1] IS TRUE OR EITHER X1 IS COLLECTIVE
               OR AT X5 CO-CONJ OBJECT IS OCCURRING IN ANDSTG.
* WAGREE4:  LN AND N AGREE IN NUMBER .
WAGREE4 [W32 - N-LN] =
               IN LNR AFTER NVAR: BOTH $SING AND $PLUR ARE TRUE   .
```

```
$SING = IF EITHER CORE X1 IS SINGULAR
              OR X1 IS VING WHERE IT IS NOT PLURAL
            THEN IN THE LEFT-ADJUNCT OF X1 NEITHER $PLURT
                                          NOR $PLURQ IS TRUE.
         $PLURT = AT ELEMENT- TPOS BOTH $LAST-ONE,
                                    AND $TPLUR-TEST[WAGREE1-THIS GREEN AND
                                                THOSE RED UMBRELLAS].
            $LAST-ONE = IF $POSTCONJ[STARTAT],
                        THEN EITHER ITERATE $POSTCONJ
                            OR TRUE.
         $PLURQ = AT ELEMENT- QPOS BOTH $LAST-ONE, AND $QPLUR-TEST[
                                    WAGREE1-ONE GREEN AND TWO RED
                                    APPLES].
         $SINGT = AT ELEMENT- TPOS BOTH $LAST-ONE, AND $TSING-TEST[
                                    WAGREE1-THESE GREEN AND THIS RED
                                    UMBRELLA].
    $PLUR = IF X1 IS PLURAL
            THEN IN THE LEFT-ADJUNCT OF X1 EITHER NEITHER $SINGT
                                          NOR $SINGQ IS TRUE
                                  OR $A-HUNDRED [WAGREE1] .
         $SINGQ = AT ELEMENT- QPOS BOTH $LAST-ONE, AND $QSING-TEST[
                                    WAGREE1-TWO RED AND ONE GREEN
                                    APPLE].
* WAGREE5:   HOST AND APPOSITION NOUN AGREE IN NUMBER .
WAGREE5 [W78 - HOST AND APPOS] =
       IN () RN AFTER APPOS:
       IF HOST X1 EXISTS
       THEN AT CORE X3 OF APPOS  EITHER BOTH $SINGX1 AND $PLURX1
                                OR $MIXED[WAGREE2].
  $SINGX1 = IF AT X1 BOTH $SINGN [WAGREE1] AND $ANDSING[WAGREE1]
            THEN AT X3 NOT $PLURN[WAGREE1].
   $PLURX1 = IF AT X1 $PLURN[WAGREE1] IS TRUE
            THEN AT X3 NOT $SINGN[WAGREE1].
* WAGREE6:  IN SAWHICHSTG, IF THE SUBJECT HAS BEEN OMITTED, THE TENSED VERB IS
* NOTPLURAL (THEY,RE NOT HERE, WHICH IS SURPRISING).
  WAGREE6 [W21 - SAWHICHSTG] =
       IN SAWHICHSTG:  IN ASSERTION, IF SUBJECT X10 IS EMPTY ,
                    THEN AT X10 CORE OF COELEMENT
       VERB IS NOT PLURAL.
* WAGREE7:  AGREEMENT OF ROVING QUANTIFIERS AND REFLEXIVES WITH THE
*           NOUN THEY ADJOIN (THEY ARE ALL IN AGREEMENT, WE WERE NOT
*           THERE OURSELVES)
WAGREE7 [W33 - RSUBJ] =
       IN RSUBJ AFTER OPTIONS 1, 2: IF BOTH THE CORE- X2 [OF RSUBJ]
       IS PRO: SINGULAR OR PLURAL AND IN THE IMMEDIATE SA X20 THE
       CORE- X1 OF COELEMENT- SUBJECT EXISTS, THEN EITHER $SUBJAGREE
       OR $OBJAGREE.
$SUBJAGREE= BOTH $SINGAGREE [WAGREE1] AND IF X2 IS PLURAL THEN
            $SUBJNOTSG.
$OBJAGREE= AT X20, IF THE CORE- X1 OF COELEMENT- OBJECT EXISTS THEN BOTH
            $SING AND $PLUR.
 $SING = IF X2 IS SINGULAR THEN AT X1 BOTH NOT $PLURN[WAGREE1] AND
            $NOTPLUROBJ.
$PLUR= IF X2 IS PLURAL THEN EITHER $NOTSINGX1 [WAGREE1] OR $ANDOBJ.
$ANDOBJ= AT X20 CO-CONJ OBJECT EXISTS WHERE IT IS OCCURRING IN ANDSTG.
$NOTPLUROBJ= BOTH NOT $ANDOBJ AND $ANDSING.
* WAGREE8: IF THE PREPOSITION IN PN, PWHN-PN OR PWHN IS +BETWEEN+ OR +AMONG+
* THEN THE NOUN MUST BE PLURAL (BETWEEN THE TREES *AMONG THE TREE).
WAGREE8 = IN PN, PWHNS, PWHNS-PN: IF ELEMENT P X20 IS +BETWEEN+ OR
            +AMONG+ THEN AT X20 EITHER $PN OR $PWH.
$PN= BOTH THE CORE- X1 OF COELEMENT- NSTGO EXISTS AND $NSTG-NOT-SING.
$PWH= BOTH THE CORE X1 OF COELEMENT- WHN EXISTS AND $WH-NOT-SING.
$NSTG-NOT-SING= EITHER $NOTSINGX1 [WAGREE1] OR AT X20 CO-CONJ
       NSTGO EXISTS WHERE IT IS OCCURRING IN ANDSTG.
```

```
$WH-NOT-SING= EITHER $NOTSINGX1 OR AT X20 CO-CONJ WHN EXISTS WHERE IT
        IS OCCURRING IN ANDSTG.
* WAGREE9: THE LEFT ADJUNCTS OF THE NOUN AGREE IN NUMBER.
WAGREE9 = IN LN AFTER QPOS:
        ALL OF $LOCATE-TPOS-QPOS, $1, $2, $3, $4.
      $LOCATE-TPOS-QPOS = BOTH ELEMENT TPOS X50 EXISTS⌐
                          AND COELEMENT QPOS X40 EXISTS.

    $1 = IF AT X50, $TSING-TEST[WAGREE1] IS TRUE
         THEN EITHER AT X40 NOT $QPLUR-TEST
           OR $A-HUNDRED[WAGREE1] IS TRUE .
    $2 = IF AT X50, $TPLUR-TEST[WAGREE1] IS TRUE
         THEN AT X40 NOT $QSING-TEST[WAGREE1].
    $3 = IF AT X40 $QSING-TEST[WAGREE1] IS TRUE
         THEN AT X50 NOT $TPLUR-TEST[WAGREE1].
    $4 = IF AT X40 $QPLUR-TEST IS TRUE
         THEN EITHER AT X50 NOT $TSING-TEST[WAGREE1]
           OR $A-HUNDRED.
$PLURT= THE CORE OF TPOS IS PLURAL.
$PLURQ= EITHER THE CORE- X4 OF QPOS IS PLURAL OR EITHER X4 IS CPDNUMBR,
        OR X4 HAS CORE-CONJUNCT.
* COMMA RESTRICTIONS
*
* DCOM1:   THE LISTED STRINGS ARE NOT TAKEN AS INSTANCES OF RN WHEN PRECEDED BY
* COMMA. (WE FOUND THE RIGHT FOOD TO EAT (RN), CONTRAST: WE FOUND THE RIGHT
* FOOD, TO EAT (SA)).
DCOM1 [D36 - RN] =
        IN ()RN RE OPTIONS S-N, TOVO, TOVO-N, FORTOVO-N, ↓WHATSOEVER↓:
        THE PRECEDING WORD IS NOT ↓,↓.
* DCOM2:  CONDITIONS FOR COMMA PRECEDING VERB
DCOM2 [D63 - BEFORE VERB] =
        IN VERB RE OPTION 1: IF THE PRECEDING WORD IS ↓,↓, THEN ONE OF
        $INCONJSTG, $PREVSA, $RN IS TRUE.
  $PREVSA = BOTH PREVIOUS-ELEMENT X1 IS SA OR SACONJ, AND X1 IS NOT          (GLOBAL)
        EMPTY.
  $RN = IF VERB IS NOT OCCURRING IN OBES THEN BOTH COELEMENT TENSE
        IS EMPTY AND CORE OF COELEMENT SUBJECT IS N OR VING OR PRO
        WHERE THE RIGHT-ADJUNCT IS NOT EMPTY.
* DCOM3: COMMA PRECEDES THESE OPTIONS UNLESS THEY ARE SENTENCE INITIAL.
DCOM3 [D23 - SA] = IN ()SA RE OPTIONS OBJBESA, SOBJBESA:
        IF THE PRECEDING WORD X1 EXISTS
        THEN X1 IS ↓,↓.
* DCOM3A: COMMA PRECEDES THESE OPTIONS UNLESS THEY ARE SENTENCE INITIAL
*        OR AFTER A NON-N OBJECT (THEY SAILED BY HEADED TOWARD SHORE).
DCOM3A = IN ()SA RE OPTIONS VINGO, VENPASS:
        IF THE PRECEDING WORD X1 EXISTS,
        THEN EITHER X1 IS ↓,↓
            OR BOTH $POST-OBJ-SA [WPOS20],
              AND CORE OF X10 [OBJ OR PASSOBJ] IS NOT N.
* DCOM3B:  TOVO AS SA SHOULD HAVE PRECEDING COMMA OR BE POST-OBJ.
DCOM3B  = IN () SA RE OPTION TOVO:
          IF THE PRECEDING WORD X1 EXISTS
          THEN EITHER X1 IS ↓,↓
              OR $POST-OBJ-SA [WPOS20].
* DCOM4: AN APPOSITION STRING NOT PRECEDED BY A COMMA IS A NAME (MY
*       FRIEND JOHN) OR ITS HOST IS A CLASSIFIER OF IT, OR ELSE IT
*       IS CONSIDERED RARE. SEE WCOM10.
DCOM4 [COMMA BEFORE APPOSITION] = IN () RN RE APPOS:
        EITHER THE PRECEDING WORD IS ↓,↓ OR ONE OF $NAME-AHEAD,
        $RARE,   $RESTRICTED-HOST IS TRUE.
  $NAME-AHEAD = THERE IS AN N:NAME AHEAD.
  $RESTRICTED-HOST = BOTH   THE HOST X1 IS N: NCLASSIFIER1 OR
        NCLASSIFIER2 AND IF X1 IS OCCURRING IN LNR ↪ THEN IN LN, TPOS
        IS NOT EMPTY.
```

```
* DCOM5: THERE SHOULD NOT BE A PUNCTUATION , IN QN BEFORE QNREP
*       (*10LBS,30OUNCES)
DCOM5 = IN () QN RE OPTION QNREP: THE PRECEDING WORD IS NOT ↓,↓ .
* DCOM6: NO PUNCTUATION COMMA BEFORE RV (*IT WAS INFECTED, LITTLE).
DCOM6 = IN RV RE OPTION 1: PRECEDING WORD IS NOT ↓,↓ .
* WCOM1: THERE IS NO COMMA IN TPOS OR QPOS UNLESS
*       HOST IS NULLN (*THESE, RESULTS ARE NEW).
  WCOM1  [W34,W40 - TPOS,QPOS]  =
                      IN NVAR AFTER OPTIONS N, VING:  IN LEFT-ADJUNCT, BOTH
                TPOS DOES NOT SUBSUME ↓,↓ , AND QPOS DOES NOT SUBSUME ↓,↓ .
WCOM1A = IN NPOS AFTER OPTIONS 1, 3 :
         IF PRESENT-ELEMENT SUBSUMES ↓,↓
         THEN IT SUBSUMES ↓AND↓ OR ↓OR↓ OR ↓BUT↓ OR ↓NOR↓ OR ↓AND/OR↓
                                      OR ↓AS↓ [FOR ↓AS≠WELL≠AS↓] .
* WCOM1B: NO COMMA BETWEEN LN AND LVINGR IN VINGOFN.
WCOM1B= IN VINGOFN AFTER LVINGR: IN LN, BOTH TPOS DOES NOT SUBSUME ↓,↓
                                      AND QPOS DOES NOT SUBSUME ↓,↓.
* WCOM2: THERE IS NO COMMA PRECEDING A NON-NULL CORE OF LNR
*       UNLESS THE CORE IS IN A CONJUNCTION STRING OR LN IS EMPTY
*       (*A LARGE, GROUP ARRIVED).
WCOM2 [D66-IN NVAR] =
         IN NVAR AFTER OPTIONS N, VING, PRO:
         IF THE WORD PRECEDING THE PRESENT NODE IS ↓,↓
         THEN $NOCOMMA-BETWN.
$NOCOMMA-BETWN = IF $LN-TO-LEFT
     [THEN NOT IN A CONJUNCT OF TYPE LN NVAR CONJ NVAR]
                 THEN X1 IS EMPTY.
  $LN-TO-LEFT = GO LEFT;
                TEST FOR LN;
                STORE IN X1 .
* WCOM2A: NO COMMA BETWEEN Q AND N .
WCOM2A = IN QN AFTER N:
         AT N , IF THE WORD PRECEDING THE PRESENT NODE IS ↓,↓
                 THEN $NOCOMMA-BETWN.
  $NOCOMMA-BETWN= BOTH     IF $Q-TO-LEFT
                           THEN X1 DOES NOT SUBSUME ↓,↓
                  AND NOT $COMMA-IN-STG.
  $Q-TO-LEFT = ITERATE GO LEFT UNTIL $Q-TEST SUCCEEDS; STORE IN X1.
  $Q-TEST = TEST FOR LQR.
  $COMMA-IN-STG= ITERATE GO LEFT UNTIL TEST FOR COMMASTG SUCCEEDS.
  $INCONJSTG = IMMEDIATE Q-NODE EXISTS.                              (GLOBAL)
* WCOM2B: NO COMMA BETWEEN LN AND LVINGR IN VINGOFN.
WCOM2B = IN VINGOFN AFTER LVINGR: AT LVINGR
           IF THE WORD PRECEDING THE PRESENT NODE IS ↓,↓
           THEN $NOCOMMA-BETWN.
  $NOCOMMA-BETWN = IF $LN-TO-LEFT THEN X1 DOES NOT SUBSUME ↓,↓.
  $LN-TO-LEFT = GO LEFT;
                TEST FOR LN;
                STORE IN X1.
* WCOM3: IF PUNCTUATION COMMA PRECEDES THESE OPTIONS THEN
*       COMMA OR ENDMARK FOLLOWS.
  WCOM3  [W43 - RN]  =
      IN ()RN AFTER OPTIONS VENPASS, VINGO, ADJINRN, APPOS :
          IF THE WORD PRECEDING THE PRESENT NODE IS ↓,↓ , THEN EITHER THE
          CURRENT WORD IS ↓.↓ OR ↓;↓ OR ↓≥↓, OR THE PRECEDING WORD IS ↓,↓.
WCOM3A = IN () SA AFTER DSTG:
          IF THE WORD PRECEDING THE PRESENT NODE IS ↓,↓ ,
          THEN EITHER THE CURRENT WORD IS ↓.↓ OR ↓;↓ OR ↓≥↓,
              OR THE PRECEDING WORD IS ↓,↓.
* WCOM4:  CONDITIONS FOR COMMA PRECEDING OBJECT.
WCOM4 [W97, D64 - COMMA BEFORE OBJ] = IN OBJECT, PASSOBJ, OBJBE:
          IF THE WORD PRECEDING THE PRESENT NODE IS ↓,↓,
          THEN ONE OF $INCONJSTG [WCOM2], $EMPTY, $PREVSA [DCOM2], $RV.
```

```
    $EMPTY = THE CORE IS NULLOBJ.
    $RV = THE RIGHT-ADJUNCT OF CORE OF VERB-COELEMENT IS NOT EMPTY.
*  WCOM5: THERE IS NOT A LONG SA BEFORE AN OBJECT UNLESS A COMMA PRECEDES.
  WCOM5  [W104 - SA, OBJ]  =
        IN ASSERTION, VINGO, VENO, TOVO, VO AFTER OBJECT:
        IF BOTH OBJECT X2 IS NOT EMPTY
           AND AT X2 PREVIOUS-ELEMENT IS SA X1,
        THEN EITHER $SASHORT
             OR $COMMA IS TRUE.
    $SASHORT = EITHER X1 HAS ELEMENT RSUBJ OR NSTGT OR INT OR PA OR DSTG,
          OR X1 IS EMPTY.
    $COMMA = IN X1, THE WORD ENDING THE PRESENT NODE IS +,+.
*  WCOM6: IF THESE OPTIONS ARE STRING INITIAL THEN A COMMA FOLLOWS.
  WCOM6  [W79 - SA-STG INITIAL]  =
      IN () SA AFTER OPTIONS OBJBESA, SOBJBESA, VINGO, VENPASS:
          IF SA IS STRING INITIAL, THEN THE WORD ENDING THE PRESENT
          NODE IS +,+.
*  WCOM8:   IN THE STRING WHENS IN RN, IF THE STRING HEAD IS NULL, THE
*          PREVIOUS WORD CANNOT BE COMMA, * WE KNOW THE DAY, HE ARRIVED.
*          IF THE STRING HEAD IS +WHEN+, +BEFORE+ OR +AFTER+ PRECEDED BY
*          A COMMA, ANALYSIS AS SA IS PREFERRED.  IF THE STRING HEAD IS
*          +WHEN+ OR +BEFORE+ OR +AFTER+ WITHOUT A PRECEDING COMMA, THEN
*          THE HOST NOUN MUST BE A TIME NOUN OR A DATE.
*          ALSO IF STRING HEAD IS NULL, THERE IS NO DEMONSTRATIVE OR
*          POSSESSIVE ARTICLE (*THIS DAY HE ARRIVED SHE WAS GONE.).[2/14/79]
  WCOM8 [D78 - BEFORE WHENS] = IN WHENS AFTER THE FIRST ELEMENT:
                                   ALL OF $1, $2, $3.
    $1 = IF THE FIRST ELEMENT X1 IS NOT +WHERE+
         THEN THE WORD PRECEDING THE PRESENT NODE IS NOT +,+.
    $2 = IF EITHER X1 IS +WHEN+ OR +BEFORE+ OR +AFTER+,
            OR X1 IS NULL,
         THEN EITHER THE HOST X2 IS NTIME1
            OR X2 IS Q OR DATE.
    $3 = IF X1 IS NULL
         THEN IN LEFT-ADJUNCT OF HOST, CORE OF TPOS IS NOT T: TDEM OR
                                                          TPOSS.
*  WCOM10:   APPOSITION IN RN IS PRECEDED BY A COMMA UNLESS: (1) THE
*          CORE N IS A PROPER NAME (MY FRIEND JOHN), OR (2)  THERE IS A
*          CLASSIFIER:CLASSIFICAND RELATION BETWEEN HOST AND ADJUNCT
*          IN WHICH CASE THE CLASSIFIER IS EITHER OF TYPE 1 OR TYPE 2, I.E.
*          EITHER A WORD LIKE +TERM+ (THE TERM +HARMFUL EFFECT+) OR ONE
*          SPECIAL TO THE SUBFIELD (THE DRUG DIGITALIS). OTHER OCCURRENCES
*          ARE TREATED AS RARE.  THE HOST OF COMMALESS APPOSITION IS
*          GENERALLY PRECEDED BY AN ARTICLE (THE DRUG DIGITALIS, +DRUG
*          DIGITALIS).
  WCOM10  [COMMA-LESS APPOSITION] = IN APPOS: ONE OF $RARE, $AFTER-COMMA,
          $NAME, $RESTRICTED-HOST IS TRUE.
    $AFTER-COMMA = THE WORD PRECEDING THE PRESENT NODE IS +,+  .
    $NAME = CORE IS N:NAME.
    $RESTRICTED-HOST = BOTH   THE HOST X1 IS N: NCLASSIFIER1 OR
          NCLASSIFIER2 AND IF X1 IS OCCURRING IN LNR + THEN IN LN, TPOS
          IS NOT EMPTY.
*  COMPARATIVE RESTRICTIONS
*  CONJUNCTION RESTRICTIONS
*  MIN-WORD RESTRICTIONS
*
DMIN1 = IN () SA, () RV, RNP, RA,OBJECT, PASSOBJ RE PN:
        IF $MINPAR THEN THE CURRENT WORD IS NOT MAT:PN: SA OR RV OR RNP
        OR RA OR OBJECT OR PASSOBJ.
  $MINPAR = THIS IS THE MIN WORD.                                  (GLOBAL)
DMIN2  = IN RW, LV, LQ  RE DSTG:
IF $MINPAR THEN BOTH THE CURRENT WORD IS NOT MAT: DSTG: RW OR LV OR LQ
     OR RV OR SA, AND THE CURRENT WORD IS NOT MAT: D: LCS.
```

```
DMIN3 = IN () RV RE OPTION DSTG:
IF $MINPAR THEN BOTH THE CURRENT WORD IS NOT MAT:DSTG:RW OR LV OR LQ
       OR RV OR SA, AND THE CURRENT WORD IS NOT MAT:D:LCS.
DMIN4 = IN () SA RE OPTION DSTG:
IF $MINPAR THEN BOTH THE CURRENT WORD IS NOT MAT:DSTG:RW OR LV OR LQ
       OR RV OR SA, AND THE CURRENT WORD IS NOT MAT:D:LCS.
DMIN5  = IN LCS RE D:
IF $MINPAR THEN BOTH THE CURRENT WORD IS NOT MAT: DSTG: RW OR LV OR LQ
       OR RV OR SA, AND THE CURRENT WORD IS NOT MAT: D: LCS.
DMIN6 = IN ( ) RN, ( ) SA RE VENPASS:
IF $MINPAR THEN THE CURRENT WORD IS NOT MAT: VENPASS: RN OR SA.
DMIN7 = IN ( ) RN, ( ) SA RE VINGO:
IF $MINPAR THEN THE CURRENT WORD IS NOT MAT: VINGO: RN OR SA.
DMIN8 = IN ( ) RN, ( ) SA RE TOVO:
IF $MINPAR THEN THE CURRENT WORD IS NOT MAT: TOVO: RN OR RA OR SA.
DMIN9 = IN () SA RE OPTION LCS :
IF $MINPAR THEN THE CURRENT WORD IS NOT MAT:LCS:SA.
DMIN10= IN ASSERTION:
IF $MINPAR THEN THE CURRENT WORD IS NOT MAT: THATS: OBJECT OR PASSOBJ.
    DMIN11 =  IN ( ) SA RE COMPAR :
             IF $MINPAR THEN THE CURRENT WORD IS NOT MAT:COMPAR:SA.
DMIN12 = IN () SA RE SAWH:
IF $MINPAR THEN THE CURRENT WORD IS NOT MAT: SAWH: SA.
DMIN13 = IN () RV RE DSTG: IF BOTH $MINPAR AND THE PREVIOUS-ELEMENT
          IS NOT OBJECT OR PASSOBJ OR OBJBE THEN THE CURRENT WORD
          IS NOT MAT:DSTG:LQ OR LA .
DMIN14 = IN () SA RE RSUBJ :
          IF $MINPAR THEN THE CURRENT WORD IS NOT MAT:RSUBJ:SA .
DMIN15 = IN () SA RE NSTGT :
          IF $MINPAR THEN THE CURRENT WORD IS NOT MAT:NSTGT:SA .
DMIN16 = IN () RV, LP RE QN:
IF $MINPAR THEN CURRENT WORD IS NOT MAT:QN:RV OR LP.
DMIN17 = IN () SA, RNP RE PDATE:
IF $MINPAR THEN CURRENT WORD IS NOT MAT:PDATE:SA OR RNP.
* NOUN PHRASE RESTRICTIONS
*
* DN1:  AMONG THE LEFT QUANTIFIERS OF NOUN, CERTAIN ARTICLES, QUANTIFIERS OR
* ADJECTIVES MAY BE USED WITHOUT A FOLLOWING NOUN IN THE STRING POSITIONS
* OCCUPIED BY NOUN (THESE WERE NOT USED, FIVE WERE REJECTED).
DN1 [D11 - CORE=0]  = IN NVAR RE OPTION NULLN:
          BOTH COELEMENT LN X10 IS NOT EMPTY
          AND AT X10 ALL OF $NNULL, $SET-UP, $OK-LN ARE TRUE.
$SET-UP = BOTH CORE X1 OF APOS X3 EXISTS
             AND BOTH COELEMENT QPOS X4 OF X3 EXISTS
                 AND CORE X2 OF COELEMENT TPOS X5 OF X3 EXISTS.
  $OK-LN =   ONE OF $ADJ, $Q, $ART IS TRUE.
  $ADJ = EITHER $ADJTEST OR $ANOTHER.
  $ADJTEST = BOTH X1 IS VEN OR VING OR ADJ: APREQ OR COMPARATIVE OR
                SUPERLATIVE OR NTH WHERE
                    BOTH $NOT-ADJ-AND-N
                    AND EITHER $RARE
                        OR VALUE OF VALUE OF X3 IS NOT ADJADJ,
             AND EITHER X2 [CORE OF TPOS] IS NS
                 OR X2 IS T: DEF OR TPOSS.
  $NOT-ADJ-AND-N = IF X1 IS ADJ: APREQ
                   THEN AT X1 WORD STARTING PRESENT NODE [ADJ] IS NOT
                     [ALSO] N. [*IN THE PAST (NULLN)]
  $ANOTHER = X1 IS +ANOTHER+ .
  $Q = BOTH X3 [APOS] IS EMPTY, AND X4 [QPOS] IS NOT EMPTY.
  $ART = BOTH X3 [APOS] IS EMPTY,
           AND BOTH X4 [QPOS] IS EMPTY
                AND EITHER X2 [CORE OF TPOS] IS NS OR T:TDEM OR TQUAN
                                                                OR TPOSS ,
                   OR X2 IS HOWQSTG.
```

```
   $NNULL = BOTH NPOS IS EMPTY AND NSPOS IS EMPTY.
* DN2: ADJPREQ IN LQ OCCURS ONLY IN QPOS, NOT IN LTR (AN ADDITIONAL
*      THREE PEOPLE, *ADDITIONAL HALF THE AMOUNT).
DN2 [D13 - PRE Q ADJ] = IN LQ RE ADJPREQ:
        IMMEDIATE-NODE OF IMMEDIATE-NODE IS QPOS.
DN3  [D45 - NSPOS] =
        IN NSPOS RE NS:
                  BOTH THE CURRENT WORD IS NOT NS:NAME, AND NOT $SCOPE.
* DN4: UNLIKELY SECOND PARSE WITH CORE EQUAL TO NULLN AND
*      CURRENT WORD A NOUN.
  DN4  [D67 - CORE=0, RARE SECOND PARSE]  =
        IN NVAR RE OPTION NULLN:  IF PARSE HAS BEEN OBTAINED , THEN THE
        CURRENT WORD IS NOT N .
* DN50: S-N IS DISQUALIFIED AS A VALUE OF RN IN A NOUN PHRASE WHOSE
*      CORE VALUE IS ZERO, UNLESS THE LEFTMOST ELEMENT OF LN IS
*      (1) A QUANTIFIER, OR (2) AN ARTICLE IN SUBCLASS TDEM (THESE,
*      THOSE), OR (3) RARELY, AN ARTICLE IN TQUAN (ANY, SUCH,
*      SOME, EITHER, NEITHER)  (MANY YOU SAW ARE NEW,
*      *JOHN↓S HE FIXED WAS A MODEL T).
* 11/78 DN50 EXTENDED TO ALL OPTIONS IN FIRST DUMMY OF RN.
DN50 [NULLN HOST] = IN RN RE OPTION 1:  IF HOST IS NULLN ↵
                        THEN IN LEFT-ADJUNCT,
                            BOTH $APOSNULL
                            AND $LEFT ARE TRUE.
  $LEFT = ONE OF $QPOS, $TPOS1, $TPOS2 IS TRUE.
  $APOSNULL = APOS IS EMPTY.                                        (GLOBAL)
  $QPOS = QPOS IS NOT EMPTY.
  $TPOS1 = BOTH THE CORE X1 OF TPOS IS TDEM AND X1 IS PLURAL.
  $TPOS2 = BOTH X1 IS TQUAN, AND THE RARE SWITCH IS ON.
* DN51  THE RIGHT ADJUNCT S-N IS CONSIDERED RARE UNLESS THE FIRST ELEMENT
*      IS (A) A NON DEFINITELY ACCUSATIVE PRONOUN (A BOOK THEY
*      RECOMMEND) OR, (B) AN ARTICLE BUT NOT ↓A↓ (THE VIEW THE MAN
*      HELD), OR (C) A PROPER OR CHEMICAL NAME (THE BOOK JOHN READS).
*      ALSO S-N MUST NOT BE WITHIN YET ANOTHER S-N, AND IF S-N ADJOINS
*      A NOUN PHRASE, THEN IN THE LEFT ADJUNCTS OF THE HOST NOUN EITHER
*      THE QUANTIFIER POSITION IS NOT EMPTY OR THERE IS AN ARTICLE.
  DN51 [D44 - S-N]  =
        IN ()RN RE OPTION S-N:  EITHER THE RARE SWITCH IS ON OR ALL OF
            $FIRST, $S-N, $HOST ARE TRUE.
    $FIRST = EITHER $SCOPE [DOPT1A]
             OR ONE OF $PRO, $T, $N IS TRUE.
    $PRO = EITHER BOTH THE CURRENT WORD X1 IS PRO, AND X1 IS NOT
           ACCUSATIVE, OR X1 IS D:DLTPRO .
    $T = BOTH X1 IS T, AND X1 IS NOT ↓A↓.
    $N = X1 IS N:NAME   OR COLLECTIVE .
    $S-N  =       PRESENT-STRING IS NOT OCCURRING IN S-N.
    $HOST  = IF HOST IS N ↵ THEN IN LEFT-ADJUNCT, EITHER QPOS IS NOT
             EMPTY OR TPOS IS NOT EMPTY.
* DN52: CERTAIN RN STRINGS ONLY ADJOIN A PRONOUN IF THE PRONOUN IS
*      INDEFINITE (SOMEONE TO DO THE JOB WILL COME ON MONDAY , *HE TO
*      DO THE JOB WILL COME ON MONDAY)  AND DO NOT ADJOIN A PROPER NAME
*      (*JOHN TO DO THE JOB IS HERE).
DN52 [D35A - RIGHT ADJUNCTS OF INDEFINITE PRONOUNS] =
        IN () RN RE OPTIONS SN, ADJINRN, S-N, TOVO-N, TOVO, VENPASS,
        VINGO, ↓WHATSOEVER↓:
        BOTH IF HOST X1 IS PRO ↵  THEN IT IS INDEFINITE, AND X1 IS NOT
        N:NAME.
* DN53: CONTINUES DN52 FOR STRINGS WITH DIFFERENT  HOUSING.
*      NOTE FOR FUTURE: THESE STRINGS NEED STRONGER RESTRICTION.
DN53 [D35B - RIGHT ADJUNCTS OF INDEFINITE PRONOUNS] =
        IN RNP RE OPTIONS PVINGSTG, PSVINGO, PSNWH:
        BOTH IF HOST X1 IS PRO ↵  THEN IT IS INDEFINITE, AND X1 IS NOT
        N:NAME.
* DN54: CERTAIN RN STRINGS ONLY ADJOIN A PRONOUN IF THE PRONOUN IS ↓WE↓
```

```
*        OR ↓YOU↓.
DN54  [D37 - RIGHT ADJUNCTS OF ↓WE↓ OR ↓YOU↓] =
         IN () RN RE APPOS: IF THE HOST IS PRO, THEN IT IS ↓WE↓ OR ↓YOU↓.
* DN55: CERTAIN RN STRINGS ONLY ADJOIN A PRONOUN IF THE PRONOUN IS
*        EITHER INDEFINITE OR ↓WE↓ OR ↓YOU↓ (EVERYONE HERE AGREES, WE HERE
*        AGREE,  *IT HERE WAS MISSING).
DN55  [D39 - RIGHT ADJUNCTS OF CERTAIN PRONOUNS] =
         IN () RN RE DSTG: IF HOST IS PRO, THEN EITHER IT IS INDEFINITE OR
         IT IS ↓WE↓ OR ↓YOU↓.
* DN56: CONTINUES DN55 FOR STRINGS WITH DIFFERENT HOUSING (SOMEONE IN
*        THE ROOM SPOKE, *HE IN THE ROOM SPOKE).
DN56  [D39A - RIGHT ADJUNCTS OF CERTAIN PRONOUNS] =
         IN RNP RE PN:
         IF HOST IS PRO, THEN EITHER IT IS INDEFINITE OR IT IS ↓WE↓ OR
         ↓YOU↓.
* DN57: NO APPOSITION ON APPOSITION
DN57  [D59 - NO APPOS ON APPOS] =
         IN () RN RE APPOS: HOST IS NOT OCCURRING AS APPOS.
DN58  =  IN RNP RE PSNWH:
            HOST IS NSENT1 OR NSENT2 OR NSENT3: AWH.
* WN1:  PERMISSIBLE QUANTIFIER-ARTICLE COMBINATIONS IN LTR (SUCH A,
*        *SUCH THE).
  WN1  [W13 - LT] =
         IN LTR:  IF BOTH CORE X1 OF LTR IS T, AND LEFT-ADJUNCT OF X1
         IS Q X2, THEN ALL OF $QMANY, $QALL, $TQ ARE TRUE.
  $QMANY      =      IF X2 IS QMANY  ,   THEN X1 IS ↓A↓ OR ↓AN↓.
  $QALL = IF X2 IS QALL, THEN X1 IS NOT ↓A↓ OR ↓AN↓ .
  $TQ = BOTH X1 IS NOT ↓NO↓, AND X1 IS NOT TQUAN.
* WN2:  PRE-ARTICLE QUANTIFIERS ARE IN ONE OF THE SUBCLASSES QHALF (HALF
*        THE DAY),QALL (ALL THE TIME), OR QMANY (MANY THE TIME).
  WN2  [W15 - PRE-ARTICLE QUANTIFIER] =
         IN LT AFTER LQR: CORE IS QHALF OR QALL OR QMANY.
* WN3:  PRE-ARTICLE ADVERBS DLTPRO CAN OCCUR WITHOUT SUCCEEDING
*        ARTICLE (ONLY HE, EVEN MEN).
  WN3  [W16 - PRE-NOUNPHRASE ADVERBS, NULLT] =
         IN LTR: IF THE CORE X1 OF LTR IS EMPTY, THEN EITHER THE CORE X2
         OF THE LEFT-ADJUNCT OF X1 IS D:DLTPRO, OR X2 IS NULL.
* WN4:  BECAUSE A NULL ARTICLE IS POSSIBLE FOLLOWING PRE-ARTICLE ADVERBS
*        DLTPRO (ONLY CHILDREN) AND SOME OF THESE ADVERBS ARE ALSO IN LQ
*        IN LTR ( ONLY HALF), A SPURIOUS READING ARISES WHEN DQ OCCURS
*        WITHOUT A PRECEDING ARTICLE ( ONLY FIVE). THE ADVERB IN THIS CASE
*        IS DIRECTED TO THE LQ SLOT NEAREST Q.
  WN4 [W17-CHOOSE LQ NEAR Q ] =
         IN QPOS AFTER LQR : IN LQR IF LQ IS EMPTY THEN IT IS NOT THE
         CASE THAT IN COELEMENT TPOS BOTH CORE X1 IS EMPTY, AND BOTH
         THE CORE X2 OF THE LEFT-ADJUNCT OF X1 IS DLTPRO AND
         X2 IS DLQ .
* WN5:  PRE-QUANTIFIER A, VING OR VEN IS APREQ OR SUPERLATIVE (AN
*        ADDITIONAL THREE PEOPLE, THE TALLEST THREE BOYS).
  WN5  [W29 - LQ] =
         IN ADJPREQ: THE CORE OF THE SECOND ELEMENT IS APREQ OR
         SUPERLATIVE.                                  .
* WN6: THE VERB ↓HAVE↓ DOES NOT OCCUR ADJECTIVALLY (*HAD MEASLES).
WN6 = IN AVAR: CORE IS NOT VHAVE.
WN7  [W30 - NON-PLURAL NOUN IN COMPOUND ADJECTIVE] =
         IN LCDA, LCDVA AFTER N: N IS NOT PLURAL.
* WN8:  NOUN LEFT ADJUNCT OF NOUN IS (USUALLY) NOT PLURAL DESPITE
*        ↓THE ESTATES GENERAL↓      .
*        ALSO, A WORD WHICH IS BOTH ADJECTIVE AND NOUN, WHEN IN LN IS
*        USUALLY AN ADJECTIVE, NOT A NOUN, E.G. ↓A FUNDAMENTAL PRINCIPLE↓.
WN8 = IN NPOS AFTER OPTIONS 1, 3:
            IF THE CORE IS N X1 THEN EITHER BOTH X1 IS NOT PLURAL
```

```
                    AND AT X1 WORD STARTING PRESENT NODE IS NOT ADJ, OR $RARE.
*  WN9:   A COUNT NOUN REQUIRES A PRECEDING ARTICLE, WH-WORD, QUANTIFIER
*         OR NS.  BUT IF THE COUNT NOUN IS ALSO SUBCLASSIFIED NCOUNT2,
*         N IN PN FOR APPROPRIATE P IS EXEMPTED; IF NCOUNT3, N IN OBJBE
*         IS EXEMPTED.
WN9  [W35 - COUNT NOUN] =
          IN LNR AFTER NVAR: IF BOTH THE CORE X1 IS SINGULAR AND X1 IS
          NCOUNT1 THEN ONE OF $TPOS, $QPOS,$APOS,$COUNT2,$COUNT3,$COUNT4
          IS TRUE.
  $TPOS  =
          IN TPOS X3 OF LEFT-ADJUNCT X2 OF X1
          EITHER $CHECK-TPOS
          OR BOTH X3 HAS VALUE NULLC WHERE IT HAS NODE ATTRIBUTE LINKC X3
          AND $CHECK-TPOS.
   $CHECK-TPOS  =               EITHER
          THE CORE OF X3 IS T OR NS, OR X3 HAS VALUE WHLN.
  $QPOS= IN X2, CORE OF QPOS IS +ONE+.
  $APOS= BOTH IN X2 CORE OF APOS IS +ANOTHER+ AND THE  WORD STARTING THE
          PRESENT NODE [LNR] IS +ANOTHER+.
$COUNT2 = BOTH X1 IS NCOUNT2 X2, AND $PNTEST IS TRUE.
$COUNT3 = BOTH X1 IS NCOUNT3, AND LNR IS OCCURRING AS OBJBE.
 $COUNT4= X1 IS NCOUNT4 .
 $PNTEST = BOTH LNR  IS OCCURRING IN PN+  AND LISTS P AND X2 HAVE A
          COMMON ATTRIBUTE.
*  WN10:   CONDITIONS FOR NOUN CORE = VING.
WN10 [W41 - CORE N = VING] =
          IN NVAR AFTER OPTION VING: EITHER VING X1 IS PLURAL
          OR BOTH X1 HAS ATTRIBUTE OBJLIST: NSTGO
          AND IN LEFT-ADJUNCT OF X1 CORE OF NPOS IS N.
*  WN11:  NAMES AND PRONOUNS TAKE LIMITED LEFT ADJUNCTS OF N ( A
*         CERTAIN MR. AND MRS. JONES, ONLY HE KNOWS)
*         FOR NAMES THESE ADJUNCTS ARE RARE .
WN11 = IN LNR AFTER NVAR: BOTH $NAME AND $PRO .
  $NAME = IF CORE X4 IS N: NAME
             THEN IN LN ALL OF $NSPOSNULL [WSN11],
                               $NPOSNULL [WSN11],
                               $UNLIKELY.
  $UNLIKELY = EITHER BOTH TPOS IS EMPTY AND BOTH $QPOSNULL AND
          $APOSNULL OR $RARE .
  $PRO = IF X4 IS PRO
          THEN IN LEFT-ADJUNCT OF X4 ALL OF $QPOSNULL, $APOSNULL,
                                            $NSPOSNULL, $NPOSNULL,
                                            $LPRO ARE TRUE .
  $LPRO = BOTH CORE OF TPOS IS NULL+ AND EITHER LEFT-ADJUNCT X1
          IS NULL OR X1 IS D:DLTPRO .
WN12  =   IN NVAR AFTER N:
          N DOES NOT HAVE ATTRIBUTE NAME.
*  WN13  A NAME WITH SEVERAL PARTS (JOHN JONES) DOES NOT HAVE A
*        SECOND READING WITH THE LAST NAME IN APPOSITION TO THE
*        PRECEDING PARTS.
WN13 = IN APPOS: IF CORE IS NAME THEN HOST IS NOT NAME OR  NTITLE .
*  WN14: THE OPTIONAL TITLE BEFORE A NAME IS EITHER NTITLE (PROF.; DR.)
*        OR NCOUNT3 (PRESIDENT TRUMAN; AMBASSADOR JONES).
WN14 = IN TITLE RE OPTION N:
          CURRENT WORD IS N:NTITLE OR NCOUNT3 .
*  WN15: THE NOUNS IN THE LEFT PART OF A PROPER NAME ARE IN  THE
*        SUBCLASS NAME.
WN15 = IN () NAMEPART RE OPTION N:
          CURRENT WORD IS N:NAME .
*  WN16: THE RIGHTMOST NOUN IN A PROPER NAME IS IN SUBCLASS NAME.
WN16 [WELLFORMED CORE OF NAMESTG] = IN LNAMER AFTER LNAME:
          IF IMMEDIATE-NODE- IS NAMESTG THEN CURRENT WORD IS N:NAME .
```

```
WN16A = IN LNAMESR:
        CORE IS NS: NAME.
WN17 = IN LNSR AFTER NS: CORE IS NOT N:NAME.
* WN50: AN ADJECTIVE OCCURS TO THE RIGHT OF N ONLY IF IT HAS
*       MODIFIERS, OR IS IN THE SUBCLASS AINRN, OR THE HOST
*       IS AN INDEFINITE PRONOUN (A STUDENT GOOD AT MATH, STUDENTS
*       PRESENT, SOMETHING GOOD).
WN50 [W5 - ADJ IN RN] = IN ()RN AFTER ADJINRN:
        BOTH THE CORE- X1 OF ADJINRN IS NOT VEN OR VING
        AND ONE OF $LEFTADJ, $RIGHTADJ, $AINRN, $INDEF,
                    $CONJOIN, $QNSTG IS TRUE.
  $LEFTADJ  =  BOTH X1 HAS LEFT-ADJUNCT X2,
                AND X2 IS NOT EMPTY.
  $RIGHTADJ = BOTH X1 HAS RIGHT-ADJUNCT X2, AND X2 IS NOT EMPTY.
  $CONJOIN = AT X1 BOTH IMMEDIATE AVAR EXISTS,
                    AND ITERATE GO RIGHT UNTIL TEST FOR C-NODE SUCCEEDS.
  $QNSTG = X1 IS QN.
  $AINRN = X1 IS AINRN.
  $INDEF = THE HOST IS PRO:INDEFINITE.
* WN51:  RESTRICTION ON PN AS RIGHT ADJUNCT OF N:
*                   IF P  IS ↓INTO↓ THEN THE HOST IS NOT HUMAN (* THE
*       CHILDREN INTO THE HOUSE ARE NOISY).  IF P IS ↓SINCE↓, THE HOST
*       IS A TIME NOUN (THE TIME SINCE HIS ARRIVAL).  IF THE HOST IS A
*       NAME, THEN P IS ↓OF↓, ↓IN↓, ↓FROM↓ OR ↓AT↓.
* IF P IS ↓BECAUSE OF↓, PN IS SA.
WN51 [PN AS RN] = IN RNP AFTER PN:
        AT PN, BOTH $HOST-OF-PN AND $SA-PREP.
  $HOST-OF-PN = IF BOTH P X1 EXISTS
                    AND HOST X2 EXISTS
                THEN ALL OF $1, $2, $3.
   $1 = IF X1 IS ↓INTO↓
        THEN X2 IS NOT NHUMAN.
   $2 = IF X1 IS ↓SINCE↓ OR ↓AWAY↓ OR ↓PRIOR,TO↓
        THEN X2 IS NTIME1 .
   $3 = IF X2 IS NAME,
        THEN X1 IS ↓OF↓ OR ↓IN↓ OR ↓FROM↓ OR ↓AT↓.
  $SA-PREP = P IS NOT ↓BECAUSE↓,↓OF↓.
* WN52: AN APPOSITION  STRING DOES NOT HAVE A NULL CORE.
WN52 =  IN APPOS: CORE IS NOT NULLN.
* WN53: CONSTRUCTIONS LIKE ↓THE MAN TO SEE↓ DON↓T OCCUR IN SUBJECT
*       POSITION UNLESS THE VERB IS BE ( THE MAN TO SEE IS JOHN).
WN53 = IN () RN AFTER TOVO-N:
        EITHER HOST IS NOT OCCURRING IN SUBJECT
        OR CURRENT WORD IS TV OR V:VBE OR BEREP.
* OPTIMIZATION RESTRICTIONS
*
* DOPT1, COUNTERPART OF WPOS1: CURRENT WORD IS ADVERB WITH
*       CORRECT SUBCLASSIFICATION FOR STARTING ADVERB STRING IN GIVEN
*       SYNTACTIC POSITION (MOST ADVERBS CAN BE LEFT ADJOINED BY ADVERBS
*       DSA, DLP, AND DVERY (HE RAN VERY SWIFTLY)).
DOPT1A = IN () SA RE OPTION DSTG: EITHER CURRENT WORD IS D:DSA OR DLP
                                    OR DVERY OR DRW OR DMANNER,
                                    OR $SCOPE.
  $SCOPE = CURRENT WORD IS SCOPEWORD.                          (GLOBAL)
DOPT1B = IN () RN RE OPTION DSTG:
        EITHER CURRENT WORD IS D:DSA OR DLP OR DVERY OR DRN OR DLOC1
            OR  DLOC3 OR DMANNER,
            OR $SCOPE.
DOPT1C = IN RW RE OPTION DSTG:
        EITHER CURRENT WORD IS D:DSA OR DLP OR DVERY OR DRW OR DMANNER,
        OR $SCOPE.
DOPT1D = IN LV RE OPTION DSTG:
```

```
                     EITHER CURRENT WORD IS D:DSA OR DLP OR DVERY OR DLV OR DRV,
                     OR $SCOPE.
DOPT1F =IN LCS RE OPTION D: EITHER CURRENT WORD IS D:DLCS, OR $SCOPE.
DOPT1G =IN LT RE OPTION D: EITHER CURRENT WORD IS D:DLT OR DLTPRO, OR
          $SCOPE.
  DOPT1H = IN OBJBE, () OBES RE OPTION DSTG:
                       EITHER CURRENT WORD IS D:DSA OR DLP OR DVERY OR DPRED
                            OR DMANNER,
                       OR $SCOPE.
DOPT1I= IN LW RE OPTION D: EITHER CURRENT WORD IS D:DLW, OR $SCOPE.
DOPT1J =IN LQ RE OPTION DSTG: EITHER CURRENT WORD IS D:DSA OR DLP
          OR DVERY OR DLQ, OR $SCOPE.
DOPT1K = IN LP RE OPTION DSTG:
             EITHER CURRENT WORD IS D:DSA OR DLP OR DVERY OR DMANNER,
             OR $SCOPE.
DOPT1L = IN () TSUBJVO RE OPTION DSTG:
                 EITHER CURRENT WORD IS D:DSA OR DLP OR DVERY  OR DPERM
                     OR DMANNER,
                 OR $SCOPE.
DOPT1N =IN LVSA RE DSTG:  EITHER CURRENT WORD IS D:DSA OR DLP OR
          DVERY, OR $SCOPE.
DOPT1P = IN OBJECT RE DSTG:
                 EITHER CURRENT WORD IS D:DSA OR DLP OR DVERY OR DEVAL,
                 OR $SCOPE.
DOPT1Q = IN ()RV RE OPTION DSTG:
                 EITHER CURRENT WORD IS D:DSA  OR DLP OR DVERY OR DRV
                     OR DMANNER,
                 OR $SCOPE.
DOPT1R = IN LA RE OPTION DSTG:
                 EITHER CURRENT WORD IS D:DSA OR DLP OR DVERY OR DRV
                     OR DLA OR DLCOMP OR DMANNER,
                 OR $SCOPE.
* DOPT2:  THERE ARE AT LEAST 2 WORDS AHEAD IN THE SENTENCE.
DOPT2 [2 WORDS] = IN () SA RE OPTION LCS:  THERE ARE AT LEAST 2 WORDS
                                               AHEAD.
* DOPT3:  THERE ARE AT LEAST 3 WORDS AHEAD IN THE SENTENCE.
 DOPT3 = IN SN RE OPTIONS 1, 2:
          THERE ARE AT LEAST 3 WORDS AHEAD.
* DOPT4: LOOK AHEAD FOR CONTAINER VERB.
  DOPT4 [D16 - VSENT] =
       IN SUBJECT RE SN:  THERE IS A V OR TV OR VEN : VBE OR BEREP OR
       VSENT1 OR VSENT2 OR VSENT3 OR VMOD OR VEXP AHEAD.
* DOPT5:  +AS+ LIES AHEAD.
  DOPT5 [D54 - AS] =
       IN SASOBJBE:  THERE IS AN +AS+ AHEAD.
* DOPT6:  FOR NSTGT OPTION OF SA, THERE MUST BE A NTIME1 OR NTIME2 AHEAD.
*         (TWO DAYS AGO, YESTERDAY).  IF THE NOUN IS AN NTIME1
*         THEN A T OR P OR D OR ADJ:TIMETAG MUST PRECEDE IT, OR A P OR D:
*         TIMETAG MUST IMMEDIATELY FOLLOW.
*         SEE WPOS10 FOR WELLFORMEDNESS.
DOPT6 = IN () SA RE NSTGT:
       PRESENT-ELEMENT- X4 EXISTS;
       CURRENT WORD EXISTS;
       STORE IN X1;
       DO $N-AHEAD;
       EITHER $TIMETAG-TEST OR BOTH $NEXTN-AHEAD AND $TIMETAG-TEST .
  $N-AHEAD = ITERATET GO TO THE NEXT WORD
             UNTIL VERIFY $N-TEST SUCCEEDS;
       STORE IN X3 .
  $N-TEST = PRESENT-ELEMENT- IS N X2 .
  $NEXTN-AHEAD = AT X3 , GO TO THE NEXT WORD;
                   DO $N-AHEAD .
```

```
 $TIMETAG-TEST = X2 IS NTIME1 OR NTIME2 ;
                  IF X2 IS NTIME1
                  THEN ONE OF $PREV-TIMETAG , $NEXT-TIMETAG.
  $PREV-TIMETAG = ITERATET $NXT-WORD UNTIL $TIMEATT SUCCEEDS.
 $TIMEATT = X1 IS T OR P OR D OR ADJ:TIMETAG .
 $NXT-WORD = AT X1, NOT TEST FOR X3;
             GO TO THE NEXT WORD;
             NOT TEST FOR X3;
             STORE IN X1 .
  $NEXT-TIMETAG = AT X3 , GO TO THE NEXT WORD;
                  STORE IN X1;
                  EITHER X1 IS P OR D:TIMETAG
                  OR X1 IS +WHEN+ OR +THAT+.
* DOPT7:FOR THE SVINGO,NSVINGO ,VINGO OR VINGOFN STRING THERE MUST BE A
* VING AHEAD.
 DOPT7 [D57 - VING] =
         IN VINGO, SVINGO, NSVINGO, VINGOFN:  THERE IS A VING AHEAD.
* DOPT8 IS AN IMPROVED VERSION OF DOPT26 WHICH REPLACES THE OLD DOPT8.[7/79]
DOPT8 = IN NPOS RE OPTIONS 1,3:
         ONE OF $1-WORD, $2-WORD, $SCOPE.
$1-WORD = CURRENT WORD IS N OR VING.  [HEAD WOUND, SLEEPING SICKNESS]
$2-WORD = BOTH CURRENT WORD IS ADJ OR Q
          AND NEXT WORD IS N OR VING  [FRESH WATER FISH, 3 BEDROOM APT,
                                           DEEP SHAFT MINING].
DOPT8A= IN NPOS RE OPTION 1:
          BOTH CURRENT WORD X1 EXISTS
          AND AT X1 , NEXT WORD IS NOT SPWORD .
DOPT8B = IN NPOS RE OPTION 3:
          BOTH CURRENT WORD X1 EXISTS
          AND AT X1 , NEXT WORD IS SPWORD .
* DOPT9:  THERE IS A +TO+ AHEAD IN THE SENTENCE.
 DOPT9 [D70 - TO] =
         IN TOVO, FORTOVO, NTOVO:  THERE IS A +TO+ AHEAD.
* DOPT10:  THERE IS A +BE+ VERB AHEAD.
 DOPT10 [D73 - BE] =
         IN PERMUTATION RE OBES:  THERE IS A TV OR VEN OR V : VBE AHEAD.
* DOPT11:  Q LIES AHEAD IN THE SENTENCE OR QPOS CANNOT BE TRIED.
DOPT11 [SEE WN5] =  IN QPOS RE LQR:
                    ONE OF $Q-CHECK, $D-CHECK, $ADJPREQ, $SCOPE, $Q-OF.
  $Q-OF = CURRENT WORD IS +TENS+ OR +DOZENS+ OR +HUNDREDS+
          OR +THOUSANDS+ OR +MILLIONS+ OR +BILLIONS+ OR +LOTS+ .
  $Q-CHECK = CURRENT WORD IS Q.
  $D-CHECK = CURRENT WORD IS D:DLQ.
  $ADJPREQ = EITHER CURRENT WORD IS ADJ OR VING
                              OR VEN: APREQ OR SUPERLATIVE,
             OR CURRENT WORD IS +VERY+ [THE VERY THREE].
* DOPT12:  NS LIES AHEAD IN THE SENTENCE FOR LNSR TO BE TRIED.
DOPT12 = IN LNSR, LNAMESR, QNS:
          THERE IS AN NS AHEAD.
* DOPT13: IF ASSERTION IS NOT IN THE SCOPE OF A CONJUNCTION THEN ONE OF
*     THE VERB FORMS W OR TV MUST BE AHEAD IN THE SENTENCE.
DOPT13 = IN ASSERTION:
          IF BOTH PRESENT-STRING IS NOT OCCURRING IN C1SHOULD
             AND IMMEDIATE-NODE- IS NOT Q-CONJ
          THEN THERE IS A W OR TV AHEAD.
* DOPT17:  A QUESTIONMARK FOLLOWS A QUESTION.
 DOPT17 [D27A] =
         IN CENTER RE QUESTION:  THERE IS A +?+ AHEAD.
DOPT18 = IN NSTG RE LNR:
          EITHER THE CURRENT WORD X1 IS PRO OR T OR Q OR ADJ OR D
                                      OR NS OR N OR VEN OR VING
                                      OR INITIAL OR SCOPEWORD,
```

```
                OR X1 IS ↓HOW↓ OR ↓WHICH↓ OR ↓WHAT↓ OR ↓WHOSE↓.
DOPT19 = IN RV, RN RE OPTION 1: THE CURRENT WORD IS NOT ↓;↓ OR ↓.↓
                OR ↓≥↓.
DOPT19A = IN SA RE OPTION 2: THE CURRENT WORD IS NOT ↓;↓ OR ↓.↓ OR ↓≥↓.
DOPT19B = IN RA RE SN, ASSERTION, PN, PVINGSTG, PSVINGO, TOVO-N,
        FORTOVO-N, TOVO:
        CURRENT WORD IS NOT ↓;↓ OR ↓.↓ OR ↓≥↓.
DOPT19C = IN RN RE OPTION 1: IF CURRENT WORD X1 IS TV
                             THEN X1 IS [ALSO] VEN OR N OR ADJ OR D
                             OR P.
DOPT19D = IN SA RE OPTION 2: IF CURRENT WORD X1 IS TV
                             THEN X1 IS [ALSO] VEN OR N OR ADJ OR D
                             OR P.
DOPT19E = IN OBJECTBE RE OBJBE: IF CURRENT WORD X1 IS TV
                             THEN X1 IS [ALSO] VEN OR N OR ADJ OR D
                             OR P.
* DOPT20:  CURRENT WORD IS CS0-8 OR D:DLCS.
* ADD ↓SHOULD↓.  2/79
DOPT20 [D53-CURRENT CS0] = IN () SA RE OPTION LCS:
        EITHER THE CURRENT WORD X1 IS CS0 OR CS1 OR CS2 OR CS3 OR
        CS4 OR CS5 OR CS6 OR CS7 OR CS8 OR SCOPEWORD, OR EITHER X1 IS
        ↓THAN↓ OR ↓AS↓ OR ↓SHOULD↓ OR X1 IS D:DLCS .
$RARE = THE RARE SWITCH IS ON.                                    (GLOBAL)
$REP = THE REP SWITCH IS ON.                                      (GLOBAL)
DOPT20A [DOPT20 FOR SA SET IN ASSERTIONZ] = IN SAZ RE OPTION LCS:
        EITHER THE CURRENT WORD X1 IS CS0 OR CS1 OR CS2 OR CS3
        OR CS4 OR CS5 OR CS6 OR CS7 OR CS8 OR SCOPEWORD, OR EITHER X1 IS
        ↓THAN↓ OR ↓AS↓ OR ↓SHOULD↓, OR X1 IS D:DLCS .
* DOPT21: WHN BEGINS WITH A WH-WORD NAMED AS AN OPTION OF WHLN IN TPOS.
DOPT21 = IN WHN: CURRENT WORD IS
        ↓WHOSE↓ OR ↓WHICH↓ OR ↓WHAT↓ OR ↓WHATEVER↓ OR ↓WHICHEVER↓ OR
        ↓WHOSEVER↓ OR ↓HOW↓.
DOPT23  =  IN QN, QNREP, QNS:
            EITHER CURRENT WORD IS Q
        OR EITHER BOTH CURRENT WORD IS D: DLQ
                    AND NEXT WORD IS Q
            OR $SCOPE.
DOPT24 [SEE WN12] = IN NQ:
                    EITHER $TEST OR $SCOPE.
 $TEST = EITHER CURRENT WORD IS N: NPREQ  OR NAME
        OR NEXT WORD IS N: NPREQ OR NAME.
DOPT25 [SEE WPOS3] = IN APOS RE ADJADJ:
            ONE OF $AVAR-CORE, $COMPOUND, $D-IN-LA, $LQNR, $SCOPE.
   $AVAR-CORE = CURRENT WORD IS ADJ OR VING OR VEN.
    $COMPOUND = BOTH CURRENT WORD IS N
                AND NEXT WORD IS ADJ OR VING OR VEN.
  $D-IN-LA = CURRENT WORD IS D:DSA OR DRV OR DLA OR DLCOMP OR DMANNER.
   $LQNR = ONE OF $QN, $NQ, $LQ.
   $QN = CURRENT WORD IS Q.
   $NQ = CURRENT WORD IS N: NPREQ OR NAME.
   $LQ = CURRENT WORD IS D: DLQ.
DOPT27 = IN RSUBJ:
        EITHER CURRENT WORD IS Q OR T:QROVING
        OR EITHER CURRENT WORD IS PRO: PROSELF
            OR $SCOPE.
DOPT28 = IN SCALESTG RE PN:
            EITHER THERE IS AN N:NSCALE AHEAD
            OR THERE IS AN ADJ: ASCALE AHEAD.
* WOPT1: THIS SUPPLEMENTS DOPT13 . IN ASSERTION AFTER SUBJECT THERE MUST
*       BE A TENSE MARKER EXCEPT IN C1SHOULD.
* ADD SVO.  2/79
WOPT1 = IN SUBJECT: IF IMMEDIATE-NODE IS ASSERTION X1
```

```
                     THEN EITHER THERE IS A W OR TV AHEAD
                        OR AT X1 IMMEDIATE-NODE- IS C1SHOULD OR SVO.
*  POSITION RESTRICTIONS
*
*  QUANTITIFIER RESTRICTIONS
*
*  DQ2: QN DOES NOT CONTAIN PN IF IT IS OCCURRING IN LN (* A THREE INCH
*       IN LENGTH LINE).
   DQ2  [D47 - QN HAS NO PN SCALESTG IN LN]  =
            IN SCALESTG RE OPTION PN:  IMMEDIATE-STRING IS NOT OCCURRING IN
            APOS.
*  DQ3:  THE QN STRING IN ADJECTIVAL POSITION CAN BE FOLLOWED BY ADJ OR
*        PN ONLY IF N IN QN IS NUNITS (A TWO INCH LONG LINE, * A TWO
*        FAMILY LARGE HOUSE).  IN RV AND LP QN DOES NOT OCCUR WITH ADJ
*        OR PN (* HE THREW IT FIVE FEET LONG).
   DQ3 [D49 - QN WITH SCALESTG] = IN SCALESTG RE OPTIONS PN, ADJ:
            BOTH IF COELEMENT N EXISTS ↱
                 THEN IT IS NUNIT,
            AND IMMEDIATE-NODE OF IMMEDIATE-NODE [QN] IS NOT LP.
*  DQ4: RV=QN ONLY POST OBJECT (↓HE HIT THE BALL 300 FT.↓)
   DQ4 = IN ()RV RE QN:
            IMMEDIATE-NODE IS NOT VERB OR LVINGR OR LVENR OR LVR OR LTVR.
*  WQ1:  IN QN, N IS A NOUN OF MEASURE NUNIT (TWO INCHES).  WHEN QN
*        OCCURS AS LN, N IS SINGULAR (A TWO INCH LINE), BUT
*        IN RV, RN AND THE PREDICATE, Q AGREES WITH N IN NUMBER
*        (THE LINE IS TWO INCHES LONG).
*        WE DISALLOW TIME NOUN AS VALUE OF N IN QN IN RV BECAUSE
*        NSTGT COVERS THIS CASE.
   WQ1 [W18 - QN NOUN SUBCLASS, AGREEMENT] = IN QN:
            IF ELEMENT N X1 EXISTS THEN ALL OF $RV-TIME, $UNIT, $AGREE.
     $UNIT = EITHER X1 IS NUNIT OR BOTH QN IS OCCURRING IN APOS AND $RARE.
   $AGREE=   BOTH $LN AND $PRED.
     $LN = IF PRESENT-STRING [QN] IS OCCURRING IN APOS,
           THEN EITHER X1 IS NOT PLURAL
                OR X1 IS ↓HOURS↓.
     $PRED = IF QN IS NOT OCCURRING IN APOS, THEN BOTH $NSING AND $NPLUR
             ARE TRUE.
     $NSING = IF X1 IS SINGULAR, THEN IT IS NOT THE CASE THAT $QPLUR1.
     $QPLUR1 = EITHER AT X1 THE CORE X4 OF COELEMENT LQR IS PLURAL,
               OR EITHER X4 IS CPDNUMBR,
                  OR X1 HAS CORE-CONJUNCT.
     $NPLUR = IF X1 IS PLURAL, THEN IT IS NOT THE CASE THAT $QSING1.
     $QSING1 = BOTH AT X1 THE CORE X4 OF COELEMENT LQR IS SINGULAR,
               AND X4 DOES NOT HAVE CORE-CONJUNCT.
     $RV-TIME = IF PRESENT-ELEMENT IS OCCURRING IN RV THEN X1 IS NOT
                                                      NTIME1 OR NTIME2.
*  WQ1A: THE N IN PERUNIT IS NUNIT (↓PER DAY↓, ↓PER MG↓).
   WQ1A = IN PERUNIT: IF N EXISTS ↱
                      THEN IT IS NUNIT.
*  WQ1B:  THE NS IN QNS IS NUNIT (4 MONTH↓S HISTORY)
   WQ1B = IN QNS AFTER NS: ELEMENT N IS NUNIT.
*  WQ2:  IN QN, IF SCALESTG IS A, THEN A IS ASCALE (LONG, WIDE) OR
*        COMPARATIVE (LARGER) (TWO INCHES LONG OR WIDE, A SHADE DARKER
*        OR LIGHTER).
   WQ2  [W54 - QN]  =
            IN SCALESTG AFTER ADJ:  ADJ IS ASCALE OR COMPARATIVE .
*  WQ3:  IN THE PN OPTION OF SCALESTG, THE N IS NSCALE (TWO INCHES IN LENGTH).
   WQ3  [W52 - SCALESTG]  =
            IN SCALESTG AFTER PN:  IN PN, CORE OF NSTGO IS NSCALE.
*  WQ4:  AMONG QUANTIFIERS, ONLY NUMBERS REPEAT, EXCEPT THAT THE LAST
*        QUANTIFIER IN A SEQUENCE OF REPEATED QUANTIFIERS MAY BE
*        COMPARATIVE MARKED (MORE LESS) OR THE  WORD       ↓SUCH↓ (THREE
```

```
    *        HUNDRED MORE; THREE HUNDRED SUCH).
    WQ4  [W73A - QVAR    COMPOUND NUMBER]  =
             IN QVAR, NUMBRSTG AFTER CPDNUMBR:   IN CPDNUMBR, BOTH $QNUMCOM
             AND $REPEAT ARE TRUE.
    $QNUMCOM = EITHER VALUE IS FRACTION
                   OR EITHER THE CORE OF THE SECOND ELEMENT X1 IS QNUMBER
                        OR COMPARATIVE , OR X1 IS +SUCH+ .
    $REPEAT=  IF X1 EXISTS ↵
              THEN BOTH IN X1, IF PREVIOUS-ELEMENT IS Q ↵
                        THEN Q IS QNUMBER,
                   AND IF IN X1, THE PREVIOUS-ELEMENT IS CPDNUMBR ↵
                        THEN BOTH THE SECOND ELEMENT X1 IS QNUMBER,
                             AND $REPEAT IS TRUE .
    WQ5  [W73B - NUMBRSTG]  =
             IN NUMBRSTG AFTER Q:   Q IS QNUMBER.
 *  WQ6:  ONLY THOSE ARTICLES AND QUANTIFIERS WHICH
 *        ARE IN THE SUBCLASS QROVING (BOTH, ALL) OCCUR AS RSUBJ
 *        (ROVING ADJUNCTS OF SUBJECT). IF Q OR T
 *        IS FOLLOWED BY PN, THEN P = +OF+ (THEY ARE ALL OF THEM AGREED,
 *        THEY ARE EACH A GOOD THEORY).
    WQ6 [W45 - RSUBJ]  =  IN RSUBJ AFTER OPTION 1:
             BOTH THE CORE OF THE FIRST ELEMENT IS QROVING,
             AND IF THE SECOND ELEMENT IS PN ↵
                   THEN P IS +OF+.
 *  WQ7:  THE QN OPTION OF LP CAN BE CHOSEN ONLY WITH AN APPROPRIATE PREPOSITION.
    WQ7  [W109 - QN IN LP ONLY BEFORE CERTAIN P]  =
             IN LP AFTER QN:     THE WORD FOLLOWING THE PRESENT NODE IS
             +OFF+ OR +INTO+
             OR +OVER+ OR +BELOW+ OR +AFTER+ OR +SINCE+ OR +FROM+ OR +DOWN+
             OR +UNDER+ OR +ABOVE+.
 *  WQ8:  SINCE QN (3 INCHES) IS IN THE ASTG OBJECT OF +BE+, AVOID
 *        REDUNDANCY IN OBJBE BY EXCLUDING NSTG WITH CORE NUNIT
 *        IMMEDIATELY PRECEDED  BY Q.
    WQ8  = IN OBJBE AFTER NSTG:  IF CORE X1 IS N:NUNIT,
                                 THEN IN LEFT-ADJUNCT OF X1
             EITHER $QPOSNULL [WSN11] OR NOT ALL OF $APOSNULL, $NSPOSNULL,
             $NPOSNULL.
 *  WQ9:  WE FORCE CONTIGUOUS QN OCCURRENCES TO BE TAKEN AS QN + QNREP
 *        (+8 POUNDS 9 OUNCES+).
    WQ9  = IN QN:
             IF ELEMENT NULL EXISTS
             THEN IT IS NOT THE CASE THAT BOTH CURRENT WORD IS Q
                                     AND  NEXT WORD IS N: NUNIT.
 *  WQ10:  IN NQ THE NOUN IS NPREQ OR NAME (+A MODEL 6 RADIO+). THIS
 *         RESTRICTION WAS FORMERLY WN6 IN THE EG.
    WQ10  = IN NQ:
             BOTH THE FIRST ELEMENT IS N:NPREQ OR NAME,
             AND IF THE SECOND ELEMENT IS N ↵
                   THEN N IS NLETTER.
 *  WQ11:  TO CORRECTLY SEGMENT THE SEQUENCE NQN (+WEIGHT 17 POUNDS+) AS
 *         N + QN AND NOT NQ + N, REJECT NQ STRING IF THE CURRENT WORD
 *         (AFTER NQ) IS NUNIT.
    WQ11  = IN NQ: CURRENT WORD IS NOT N: NUNIT.
 *  WQ12:  NQ SEQUENCES SHOULD NOT BE SPLIT BETWEEN N AND Q.  NOTE: Q POSITION
 *  HERE ALSO INCLUDES NLETTER.  +TYPE B+.
    WQ12  = IN NVAR:
             IF EITHER CURRENT WORD IS N: NLETTER
                OR CURRENT WORD IS Q
             THEN N IS NOT NPREQ OR NAME.
 *  WQ13:  REPLACES DQ1 FOR EFFICIENCY OF SAVING .
 *         THE DIMENSIONAL SEQUENCE QN DOES NOT OCCUR AS ADJINRN UNLESS
 *         THERE IS AN A OR PN IN QN ( A PORTICO 100 FEET LONG WAS SEEN,
```

```
*       * A PORTICO 100 FEET WAS SEEN) .
WQ13= IN ADJINRN AFTER LQNR: ELEMENT SCALESTG OF QN OF QNPOS OF LQNR
        IS NOT EMPTY .
* WQ14: IF WORD AFTER ↓PERCENT↓ IS NOT A NOUN THEN ↓PERCENT↓ SHOULD
*       FILL NOUN SLOT IN QN, AND PERUNIT SHOULD BE EMPTY.
WQ14= IN PERUNIT AFTER OPTIONS ↓PERCENT↓, ↓PER↓ [FOR ↓PER CENT↓] :
        THE CURRENT WORD IS N .
* SELECTION RESTRICTIONS
*
* WSEL1:  SUITABLE OBJECT N FOR GIVEN VERB.
  WSEL1 [W100] =
          IN OBJECT AFTER NSTGO: IF ALL OF $OBJECT-NOUN, $GOVERNING-VERB,
          $FORBIDDEN-NOUN-LIST ARE TRUE, THEN $NO-COMMON IS TRUE .
  $OBJECT-NOUN = THE EXTENDED-CORE X3 OF THE OBJECT X10 IS N OR PRO .
  $GOVERNING-VERB = AT X10 THE VERB-COELEMENT X4 EXISTS.
  $FORBIDDEN-NOUN-LIST = THE CORE OF X4 HAS THE ATTRIBUTE NOTNOBJ X5.
  $NO-COMMON = LISTS X3 AND X5 HAVE NO COMMON ATTRIBUTE .                   (GLOBAL)
* WSEL2:  SUITABLE SUBJECT N FOR GIVEN VERB.
WSEL2 [W26] =
    IN ASSERTION, YESNOQ, SVINGO, FORTOVO, NTOVO, SVO, STOVO-N,TSUBJVO,
    OBES:
    IF ALL OF $SUBJECT-NOUN, $FORBIDDEN-SUBJN, $NOTPASS ARE TRUE,
    THEN $NOCOMMON.
  $SUBJECT-NOUN = THE EXTENDED-CORE X1 OF THE SUBJECT X10 IS N OR PRO .
  $FORBIDDEN-SUBJN = AT X10,THE CORE OF THE DEEPEST-COVERB X2 HAS
        ATTRIBUTE NOTNSUBJ X5.
  $NOTPASS = X2 IS NOT OCCURRING IN VENPASS.
$NOCOMMON = LISTS X1 AND X5 HAVE NO COMMON ATTRIBUTE .
* WSEL3:   IN COMPOUND NOUNS NVING (HAT WEARING) THE MOST PRODUCTIVE SUBTYPE
*       IS ONE WHERE THE NOUN IS A POSSIBLE OBJECT OF THE VING VERB
*       (CF. WSEL1).
  WSEL3 [W71] =
          IN NVAR AFTER VING:  IF BOTH IN LEFT-ADJUNCT, CORE X2 OF NPOS IS
          N, AND    VING HAS ATTRIBUTE NOTNOBJ X3 , THEN LISTS X2 AND X3
          HAVE NO COMMON ATTRIBUTE .
* WSEL4: SIMILAR TO WSEL3 EXCEPT APPLIES TO NVING AS COMPOUND
*       ADJECTIVE (A HAT WEARING PERSON, *AN EVIDENCE LEADING MACHINE).
  WSEL4 [W71A]  =
          IN AVAR AFTER OPTION 2:IF BOTH LCOVA X10 HAS VALUE N X2,AND
          AT X10 CORE OF COELEMENT AVAR IS
                   VING:NOTNOBJ X3, THEN LISTS X2 AND X3 HAVE NO COMMON
          ATTRIBUTE.
* WSEL5:  IF RN = VENPASS, THEN THE HOST NOUN IS NOT ON THE FORBIDDEN
*       OBJECT LIST OF THE VERB (IF ↓HE QUOTED A VERSE↓ THEN ↓THE VERSE
*       QUOTED↓ , IF *↓HE ATE A FACT↓ THEN *↓THE FACT EATEN↓).
* WSEL5: OPTIMIZES OLD WSEL5 BY HOUSING IT LOWER.
WSEL5 [W83] = IN VENPASS AFTER LVENR:
          IF BOTH IMMEDIATE-NODE IS RN WHERE HOST X3 IS N OR PRO,
          AND CORE OF LVENR HAS ATTRIBUTE NOTNOBJ X5
          THEN $NO-COMMON [WSEL1] IS TRUE.
* WSEL6: FOR VINGO IN RN, HOST IS SUITABLE SUBJECT FOR VING.
*       (A GENTLEMAN DINING HERE).
WSEL6  =  IN ()RN AFTER VINGO:
              IF BOTH HOST X3 IS N OR PRO
                 AND IN VINGO THE CORE OF LVINGR HAS ATTRIBUTE NOTNSUBJ X5
              THEN $NO-COMMON [WSEL1] IS TRUE.
* WSEL7:IF APOS CONTAINS VING/VEN THEN HOST N IS SUITABLE SUBJECT/OBJECT
*       OF ROOT VERB IN VING/VEN. (WAS DSEL1).
*      PREVENTS VING FROM BEING TREATED AS ADJ IN EXAMPLES SUCH AS
*      ↓IMPRESSION OF MENINGITIS WAS CONFIRMED BY FINDING CLOUDY
*      CEREBROSPINAL FLUID↓, WHERE ↓FLUID↓ IS NOT AN OK SUBJECT OF
*      ↓FIND↓ .
```

```
*       ALSO CHECKS SELECTION OF ADJECTIVAL VEN WITH RESPECT TO HOST N:
*       N IS OK OBJECT OF VEN (↓A TRANSFUSED PATIENT↓, BUT NOT
*       ↓A TRANSFUSED DIAGNOSIS↓) OR ELSE VEN IS VVERYVING
*       (↓A DETERMINED PERSON↓, BUT NOT  ↓THEY DETERMINED THE PERSON↓).
WSEL7 [VING OR VEN AS ADJ] = IN NVAR AFTER N:
   IF BOTH LEFT-ADJUNCT X2 SUBSUMES VING OR VEN
      AND ELEMENT N X3 EXISTS
   THEN AT APOS X7 OF X2
         BOTH ITERATET $VING-IS-ADJ UNTIL $ADJADJ FAILS
         AND  ITERATET $VEN-IS-ADJ UNTIL $ADJADJ FAILS.
  $VEN-IS-ADJ = IF CORE OF X7 IS VEN X8
                   THEN EITHER X8 IS VVERYVING
                      OR IF X8 HAS ATTRIBUTE NOTNOBJ X5
                         THEN $NO-COMMON [WSEL1] IS TRUE.
   $VING-IS-ADJ = IF CORE OF X7 IS VING WHERE BOTH VING HAS ATTRIBUTE
                                                     NOTNSUBJ X5
                                          AND COELEMENT LCOVA IS EMPTY
                  THEN $NO-COMMON IS TRUE.
   $ADJADJ = VALUE IS ADJADJ X7.
* WSEL8: THE SUBJECT OF A PASSIVE MUST BE A POSSIBLE [NON-PASSIVE] OBJECT
* ↓THE CHILD WAS SEEN.↓ ↓*THE CHILD WAS AGREED.↓ [MED UD 7/79]
WSEL8 = IN PASSOBJ: BOTH $SUBJ-CAN-BE-N AND $N-SUBCLASS-OK.
$SUBJ-CAN-BE-N = IF BOTH VALUE [OF PASSOBJ] IS NULLOBJ
                    AND CORE X1 OF ULTIMATE-SUBJECT IS N
                    THEN CORE X2 OF COELEMENT LVENR [OF PASSOBJ] HAS
                    ATTRIBUTE OBJLIST: NSTGO.
$N-SUBCLASS-OK = IF X2 HAS ATTRIBUTE NOTNOBJ: X3
                    THEN LISTS X1 AND X3 HAVE NO COMMON ATTRIBUTE.
* SENTENCE NOMINALIZATION RESTRICTIONS
*
* DSN1: CORRECT SUBJECT FOR SN OR ASSERTION OBJECT OF ↓BE↓
*        (THE TRUTH IS WE NEED MONEY).
DSN1[D1-SN AS OBJECT OF BE]=
         IN OBJECTBE RE SN, ASSERTION: ONE OF $SUBJN,
                                              $PRO,
                                              $STRING IS TRUE.
  $SUBJN = THE CORE X1 OF THE ULTIMATE-SUBJECT IS NSENT1 OR
         NSENT2 OR NSENT3.
  $PRO    =      BOTH X1 IS PRO, AND X1 IS NOT NHUMAN.
$STRING= EITHER X1 IS NULLN, OR X1 IS FORTOVO OR TOVO [SEE WSN3].
* DSN2:  AN SN STRING OR ASSERTION OCCURS AS THE RIGHT ADJUNCT OF AN
*         ADJECTIVE ONLY FOR CERTAIN
*         SUBCLASSES OF ADJECTIVES (IT IS TRUE THAT HE CAME, * IT IS
*         ROUND THAT HE CAME).
*         ALSO: ↓SHE IS ANXIOUS FOR YOU TO KNOW↓ (ASENT3).
DSN2   [D2 - SN AS RA] =
         IN RA RE SN, ASSERTION:  ALL OF $HOST, $NOCOMMA, $NOT-ADJINRN,
         $IT, $HUMAN ARE TRUE.
  $HOST      =      HOST X1 IS ASENT1 OR ASENT3 OR VSENT1.
$NOT-ADJINRN = RA IS NOT OCCURRING IN ADJINRN.
$NOCOMMA = THE PRECEDING WORD IS NOT ↓,↓.
$IT =   IF EITHER X1 IS VSENT1 OR BOTH X1 IS ASENT1 AND X1 IS NOT
         ASENT3, THEN $SUBJIT.
$SUBJIT = THE CORE X3 OF THE ULTIMATE-SUBJECT X10 IS ↓IT↓.              (GLOBAL)
$HUMAN = IF X1 IS ASENT3 THEN AT THE CORE X9 OF THE ULTIMATE-SUBJECT
         $NHUMAN [WPOS22] IS TRUE.
* DSN3:  SELECTION OF PARTICULAR SN STRING AS RIGHT ADJUNCT OF
*         PARTICULAR ASENT ADJECTIVE (IT IS EASY FOR HIM TO LEAVE,
*         *IT IS PROVABLE FOR HIM TO LEAVE). ALSO SIMILAR SELECTION
*          WHERE HOST IS NOUN NSENT1 (THE DEMAND THAT HE GO,
*          *THE FACT THAT HE GO)
DSN3   [D3,D7  -CHOICE OF SN OPTION ] =
```

```
        IN SN RE OPTION 1:
                IF BOTH SN IS OCCURRING IN RA OR RN AND HOST IS
                ASENT1 OR ASENT3 OR NSENT1 X2 WHERE X2 IS ANYTHING THEN EDIT
                [OPTIONS OF SN] BY $1.
     $1 = ALL OF $THATS, $FORSHOULD, $WH ARE TRUE .
     $THATS= IF TEST FOR THATS OR ASSERTION THEN X2 IS ATHAT.
     $FORSHOULD = IF TEST FOR FORTOVO OR TOVO OR C1SHOULD THEN X2 IS
             AFORTO OR ASHOULD.
     $WH = IF TEST FOR SNWH THEN X2 IS AWH.
* DSN4: CONDITIONS FOR ACCEPTING SN FOLLOWING VSENT1 (IT SURPRISED
*       HIM THAT SHE LEFT) OR FOLLOWING A PASSIVE VSENT3 (IT WAS
*       KNOWN THAT SHE LEFT).
DSN4 [↓IT↓ FORM FOR SENTENTIAL VERBS ] =
                IN () RV RE SN: BOTH $VSENT13 AND $SUBJIT [DSN2] ARE TRUE.
     $VSENT13=       EITHER BOTH THE CORE X9 OF THE VERB-COELEMENT IS
                VSENT3 X8 AND THE PREVIOUS-ELEMENT IS PASSOBJ WHERE CORE IS
                NULLOBJ OR BOTH X9 IS VSENT1 AND THE PREVIOUS-ELEMENT
                IS OBJECT WHERE VALUE IS NSTGO OR PN OR PSTG.
* DSN5:  AN SN STRING IS ACCEPTABLE AS RIGHT ADJUNCT OF N ONLY IF N IS
*       NSENT1, NSENT2 OR NSENTP.  IF N IS NSENTP, N IS IN PN WITH
*       APPROPRIATE P AND THE ULTIMATE SUBJECT IS ↓IT↓
*       (THE FACT THAT HE EXISTS, IT IS OF INTEREST THAT HE EXISTS).
*       IF NSENT WITH ADJUNCT SN IS IN THE PREDICATE, THEN THE
*       ULTIMATE SUBJECT IS ↓IT↓ (IT IS TRUE THAT HE EXISTS). IF SN IS
*       POST-OBJECT THEN THE SUBJECT CANNOT ALSO HAVE A CONTIGUOUS SN
*       RIGHT ADJUNCT (A REPORT EXISTS THAT HE LEFT,* A REPORT THAT HE
*       LEFT EXISTS THAT HE  RETURNED).
DSN5 [D5 - SN AS RN] =
          IN () RN, RNSUBJ RE SN: ALL OF $NSENT, $NSENTP, $RNSUBJ.
     $NSENT = BOTH HOST X1 IS NSENT1 OR NSENT2 OR NSENT3 OR NSENTP
                AND IF EITHER X1 IS NSENT3
                            OR X1 IS OCCURRING IN OBJBE
                THEN $SUBJIT [DSN2] IS TRUE.
     $NSENTP = IF X1 IS NSENTP X2 THEN BOTH X1 IS OCCURRING IN PN X8
                WHERE $SUBJIT IS TRUE AND IN X8, LISTS P  AND X2 HAVE A
                COMMON ATTRIBUTE.
     $NINPN = X1 IS OCCURRING IN PN X3.
     $CORRECTP = IN X3, LISTS    P AND X2 HAVE A COMMON ATTRIBUTE .
     $RNSUBJ = IF RNSUBJ EXISTS, THEN AT X1 THE RIGHT-ADJUNCT IS NOT
                OCCURRING IN SN.
* DSN6:  IF THE TOVO-N OPTION OF RA IS TAKEN THEN THE HOST ADJECTIVE MUST
*       EITHER BE ADJ OF SUBCLASS ASENT1:AFORTO OR VING OF SUBCLASS
*       VSENT1. (THE PROBLEM IS EASY TO SOLVE, THAT IS ASTONISHING TO
*       HEAR ). AASP IS ALSO ACCEPTED BUT ONLY A FEW WORK (THE RESULTS
*       ARE READY TO PUBLISH, *THE RESULTS ARE LUCKY TO PUBLISH).
DSN6 [D6] =
     IN RA RE TOVO-N:  EITHER HOST X1 IS VSENT1
                            OR X1 IS ASENT1: AFORTO.
* DSN7: TOVO AS NON-SENTENTIAL RA ADJOINS ONLY ADJ:AASP (HE IS APT TO
*       DO IT) OR ASENT1:AFORTO (HE IS NOBLE TO DO IT), AND IN THE LATTER
*       CASE  HAS A HUMAN SUBJECT. AASP ↓TOVO CAN BE RN (NOONE ABLE TO
*       DO IT WAS FOUND, *NOONE NOBLE TO DO IT WAS FOUND).
DSN7 [D62 - ASPECTUAL ADJ WITH TOVO] =
     IN RA RE TOVO: BOTH $HOST AND $HOST-OF-HOST.
$HOST  = EITHER THE HOST X5 IS AASP, OR X5 IS ASENT1:AFORTO X7   WHERE
             AT THE CORE X9 OF THE ULTIMATE-SUBJECT OF X5
                        $NHUMAN [WPOS22] IS TRUE.
$HOST-OF-HOST = IF X7 EXISTS THEN THE HOST OF X5 IS NOT OCCURRING IN
             LNR.
* DSN8:  A STRING IN SN RARELY IF EVER OCCURS AS THE VALUE OF THE SUBJECT OF
*         A STRING IN SN OR RELATED STRINGS.
DSN8 [D24] =
```

```
          IN SUBJECT RE OPTION SN:  EITHER THE RARE SWITCH IS ON, OR BOTH
               $SN1 AND $SN2 ARE TRUE.
   $SN1 = THE NONSEG-IMMEDSTG X5 IS NOT S-N OR FORTOVO OR NTOVO OR
          NTOBE OR SOBJBE OR SASOBJBE OR SVEN OR STOVO-N OR THATS OR
          C1SHOULD OR SVO .
   $SN2 = X5 IS NOT OCCURRING IN SNWH.
 * DSN9: NO LV IN VINGOFN (*THE FREQUENTLY WRITING OF LETTERS).
 DSN9 = IN LV RE DSTG: IMMEDIATE-STRING IS NOT VINGOFN.
 * DSN10:  THE SPECIAL OBJECT STRING DPOFN OCCURS ONLY IN VINGOFN (THE
 *          WRITING DOWN OF THE RESULT).
  DSN10  [D74 - DP4 IN VINGOFN]  =
          IN DP4  :  DP4   IS OCCURRING IN VINGOFN.
 * DSN11:  TV IS NOT AN ELEMENT OF C1SHOULD OR SVO; W  IS NOT AN ELEMENT OF
 *         SVO; V IS AN ELEMENT OF C1SHOULD OR SVO (ASK THAT JUSTICE BE
 *         DONE, INSIST THAT HE SHOULD DO IT). SEE ALSO WVC1.
 DSN11A [D12A] =
          IN VVAR RE TV: BOTH IMMEDIATE-STRING IS NOT TOVO OR TOBE
          AND  NONSEG-IMMEDSTG IS NOT C1SHOULD OR SVO.
 DSN11B [D12B] =
          IN TENSE RE OPTION 1: NONSEG-IMMEDSTG IS NOT SVO.
 *  DSN12:  A QUESTION CENTER PRECEDED BY ↓:↓ CAN OCCUR AS THE RIGHT
 *      ADJUNCT OR PREDICATE OF THE WORD ↓QUESTION↓ AND AS THE OBJECT
 *      OF PARTICULAR VERBS, E.G., ↓ASK↓ (WE ASK:  IS IT CHANCE.).
 DSN12 = IN EMBEDDEDQ RE OPTION 1: ALL OF $SUBJ-OR-OBJ, $RN, $OBJECTBE.
  $SUBJ-OR-OBJ = EITHER PRESENT-STRING X1 IS OCCURRING AS SUBJECT OR
          OBJECT, OR HOST OF X1 IS OCCURRING AS SUBJECT OR OBJECT.
   $RN = IF PRESENT-STRING IS OCCURRING AS RN ⇏ THEN HOST IS NSENT1:AWH.
   $OBJECTBE = IF PRESENT-STRING IS OCCURRING AS OBJECTBE ⇏ THEN THE
          CORE OF THE ULTIMATE-SUBJECT IS NSENT1:AWH.
 * DSN13: THE VERBS IN THE SMALL (ABERRENT) CLASS VSENT4 CONTAINING
 *      ↓SEEM↓, ↓APPEAR↓ ↓HAPPEN↓ ETC.  TAKE THE FORM: IT VSENT4 SN
 *      THOUGH THEY DO NOT OCCUR IN: SN VSENT4 OBJECT (IT SEEMS THAT HE
 *      LEFT, *THAT HE LEFT SEEMS).
 DSN13 [ABERRENT ↓IT VSENT4 SN↓] =  IN OBJECT RE THATS, FORTOVO,
          ASSERTION:
          IF THE CORE OF THE VERB-COELEMENT IS VSENT4
          THEN THE ULTIMATE-SUBJECT IS ↓IT↓ .
 * WSN1:  CORRECT VERB OR PREDICATE FOR SN SUBJECT (THAT HE SPOKE IS
 *          TRUE, *THAT HE SPOKE IS BLUE).
 WSN1    [W113,W1,W95 - SN AS SUBJECT] =
          IN ASSERTION, YESNOQ, SVINGO, FORTOVO, NTOVO,  NTOBE, SOBJBE,
          SASOBJBE, SVO, STOVO-N, SAWHICHSTG:
          IF EITHER ELEMENT SUBJECT X10 HAS VALUE SN,     OR PRESENT-STRING
          IS SAWHICHSTG X100 WHERE X10 HAS VALUE NULLWH, THEN
          ONE OF $PREDICATE, $SENTENTIAL-VERB, $EVENT-VERB  IS TRUE.
    $PREDICATE = AT X10 BOTH CORE X1 OF DEEPEST-COPRED IS NOT OCCURRING
             IN SN, AND ONE OF $ADJPRED, $VINGPRED, $NPRED, $PNPRED, $RAKE
                   IS TRUE  .
 $ADJPRED = X1 IS ADJ: ASENT1 OR ASENT2.                  [ IS TRUE ]
 $VINGPRED = X1 IS VING: VSENT1.                          [IS SURPRISING]
 $NPRED = X1 IS N: NSENT1 OR NSENT2 OR NSENT3.            [IS A FACT]
 $PNPRED= BOTH X1 IS PN WHERE CORE OF ELEMENT NSTGO IS NSENTP X12
          AND IN X1 LISTS P AND X12 HAVE  A COMMON ATTRIBUTE
                                                [IS OF INTEREST].
 $SENTENTIAL-VERB = ALL OF $VSENT, $PASSIVE, $WHICH-STRING.
  $VSENT = EITHER CORE X2 OF X7[DEEPEST-COVERB IS STORED IN X7 BY
                          DEEPEST-COPRED]
             IS VSENT1 OR VSENT2 OR VSENT3 OR VMOD OR VEXP,
          OR X2 IS VBE WHERE BOTH CORE OF COELEMENT OBJECT OF X7 IS TOVO⇏
                          AND  IT IS OCCURRING IN SN[SURPRISED US,
                                   IS KNOWN, HAS MERIT,
                                   TO LIVE IS TO SUFFER].
```

```
$PASSIVE= IF BOTH X2 IS VSENT3 AND X2 IS NOT VSENT2, THEN X2 IS
         OCCURRING IN VENPASS    [IS KNOWN, WAS SHOWN] .
$WHICH-STRING = IF X100 EXISTS WHERE X2 IS VSENT1 THEN FIRST
         ELEMENT [OF SAWHICHSTG] IS +WHICH+
                                          [WHICH SURPRISED US, *AS SURPRISED
                                                                US] .
 $EVENT-VERB = BOTH X100 EXISTS AND X2 IS VEVENT [WHICH HAPPENS OFTEN].
* WSN2:  (EDIT TEST FROM DSN4) CONDITION FOR ACCEPTING SN AS RV FOLLOWING
* PASSIVE VSENT3 (IT WAS KNOWN THAT SHE LEFT).  THIS TEST COMPLETES
* $VSENT13 IN DSN4.
WSN2  [+IT+ FORM FOR SENTENTIAL VERBS] =
           IN () RV AFTER SN: IF BOTH THE CORE X9 OF THE VERB-COELEMENT
           IS VSENT3    AND THE PREVIOUS-ELEMENT IS PASSOBJ WHERE CORE
           IS NULLOBJ,THEN IF X9 HAS ATTRIBUTE OBJLIST: ANYTHING X1,
           THEN THE VALUE OF SN IS X1.
* WSN3:  IN THE CASE WHERE THE OBJECT OF THE VERB +BE+ IS AN SN STRING,
*        IF THE SUBJECT OF +BE+ IS TOVO THEN THE OBJECT OF +BE+ IS ALSO
*        TOVO, AND IF THE SUBJECT OF +BE+ IS FORTOVO THEN THE OBJECT OF
*        +BE IS ALSO FORTOVO (TO ASK THE QUESTION IS TO ANSWER IT).
  WSN3  [WD1 - SN] =
           IN OBJECTBE AFTER OPTION SN: BOTH IF THE CORE X1 OF THE
           ULTIMATE-SUBJECT IS TOVO, THEN THE CORE OF OBJECTBE IS TOVO, AND
           IF X1 IS FORTOVO, THEN THE CORE OF OBJECTBE IS FORTOVO.
* WSN4:  THE C1SHOULD STRING HAS NO TENSE OR ELSE THE
*        AUXILIARY IS +SHOULD+ (DEMAND THAT HE DO IT, DEMAND
*        THAT HE SHOULD DO IT).
WSN4[W84 - SHOULD] =
           IN TENSE: IF TENSE IS OCCURRING IN C1SHOULD, THEN EITHER
           VALUE IS NULL OR CORE IS +SHOULD+.
* WSN5:  C1SHOULD STRING WITHOUT +THAT+ IS NOT TAKEN AS SUBJECT (THAT HE
*        SHOULD LEAVE WAS TO BE EXPECTED, *HE SHOULD LEAVE WAS TO BE
*        EXPECTED).
  WSN5  [WD22] =
           IN C1SHOULD AFTER THE FIRST ELEMENT:  IF THE FIRST ELEMENT
           IS EMPTY, THEN C1SHOULD IS NOT OCCURRING AS SUBJECT .
* WSN6:  IN WHETHS,  IF THE FIRST ELEMENT IS +IF+,
* THEN WHETHS IS NOT OCCURRING AS SUBJECT OR SA.
  WSN6  [W49 - WHETHS] =
           IN ( ) WHETHS AFTER +IF+: WHETHS IS NOT OCCURRING
           AS SUBJECT OR SA .
* WSN7:  WHEN WHETHS OCCURS AS SENTENCE ADJUNCT, IT IS CONJOINED BY AN
*        OR-STRING OR BY ≠OR NOT≠ (WHETHER OR NOT YOU GO I WILL GO,
*        *WHETHER YOU GO, I WILL GO).
  WSN7  [W50 - WHETHS AS SA] =
           IN SAWH AFTER WHETHS:  BOTH ONE OF $ORNOT1, $ORNOT2,
           $OR IS TRUE AND $NOTBOTH IS TRUE.
 $ORNOT1 = IN WHETHS, THE SECOND ELEMENT IS NOT EMPTY.
 $ORNOT2 = IN WHETHS, THE 4TH    ELEMENT IS NOT EMPTY.
 $OR = WHETHS SUBSUMES +OR+ .
 $NOTBOTH = IT IS NOT THE CASE THAT BOTH $ORNOT1 AND $ORNOT2 ARE TRUE.
* WSN8:  SOME OBJECT NOMINALIZATION STRINGS CONTAIN AS THEIR FIRST
*        PART A HUMAN OBJECT (I TOLD HIM THAT IT WORKS).
WSN8 [HUMAN OBJECT IN NOMINALIZATION STRINGS] =
           IN NTHATS, NSNWH, PNTHATS, PNTHATSVO,PNSNWH AFTER NSTGO:
           AT CORE X9 OF NSTGO $NHUMAN [WPOS22] IS TRUE .
* WSN9:  SVINGO AS SUBJECT (WHICH IS RARE) DOES NOT START WITH PRONOUN.
  WSN9  [W55 - SVINGO] =
           IN SVINGO:  IF SVINGO IS OCCURRING AS SUBJECT, THEN CORE OF
           FIRST ELEMENT IS NOT PRO.
* WSN10: NSVINGO AND VINGOFN CONTRAST WHEN AN OBJECT BEGINNING WITH
*        N IS PRESENT, OR WHEN LN CONTAINS +A+ OR +THE+ OR ADJECTIVES.
*        NSVINGO AND    VINGOFN PARSE THE SAME SEQUENCES
```

```
*         WHERE VING HAS NO OBJECT OR AN OBJECT NOT BEGINNING WITH
*         N, AND WHERE THE LEFT MODIFIERS OF VING ARE NOT DEFINITELY
*         ADJECTIVAL [HIS TALKING].  UNTIL DISAMBIGUATING
*         RESTRICTIONS ON PREDICATES CAN BE WRITTEN (E.G. HIS
*         TALKING WAS LOUD VS. HIS TALKING TOOK COURAGE), THESE
*         SEQUENCES ARE TAKEN AS NSVINGO.
WSN10 [W56 - NSVINGO] = IN NSVINGO AFTER TPOS: NOT $TAKE-AS-VINGOFN.
$TAKE-AS-VINGOFN = EITHER CORE X4 OF TPOS IS ↓A↓ OR ↓AN↓ OR
         ↓THE↓, OR X4 IS TQUAN OR EACHEVRY.
* WSN11: SEE *WSN10. ALSO WELLFORMEDNESS OF VINGOFN REQUIRES
*         THAT NPOS BE EMPTY (* THE ROAD BUILDING OF HIGHWAYS),
*         AND THAT OBJECTS OF VING WHICH BEGIN WITH N BE PRECEDED BY
*         ↓OF↓  (THE WRITING OF LETTERS).
WSN11[W57-VINGOFN] =
         IN VINGOFN AFTER OBJECT: ALL OF $NO-COMPOUND-NOUN,
         $OF-BEFORE-N-OBJ, $NO-OF-CASE .
$NO-COMPOUND-NOUN = IN LN X5, NPOS IS EMPTY  .
 $OF-BEFORE-N-OBJ = BOTH IF THE THIRD ELEMENT X10 IS ↓OF↓ THEN
         $NSTART, AND IF $NSTART THEN X10 IS ↓OF↓.
 $NSTART = AT X10 EITHER VALUE OF COELEMENT OBJECT X20 IS
         NSTGO OR NPN OR NN OR NA OR ND OR DP3 OR DP3PN OR VINGOFN OR
         NSVINGO , OR BOTH $RARE AND VALUE OF X20 IS
         NTOVO OR NTHATS OR NSNWH OR NPVINGO OR NPVINGSTG OR
         NPSVINGO OR NPSNWH .
$NO-OF-CASE = IF X10 IS NOT ↓OF↓ THEN EITHER AT X10 CORE X11 OF
         COELEMENT OBJECT X20 IS DP4
         OR DP4PN [THE HANDING OVER OF THE PRISONERS], OR BOTH $OVERLAP
                        AND IN X5 [LN] EITHER NOT ALL OF
         $QPOSNULL, $APOSNULL, $NSPOSNULL ARE TRUE OR
         EITHER CORE X4 OF TPOS IS ↓A↓ OR ↓AN↓ OR ↓THE↓ , OR X4 IS
         TQUAN OR EACHEVRY .
$OVERLAP = EITHER X11 IS NULLOBJ OR NULLRECIP [ THE SINGING ] , OR
         X11 IS PN .
$QPOSNULL = QPOS IS EMPTY.                                       (GLOBAL)
$NSPOSNULL = NSPOS IS EMPTY.                                     (GLOBAL)
$NPOSNULL = NPOS IS EMPTY.                                       (GLOBAL)
* VERB AND CENTER STRING RESTRICTIONS
*
* DVC1: ALLOW OPTIONS OF OBJECT THAT ARE ON OBJLIST OF VERB COELEMENT OF
* OBJECT. IF OBJLIST HAS PN, NPN OR PNN OPTION, LOOK AHEAD IN SENTENCE
* TO CHECK WHETHER IT CONTAINS A P WHICH IS ON PVAL LIST OF OPTION.
* HOWEVER, DO NOT CHECK FOR P IF OBJECT IS IN PN-OMITTING-WH-STG.
DVC1    [DEDIT1] =  IN OBJECT RE OPTION 1:
                    IF THE CORE OF THE VERB-COELEMENT HAS ATTRIBUTE
                       OBJLIST X10 WHERE X10 HAS ATTRIBUTE ANYTHING X1
                    THEN BOTH PRESENT-ELEMENT- X3 EXISTS
                         AND EDIT BY $1.
 $1 = EITHER $IS-X1 OR TEST FOR NULLC.
 $IS-X1 = TEST FOR X1;
         IF PRESENT-ELEMENT- IS PN OR NPN OR PNN X11
         THEN AT X3 EITHER $IN-PN-OMITSTG
                      OR $PROPER-P-AHD.
$IN-PN-OMITSTG = IMMEDIATE-NODE OF IMMEDIATE-NODE IS OF TYPE
                 PN-OMITTING-WH-STG.
$PROPER-P-AHD = X10 HAS ATTRIBUTE X11: PVAL X2; DO $P-CHECK.
$P-CHECK = GO TO CURRENT WORD; ITERATET GO TO NEXT WORD UNTIL
          $P-WORD SUCCEEDS.
$P-WORD = TEST FOR P; STORE IN X12;
          LISTS X2 AND X12 HAVE A COMMON ATTRIBUTE.
DVC2    [DEDIT2]  =
         IN PASSOBJ RE OPTION 1: IF CORE OF COELEMENT LVENR HAS ATTRIBUTE
         POBJLIST:ANYTHING X1, THEN EDIT BY $1.
```

```
$1 = TEST FOR X1.
* DVC3:  IN YESNOQ AND TSUBJVO, V OCCURS IN VERB2 POSITION ONLY IF W OCCURS IN
* VERB1 POSITION (WILL YOU CHOOSE THIS, HAS HE ANSWERED, *HAS HE ANSWER IT).
DVC3 [D71 - VERB2 IN PERM STRINGS] =
       IN VERB2 RE OPTION 1: COELEMENT VERB1 HAS VALUE TENSE.
* DVC4:  IN YESNOQ AND TSUBJVO THE POST-SUBJECT VERB POSITION (VERB2)
*        IS NULL ONLY IF THE PRE-SUBJECT VERB POSITION (VERB1) IS FILLED
*        BY A TENSED FORM OF +HAVE+ OR +BE+.
DVC4 = IN VERB2 RE OPTION 2: COELEMENT VERB1 HAS VALUE LTVR.
* DVC5:  +HAD+ IS VIRTUALLY EXCLUDED AS A PASSIVE VERB IN SCIENTIFIC
*        ENGLISH [CF. WVC4]. [MADE STRONGER 7/79]
DVC5  =  IN VENPASS RE OPTION 1:
            THE CURRENT WORD IS NOT +HAD+.
* WVC1: NO TENSE WORD PRECEDES A TENSED VERB.
WVC1 = IN VVAR: BOTH IF CORE X1 IS TV THEN IN IMMEDIATE VERB COELEMENT
            TENSE IS EMPTY, AND IF X1 IS V THEN EITHER IMMEDIATE VERB
            X2 IS OCCURRING IN TOVO OR TOBE , OR AT X2 EITHER
            COELEMENT TENSE IS NOT EMPTY OR NONSEG-IMMEDSTG IS SVO OR
            C1SHOULD.
* WVC2: UNLIKE OTHER VERBS THE INFINITIVE +BE+ DOES NOT OCCUR PRECEDED
*        BY TV +DO+ (THEY DON+T LIVE HERE, *THEY DON+T BE HERE).
WVC2 [W37 - NO +DO+ BEFORE +BE+] =
       IN VERB: IF CORE IS V:VBE THEN IF CORE X1 OF COELEMENT TENSE
       EXISTS ↱ THEN X1 IS NOT VDO.
* WVC3: VENO IS NOT AN ACCEPTABLE VALUE OF OBJECT IN VENO;  ALSO,NOT OF VINGO
* IF VINGO FOLLOWS +BE+ (*HE HAS HAD HAD GOOD LUCK).
 WVC3 [W38 - NON-PASSIVE VEN] =
       IN VENO:  BOTH $VENO AND $VINGBE ARE TRUE.
 $VENO = VENO IS NOT OCCURRING IN VENO.
 $VINGBE = IF VENO IS OCCURRING IN VINGO ↱ THEN VINGO IS NOT
           OCCURRING AS OBJECTBE .
* WVC4:  ONLY VERBS WITH PASSIVE-OBJECT-LIST CAN OCCUR AS VEN IN THE
*        PASSIVE STRING.
WVC4 = IN LVENR AFTER VEN: IF IMMEDIATE-NODE IS VENPASS
                             THEN BOTH THE CORE X1 [OF LVENR] HAS ATTRIBUTE
                                                             POBJLIST
                             AND X1 IS NOT +HAD+.
* WVC5: IN YESNOQ AND TSUBJVO,ONLY +BE+, +HAVE+ OR W CAN OCCUR IN VERB1 POSITION
* (IS HE WORKING ON THE BOOK, *WORKS HE ON THE BOOK).
WVC5 = IN VERB1:
       BOTH VERB1 IS NOT EMPTY
       AND IF VERB1 HAS VALUE LTVR,
            THEN THE CORE IS VHAVE OR VBE.
* WVC6:  THE VERB IN THE INVERTED +BE+ STRING IS +BE+ (AT STAKE IS THE
*        FUTURE OF PUBLIC EDUCATION).
WVC6  [W99 - VERB IN OBES IS +BE+] =
       IN OBES AFTER VERB: CORE OF VERB IS VBE.
* WVC7: TSUBJVO BEGINS WITH NEGATIVE MARKER.
 WVC7  [W88 - TSUBJVO]  =
       IN TSUBJVO:  IF THE FIRST ELEMENT X1 IS PN OR DSTG,
          THEN X1 SUBSUMES T OR ADJ OR D OR W : NEGATIVE.
* WVC8:  PN AS THE OBJECT OF +BE+ CANNOT HAVE P = +SINCE+ UNLESS THE ULTIMATE
* SUBJECT IS +IT+. (IT IS SINCE SUNDAY THAT THEY ARE HERE, *THE JOB WAS SINCE
* SUNDAY)
 WVC8  [ D58 - +IT+ EXTRACTION WITH PN: P = +SINCE+ ] =
          IN OBJBE AFTER PN:  IN PN, IF P IS +SINCE+, THEN THE
          ULTIMATE-SUBJECT IS +IT+.
* WVC9:  IF THE SUBJECT IS +THERE+, THEN THE VERB IS +BE+ OR +BE+ REPLACER.
*        AND THE OBJECT IS A NOUN PHRASE (*THERE IS MILD) .
WVC9 = IN ASSERTION, YESNOQ, TSUBJVO AFTER OBJECT :
                    IF THE CORE OF THE SUBJECT X10 IS +THERE+
                    THEN BOTH AT X10 THE CORE OF THE DEEPEST-COVERB X11 IS
```

```
                                         VBE OR BEREP
                      AND AT COELEMENT OBJECT OF X11 THE VALUE OF THE
            VALUE OF THE VALUE IS NSTG [ OBJECT↦OBJECTBE↦OBJBE↦NSTG ] .
* WVC9A: SAME AS WVC9, FOR SVINGO, FORTOVO, NTOVO OR NTOBE.
WVC9A = IN VINGO, TOVO, TOBE AFTER OBJECT:
      IF IMMEDIATE-NODE X2 IS SVINGO OR FORTOVO OR NTOVO OR NTOBE
        THEN IF THE CORE OF THE SUBJECT OF X2 [SVINGO OR FORTOVO OR NTOVO
              OR NTOBE] IS ↓THERE↓
               THEN BOTH AT OBJECT THE CORE OF THE DEEPEST-COVERB X11 IS
                           VBE OR BEREP
                    AND AT COELEMENT OBJECT OF X11 THE VALUE OF THE VALUE
                       OF THE VALUE IS NSTG [OBJECT↦OBJECTBE↦OBJBE↦NSTG].
* WVC10:  NO INTRODUCER IN A CONJUNCT.
WVC10 = IN INTRODUCER:
          IMMEDIATE-NODE- IS NOT Q-CONJ.
* WH-STRING RESTRICTIONS
*
* DWH1:  SET MUSTOMIT FLAG IN OMITTING WH-STRINGS .
DWH1 = IN N-OMITTING-WH-STRING: ASSIGN PRESENT STRING NODE ATTRIBUTE
        MUSTOMIT .
DWH1A = IN PN-OMITTING-WH-STG: ASSIGN PRESENT STRING NODE ATTRIBUTE
        MUSTOMPN .
* DWH1B = SET MUSTOMIT FLAG IN CONJUNCTION STRING WITHIN SCOPE OF
*         OMISSION. NOTE IN REGARD TO $HIGHER-UP THAT CONJOINING IS AT A
*         HIGHER LEVEL WHEN CONJ-STRING REPEATS WH-WORD (THOSE WHO BET AND
*         WHO WIN). REGARDING THE TEST $1, IT RULES OUT VERB+OBJECT CONJ
*         VERB+OBJECT WHERE THE FIRST VERB HAS A NULLWH SUBJECT AND THE
*         SECOND VERB HAS A NULLWH OBJECT, THE WRONG READING FOR ↓THE MAN
*         WHO WAS HERE AND LEFT↓.
DWH1B [SET MUSTOMIT FLAGS IN Q-CONJ] = IN Q-CONJ RE OPTION 1:
            EITHER PRESENT-ELEMENT IS OF TYPE LXR
            OR IF ONE OF $A, $B, $C [CHECK FOR MUSTOMIT]
                THEN BOTH $CHECK-FOR-OMIT [IF CONJUNCT IS AFTER OBJECT]
                        AND IF $HAS-DIDOMIT
                            THEN EITHER $N-OMISSION [ASSIGN MUSTOMIT]
                                 OR $PN-OMISSION [ASSIGN MUSTOMPN].
  $A  = NONSEGWH X5 HAS NODE ATTRIBUTE MUSTOMIT X10.
  $B  = X5 HAS NODE ATTRIBUTE MUSTOMPN X20.
  $C  = BOTH ULTIMATE-OBJECT EXISTS ↦
        AND EITHER $A OR $B IS TRUE.
  $CHECK-FOR-OMIT  =
        IF AT IMMEDIATE-NODE- [C-NODE] PREVIOUS-ELEMENT- X6 IS OBJECT
        THEN EITHER $DIDOMIT-N
            OR $DIDOMIT-PN IS TRUE.
  $HAS-DIDOMIT = BOTH ONE OF $OMISSION-CHECKED,
                            $DIDOMIT-N,
                            $DIDOMIT-PN
                AND $EDIT-IF-SUBJNULLWH.
  $EDIT-IF-SUBJNULLWH = IF X11 IS OCCURRING IN SUBJECT
                         THEN EDIT [Q-CONJ] BY $1.
  $DIDOMIT-N = X5 HAS NODE ATTRIBUTE DIDOMIT X11.
  $DIDOMIT-PN = X5 HAS NODE ATTRIBUTE DIDOMPN X11.
  $OMISSION-CHECKED = X11 EXISTS.
 $HIGHER-UP = X6 IS ASSERTION OR YESNOQ.
 $1 = TEST FOR SUBJECT .
  $N-OMISSION = BOTH X10 EXISTS
                AND ASSIGN [Q-CONJ] THE NODE ATTRIBUTE MUSTOMIT.
  $PN-OMISSION = BOTH X20 EXISTS
                 AND ASSIGN [Q-CONJ] THE NODE ATTRIBUTE MUSTOMPN.
* DWH51: ↓WHAT↓ IS NOT AN ACCEPTABLE STRING HEAD IN WH-N, PWH-PN, AND PWH
*        WHEN THESE STRINGS OCCUR IN RN OR RN SUBJ (* THE BOOK WHAT I
*        READ, * THE BOOK TO WHAT I REFERRED).
```

```
DWH51 = IN ()WHS-N, ()PWHS-PN, ()PWHS AFTER ↓WHAT↓:
          THE IMMEDIATE-NODE IS NOT RNWH.
*  WWH1:   A COMPLETED OMITTING WH-STRING SHOULD HAVE THE NODE-ATTRIBUTE
*          WHICH SHOWS THAT THE PROPER OMISSION WAS MADE .
WWH1 = IN N-OMITTING-WH-STRING: PRESENT-STRING HAS NODE ATTRIBUTE
          DIDOMIT .
   WWH1A = IN PN-OMITTING-WH-STG:   PRESENT-STRING HAS NODE ATTRIBUTE
          DIDOMPN .
WWH1B = IN Q-CONJ:   BOTH $N-OMISSION AND $PN-OMISSION.
$N-OMISSION = IF Q-CONJ HAS ATTRIBUTE MUSTOMIT
             THEN IT- HAS NODE ATTRIBUTE DIDOMIT.
$PN-OMISSION = IF Q-CONJ HAS NODE ATTRIBUTE MUSTOMPN
             THEN IT- HAS ATTRIBUTE DIDOMPN.
*  WWH2:   CONDITIONS FOR ACCEPTING NULLWH AS VALUE OF SUBJECT ( A BOOK
*          WHICH IS INTERESTING, A BOOK THEY SAY IS INTERESTING ) .
WWH2 [NULLWH VALUE OF SUBJECT]  =  IN SUBJECT AFTER NULLWH:
          IN SUBJECT X3 ALL OF $PRETEST1, $PRETEST2, $PATH,
                      $POSTEST, $ACCEPT ARE TRUE.
$PRETEST1 = BOTH NONSEGWH X5 EXISTS AND X5 IS NOT FORTOVO OR
          THATS OR WHETHS OR S-N .
 $PRETEST2 = IF X5 IS C1SHOULD ⊅ THEN THE FIRST ELEMENT IS EMPTY .
$PATH = EITHER $HERE OR $NESTED .                              [GLOBAL]
  $HERE = X5 HAS NODE ATTRIBUTE MUSTOMIT .
  $NESTED  =  BOTH X5 IS OF THE TYPE OMITTING-OBJECT-STG
              AND IN THE NONSEGWH X5 OF THE ULTIMATE-OBJECT,
                  PRESENT-ELEMENT HAS THE NODE ATTRIBUTE MUSTOMIT.
$POSTEST = AT X5, BOTH $NOTAG AND $IFRN ARE TRUE.
$NOTAG  =  IT IS NOT THE CASE THAT X5 HAS THE NODE ATTRIBUTE DIDOMIT.  (GLOBAL)
$NOTWHOM = IN X5 THE CORE X1 OF THE FIRST ELEMENT IS NOT ↓WHOM↓ OR     (GLOBAL)
          ↓WHOMEVER↓.
  $IFRN = IF X5 IS OCCURRING AS RN WHERE HOST X9 IS NOT EMPTY, THEN IF  (GLOBAL)
          THE FIRST ELEMENT [OF X5] IS ↓WHICH↓ OR ↓WHO↓ OR ↓WHOM↓
          X30 THEN EITHER $WHICH-NONHUMAN OR $WHO-HUMAN IS TRUE.        (GLOBAL)
  $WHICH-NONHUMAN = BOTH X30 IS ↓WHICH↓ AND AT X9 IT IS NOT THE CASE THAT
        $NHUMAN [WPOS22] IS TRUE.
  $WHO-HUMAN = BOTH X30 IS ↓WHO↓ OR ↓WHOM↓
             AND X9 IS NOT NONHUMAN .
  $ACCEPT  =  BOTH PRESENT-ELEMENT- HAS VALUE NULLWH X0,                (GLOBAL)
          AND IN X5 ASSIGN PRESENT STRING THE NODE ATTRIBUTE DIDOMIT.
*  WWH3:   CONDITIONS FOR ACCEPTING NULLWH AS VALUE OF NSTGO FOR NSTGO
*          OCCURRING AS OBJECT OR AS PART OF OBJECT ( A BOOK I READ AND
*          CAN LEND YOU ) ; AND CONDITIONS FOR ACCEPTING NULLWH AS VALUE
*          OF NSTGO , FOR NSTGO OCCURRING AS N IN AN ADJUNCT PN (THE
*          CHART WHICH WE NEED A COPY OF , THE CHART WHICH WE HAVE A COPY
*          OF A COPY OF ) .
WWH3 [NULLWH VALUE OF NSTGO]  =  IN NSTGO AFTER NULLWH:
          EITHER $ADJ OR $OBJ IS TRUE.
  $ADJ = ALL OF $ADJ-PRETEST, $STARTPATH, $PATH[WWH2], $ADJ-POSTEST,
          $ACCEPT[WWH2] ARE TRUE.
  $ADJ-PRETEST = BOTH NSTGO X3 IS OCCURRING IN PN X4 AND EITHER BOTH
          $PN-IN-RN AND $RN-IN-OBJECT ARE TRUE OR $RV IS TRUE.
  $PN-IN-RN = BOTH COELEMENT P IS ↓OF↓ OR ↓FOR↓ AND X4 IS OCCURRING IN RN
          WHERE HOST X3 IS N OR VING.
  $RN-IN-OBJECT = EITHER X3 IS OCCURRING AS OBJECT OR PASSOBJ, OR THE
          ULTIMATE-HOST X3 OF X4 IS OCCURRING AS OBJECT OR PASSOBJ
                              [WHICH WE HAVE A COPY (OF A COPY) OF].
  $STARTPATH = NONSEGWH X5 OF X3 EXISTS.
  $RV = BOTH COELEMENT P IS ↓WITH↓ AND X4 IS OCCURRING AS RV WHERE THE
          PREVIOUS-ELEMENT X3 IS OBJECT OR PASSOBJ
                              [WHICH HE CUT THE MEAT WITH].
  $ADJ-POSTEST = AT X5, BOTH $NOTAG [WWH2] AND $IFRN [WWH2] ARE TRUE.
  $OBJ = ALL OF $OBJ-PRETEST, $PATH [WWH2], $POSTEST, $ACCEPT [WWH2] ARE
```

```
         TRUE.
$OBJ-PRETEST = BOTH X3 IS NOT OCCURRING AS ADJSET AND EITHER X3
         IS OCCURRING AS OBJECT OR PASSOBJ WHERE NONSEGWH X5 EXISTS
         OR $OBJPART IS TRUE.
$OBJPART = BOTH NONSEGWH X5 IS NOT OCCURRING AS ADJSET WHILE X5 IS
         OCCURRING IN OBJECT OR PASSOBJ, AND IF X5 IS NN THEN X3 IS
         NOT STRING INITIAL.
$POSTEST = AT X5, ALL OF $NOTAG [WWH2], $IFRN [WWH2], $QUESTION ARE
         TRUE.
$QUESTION = IF X5 IS WHQ-N OR WHNQ-N , THEN X5 DOES NOT HAVE ELEMENT
         ASSERTION .
*                                                          [GLOBAL]
* WWH4:  CONDITIONS FOR ACCEPTING NULLWH AS VALUE OF OBJBE ( THE
*        MAN YOU ARE AND HOPE TO REMAIN (N), WHAT SHE IS IS PRETTY (A),
*        NEARBY IS WHERE SHE IS (D) ).
WWH4 [NULLWH VALUE OF OBJBE]  =  IN OBJBE AFTER NULLWH:
         ALL OF $PRETEST1, $PRETEST2, $PATH [WWH2], $NOTAG [WWH2],
            $NOTWHOM [WWH2], $ACCEPT [WWH2] ARE TRUE.
$PRETEST1 = PRESENT-ELEMENT IS OCCURRING AS OBJECT WHERE CORE OF
         COELEMENT VERB IS VBE OR BEREP .
$PRETEST2 = NONSEGWH X5 EXISTS.
* WWH5:  CONDITIONS FOR ACCEPTING NULLWH AS VALUE OF PN IN OBJECT ( A
*        MAN ON WHOM YOU CAN RELY ) .
WWH5 [NULLWH VALUE OF PN]  =  IN PN AFTER NULLWH:
         ALL OF $OPTIMIZE, $PRETEST, $PNPATH, $NOPNTAG, $ACCEPTPN
                                                     ARE TRUE.
 $OPTIMIZE = GO TO CURRENT WORD;
         ITERATE GO TO THE PRECEDING WORD UNTIL TEST FOR P SUCCEEDS;
         GO TO THE NEXT WORD;
         IT- IS ↓WHICH↓ OR ↓WHAT↓ OR ↓WHOM↓ OR ↓WHOSE↓ OR ↓WHATEVER↓
             OR ↓WHICHEVER↓ OR ↓WHOSEVER↓ OR ↓HOW↓.
 $PRETEST = BOTH PN X3 IS NOT OCCURRING IN ADJSET
                             WHERE X3 IS NOT [ALSO] OCCURRING IN OBJBE
                 AND EITHER X3 IS OCCURRING AS OBJECT OR PASSOBJ,
                    OR NONSEGWH X3 IS OCCURRING AS OBJECT OR PASSOBJ WHERE
                                                     X3 IS NPN.
$PNPATH = EITHER $HERE OR $NESTED.
$HERE = IN X3 NONSEGWH X5 HAS NODE ATTRIBUTE MUSTOMPN.
 $NESTED = AT X3 BOTH THE PRESENT-ELEMENT- IS OF THE TYPE
         OMITTING-OBJECT-STG AND THE NONSEGWH X5 OF THE ULTIMATE-OBJECT
         HAS THE NODE ATTRIBUTE MUSTOMPN.
$NOPNTAG = NOT $HASPNTAG .
$HASPNTAG = X5 HAS NODE ATTRIBUTE DIDOMPN.
 $ACCEPTPN =
         BOTH PRESENT-ELEMENT- HAS VALUE NULLWH X0,
         AND IN X5 ASSIGN PRESENT STRING THE NODE ATTRIBUTE DIDOMPN.
* WWH51:  IN LNR OR VINGOFN, TPOS HAS THE VALUE ↓WHOSE↓, ↓WHICH↓, ↓WHAT↓
*         ONLY IF TPOS IS OCCURRING IN A WH QUESTION OR WH STRING (WHICH BOOK
*         DID YOU CHOOSE, IN WHOSE BASE AND WHOSE STEM THE LEAVES ARE FOUND).
* WWH53:  IN WHQ-N, IF VERB IS HAVE, BE, DO THE YESNOQ OPTION MUST BE USED.
WWH51 [W53 - WH IN TPOS IN WHNS STGS] =
         IN LNR, VINGOFN:  IF IN LN, TPOS HAS VALUE WHLN OR HOWQSTG,
         THEN THE PRESENT-STRING IS OCCURRING IN WHN.
WWH52 [W53 - WH IN TPOS IN WHNS STGS] =
         IN WHN AFTER OPTIONS LNR, VINGOFN:  IN THE VALUE OF WHN, IN LN,
         TPOS HAS VALUE WHLN OR HOWQSTG.
* WWH53:  N-OMITTING WH QUESTIONS USE ASSERTION OPTION IFF SUBJECT IS
*     OMITTED.
WWH53 = IN WHQ-N, WHNQ-N:
    BOTH IF ASSERTION EXISTS ⊅THEN CORE OF SUBJECT IS NULLWH
    AND IF YESNOQ EXISTS ⊅THEN CORE OF SUBJECT IS NOT NULLWH.
* WWH54:  IN WHQ-N, THE ASSERTION OPTION DOES NOT FOLLOW ↓WHOM↓.
```

```
WWH54[D28] =
        IN WHQ-N:IF THE SECOND ELEMENT X10 IS ASSERTION,THEN AT X10
                THE PREVIOUS-ELEMENT IS NOT +WHOM+.
* ZEROING RESTRICTIONS
*CLOSE()
```

Appendix 2   A Guide to Finding LSP BNF Definitions in the Grammar

A Guide to Finding LSP BNF Definitions [*]

Name of BNF Definition	Explanation of mnemonics of Definition	Number of BNF Definitio
ADJADJ	Adjective + Adjective	12.12A
ADJINRN	Adjective In RN(right adjuncts of the noun)	11.6
ADJN	Adjective + N(noun phrase)	8D.4
ADJPREQ	Adjective Pre(i.e. before) Q(quantifier)	14.3A
ANDSTG	and string	16.1
AND-ORSTG	and/or string	16.16
APOS	Adjective Position of the ordered left adjuncts of a noun	12.12
APPOS	Appositive	11.7
ASOBJBE	as + Object of be	8D.7

[*] Prepared by Cynthia Insolio Benn

ASSERTION	Subject + Tense + Verb + Object, with optional Sentence Adjuncts between these elements	2.1
ASSERTIONZ	Null Assertion + Sentence Adjunct	2.5
ASSTG	<u>as</u> string	16.8
ASTG	Adjective string	8.8
AS-WELL-AS-STG	<u>As well as</u> string	16.17
AVAR	Adjective variant	12.14
BEINGO	<u>being</u> + Object (as object of <u>be</u>, e.g., He is <u>being difficult</u>.)	8.5
BOTHSTG	<u>both</u> string	16.5
BUTSTG	<u>but</u> string	16.9
CENTER	CENTER string of ^{SENTENCE}	1.3
COMMASTG	Comma string	16.10
COMPAR	Comparative complement (e.g., It is so old <u>that it is decaying</u>.)	9.1B
CPDNUMBR	Compound number (e.g., <u>one hundred</u>)	12.11
CSSTG	CS(subordinate conjunction) string	9.7
C1SHOULD	Subjunctive form of ASSERTION	6.4
DASHSTG	Dash string	16.12A
DATEPREP	Date preposition (e.g., <u>on</u>, <u>in</u>, <u>until</u>, <u>since</u>, etc.)	9.1E
DAYYEAR	Various forms of date	9.1G
DPSN	Particle(e.g., <u>up</u>, <u>out</u>) + SN(embedded sentence), (e.g., He found <u>out that we went</u>.)	8B.5
DP1	Particle(e.g., carry <u>on</u>, find <u>out</u>)	8B.1
DP2	DP(particle) + N(noun phrase)	8B.2
DP3	N(noun phrase) + DP(particle)	8B.3
DP4	<u>of</u>-permutation of DP3	8B.4

DP1P	DP1(particle) + P(preposition)	8B.10
DP1PN	DP1(particle) + PN(prepositional phrase)	8B.6
DP2PN	DP2(particle + noun phrase) + PN(prepositional phrase)	8B.7
DP3PN	DP3(noun phrase particle) + PN(prepositional phrase)	8B.8
DP4PN	of-permutation of DP3 + PN(prepositional phrase)	8B.9
DSTG	Adverb string	9.2
EITHERSTG	either string	16.6
EMBEDDEDQ	Embedded Question	8.10
ENDMARK	Punctuation at end of CENTER string of SENTENCE	1.4
ESPECIALLY-STG	Especially string	16.18
FORTOVO	for + Subject + to Verb(infinitive) + Object (e.g., For John to see her is important.)	6.2
FORTOVO-N	for + to + Verb + Object (less one noun phrase in Object, e.g., the person for John to see)	11.5
FRACTION	Fraction	12.11A
HOWQASTG	how + Quantifier(much, many) or Adjective + [of] + article (e.g., how much of the cake, how good an argument)	12.6
HOWQSTG	how + Quantifier(much, many)	12.7
IMPERATIVE	Imperative sentence in CENTER string	2.6
INTRODUCER	Pre-CENTER connective to preceding sentence (e.g., and, or, nor, for)	1.2
LA	Left adjunct of Adjective	14.4
LAR	Left adjunct of adjective(optional) + Adjective + Right adjunct of adjective (optional)	8.9
LAR1	LAR with limited Right adjuncts, as it occurs to the left of a noun	12.13

LDATE	Left adjunct of date	14.12
LDATER	Left adjunct of date + Date + right adjunct of date	9.1G
LCDA	Left part of Compound Adjective	14.9
LCDN	Left part of Compound Noun	14.11
LCDVA	Left part of Compound Verbal Adjective (e.g., a <u>hog</u> raising farm)	14.10
LCS	Left adjunct of CS(subordinate conjunction)	14.6
LN	Left adjuncts of the Noun	12.1
LNAME	Left adjunct of a Name (e.g., <u>Dr.</u> Jones)	14.13
LNAMER	Left adjunct of a name + Name + right adjunct of name	5.7
LNAMESR	Left adjunct of name + possessive form of name	12.3A
LNR	Left adjuncts of the noun + N(noun) + Right adjuncts of the noun	5.3
LNSR	Left adjuncts of the noun + N's (possessive-case noun) + limited Right adjuncts of the noun	12.4
LP	Left adjunct(e.g., Adverb) of Preposition	14.5
LPRO	Left adjunct(e.g., Adverb) of Pronoun (e.g., <u>only</u> he)	14.7
LQ	Left adjunct of Quantifier	14.3
LQNR	Left adjunct of quantifier + QN string + Right adjunct of quantifier	12.15
LQR	Left adjunct of quantifier + Quantifier + Right adjunct of quantifier	12.9
LT	Left adjunct of T + T(determiner, e.g., <u>the</u>)	14.8
LTR	Left adjunct of T + T(determiner) + Right adjunct of T	12.3
LTVR	Left adjunct of tense + Tensed form of <u>be</u> or <u>have</u> + Right adjunct of tense (e.g., in question: <u>Hasn't</u> he come yet?) See also VERB	7.2

LV	Left adjunct of V(verb)	14.2
LVENR	Left adjunct of V + VEN(past participle of verb) + Right adjunct of V	7.6
LVINGR	Left adjunct of V + VING(-ing form of verb) + Right adjunct of V	7.10
LVR	Left adjunct of V + Verb(infinitive) + Right adjunct of V	7.4
LVSA	Sentence Adjunct occurring to the Left of VING or VEN in the adjunct strings VINGO and VENPASS	7.8
LW	Left adjunct of W + W(the tense or a modal) (e.g., just can't)	14.1
NA	Noun phrase + Adjective (as object)	8D.3
NAMEPART	Name part (all parts of proper name preceding surname)	14.15
NAMESTG	Name string (as value of NVAR)	5.6
NASOBJBE	Noun phrase + as + Object of be	8D.8
ND	Noun phrase + Adverb (as object, e.g., put it here)	8D.5
NEITHERSTG	neither string	16.7
NN	N(indirect object noun phrase) + Noun phrase	8.7
NNN	Nouns occurring as left adjuncts of a head noun (e.g., herring gull colony)	12.22A
NORSTG	nor string	16.3
NOTOPT	Optional not	16.10A
NPN	Noun phrase + Prepositional phrase (as object)	8A.8
NPOS	Noun Position of the ordered left adjuncts of a noun	12.22
NPSNWH	Noun phrase + Preposition + SNWH (wh-string as a Sentence Nominalization)	8A.15
NPSVINGO	Noun phrase + Preposition + Subject + VING(-ing form of verb) + Object	8A.13

NPVINGO	Noun phrase + Prepositional phrase + VING(-ing form of verb) + Object	8A.14
NPVINGSTG	Noun phrase + Prepositional phrase + VINGSTG (either VINGOFN or NSVINGO)	8A.12
NQ	Noun phrase + Quantifier/Letter (e.g., the Mark 2 analyzer, the Model B spectro-photometer)	12.20
NSNWH	Noun phrase + SNWH(wh-string as Sentence Nominalization)	8C.4
NSPOS	Possessive Noun of type position of the ordered left adjuncts of a noun (e.g., one lost children's bicycle)	12.21
NSTG	Noun string	5.2
NSTGO	Noun string as Object	8.6
NSTGT	Noun string of Time	9.4
NSVINGO	N's (possessive-case noun or pronoun) + VING(-ing form of a verb) + Object	5.9
NTHATS	Noun phrase + that + ASSERTION	8C.3
NTOBE	Noun phrase + to + be + Object of be	8C.1A
NTOVO	Noun phrase + to + V(infinitive verb) + Object	8C.1
NUMBRSTG	Number string	12.18
NVAR	Noun variant	5.4
NVSA	Noun + Verb Sequence of the type: we know in, e.g., It is, we know, unusual.	9.11
NWHSTG	Noun position wh-strings (e.g., What he cooks tastes good). Contrast with wh-complements, i.e., sentence nominalizations SNWH, e.g., What he cooks depends on what's on sale.	5.5
OBES	Object of be + tensed form of be + Subject of be	4.2
OBJBE	Predicate noun phrase or adjective phrase or PN or adverb	8.4
OBJBESA	OBJBE occurring as Sentence Adjunct	9.8

OBJECT	The set of Object strings of verbs in active voice	8.1
OBJECTBE	OBJBE + verbal objects of be	8.3
ORNOT	or not	**3.2**
ORSTG	or string	16.2
P1	Preposition as passive object (see PASSOBJ; e.g., They can be relied on.)	8A.1
PA	Preposition + Adjective (e.g., at last)	9.3
PARENSTG	Parenthesis string	16.12B
PARTICULARLY-STG	Particularly string	16.19
PASSOBJ	Object strings in passive	8.2
PDATE	Date preposition + Date	9.1D
PERMUTATION	Permuted forms of the CENTER ASSERTION string	2.4
PERUNIT	Per + unit (per hour, per cent)	12.17A
PN	Prepositional phrase (Preposition + Noun phrase)	8A.3
PNN	Prepositional phrase + Noun phrase (permuted form of NPN)	8A.9
PNSNWH	Prepositional phrase + SNWH(wh-string as Sentence Nominalization)	8C.7
PNTHATS	Prepositional phrase + THATS(that + ASSERTION)	8C.5
PNTHATSVO	Prepositional phrase + that tenseless ASSERTION	8C.6
PNVINGSTG	Prepositional phrase + VINGSTG(either VINGOFN or NSVINGO)	8A.11
PROSENT	Pronoun that refers to a preceding sentence	2.3
PSNWH	Preposition + SNWH(wh-string as Sentence Nominalization)	8A.7
PSTG	A subset of prepositional object strings used in the lexicon	8A.2
PSVINGO	Preposition + SVINGO(Subject + VING(-ing form of verb) + Object)	8A.5

PVINGO	Preposition + VINGO(VING + Object)	8A.6
PVINGSTG	Preposition + VINGSTG(either VINGOFN or NSVINGO)	8A.4
PWHNQ	Preposition + wh-containing Noun phrase + yes-no Question (e.g., From which side did they enter?)	3.9
PWHNQ-PN	Preposition + wh-containing Noun phrase + yes-no Question less a PN(prepositional phrase) in Object (e.g., To whom is it attributed?)	3.8
PWHNS	Preposition + wh-containing Noun phrase +ASSERTION (e.g., the girl from whose apartment it was taken)	15.7
PWHNS-PN	Preposition + wh-containing Noun phrase + ASSERTION less a PN in object (e.g., the artist to whom it is attributed)	15.8
PWHQ	Preposition + wh-word yes-no Question (e.g., For whom was it ordered?)	3.6
PWHQ-PN	Preposition + wh-word + yes-no Question less a PN in Object (e.g., On what is it based?)	3.5
PWHS	Preposition + wh-word + ASSERTION	15.4
PWHS-PN	Preposition + wh-word + ASSERTION less a PN in object	15.5
Q-ASSERT	Assertion used in analyzing comparative	16.13
Q-CONJ	Body of conjunction string following a coordinate. Generated during processing.	16.4
Q-INVERT	Inverted assertion used in analyzing comparative	16.14
QN	Quantifier + Noun (where Noun = name of a unit; e.g., a 3-inch line)	12.17
QNREP	Repeated QN sequence (4 lb. 2 oz.)	12.17B
QNS	Quantifier + possessive unit noun (a 4 month's history of headaches)	12.16A
Q-OF	Q-word (e.g., tens, dozens, lots, hundreds + of)	12.11B

QNPOS	Position of the QN string and NQ string in the ordered left adjuncts of a noun	12.16
Q-PHRASE	<u>ever</u>, <u>usual</u>, <u>necessary</u> in comparative (e.g., We will wait as long <u>as usual</u>.)	16.15
QPOS	Quantifier Position of the ordered left adjuncts of a noun.	12.8
QUESTION	Question as CENTER string of a SENTENCE	2.2
QVAR	Quantifier Variant	12.10
RA	Right adjuncts of an Adjective	13.3
RA.1	<u>enough</u> or NULL as Right adjunct of an Adjective occurring as left adjunct of a noun	13.4
RD	Right adjunct of an Adverb	13.6
RDATE	Right adjunct of Date	14.12
RNAME	Right adjunct of a Name	13.7
RNP	Strings beginning with a Preposition as Right adjuncts of a Noun phrase	11.2
RN*R	Right adjuncts of a Noun phrase (*R indicates adjunction is repeatable)	11.1
RNSUBJ	Right adjuncts of a Noun Subject at a distance (e.g., A procedure is described <u>which</u>...)	9.6
RNWH	Relative clause, i.e., <u>wh</u>-string, as Right adjunct of a Noun	11.3
RQ	Right adjunct of a quantifier	13.2
RSUBJ	Roving adjuncts of the Subject (or a more proximate noun) of quantifier type (e.g., We are <u>all</u> amazed.)	9.5
RV*R	Right adjuncts of a Verb (*R indicates adjunction is repeatable)	13.5
RW	Right adjunct of W(the tense or a modal) (e.g., He is <u>not</u> coming; she will <u>not</u> be here)	13.1
SACONJ	Sentence Adjunct following a coordinate Conjunction	9.1C

SA*R	Sentence Adjuncts (*R indicates adjunction is repeatable)	9.1
SASOBJBE	Subject + as + Object of be	8D.6
SAWH	Wh-strings in the set of Sentence Adjuncts	9.10
SAWHICHSTG	Which-string(relative clause) as Sentence Adjunct (e.g., She left, which surprised him.)	15.14
SAZ	Adjunct of a zeroed Sentence under conjunction (e.g., He left, and fast.)	9.1A
SCALESTG	Scale string	12.19
SENTENCE	Introducer + center + endmark	1.1
SN	Sentence Nominalization	5.11
S-N	Assertion less one Noun phrase (i.e., headless relative clause)	15.13
SNWH	wh-string as a Sentence Nominalization (i.e., wh-complement)	6.5
SOBJBE	Subject + Object of be	8D.1
SOBJBESA	Subject + Object of be occurring as Sentence Adjunct	9.9
STOVO-N	Subject + TOVO-N string as object of have	8C.8
SUBJECT	Subject of verb in the same string	5.1
SUB0	Subordinate conjunction + Object of be	10.1
SUB1	Subordinate conjunction + assertion	10.2
SUB2	Subordinate conjunction or as or than + VENPASS (passive verb with its passive object)	10.3
SUB3	Subordinate conjunction + VING('-ing form of verb) + Object	10.4
SUB4	Subordinate conjunction + VING string (either VINGOFN or NSVINGO)	10.5
SUB5	Subordinate conjunction + SVINGO	10.6
SUB6	Subordinate conjunction + SOBJBE	10.7
SUB7	Subordinate conjunction + SVEN	10.8

SUB8	Subordinate conjunction (as) + inverted Assertion	10.9
SUB9	Should + SVO, subjunctive adjunct (should she accept, she can start tomorrow.)	10.10
SVEN	Subject + passive verb with its passive object (VENPASS)	8D.2
SVINGO	Subject + VING(-ing form of verb) + Object	6.3
SVO	Subject + Verb(tenseless) + Object	8C.2
TENSE	Position for tense-word(modal)	7.3
THANSTG	than string	16.11
THATS	that + ASSERTION	6.1
THATS-N	that + ASSERTION less one Noun phrase (relative clause with word that instead of wh-word)	15.12
TITLE	A Title used as part of a name (e.g., Mr., Ms.)	14.14
TOBE	to + be as tenseless Verb + Object	7.12A
TOSTG	to string (from 3 to 4 hours)	6.12
TOVO	to + tenseless Verb + Object	7.12
TOVO-N	to + tenseless Verb + Object less one Noun phrase in Object	11.4
TPOS	T(definer) Position of left adjuncts of noun phrase	12.2
TSUBJVO	Tense + Subject + tenseless Verb + Object	4.1
VENO	VEN(past participle of a verb) + Object	7.5
VENPASS	VEN(past participle of a verb) + Passive object	7.7
VERB	tensed or tenseless Verb with optional left and right adjuncts	7.1
VERB1	tense-word or tensed be or have in Question	7.13
VERB2	2nd Verb position in Question	7.14
VINGO	VING(-ing form of Verb) + Object	7.9

VINGOFN	Ving + of + Noun phrase	5.10
VINGSTG	VING string (NSVINGO or VINGOFN)	5.8
VINGSTGPN	VING string + PN(prepositional phrase)	8A.10
VO	tenseless Verb + Object	7.11
VVAR	Verb Variant (tensed or tenseless verb)	7.1A
WHATS-N	what + ASSERTION less one Noun phrase	15.9
WHENS	when or where or NULL + ASSERION (when can be NULL if string adjoins time noun)	15.11
WHERES	where + ASSERTION	15.10
WHETHS	whether or where or when or how or why or if + ASSERTION + optional or not	15.1
WHETHTOVO	whether (or other wh-words) + to + Verb + Object	15.2
WHEVERS-N	wh-ever (whoever, whenever, whichever, whatever) + ASSERTION	15.15
WHLN	wh-word (whose, which, what, how string) as a Left adjunct of a Noun	12.5
WHN	Noun phrase or VINGOFN string carrying a wh-word (e.g., whose book was lost)	3.7A
WHNQ-N	wh-containing Noun phrase + yes-no QUESTION less one Noun phrase (e.g., whose book have you?)	3.7
WHNS-N	wh-containing Noun phrase + ASSERTION less one Noun phrase	15.6
WHQ	wh-word + yes-no QUESTION	3.4
WHQ-N	wh-word + yes-no QUESTION or ASSERTION less one Noun phrase	3.3
WHS-N	wh-word + ASSERTION less one Noun phrase	15.3
YESNOQ	Yes-No QUESTION (e.g., Have you a book? Did she leave?)	3.1

Appendix 3   The Lexical Subclasses of the LSP English Grammar

The Lexical Subclasses of the LSP English Grammar

Eileen Fitzpatrick and Naomi Sager

This appendix defines adjective, noun and verb subclasses. These subclasses, as well as others not presented here, are defined in such a way that they can be used as a guide for classifying new entries to the LSP lexicon and as a linguistic reference tool. Each definition includes a statement of the intent of the subclass, a diagnostic frame, sentence examples, and a word list drawn from the present dictionary. The subclasses are defined to reflect precisely the grammatical properties tested for by the restrictions of the grammar. Where necessary for clarifying the intent of the subclass, three additional criteria are employed: excision, implicit and co- reference, and paraphrase. The subclasses have been defined so as to be consistent with a subsequent stage of transformational analysis.

The notational conventions used in the subclass definitions and frames are as follows:

ϕ - an ungrammatical sequence

<u>x</u> - x (the underlined term) is the class being subclassed in the frame or a particular lexical item used in the frame.

<u>x̲</u> - x (the double underlined term) is the class being subclassed in the frame where the frame also contains a particular lexical item

(X) - in a frame, an optional element

(X) - in a definition, a further subdivision of a subclass

X/Y – either X or Y

$$\begin{bmatrix} X \\ Y \\ Z \end{bmatrix}$$ – either X or Y or Z

T – article

D – adverb

OBJ – a cover term for all the object strings (see object string reference guide)

SN – an embedded sentence of the following types:

> THATS – <u>That John was here</u>
> FORTOVO – <u>for Mary to go</u>
> TOVO – <u>to live</u>
> SVINGO – <u>them working overtime</u>
> C1SHOULD – <u>that John be here</u>
> SNWH – <u>whether/why/how. . .he went</u>

It should also be noted that the specified frame which delimits a word is not the only frame in which that word can occur; it serves merely as the test frame when classifying words.

Object String (OBJLIST) Reference Guide

ADJN = Adjective + N (noun phrase)
ASOBJBE = <u>as</u> + Object of <u>be</u>
ASSERTION = Subject + Tense + Verb + Object
ASTG = Adjective String
C1SHOULD = Subjunctive form of ASSERTION
DPSN = Particle + SN
DP1 = Particle (e.g. carry <u>on</u>)
DP1PN = DP1 + PN
DP2 = DP + N
DP2PN = DP2 + PN
DP3 = N + DP
DP3PN = DP3 + PN
DP4 = <u>of</u>-permutation of DP3
DP4PN = DP4 + PN
DSTG = Adverb string
FORTOVO = <u>For</u> + Subject + <u>to</u> + Object
NA = N + Adjective
NASOBJBE = N + <u>as</u> + Object of <u>be</u>
ND = N + Adverb
NN = N(indirect object) + N
NPN = N + PN
NPSNWH = N + P + <u>wh</u>-complement
NPSVINGO = N + P + SVINGO
NPVINGO = N + P + VINGO
NPVINGSTG = N + P + VINGSTG *
NSNWH = N + SNWH
NSTGO = Object N
NSVINGO = N's + VINGO
NTHATS = N + <u>that</u> + ASSERTION

NTOBE = N + <u>to</u> + <u>be</u> + Object of <u>be</u>
NTOVO = N + <u>to</u> + V(infinitive) + Object
NULLOBJ = Null object for intransitive verbs
NULLRECIP = Null object for reciprocal verbs
OBJBE = predicate N or adjective or PN or adverb
OBJECTBE = OBJBE + verbal objects of <u>be</u>
PN = prepositional phrase
PNHOWS = PN + <u>how</u> + ASSERTION
PNN = PN + N inverted NPN string
PNSNWH = PN + SNWH
PNTHATS = PN + THATS
PNTHATSVO = PN + <u>that</u> + tenseless ASSERTION
PNVINGSTG = PN + VINGSTG *
PSNWH = P + SNWH
PSVINGO = P + SVINGO
PVINGO = P + VINGO
PVINGSTG = P + VINGSTG *
SASOBJBE = Subject + <u>as</u> + OBJBE
SNWH = <u>wh</u>-complement
SOBJBE = Subject + OBJBE
STOVO-N = Subject + TOVO less one object N
SVEN = Subject + passive verb phrase
SVINGO = Subject + <u>Ving</u> + Object
SVO = Subject + tenseless V + Object
THATS = <u>that</u> + ASSERTION
TOVO = <u>to</u> + tenseless V + Object
VENO = past participle + Object
VINGO = <u>Ving</u> + Object
VINGOFN = (N's) <u>Ving of</u> Object
VINGSTGPN = VINGSTG + PN

*VINGSTG = VINGOFN/ NSVINGO

I. Adjective Subclasses.

AASP:

an adjective is in AASP if it occurs only with the non-sentential (non-SN) right adjunct to V OBJ (SN = an embedded, or contained, sentence) (DSNG, 7):

John is able to walk.
∅ John is able for Bill to walk.
∅ John is able that Bill walks.
∅ John is able whether Bill walks.

Adjectives which occur with both non-sentential and sentential right adjuncts are not in AASP (see ASENT1, ASENT3), e.g.:

John is certain to go.
John is certain that he will go.
John is not certain whether to go.
John is eager to go.
John is eager for Mary to go.

WORD LIST: able, fit, free, quick, ready, set, slow.

Frame:

N be Adj to V OBJ

Examples:

John is free to leave.

She is fit to work.

The book is apt to fall.

You are apt to be asked for money.

It is apt to be assumed that John left.

She is due to arrive at five.

She was right to object.

NOT AASP:

John is certain to go. (ASENT1)

He is anxious to leave. (ASENT3)

AINPA:

an adjective is in subclass AINPA if it occurs in the adjective position in the sentence adjunct string PA (P = in or at); e.g.: in general, at present, in particular (WPOS11).

The particular P must be specified for each adjective.

Frame:

in
      Adj,
at

Examples:

In general, we can maintain the following.

We do not, at present, know the answer.

We cannot say, in advance, what tomorrow will bring.

We didn't know what to think about her statement at first.

Dictionary Entry:

GENERAL.
ADJ: (.10), ...
.10 =   AINPA: (∗ IN∗).

WORD LIST: advance (in), best (at), first (at), full (in), general (in), last (at), least (at), particular (in), present (at), short (in).

AINRN:

an adjective is in the small subclass AINRN if it can occur as a single-word right adjunct of a noun (WN50):

the people present
the conclusions possible

Non-AINRN adjectives in RN require an adjunct or conjunct (WN50):

an item worthy of your attention
∮ an item worthy
a sum greater than they expected
∮ a sum great (er)
a man courageous and true
∮ a man courageous

Frame:

N Adj X   (X ≠ adjunct or conjunct of adj)

Examples:

The figure above illustrates this point.

The people absent represent the dissenting opinion.

This man alone understands the consequences.

The arguments necessary have been listed below.

WORD LIST: above, absent, alone, apparent, available, available, due, necessary, observable, obtainable, possible, present, relevant, responsible, visible.

APREQ:

an adjective (or Ving or Ven form of the verb) is in APREQ if it occurs before a quantifier which is a left adjunct of N (WN5), e.g.:

an additional five people
the following three items

The occurrence of superlative adjectives before Q N (the tallest three boys) is accounted for by a separate statement in WN5; therefore, superlative forms should not be listed as APREQ.

Frame:

(T) Adj Q N

Examples:

An additional five people were found.

The following three items were mentioned.

Please make the next several payments on time.

We chose the first few people to welcome him.

The next ten people will constitute the control group.

WORD LIST: above, additional, another, bottom, first, good, last, necessary, next, other, own, particular, previous, representative, same, top, usual, very, wrong.

ASCALE:

an adjective is in ASCALE if it can occur to the right of the measure sequence QN in which N is in subclass NUNIT (inches, feet, pounds, years, etc.) (WQ2), e.g., long in

The line is 10 inches long.
a ten inch long line.

ASCALE includes long, wide, deep, broad, tall, thick, high, old.
Since both ASCALE and non-ASCALE adjectives can occur in Q N ADJ in their

comparative form (three shades darker), the Q N + Comparative Adj. is accounted for by a separate statement in WQ2. Therefore, comparative forms need not be listed as ASCALE.

Frame:

Q N Adj (Adj is not comparative)

Examples:

The line is ten inches long.

This is a ten inch long line.

He is five years old.

He is a five year old child.

This area is 200 feet square.

This is a 200 foot square area.

WORD LIST: broad, deep, high, long, old, premature, square, tall, wide.

ASENT1:

an adjective is in the subclass ASENT1 (similar to noun subclass NSENT1) if it can occur as the object of the verb be when the subject of be is a string from the set SN (i.e., THATS, (FOR)TOVO, C1SHOULD, SNWH) (WSN1):

> That he sold books is probable.
> Whether he will come is uncertain.

As the object of the verb be, an adjective in ASENT1 may have a string from SN as its right adjunct, provided the subject of be is it (DSN2):

> It is probable that he sold books.
> ∮ John is probable that he sold books.

Several adjectives which occur as ASENT1 also occur as ASENT3, e.g.:

> John is certain that he sold books (ASENT3)
> It is certain that he sold books. (ASENT1)

Therefore, such adjectives should be listed as both ASENT1 and ASENT3.

ASENT1 is subdivided according to the type of SN string with which the particular ASENT1s occur; i.e.,

1) ASENT1: (AFORTO)
   For us to leave now would be easy.
   It would be easy for us to leave now.
2) ASENT1: (ASHOULD)
   That he return is imperative.
   It is imperative that he return.
3) ASENT1: (ATHAT)
   That they lied is obvious.
   It is obvious that they lied.
4) ASENT1: (AWH)
   Whether he will come is uncertain.
   It is uncertain whether he will come.

ASENT1: (AFORTO) is further subdivided into three classes according to the type of extraction from the embedded sentence which occurs with a particular adjective; viz.:

1) ASENT1: (AFORTO: (OBJEXT)) occurs in N_2 t be -- (for N_1) to V -N_2:

> The problem will be easy for John to solve.

Frame:

SN be Adj

Examples:

For John to leave now would be bad.

It would be bad for John to leave now.

That we solve the problem immediately is crucial.

It is crucial that we solve the problem immediately.

That they lied is obvious.

It is obvious that they lied.

Whether they will come isn't clear.

It isn't clear whether they will come.

Dictionary Entry:

     CLEAR.
     ADJ: .10 .
.10 =   ASENT1: (AWH, ATHAT).

related to

> For John to solve the problem will
> be easy.

2) ASENT1: (AFORTO: (SUBJEXT))
occurs in N₁ t be -- to V OBJ:

> John was kind to invite me.

related to

> For John to invite me was kind.

3) ASENT1: (AFORTO: (NOEXT))
occurs with neither type of extraction:

> For John to write a letter now would
> be curious.
> ⌀ A letter would be curious for John to
> write now.
> ⌀ John would be curious to write a let-
> ter now.

> All three subclasses of ASENT1:
> (AFORTO) can occur with a PN adjunct:

> For us to leave now would be bad for
> John.
> For John to invite me was kind of him.
> For us to leave now would seem curi-
> ous to John.

WORD LIST: AFORTO: OBJEXT: bad, base, convenient, difficult, easy, simple; AFORTO:
SUBJEXT: gross, just, kind, original, rash, wrong; AFORTO: NOEXT: curious, justifiable,
permissible, possible, practical, usual; ASHOULD: crucial, desirable, essential, important,
right; ATHAT: apparent, bad, certain, crucial, curious, good, important, just, likely, natural,
peculiar, possible, significant, understandable, wrong: AWH: clear, insignificant, doubtful,
uncertain, unclear.

ASENT3:

> an adjective is an ASENT3 if, as the object of be, it can have a sentential right adjunct SN while the subject of be is not necessarily it (see ASENT1); i.e., ASENT3 can occur in the environment N t be -- SN:

> He is certain that they passed his
> doorway.
> ⌀ He is tall that they passed his doorway.

> ASENT3 is subdivided according to the type of SN string within which the particular ASENT3s occur; i.e.,
> 1) ASENT3: (AFORTO)
>   I would be happy for you to come.
> 2) ASENT3: (ASHOULD)
>   I am insistent that you go alone.
> 3) ASENT3: (ATHAT)
>   I am certain that John will come.
> 4) ASENT3: (AWH)
>   We are uncertain why he left.

Frame:

N t be Adj SN   (N ≠ expletive it)

Examples:

I would be happy for you to come.

They were eager for the speaker to address the crowd.

I am insistent that you go alone.

I am certain that John will come.

I'M grateful that the stuff arrived on time.

We're happy that you can come.

He is doubtful whether the plans will come off.

I'm not sure whether they will come.

We are uncertain why he left.

Dictionary Entry:

HAPPY
ADJ: .10 .
.10 =   ASENT3: (AFORTO, ATHAT).

WORD LIST: AFORTO: anxious, eager, happy, impatient, ready; ASHOULD: emphatic, insistent; ATHAT: certain, doubtful, grateful, happy, hopeful, impressed, lucky, proud, sad, sorry; AWH: doubtful, uncertain.

ATIMETAG:

adjectives (and articles) classified as TIMETAG may occur in the sentence adjunct position as left adjuncts of NTIME1 (NTIME1 includes week, year, day, etc.) (WPOS10).

Frame:

Adj/T NTIME1

Examples:

Last week, John told Mary the news.

∌ Good week, John told Mary the news.

I will see him next year.

He looked better this time.

WORD LIST: last, next, this.

COMPARATIVE:

an adjective is in the subclass COMPARATIVE if it can occur in the environment N_1 t be -- than N_2:

John is happier than Bill.
∌ John is tender than Bill.

Frame:

N_1 t be Adj than N_2

Examples:

John is happier than Bill.

Adjectives listed as COMPARATIVE also occur to the right of the measure sequence QN in which N is in subclass NUNIT (cf. ASCALE) (WQ2), (e.g.: three shades darker, one pound lighter).
COMPARATIVE adjectives are listed separately from their positive forms.

This light is dimmer than that one.

My left hand is number than my right.

A is higher than B.

WORD LIST: abler, deeper, earlier, greater, higher, larger, narrower, number, rougher, simpler, smaller, straighter, stranger, stronger, sweeter, weaker.

SUPERLATIVE:

an adjective is in the subclass SUPERLATIVE if it occurs with the suffix -(e)st before a quantifier which is a left adjunct of N (WN5), e.g.:

the worst ten days
the tallest three boys

Cf. APREQ.

Frame:

T Adj Q N

Examples:

Those were the worst ten days of my life.

The longest five minutes of my life were spent waiting for this.

Give me the tallest five boys.

WORD LIST: ablest, deepest, greatest, highest, lightest, longest, lowest, narrowest, roughest, simplest, straightest, strangest, sweetist, tallest.

II. <u>Noun Subclasses.</u>

<u>AGGREGATE:</u>

a singular noun is in AGGREGATE if
it can occur as the subject of both definitely
singular verbs and definitely plural verbs,
(WAGREE1): e.g.:

> The group has changed its mind.
> The group have changed their minds.

An AGGREGATE noun cannot occur
as a predicate of <u>be</u> when the subject of the
sentence is singular (WAGREE2):

> ⊘ He is a group.

In the construction <u>Q of N,</u> if N is
singular, it is AGGREGATE (WN53):

> five of the group
> ⊘ five of the book

Also AGGREGATE nouns can occur
as the subject of collective and reciprocal
verbs (WAGREE3):

> The group gathered.
> ⊘ He gathered.
> The group met.
> ⊘ He met.

Tests for NHUMAN allow for AGGRE-
GATE nouns in the NHUMAN position:

> The group who call themselves the
> rangers are waiting. (WWH3)
> He brought the group a present.
> (WPOS22).

WORD LIST: aggregate, assembly, block, board, couple, ensemble, family, group, government,
majority, minority, pair, public, remainder, segment.

<u>Frame:</u>

<u>N</u> tV (sing/pl)

<u>Examples:</u>

The <u>group</u> has changed its mind.

The <u>group</u> have changed their minds.

The <u>couple</u> is of one mind.

The <u>couple</u> are of one mind.

The <u>public</u> disapproves of it.

The <u>public</u> disapprove of it.

A <u>minority</u> is in favor of the action.

A <u>minority</u> are in favor of the action.

<u>INITIAL (atomic class):</u>

used for abbreviation of proper names
(Harry <u>S</u>. Truman), names of organizations
(A. F. of L.), etc.

The 26 letters of the English alphabet
must appear in the dictionary each followed
by a period.

<u>NAME:</u>

A noun is in NAME if it can occur in
the environment

> $\begin{Bmatrix} \text{NTITLE} \\ \text{NCOUNT3} \end{Bmatrix}$ --

or in the environment

> $\begin{Bmatrix} \text{INITIAL} \\ \text{NAME} \end{Bmatrix}$ --

<u>Frames:</u>

$\begin{bmatrix} \text{NTITLE} \\ \text{NCOUNT3} \\ \text{INITIAL} \\ \text{NAME} \end{bmatrix}$ <u>N</u>

<u>Examples:</u>

Prof. <u>Mary</u> T. <u>Jones</u>

for example:

    Prof. Jones
    President Nixon
    John P. Jones
    Mary Smith

    Mr. Smith

    Associate Director Robert Brown

    Secretary of State Kissinger

The subclass NAME also shares restrictions with the other non-NCOUNT1 nouns, i.e.:

1) it cannot occur as the host of a relative clause S-N (DN53):

    ∅ Charles you slapped was a mere child

2) it is a more likely subject of the relative clause S-N than are most other nouns (DN51):

    The report John presented . . .
    ?The report writers presented . . .

3) it can occur in commaless apposition to a host noun (WCOM10):

    My friend John

WORD LIST: Abe, Acheson, Friedman, John, Jones, Mary, Maurey, Ringer, Solomon.

NCLASSIFIER:

A noun is in NCLASSIFIER if it occurs as the host of another noun, N_2, where N_2 occurs in commaless apposition to NCLASSIFIER, e.g.:

    the term revolution
    the element hydrogen

All NCLASSIFIERS are NONHUMAN; for N NHUMAN apposition (my friend John) see NAME and NCOUNT3).

An NCLASSIFIER is in either:
1) NCLASSIFIER1, which includes metalinguistic words that introduce terminology, e.g. term, symbol,
or   2) NCLASSIFIER2, which includes classifier words specific to the subject matter area (supplied by the user), e.g.: element, drug, acid, enzyme, extract, hormone, ion, mineral, coefficient, factor, etc.

Note: An NCLASSIFIER noun should not be confused with the host of a relative clause S - N construction. If a noun can occur as N_1 in the string

    The N_1 N_2 be . . .

then N_1 is a NCLASSIFIER. For example:

    The element hydrogen is the lightest
    substance.

Frame:

The N_1 N_2 t be. . .
             ($N_2 \neq$ NHUMAN)

Examples:

NCLASSIFIER1:

The symbol Σ is interpreted as the subject of a sentence.

Linguists often confuse the terms string and sequence.

The expression Rarified grammar will be used to refer to the grammar in Appendix II.

NCLASSIFIER2:

The element hydrogen is the lightest substance.

The drug digitalis promotes undesirable side effects.

The feature +singular is necessary here.

Therefore <u>element</u> is an NCLASSIFIER.
However,

> The reaction digitalis produces is
> dangerous.
> ∮ The reaction digitalis is dangerous.

Therefore, <u>reaction</u> is not an NCLASSIFIER.

WORD LIST: NCLASSIFIER1: expression, symbol, term.

   NCLASSIFIER2: acid, amphibian, chemical, carrier, compound, drug, enzyme, extract, fibre, hormone, ion, isolate, mineral, molecule.

<u>COLLECTIVE:</u>

   a noun is in NCOLLECTIVE if it occurs as the non-plural subject of a collective verb when that verb has a null object, e.g.:

> Dust gathered in the corners.
> ∮ A book gathered in the corners.

or as the non-plural object of a collective verb, (WAGREE3), e.g.:

> The shelf will gather dust.
> ∮ The shelf will gather a book.

   Cf. AGGREGATE.

<u>Frame:</u>

<u>N</u> tV.

N tV <u>N</u>.

tV = VCOLLECTIVE

<u>Examples:</u>

In the corners, <u>dust</u> collected.

While he was away, the <u>fortune</u> accumulated.

The cell accumulates <u>sodium</u>.

These books will only gather <u>dust</u>.

He accumulated a <u>fortune</u>.

WORD LIST: acid, alcohol, ammonium, blood, calcium, change, digitalis, down, energy, evidence, fluid, hydrogen, interest, knowledge, plasma, salt, sweat.

<u>NCOUNT1:</u>

   occurs in the environment <u>A (n) -- tV</u>
<u>OBJ</u>, and not in the environment <u>-- tV OBJ</u>.
(WN9).

   Nouns not classified as NCOUNT1 (i.e. mass nouns and many abstract nouns) can begin a headless relative clause S-N (DN51):

The reaction $\begin{Bmatrix} \text{digitalis} \\ \cancel{\text{drug}} \end{Bmatrix}$ produces . . .

<u>Frame:</u>

T <u>N</u>

<u>Examples:</u>

A <u>book</u> fell.

A <u>series</u> of coincidences occurred.

∮ Book fell.

∮ A <u>blood</u> flows.

WORD LIST: act, advance, agent, amount, amphibian, analogue, animal, antidiuretic, associate, auricle, author, back, can, case, cat, cation, cause, chemical, chief, claim, collaborator, complex, compound, conclusion, controversy, correlate, cortex, couple, covering, decrease, degree, difference, dog, draw, drug, enzyme, equation, essential, event, example, explanation, factor, foot, fit, fraction, gradient, gross, group, human, hypothesis, inhibitor, investigator, ion, isolate, junction, king, lead, length, limit, look, make, maximum, mean, meeting, negative, nucleus, number, original, peak, period, point, preliminary, president, problem, question, relation, relative, say, significance, source, subject, synthesis, test, thing, total, try, whole, worker, year.

<u>NCOUNT2:</u>

   an NCOUNT1 which, as the object of a specified preposition P, occurs without a preceding article (WN9). The particular P which occurs with a given NCOUNT2 is specified in the dictionary entry of that NCOUNT2.

<u>Frame:</u>

P <u>N</u>

<u>Examples:</u>

He came by <u>car</u>.

Note: It is not necessary to apply the NCOUNT2 test to a word not classified as NCOUNT1.

The solution is at <u>hand</u>.

In <u>conclusion</u>, . . .

His illness was of pancreatic <u>origin</u>.

He stayed at <u>home</u>.

What is at <u>issue</u> here ?

Dictionary Entry:

(NSIX) CONCLUSION.
.11 = NCOUNT1, NCOUNT2: (↓IN↓), . . .

WORD LIST: amount (in), answer (in), approach (in), assumption (in, by), bed (in), case (in), charge (in), conclusion (in), contract (against, by, from, in, into, on), course (in, of, on), degree (in, of), end (without), estimate (according to, beyond, by), example (by, for), foot (on), focus (in, into, out of), gross (in), hand (at, by, in, on, out of), kind (in), length (at, in), limit (beyond, within, without), line (in, on, off), mark (of), measure (beyond, to), number (according to, beyond, by, in, of, without), parallel (in, without), phase (in, out of), place (according to, in, into, of, out of), point (in), position (in), process (in), question (beyond, in, into, under, without), ratio (in), reach (beyond, in, into, out of, within), show (for, in, on), significance (of), turn (in), view (from, in, into, on), way (by).

NCOUNT3:

NCOUNT1s which can occur without a preceding article after <u>be</u> or in the object position in SOBJBE and OBJBE (see OBJLIST: (SOBJBE), (OBJBE)) (WN9):

>   He is president.
>   We elected him president.
>   He remained president.

Frame:

N t <u>be</u> <u>N</u>

Examples:

He is <u>president</u>.

I am <u>treasurer</u>.

He is chief <u>investigator</u>.

We elected him <u>president</u>.

They appointed me <u>treasurer</u>.

WORD LIST: collector, director, head, investigator, judge, president, secretary.

NHUMAN:

Can occur as the first noun in the string NN -- i.e., as indirect object -- (WPOS22):

>   She bought the boy a book.

(cf. AGGREGATE) or as the host of a right adjunct WH string (relative clause) headed by <u>who</u>/<u>whom</u> (WWH2):

>   The man who ate the cheese left.

NHUMAN does not occur as the host N of a right adjunct PN string with P = <u>into</u> (WN51):

>   ∅ The children into the house are noisy.

or as the subject of the sentential predicate <u>be</u> + SN (DSN1):

>   ∅ The man is that we need money.

Frames:

$\underline{N_1}$ $\underline{N_2}$ (N₁ = indirect object)

<u>N</u> <u>who</u>

Examples:

She bought the <u>boy</u> a book.

She wrote the <u>workers</u> a letter.

She showed her <u>relations</u> the present.

The <u>man</u> whom you saw was Bob.

She needs a <u>friend</u> who can care for her.

WORD LIST: agent, boy, chemist, doctor, German, host, independent, judge, man, neighbor, native, neighbor, observer, parent, person, president, relation, representative, sister, student, subject, woman, worker.

NLETTER:
a noun subclass which contains all the letters of the English alphabet. It is used in the NQ string as a variant of Q (WN12):

> Table 1
> Table A
> size 5
> size B

NONHUMAN:
a noun is in NONHUMAN if it cannot occur as the subject of a verb in VSENT3 (e.g.: believe, deny, discover, know, read) and other verbs which require a human subject (e.g.: hand, laugh, long, skin) (WSEL2). Cf. NOTNSUBJ.

Frame:

∅ N tV (V = NOTNSUBJ: NONHUMAN)

Examples:

∅ The clock believes that this is so.

∅ The account knows that he is wrong.

∅ The apparatus laughed.

WORD LIST: ability, act, assumption, balance, can, day, dose, enzyme, feature, frog, gland, hypothesis, interaction, junction, London, mean, need, organ, pathway, peak, position, property, range, saturation, tension, use, wonder.

N:PLURAL:
a noun is in the subclass N:PLURAL if it occurs in the environment These -- tV OBJ and not in This -- tV OBJ (WAGREE4); e.g.:

> These groups answered quickly.
> ∅ This groups answered quickly.

Frame:

These N tV OBJ.

Examples:

These men love Mary.
∅ This men love Mary.

WORD LIST: abilities, ages, combinations, data, effects, groups, measures, mucosae, observations, parallels, problems, rises, seconds, tries, uncertainties, uses, valencies, wants, years.

NPREQ:
a noun which is not also a proper name is in NPREQ if it occurs as the N of the sequence NQ (Q = quantifier, here restricted to numbers) in the left adjunct of a N, i.e., if it occurs in the environment T -- Q N (WN12).

Frame:

T N Q N

Examples:

a size ten dress

a pH 7 solution

a model six radio

a table 6 calculation

WORD LIST: area, base, figure, model, pattern, pH, phase, section, site, stage, table, type.

NSCALE:

Subclass NSCALE can almost be de-fined extensionally. It contains the words length, width, depth, height, breadth, thickness, age, weight, volume, area, and perhaps a few others. These words occur as N_2 in the sequence $Q\ N_1\ P\ N_2$ where N_1 = NUNIT (inches, years, etc.) and Q = quantifier, including numbers (WQ3).

In the case of length sequence (two inches) a class of nouns, also classified as NSCALE, can occupy the place of length in P NSCALE: two inches in diameter, in circumfrence, along the diagonal, etc.

(The adverbs across and around can also occupy the P NSCALE position.)

WORD LIST: age, altitude, area, breadth, height, intensity, length, luminosity, strength, volume, wavelength, width, circumfrence, diameter, thickness.

Frame:

Q N P $\underline{N}$

Examples:

The line is two inches in length.

He is five years of age.

The area measures twenty feet in width.

The rectangle is two inches along the diameter.

NSENTP:

occurs in the environment It be P -- SN, where P is of or to (DSN5). The choice of of or to must be indicated in the dictionary entry of each NSENTP.

P + NSENTP functions like sentential adjectives: It is of interest that he came, similar to It is interesting that he came; It is to his advantage (for him) to be here, similar to It is advantageous for him to be here.

Frame:

It be P $\underline{N}$ SN.

Examples:

It is of interest whether he came.

It is of significance that he was here.

It is to your advantage (for you) to be here.

Dictionary Entry:

        INTEREST.
        N: .11, ...
.11 =   NSENTP: (↓ OF↓), ...

WORD LIST: account, advantage, concern, consequence, essence, importance, interest, moment, necessity, note, value, weight.

NSENT1:

occurs with a right adjunct SN (SN = an embedded, or contained, sentence) or a predicate be + SN, but not with both in the same string (DSN5):

> The fact that he left surprised me.
> The fact is that no one wants to come.
> ∫ The fact that he left is that no one wants to come.

Note: To avoid confusion between NSENT1 + SN and the relative clause N + THATS-N (e.g., The book that he wrote) use an intransitive verb in the contained, or embedded, clause of the test sentence, viz.,

> The fact that the atom exists is clear.
> ∫ The book that the atom exists is clear.

Frames:

(T) $\underline{N}$ SN tV OBJ.

(T) $\underline{N}$ be SN.   (OBJ ≠ SN)

Examples:

The demand that salaries be raised was rebuffed.

The plan for him to go to college was foremost in their minds.

His attempts to leave were noticed.

The fact that they enrolled is known.

The question whether or not to vote was posed.

NSENT1 is subdivided according to the type of SN string with which the particular NSENT1s occur; i.e.,

1) NSENT1: (A FORTO)
   <u>The plan for him to go</u>
   <u>His attempts to leave</u>
2) NSENT1: (ASHOULD)
   <u>The demand that salaries be raised</u>
3) NSENT1: (ATHAT)
   <u>The fact that they enrolled</u>
4) NSENT1: (AWH)
   <u>The question whether to vote</u>

WORD LIST: demand, move, notice, order, suggestion, direction, analysis, assumption, charge, claim, conclusion, criticism, doubt, estimate, fact, finding, hypothesis, idea, interpretation, knowledge, observation, position, postulate, report, representation, response, theory, thought, view, alternative, question.

<u>NSENT2:</u>

A noun is in NSENT2 if it can occur in the environment <u>T -- SN is SN</u> (DSN5).

Note: NSENT2s are automatically allowed by the grammar in the environment specified for NSENT1s (i.e. <u>T -- SN tV OBJ:</u> <u>The evidence that he murdered her surprised me</u>); therefore, NSENT2s need not also be classified as NSENT1s.

WORD LIST: evidence, indication, reason.

Frame:

T <u>N</u> SN be SN

Examples:

The <u>evidence</u> that he remained is that someone saw him there.

The <u>reason</u> that he didn't tell the truth was that he loved her.

<u>NSENT3:</u>

occurs as the subject of <u>be + SN</u> (DSN1), but not with a right adjunct SN (DSN5).

Note: NSENT1s and NSENT2s are automatically allowed by the grammar in the environment specified for NSENT3s, thus

The fact is that he came.
The reason was that he loved her.

Therefore, NSENT1s and NSENT2s need not also be classified as NSENT3s.

Frame:

(T) <u>N</u> <u>be</u> SN

Examples:

The <u>trouble</u> is that we have no money.

∄ The trouble that we have no money bothers us.

The <u>truth</u> is that we need money.

∄ The truth that we need money bothers us.

The <u>basis</u> for this theory is that the two factors are the same.

∄ The basis that the two factors are the same is untenable.

WORD LIST: approach, basis, change, conflict, connection, consideration, deal, detail, development, difficulty, ending, error, point, problem, procedure, reason, result, reverse, rule, significance, situation, solution, thing, trouble, wonder.

<u>N:SINGULAR:</u>

a noun is in the subclass N:SINGULAR if it occurs in the environment <u>This -- tV OBJ</u> and not in <u>These -- tV OBJ</u> (WAGREE4), e.g.:

This book fell.
∄ These book fell.

Frame:

<u>This</u> <u>N</u> tV OBJ.

Examples:

This <u>boy</u> is happy.

∄ These boy is happy.

Note: words like <u>fish</u>, <u>series</u>, etc. are in neither N:PLURAL nor N:SINGULAR.

WORD LIST: ability, age, combination, data, digitalis, excitability, group, Gunther, lactone, liberation, measure, mucosa, observation, plasma, rise, sodium, try, uncertainty, use, valency, want, year.

NTIME1:

a noun is in NTIME1 if it cannot occur alone as a sentence adjunct. It occurs as a sentence adjunct with appropriate left or right adjuncts. Its left adjuncts include <u>last</u>, <u>next</u>, <u>each</u>, <u>every</u>, etc. (i.e., adjectival TIMETAGs). Its right adjuncts include <u>hence</u>, <u>ago</u>, <u>later</u>, etc. (i.e. adverbial TIMETAGs) (WPOS10).

If in the PN right adjunct of N, P = <u>since</u>, the host noun is an NTIME1 (WN51):

The week since his arrival has been hectic.

A noun in NTIME1 can also occur as the host of <u>when + S</u> (WCOM8):

I remember the day when he arrived.

Frames and examples:

LN <u>N</u> Sentence (LN = adjectival TIMETAG)

Sentence LN <u>N</u>

We'll finish the work next <u>time</u>.

Last <u>week</u>, we met in New York.

They eat eggs every <u>day</u>.

BUT NOT:
Last meal, the meat was overdone.
(requires special context)

<u>N</u> RN Sentence (RN = adverbial TIMETAG)

Sentence <u>N</u> RN

An <u>hour</u> hence, the place will be deserted.

I saw him two <u>days</u> ago.

ɫ Five sentences ago I understood you.

ɫ A report later they show how it works.

WORD LIST: century, day, evening, Fall, generation, hour, minute, moment, month, morning, night, second, term, time, week, year.

NTIME2:

a noun is in NTIME2 if it can occur alone as a sentence adjunct (WPOS10). NTIME2 is a closed class including <u>yesterday</u>, <u>today</u>, <u>tomorrow</u>, <u>Sunday</u>, <u>Monday</u>, etc.

NTIME2s (but not NTIME1s) may also occur alone as possessive nouns in noun phrases:

Yesterday's meeting was cancelled.
ɫ Hour's meeting took place on Tuesday.
(<u>hour</u> = NTIME1)

Frame:

<u>N</u> Sentence.

Sentence <u>N</u>.

Examples:

Yesterday I went to the movies.

Sunday he will run the race.

They will sail for Europe tomorrow.

He'll be here Tuesday.

WORD LIST: yesterday, tomorrow, Sunday, Tuesday.

NTITLE:

A noun is in NTITLE if it is a title which can precede names of persons, e.g.: <u>Dr.</u>, <u>Mrs.</u>, <u>Mr.</u>, <u>Ms.</u>, <u>Prof.</u>, <u>Professor</u> (WPOS24).

Nouns in NCOUNT3 (e.g. <u>President</u>) need not be classified as NTITLE.

Frame:

<u>N</u> NAME (INITIAL) (NAME)

Examples:

<u>Dr.</u> John Smith

<u>Prof.</u> Mary Jones

WORD LIST: Dr., Doctor, Mr., Ms.

NUNIT:

a noun is in NUNIT if it can occur as the N of the measure sequence Q N followed by a P N or A of dimension (in length, of age, long, old; see ASCALE) (DQ3).

In the predicate position, NUNIT agrees in number with Q (WQ1):

He is five years old.
∅ He is one years old.
He is five years of age.
∅ He is one years of age.

in the LN position, NUNIT is singular (WQ1) and Q N is not followed by a PN (DQ2):

a five year old child
∅ a five years old child
∅ a five years in age child.

Nouns which are not NUNIT by the above criteria, but which occur in Q N of an LN sequence (e.g., a three act play) will be accepted in the N of Q N if the rare switch is on.

WORD LIST: block, centimeter, century, column, day, foot, hand, hour, inch, kg., mile, millisecond, moment, morning, nights, pound, row, section, segment, week, yars.

Frames and Examples:

Q N̲ P N

It is two inches in width.

He is five years of age.

The play is two hours in length.

Q N̲ A   (A = ASCALE)

It is two inches long.

He is five years old.

The play is two hours long.

a two inch (long) line

a five year old child

a two hour play

III. Selection Attributes of the Verb

NOTNOBJ:

applies to verbs restricted in terms of the noun objects with which they can occur in scientific writing. The noun subclasses with which the verb cannot occur are listed as NOTNOBJ attributes of the verb (WSEL1); e.g., since NSENT1 nouns do not occur as the object of eat (∅ He eats the fact), eat is classified as NOTNOBJ: (NSENT1).

The noun subclasses considered in NOTOBJ are NHUMAN, NONHUMAN, NSENT1, NSENT2, NSENT3, NTIME1, NTIME2.

NOTNOBJ classes also apply to the compound noun N Ving (hat wearing), the compound adjective N Ving (a hat wearing man) and the passive Ven as an RN (the verse quoted): If for any given verb N_1 tV N_2 does not occur then N_2 Ving and N_2 Ven do not occur: (WSEL3, 4 and 5 respectively):

That man wears a hat.
Hat wearing
A hat wearing man
He quoted the verse.

Examples:

NOTNOBJ: (NHUMAN)
∅ The government abolished the boy.

NOT NOBJ: (NONHUMAN)
∅ John surprised the enzyme.

NOTNOBJ: (NSENT1)
∅ John ate the fact.

NOTNOBJ: (NSENT2)
∅ John fished the reason.

NOTNOBJ: (NSENT3)
∅ John dried the trouble.

NOTNOBJ: (NTIME1)
∅ John convinced the week.

NOTNOBJ: (NTIME2)
∅ John convinced yesterday.

Dictionary Entry:

EAT.
TV: (NOTNOBJ: .2 . . . .)
.2 =   NSENT1, NSENT2, NSENT3,
NTIME1, NTIME2.

The verse quoted

vs. ∅ He eats the fact.
∅ Fact eating
∅ A fact eating man
∅ The fact eaten

WORD LIST: NOTNOBJ:(NHUMAN): abolish, assume, compress, edit, fish, fraction, interpret,

learn, paper, peak, smooth, summarize; NOTNOBJ: (NONHUMAN): convince, surprise;
NOTNOBJ: (NSENT1): act, content, decrease, inactivate, lower, prevent, tend, work;
NOTNOBJ: (NSENT2): act, content, decrease, inactivate, further, lower, maintain, tend, work;
NOTNOBJ: (NSENT3): act, content, extract, inactivate, learn, lower, tend, work;
NOTNOBJ: (NTIME1): achieve, diminish, oppose, restore; NOTNOBJ: (NTIME2): achieve,
analyze, diminish, oppose.

NOTNSUBJ:

applies to verbs restricted in terms of the noun subjects with which they can occur. Similar to NOTNOBJ in form, the value of the NOTNSUBJ attribute is a list of noun subclasses which cannot, (in scientific writing, at least) occur as the subject of the verb in question (WSEL2).

Also, for occurrences of adjectival Ving N (the dining gentleman), if for any given verb N tV OBJ does not occur then Ving N does not occur (DSEL1):

The gentleman dined.
The dining gentleman
∅ The gentleman occurred
∅ The occurring gentleman

Examples:

NOTNSUBJ: (NHUMAN)
∅ The gentleman occurred.

NOTNSUBJ: (NONHUMAN)
∅ The clock believed it.

NOTNSUBJ: (NSENT1)
∅ The fact cares.

NOTNSUBJ: (NSENT2)
∅ The reason knows.

NOTNSUBJ: (NSENT3)
∅ The trouble studied.

NOTNSUBJ: (NTIME1)
∅ The week designed the plan.

NOTNSUBJ: (NTIME2)
∅ Yesterday designed the plan.

Dictionary Entry:

```
          BELIEVE
          TV: (NOTNSUBJ: .1, . . . .)
.1 =      NONHUMAN, NSENT1, NSENT2,
          NSENT3, NTIME1, NTIME2.
```

WORD LIST: NOTNSUBJ: (NHUMAN): bound, occur, peak, result; NOTNSUBJ: (NONHUMAN): assess, believe, care, hand, long, skin, stage, wonder; NOTNSUBJ: (NSENT1): believe, care, consider, design, discover, dose, drug, eat, last, learn, occur, publish, sight, sleep, think, understand, wonder; NOTNSUBJ: (NSENT2): accelerate, consider, doubt, interpret, occur, sense, sight, summarize, think, understand, wonder; NOTNSUBJ: (NSENT3): associate, care, consider, initiate, learn, publish, question, rate, think, understand, wonder; NOTNSUBJ: (NTIME1): compound, diminish, initiate, occur, refer; NOTNSUBJ: (NTIME2): compound, diminish, initiate, occur, refer.

IV. Object Attributes of the Verb.

OBJLIST:ADJN:

The object string ADJN is a permutation of NA (e.g., Paint the house red; see OBJLIST: (NA)). Therefore the OBJLIST of a verb which includes one must also include

Frame:

N tV N ADJ

N tV ADJ N

the other.

ADJN is marginal if N is not followed by a right adjunct of N:

?I painted red the house.
I painted red the house which you
saw last Tuesday.

WORD LIST: bind, color, draw, grind, keep, make, mark, plate, pound, pump, split, stretch, tie

OBJLIST: (ASOBJBE):

The object string ASOBJBE must be distinguished from the adjunct sequence as + NSTGO. The two may be distinguished by the fact that the as of the ASOBJBE string is paraphrasable as 'in the capacity or character of', e.g.,

They served as messengers.
=in the capacity of messengers

whereas the as of the adjunct sequence is paraphrasable as 'when' or 'while' e.g.,

They served as young men.
=when they were young men

The two may also be distinguished by the fact that in sentences containing the ASOBJBE string, the primary stress of the sentence falls on the head noun of the noun phrase functioning as the OBJBE, e.g.,

Enzymes function as cátalysts.
∅ Enzymes function as catalysts.

whereas, in sentences containing the adjunct sequence, the primary sentence stress falls on the verb, e.g.,

John chánged as a lieutenant.
∅ John changed as a lieuténant.

Note 1: a large number of verbs occur with both the object string and the adjunct, e.g., serve (above).

Note 2: An occurrence of ASOBJBE can frequently be related to an occurrence of NASOBJBE:

They served (the king) as messengers.

Cf. NASOBJBE.

Examples:

He painted red the house on the corner.

He bound tight the ropes which were slipping off the deck.

She made secure the rattling windows.

He marked "fragile" the package we sent.

You've already pumped dry the source you were planning to count on.

We split open the package marked "fragile".

Frame:

N tV as N

Examples:

They served as messengers.

Enzymes function as catalysts.

He can act as bartender.

This idea originated as a vague possibility.

That invention began as a joke.

John applied as a mechanic.

He will continue as a private.

He ran as a sprinter.

The reaction occurred as an after-effect.

The fact exists as an anomaly.

NOTOBJLIST: (ASOBJBE):

John changed as a lieutenant.

John ate well as a young man.

I didn't go to school as a child.

He lived in England as a schoolboy.

WORD LIST: appear, apply, arise, begin, continue, enter, exist, fail, function, go, occur, originate, participate, remain, train.

OBJLIST: (ASSERTION):

The verbs classified as OBJLIST: (ASSERTION) are a subset of the verbs classified as OBJLIST: (THATS), i.e.:

> She knows John is an "A" student.
> She knows that John is an "A" student.
>   (know OBJLIST ⊃ ASSERTION, THATS)
> ∅ She reported John is an "A" student.
> She reported that John is an "A" student. (report OBJLIST ⊃ THATS
>   ⊅ ASSERTION)

It should be noted that the computational treatment of forms like It seems that he was here is to define a small subclass, VSENT4 (= appear, happen, remain, seem, turn out), which can take OBJLIST: (ASSERTION), (THATS) where applicable, provided the subject of the VSENT4 is the expletive It.

Frame:

SUBJ tV (that) S

Examples:

I assume you will arrive on time.

They feel they are being abused.

He believes the earth is flat.

She discovered he was an excellent cook.

We said we knew a better solution.

It seems he is happier away from home.

NOT OBJLIST: (ASSERTION):

∅ He added John was a witness.

∅ He argued their approach was metaphysical.

∅ She reported John was an "A" student.

WORD LIST: appear, assume, believe, discover, feel, figure, find, imply, know, learn, maintain, mean, note, say, seem, sense, show, state, suggest, suppose, think, understand.

OBJLIST: (ASTG):

Verbs which occur with the object string ASTG each occur with a limited set of adjectives in the adjective position:

> This rings true.
> ∅ This rings red.

This limitation on the set of adjectives which occur with verbs specified as OBJLIST: (ASTG) distinguishes these verbs from those specified as OBJLIST: (OBJBE) for which no such limitation exists:

> She remains true.
> She remains red.
> She remains sick.
> She remains intelligent.

Frame:

SUBJ tV ADJ

Examples:

That story rings true.

She remained red in the face.

They fell sick.

He lay still.

John turned purple.

Math comes easy to him.

Mary went crazy.

The rope worked loose.

The ore assayed high in silver.

This class tested low in reading.

NOTOBJLIST: (ASTG):

She remains true.

John looks happy.

WORD LIST: assay, break, come, glow, go, hold, lay, rest, ring, stand, test, turn, work.

OBJLIST: (C1SHOULD):

The verb of the SN is not tensed.

Verbs which satisfy the frame occur with should V as well as with V.

Frame:

SUBJ tV that N V OBJ

Examples:

I demand that he come.

The plan provides that he be on time.

It necessitates that he be on time.

WORD LIST: ask, demand, direct, mean, move, order, prefer, propose, provide, require, suggest.

OBJLIST: (DPSN):

It is necessary to define this as an object string (in place of treating it as an adverbial adjunct plus SN) since some sequences have no analysis in terms of an SN string plus optional adjunct, e.g.:

He pointed out that this was the best approach.

∅ He pointed that this was the best approach.

The particular Dp must be specified for each verb.

Frame:

N tV Dp SN

Examples:

I found out whether he was coming.

He pointed out that this was the best approach.

They often make out to be villains.

Dictionary Entry:

	FIND
	TV: (OBJLIST: .3, ...).
.3 =	DPSN: .17, ...
.18 =	DPVAL: (↓ OUT↓).

WORD LIST: bring (out, up), figure (out), find (out), leave (in, out), let (on), make (out), mark (down), point (out), write (down).

OBJLIST: (DP1):

Applies to strings in which the adverb-preposition (or particle), DP, cannot be analyzed as an adverbial adjunct, e.g.:

They lined up.

∅ They lined.

Or, if the verb also occurs without a DP or other object, then it occurs in a different sense than with the DP, as is often indicated by a difference in subject selection:

John carried on.

∅ John carried.

The point carried.

Some of the constructions classified as OBJLIST: (DP1) are the result of 'mid-

Frame:

N tV DP.

Examples:

They carried on.

He showed off.

We give up.

The plane took off.

NOT OBJLIST: (DP1):

She drove in.

He went out.

They walked down.

dling', i.e., they are related to a class of
V N DP constructions:

> They blew the house up.
> The house blew up.

> The particular DP must be specified
for each verb.

> ACT.
> TV: (OBJLIST: .3 . . . .)
> .3 =   DP1: .16, ...
> .16 =   DPVAL: (↓UP↓).

WORD LIST: act (up), add (up), back (down, off, out), come (shout, around, to, up), carry (on),
clear (out, up), cool (down, off), couple (up), cover (up), double (back, up), draw (back, up), dry
(out, up), fall (away, in, off, out), follow (through), give (in, out, up), level (off, out), look (up),
lose (out), measure (up), phase (out), run (down, on, out, over, up), show (off, up), sleep (in,
over), slow (down, up), split (away, off, up), start (in, out, up), stop (by, in, off, over, up), take
(off), test (out), try (out), turn (out, up), warm (up), work (out).

OBJLIST: (DP1 PN):

It is necessary to define this as an
object string (in place of treating it as an
adverbial adjunct plus PN) since some
sequences have no analysis in terms of a
PN string plus optional adjunct, e.g.:

> She moved in on him.
> ⌀ She moved on him.

In place of N, a _Ving_ string is sometimes
possible and is allowed by the grammar:

> It boils down to their having taken
a bribe.

> The particular Dp and P must be
specified for each verb.

> In the WORD LIST, the arrow (→)
follows the set of DPs specified for each
verb and precedes the set of Ps specified
for that verb.

Frame:

N _tV_ Dp PN

Examples:

I _found_ out about his coming.

They _settled_ down to the job at hand.

It all _adds_ up to nothing.

NOT OBJLIST: (DP1 PN):

He went down to Washington.

He walked around to the bus station.

He sped on past the exit.

Dictionary Entry:

> MOVE.
> TV: (OBJLIST: .3, ...).
> .3 =   DP1PN: .18, ...
> .18 =   DPVAL: (↓IN↓), PVAL: (↓ON↓).

WORD LIST: add (up → to), build (up→ to), come (up, around, back→ to, with), double (up→
with), face (up→ to), feel (up→ to), fit (in→ with), go (along, down, in, off, out→ for, in, of, with),
keep (away, up→ from, to), lead (up→ to), link (up→ to, with), live (up→ to), look (down, in,
out, up→ for, on, to), measure (up→ to), own (up→ to), pair (up, off→ with), play (up→ to),
put (up→ with), reach (out→ for), speak (out, up→ for), stand (up→ to, for), try (out→ for).

OBJLIST: (DP2 PN), (DP3 PN), (DP4 PN):

applies to strings in which the adverb-
preposition, (or particle), DP, cannot be
analyzed as an adverbial adjunct; i.e., _mix
up the last name with the first_ ≠ _mix the
last name with the first_ + _up_.

As the object of _Ving_ in certain
strings where _Ving_ usually is followed
by _of N_ there is an object form of the

Frame:

N _tV_ DP N P N   (DP2 PN)

N _tV_ N DP P N   (DP3 PN)

Examples:

I _mixed_ up the last name with the first.
I _mixed_ the last name up with the first.

DPN PN string where the of occurs between DP and NPN (the splitting up of the project into three parts). This form is DP4PN.

Any verb which takes DP2PN takes all the variants: OBJLIST: (DP2PN), (DP3PN), (DP4PN). The particular DP and P must be specified for each verb.

In the WORD LIST, the arrow (→) follows the set of DPs specified for each verb and precedes the set of Ps specified for that verb.

The mixing up of the last name with the first.

He split up the project into three parts.

They bound up the old wheat with the new.

He is linking up the defendants with this new crime.

Dictionary Entry:

BIND.
TV: (OBJLIST: .3, ...)
.3 = DP2PN; .19, DP3PN: .19,
DP4PN: .19, ...
.19 = DPVAL: (↓ UP↓), PVAL: (↓ WITH↓).

WORD LIST: add (in→ with), bind (up→ with), call (away→ to), chain (down, up→ to), divide (up→ with), end (up→ in, with), follow (up→ with), link (up→ to, with), pair (up, off→ with, into), play (off→ against), separate (out, off→ from), sign (over→ to), single (out→ for), take (up→ with), trace (back→ to), yield (up→ to).

OBJLIST: (DP2 , DP3 , DP4):

DP2 may be distinguished from a prepositional phrase PN by the fact that the DP and N permute:

He looked the number up.
He looked up the number.

whereas the P and N of the prepositional phrase do not permute:

He looked up the shaft.
✗ He looked the shaft up.

For some verbs which take DP N objects, the N position may be filled by a Ving string (They kept up their writing to the President). In the machine grammar, a Ving string is allowed freely in place of N in DP N, and is considered rare as a replacement of N in N DP.

As the object of Ving in certain strings where Ving usually is followed by of N there is an object form of the DP string where the of occurs between DP and N (the sending in of the entry). This form is DP4.

Any verb which takes DP2 takes all the variants: OBJLIST: (DP2 , DP3 , DP4).

The particular DP(s) must be specified for each verb.

Frame:

N_1 tV DP N_2 (DP2)
    ($N_2 \neq$ PRO)

N tV N DP (DP3)

Examples:

He looked up the number.
He looked the number up.

He sent back the gift.
He sent the gift back.

He sent in his entry.
He sent his entry in.

He took off his coat.
He took his coat off.

He put on his coat.
He put his coat on.

He looked over his notes.
He looked his notes over.

Dictionary Entry:

LOOK.
TV: (OBJLIST: .3 . . . .)
.3 = DP2: .17, DP3: .17, DP4: .17, ...
.17 = DPVAL: (↓ OVER↓), (↓ UP↓).

WORD LIST: act (out), add (in, on, up), ask (in, out, over, up), back (up), beat (up), bend (back, up), bind (down, off, over, up), block (in, off, out, up), bring (about, off, out, up), carry (out, through), clear (away, off, out, up), cool (down, off), cover (up), deal (out), divide (up), draw (back, down, in, off, out, up), dry (off, out), drive (in, off, out), eat (away, up), factor (out), figure (out), find (out), fish (out, up), fit (in), follow (up), give (away, back, in, out, over, up), hand (around, back, down, in, on, out, over), lead (in), leave (in, out), level (down, off, out), line (up), live (down), look (over, up), make (out, over, up), mark (down, off, up), move (in, out), paper (over), point (off, out, up), pump (in, off, out, up), read (over), reason (out), regain (back), rule (out), save (up), show (in, off, out, up), sleep (off), slice (off), slow (down, up), smooth (away, back, down, off, out), space (out), split (away, off, up), stop (up), store (up), strip (off), switch (off, on), take (off, out, up), think (out, over), try (on, out), turn (down, off, on, over), use (up), warm (up), wash (away, down, off), weigh (down), work (off, out, over), write (down, in, off, out, up).

OBJLIST: (DSTG):

applies to small subclasses of verbs which occur with particular adverb subclasses. E.g., <u>act</u>, <u>do</u>, <u>mean</u>, <u>behave</u>, require an 'evaluative' adverb (<u>He behaves badly but he means well</u>. ∮ <u>He behaves but he means</u>); other verbs require an adverb of motion (<u>He glanced up</u>, <u>He glanced about</u>, ∮ <u>He glanced</u>); still others require a locative adverb (<u>He resides here</u>).

The verbs which require a locative adverb also occur with other locative strings –

He resides on Prince St.
He resides where he pleases.

– although a set of locative object strings is not in the present grammar.

Frame:

N <u>tV</u> D

Examples:

He <u>meant</u> well.

∮ He meant.

He <u>did</u> poorly.

∮ He did.

He <u>resides</u> here.

∮ He resides.

WORD LIST: compare, do, handle, head, lie, place, range, rate, tunnel.

OBJLIST: (FORTOVO):

The computational treatment of forms like <u>It remains for us to make the final decision</u> is to define a small subclass, VSENT4 (=<u>appear</u>, <u>happen</u>, <u>remain</u>, <u>seem</u>, <u>turn out</u>) which can take OBJLIST: (FORTOVO) where applicable, provided the subject of the VSENT4 is the expletive <u>it</u>.

Note: To distinguish between FORTOVO and the object <u>for N</u> + <u>to V</u> (OBJ) where <u>to V</u> (OBJ) is an adjunct (<u>He is looking for an assistant to aid him in his work</u>), use <u>there</u> as the subject of the FORTOVO:

He plans for there to be five people on the committee.
I asked for there to be a proctor at the exam.

Frame:

N <u>tV</u> for N <u>to</u> V (OBJ)

Examples:

I <u>prefer</u> for him to go to college.

It <u>remains</u> for us to make the final decision.

I <u>plan</u> for him to do it.

I <u>asked</u> for there to be a proctor at the exam.

He is <u>longing</u> for her to ask him.

She <u>moved</u> for the meeting to adjourn.

WORD LIST: appeal, arrange, ask, cry, demand, fight, hope, intend, like, long, mean, motion, pay, plan, prefer, press, provide, remain, wait, wish.

OBJLIST: NA:

     Verbs which occur with the object string NA each occur with a limited set of adjectives in the adjective position in NA:

     He painted the house red.
     ∅ He painted the house strange.

This selectional dependency between the verb and the adjective distinguishes the verbs which occur with NA, such as <u>paint</u>, from sentence-container verbs, such as <u>think</u>, <u>consider</u>, <u>judge</u>, etc. (classified as OBJLIST: SOBJBE), which exhibit no selectional dependencies between the verb and the adjective:

     I consider the house red.
     I consider the house strange.

     Verbs which occur with the object string NA also differ from verbs which occur with the sequence NSTGO + adjectival adjunct (e.g., <u>She ate the apple green</u>). These two sequences differ in that the noun and adjective of NA permute while the noun and adjective of NSTGO + adjunct do not:

     He painted red the house on the corner.
     ∅ He ate green the apple on the table.

     Some verbs which occur with NA require an NA object, i.e., they do not also occur with a N object:

     The blow knocked him senseless.
     ∅ The blow knocked him.

Some border on the idiomatic:

     Strike him dumb.
     Pump it dry.

Frame:

N $\underline{tV}$ N ADJ

N $\underline{tV}$ ADJ N

Examples:

He <u>painted</u> the house red.

He <u>bound</u> the ropes tight.

She <u>made</u> the rattling windows secure.

He <u>marked</u> the package "fragile".

Don't <u>pump</u> your sources dry.

We <u>split</u> the package open.

Not OBJLIST: NA:

He considers this book worthless.

She thought the question absurd.

He drinks his coffee black.

She prefers her men tall and thin.

WORD LIST: bind, color, draw, grind, keep, make, mark, plate, pound, pump, split, stretch, tie.

OBJLIST: (NASOBJBE):

     A verb is classified as occurring with OBJLIST: (NASOBJBE) if it occurs in the frame

     N_1 $\underline{tV}$ N_2 <u>as</u> N_3

where N_3 is a predicate of — or refers to — N_1. For example, in <u>They served the king as messengers</u>, <u>messengers</u> is predicated of <u>they</u>.

     This distinguishes sentences occurring with the object string NASOBJBE from

Frame:

N_1 $\underline{tV}$ N_2 <u>as</u> N_3

N_3 is a predicate of N_1

Examples:

They <u>served</u> the king as messengers.

He <u>entered</u> the army as a private.

She <u>interpreted</u> it as a linguist.

He <u>ran</u> the race as a sprinter.

those occurring with the object string SASOBJBE, in which N_3 is a predicate of N_2 (They treated him as a lackey).

The object string NASOBJBE must also be distinguished from the sequence N + as + N, where as + N is a sentence adjunct. These two may be distinguished by the fact that the as of NASOBJBE is paraphrasable as 'in the capacity or character of', e.g.,

> They served the king as messengers.
> = in the capacity of messengers

whereas the as of the sequence N + as + N is paraphrasable as 'when' or 'while', e.g.,

> They served the king as young men.
> = when they were young men.

Cf. OBJLIST: (ASOBJBE).

Note: a number of verbs occur with both the object string and the adjunct sequence, e.g., serve (above).

WORD LIST: begin, continue, enter, interpret, run, serve.

NOTOBJLIST: (NASOBJBE):

They treated him as a lackey. (SASOBJBE)

We will consider John as our (")
preferred candidate.

He established it as a fact. (")

They served the king as young men. (adjunct)

He discovered the enzyme as a student. (")

OBJLIST: (ND):

applies to strings in which the adverb (D) cannot be analyzed as an adjunct, e.g.:

> He put it there.
> ∅ He put it.

Or, if the verb also occurs with a noun object alone, it occurs in a different sense than with the N + D:

> They treated them.
> They treated them well.

There is a selectional dependency between the verb and the adverb such that verbs specified as OBJLIST: (ND) can occur only with either locative adverbs and adverbs of motion (here, there, nearby, up, down) or with 'evaluative' adverbs (well, badly, poorly) (WPOS1M):

> He put it there.
> ∅ He put it about.
> He bore the news well.
> ∅ He bore the news there.

The particular adverb subclass (whether DLOC1 or DLOC3 or DEVAL) with which each verb occurs is not at present checked by the grammar.

Frame:

N tV N D

Examples:

They treat them well/badly.

He put it there.

He bore the news well.

She wears her age well.

WORD LIST: bear, put, treat, wear.

OBJLIST: (NN):

In sentences occurring with OBJLIST: (NN) either the verb is <u>give</u> in its modal use (He gave the door a kick) or N_2 (the indirect object) is NHUMAN or AGGREGATE:

I gave him a book.
He bought his family presents.
(WPOS22).

A majority of the verbs classified as OBJLIST: (NN) enter into the transformation

$$N \ tV \ N_2 \ P \ N_3 \ \leftrightarrow \ N \ tV \ N_3 \ N_2$$

where N_3 = NHUMAN or AGGREGATE.

Others occur with idiomatic extensions of the transformation:

I showed him a good time.

or with quantity expressions of the NQN type:

It cost him five dollars.

<u>Frame:</u>

N <u>tV</u> N N

<u>Examples:</u>

I <u>gave</u> him a book.

They <u>bought</u> John a present.

I <u>showed</u> him a good time.

They <u>allowed</u> the patient a cigar.

It <u>cost</u> him five dollars.

He <u>gave</u> the door a kick.

WORD LIST: allow, ask, bring, cause, charge, choose, deal, deny, design, do, draw, find, gain, give, hand, leave, make, net, order, prepare, read, save, show, take, tell, will, write.

OBJLIST: (NPN):

There are at least several types of verbs which occur with the object string NPN:

1) Those which require the complete NPN object:

They attributed the painting to Massaccio.
∅ They attributed the painting.
I referred him to the librarian.
∅ I referred him.

2) Those for which the PN is droppable –

They liberated the city from the enemy.
They liberated the city.

– but which exhibit a strong selectional dependency between the verb and the pre-position:

∅ They liberated the city to the enemy.
I filled it with water.
∅ I filled it around the edge.
I bought a gift for Mary.
∅ I bought a gift to Mary.

<u>Frame:</u>

N <u>tV</u> N P N

particular P for each tV

<u>Examples:</u>

They <u>attributed</u> the painting to Massaccio.

I <u>fed</u> his lunch to him.

I <u>entered</u> him into school.

I <u>continued</u> him in school.

I <u>directed</u> my attention to the blackboard.

I <u>brought</u> a gift to John.

One can <u>transform</u> X into Y.

I <u>emptied</u> the water into the sink.

He <u>concerned</u> himself with the issue.

I <u>incorporated</u> your suggestion into the paper.

I <u>applied</u> my solution to our problem.

I <u>connected</u> the plug to the outlet.

This dependency helps to distinguish the object string NPN from the sequence noun object plus P N adjunct (e.g., They liberated the city on Sunday). Many verbs can occur with either the NPN object string and the noun object plus P N adjunct, where the preposition is the same in both cases:

> They liberated the city from the enemy. (NPN)
> They liberated the city from motives of political advantage. (N + PNadjunct)

The particular P must be specified for each verb.

I dipped my donut into my coffee.

I divided the pie into five parts.

He fastened the chain to the door.

WORD LIST: accelerate (to), attract (to), add (to), apply (to), ask (into, to), associate (with), attribute (to), balance (against, on), beat (into, to), bring (into, to), catalyse (into), charge (to), clear (of), combine (with), correlate (with), demonstrate (to), deprive (of), direct (against, at, to, toward), enter (in), expel (from), give (to), identify (with), limit (to), make (of), obtain (from), pattern (after), present (to, with), slice (from, off), subject (to), take (from, to), turn (against, from, into, on, to), view (with).

OBJLIST: (NPSNWH):

The particular Prep must be specified for each verb.

The P is restricted in terms of the container verb, not in terms of the contained SNWH. This is evidenced by the fact that the P of NPSNWH does not permute to the end of the SNWH string, e.g.:

> John asked me about what he should do.
> ⌿ John asked me what he should do about.

Cf. OBJLIST: SNWH.

Note: Avoid use of what S as the SNWH in the test frame since what S may be the replacement of a given N_2 in N_1PN_2, e.g.:

> I covered it with what you gave me.

Frame:

SUBJ tV N P SNWH

Examples:

I asked him about whether my passport would be stamped.

He interested her in what he was planning to do.

I will base my opinion on whether she shows up.

I saw the organizer about whose car we should take to the picnic.

They made a big deal of whether you came on time.

Dictionary Entry:

      INTEREST
      TV: (OBJLIST: .3 . . . .).
.3 = NPSNWH: .17, . . .
.17 = PVAL: (⸢IN⸣).

WORD LIST: ask (about), base (on, upon), brief (on, about), contact (about), interest (in), make (of), question (about), see (about), trace (to).

OBJLIST: (NPSVINGO):

As distinct from the object string NPVINGSTG, the N_3 of NPSVINGO is not possessive:

> I asked him about John's having been there. (NPVINGSTG)

Frame:

N_1 tV N_2 P N_3 Ving (OBJ)

Examples:

I asked him about no one having been there.

I asked him about no one having been there. (NPSVINGO)

If N_3 is a pronoun, it is accusative (WPOS5).

Note: to avoid confusion of the object string NPSVINGO with the sequence N P N plus a right adjunct Ving (He kissed Mary near the door opening on to the balcony), use the expletive there as N_3:

I asked him about there having been no witnesses.

The particular preposition(s) must be specified for each verb. (WPOS15).

I charge his acquittal to there having been no witnesses.

He attributes his success to there having been no competitors.

He told us about there being no doubt in his mind.

Dictionary Entry:

   ASK.
   TV: (OBJLIST: .3, ...).
.3 = NPSVINGO: .16, ...
.16 = PVAL: (ABOUT)

WORD LIST: ask (about), attribute (to), base (on, upon), brief (about, on), caution (about), center (on, about, around, upon), charge (to), compare (to, with), contact (about), contrast (to, with), correlate (with), deduce (from), identify (with), limit (to), make (of), question (about), relate (to), tell (about), trace (to).

OBJLIST: (NPVINGO):

The noun object (N_2) of tV is understood to be the subject of Ving.

The particular preposition(s) must be specified for each verb (WPOS15).

Frame:

N_1 tV N_2 P Ving (OBJ).

Examples:

I prevented him from ruining his health.

I cautioned him against ruining his health.

I talked him into going to Chicago.

I cured him of stuttering.

I converted him to smoking cigars.

Dictionary Entry:

   CONVERT.
   TV: (OBJLIST: .3, ...).
.3 = NPVINGO: .16, ...
.16 = PVAL: (↓TO↓)

WORD LIST: attract (to), charge (with), clear (of), condition (to), drive (to), end (by), expose (to), fit (for), inhibit (from), interest (in), limit (to), prevent (from), release (from), restrict (to, from), stop (from).

OBJLIST: (NPVINGSTG):

In the object string NPVINGSTG, the left adjunct of Ving (specified in the frame as N_3's) is either an overt subject - -

I told him about Mary's leaving.

-- an article --

I told him about the singing of the anthem.

-- or null --

I told him about writing programs.

Frame:

N_1 tV N_2 P N_3's Ving (OBJ).

Examples:

I asked him about their offering him more money.

I told him about Mary's leaving.

She asked him about writing programs.

I attributed my success to changing my plans.

Don't subject me to John's singing.

However, a verb classified as occurring with the object string NPVINGSTG must be capable of occurring with a sequence N P Vingstg in which the Ving has an overt subject and in which this overt subject is not

Dictionary Entry:

ASK.
TV: (OBJLIST: .3, ...).
.3 =   NPVINGSTG: .17, ...
.17 = PVAL: ($\downarrow$ABOUT$\downarrow$)

coreferential with either the subject $\setminus(N_1)$ or the noun object (N_2) of the tV.

Note that VINGSTG here refers to either the object string NSVINGO or the object string VINGOFN.

The particular preposition(s) must be specified for each verb (WPOS15).

WORD LIST: ask (about), attach (to), attribute (to), base (on, upon), compare (to, with), connect (with), deduce (from), identify (with), link (with), make (of), pattern (after), prepare (for), question (about), relate (to), separate (from), set (on), subject (to), tell (about), trace (to).

OBJLIST: (NSNWH):

N_2 is NHUMAN (WSN8).

Note: Avoid the use of what S as the SNWH in the test frame since what S may be the replacement of a given N_2 in N_1N_2 (e.g., I gave him what he needed).

Frame:

N_1 tV N_2 SNWH.

Examples:

He told me whether they were coming.

They wrote him who was coming.

I asked him why he did it.

I taught him how to do it.

WORD LIST: ask, teach, tell, write.

OBJLIST: (NSTGO):

verbs classified as occurring with the object string NSTGO include

1) the pure transitives (He accomplished his mission) including those which drop the N object (He reads books; He reads).

2) verbs which occur with an NPN object where the PN is droppable (He fastened the chain to the door; He fastened the chain). (Dropping of PN is not an automatic process of the grammar).

3) verbs which require either a conjoined or plural object (He equated A and B; He correlated the two sets of values) or a collective noun object (It gathers dust).

4) verbs which require reflexive objects: (He absented himself).

5) measure verbs (The line measures two inches; It costs five dollars).

Note: due to their relatively infrequent occurrence with noun objects, verbs which

Frame:

N tV N.

Examples:

He analyzed the compound.

John met Mary.

He amassed a fortune.

He equated A and B.

This key opens the door.

They perjured themselves.

It costs five dollars.

He fastened the chain.

occur only with special noun objects (usually
nominal transforms of the verb of the sentence: He slept a good sleep) are classified
as OBJLIST: (NULLOBJ) only.

WORD LIST: ask, believe, combine, divide, eat, face, fish, group, like, mean, number, order,
part, place, prefer, provide, question, run, relax, require, say, skin, substitute, suppose, take,
tell, try, underestimate, vary, want, work, write.

OBJLIST: (NSVINGO):

The Ving in the object string NSVINGO
may occur with either an overt or a zeroed
subject:

> She favors doing it.
> She favors their doing it.

The subject of Ving need not be the
same as the subject of the container sentence; e.g., in

> John described his studying.

his = John or, alternatively, his = some
other person. Cf. VINGO.

Since NSVINGO is more sentencelike in its form than the VINGOFN string
it is helpful to include in the test frame for
NSVINGO features which are characteristic
of sentences, e.g.:

1) an object after Ving: We discussed
   writing novels.
2) an adverb after the object: She
   prefers doing it quickly.
3) a negative element before the Ving:
   She favors not doing it.

Note: to avoid possible confusion, do
not use in the test frame for OBJLIST:
(NSVINGO) a Ving which can function as a
noun modifier (see VVERYVING). I.e., you
don't want He needs designing women classified as a case of NSVINGO.

Frame:

N tV (N's) Ving (OBJ)

Examples:

He described (his) studying at night.

He decided to accelerate their advertising.

The group discussed writing novels.

In their program of exercise, they include
climbing a mountain.

The nurse has limited (her) seeing visitors
so frequently.

He mentioned (his) seeing Mary.

They opposed (their) adjourning early.

She prefers doing it her way.

They proposed sending another letter.

He questioned having to arrive at 8 P.M.

The doctor has restricted his seeing visitors.

He suggested swimming more slowly.

I understand his wanting to leave so early.

WORD LIST: abolish, accelerate, allow, choose, complicate, describe, determine, discuss,
evidence, facilitate, include, infer, limit, mean, mention, notice, oppose, prefer, prevent,
propose, question, restrict, suggest.

OBJLIST: (NTHATS):

The noun object of tV is NHUMAN
(WSN8).

Note: a verb which takes a sentence
string as its subject (That no one wants to
come troubles her) may appear to take the
sentence string in its object when the subject is the expletive it (It troubles her that
no one wants to come); but these are not
considered to be object strings or parts of
object strings. The one exception is the
closed class VSENT4.

Frame:

N tV OBJ (that) SN

Examples:

I told you that he came.

I taught him that honesty is the best policy.

WORD LIST: advise, caution, content, convince, interest, promise, satisfy, show, teach, tell, write.

OBJLIST: (NTOBE):

verbs classified as OBJLIST: (NTOBE) can occur with the following object strings:

N to be OBJBE
N to have N
N to have Ven

e.g.:

They discovered him to be in error.
We consider Dr. Smith to have the best solution.
John was found to have left early.

Verbs classified as occurring with the object string NTOBE cannot occur with an NTOVO object string:

∮ They discovered him to cross the street.

However, when tV occurs in the passive, any verb is allowed in the infinitive:

John was found to frequent houses of ill repute.
vs. ∮ They found John to frequent houses of ill repute.

The to of OBJLIST: (NTOBE) does not equal in order to; i.e., sequences such as They introduced this plan to be controversial (=They introduced this plan in order to be controversial) should not be considered as cases of OBJLIST: (NTOBE).

If N_2 is a pronoun, it is accusative (WPOS5).

Frame:

N_1 tV N_2 to be OBJ

(not: N tV N to V(≠ be, have) OBJ)

Examples:

They showed him to be a fool.

∮ They showed him to cross the street.

We found him to be an excellent companion.

∮ We found him to eat hamburgers.

We noticed this to be the case.

They demonstrated the solution to be correct.

They showed us to be in error.

We consider Dr. Smith to have the best solution.

NOT OBJLIST: (NTOBE):

They allow him to be impolite. (cf. NTOVO)

They asked him to be quiet. (cf. NTOVO)

WORD LIST: assume, believe, claim, confirm, consider, demonstrate, determine, discover, establish, feel, find, know, observe, note, notice, report, show, suppose, think.

OBJLIST: (NTOVO):

The V of the object string NTOVO includes be and have but also other V:

They expected him to go home.
They expected him to be on time.
They expected him to have the best solution.

(See OBJLIST: (NTOBE)).

The to of OBJLIST: (NTOVO) does not equal in order to; i.e., sequences such as He drinks milk to keep thin (= He drinks milk in order to keep thin) should not be considered as cases of OBJLIST: (NTOVO).

Frame:

N tV N to V (OBJ)

Examples:

They allowed him to go.

I asked him to do it yesterday.

They conditioned them to beg for food.

I like him to come home early.

I told him to do it over.

They forced him to sign.

Note: do not classify verbs which occur with the expletive <u>it</u> as subject (<u>It</u> <u>contents him to know that she is here</u>) as NTOVO (see OBJLIST: (NTHATS)).

If N_2 is a pronoun, it is accusative (WPOS5).

They are <u>requiring</u> yout to show your I.D.

WORD LIST: advise, allow, ask, cause, caution, challenge, choose, condition, convince, designate, detail, employ, engage, expect, forbid, force, induce, influence, intend, like, mean, motion, motivate, order, pay, permit, prefer, prepare, press, pressure, require, stimulate, suffer, teach, tell, trouble, trust, want, write.

OBJLIST: (NULLOBJ):

verbs classified as occurring with the object string NULLOBJ include

1) verbs which do not also occur with N or PN or other object strings (<u>disappear</u>, <u>vegetate</u>, <u>ache</u>).

2) verbs which can occur with special N objects (<u>He slept</u>) (see OBJLIST: (NSTGO) note).

3) normally transitive verbs which may occur without their N objects (<u>He reads</u>; <u>He reads books</u>).

4) a VCOLLECTIVE if it occurs with a non-singular or collective subject (<u>Dust</u> <u>gathers</u>).

5) verbs with droppable PN or adverb objects:

He worked on the problem.
He worked.
He walked by.
He walked.

<u>Frame:</u>

N t<u>V</u>.

<u>Examples:</u>

The book has <u>disappeared.</u>

He <u>slept</u>

He <u>ate</u>.

Knowledge <u>accumulates</u>.

He <u>acted</u>.

John <u>came</u>.

WORD LIST: accelerate, act, age, appear, care, change, come, compete, compound, continue, decrease, demonstrate, diminish, draw, eat, enter, exist, fail, fish, follow, go, happen, homogenize, know, last, lengthen, live, look, matter, move, occur, point, provide, publish, ran, read, relax, remain, rest, result, return, ring, see, sleep, start, study, sweat, take, think, try, wonder, work, write.

OBJLIST: (NULLRECIP):

a verb is classified as occurring with the object string NULLRECIP if, when it occurs with no overt object and with a noun subject which is not singular (i.e., is AGGREGATE, PLURAL, or conjoined) it would be natural to reconstruct the object <u>each other</u> or P <u>each</u> <u>other</u> (on at least one reading); e.g.:

The couple fought (with each other), (with me).
The parties conferred (with each other).

<u>Frame:</u>

N_1 <u>and</u> N_2 t<u>V</u> (P) <u>each</u> <u>other</u>.

<u>Examples:</u>

John and Mary <u>met</u> each other at school.

X and Y <u>differ</u> (from each other) as to structure.

Your claim and my claim <u>conflict</u> (with each other) .

Bill and Bob <u>fought</u> (with each other).

John and Mary agree (with each other),
(to your plan).
⌿ John met.
⌿ John fought with each other.

The groups _separated_ (from each other).

The lines _parallel_ each other.

WORD LIST: agree, argue, associate, combine, confer, conflict, correlate, differ, link, meet, part, parallel, separate.

OBJLIST: (OBJBE):

In the object strong OBJBE, the OBJBE is the predicate of N$_1$. The machine grammar allows four possible values for OBJBE:

1) NSTG (noun string):

John appeared an idiot.
He seemed a happy man.

The restriction on number agreement between subject and object (WAGREE2) applies here.

Note: if the sequences N:SINGULAR tV N:PLURAL and/or N:PLURAL tV N: SINGULAR occur, the tV is not classified as

OBJLIST: (OBJBE).

2) ASTG (adjective string), including adjectival _Vens_ and _Vings_ (see VENDADJ and VVERYVING):

They look happy to be here.
We felt satisfied.
The results might seem surprising.

Note: verbs which occur with only a limited set of adjectives (ring true, blush red, etc.) are classified as OBJLIST: (ASTG), not OBJLIST: (OBJBE).

3) DSTG (adverb string):

I feel down.
He seems down and out.
They looked well.

A restriction limiting adverbs to those which occur after _be_ (WPOS1H) applies here.

Note: verbs which occur with a wider range of adverbs, i.e. which occur with adverbs of motion, manner, etc., are not classified as occurring with the object string OBJBE: (DSTG), e.g. _He came here_, up, down, quickly, etc.

4) P N:

This appears of great significance.
The matter seems in dispute.

Note: Verbs classified as occurring with OBJBE: PN, as opposed to those classified as occurring with PN, can occur with a

Frame:

N$_1$ _tV_ OBJBE

OBJBE = noun, adjective, adverb, P N

Examples:

John _acted_ strange.

They _appear_ happy to be here.

He _became_ ecstatic when I told him.

They _feel_ able to assume the responsibility.

She _looks_ capable.

Whether they will come _remains_ unclear.

She _seems_ right for the job.

The eggs _smell_ bad.

John _appeared_ an idiot.

He _became_ president a year ago.

She _remains_ a strong woman.

He _seemed_ a happy man.

John _appeared_ down and out.

Bill _felt_ apart from the rest of us.

They _looked_ well.

They _seem_ well.

The matter _appears_ in dispute.

It will _remain_ to his advantage to see them.

The cake _smells_ of anisette.

range of P + NSENTP (to his advantage, of
value, of interest, of significance) constructions. Therefore, verbs which can occur with
this range of constructions should be classified as OBJBE: (PN), although other PN constructions are also possible here.

WORD LIST: ASTG: act, appear, become, feel, look, remain, seem; DSTG: appear, feel, look,
seem; NSTG: appear, become, remain, seem; PN: appear, remain, seem.

OBJLIST: (OBJECTBE):
      applies only to the verb be in all its forms
(am, are, be, been, being, is, was, were).
      The sequences which are treated as objects
of be include:
      1) Ving (OBJ) (He is looking into the
matter). This is the same string as the object string VINGO. As object of be, the string
represents a treatment of the progressive
tense; it is therefore restricted so as to exclude non-well-formed verbal sequences:

      ∮ He is having gone.
      ∮ She was being going, etc.

      2) passive Ven + (OBJ) (War was never
declared). Because of the frequent occurrence
of the passive construction in scientific writing,
it is more economical to list the passive objects
for each verb in   the word dictionary than to
compute them by a rule of passive omission.
The correspondences between active and passive objects used in the preparation of dictionary
entries is given in POBJLIST below.
      3) OBJBE, i.e., a noun, adjective, ad-
verb or PN string (cf. OBJLIST: (OBJBE):

      He is a carpenter.
      He is happy.
      He is here.
      The matter is in dispute.

      4) SN (an embedded sentence):

      The trouble is that no one knew.
      To ask the question is to answer it.
      It is not that there was nothing to do.

      5) Ving strings (see OBJLIST: (NSVINGO)
and OBJLIST: (VINGOFN)):

      An added burden is filling out innumerable
forms.

      6) TOVO (John is to start Monday).
      7) ASSERTION (The trouble is John wants
to go).
      8) BEINGO (John is being a fool).
      9) EMBEDDEDQ (The question is: why
did John go ?)

OBJLIST: (PN):
        verbs which occur with OBJLIST:
(PN) exhibit a strong selectional dependency
with the preposition:

        He depends on Mary.
        ∮ He depends with Mary.
        It matters to me.
        ∮ It matters with me.

and, for the most part, do not also occur
(with the same meaning) with a zeroed object:

        You can rely on John.
        ∮ You can rely.
        He stands for justice.
        He stands.

        Verbs which occur with the object string
NPN from which the leftmost N can be dropped
(He gives (money) to charity) are also included
here.
        In the case of some verbs, a middle form
of the verb takes both NPN and PN objects:

        One can transform X into Y.
        X transforms into Y.

        The particular preposition(s) must be
specified for each verb (WPOS15).

Frame:

N tV P N

Examples:

I looked at him.

It consists of protein.

He happened across a new solution.

He accounts for the exceptions.

This adds to our problems.

He ran for president.

He is referring to the latest debate.

The pie divided into five parts.

Dictionary Entry:
        DEPEND.
        TV: (OBJLIST: .3, ...).
.3 = PN: .15, ...
.15 = PVAL: (↓ON↓ , ↓UPON↓).

WORD LIST: account (for), act (on), add (to), agree (on, to), amount (to), answer (for), ask (about, for), associate (with), balance (on), believe (in), care (about, for), change (into, to), compare (to, with), consist (in, of), deal (with), depend (on, upon), differ (from, in, with), divide (into), draw (from, on, to, upon), drive (at), enter (in upon), focus (on), give (of, to), happen (across, on, upon), identify (with), long (for), look (at, after, for, into, upon), meet (with), reduce (to), run (for), substitute (for), tell (of), transfer (to), wonder (about).

OBJLIST: (PNHOWS):
        includes those verbs which occur with
how S but not with SNWH, e.g.:

        He liked how it was done.
        ∮ He liked whether it was done.

        Many of these verbs also occur with
PN how S which is included in this string.

For these verbs the particular preposition(s)
must be specified (WPOS15).

Frame:

N tV (PN) how S (and not N tV whether S)

Examples:

This will complicate how it is to be done.

They demonstrated (to us) how the situation
was handled.

NOT OBJLIST: (PNHOWS):

This concerns [how / whether] we are to escape.
(= OBJLIST:(SNWH)).

Dictionary Entry:

        DEMONSTRATE.
        TV: (OBJLIST: .3, ...).
.3 =   PNHOWS: .18, ...
.18 =   PVAL: (↓FOR↓ , ↓TO↓).

WORD LIST: complicate, correct, define (for), demonstrate (for, to), describe (for, to), expose (to), film, infer, like, mention (to), restrict, review (for), summarize (for), understand.

OBJLIST: (PNN):

    Since PNN is a permutation of NPN, any verb specified for one must be specified for the other.

    PNN, however, usually occurs only when $N_3 = N + RN$:

    ?Mary gave to John the book.
    Mary gave to John the book which he needed for his exams.

    The particular preposition(s) must be specified for each verb (WPOS15)

Frame:

N_1 $\underline{tV}$ P N_2 N_3

N_1 $\underline{tV}$ N_3 P N_2

Examples:

He gave to her the book which he himself needed.

They attribute to Massaccio the introduction of perspective into medieval art.

They correlated with speech variation several factors which are usually considered sociological.

They have depleted of its riches the soil which we cared for so lovingly.

Dictionary Entry:

    ATTRIBUTE.
    TV: (OBJLIST: .3, ...).
.3 =   NPN: .17, PNN: .17,. . . .
.17 = PVAL: (↓TO↓).

WORD LIST: see OBJLIST: (NPN).

OBJLIST: (PNSNWH):

    The noun of PN is NHUMAN (WSN8). The P is from, to or of.

    Verbs which can occur only with PN how S and not with the full range of SNWH strings--

    He described to me how to go.
    ∅ He described to me whether to go.

--are classified as OBJLIST: (PNHOWS) and not as OBJLIST: (PNSNWH).

    Note: avoid use of what S as the SNWH in the test frame since what S may be the replacement of a given N_2 in P N_1 N_2 (e.g. I will give to him what he needs).

    Note: do not classify verbs which occur with the expletive it as subject (It matters to me whether he comes) as PNSNWH (see OBJLIST: (NTHATS)).

    The particular preposition(s) must be specified for each verb (WPOS15).

Frame:

N $\underline{tV}$ P N SNWH

Examples:

They inquired of him whether he was coming.

It matters to me whether he comes.

He didn't mention to me whether he was interested.

WORD LIST: admit (to), communicate (to), conceal (from), explain (to), hint (to), indicate (to), learn (from), mention (to), prove (to), relate (to), say (to), write (to).

OBJLIST: (PNTHATS):
    The noun of PN is NHUMAN (WSN8).
The P is <u>from</u>, <u>to</u> or <u>of</u>.
    The computational treatment of forms
like <u>It appeared to John that Mary was here</u>
is to define a small subclass, VSENT4 (= <u>ap-</u>
<u>pear</u>, <u>happen</u>, <u>remain</u>, <u>seem</u>, <u>turn out</u>) which
can take the object string PNTHATS, where
appropriate, provided the subject is <u>it</u>.
    Note: do not classify verbs which oc-
cur with the expletive <u>it</u> as subject and which
also occur with a sentence string as subject
(<u>It occurred to John that he was needed</u>. <u>That</u>
<u>he was needed occurred to John</u>) as PNTHATS.
(see OBJLIST: (NTHATS)).
    PN can be accompanied by an adjunct,
in which case the subject of SN is usually a
pronoun:

        They reported to him (about his leaving)
        that it had not been voluntary.

    The particular preposition (s) must be
specified for each verb (WPOS15)

Frame:

N <u>tV</u> P N SN

Examples:

I <u>learned</u> from John that the matter was under
discussion.

I <u>demonstrated</u> to them that the hypothesis
accounted for several dispararate facts.

It <u>appeared</u> to him that Mary was here.

Dictionary Entry:

    DEMONSTRATE.
    TV: (OBJLIST: .3, ...).
.3 = PNTHATS: .5, ...
.5 = PVAL: (↓TO↓).

WORD LIST: admit (to), announce (to), assert (to), cry (to), communicate (to), demonstrate (to),
disclose (to), explain (to), hint (to), illustrate (to), indicate (to), intimate (to), learn (from),
    mention (to), motion (to),   prove (to), remark (to), require (of), reveal (to), say (to),
        suggest (to), write (to).

OBJLIST: (PNTHATSVO):
    the verb of the embedded sentence is
not tensed. (cf. OBJLIST: (C1SHOULD)).
    Verbs which satisfy the frame occur
with <u>should</u> V as well as with V.
    The noun of PN is NHUMAN (WSN8).
    The particular preposition (s) must be
specified for each verb (WPOS15).

Frame:

N <u>tV</u> P N <u>that</u> N V (OBJ).

Examples:

They <u>suggested</u> to him that he curtail his
remarks.

They <u>demanded</u> of her that she remain.

They <u>required</u> of John that he attend.

Dictionary Entry:

    REQUIRE.
    TV: (OBJLIST: .3, ...).
.3 = PNTHATSVO: .6, ...
.6 = PVAL: (↓OF↓).

WORD LIST: ask (of), demand (of), expect (of), propose (to), require (of), suggest (to).

OBJLIST: (PNVINGSTG):
    Since PNVINGSTG is a permutation of
VINGSTGPN, any verb specified for one must
be specified for the other.

Frame:

N_1 <u>tV</u> P N_2 VINGSTG

N_1 <u>tV</u> VINGSTG P N_2

Usually, however, the acceptability of the PNVINGSTG permutation depends on the presence of one or more adjuncts within the VINGSTG:

> ?He prefers to going out with Mary staying home.
> He prefers to going out with Mary staying home with someone else.

The particular preposition(s) must be specified for each verb (WPOS15).

Examples:

They <u>limited</u> to certain hours his seeing visitors.

They <u>reported</u> to the nurse his seeing visitors.

They <u>attributed</u> to his wife's business acumen his succeeding where everyone else had failed.

He <u>charged</u> to a heavy workload his going home late.

Dictionary Entry:

    ATTRIBUTE.
    TV: (OBJLIST: .3, ...)
.3 = VINGSTGPN: .15, PNVINGSTG: .15, ...
.15 = PVAL: (↓TO↓).

WORD LIST: see OBJLIST: (VINGSTGPN).

OBJLIST: (PSNWH):

The P of the object string PSNWH is restricted in terms of the container verb, not in terms of the contained SNWH. This is evidenced by the fact that the P of PSNWH does not permute around the SNWH (Cf. OBJLIST: (SNWH)):

> John asked about whether he should go.
> ∅ John asked whether he should go about.

Note: avoid use of <u>what S</u> as the SNWH in the test frame since <u>what S</u> may be the replacement of a given N in PN (e.g., <u>John landed on what he had been looking for</u>).

The particular preposition(s) must be specified for each verb (WPOS15).

Frame:

N <u>tV</u> P SNWH

Examples:

I <u>asked</u> about whether he would come.

I <u>inquired</u> into whether he would come.

They <u>pondered</u> over whether he would come.

John <u>wondered</u> about why she did it.

Dictionary Entry:

    ASK.
    TV: (OBJLIST: .3, ...).
.3 = PSNWH: .13, ...
.13 = PVAL: (↓ABOUT↓)

WORD LIST: ask (about), care (about), check (on, into), depend (on), figure (out), hear (about), hint (at), knew (about), look (into), pertain (to), read (about), refer (to), reflect (on, upon), remark (on, about), report (on), speak (about), talk (about), tell (about), think (of, about), touch (on, upon), wonder (about), write (about).

OBJLIST: (PSVINGO):

As distinct from the object string PVINGSTG, the N_2 of PSVINGO is not possessive; however, the two object strings overlap extensively:

> They worried over [his/him] drinking so much.

If N_2 is a pronoun, it is accusative (WPOS5).

Note: to avoid confusion of the object string PSVINGO with the sequence PN plus a right adjunct <u>Ving</u> (<u>He looked at the door opening on to the balcony</u>), use the expletive <u>there</u> as the N_2:

Frame:

N_1 <u>tV</u> P N_2 Ving (OBJ)

Examples:

They <u>worried</u> over him drinking so much.

He <u>focused</u> on the president flying to Florida in a private plane.

We <u>asked</u> about there being no food.

He <u>writes</u> about John's absence disturbing Mary.

We asked about there being no food.

The particular preposition(s) must be specified for each verb (WPOS15).

WORD LIST: account (for), amount (to), answer (for), approve (of), argue (about), ask (about), began (with), center (on, about, around, upon), come (to, of, from), care (about, for), compare (to, with), depend (on, upon), end (in, with), explain (about), focus (on), hear (of, about), lie (about), plan (on), point (to), read (about), remark (on, about). remember (about), speak (of, about), talk (of, about), think (about), wonder (about), write (about).

OBJLIST: (PVINGO):
There is no overt subject of Ving (∅ He refrained from his pressing the point). The subject of tV (N₁) is understood to be the subject of Ving.

The particular preposition(s) must be specified for each verb (WPOS15).

Dictionary Entry:

    FOCUS.
    TV: (OBJLIST: .3, ...).
.3 = PSVINGO: .18, ...
.18 = PVAL: (∤ ON∤).

Frame:

N_1 tV P Ving (OBJ)

Examples:

I can't keep from smoking.

He refrained from pressing the point.

She succeeded in passing.

She is engaged in writing a novel.

He left off seeing her.

NOT OBJLIST: (PVINGO):

He relies on (our) making an impression. (PVINGSTG).

He couldn't account for (their) making a mistake. (PVINGSTG).

Dictionary Entry:

    KEEP.
    TV: (OBJLIST: .3, ...).
.3 = PVINGO: .19, ...
.19 = PVAL: (∤ FROM∤).

WORD LIST: admit (to), convert (to), delay (in), engage (in), fail (in), go (without), keep (from), specialize (in).

OBJLIST: (PVINGSTG):
In the object string PVINGSTG the left adjunct of Ving (specified in the frame as N_2's) is either an overt subject—

He asked about their writing programs.

—an article—

He asked about the writing of programs.

—or null—

He asked about writing programs.

Frame:

N_1 tV P N_2's Ving (OBJ)

Examples:

Mary couldn't account for (John's) losing the key.

Mary couldn't account for the losing of the key.

This amounts to (his) writing a new program.

This amounts to the writing of a new program.

They asked about (his) leaving early.

However, a verb classified as occurring with the object string PVINGSTG must be capable of occurring with a sequence P Vingstg in which the Ving has an overt subject and in which this overt subject is not coreferential with the subject of the tV.

Note that VINGSTG here refers to either the object string NSVINGO or the object string VINGOFN.

The particular preposition(s) must be specified for each verb (WPOS15).

They asked about John's reading of the passage.

Dictionary Entry:

ASK.
TV: (OBJLIST: .3, ...).
.3 = PVINGSTG: .15, ...
.15 = PVAL: (↓ABOUT↓).

WORD LIST: account (for), agree (on), amount (to), answer (for), argue (about, against, for), ask (about), come (from, of), compare (with), focus (on), long (for), look (into), point (to), provide (against, for), read (about), test (for), think (about), wonder (about), write (about).

OBJLIST: (SASOBJBE):

a verb is classified as occurring with OBJLIST: (SASOBJBE) if it occurs in the frame

$$N_1 \text{ -- } N_2 \underline{\text{ as }} N_3$$

where N_3 is a predicate of N_2. For example, in They treated him as a lackey, lackey is predicated of him, not they (cf. OBJLIST: (NASOBJBE)).

Unlike the sentence adjunct as + N (They treated him as a reward), the as + N of SASOBJBE cannot be preposed to the beginning of the sentence:

⌿ As a lackey, they treated him.
  As a reward, they treated him.
⌿ As a fact, he established it.

An object string VINGO (cf. OBJLIST: (VINGO)) may also occur as the predicate of N_2:

They established it as following from the premises.
She described them as sharing her opinion.

Note: a number of verbs occur with both the object string and the adjunct sequence, e.g., treat (above).

Frame:

$$N_1 \underline{\text{ tV }} N_2 \text{ as } [\begin{smallmatrix} N_3 \\ \text{VINGO} \end{smallmatrix}]$$

N_3, VINGO are predicates of N_2

Examples:

They treated him as a lackey.

He established it as a fact.

They entered it as a business expense.

He designed the building as a refuge.

She described them as sharing her opinion.

They established it as following from the premise.

NOT OBJLIST: (SASOBJBE):

They served the king as messengers. (NASOBJBE)

He discovered the enzyme as a student (adjunct)

WORD LIST: accept, acknowledge, administer, advance, characterize, choose, consider, depict, describe, designate, discontinue, employ, engage, enter, establish, expose, identify, include, intend, interpret, isolate, know, label, mean, mention, plan, present, propose, provide, put, receive, recognize, regard, represent, see, separate, suggest, train, try, undertake, use, utilize, view, visualize.

OBJLIST: (SNWH):

Note: a P may occur at the beginning or end of the SNWH string:

I wonder to whom he is referring.
I wonder whom he is referring to.
I don't know from whom he obtained the information.
I don't know whom he obtained the information from.

This P in SNWH is not to be confused with the P which is dependent on the container verb (cf. OBJLIST: (PN), (PSNWH)). This latter P does not occur at the end of the SNWH string:

I wondered about whether to go.
∅ I wondered whether to go about.

Note: avoid use of what S as the SNWH in the test frame since what S may be the replacement of a given N in NSTGO (e.g., I ate what he gave me).

Note: do not classify verbs which occur with the expletive it as subject (It doesn't matter whether he comes) as SNWH (see OBJLIST: (NTHATS)).

Frame:

N tV WH $\begin{bmatrix} \text{ASSERTION} \\ \text{to V(OBJ)} \end{bmatrix}$

WH = Whether, if, where, when, how, why, who, whom, which, what, whose

Examples:

The results will affect whether or not we will continue.

I asked whether I should go.

I don't care who you got it from.

This statement concerns why he chose to leave.

She is trying to discover whether he killed the woman.

They are discussing whether to leave.

I doubt if he can do it.

We cannot establish how this process works.

WORD LIST: affect, ascertain, ask, calculate, check, contemplate, choose, concern, consider, control, decide, deduce, denote, discern, discuss, doubt, establish, examine, hear, indicate, influence, investigate, judge, know, learn,   measure, mention, mind, note, observe, predict, prove, question, remember, report, reveal, say, see, show, state, tell, verify, wonder, write.

OBJLIST: (SOBJBE):

In the object string SOBJBE the OBJBE is the predicate of N_2. The machine grammar allows four possible values for OBJBE:

1) NSTG (noun string):

They considered him their savior.
They elected him president.
They call him a genius.

The restrictions on number agreement between subject and object (WAGREE2) apply here.

2) ASTG (adjective string), including adjectival Vens and Vings (see VENDADJ and VVERYVING; also OBJLIST: (SVEN)):

He considers them foolish.
I found it well-designed.
We thought him interesting.

3) DSTG (adverb string):

They mistakenly thought him here.
We prefer a meeting today.

Frame:

N_1 tV N_2 OBJBE

OBJBE = noun, adjective, adverb, P N

Examples:

They consider him their savior.

They termed him a genius.

She thought him a good man.

He considers them foolish.

I found it well-designed.

We thought him interesting.

I believe it possible.

I prefer him here.

I supposed it nearby.

They assumed him on the premises.

They find it of slight interest.

A restriction limiting adverbs to those which occur after be (WPOS1H) applies here.

4) P N:

For legal purposes, they assumed him on the premises.
They find it of slight interest.

The particular values of OBJBE must be specified for each verb.

They ruled him out of order.

I consider the matter in dispute.

We thought it to his advantage to see you.

Dictionary Entry:

CONSIDER.
   TV: (OBJLIST: .3, ...)
.3 = SOBJBE: .19, ...
.19 = BVAL: (ASTG, NSTG, PN).

WORD LIST: believe (ASTG, DSTG, NSTG, PN), consider (ASTG, NSTG, PN), find (ASTG, DSTG, NSTG, PN), judge (ASTG,NSTG), label (ASTG, NSTG, PN), prefer (ASTG, DSTG, PN), pronounce (ASTG, PN), prove (ASTG, DSTG), report (ASTG, DSTG, PN), show (ASTG), suppose (ASTG, DSTG, PN), term (ASTG, NSTG, PN), think (ASTG, DSTG, NSTG, PN).

OBJLIST: (STOVO-N):

The verbs classified as OBJLIST: (STOVO-N) are be and have.

If the to V is deleted from an occurrence of STOVO-N either the remaining sentence is unacceptable:

He has paying his workers to consider.
∅ He has paying his workers.
There is not a moment to lose.
∅ There is not a moment.

or the sense of the remaining sentence is changed:

I have a guy to see.
I have a guy.
It is nothing to sneeze at.
It is nothing.

The N_2 or Vingstg functions as the logical object of the verb of the embedded sentence.

Frame:

N_1 tV [$\begin{smallmatrix} N_2 \\ \text{Vingstg} \end{smallmatrix}$] to V.

Examples:

He has paying his workers to consider.

I have some stuff to deliver.

He has money to burn.

There is not a moment to lose.

There is paying the workers to consider.

That is the right principle to maintain.

OBJLIST: (SVEN):

The object string SVEN (as in I got the papers duplicated) must be distinguished from (1) the sequence noun plus adjunct (I delivered the papers duplicated) and (2) the object string SOBJBE (I considered the house well-designed).

SVEN may be distinguished from the noun plus adjunct sequence by the fact that if the Ven is deleted from an occurrence of SVEN either the remaining sentence is un- acceptable:

He wishes the tapes destroyed.

Frame:

N_1 tV N_2 Ven

Examples:

I got the papers duplicated.

I saw him robbed.

He had John punished.

We want the problems eliminated.

The king ordered them beheaded.

∦ He wishes the tapes.

or the sense of the main verb is changed:

I got the papers duplicated.
I got the papers.

whereas if the Ven is deleted from the noun plus adjunct sequence the remaining sentence is acceptable and the sense of the verb remains the same:

I delivered the papers duplicated.
I delivered the papers.

SVEN may be distinguished from SOBJBE by the fact that the Ven of SVEN is a true passive, whereas the Ven of SOBJBE is adjectival:

I got the papers duplicated.
∦ I got the papers beautiful.
I consider the house well-designed.
I consider the house beautiful.

Note: In distinguishing verbs which occur with SVEN from those which occur with SOBJBE : (1) add an adverbial left adjunct (well, badly, very, etc.) to the Ven. If this addition is acceptable, the verb being tested should be classified as SOBJBE:

I thought the house well-designed.
I consider him very reserved.

if the addition is marginal, the verb should be classified as SVEN:

?I ordered the house well-designed.
∦ I got the papers very duplicated.

(2) replace the Ven with a pure adjective (happy, small, intelligent, etc.). If the sentence is still acceptable, the verb being tested should be classified as SOBJBE, not SVEN.

∦ I ordered the house beautiful.
I considered the house beautiful.

If N_2 is a pronoun, it is accusative (WPOS5).

WORD LIST: assume, had, like, order, require, see, want, wish.

OBJLIST: (SVINGO):
The object string SVINGO must be distinguished from (1) the sequence noun plus adjunct and (2) the object string SOBJBE.
SVINGO may be distinguished from the noun plus adjunct sequence by the fact that

NOT OBJLIST: (SVEN):

I delivered the papers duplicated. (N + adjunct)

I considered the house well-designed. (OBJLIST: (SOBJBE))

Frame:

N_1 tV N_2 Ving (OBJ).

Examples:

They kept John waiting.

if the <u>Ving</u> is deleted from an occurrence of SVINGO either the remaining sentence is unacceptable:

> I left the book lying on the table.
> ∮ I left the book.

or the sense of the main verb is changed:

> John kept Mary waiting.
> John kept Mary.

Note: verbs such as <u>sketch,</u> <u>illustrate,</u> <u>photograph</u> may be ambiguous between the noun plus adjunct reading and the SVINGO reading, e.g.:

> He photographed the girl laughing.

(SVINGO = He photographed her laughing, not crying; N + adjunct = He photographed the girl who was laughing).
    SVINGO may be distinguished from SOBJBE by the fact that the <u>Ving</u> of SOBJBE is adjectival whereas the <u>Ving</u> of SVINGO is not (cf. OBJLIST: (SVEN)). Therefore, the <u>Ving</u> of SOBJBE occurs with certain adverbial left adjuncts (<u>quite,</u> <u>very,</u> etc.):

> I consider him very interesting.

whereas the <u>Ving</u> of SVINGO does not:

> ∮ They kept him very waiting.

    If N_2 is a pronoun, it is accusative (WPOS5).

WORD LIST: detect, discern, display, feel, find, have, illustrate, keep, leave, mind, observe, photograph, remember, sketch, start, watch, visualize.

He <u>has</u> the clock working now.

I <u>left</u> the book lying on the table.

We <u>observed</u> their intellect and their moral sense expanding.

I've <u>started</u> the machine going.

NOT OBJLIST: (SVINGO):

PBS covered the investigations involving Watergate. (N + adjunct).

I consider him interesting. (OBJLIST: (SOBJBE)).

OBJLIST: (SVO):
    If N_2 is a pronoun, it is accusative (WPOS5).
    Note: to avoid confusion with OBJLIST: (C1SHOULD) (<u>Suggest he go</u>), use pronouns for N_2 in the test frame for SVO.

Frame:

SUBJ <u>tV</u> N_2 V (OBJ)

Examples:

I <u>let</u> him go.

I <u>made</u> him sign a statement.

I <u>watched</u> him do it.

I <u>had</u> him pick up Mary at the station.

WORD LIST: have, let, make, observe, see, watch.

OBJLIST: (THATS):
    The verb of the embedded sentence is tensed.

Frame:

N <u>tV</u> <u>that</u> S   (V of embedded S = tV)

Both the verbs for which the <u>that</u> is optional (<u>He believes (that) the earth is flat</u>) and those for which it is obligatory (<u>He argues that it is impossible</u>) must be classified as occurring with OBJLIST: (THATS) (cf. OBJLIST: (ASSERTION)).

It should be noted that the computational treatment of forms like <u>It appears that John has left</u> is to define a small subclass, VSENT4 (=<u>appear</u>, <u>happen</u>, <u>remain</u>, <u>seem</u>, <u>turn out</u>), which can take OBJLIST: (THATS) where applicable, provided the subject of the VSENT4 is the expletive <u>It</u>.

Examples:

He <u>added</u> that they were happy.

He <u>wrote</u> that John was returning.

We <u>agree</u> that the matter should be settled.

I <u>know</u> that he was here.

We <u>estimate</u> that it will take five months.

It <u>appears</u> that John has left.

WORD LIST: add, agree, allow, answer, appear, argue, assume, believe, calculate, charge, claim, conclude, confirm, consider, demonstrate, deny, denote, detect, determine, discover, doubt, establish, estimate, evidence, expect, explain, feel, figure, find, follow, happen, imply, infer, intimate, know, learn, maintain, matter, mean, mention, note, notice, observe, provide, read, reason, report, rule, say, see, seem, sense, show, state, suggest, think, understand, write.

OBJLIST: (TOVO):

verbs classified as occurring with the object string TOVO include the aspectual verbs (those verbs which never occur with an overt subject in the contained sentence:

John tried to go.)

and those container verbs which occur with either an overt or a zeroed subject:

I want Mary to go.
I want to go.

Note: The <u>to</u> of OBJLIST: (TOVO) does not equal <u>in order to</u>; i.e., sequences such as <u>She washed to please her mother</u> (= <u>She washed in order to please her mother</u>), should not be considered as cases of OBJLIST: (TOVO)=

Frame:

N <u>tV</u> <u>to</u> V   (OBJ)

Examples:

He <u>appears</u> to like her.

He <u>attempted</u> to meet her.

He <u>claims</u> to know her.

He <u>agreed</u> to meet him.

She <u>expected</u> to leave.

She would <u>like</u> to see him.

WORD LIST: affect, agree, appear, ask, attempt, choose, claim, come, continue, demand, determine, expect, fail, happen, have, learn, like, long, mean, need, prefer, prepare, propose, seem, start, tend, use, want.

OBJLIST: (VENO):

The verb <u>have</u> (<u>has</u>, <u>had</u>) is classified as OBJLIST: (VENO) for its occurrence with the past participle:

John has gone.
We have been satisfied.

OBJLIST: (VINGO):

The <u>Ving</u> of the object string VINGO may occur either with an overt subject--

Frame:

N_1 <u>tV</u> (N_2's) Ving (OBJ)

He delayed his writing for two years.

--or a zeroed subject--

He delayed writing for two years.

In either case, the subject of <u>Ving</u> is understood exclusively as referring to the subject of <u>tV</u>. Cf. OBJLIST: (NSVINGO). Thus <u>She began doing it</u> is a case of OBJLIST: (VINGO) while <u>She favors doing it</u> is not.

<u>Examples:</u>

She <u>began</u> doing it.

He <u>delayed</u> writing the book for two years.

She has <u>continued</u> working.

They <u>started</u> eating at five o'clock.

They <u>stopped</u> eating at nine.

<u>NOT OBJLIST: (VINGO)</u>:

She favors doing it.

These new glasses will facilitate reading fine print.

He explained seeing to the blind man.

Simon opposes rationing gasoline.

He proposed boycotting grapes.

He really understands teaching.

WORD LIST: attempt, continue, delay, start, stop, try.

<u>OBJLIST: (VINGOFN)</u>:

The <u>Ving</u> in the object string VINGOFN may occur with either a possessive noun subject--

They imitated his singing of the song.

--or an article--

They imitated the singing of the song.

Since VINGOFN is more noun-like in its form than the NSVINGO object string, it is also helpful to include those phenomena which are characteristic of noun strings in the test frame, e.g.:

1) an adjective before the <u>Ving</u>:

You could not duplicate his tactful handling of the situation.

2) a plural <u>Ving</u> form:

They covered the bombings of Siagon.

<u>Frame:</u>

N tV $[^{N's}_{T}]$ (Adj) Ving <u>of</u> OBJ

<u>Examples:</u>

You could not <u>duplicate</u> his tactful handling of the situation.

They <u>imitated</u> his singing of the song.

They <u>covered</u> the bombing of Saigon.

They have <u>decreased</u> the sending of supplies.

They <u>delayed</u> the signing of the contract.

These factors <u>determine</u> the stating of the conditions.

He <u>directed</u> the editing of the manuscript.

The full ashtrays <u>evidence</u> the smoking of many cigars.

This will <u>facilitate</u> my understanding of the matter.

John <u>influenced</u> his handling of the situation.

He <u>noticed</u> the wording of the passage.

They have <u>restricted</u> the selling of gas.

WORD LIST: advance, affect, assess, block, cause, concern, consider, control, cover, decrease, denote, describe, direct, discuss, expect, explain, facilitate, film, follow, further, include, infer, influence, inhibit, investigate, limit, mention, notice, oppose, order, propose, question, report, restrict, review, study, time, vary.

OBJLIST: (VINGSTGPN):

As with verbs which occur with the object string NPN, those which occur with VINGSTGPN either require the complete VINGSTGPN object:

> They attributed his succeeding in business to his wife's business acumen.
> ∌ They attributed his succeeding in business.

or exhibit a strong selectional dependency between the verb and the preposition of VINGSTGPN:

> He charged his going home late to a heavy workload.
> ∌ He charged his going home late for a heavy workload.

This dependency helps to distinguish the object string VINGSTGPN from the sequence VINGSTG plus P N adjunct, e.g.:

> He described his frequent writing of letters with reluctance.
> He described his frequent writing of letters during his absence.
> He described his frequent writing of letters for money.

Note that VINGSTG here refers to either the object string NSVINGO or the object string VINGOFN.

The particular preposition(s) must be specified for each verb (WPOS15).

Frame:

N_1 $\underline{tV}$ P N_2 VINGSTG

N_1 $\underline{tV}$ VINGSTG P N_2

Examples:

They attributed his succeeding in business to his wife's business acumen.

He charged his going home late to a heavy workload.

They reported his seeing visitors to the nurse.

They limited his seeing visitors to certain hours.

He correlated the sinking of the ships with the bad weather in Pyraeus.

Dictionary Entry:

    ATTRIBUTE.
    TV: (OBJLIST: .3, ...)
.3 = VINGSTGPN: .15, PNVINGSTG: .15, ...
.15 = PVAL: (↓TO↓).

WORD LIST: add (to), associate (with), attribute (to), base (on, upon), charge (to), combine (with), compare (to, with), equate (with), exclude (from), identify (with), isolate (from), limit (to), mention (to), pattern (after), prefer (to), report (to, view (with).

V. Passive-Object Attributes of the Verb.

POBJLIST:

Because of the frequent occurrence of the passive construction in scientific writing, it is more economical to list the passive objects for each verb V in the word dictionary, than to compute them by a rule of passive 'omission'. The POBJLIST values of a given verb are listed under the past participle (Ven) form of the verb. The correspondence between active and passive objects used in the preparation of dictionary entries is as follows:

V has passive object	if V has one of the active objects
NULLOBJ	NSTGO, THATS, C1SHOULD, SNWH, FORTOVO, NSVINGO, VINGOFN, VINGO
P *	PN, PVINGSTG, PSNWH

VINGO	SVINGO
TOVO	NTOVO, NTOBE
NSTGO	NN (for N_1 or N_2), NTHATS, NSNWH
THATS	NTHATS
SNWH	NSNWH
PN*	NPN, PNTHATS, PNTHATSVO, PNSNWH, PNVINGSTG, PNHOWS
PVINGSTG*	NPVINGSTG
PVINGO*	NPVINGO
PSVINGO*	NPSVINGO
PSNWH*	NPSNWH
OBJBE	SOBJBE
ASOBJBE	SASOBJBE
VENPASS	SVEN
ASTG	NA
DSTG	ND
VO	SVO
DP1*	DP2, DP3, DP4, DPSN
DP1PN*	DP2PN, DP3PN, DP4PN
DP1P*	DP1PN

*Same P (or DP) subclass as in corresponding active object for given verb.

VI. Verb subclasses.

VBEREP:

A verb is in VBEREP if it occurs in the environments

SN--OBJ
It-- OBJ SN

where OBJ is either an NSENT1, an NSENT3, or ASENT1 (DOPT4, ultimate subject routine used in SN restrictions):

That the earth might revolve around the sun seemed an unlikely hypothesis.
It seemed an unlikely hypothesis that the earth might revolve around the sun.
For John to solve that problem remains easy.
It remains easy for John to solve that problem.

Most of these verbs also occur in other environments of be, but the one defined here is the only one used in restrictions.

Frame:

SN tV OBJ
It tV OBJ SN

(OBJ = NSENT1, NSENT3 ASENT1)

Examples:

That the earth might revolve around the sun seemed an unlikely hypothesis.

It seemed an unlikely hypothesis that the earth might revolve around the sun.

That John will arrive too soon appears a problem.

It appears a problem that John will arrive too soon.

To live here becomes easier as time goes on.

It becomes easier to live here as time goes on.

WORD LIST: appear, become, remain, seem.

VCOLLECTIVE:

a verb is in VCOLLECTIVE if it occur with a noun object which is PLURAL or conjoined, but does not occur with a noun object which is SINGULAR, unless the singular noun is NCOLLECTIVE (e.g., dust) or AGGREGATE (e.g., group) (WAGREE3):

> He collected his tools.
> He collected a pen, pencil and pad.
> The bookshelf collects dust.
> He collected a group around him.
> ∌ He collected a pen.

Also a verb is in VCOLLECTIVE if, when it occurs with a null object (see OBJ-LIST: NULLOBJ), its subject is either PLURAL or conjoined or, if SINGULAR, then AGGREGATE or NCOLLECTIVE (WAGREE3):

> People gathered at street corners.
> John, Mary and Bill gather in the Commons Room at noon.

> A group gathered around him.
> Dust gathered in the corner.
> ∌ A book gathered in the corner.

FRAME:

$$N \; \underline{tV} \; \begin{bmatrix} \text{NCOLLECTIVE} \\ \text{N: PLURAL} \\ \text{N:AGGREGATE} \\ \text{N and N} \end{bmatrix}$$

$$\begin{bmatrix} \text{NCOLLECTIVE} \\ \text{N:PLURAL} \\ \text{N:AGGREGATE} \\ \text{N and N} \end{bmatrix} \; \underline{tV} \; \text{NULLOBJ}$$

Examples:

Dust gathered in the corners.

These books will only gather dust.

∌ A book gathered in the corner.

The fortune accumulated while he was away.

He accumulated a fortune.

∌ Mary accumulated while he was away.

Blood collected in the sac.

The sac collected blood.

∌ A sponge collected in the sac.

WORD LIST: accumulate, cluster, collect, diffuse, gather, mass, scatter.

VEXP:

a verb is in VEXP if it does not ordinarily occur with a sentential SN subject, but in particular expressions specific to each verb, may occur with such a subject (WSN1, DOPT4) e.g.:

> ∌ That Mary has left has come.
> That Mary has left has come to his attention.

Note: verbs classed as VMOD are only those verbs which cannot be classed as VSENT2 (That he would think of running confirms my suspicions) or VMOD (That John was here presents a problem).

Frame:

SN tV + expression
∌ SN tV.

Examples:

That Mary has left has come to his attention.

For him to do that goes against the grain.

That he would make such a claim merits attention.

WORD LIST: come, go, merit.

VENDADJ:

a verb is in VENDADJ if its past participle Ven occurs adjectivally with an im-

Frames and Examples:

D Ven N

mediately preceding adverbial left adjunct other than <u>very</u> (WPOS12), e.g., <u>well-spoken</u> Cf. VVERYVING.

He was a well-<u>spoken</u> man.

⌀ He was a spoken man.

He is a high-<u>strung</u> fellow.

⌀ He is a strung fellow.

N <u>be</u> D <u>Ven</u>.

That man was well-<u>spoken</u>.

That fellow is high-<u>strung</u>.

WORD LIST: argue, place, read, regard, speak, tell, try.

VMOD:

a verb is in VMOD if it can occur in at least one of the following environments:

SN -- N_X
SN -- N_X P N
SN -- N N_X

where N_X is an NSENT3, e.g.:

That John was here presents a problem.
That John was here will give trouble for us.
That John was here will give us trouble.

VMOD can almost be defined extensionally for the verbs occurring with both N_XPN and NN_X (i.e., <u>make</u>, <u>present</u>, <u>give</u>). The class also includes <u>have</u> and such verbs as <u>compound</u>, <u>accentuate</u>, <u>augment</u>, etc.

Frame:

$$\text{SN } \underline{tV} \begin{bmatrix} N_X \\ N_X \text{ P N} \\ N \ N_X \end{bmatrix} \quad (N_X = \text{NSENT3})$$

Examples:

That John was here <u>presents</u> a problem (for us).

For John to leave now would only <u>compound</u> our difficulties.

For us to give up now would <u>make</u> trouble for those who will follow us.

That he would propose such a solution when planning to leave <u>has</u> inherent difficulties.

WORD LIST: give, have, make, present, augment, compound, complicate, increase, limit, modify, restrict.

VMOTION:

a verb is in VMOTION if it occurs with a right adjunct locative adverb (e.g.: <u>out</u>, <u>down</u>, <u>in</u>, <u>up</u>, <u>over</u>) (WPOS2).
The sequence VMOTION + locative adverb (<u>John walked up</u>) may be distinguished from the sequence tV + DP (<u>John measured up</u>) by the fact that the locative adverb permutes with the verb (<u>In walked John</u>) while the DP does not (⌀ <u>Up measured John</u>).

Frame:

N <u>tV</u> DLOC3

DLOC3 <u>tV</u> N

Examples:

John <u>climbed</u> down.

The rock <u>fell</u> down.

John <u>walked</u> out.

John <u>sauntered</u> in.

WORD LIST: come, drive, fall, flow, jump, run, shuttle, speed, swim, travel, walk.

V:PLURAL:

a tensed verb <u>tV</u> is in the subclass PLURAL if, in the defining environment for

Frame:

N:PLURAL <u>tV</u> (OBJ)

tV, N -- OBJ, it occurs with a PLURAL noun and not with a SINGULAR noun (WAGREE1). The verb subclass PLURAL, then, includes present tense verbs which lack the suffix -s (i.e., 3rd person plural present tense) and were.

VSENT1:

a verb is in VSENT1 if it occurs in both of the environments

SN -- OBJ
It -- OBJ SN

where OBJ is N or PN (NHUMAN), (DSN2, ultimate subject routine used in SN restrictions):

That no one answered alarmed him.
It alarmed him that no one answered.

Also, if a Ving occurs in the environments

It be Ving to V N.
N be Ving to V.

then the Ving is in VSENT1 (DSN6):

It is surprising to hear such allegations.
Such allegations are surprising to hear.

Cf. ASENT1: (AFORTO: (OBJEXT)).

Examples:

The men disregard the rules.
∅ The man disregard the rules.

Frames:

SN tV OBJ

It tV OBJ SN

Examples:

It concerned him that no one came.

That no one came concerned him.

It contents her that she is accepted by the family.

That she is accepted by the family contents her.

It disturbs him that she didn't come.

That she didn't come disturbs him.

It doesn't matter to him that he failed.

That he failed doesn't matter to him.

It has occurred to me that this is a non-problem.

That this is a non-problem has occurred to me.

WORD LIST: affect, antagonize, concern, confound, content, disturb, encourage, excite, interest, intrigue, matter, move, occur, shock, suit, surprise, trouble.

VSENT2:

A verb is in VSENT2 if its tensed form occurs in the environment SN -- SN (DOPT4, WSN1):

That he lied proves that he doesn't care.
∅ That he lied alarmed that he doesn't care.

Frame:

SN tV SN

Examples:

That John left shows that he doesn't care.

For him to say that means that he understands the problem.

How he did it explains why he did it.

That he ran the mile in 4 minutes demonstrates that it can be done.

WORD LIST: confirm, demonstrate, establish, explain, imply, indicate, mean, obscure, predict, prove, reveal, say, show.

VSENT3:

a verb is in VSENT3 if its tensed form occurs in the environment N -- SN and not in the environment SN -- SN:

Frame:

N tV SN   (where ∅ SN tV SN)

He knows that we are ready.

ɟ That time is running short knows that
we are ready.

    The passive form of a VSENT3 can occur
in the environment It -- SN (WSN2, ultimate
subject routine used in SN restrictions):

It was known that she left.

and in the environment SN -- (WSN1):

That she left was known.

Cf. VSENT1.

WORD LIST: add, argue, ask, believe, care, claim, conclude, consider, deny, determine, discover,
doubt, expect, find, know, learn, long, maintain, mention, note, notice, observe, propose, read,
reason, report, require, rule, state, suggest, think, understand.

VSENT4:

    a verb is in VSENT4 if it occurs in the
environment It -- SN but does not occur in
the environment SN -- (DSN13):

It seems that he left.

ɟ That he left seems.

It appears that they don't want to come.

ɟ That they don't want to come appears.

Cf. VSENT1.

Note: The computational treatment of
VSENT4 requires that the particular SN
strings (i.e., THATS, ASSERTION, etc.) that
occur with a given VSENT4 verb must be
named on the OBJLIST of that verb. Cf.
OBJLIST: ASSERTION, THATS, FORTOVO,
TOVO).

WORD LIST: appear, happen, remain, seem, turn out.

V:SINGULAR:

    a tensed verb tV is in subclass
SINGULAR if, in the environment N -- OBJ,
it occurs with a SINGULAR noun and not a
PLURAL noun (WAGREE1). The verb subclass SINGULAR, then, includes tensed verbs
carrying the suffix -s (3rd person singular
present tense) and was, am.

VVERYVING:

    a verb is in VVERYVING if either its
present participle Ving or its past participle

Examples:

He knows that we are ready.

We asked for the mail to be sent here.

They claim that the experiment is invalid.

I still maintain that this is correct.

Frame:

It tV SN   (where ɟ SN tV)

Examples:

It seems that he left.

ɟ That he left seems.

It appears that they don't want to come.

ɟ That they don't want to come appears.

It happens that she believes in this.

ɟ That she believes in this happens.

It turned out that he was innocent.

ɟ That he was innocent turned out.

It remains for us to find the cure.

ɟ For us to find the cure remains.

Frame:

N:SINGULAR tV (OBJ)

Examples:

The earth revolves on its axis.

ɟ The earth revolve on its axis.

Frames and Examples:

Ving:

Ven can occur in adjectival positions (i.e., as LN or as an object of be) with a left adjunct very (WPOS13):

> A very surprising result
> The result was very surprising.
> A very reserved man
> The man was very reserved.

Verbs occurring in their Ving form in predicate position which are not classed as VVERYVING are analyzed only as part of the is Ving (progressive tense) verb sequence (see OBJLIST: (OBJECTBE)).

Verbs occurring in their Ven form in predicate position which are not classed as VVERYVING (or VEND ADJ) are analyzed only as part of the passive construction (see OBJLIST: (OBJECTBE)).

Note: if both the Ving and the Ven forms of the verb must be specified for the subclass VVERYVING, then the subclass is assigned to the main entry of the verb (the infinitive). If only one form of the verb must be specified for VVERYVING, then the subclass is assigned to the appropriate form.

T (very) Ving N/ N be (very) Ving.

a very surprising result

a very becoming dress

a very interesting speaker

∅ a very walking business

The result was very surprising.

That dress is very becoming.

This speaker will be very interesting.

∅ That business is very walking.

Ven:

T (very) Ven N / N be (very) Ven.

a very reserved man

a very determined man

a very inhibited personality

∅ a very killed person

That man is very reserved.

That man is very determined.

His personality is very inhibited.

∅ That person was very killed.

WORD LIST: Ving: becoming, conflicting, designing, fitting, incriminating, intriguing, knowing, lasting, moving, stimulating, trying, understanding. Ven: concerned, contented, determined, involved, isolated. Both Ving and Ven: affect, antagonize, disturb, excite, inhibit, interest, limit, relax, surprise, trouble.

Appendix 4   Restriction Short Index

```
*  RESTRICTION SHORT INDEX
*
*
*  AGREEMENT RESTRICTIONS
*
*  WAGREE1        SUBJECT-VERB
*  WAGREE1A       SUBJECT-VERB IN QUESTION
*  WAGREE1B       SUBJECT-VERB IN OBES (PERMUTED BE-STRING)
*  WAGREE2A       SUBJECT-PREDICATE IN SOBJBE
*  WAGREE2B       SUBJECT-PREDICATE IN SASOBJBE
*  WAGREE2        SUBJECT-PREDICATE
*  WAGREE3        RECIPROCAL AND COLLECTIVE VERBS
*  WAGREE4        N-LN
*  WAGREE5        HOST AND APPOSITION N
*  WAGREE6        SAWHICHSTG: VERB IS SINGULAR
*  WAGREE7        RSUBJ IN SA AGREES WITH SUBJECT
*  WAGREE8        *AMONG*, *BETWEEN* REQUIRE PLURAL N
*  WAGREE9        ADJUNCTS OF N AGREE IN NUMBER
*
*  FCR AGREEMENT SEE ALSO:
*  WG1
*
*
*
*  CCMMA RESTRICTIONS
*
*  DCOM1          NO COMMA BEFORE CERTAIN RN STRINGS
*  DCOM2          CONDITIONS ON COMMA BEFORE VERB
*  DCOM3          SA STRINGS OBJBESA, SOBJBESA REQUIRE COMMA
*  DCOM3A         SA STRINGS VINGO, VENPASS REQUIRE COMMA - WITH EXCEPTIONS
*  DCOM3B         TOVO AS SA REQUIRES COMMA IF NOT POST-OBJ
*  DCOM4          COMMA BEFORE APPOSITION
```

Naomi Sager, Natural Language Information Processing: A Computer Grammar of English and Its Applications
Copyright © 1981 by Addison-Wesley Publishing Company, Inc., Advanced Book Program.   ISBN 0-201-06769-2

```
*  DCOM5          NO PUNCTUATION COMMA IN QN BEFORE QNREP
*  DCOM6          NO COMMA BEFORE RV
*
*  WCOM1          NO COMMA IN TPOS
*  WCOM1A         NO COMMA IN NPOS EXCEPT WITH CONJ
*  WCOM2          NO COMMA BEFORE NON-NULL CORE OF LNR
*  WCOM2A         NO COMMA IN QN BETWEEN Q AND N EXCEPT WITH CONJ
*  WCOM2B         NO COMMA BETWEEN LN AND LVINGR IN VINGOFN
*  WCOM3          COMMA REQUIRED AFTER SOME RN STRINGS IF COMMA PRECEDES
*  WCOM3A         COMMA OR ENDMARK REQUIRED AFTER DSTG IN SA IF COMMA
*                 PRECEDES
*  WCOM4          NO COMMA BEFORE OBJ UNLESS IN CONJ STRING OR AFTER ADJUNCT
*  WCOM5          COMMA REQUIRED AFTER LONG SA BEFORE OBJECT
*  WCOM6          COMMA REQUIRED AFTER SOME STRING INITIAL SA
*  WCOM8          NO COMMA BEFORE HEADLESS WHENS IF HOST IS TIME NOUN
*  WCOM10         COMMA REQUIRED BEFORE APPOSITION EXCEPT AS STATED (SEE DCOM6)
*
*  FOR CCMMA SEE ALSO
*  DSN2
*  DPOS5
*
*
*
*  CCMPARATIVE RESTRICTIONS
*
*  DCOMP1
*  DCOMP2         Q-ASSERT OPTION IS ONLY IN LAR (↓ A MAN RICHER THAN HE IS...↓)
*  DCOMP3         NO OPTION BUT Q-CONJ AFTER EMPTY NODE; REDUNDANT, OF WCONJ3
*  DCOMP4         Q-PHRASE OPTION IN CENTER-LIKE STRING ONLY
*  DCOMP5         Q-INVERT OPTION IN ASSERTION ONLY
*  DCOMP6         COMP-MARKER HAS LOCAL SCOPE (↓MORE↓ ON X ONLY IN ↓MORE X THAN Y↓)
*
*  WCOMP1         RESTRICT VERB AND OBJECT IN Q-ASSERT
*  WCOMP2         Q-INVERT- CERTAIN VERBS ONLY
*  WCOMP3         RESTRICT PRECOMPARATIVE TENSE IF TENSE IN Q-INVERT IS
*                 NOT EMPTY
*  WCOMP4         Q-ASSERT IN ADJINRN
*  WCOMP-ADJ      ASSIGN NODE ATTRIBUTE COMP-MARKER OR AS1-MARKER FOR
*                 COMPARATIVE ADJ OR LA=↓AS↓
*  WCOMP-D        ASSIGN COMP-MARKER FOR COMPARATIVE D OR AS1-MARKER FOR
*                 D=↓AS↓
*  WCOMP-Q1       ASSIGN COMP-MARKER FOR COMPARATIVE Q OR AS1-MARKER FOR
*                 LQ=↓AS↓
*  WCOMP-Q1A      ASSIGN COMP-MARKER FOR COMPARATIVE Q IN CPDNUMBER
*  WCOMP-Q2       CONDITIONS FOR MOVING COMP-MARKER OR AS1-MARKER UP IN LAR1
*  WCOMP-Q2A      CONDITIONS FOR MOVING COMP-MARKER OR AS1-MARKER UP IN
*                 CPDNUMBER
*  WCOMP-Q2B      CONDITIONS FOR MOVING COMP-MARKER OR AS1-MARKER UP IN
*                 LQR
*  WCOMP-Q2C      CONDITIONS FOR MOVING COMP-MARKER OR AS1-MARKER UP IN
*                 LNR OR LAR
*  WCOMP-Q2D      CONDITIONS FOR MOVING COMP-MARKER OR AS1-MARKER UP IN
*                 STRING
*  WCOMP5         NODE ABOVE THANSTG MUST HAVE COMP-MARKER
*  WCOMP5A        ↓THAN↓ IN SAWHICHSTG SUB2: NODE ABOVE HAS COMP-MARKER
*  WCOMP5B        ↓THAN↓ IN WHS-N: CHECK IMMEDIATE LNR OR STRING FOR
*                 COMP-MARKER
*  WCOMP5C        NODE ABOVE ASSTG HAS AS1-MARKER
*  WCOMP5D        STRING ABOVE SAWHICHSTG OR SUB2 HAS AS1-MARKER
*  WCOMP5E        STRING OR LNR ABOVE WHS-N HAS AS1-MARKER
*  WCOMP6         THANSTG: CHECK FOR COMP-MARKER AND ASSIGN THAN MARKER TO
*                 COMPARATIVE
*  WCOMP6A        ↓THAN↓ IN SAWHICHSTG, SUB2: SEE WCOMP6
```

```
* WCOMP6B      +THAN+ IN WHS-N: SEE WCOMP6
* WCOMP6C      ASSTG: CHECK FOR AS1-MARKER AND ASSIGN AS2-MARKER TO
               FIRST +AS+
* WCOMP6D      +AS+ IN SAWHICHSTG, SUB2: SEE WCOMP6C
* WCOMP6DD     GET SUB2 WHEN NOT IN COMPARATIVE STRING
* WCOMP6E      +AS+ IN WHS-N: SEE WCOMP6C
* WCOMP7       [W94] FOR +THAN+/+AS+ IN SUB2: RESTRICT VERB IN SUB2
* WCOMP7A      FOR +THAN+/+AS+ IN SAWHICHSTG ALLOW VERBS OR OBJECTS
* WCOMP8       THANSTG, ASSTG: RESTRICTS PRECOMPARATIVE VERB DEPENDING
               ON POSTCOMPARATIVE VERB
*
*
*
* CONJUNCTION RESTRICTIONS
*
* DCONJ0       ELIMINATE REDUNDANCY WHEN CONJOINING ON HIGHER LEVEL
* DCONJ0A      ELIMINATE REDUNDANCY WHEN CONJOINING VENPASS
               OBJECTS OF +BE+
* DCONJ0B      ELIMINATE REDUNDANCY WHEN CONJOINING VINGO
               OBJECTS OF +BE+
* DCONJ0I      ELIMINATE REDUNDANCY WHEN CONJOINING LAR
               OBJECTS OF +BE+
* DCONJ0J      ELIMINATE REDUNDANCY WHEN CONJOINING LQNR
               OBJECTS OF +BE+
* DCONJ0K      ELIMINATE REDUNDANCY WHEN CONJOINING PN
               OBJECTS OF +BE+
* DCONJ1       DON+T CONJOIN TO EMPTY STRING OR NULL OPTION OF COMMASTG
* DCONJ2       DON+T ATTACH CONJUNCTION TO RIGHT OF ANOTHER CONJUNCTION
* DCONJ2A      DON+T ATTACH CONJUNCTION +,+ TO THE RIGHT OF ANOTHER
               CONJUNCTION
* DCONJ3       SACONJ=SA WHEN RARE SWITCH IS OFF
* DCONJ4       GENERATE OPTIONS FOR Q-CONJ
* DCONJ5       ATTACH CONJUNCTION IN LXR OR STRING
* DCONJ5A      ATTACH CONJUNCTION IN LXR OR CERTAIN STRING
* DCONJ5B
* DCONJ5C      NO CONJOINING AFTER EMPTY SA
* DCONJ5D      ATTACH CONJUNCTION COMMA IN LXR OR CERTAIN STRINGS
* DCONJ6       ALLOW SUBJ CONJ SUBJ FOR CERTAIN VALUES OF SUBJ
* DCONJ7       ALLOW OBJ CONJ OBJ FOR CERTAIN VALUES OF OBJ
* DCONJ8       DON+T ALLOW CONJUNCTION +,+ IF NEXT OR PREVIOUS WORD
               A CONJUNCTION
* DCONJ8A      ALLOW PUNCTUATION +,+ IF NEXT TO NONEMPTY ATOMIC
* DCONJ9       RESTRICTS CONJUNCTION COMMA
* DCONJ10      CONJUNCTION +TO+ ALLOWED IN CERTAIN STRINGS
* DCONJ10A     CONJUNCTION +-+ ALLOWED IN CERTAIN STRINGS
* DCONJ11      ALLOW PARENTHESES NEXT TO NONEMPTY ATOMIC
* DCONJ13      ONLY COMPATIBLE RN+S CAN BE CONJOINED TO EACH OTHER
* DCONJ14      NSTGT IS NOT ALLOWED IN SACONJ IN LNR
*
* WCONJ1       Q-CONJ CANNOT BE EMPTY
* WCONJ2       TWO RIGHT ADJUNCTS CANNOT BE CONJOINED TO EACH OTHER
               WHEN EMPTY
* WCONJ3       RULE OUT REDUNDANCY WHEN CONJOINED STRINGS HAVE FIRST
               OR LAST ELEMENTS BOTH NULL
* WCONJ3A      RULES OUT REDUNDANCY WHEN TWO LN+S ARE CONJOINED
* WCONJ4       RESTRICTS CONJOINING IN LN
* WCONJ6       ASSIGNS SCOPE MARKER
* WCONJ7       SCOPE MARKER MUST BE MATCHED BY CONJUNCTION
* WCONJ8       CONJUNCTION +,+ ALLOWED IN CERTAIN CONSTRUCTIONS
* WCONJ9       TWO CONJOINED NOUNS MUST HAVE COMPATIBLE SUBCLASSES
* WCONJ10      TWO OBJECTS OF +BE+ MUST BE COMPATIBLE WHEN CONJOINED
               TO EACH OTHER
* WCONJ11      DISQUALIFY Q-CONJ=NVAR=NULLN
```

```
*  WCONJ12      ADJUNCTS ARE LOCAL IN CONJOINED NOUN PHRASES
*  WCONJ50      ASSIGN PRE AND POST CONJUNCTION NODE ATTRIBUTES
*
*
*
*
*  MIN-WORD RESTRICTIONS
*
*  DMIN1        PN IN RNP, ()SA, ()RV, RA, OBJECT, PASSOBJ: NOT PREVIOUSLY SAME
*  DMIN2        DSTG IN RW, LV, LQ: NOT PREVIOUSLY RW, LV, LQ, RV, SA
*  DMIN3        DSTG IN ()RV: NOT PREVIOUSLY RW, LV, LQ, RV, SA
*  DMIN4        DSTG IN ()SA: NOT PREVIOUSLY RW, LV, LQ, RV, SA
*  DMIN5        D IN LCS: NOT PREVIOUSLY RW LV, LQ, RV, SA
*  DMIN6        VENPASS IN ()RN, ()SA: NOT PREVIOUSLY RN, SA
*  DMIN7        VINGO IN ()RN, ()SA: NOT PREVIOUSLY RN, SA
*  DMIN8        TOVO IN ()RN, ()SA: NOT PREVIOUSLY RN, SA, RA
*  DMIN9        LCS CSSTG IN ()SA: NOT PREVIOUSLY SA
*  DMIN10       ASSERTION: NOT PREVIOUSLY AS THATS IN OBJECT OR PASSOBJ
*  DMIN11       COMPAR IN ()SA: NOT PREVIOUSLY SA
*  DMIN12       SAWH IN ()SA: NOT PREVIOUSLY SA
*  DMIN13       DSTG IN ()RV [INLXR]: NOT PREVIOUSLY LQ, LA
*  DMIN14       RSUBJ IN () SA:  NOT PREVIOUSLY SA
*  DMIN15       NSTGT IN () SA:  NOT PREVIOUSLY SA
*  DMIN16       QN IN () RV, LP:  NOT PREVIOUSLY RV OR LP
*  DMIN17       PDATE IN () SA, RNP:  NOT PREVIOUSLY SA OR RNP
*
*  NOUN PHRASE RESTRICTIONS
*  1-49 LN AND CORE, 50-99 RN
*
*  DN1          CORE=NULLN: CONDITIONS ON LN
*  DN2          PRE-Q ADJ IS ONLY IN QPOS, NOT IN LTR [*THE LAST 3*]
*  DN3          NSPOS HAS NO NAMES
*  DN4          CORE=NULLN, SECOND PARSE RARE IF CURRENT WORD=N, CF WMED2 1979
*  DN50         S-N: CONDITIONS ON STARTING LN
*  DN51         S-N: CONDITIONS ON HOST*S LN IF HOST*S CORE IS NULLN
*  DN52         RIGHT ADJUNCTS OF INDEFINITE PRONOUNS AND NAMES
*  DN53         MORE ON RIGHT ADJUNCTS OF INDEFINITE PRONOUNS AND NAMES
*  DN54         RIGHT ADJUNCTS OF *YOU* AND *WE*
*  DN55         RIGHT ADJUNCT OF *YOU*, *WE* AND INDEFINITE PRONOUNS
$  DN56         MORE ON ADJUNCTS OF *YOU*, *WE* AND INDEFINITE PRONOUNS
*  DN57         NO APPOS ON APPOS
*  DN58         PSNWH AS RN: HOST IS NSENT OF AWH TYPE
*
*  WN1          Q-T COMBINATIONS IN TPOS
*  WN2          PRE-ARTICLE Q IN TPOS
*  WN3          PRE-NOUNPHRASE ADVERBS, NULL T
*  WN4          CHOOSE LQ NEAR Q
*  WN5          PRE-ADJ: SUBCLASS IS APREQ OR SUPERLATIVE [*THE BEST*]
*  WN6          *HAD* NEVER IN APOS [*THE HAD MEASLES]
*  WN7          NO PLURAL N IN COMPOUND ADJECTIVE (LCDA, LCDVA)
*  WN8          NO PLURAL N IN COMPOUND NOUN (NPOS)
*  WN9          COUNT NOUN CONSTRAINTS
*  WN10         IF CORE OF LNR=VING, IT IS PLURAL OR HEAD OF COMPOUND NOUN
*  WN11         NAMESTG AND PRO IN NVAR HAVE RESTRICTED LN
*  WN12         N IN NVAR IS NOT NAME [NAMES ARE DONE BY NAMESTG]
*  WN13         TWO-PART NAME IS NOT ALSO N WITH APPOS
*  WN14         TITLE N (IN LNAME) IS NTITLE OR NCOUNT3
*  WN15         NAME-PART N (IN LNAME) IS N:NAME
*  WN16         CORE OF NAMESTG IS N:NAME
*  WN16A        CORE OF LNAMESR IS NS: NAME
*  WN17         CORE OF LNSR IS NOT N:NAME [DONE BY LNAMESR]
*  WN50         ADJ IN RN
```

```
*  WN51        PN AS RN
*  WN52        CORE OF APPOS IS NOT NULLN
*  WN53        TOVO-N AS RN IN SUBJECT OCCURS WITH VERB +BE+ ONLY
*
*  FOR NOUN PHRASE SEE ALSO:
*  DG2
*  DG3
*  DCOM4
*  WCOM10
*
*
*
*  OPTIMIZATION RESTRICTIONS
*
*  DOPT1        DOPT1 CHECKS WORD STARTING ADVERB STRING [WPOS1]
*  DOPT1A       DSTG IN ()SA
*  DOPT1B       DSTG IN ()RN
*  DOPT1C       DSTG IN RW
*  DOPT1D       DSTG IN LV
*  DOPT1F       D IN LCS
*  DOPT1G       D IN LT
*  DOPT1H       DSTG IN OBJBE, ()OBES
*  DOPT1I       D IN LW
*  DOPT1J       DSTG IN LQ
*  DOPT1K       DSTG IN LP
*  DOPT1L       DSTG IN TSUBJVO
*  DOPT1N       DSTG IN LVSA
*  DOPT1P       DSTG IN OBJECT
*  DOPT1G       DSTG IN ()RV
*  DOPT1R       DSTG IN LA
*  DOPT2        2 WORDS AHEAD
*  DOPT3        3 WORDS AHEAD
*  DOPT4        SN AS SUBJECT: VSENT AHEAD
*  DOPT5        SASOBJBE: +AS+ AHEAD
*  DOPT6        NSTGT: NTIME1 WITH TIMETAG OR NTIME2 IS FIRST OR SECOND N AHEAD
*  DOPT7        VINGO, SVINGO, NSVINGO, VINGOFN: VING AHEAD
*  DOPT8        NNN: CURRENT WORD AND NEXT WORD CONSTRAINTS
*  DOPT8A       NNN AS OPTION 1 OF NPOS:   NEXT WORD IS NOT SPWORD
*  DOPT8B       NNN AS OPTION 3 OF NPOS:   NEXT WORD IS SPWORD
*  DOPT9        TOVO, FORTOVO, NTOVO: +TO+ AHEAD
*  DOPT10       OBES: +BE+ AHEAD
*  DOPT11       QPOS: CURRENT WORD IS Q OR D:DLQ OR SUITABLE ADJPREQ-WORD
*  DOPT12       LNSR, LNAMESR, QNS: NS AHEAD
*  DOPT13       ASSERTION: TV OR W AHEAD IF NOT IN CONJUNCTION OR C1SHOULD [WOPT1]
*  DOPT17       QUESTION: QUESTION MARK AHEAD
*  DOPT18       LNR: CURRENT WORD TO START LNR
*  DOPT19       NON-NULL RV, RN: CURRENT WORD IS NOT AN ENDMARK WORD
*  DOPT19A      NON-NULL SA: CURRENT WORD IS NOT AN ENDMARK WORD
*  DOPT19B      NON-NULL RA: CURRENT WORD IS NOT AN ENDMARK WORD
*  DOPT19C      IN RN VENPASS IF CURRENT WORD IS TV, IT IS ALSO VEN, V,
*               ADJ, D, OR P
*  DOPT19D      IN SA IF CURRENT WORD IS TV, IT IS ALSO VEN, N, ADJ, D,
*               OR P
*  DOPT19E      IN OBJBE IN OBJECTBE IF CURRENT WORD IS TV, IT IS ALSO
*               VEN, N, ADJ, D, OR P
*  DOPT20       LCS CSSTG: CURRENT WORD IS CS OR D:LCS
*  DOPT20A      LCS CSSTG IN SAZ: CURRENT WORD IS CS OR D:LCS
*  DOPT21       WHN: CURRENT WORD IS SUITABLE WH WORD
*  DOPT23       QN, QNREP, QNS: CURRENT WORD IS Q OR D:DLQ
*  DOPT24       NQ: CURRENT WORD IS N:NPREQ OR NAME [WN12]
*  DOPT25       ADJADJ: CURRENT WORD, CF WPOS3
*  DOPT27       RSUBJ: CURRENT WORD
*  DOPT28       PN IN SCALESTG: THERE IS ADJ:ASCALE OR N:NSCALE AHEAD
*
```

```
* WCPT1        ASSERTION: REPEATS DOPT13 FOR WORDS FOLLOWING SUBJECT
*
*
*
* POSITION RESTRICTIONS
*
* DPOS1        TREATMENT OF ↓IS TO↓: ↓HE IS TO BEGIN TOMORROW↓
* DPOS2        SUB1 - CERTAIN CS WORDS NOT STRING INITIAL
* DPOS3        RNSUBJ REQUIRES HOST SUBJECT
* DPOS4A       RSUBJ NOT STRING-INITIAL
* DPOS4B       RNSUBJ IS POST-OBJECT
* DPOS4C       SUB7 IS POST-OBJECT
* DPOS5        SAWHICHSTG WITH ↓WHICH↓ IS POST OBJECT AND NEEDS COMMA
* DPOS6        SAWHICHSTG WITH STG HEAD ↓THAN↓ IS POST OBJECT
* DPOS7        SOME SA STRINGS ONLY IN CENTERLIKE OR VERBAL STRINGS
* DPOS9        SAWHICHSTG ONLY IN CENTERLIKE OR VERBAL STRINGS
* DPOS10       D AS LVSA ONLY WHEN HOST STRING IS SA OR RN (NOT OBJECT)
* DPOS11       ↓OR NOT↓ IN QUESTION
* DPOS12       NVSA IS NOT STRING-INITIAL
* DPOS13       PROSENT IS PRECEDED BY ↓AND↓
* DPOS14       RNWH AS POST OBJECT RNSUBJ IS RARE
* DPOS15       SACONJ
* DPOS16       FORCE POST-OBJ RV TO BE IN DEEPEST NESTED OBJECT
* DPOS17       SAME AS DPOS16 FOR POST-OBJ SA
* DPOS18       OBJBE IN SUBO: NO ADJ OR D AFTER ↓AS↓
* DPOS19       PN IN SA: P≠OF EXCEPT STRING INITIAL: ↓OF 3 SAMPLES,
               1 WAS POSITIVE↓
* DPOS 20      SO/SUCH COMPARATIVE
* DPOS21       ↓BE↓ DOES NOT TAKE RV=PN
* DPOS22       TOVO PREFERRED AS PASSOBJ NOT SA WHEN PASSOBJ IS POSSIBLE
*
* WPOS1        WPOS1 CHECKS ADVERB SUBCLASS
* WPOS1A       IN () SA
* WPOS1B       IN ()RN
* WPOS1C       IN RW
* WPOS1D       IN LV
* WPOS1F       IN LCS
* WPOS1G       IN LT
* WPOS1H       IN OBJBE, OBES
* WPOS1HH      FORCES ↓NOT↓ BEFORE PREDICATE ADJ TO BE ADJUNCT OF ↓BE↓
* WPOS1I       IN LW
* WPOS1J       IN LQ
* WPOS1K       IN LP
* WPOS1L       IN TSUBJVO
* WPOS1M       IN ND
* WPOS1N       IN LVSA
* WPOS1P       IN OBJECT DSTG
* WPOS1Q       IN SAZ
* WPOS1R       IN PASSOBJ DSTG
* WPOS2        ADVERB IN RV
* WPOS3        ADVERB IN LA
* WPOS4        ADVERB IN LA AS ADJUNCT OF VING OR VEN
* WPOS5        SUBJECT PRONOUN IS NOMINATIVE EXCEPT IN STATED STRINGS
* WPOS6        OBJECT PRONOUN IS NOT NOMINATIVE
* WPOS7        PRO IN RSUBJ IS PROSELF
* WPOS8        PRO IN SUBO IF INDEFINITE THEN HAS ADJUNCT
* WPOS9A       NO PRO AS CORE OF OBJBE IN OBJBESA
* WPOS9B       PRO CORE OF OBJBE IN SUBO IS INDEFINITE
* WPOS10       WELLFORMEDNESS OF NSTGT
* WPOS11       IN PA, ADJ IS AINPA, AND P IS ↓IN↓ OR ↓AT↓
* WPOS12       VENDADJ REQUIRES LEFT ADJUNCT
* WPOS13       ADJECTIVAL VING OR VEN PREDICATE IS VVERYVING
```

```
* WPOS14        VEN TAKEN ADJECTIVALLY ONLY IF IT HAS POBJLIST
* WPOS15        IF P MATCHES P ON PVAL LIST, P-STRING IS OK OBJECT
                AND PREFERRED AS OBJECT NOT RV
* WPOS15A       SAME FOR PVINGSTG VS SUB3
* WPOS15B       SAME FOR PVINGSTG VS SUB4
* WPOS16        SIMILAR TO WPOS15 FOR DP OBJECTS
* WPOS17        PN IN RV: ONLY CERTAIN PREPOSITIONS
* WPOS18        VENPASS IN SA IS USUALLY MORE THAN ONE WORD
* WPOS19        HEAVY SA IN PROSENT
* WPOS20        TOVO AS OBJECT VS, TOVO AS SA
* WPOS21        LEFTMOST D IN ADVERB NEST
* WPOS22        OBJ=NN: FIRST N IS HUMAN (INDIRECT OBJECT) OR VERB=VMOD
* WPOS23        QUESTION CENTER NEEDS QUESTION MARK
* WPOS27        SA STRINGS DO NOT FLANK EMPTY OBJECT
* WPOS27A       SA STRINGS DO NOT FLANK EMPTY TENSE
* WPOS28        WHETHS AS SA
* WPOS29        TOVO-N NOT ALLOWED IN RN OF SUBJECT OF SOBJBE IF N
*               IS AVAILABLE IN OBJBE
* WPOS30        NO ADJUNCTS BETWEEN VERB AND SHORT DP OBJECT
* WPOS31        TOBE STRING
* WPOS32        MORE ON TOBE STRING
* WPOS33        SUB2 WITH CS2=+AS+ VS, AS-AS COMPARATIVE
* WPOS34        SUB8 WITH CS8=+AS+ VS, AS-AS COMPARATIVE
* WPOS35        N IN DAYYEAR IS NMONTH
* WPOS36        SUB1:.FOR SOME CS1 WORDS SUB1 IS NOT STRING INITIAL
*
* FOR POSITION SEE ALSO:
* WN1
* WN2
* WN3
* WN4
* WN5
* WG2
* WG7
* WCOM7
* WVC9
* WAGREE8
* WVC6
* WVC7
* WSN6
* WSN7
* WSN10
* DCPT1
*
*
*
* QUANTITIES RESTRICTIONS
*
* DG1           QN AS RN HAS NON-EMPTY SCALESTG
* DQ2           QN HAS NO PN SCALESTG IN LN [SEE ALSO WQ13]
* DG3           QN WITH SCALESTG IN LN
* DG4           QN AS RV ONLY POST-OBJECT
*
*
* WG1           QN: SUBCLASS CHECK AND AGREEMENT
* WG1A          PERUNIT
* WG1B          QNS: NS IS NUNIT
* WG2           SCALESTG ADJ IS ASCALE OR COMPARATIVE
* WG3           SCALESTG PN HAS N:NSCALE
* WG4           QVAR COMPOUND NUMBER: FRACTION OR QNUMBER SEQUENCE (W/EXC,)
* WG5           NUMBRSTG: Q IS QNUMBER
* WG6           RSUBJ: Q OR T ARE QROVING (+THEY ARE ALL COMING+)
* WG7           QN IN LP ONLY BEFORE CERTAIN P
```

```
* WQ8         FORCE Q+N IN OBJBE-POSITION TO BE QN IN ASTG, NOT LN N
* WQ9         FORCE Q+N FOLLOWING QN OCCURRENCE TO BE QNREP
* WQ10        NQ: N IS NPREQ OR NAME; +Q+ MAY NLETTER OR Q
* WQ11        FORCE N+Q+N TO BE N+QN, NOT NQ+N
* WQ12        FORCE N+Q TO BE NQ, NOT LN IN NVAR WITH NEXT WORD Q
* WQ13        QN AS RN HAS NON-EMPTY SCALESTG
* WQ14        FORCE + PERCENT + INTO REQUIRED N OF QN IF NEXT WORD IS NOT N
*
*
*
* SELECTION RESTRICTIONS
*
*
* WSEL1       SUITABLE OBJECT N FOR GIVEN V
* WSEL2       SUITABLE SUBJECT N FOR GIVEN V
* WSEL3       N+VING: N OK IN NPOS IF N IS OK OBJECT OF VING
* WSEL4       N+VING AS COMPOUND ADJECTIVE: SAME CONSTRAINT AS WSEL3
* WSEL5       VENPASS AS RN: HOST MUST BE OK OBJECT OF ACTIVE FORM OF VERB
* WSEL6       N+VING AS HOST N WITH VINGO IN RN
* WSEL7       VING+N: VING OK IN APOS IF N IS OK SUBJECT OF VING:
*             ALSO VEN+N OK IN APOS IF N IS OK OBJECT OF ACTIVE FORM OF
*             VEN
* WSEL8       SUBJECT OF PASSIVE VERB MUST BE OK OBJECT OF ACTIVE FORM
*             OF SAME VERB
*
*
*
* SENTENCE NOMINALIZATION RESTRICTIONS
*
* DSN1        SN AS OBJECT OF BE
* DSN2        SN AS RA (+IT+ SUBJECT)
* DSN3        CHOICE OF SN OPTION IN RN, RA DEPENDING ON HOST SUBCLASS
* DSN4        SN FOLLOWING VERB (+IT+ SUBJECT)
* DSN5        SN AS RN (INCLUDING +IT+ SUBJECT)
* DSN6        TOVO-N AS RA
* DSN7        ASPECTUAL ADJ WITH TOVO
* DSN8        SN AS SUBJECT IN SN STRING IS RARE
* DSN9        NO LV IN VINGOFN (+THE FREQUENTLY WRITING OF LETTERS+)
* DSN10       DP4 IN VING OF N STRING ONLY (+THE BREAKING UP OF THE GAME+)
* DSN11       CONSTRAINTS ON VERB FOR TENSELESS STRINGS. (SEE WVC1)
* DSN11A      TENSELESS TOVO, TOBE, SVO, C1SHOULD (SEE WSN4)
* DSN11B      NO MODAL IN SVO
* DSN12       EMBEDDED QUESTION: HOST IS NSENT1: AWH
* DSN13       VSENT4 IN +IT+ FORM (+IT SEEMS THAT S+)
*
* WSN1        CORRECT VERB OR PREDICATE FOR SN AS SUBJECT
* WSN2        REFINES DSN4 FOR PASSIVE VSENT3
* WSN3        TOVO AS SUBJECT AND OBJECT OF +BE+
* WSN4        TENSE IN C1SHOULD
* WSN5        C1SHOULD AS SUBJECT, NO DROPPING OF +THAT+
* WSN6        WHETHS AS SUBJECT DOES NOT BEGIN WITH +IF+
* WSN7        WHETHS AS SA CONTAINS OR-STRING OR +OR NOT+
* WSN8        HUMAN OBJECT IS SOME OBJECT NOMINALIZATION
* WSN9        SVINGO  AS SUBJECT DOES NOT BEGIN WITH PRONOUN
* WSN10       AMBIGUITY OF NSVINGO AND VINGOFN
* WSN11       WELLFORMEDNESS OF VINGOFN
*
*
*
* VERB AND CENTER STRING RESTRICTIONS
*
* DVC1        ACTIVE OBJECT: EDIT OPTIONS BY OBJLIST OF V
* DVC2        PASSIVE OBJECT: EDIT OPTIONS BY POBJLIST OF V
```

```
* DVC3         TSUBJVO, YESNOQ: PERMUTED TENSE+V IN VERB1, VERB2
* DVC4         TSUBJVO, YESNOQ: PERMUTED +HAVE+/+BE+ NULL (SEE WVC5)
* DVC5         +HAD+ NOT TAKEN AS PASSIVE
*
* WVC1         NO TENSE WORD BEFORE TENSED VERB
* WVC2         NO +DO+ BEFORE +BE+
* WVC3         WELLFORMEDNESS OF NON-PASSIVE VEN OBJECT STRING (VENO)
* WVC4         VEN IN PASSIVE HAS POBJLIST
* WVC5         LTVR IN VERB1 IS PERMUTED +HAVE+, +BE+   (SEE DVC3,4)
* WVC6         VERB IN OBES IS +BE+
* WVC7         NEGATIVE FIRST ELEMENT IN TSUBJVO CENTER
* WVC8         +SINCE+ AS P IN PN IN OBJBE ONLY WITH +IT+ SUBJECT
* WVC9         VERB IN +THERE+ STRING IS +BE+ OR BE-REPLACER
* WVC10        NO INTRODUCER IN A CONJUNCT
*
* FOR VERB AND CENTER STRING SEE ALSO:
* WPOS23
* WSN4
* WSN5
*
*
*
* WH-STRING RESTRICTIONS
* 1-49 OMISSION, 50-99 OTHER WH WELLFORMEDNESS
*
* DWH1         SET MUSTOMIT IN N-OMITTING WH STRINGS
* DWH1A        SET MUSTOMPN FLAG IN PN-OMITTING WH STRINGS
* DWH1B        SET MUSTOMIT/MUSTOMPN IN CONJUNCTION STRING IN SCOPE OF
*              OMITTING STRING
* DWH51        +WHAT+ AS STG HEAD NOT OK IN RN
*
* WWH1         COMPLETED N-OMITTING WH STRING MUST HAVE DIDOMIT FLAG
* WWH1A        COMPLETED PN-OMITTING WH-STRING MUST HAVE DIDOMPN FLAG
* WWH1B        Q-CONJ WITH MUSTOMIT MUST HAVE DIDOMIT; SAME FOR PN CASE
* WWH2         NULLWH AS VALUE OF SUBJECT
* WWH3         NULLWH AS VALUE OF NSTGO
* WWH4         NULLWH AS VALUE OF OBJBE
* WWH5         NULLWH AS VALUE OF PN
* WWH51        WH IN TPOS IN WHN ONLY
* WWH52        IN WHN, TPOS MUST HAVE WH VALUE
* WWH53        ASSERTION OPTION OF WH QUESTION IFF SUBJECT OMITTED
* WWH54        WHQ-N: NO ASSERTION OPTION AFTER WHOM
*
* FOR WH-STRING SEE ALSO:
* WSN9
*
*
*
* ZEROING RESTRICTIONS
*
* DZERO1       ZEROED ASSERTION (+HE LEFT AND FAST+)
* WZERT4       IGNORE NULLC OPTION FOR NOW
* WZERO1       TENSE ZEROING (+HE WILL GO AND SHE TOO+ ETC.)
* WZERO2       VERB ZEROING AFTER TENSE OR +TO+
* WZERO3       OBJECT ZEROING AFTER +HAVE+, +BE+, ZERO VERB, OR IN COMPARATIVE
* WZERO4       ZEROED TENSE+VERB+OBJECT NEEDS ADJUNCT SUPPORT
* WZERO5       ZEROING IN TPOS (TO DISTRIBUTE ARTICLE)
* WZERO6       CONSTRAINT ON TPOS ZEROING
*
```

Index to Symbols of the Computer Grammar in Part 2

prepared by Susanne Wolff

In the description of the computer grammar of English in Part 2, BNF definitions, routines, restrictions and attributes are written in capital letters. These symbols are indexed here. Note that all symbols beginning with $ (restriction substatements) are in one final section of the index. A page number in italics indicates that the referenced symbol appears as part of a BNF definition or routine or restriction on that page. In addition

   <X>   indicates X is a syntactic type defined in the BNF portion of the grammar;

   <*X>   indicates X is a lexical type standing for a major word class in the BNF portion of the grammar;

   *X   is the form of <*X> used in the body of the text and in parse trees not generated by the computer parsing program. In the latter no < > or * are printed.

Index

Italicized number indicates the page on which the term is defined.

n following a page number indicates "note" on cited page number.

Symbols of the computer grammar are in CAPITAL LETTERS. Those in Part 2 are separately indexed on the preceding pages.

Appendix 2 explains the computer mnemonics for the symbols in definitions.

PE 1074.5
.S3

DO NOT REMOVE

SLIP FROM POCKET

DEMCO

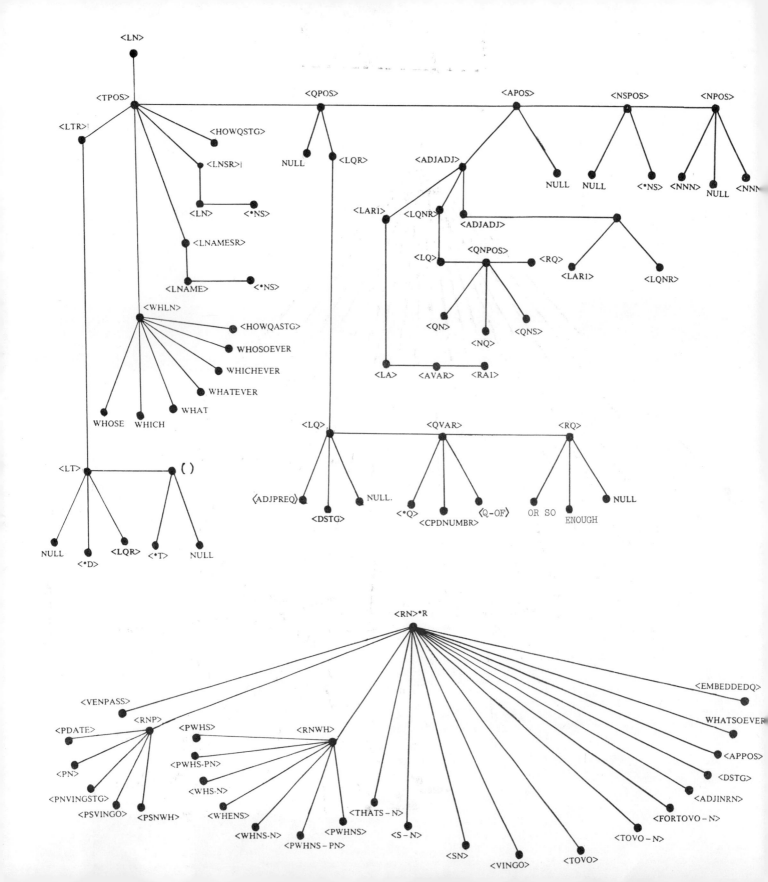